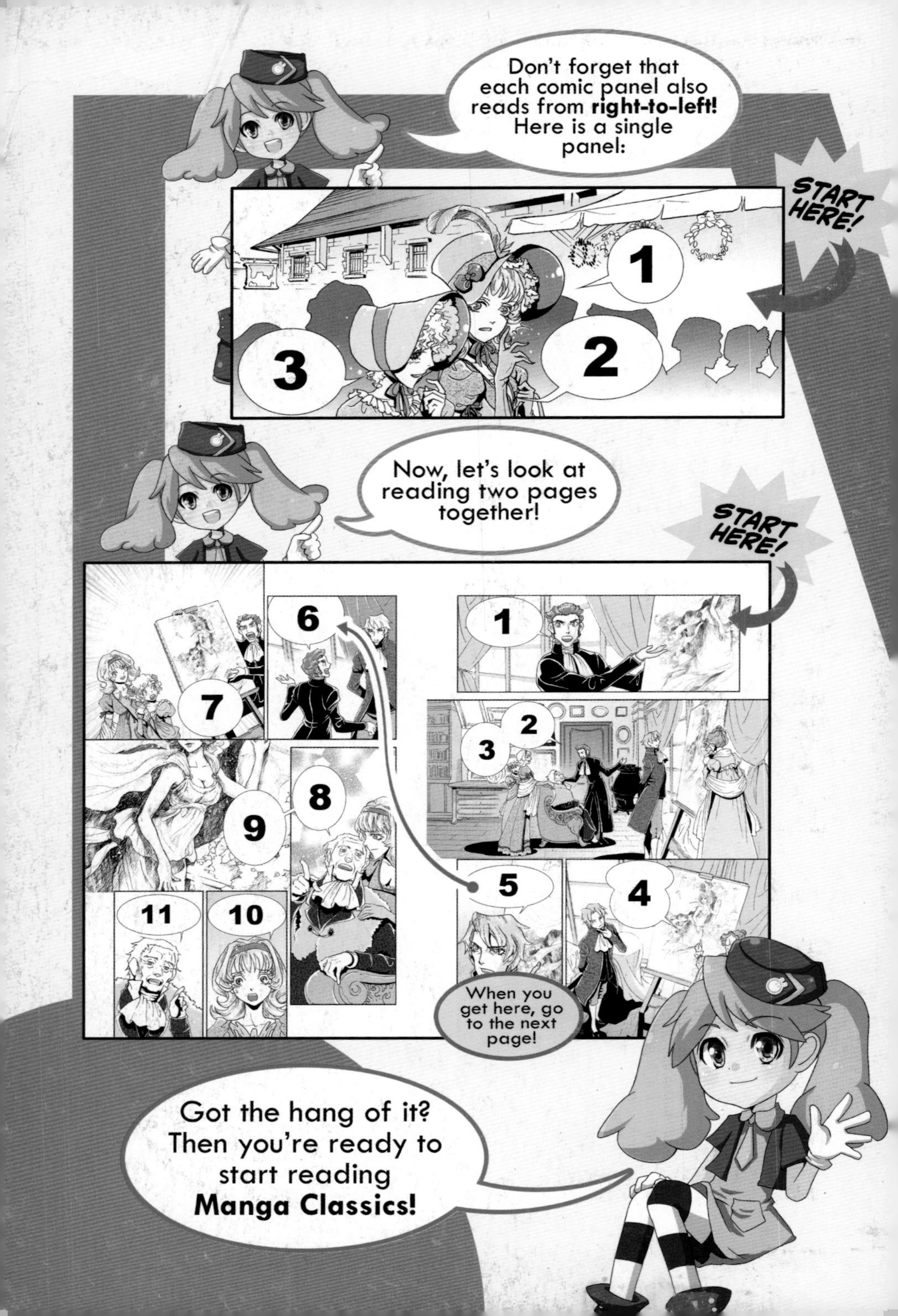
Don't forget that each comic panel also reads from **right-to-left!** Here is a single panel:
START HERE!
1
2
3
Now, let's look at reading two pages together!
START HERE!
1
2
3
4
5
6
7
8
9
10
11
When you get here, go to the next page!
Got the hang of it? Then you're ready to start reading **Manga Classics!**

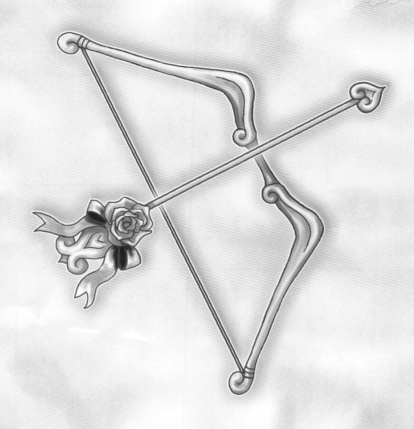

CONTENTS:

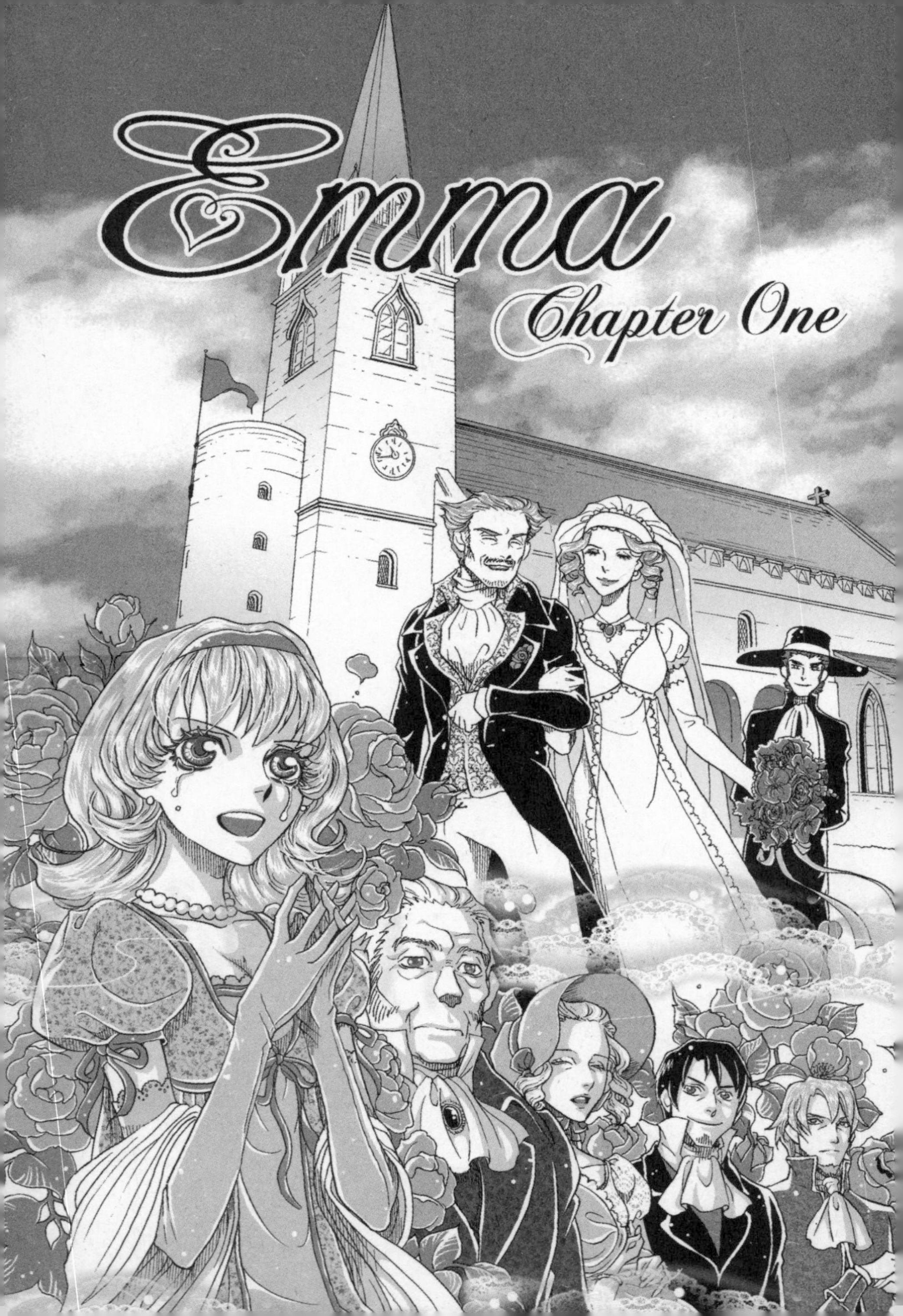
Emma
Chapter One

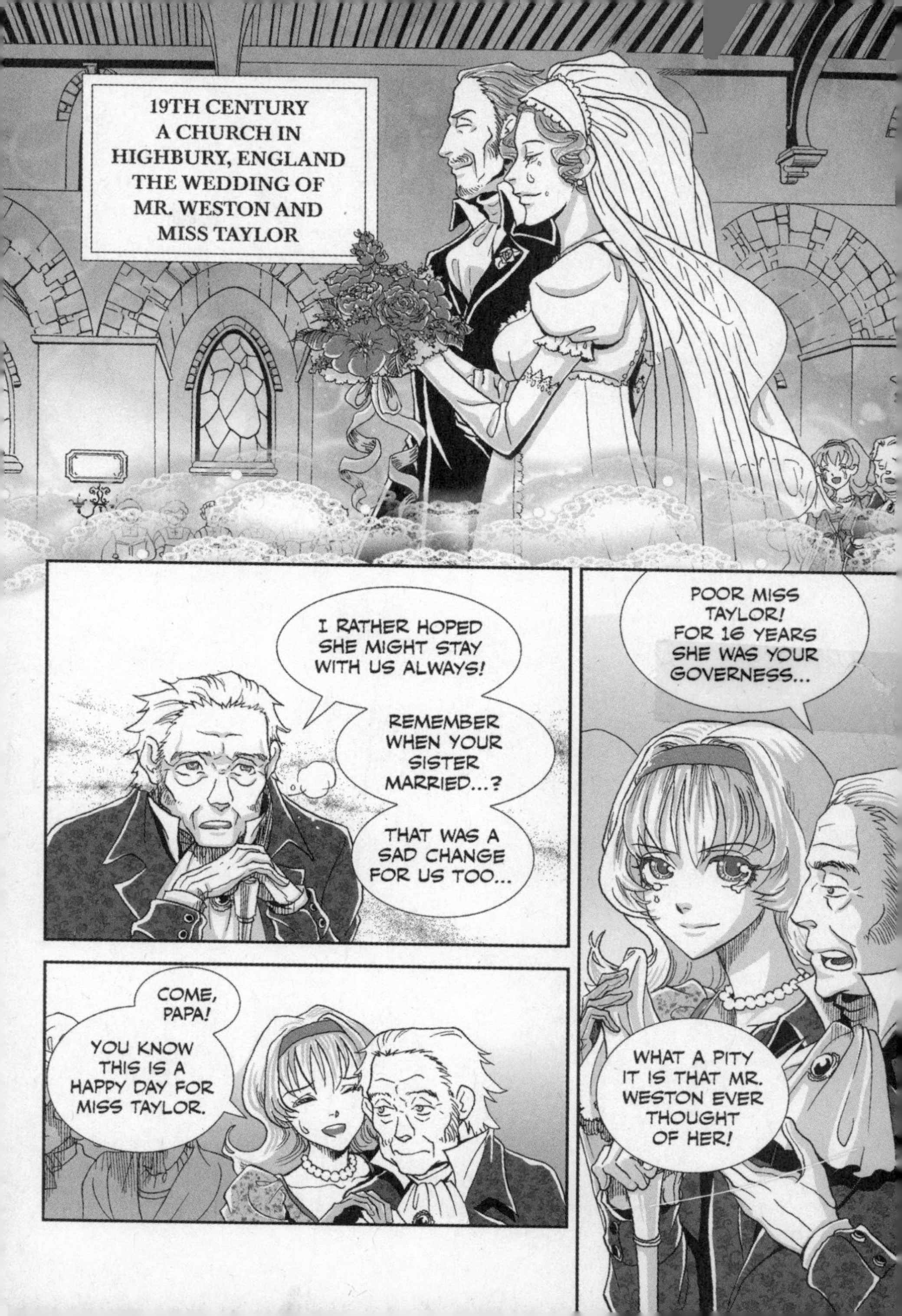
19TH CENTURY
A CHURCH IN
HIGHBURY, ENGLAND
THE WEDDING OF
MR. WESTON AND
MISS TAYLOR
POOR MISS TAYLOR! FOR 16 YEARS SHE WAS YOUR GOVERNESS...
WHAT A PITY IT IS THAT MR. WESTON EVER THOUGHT OF HER!
I RATHER HOPED SHE MIGHT STAY WITH US ALWAYS!
REMEMBER WHEN YOUR SISTER MARRIED...?
THAT WAS A SAD CHANGE FOR US TOO...
COME, PAPA!
YOU KNOW THIS IS A HAPPY DAY FOR MISS TAYLOR.

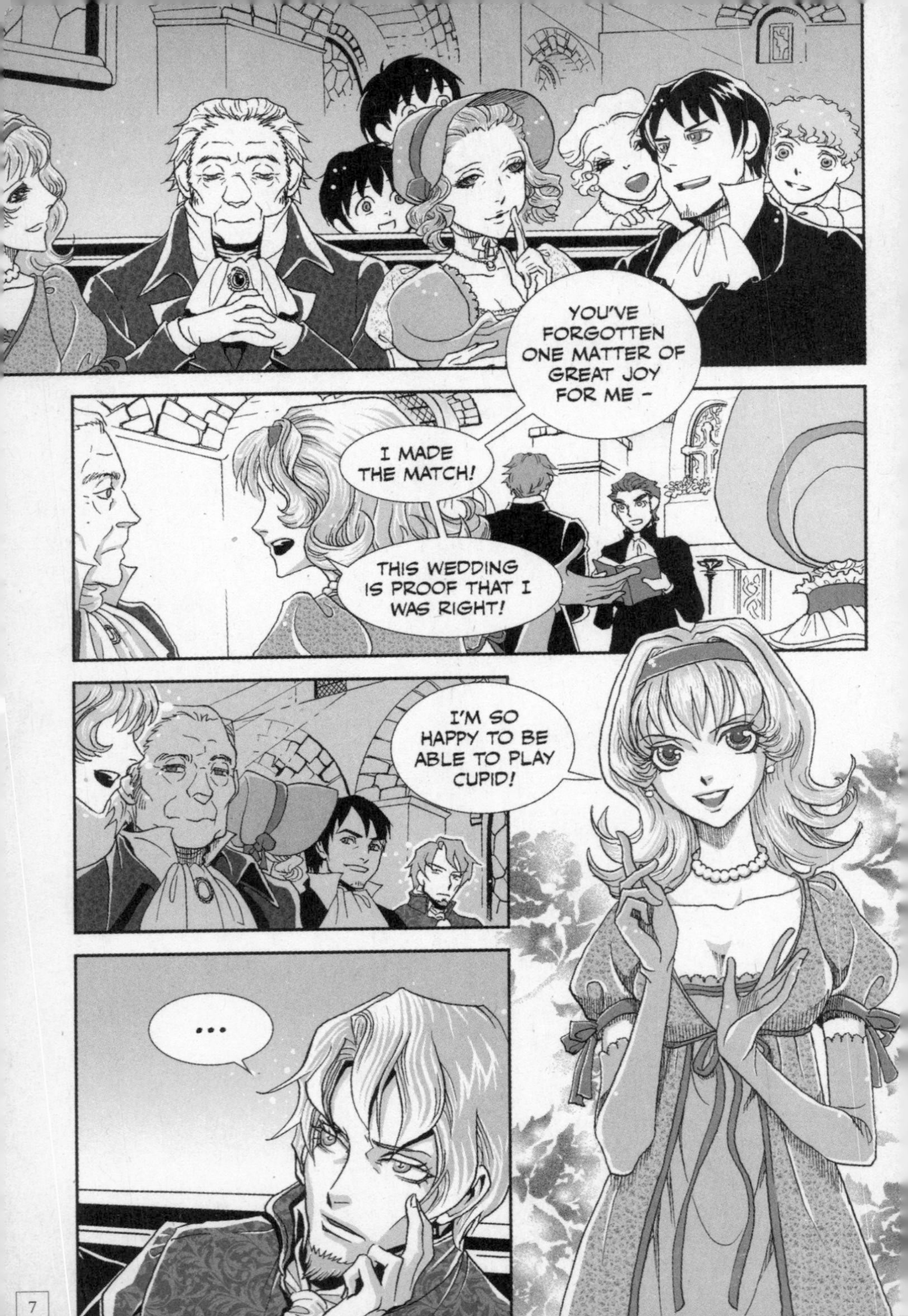
YOU'VE FORGOTTEN ONE MATTER OF GREAT JOY FOR ME –
I MADE THE MATCH!
THIS WEDDING IS PROOF THAT I WAS RIGHT!
I'M SO HAPPY TO BE ABLE TO PLAY CUPID!
...

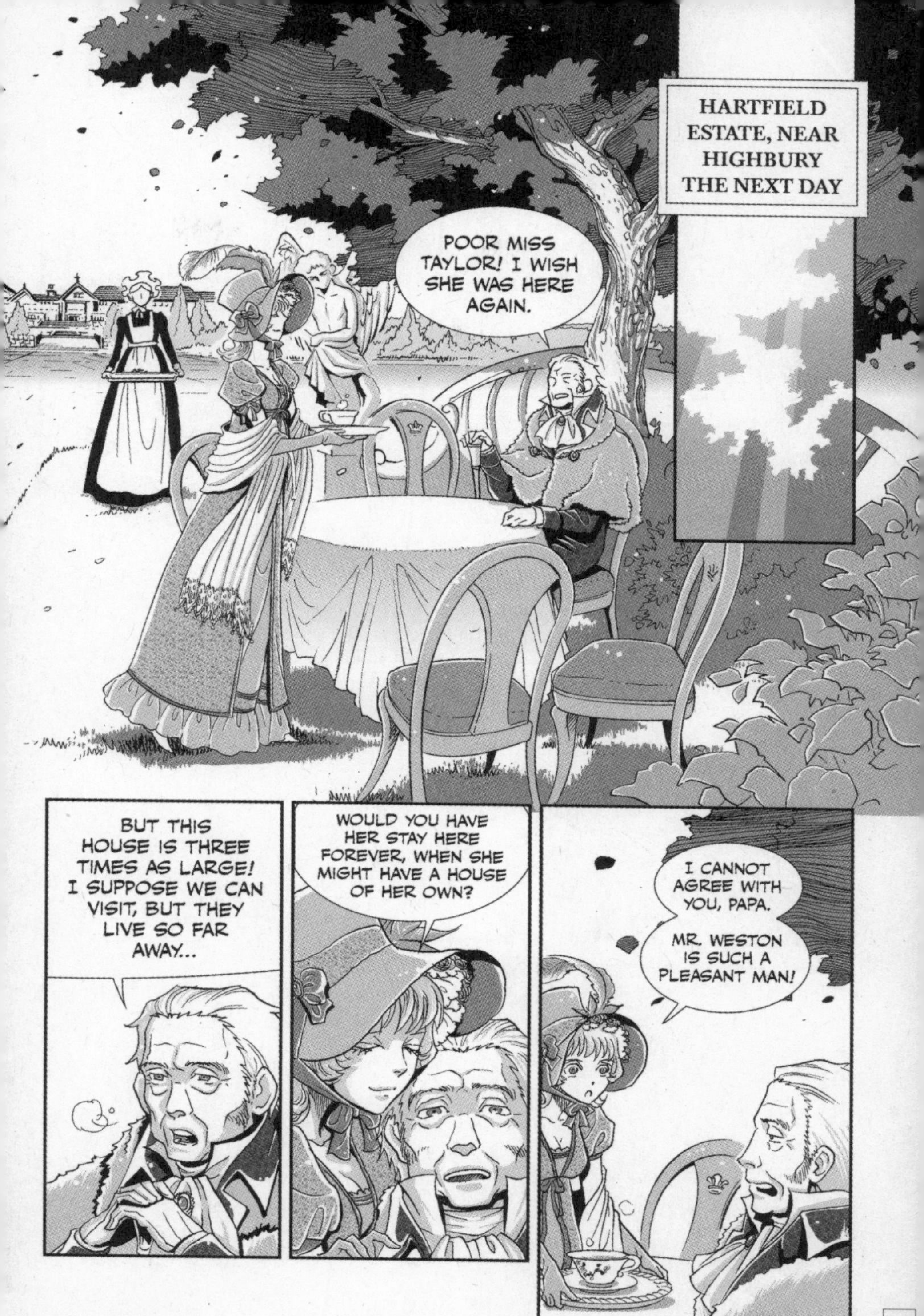
HARTFIELD ESTATE, NEAR HIGHBURY THE NEXT DAY
POOR MISS TAYLOR! I WISH SHE WAS HERE AGAIN.
I CANNOT AGREE WITH YOU, PAPA.
MR. WESTON IS SUCH A PLEASANT MAN!
WOULD YOU HAVE HER STAY HERE FOREVER, WHEN SHE MIGHT HAVE A HOUSE OF HER OWN?
BUT THIS HOUSE IS THREE TIMES AS LARGE! I SUPPOSE WE CAN VISIT, BUT THEY LIVE SO FAR AWAY...

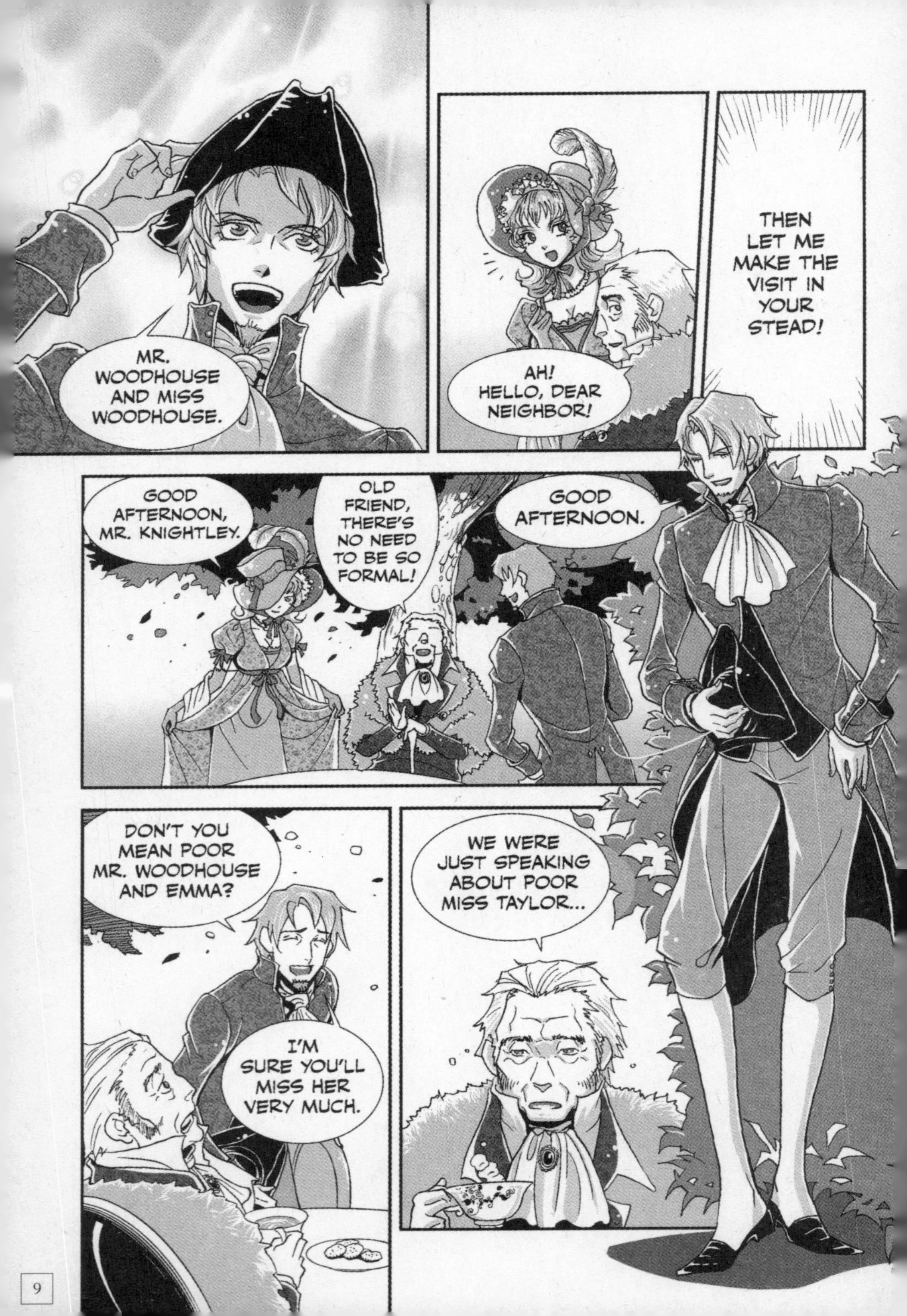
THEN LET ME MAKE THE VISIT IN YOUR STEAD!
AH! HELLO, DEAR NEIGHBOR!
MR. WOODHOUSE AND MISS WOODHOUSE.
GOOD AFTERNOON.
OLD FRIEND, THERE'S NO NEED TO BE SO FORMAL!
GOOD AFTERNOON, MR. KNIGHTLEY.
WE WERE JUST SPEAKING ABOUT POOR MISS TAYLOR...
DON'T YOU MEAN POOR MR. WOODHOUSE AND EMMA?
I'M SURE YOU'LL MISS HER VERY MUCH.

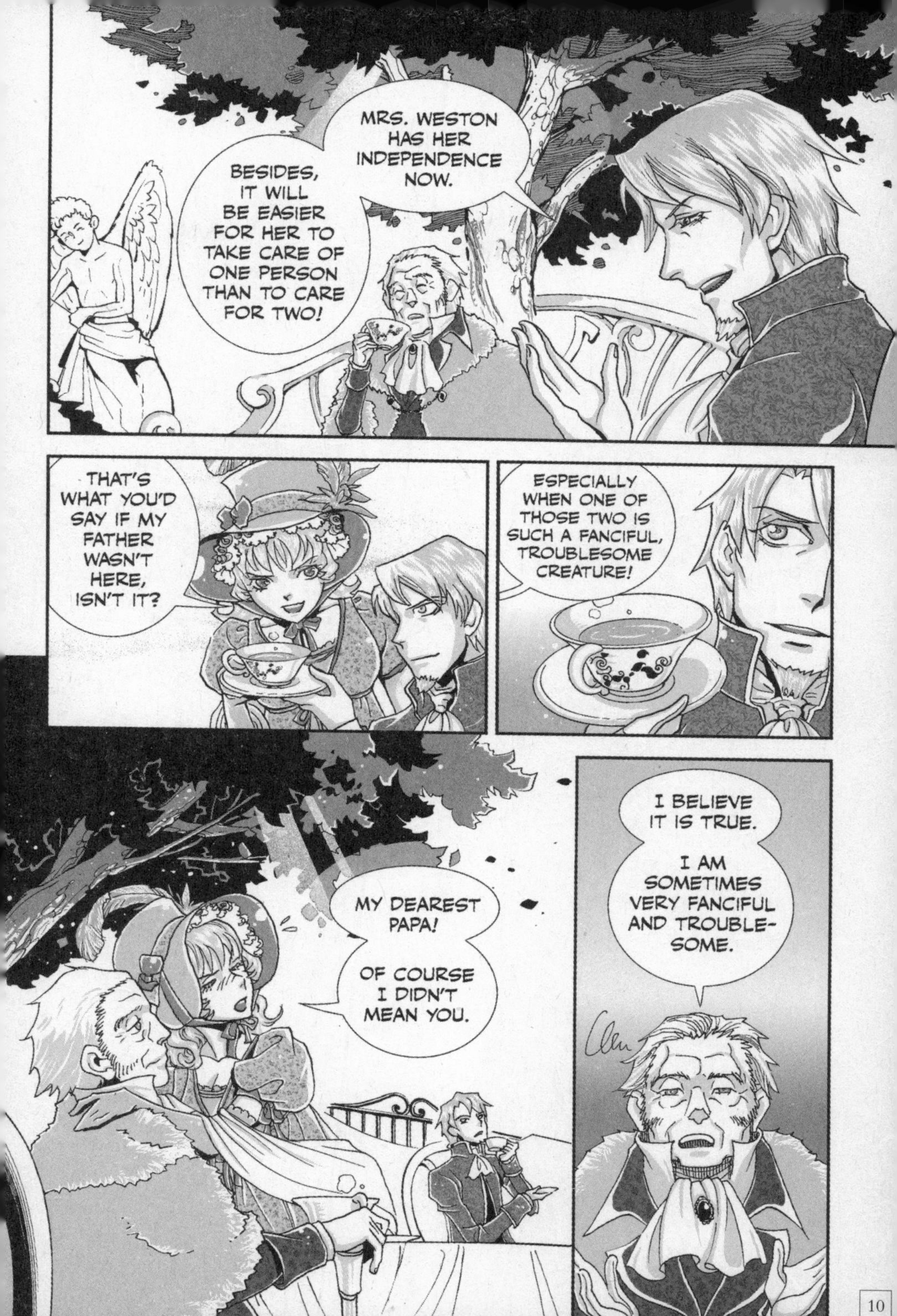
MRS. WESTON HAS HER INDEPENDENCE NOW.
BESIDES, IT WILL BE EASIER FOR HER TO TAKE CARE OF ONE PERSON THAN TO CARE FOR TWO!
ESPECIALLY WHEN ONE OF THOSE TWO IS SUCH A FANCIFUL, TROUBLESOME CREATURE!
THAT'S WHAT YOU'D SAY IF MY FATHER WASN'T HERE, ISN'T IT?
I BELIEVE IT IS TRUE.
I AM SOMETIMES VERY FANCIFUL AND TROUBLE-SOME.
MY DEAREST PAPA!
OF COURSE I DIDN'T MEAN YOU.

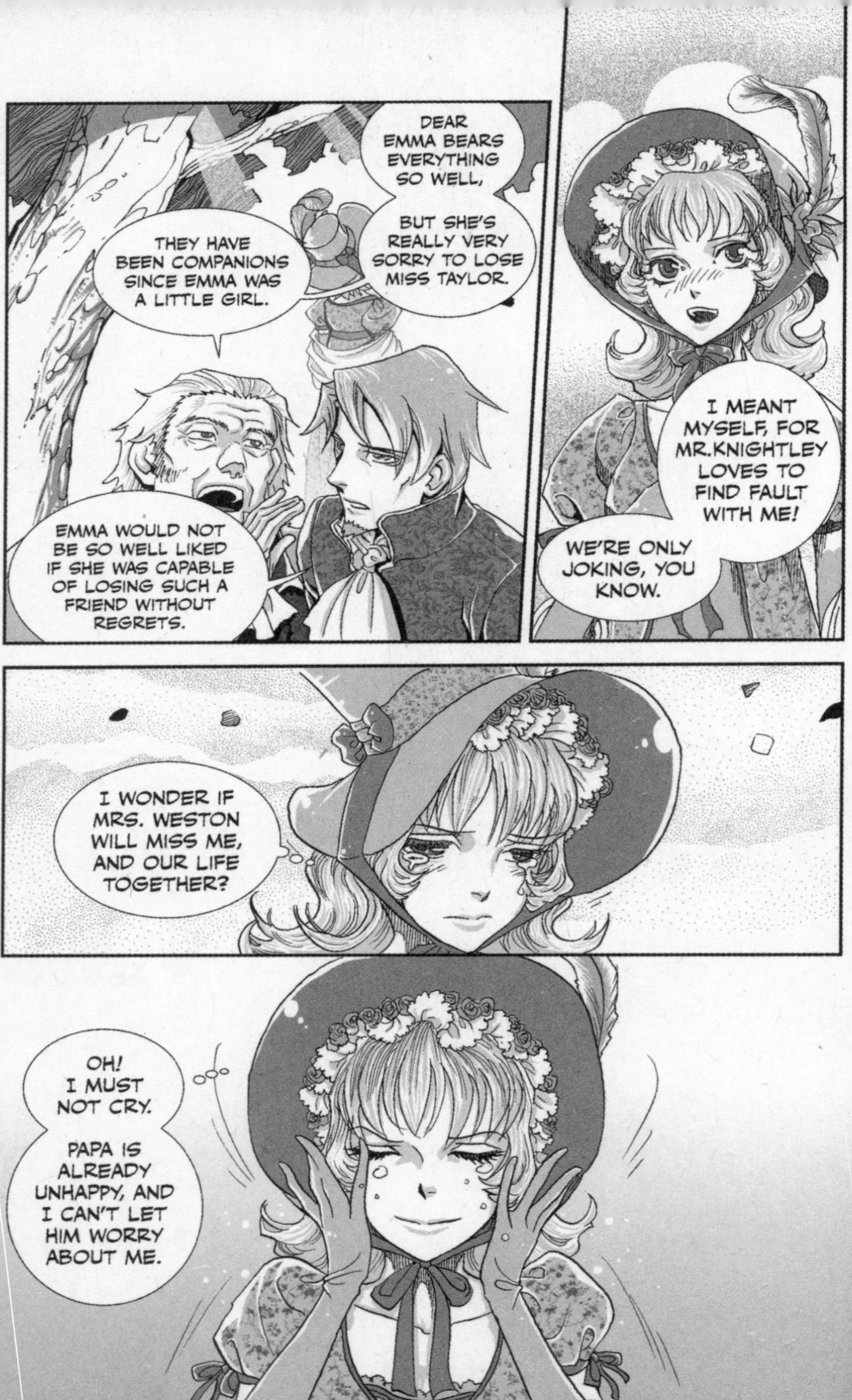
I MEANT MYSELF, FOR MR.KNIGHTLEY LOVES TO FIND FAULT WITH ME!
WE'RE ONLY JOKING, YOU KNOW.
DEAR EMMA BEARS EVERYTHING SO WELL,
BUT SHE'S REALLY VERY SORRY TO LOSE MISS TAYLOR.
THEY HAVE BEEN COMPANIONS SINCE EMMA WAS A LITTLE GIRL.
EMMA WOULD NOT BE SO WELL LIKED IF SHE WAS CAPABLE OF LOSING SUCH A FRIEND WITHOUT REGRETS.
I WONDER IF MRS. WESTON WILL MISS ME, AND OUR LIFE TOGETHER?
OH! I MUST NOT CRY.
PAPA IS ALREADY UNHAPPY, AND I CAN'T LET HIM WORRY ABOUT ME.

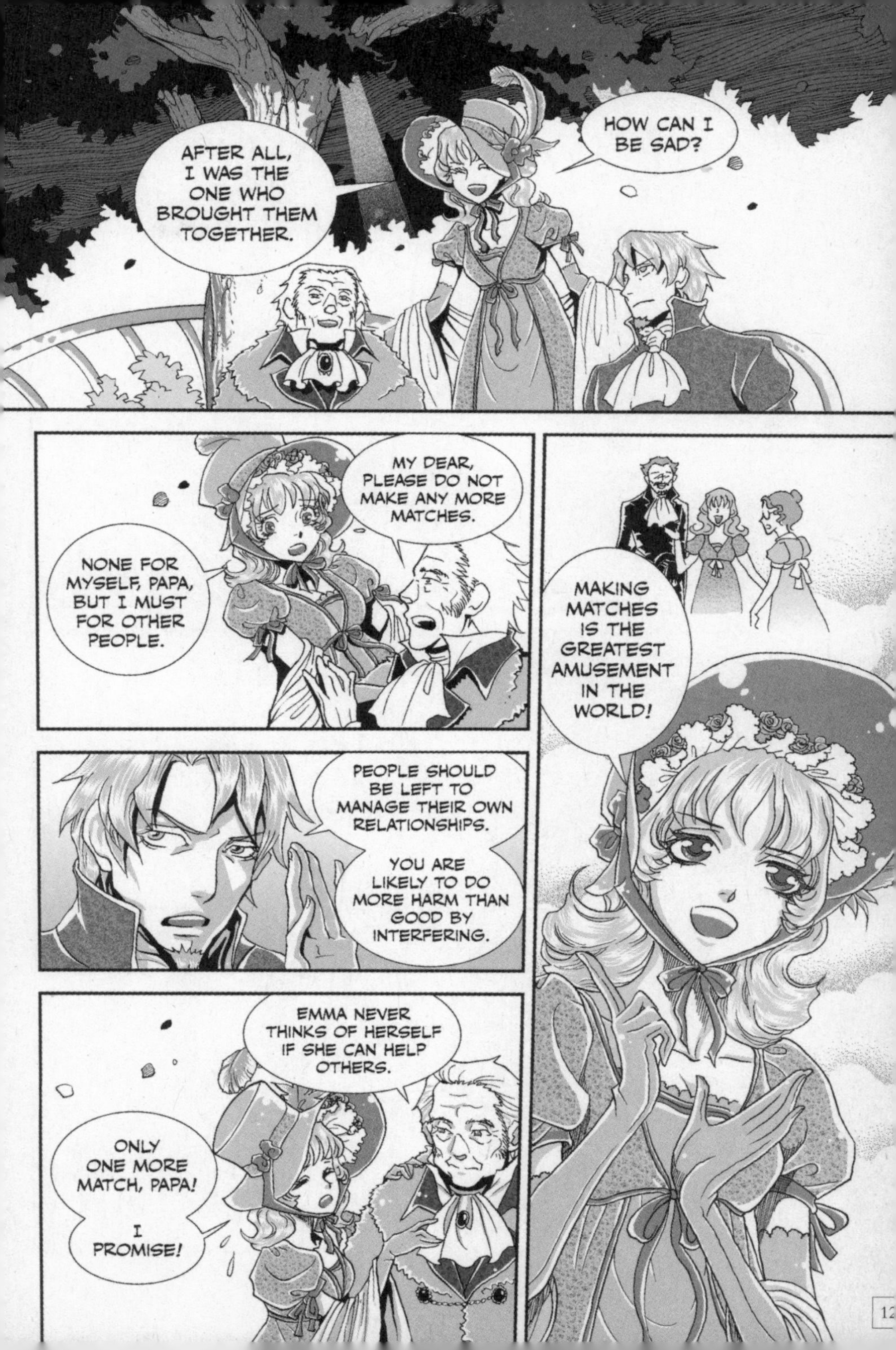
HOW CAN I BE SAD?
AFTER ALL, I WAS THE ONE WHO BROUGHT THEM TOGETHER.
MAKING MATCHES IS THE GREATEST AMUSEMENT IN THE WORLD!
MY DEAR, PLEASE DO NOT MAKE ANY MORE MATCHES.
NONE FOR MYSELF, PAPA, BUT I MUST FOR OTHER PEOPLE.
PEOPLE SHOULD BE LEFT TO MANAGE THEIR OWN RELATIONSHIPS.
YOU ARE LIKELY TO DO MORE HARM THAN GOOD BY INTERFERING.
EMMA NEVER THINKS OF HERSELF IF SHE CAN HELP OTHERS.
ONLY ONE MORE MATCH, PAPA!
I PROMISE!

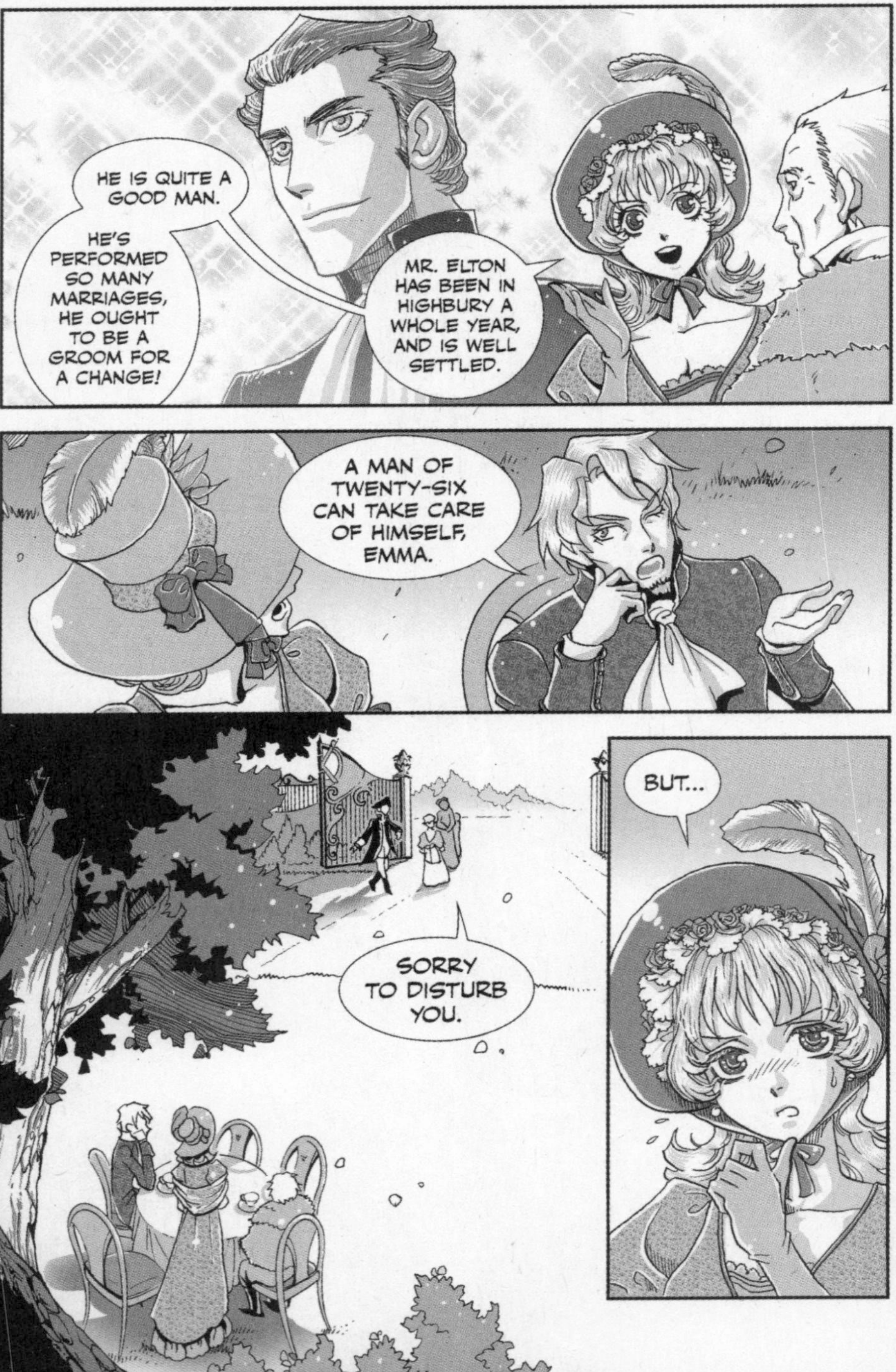
MR. ELTON HAS BEEN IN HIGHBURY A WHOLE YEAR, AND IS WELL SETTLED.
HE IS QUITE A GOOD MAN.
HE'S PERFORMED SO MANY MARRIAGES, HE OUGHT TO BE A GROOM FOR A CHANGE!
A MAN OF TWENTY-SIX CAN TAKE CARE OF HIMSELF, EMMA.
BUT...
SORRY TO DISTURB YOU.

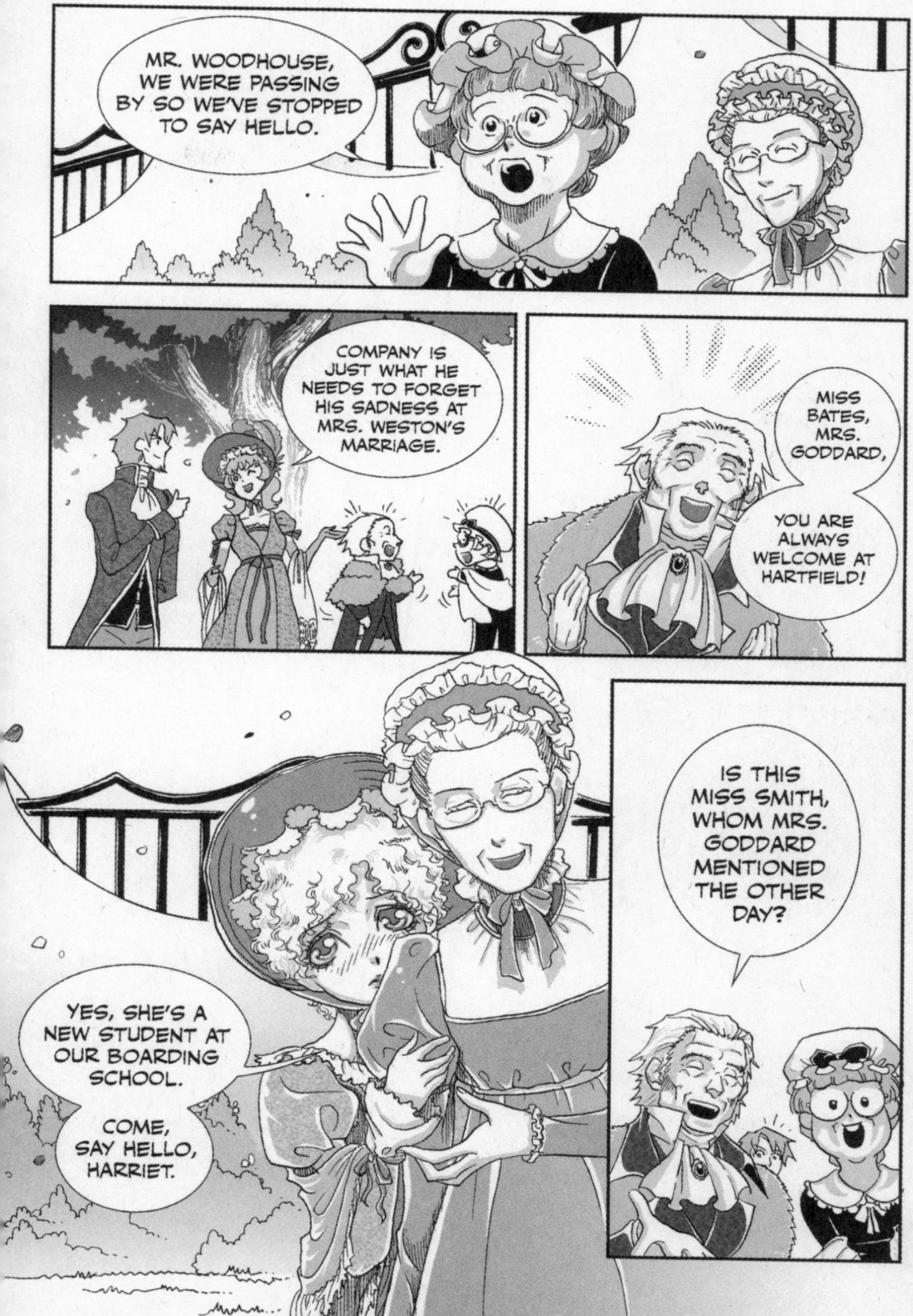
MR. WOODHOUSE, WE WERE PASSING BY SO WE'VE STOPPED TO SAY HELLO.
MISS BATES, MRS. GODDARD,
YOU ARE ALWAYS WELCOME AT HARTFIELD!
COMPANY IS JUST WHAT HE NEEDS TO FORGET HIS SADNESS AT MRS. WESTON'S MARRIAGE.
IS THIS MISS SMITH, WHOM MRS. GODDARD MENTIONED THE OTHER DAY?
YES, SHE'S A NEW STUDENT AT OUR BOARDING SCHOOL.
COME, SAY HELLO, HARRIET.

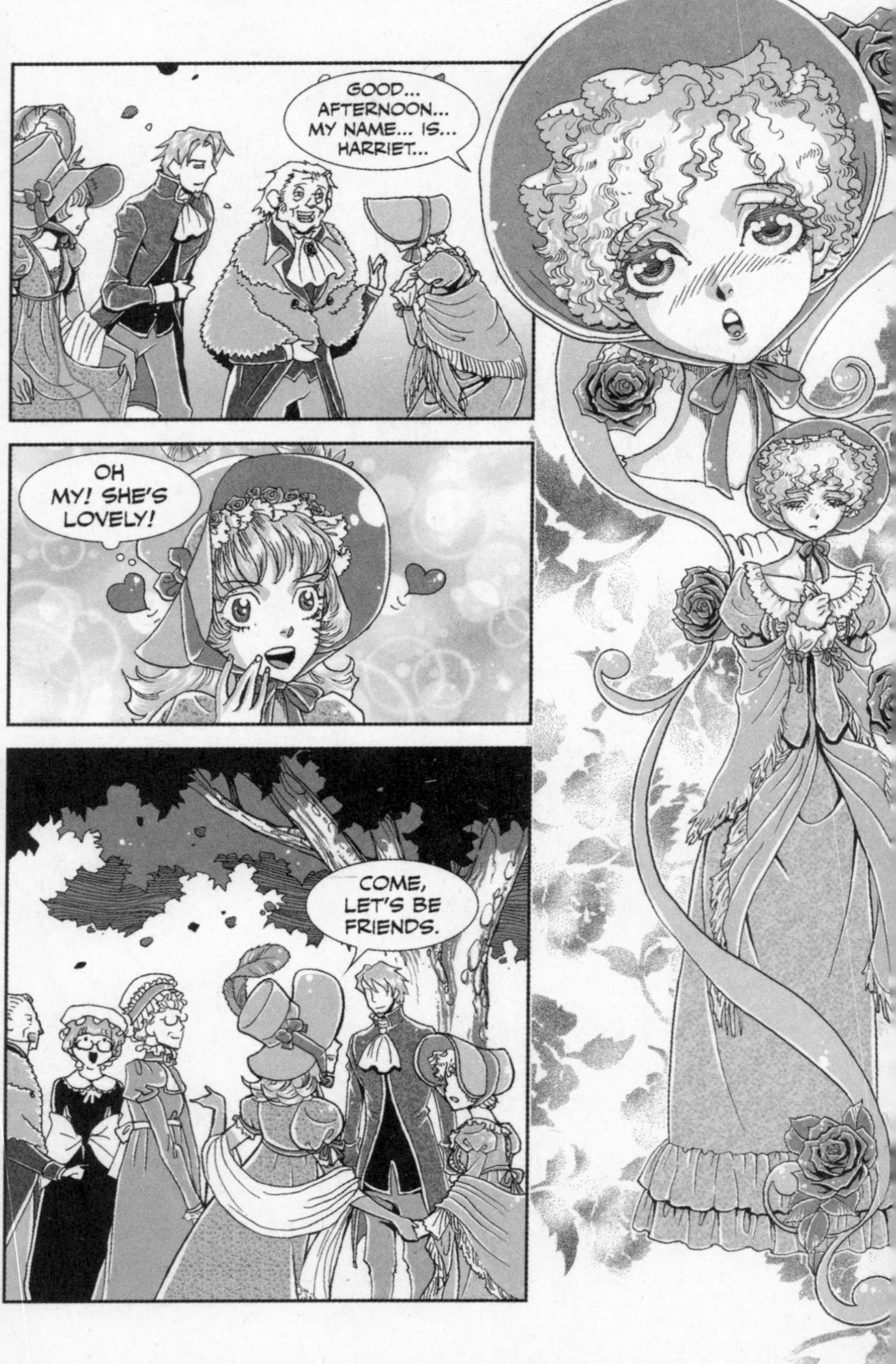
GOOD... AFTERNOON... MY NAME... IS... HARRIET...
OH MY! SHE'S LOVELY!
COME, LET'S BE FRIENDS.

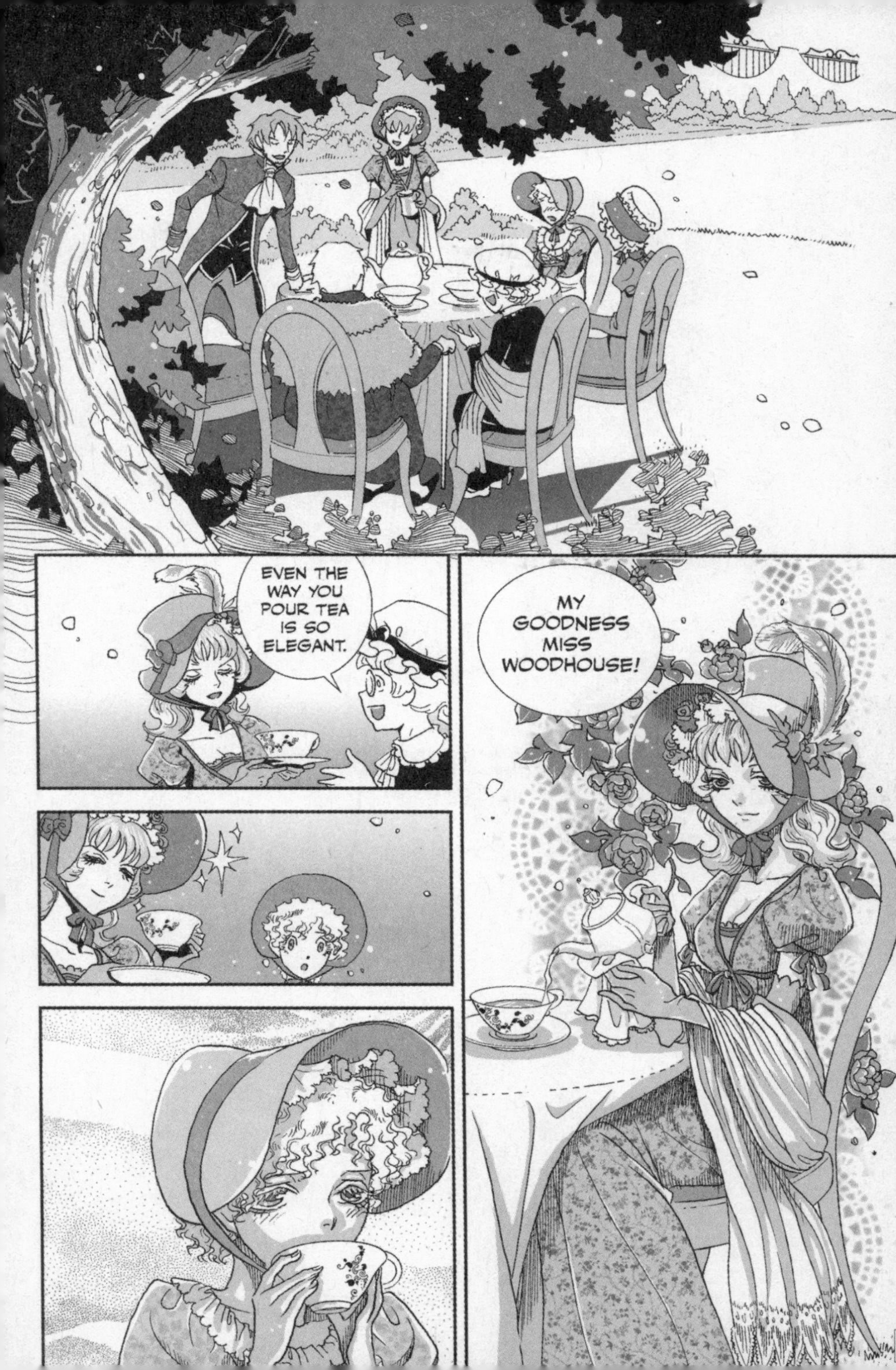
MY GOODNESS MISS WOODHOUSE!
EVEN THE WAY YOU POUR TEA IS SO ELEGANT.

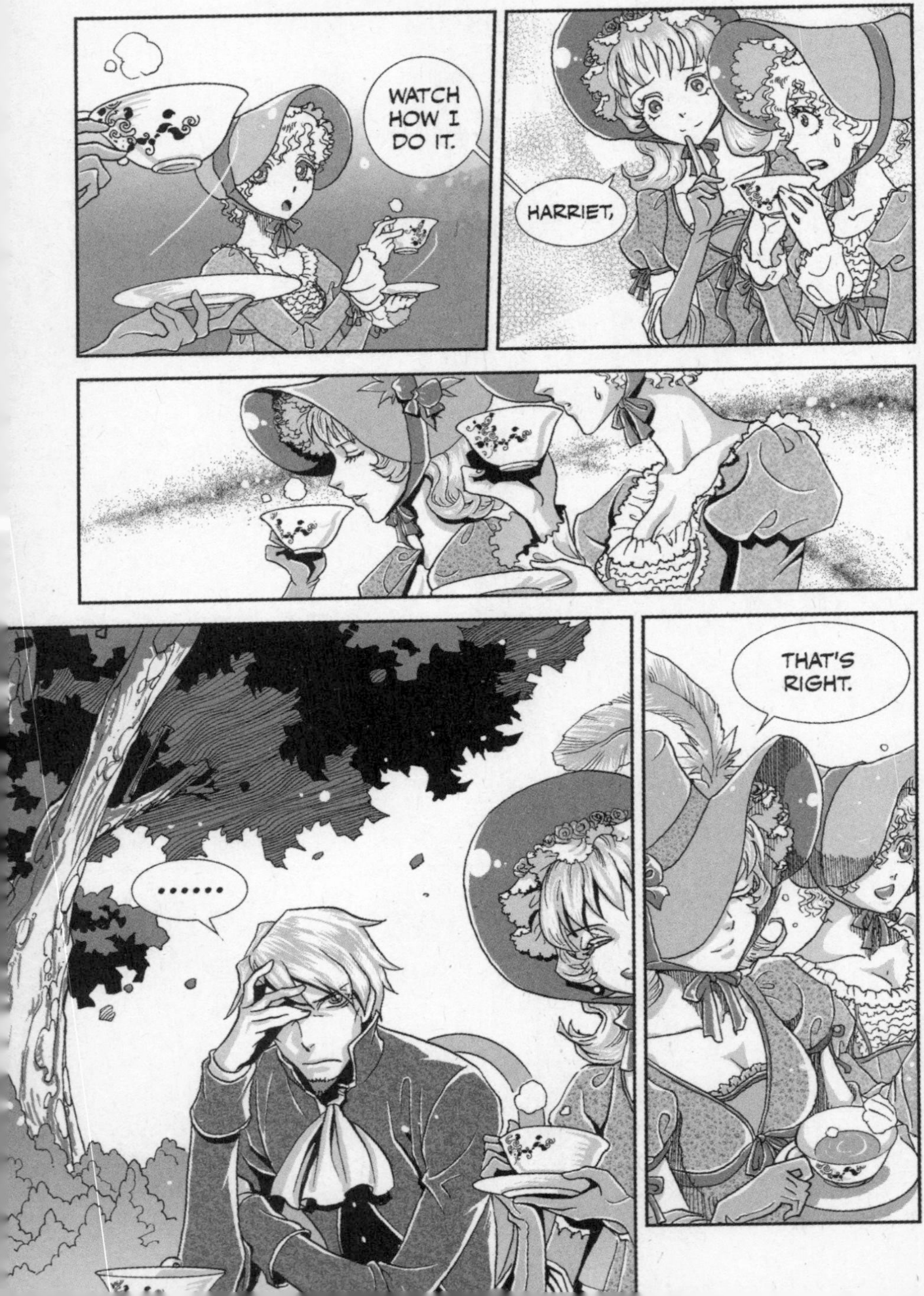
HARRIET,
WATCH HOW I DO IT.
THAT'S RIGHT.
......

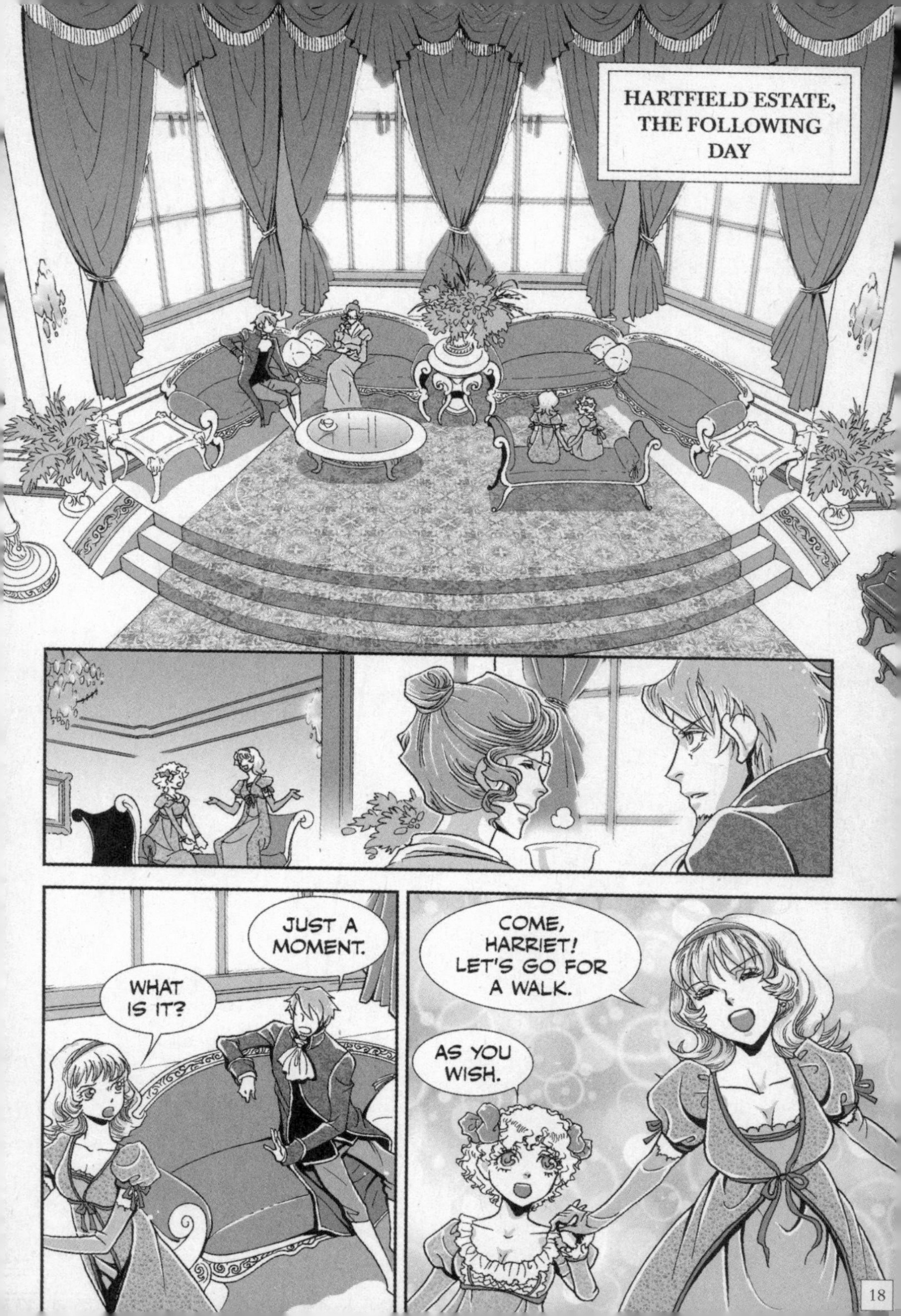
HARTFIELD ESTATE, THE FOLLOWING DAY
COME, HARRIET! LET'S GO FOR A WALK.
AS YOU WISH.
JUST A MOMENT.
WHAT IS IT?

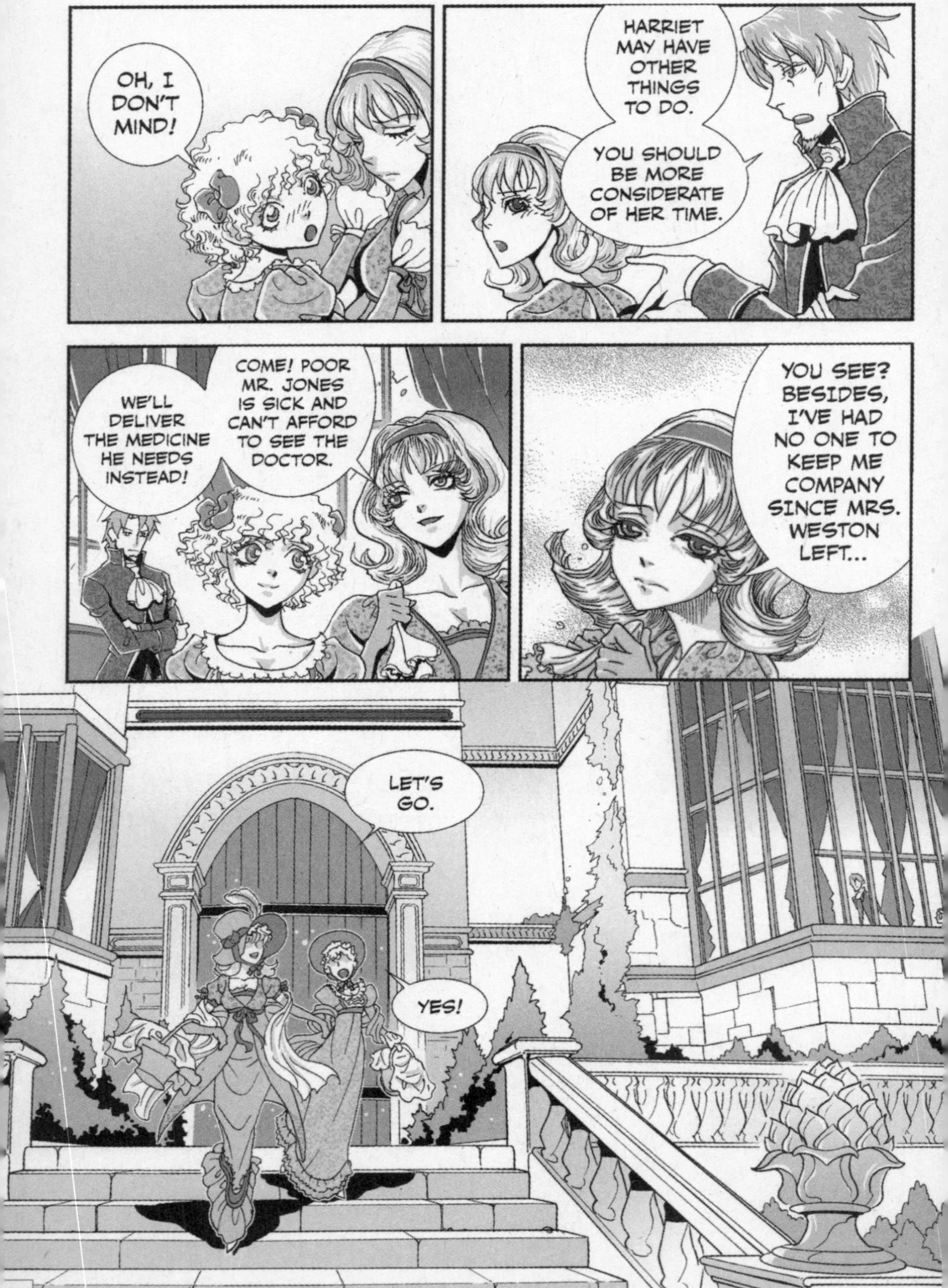
HARRIET MAY HAVE OTHER THINGS TO DO.
YOU SHOULD BE MORE CONSIDERATE OF HER TIME.
OH, I DON'T MIND!
YOU SEE? BESIDES, I'VE HAD NO ONE TO KEEP ME COMPANY SINCE MRS. WESTON LEFT...
COME! POOR MR. JONES IS SICK AND CAN'T AFFORD TO SEE THE DOCTOR.
WE'LL DELIVER THE MEDICINE HE NEEDS INSTEAD!
LET'S GO.
YES!

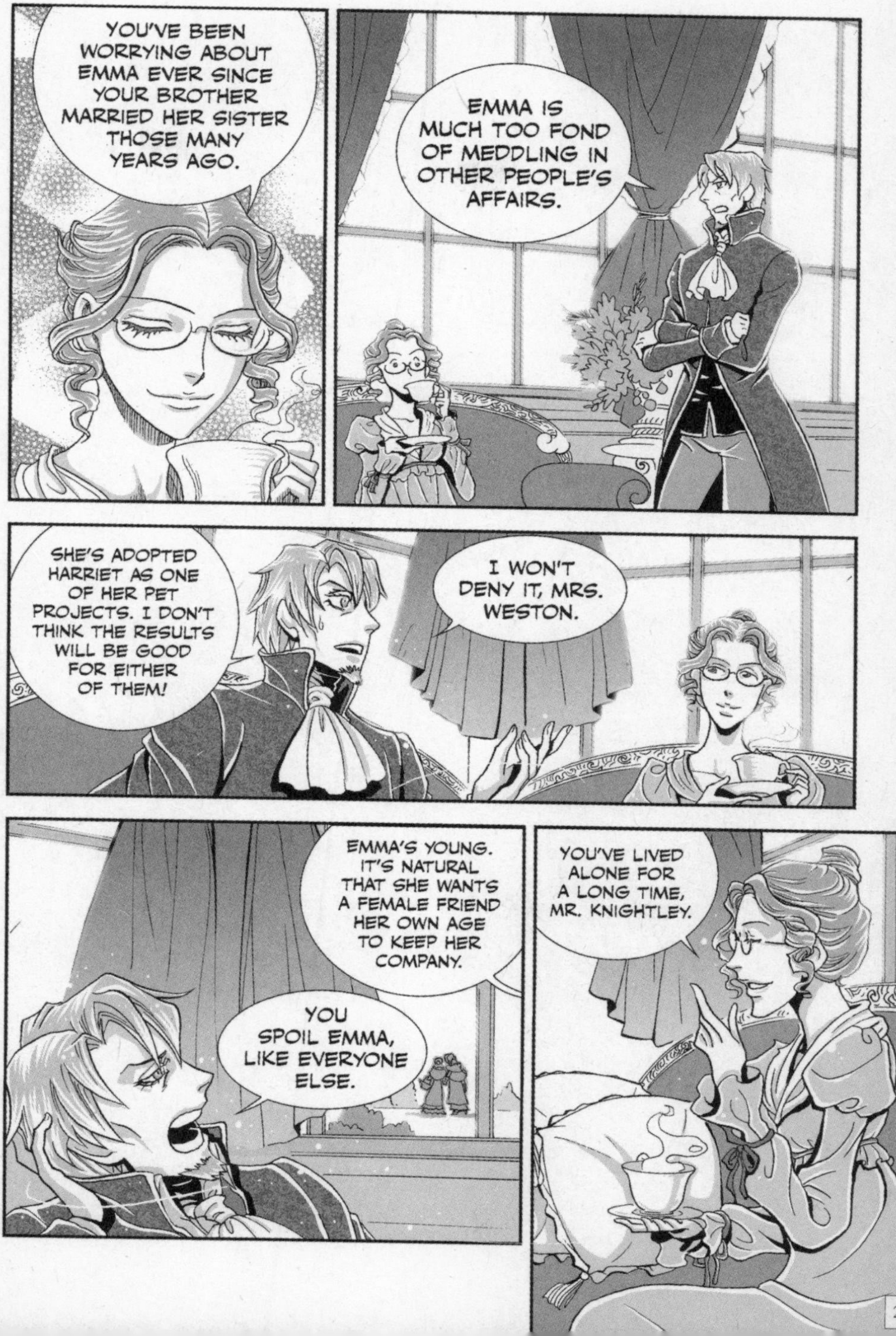
EMMA IS MUCH TOO FOND OF MEDDLING IN OTHER PEOPLE'S AFFAIRS.
YOU'VE BEEN WORRYING ABOUT EMMA EVER SINCE YOUR BROTHER MARRIED HER SISTER THOSE MANY YEARS AGO.
I WON'T DENY IT, MRS. WESTON.
SHE'S ADOPTED HARRIET AS ONE OF HER PET PROJECTS. I DON'T THINK THE RESULTS WILL BE GOOD FOR EITHER OF THEM!
YOU'VE LIVED ALONE FOR A LONG TIME, MR. KNIGHTLEY.
EMMA'S YOUNG. IT'S NATURAL THAT SHE WANTS A FEMALE FRIEND HER OWN AGE TO KEEP HER COMPANY.
YOU SPOIL EMMA, LIKE EVERYONE ELSE.

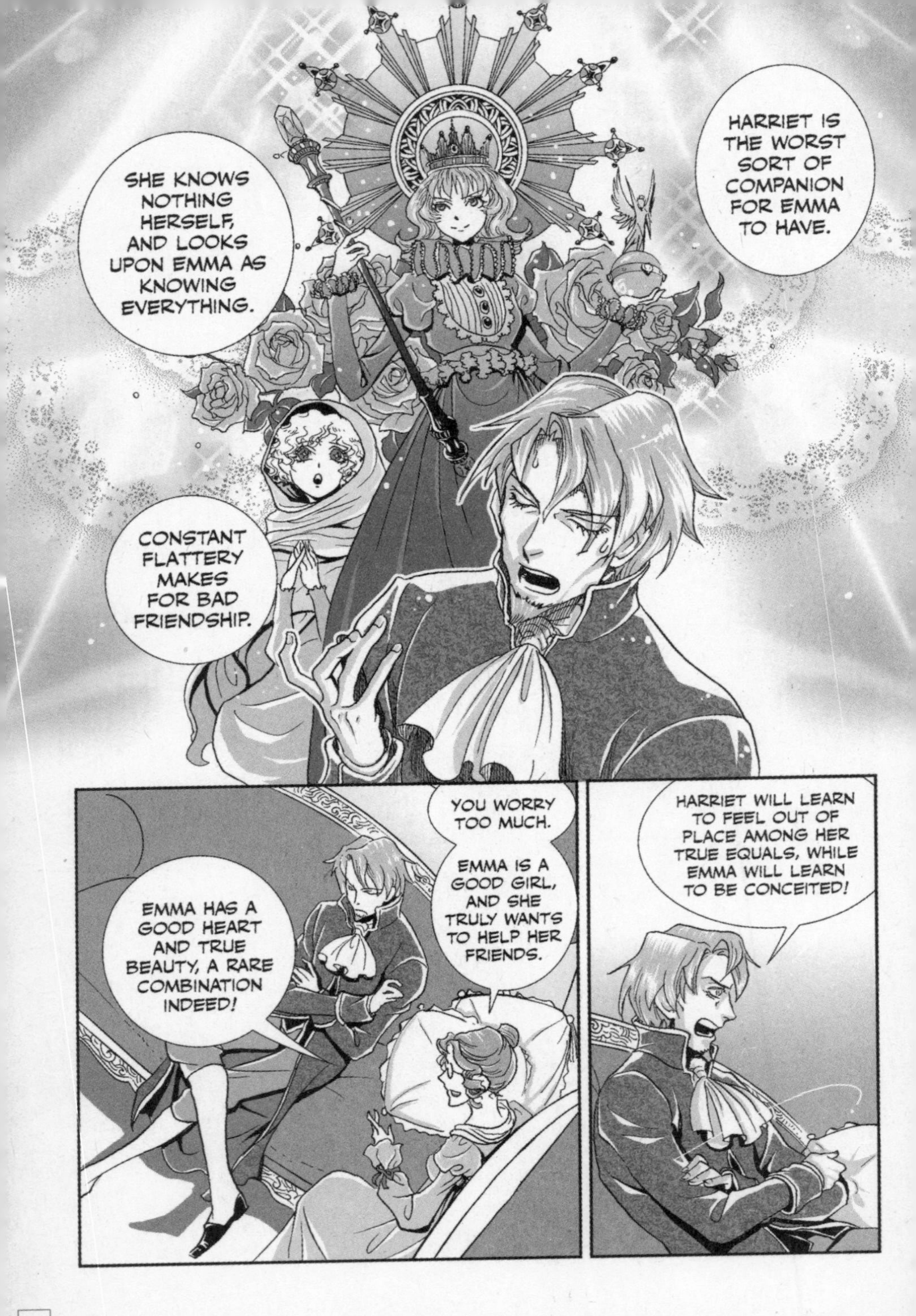
HARRIET IS THE WORST SORT OF COMPANION FOR EMMA TO HAVE.
SHE KNOWS NOTHING HERSELF, AND LOOKS UPON EMMA AS KNOWING EVERYTHING.
CONSTANT FLATTERY MAKES FOR BAD FRIENDSHIP.
HARRIET WILL LEARN TO FEEL OUT OF PLACE AMONG HER TRUE EQUALS, WHILE EMMA WILL LEARN TO BE CONCEITED!
YOU WORRY TOO MUCH.
EMMA IS A GOOD GIRL, AND SHE TRULY WANTS TO HELP HER FRIENDS.
EMMA HAS A GOOD HEART AND TRUE BEAUTY, A RARE COMBINATION INDEED!

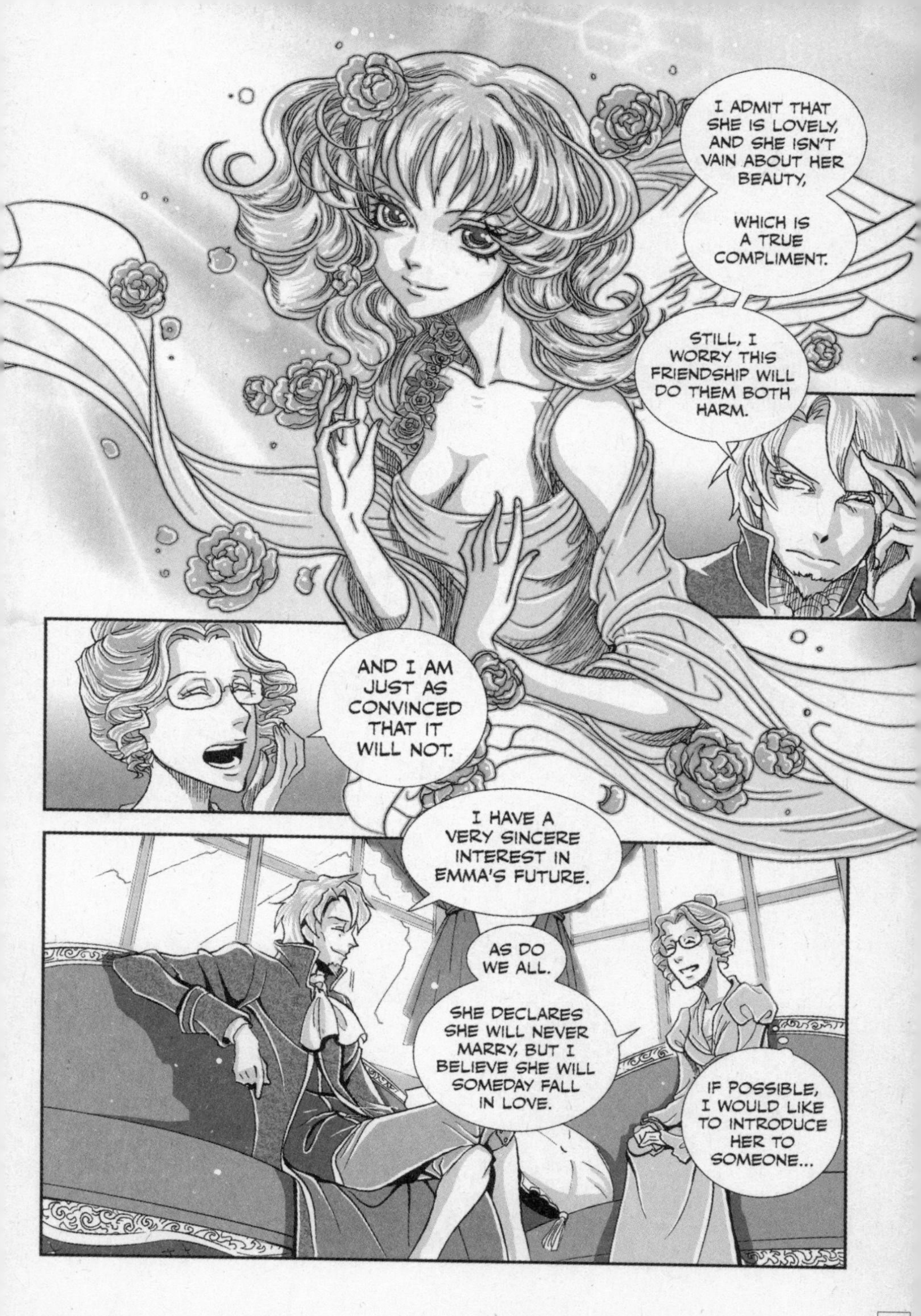
I ADMIT THAT SHE IS LOVELY, AND SHE ISN'T VAIN ABOUT HER BEAUTY,
WHICH IS A TRUE COMPLIMENT.
STILL, I WORRY THIS FRIENDSHIP WILL DO THEM BOTH HARM.
AND I AM JUST AS CONVINCED THAT IT WILL NOT.
I HAVE A VERY SINCERE INTEREST IN EMMA'S FUTURE.
AS DO WE ALL.
SHE DECLARES SHE WILL NEVER MARRY, BUT I BELIEVE SHE WILL SOMEDAY FALL IN LOVE.
IF POSSIBLE, I WOULD LIKE TO INTRODUCE HER TO SOMEONE...

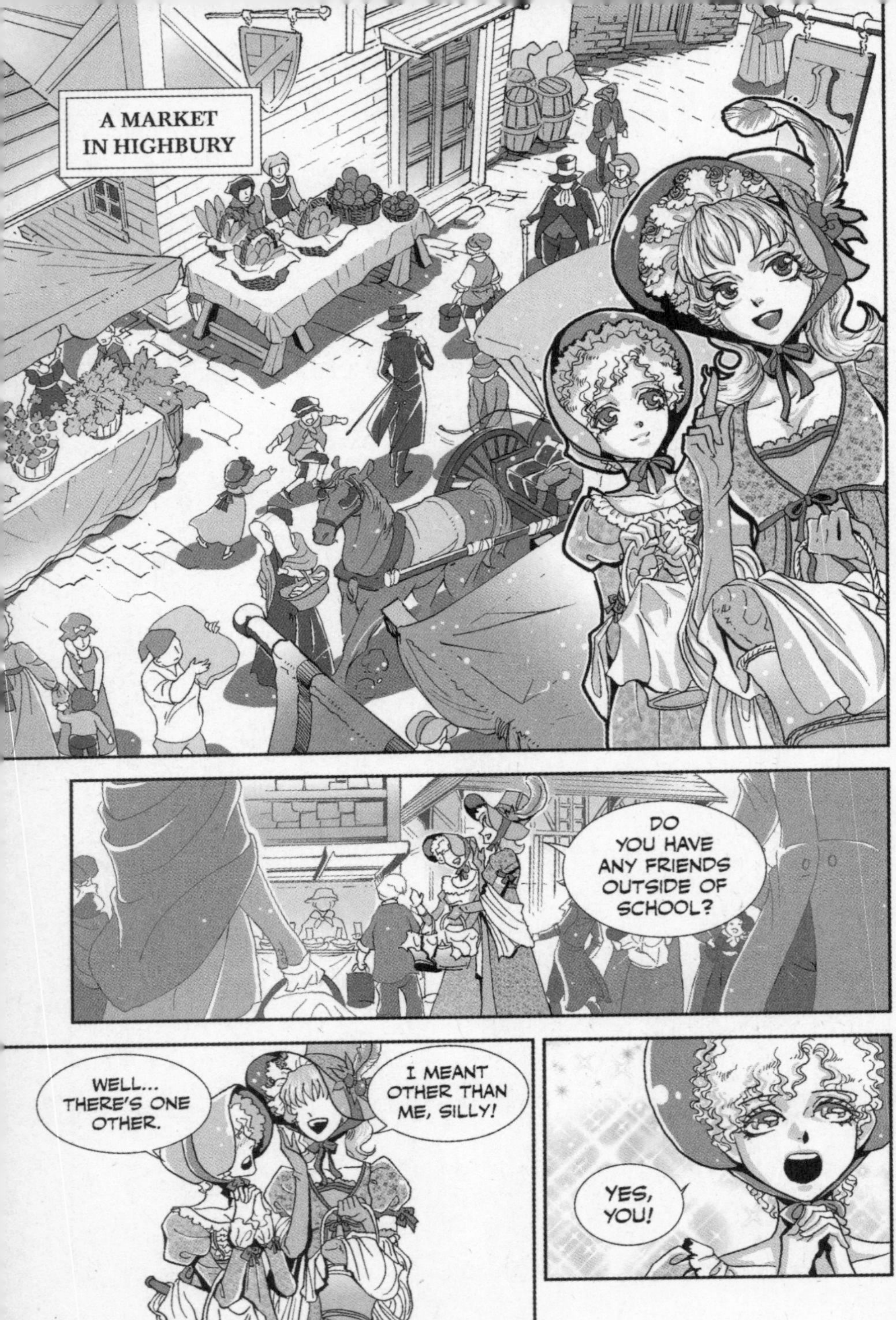
A MARKET IN HIGHBURY
DO YOU HAVE ANY FRIENDS OUTSIDE OF SCHOOL?
YES, YOU!
I MEANT OTHER THAN ME, SILLY!
WELL... THERE'S ONE OTHER.

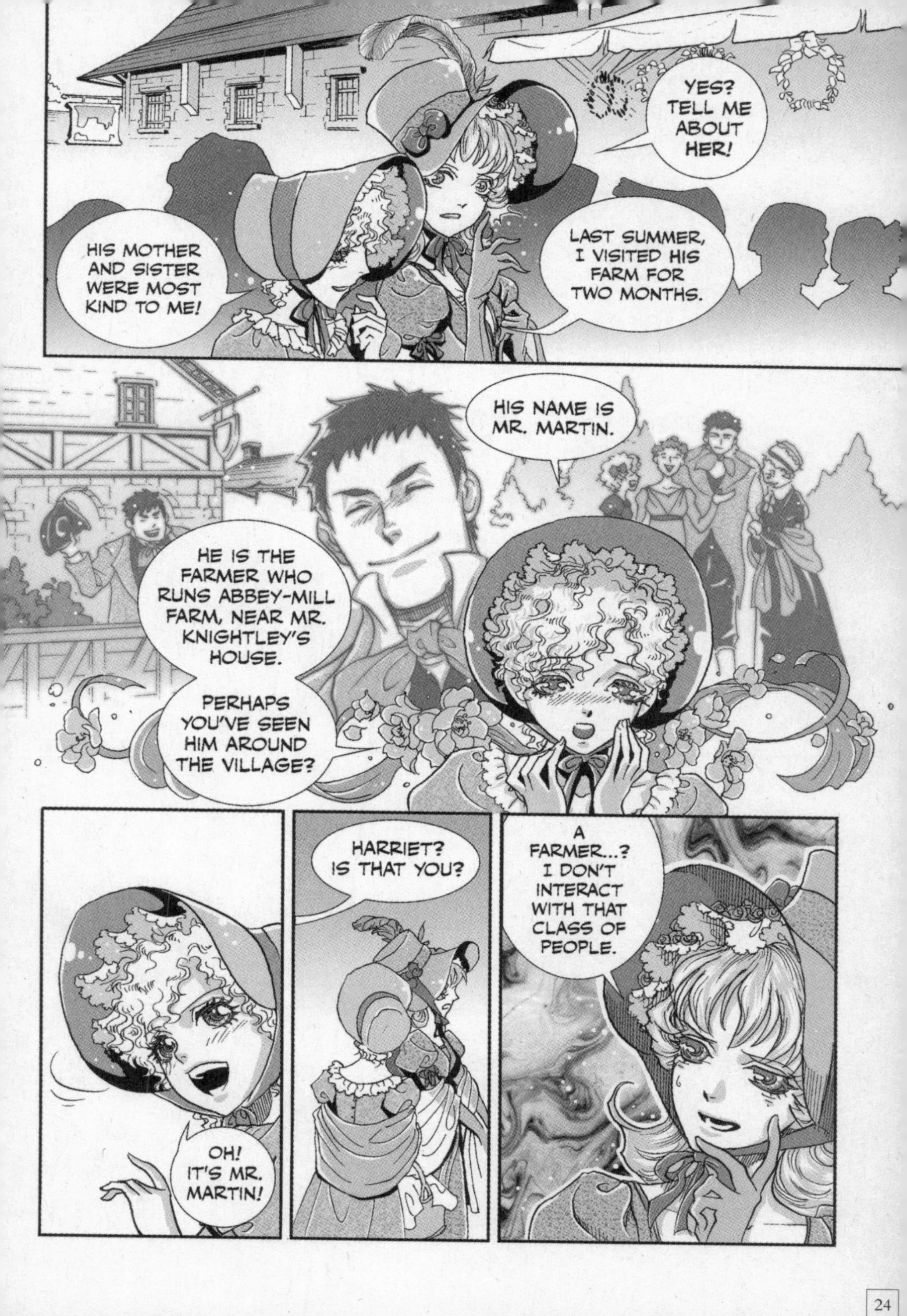
YES? TELL ME ABOUT HER!
LAST SUMMER, I VISITED HIS FARM FOR TWO MONTHS.
HIS MOTHER AND SISTER WERE MOST KIND TO ME!
HIS NAME IS MR. MARTIN.
HE IS THE FARMER WHO RUNS ABBEY-MILL FARM, NEAR MR. KNIGHTLEY'S HOUSE.
PERHAPS YOU'VE SEEN HIM AROUND THE VILLAGE?
A FARMER...? I DON'T INTERACT WITH THAT CLASS OF PEOPLE.
HARRIET? IS THAT YOU?
OH! IT'S MR. MARTIN!

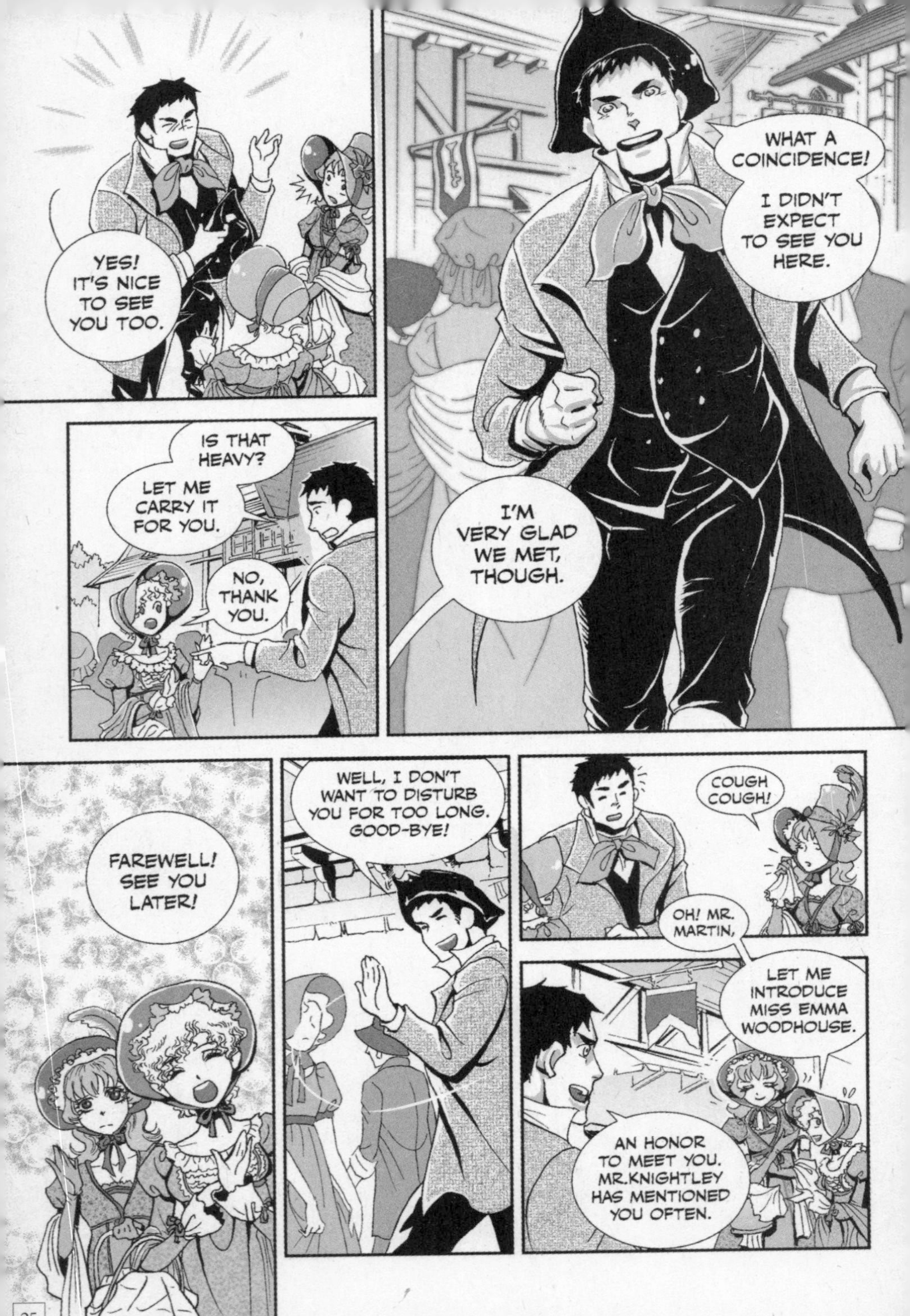
WHAT A COINCIDENCE!
I DIDN'T EXPECT TO SEE YOU HERE.
I'M VERY GLAD WE MET, THOUGH.
YES! IT'S NICE TO SEE YOU TOO.
IS THAT HEAVY?
LET ME CARRY IT FOR YOU.
NO, THANK YOU.
COUGH COUGH!
OH! MR. MARTIN,
LET ME INTRODUCE MISS EMMA WOODHOUSE.
AN HONOR TO MEET YOU. MR.KNIGHTLEY HAS MENTIONED YOU OFTEN.
WELL, I DON'T WANT TO DISTURB YOU FOR TOO LONG. GOOD-BYE!
FAREWELL! SEE YOU LATER!

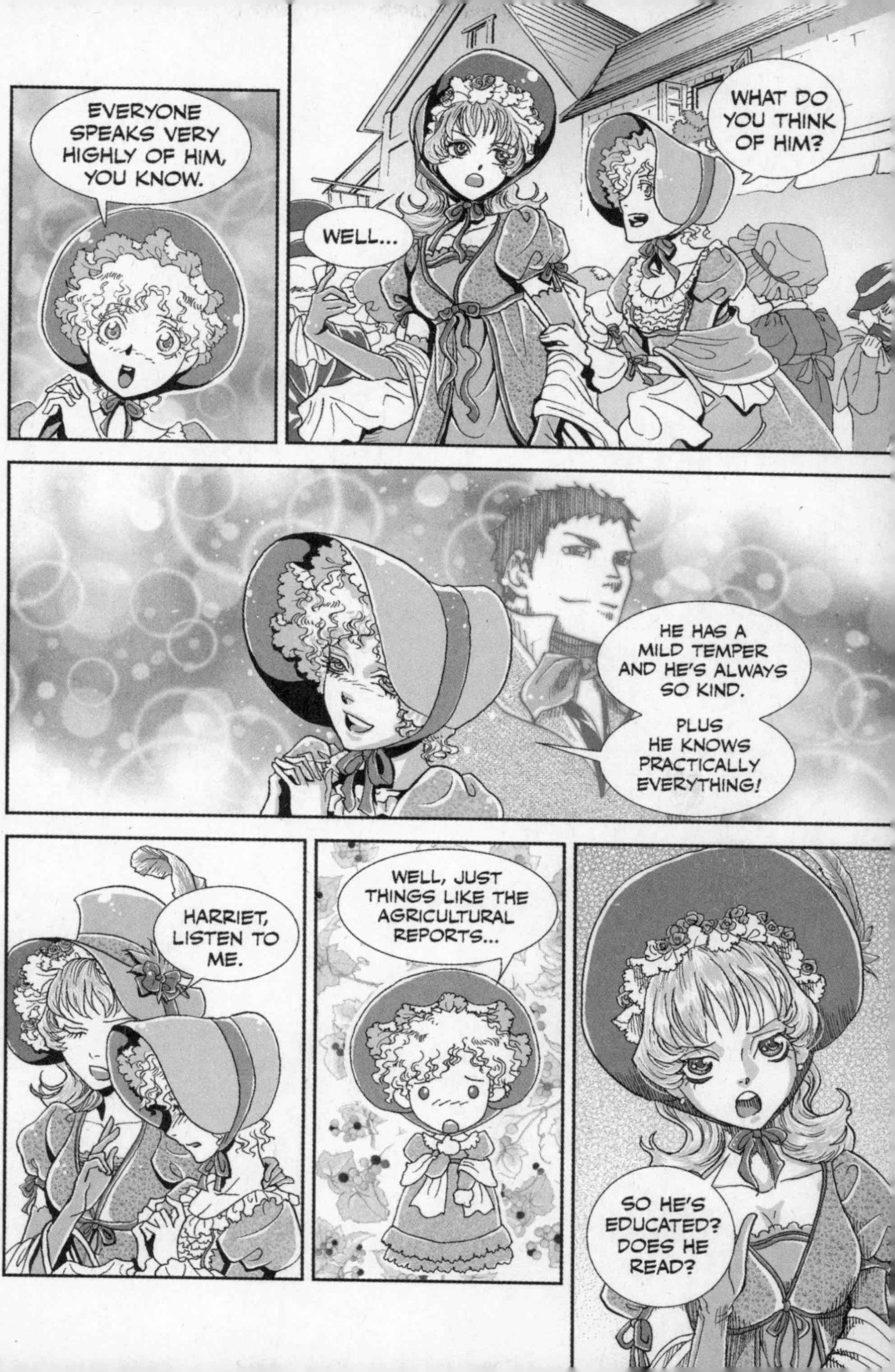
WHAT DO YOU THINK OF HIM?
WELL...
EVERYONE SPEAKS VERY HIGHLY OF HIM, YOU KNOW.
HE HAS A MILD TEMPER AND HE'S ALWAYS SO KIND.
PLUS HE KNOWS PRACTICALLY EVERYTHING!
SO HE'S EDUCATED? DOES HE READ?
WELL, JUST THINGS LIKE THE AGRICULTURAL REPORTS...
HARRIET, LISTEN TO ME.

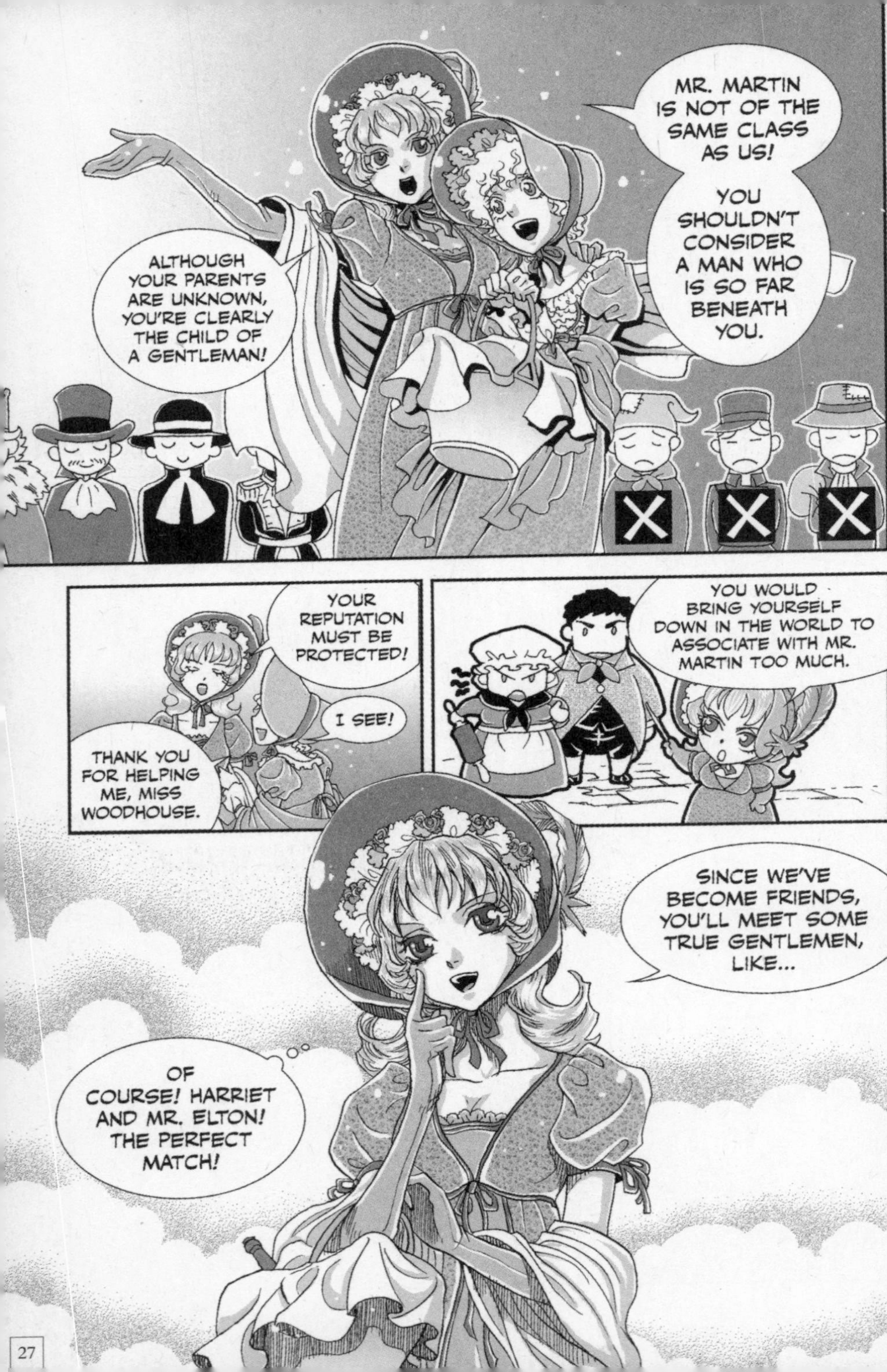
MR. MARTIN IS NOT OF THE SAME CLASS AS US!
YOU SHOULDN'T CONSIDER A MAN WHO IS SO FAR BENEATH YOU.
ALTHOUGH YOUR PARENTS ARE UNKNOWN, YOU'RE CLEARLY THE CHILD OF A GENTLEMAN!
YOU WOULD BRING YOURSELF DOWN IN THE WORLD TO ASSOCIATE WITH MR. MARTIN TOO MUCH.
YOUR REPUTATION MUST BE PROTECTED!
I SEE!
THANK YOU FOR HELPING ME, MISS WOODHOUSE.
SINCE WE'VE BECOME FRIENDS, YOU'LL MEET SOME TRUE GENTLEMEN, LIKE...
OF COURSE! HARRIET AND MR. ELTON! THE PERFECT MATCH!

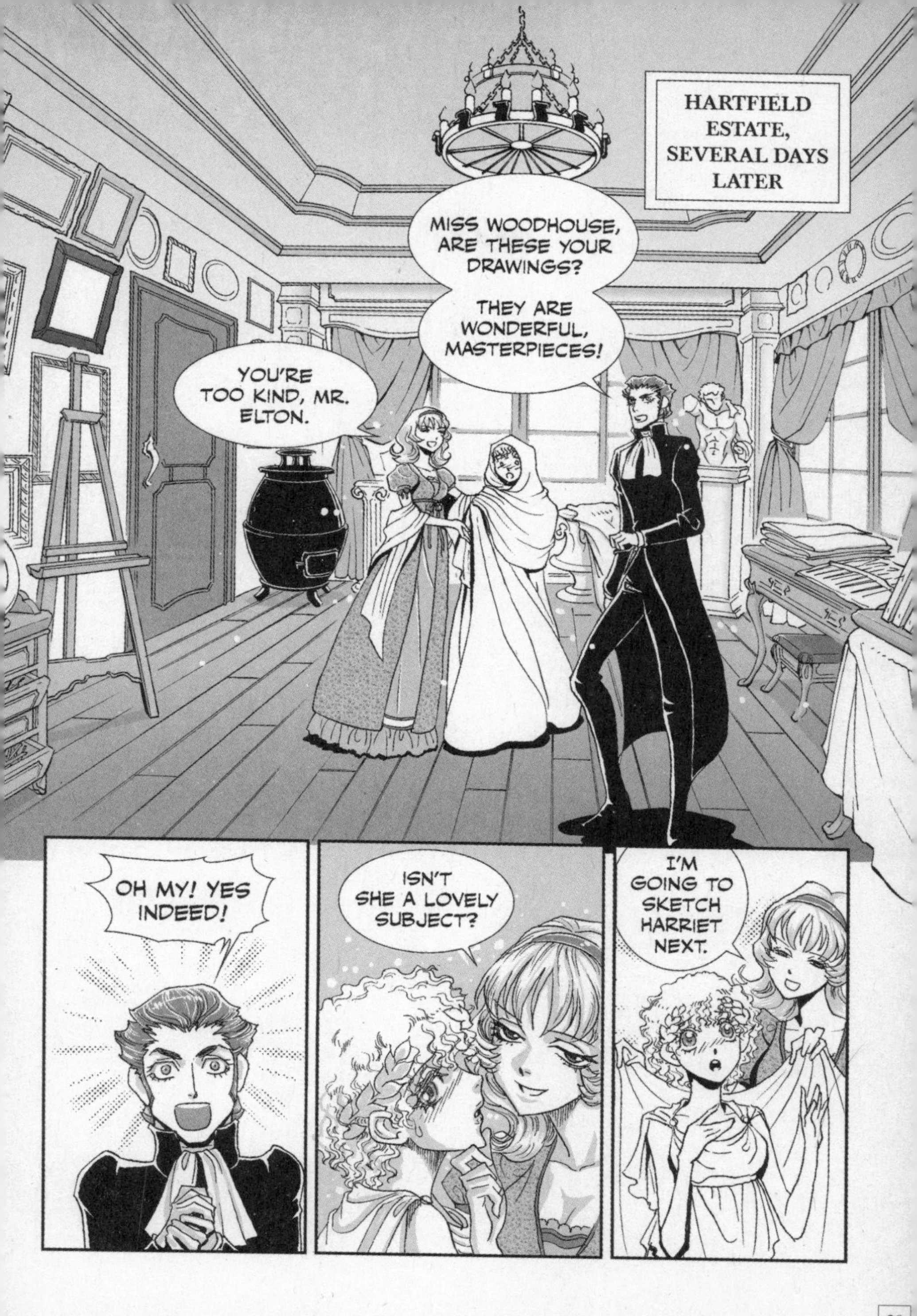
HARTFIELD ESTATE, SEVERAL DAYS LATER
MISS WOODHOUSE, ARE THESE YOUR DRAWINGS?
THEY ARE WONDERFUL, MASTERPIECES!
YOU'RE TOO KIND, MR. ELTON.
I'M GOING TO SKETCH HARRIET NEXT.
ISN'T SHE A LOVELY SUBJECT?
OH MY! YES INDEED!

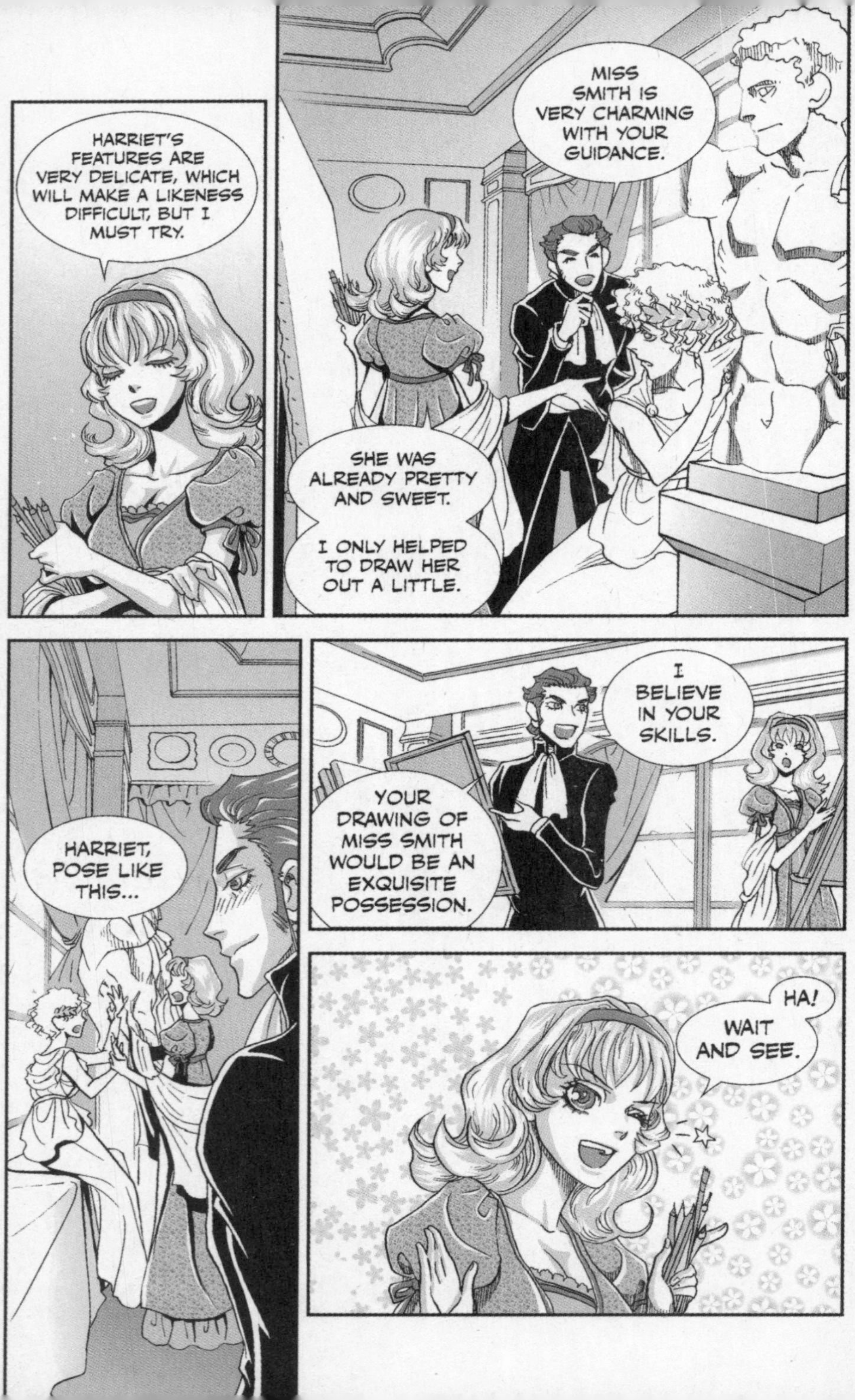
MISS SMITH IS VERY CHARMING WITH YOUR GUIDANCE.
SHE WAS ALREADY PRETTY AND SWEET.
I ONLY HELPED TO DRAW HER OUT A LITTLE.
HARRIET'S FEATURES ARE VERY DELICATE, WHICH WILL MAKE A LIKENESS DIFFICULT, BUT I MUST TRY.
I BELIEVE IN YOUR SKILLS.
YOUR DRAWING OF MISS SMITH WOULD BE AN EXQUISITE POSSESSION.
HA!
WAIT AND SEE.
HARRIET, POSE LIKE THIS...

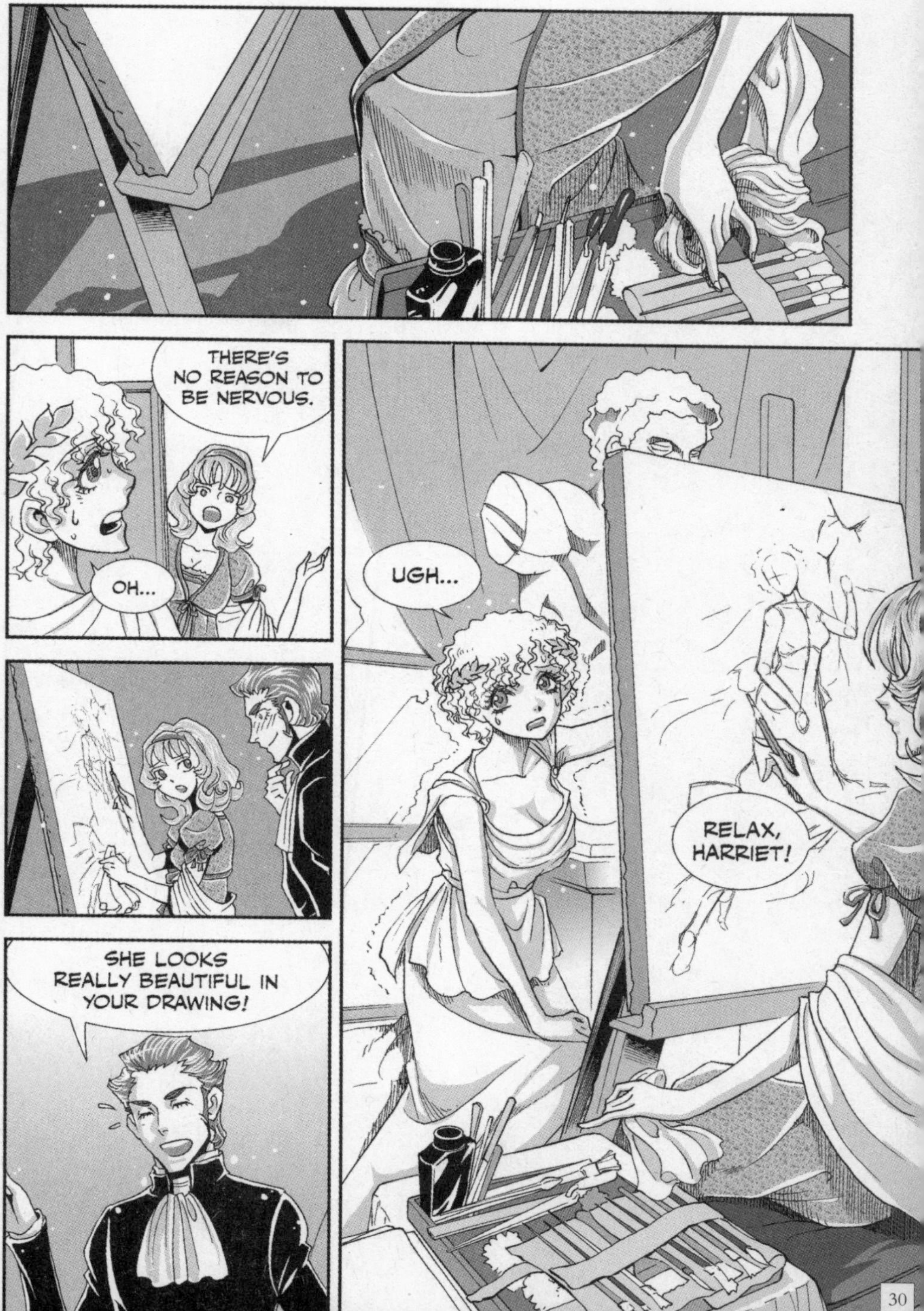
UGH...
RELAX, HARRIET!
THERE'S NO REASON TO BE NERVOUS.
OH...
SHE LOOKS REALLY BEAUTIFUL IN YOUR DRAWING!

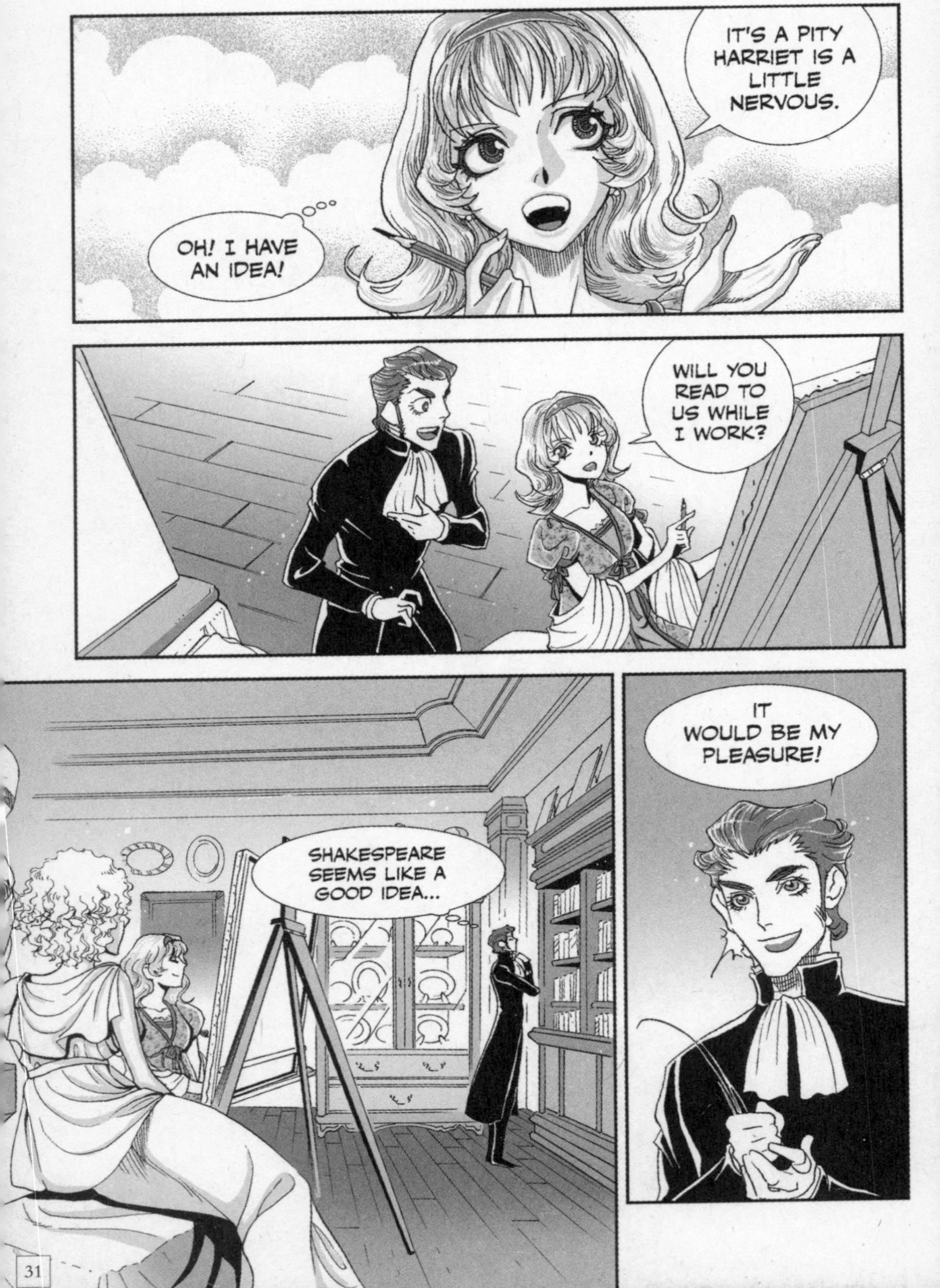
IT'S A PITY HARRIET IS A LITTLE NERVOUS.
OH! I HAVE AN IDEA!
WILL YOU READ TO US WHILE I WORK?
IT WOULD BE MY PLEASURE!
SHAKESPEARE SEEMS LIKE A GOOD IDEA...

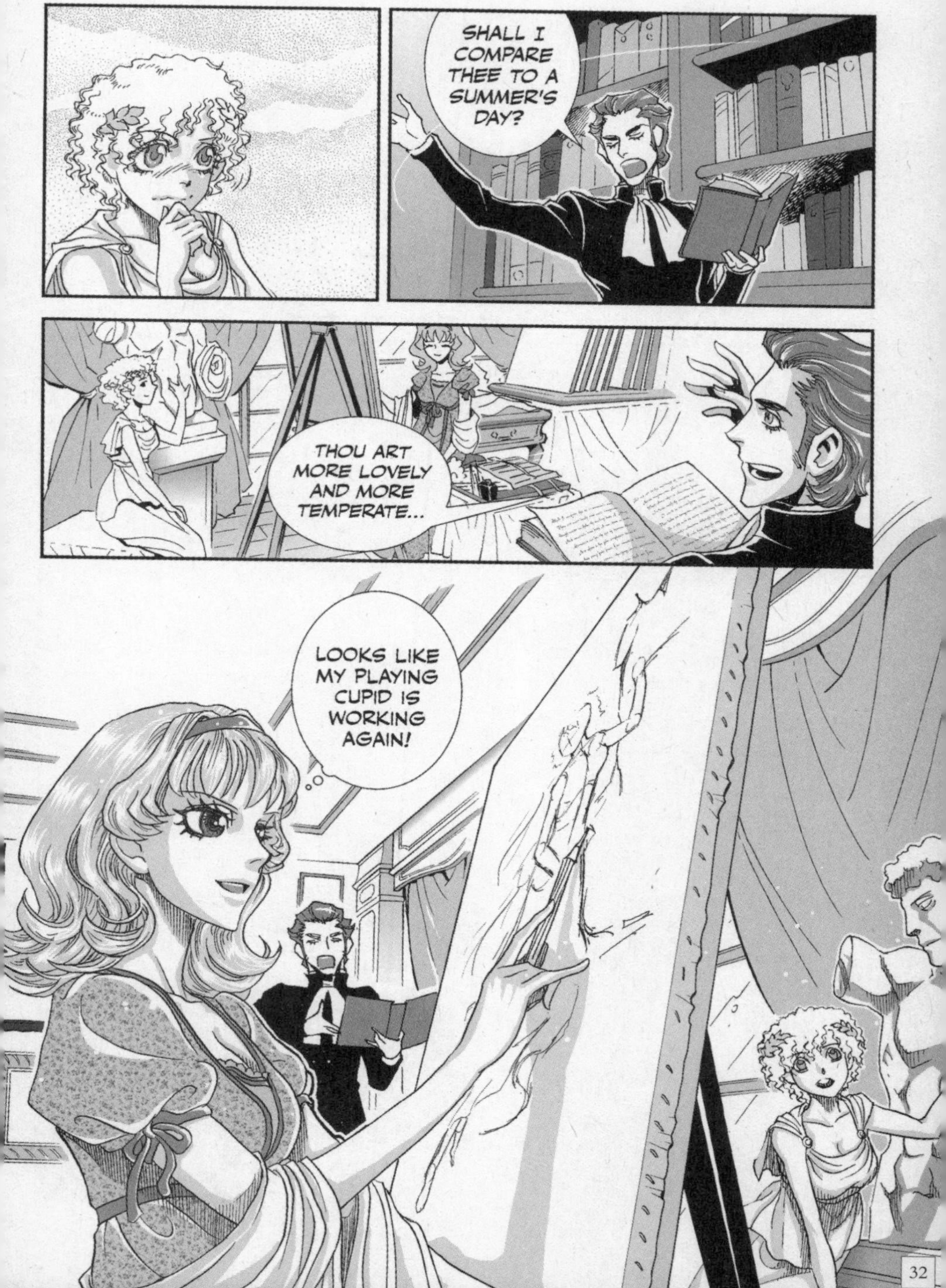
SHALL I COMPARE THEE TO A SUMMER'S DAY?
THOU ART MORE LOVELY AND MORE TEMPERATE...
LOOKS LIKE MY PLAYING CUPID IS WORKING AGAIN!

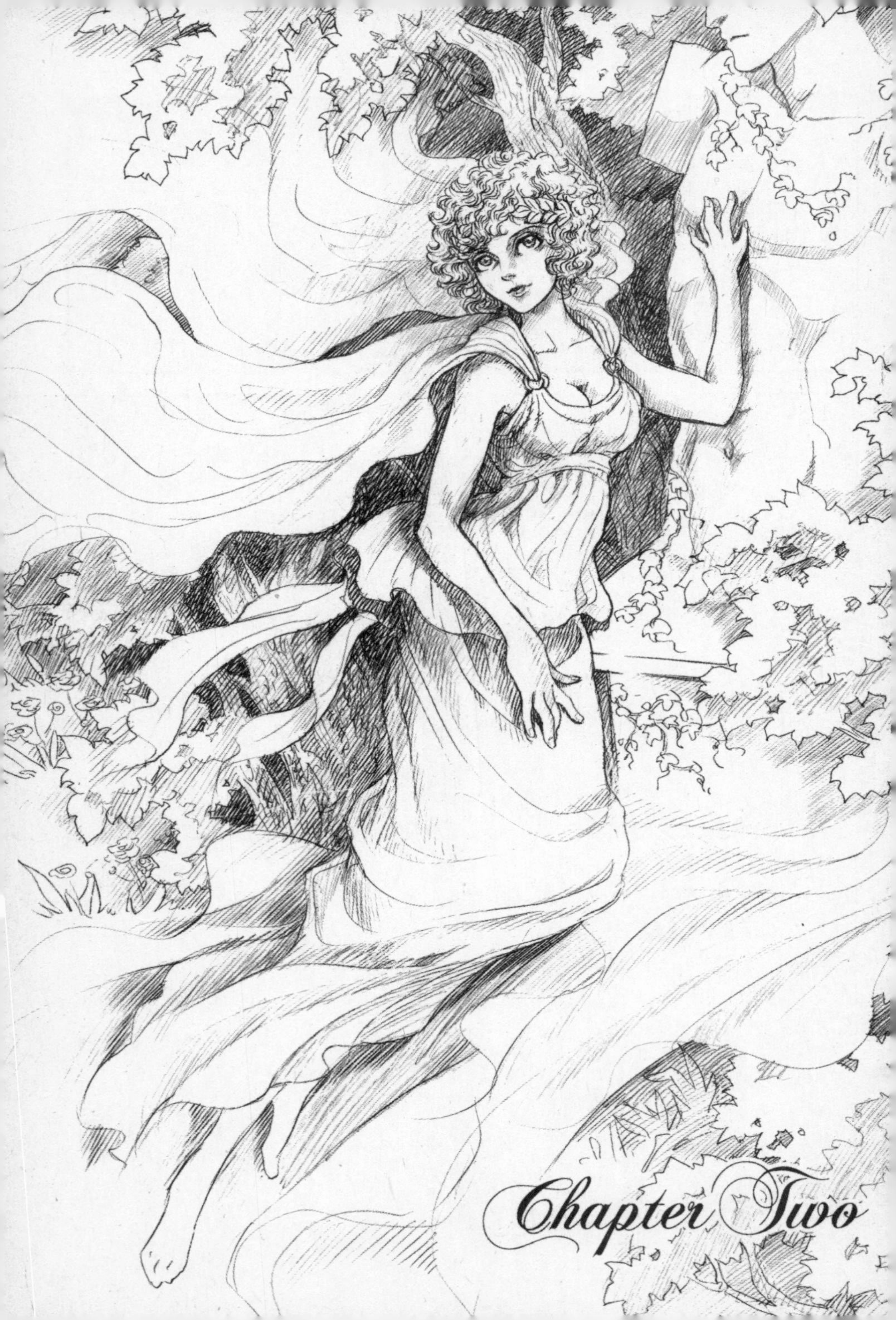

Chapter Two

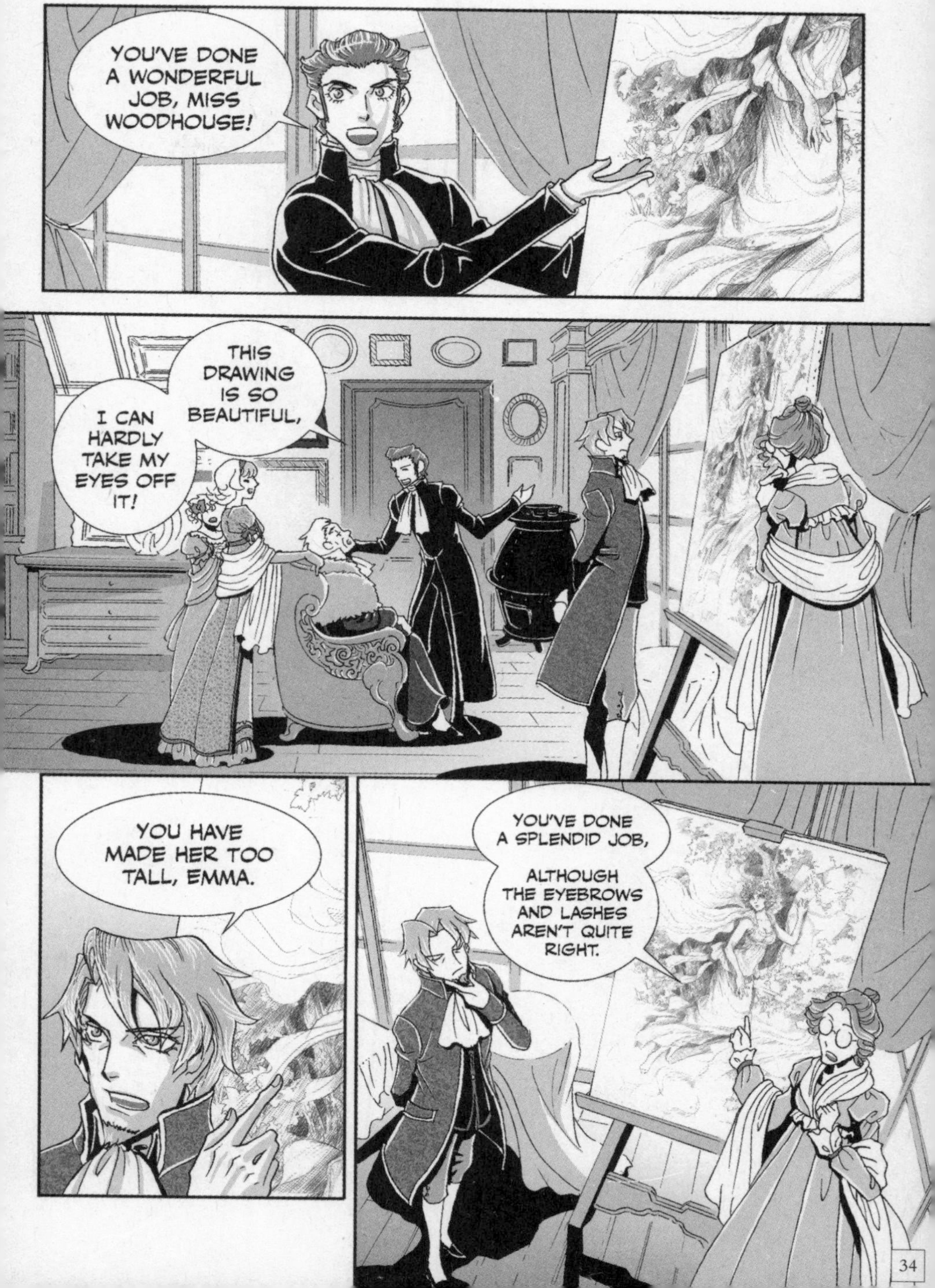
YOU'VE DONE A WONDERFUL JOB, MISS WOODHOUSE!
THIS DRAWING IS SO BEAUTIFUL,
I CAN HARDLY TAKE MY EYES OFF IT!
YOU'VE DONE A SPLENDID JOB,
ALTHOUGH THE EYEBROWS AND LASHES AREN'T QUITE RIGHT.
YOU HAVE MADE HER TOO TALL, EMMA.

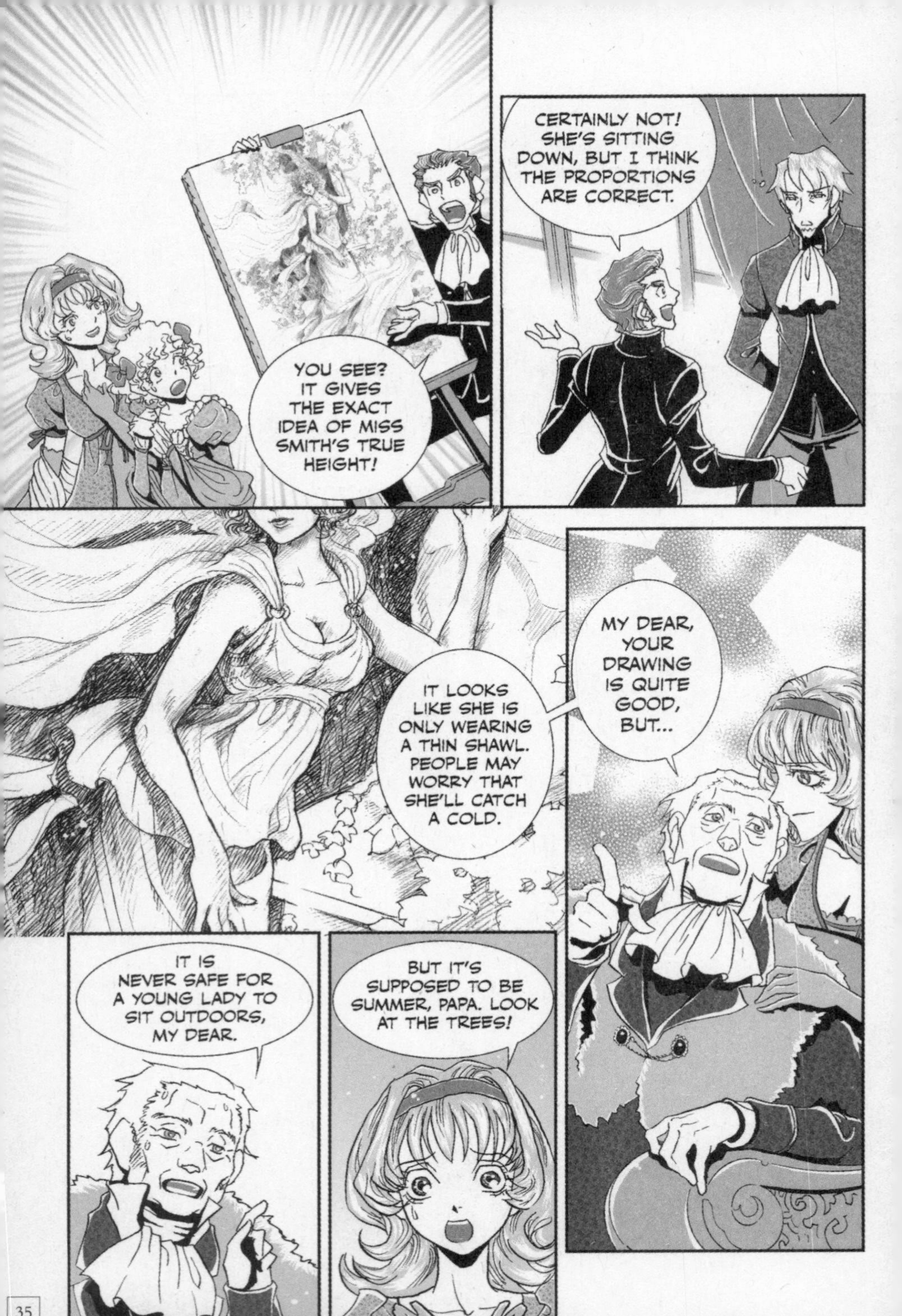
CERTAINLY NOT! SHE'S SITTING DOWN, BUT I THINK THE PROPORTIONS ARE CORRECT.
YOU SEE? IT GIVES THE EXACT IDEA OF MISS SMITH'S TRUE HEIGHT!
MY DEAR, YOUR DRAWING IS QUITE GOOD, BUT...
IT LOOKS LIKE SHE IS ONLY WEARING A THIN SHAWL. PEOPLE MAY WORRY THAT SHE'LL CATCH A COLD.
BUT IT'S SUPPOSED TO BE SUMMER, PAPA. LOOK AT THE TREES!
IT IS NEVER SAFE FOR A YOUNG LADY TO SIT OUTDOORS, MY DEAR.

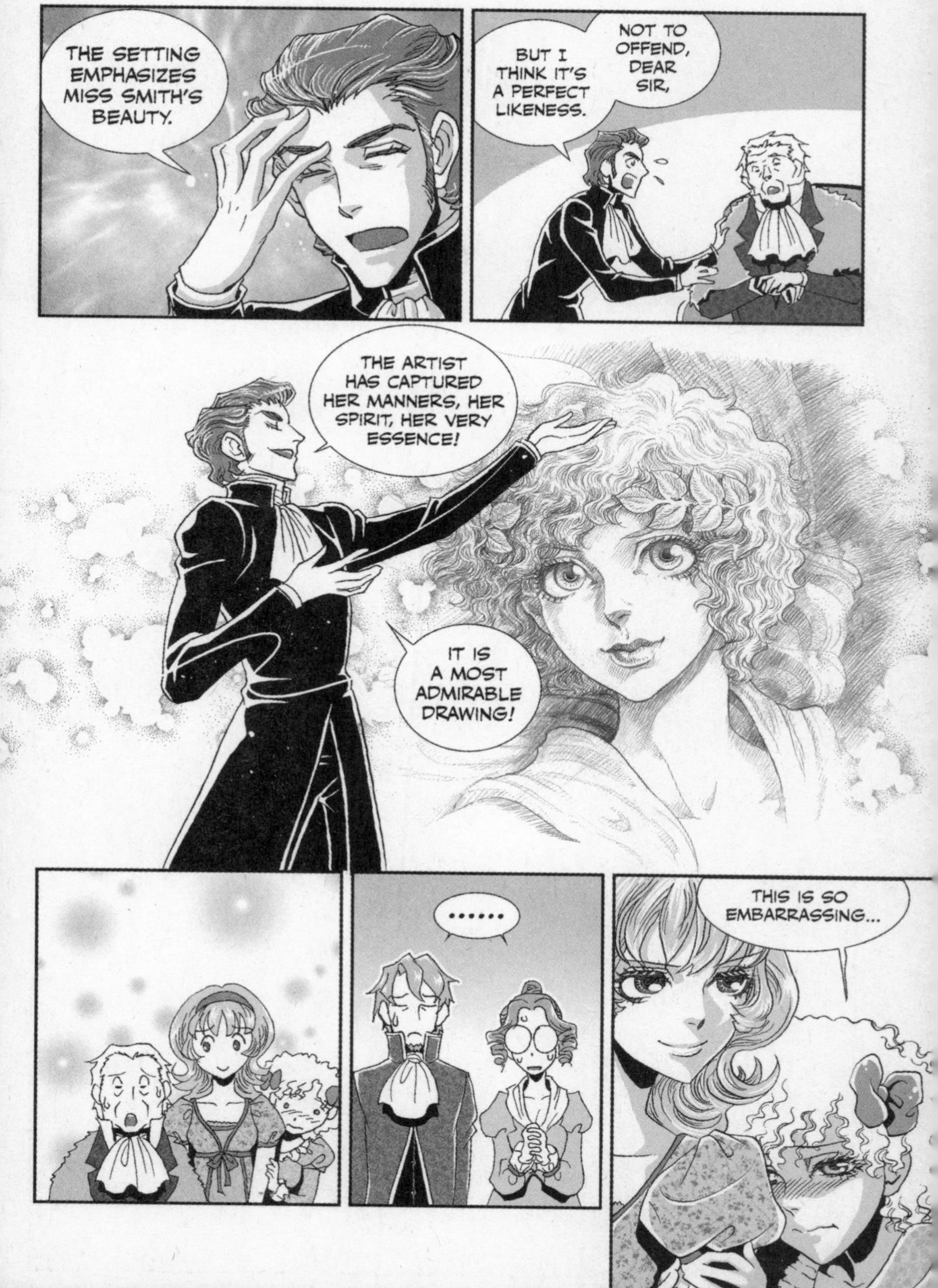
NOT TO OFFEND, DEAR SIR,
BUT I THINK IT'S A PERFECT LIKENESS.
THE SETTING EMPHASIZES MISS SMITH'S BEAUTY.
THE ARTIST HAS CAPTURED HER MANNERS, HER SPIRIT, HER VERY ESSENCE!
IT IS A MOST ADMIRABLE DRAWING!
THIS IS SO EMBARRASSING...
......

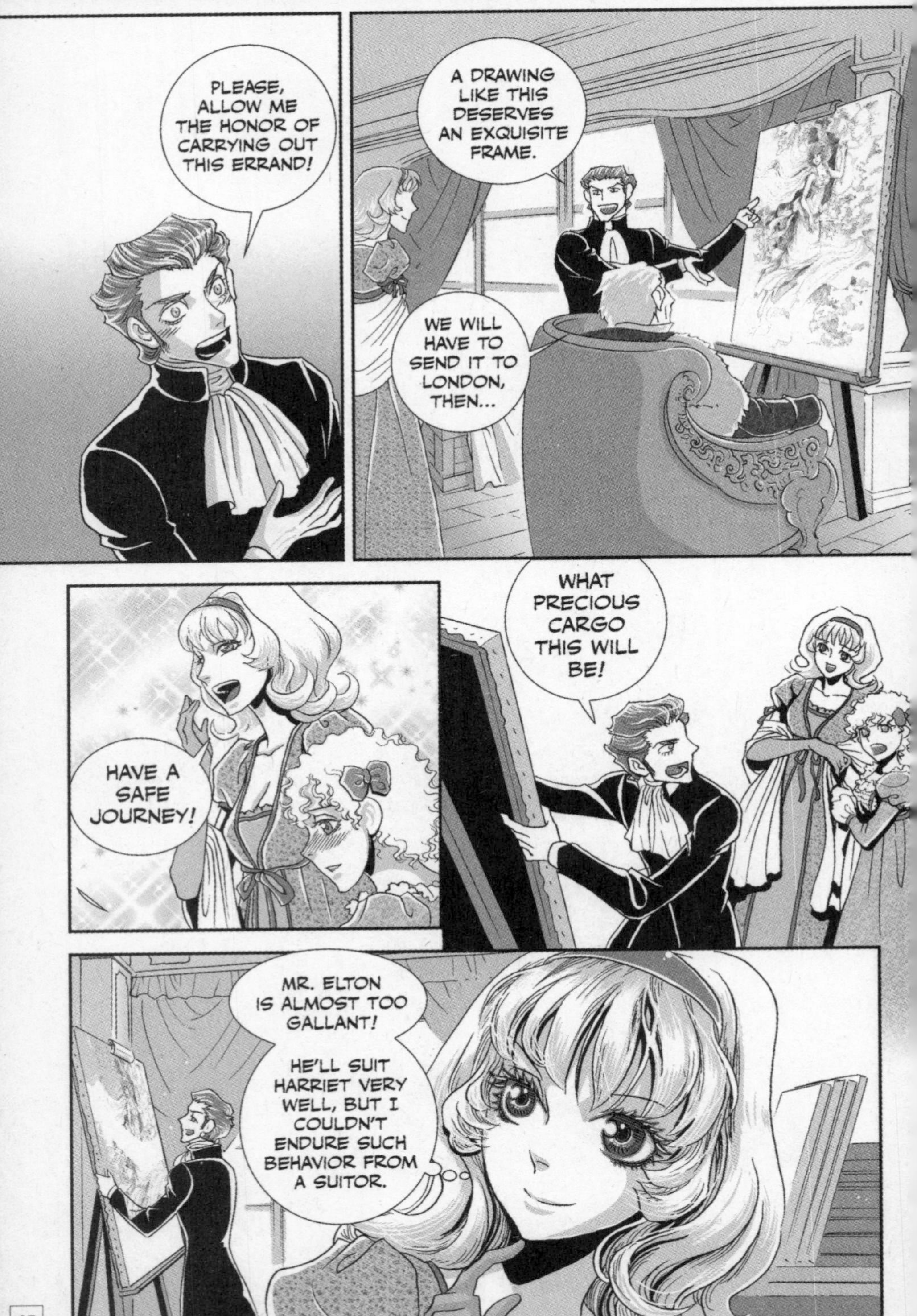
A DRAWING LIKE THIS DESERVES AN EXQUISITE FRAME.
WE WILL HAVE TO SEND IT TO LONDON, THEN...
PLEASE, ALLOW ME THE HONOR OF CARRYING OUT THIS ERRAND!
WHAT PRECIOUS CARGO THIS WILL BE!
HAVE A SAFE JOURNEY!
MR. ELTON IS ALMOST TOO GALLANT!
HE'LL SUIT HARRIET VERY WELL, BUT I COULDN'T ENDURE SUCH BEHAVIOR FROM A SUITOR.

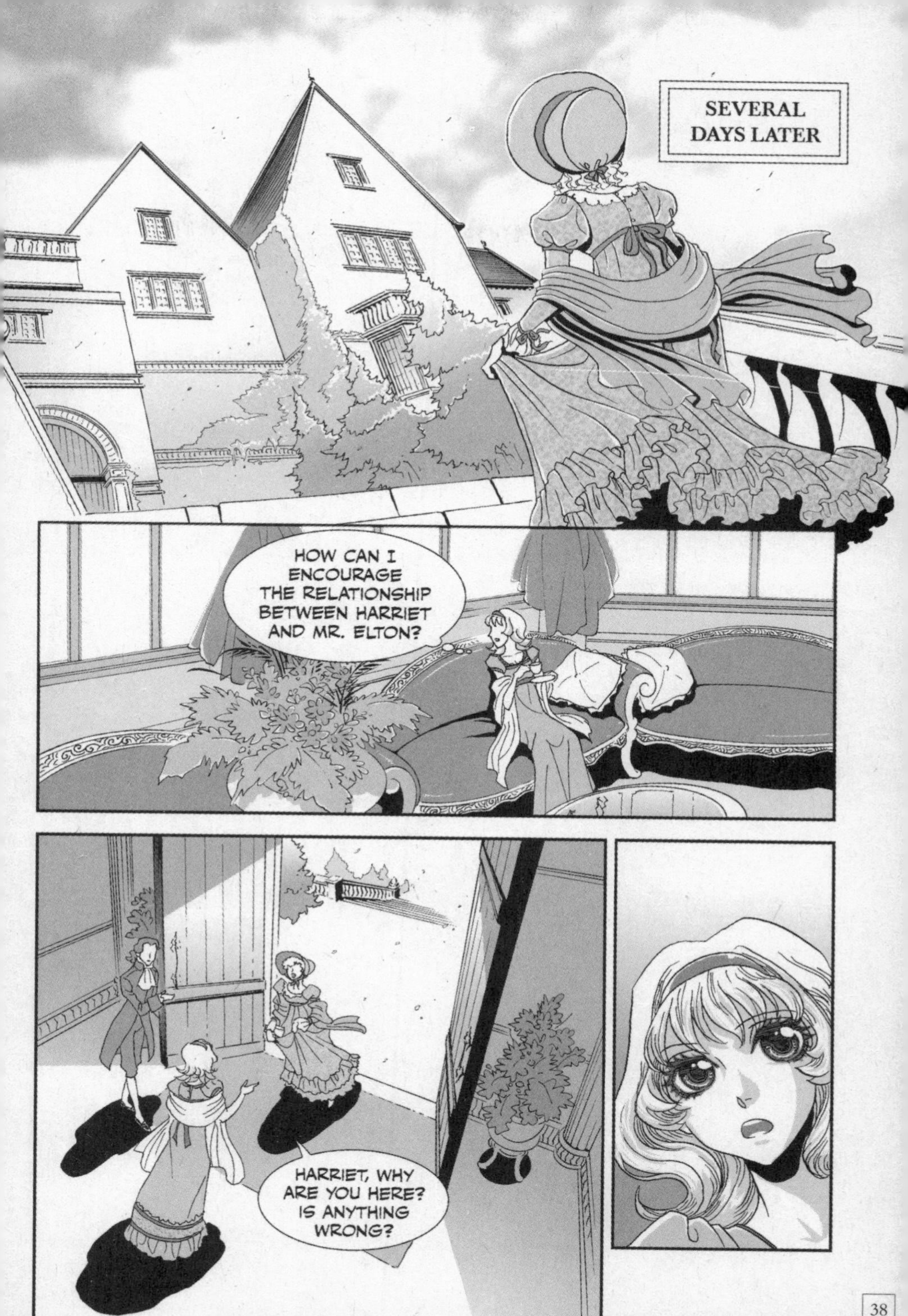
SEVERAL DAYS LATER
HOW CAN I ENCOURAGE THE RELATIONSHIP BETWEEN HARRIET AND MR. ELTON?
HARRIET, WHY ARE YOU HERE? IS ANYTHING WRONG?

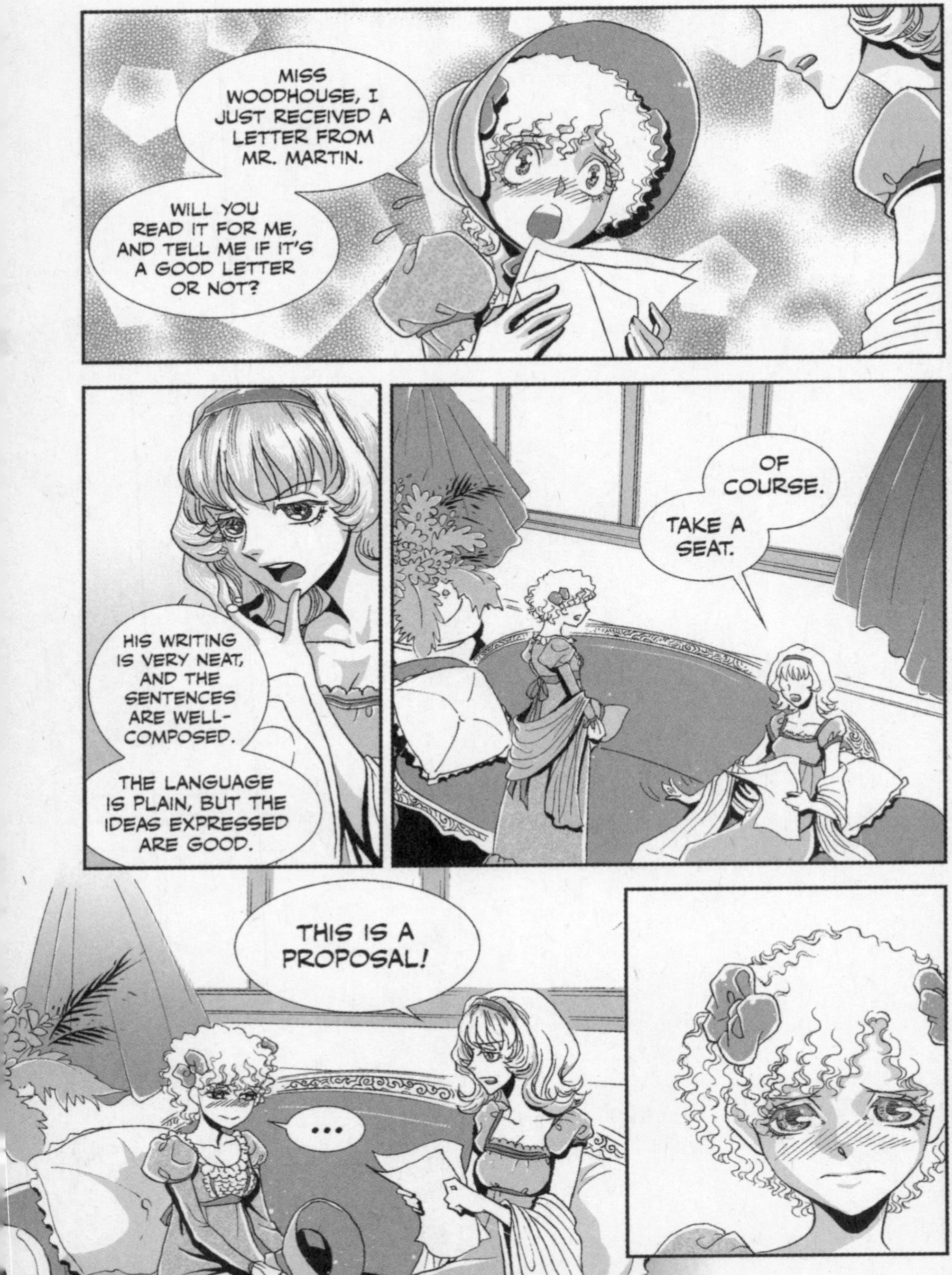
MISS WOODHOUSE, I JUST RECEIVED A LETTER FROM MR. MARTIN.
WILL YOU READ IT FOR ME, AND TELL ME IF IT'S A GOOD LETTER OR NOT?
OF COURSE.
TAKE A SEAT.
HIS WRITING IS VERY NEAT, AND THE SENTENCES ARE WELL-COMPOSED.
THE LANGUAGE IS PLAIN, BUT THE IDEAS EXPRESSED ARE GOOD.
THIS IS A PROPOSAL!
...

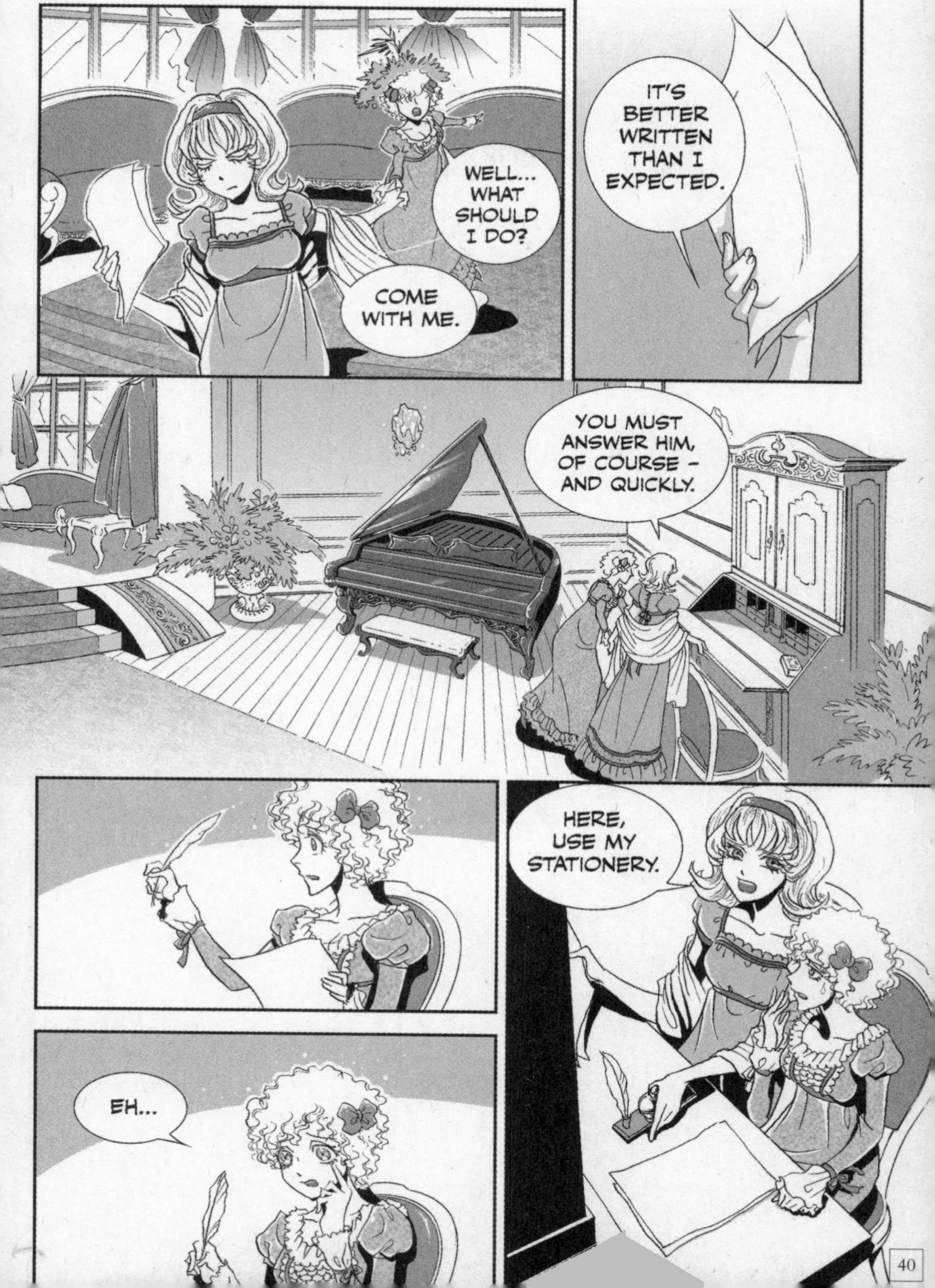
IT'S BETTER WRITTEN THAN I EXPECTED.
WELL... WHAT SHOULD I DO?
COME WITH ME.
YOU MUST ANSWER HIM, OF COURSE – AND QUICKLY.
HERE, USE MY STATIONERY.
EH...

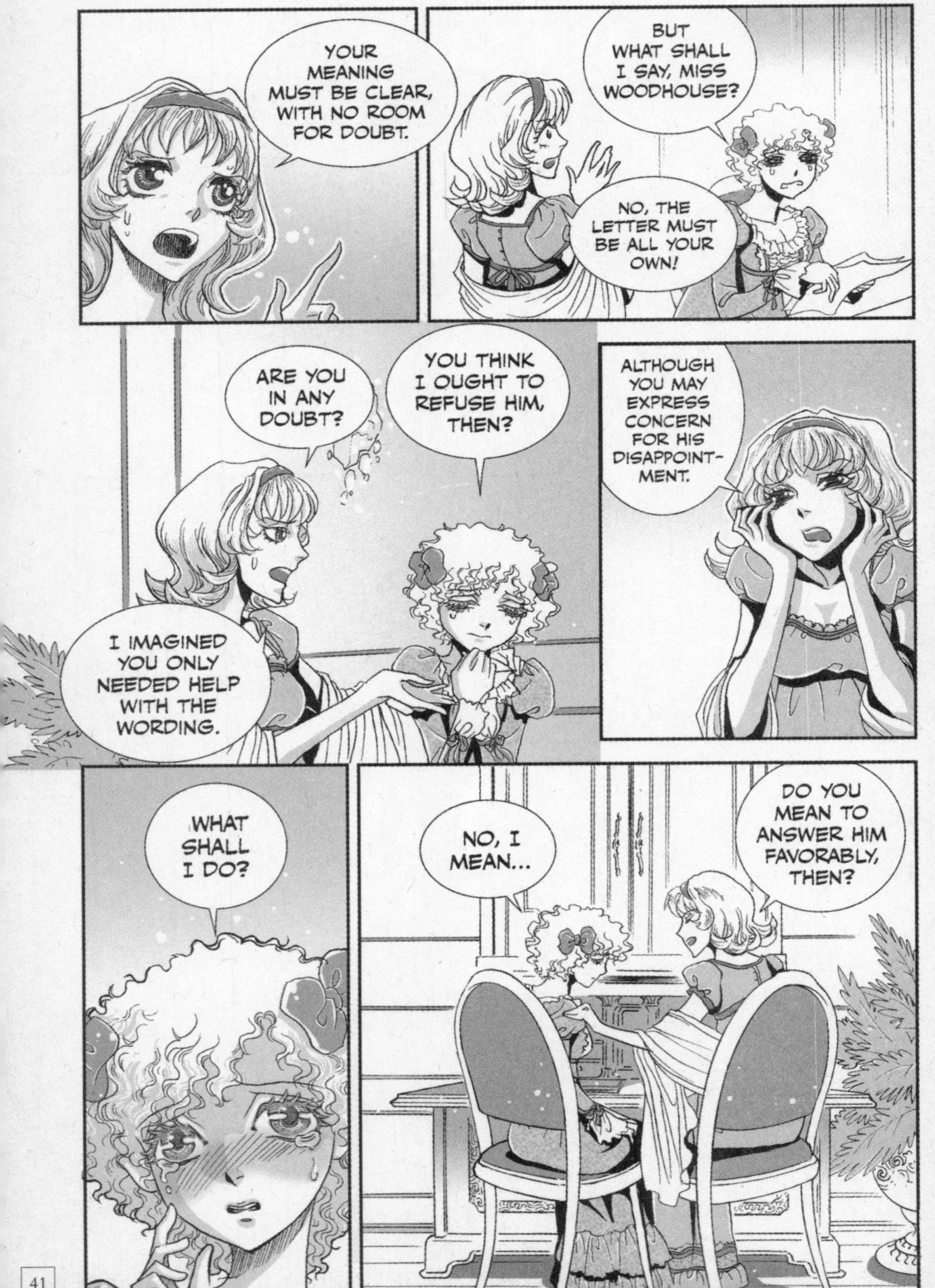
BUT WHAT SHALL I SAY, MISS WOODHOUSE?
NO, THE LETTER MUST BE ALL YOUR OWN!
YOUR MEANING MUST BE CLEAR, WITH NO ROOM FOR DOUBT.
ALTHOUGH YOU MAY EXPRESS CONCERN FOR HIS DISAPPOINTMENT.
YOU THINK I OUGHT TO REFUSE HIM, THEN?
ARE YOU IN ANY DOUBT?
I IMAGINED YOU ONLY NEEDED HELP WITH THE WORDING.
DO YOU MEAN TO ANSWER HIM FAVORABLY, THEN?
NO, I MEAN...
WHAT SHALL I DO?

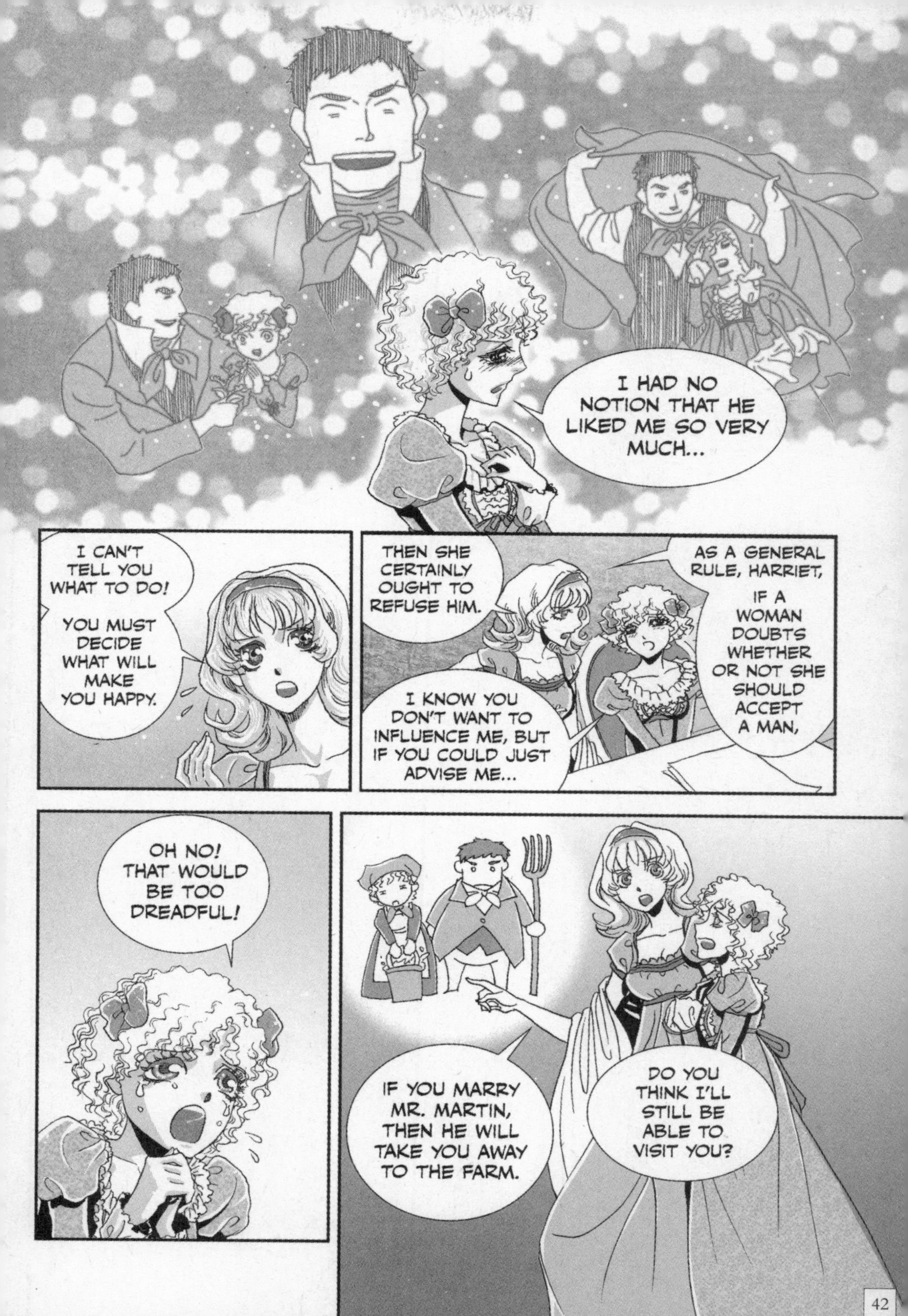

I HAD NO NOTION THAT HE LIKED ME SO VERY MUCH...
AS A GENERAL RULE, HARRIET,
IF A WOMAN DOUBTS WHETHER OR NOT SHE SHOULD ACCEPT A MAN,
THEN SHE CERTAINLY OUGHT TO REFUSE HIM.
I KNOW YOU DON'T WANT TO INFLUENCE ME, BUT IF YOU COULD JUST ADVISE ME...
I CAN'T TELL YOU WHAT TO DO!
YOU MUST DECIDE WHAT WILL MAKE YOU HAPPY.
DO YOU THINK I'LL STILL BE ABLE TO VISIT YOU?
IF YOU MARRY MR. MARTIN, THEN HE WILL TAKE YOU AWAY TO THE FARM.
OH NO! THAT WOULD BE TOO DREADFUL!

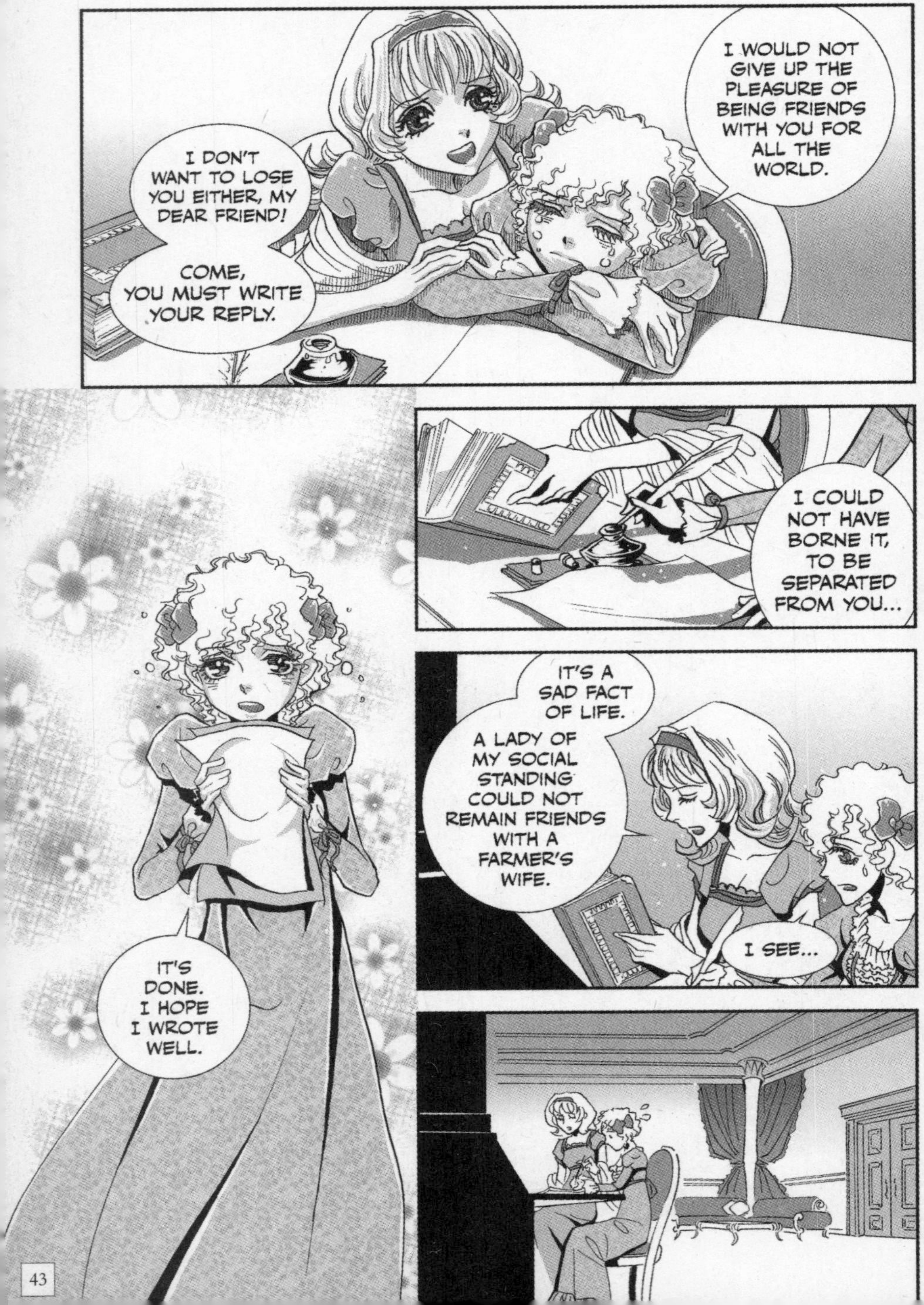
I WOULD NOT GIVE UP THE PLEASURE OF BEING FRIENDS WITH YOU FOR ALL THE WORLD.
I DON'T WANT TO LOSE YOU EITHER, MY DEAR FRIEND!
COME, YOU MUST WRITE YOUR REPLY.
I COULD NOT HAVE BORNE IT, TO BE SEPARATED FROM YOU...
IT'S A SAD FACT OF LIFE.
A LADY OF MY SOCIAL STANDING COULD NOT REMAIN FRIENDS WITH A FARMER'S WIFE.
I SEE...
IT'S DONE. I HOPE I WROTE WELL.

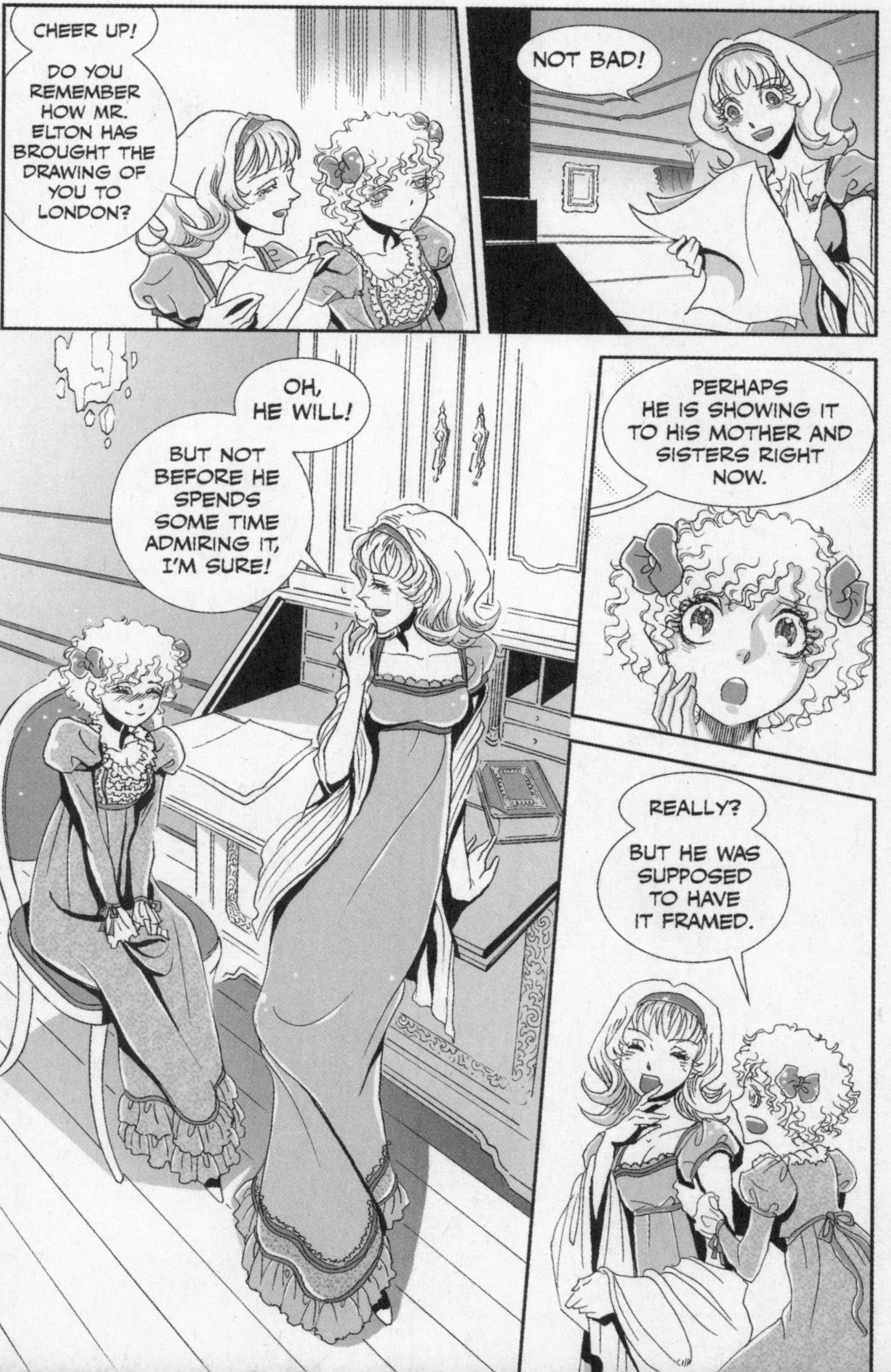
NOT BAD!
CHEER UP!
DO YOU REMEMBER HOW MR. ELTON HAS BROUGHT THE DRAWING OF YOU TO LONDON?
PERHAPS HE IS SHOWING IT TO HIS MOTHER AND SISTERS RIGHT NOW.
REALLY?
BUT HE WAS SUPPOSED TO HAVE IT FRAMED.
OH, HE WILL!
BUT NOT BEFORE HE SPENDS SOME TIME ADMIRING IT, I'M SURE!

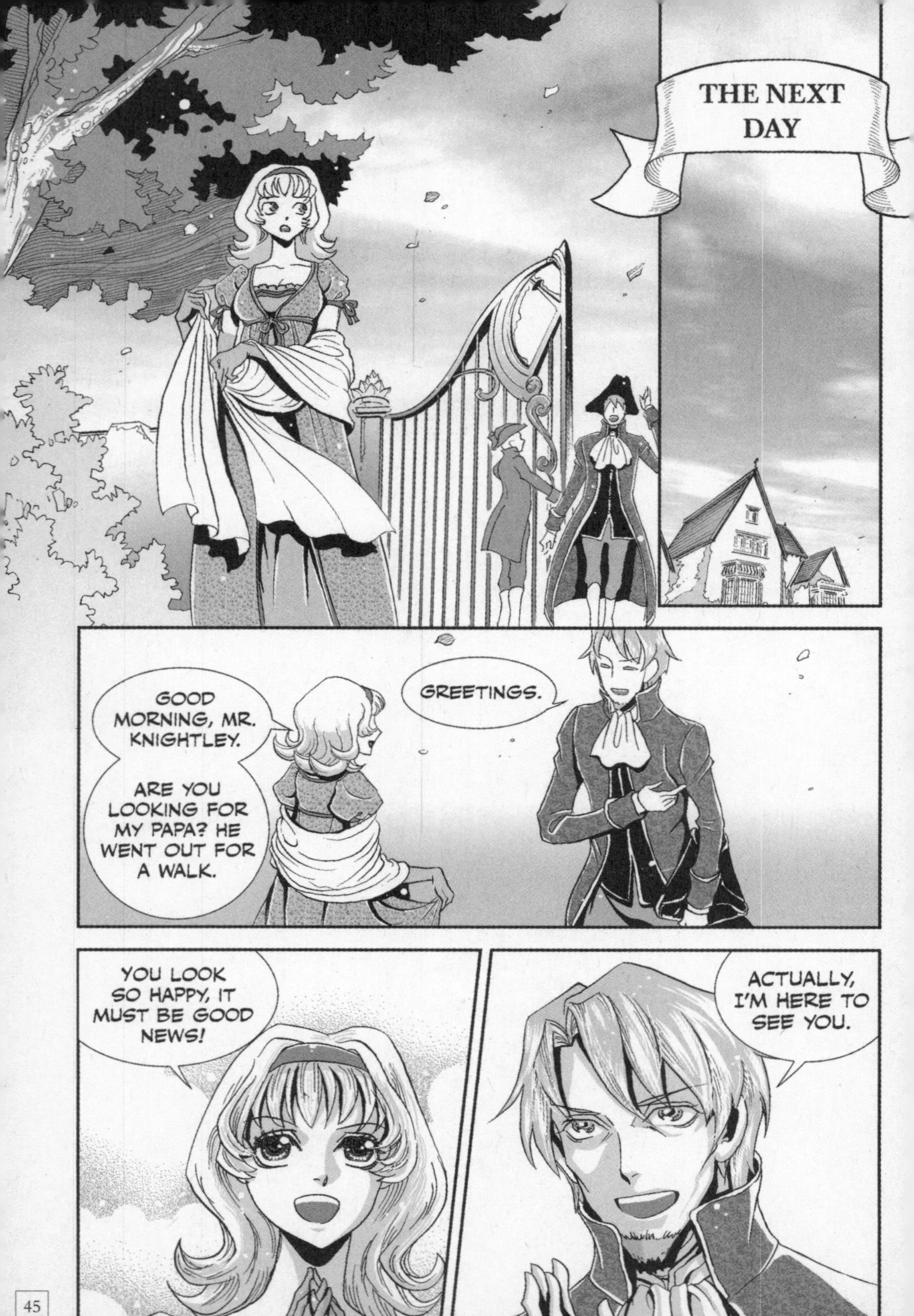
THE NEXT DAY
GREETINGS.
GOOD MORNING, MR. KNIGHTLEY.
ARE YOU LOOKING FOR MY PAPA? HE WENT OUT FOR A WALK.
ACTUALLY, I'M HERE TO SEE YOU.
YOU LOOK SO HAPPY, IT MUST BE GOOD NEWS!

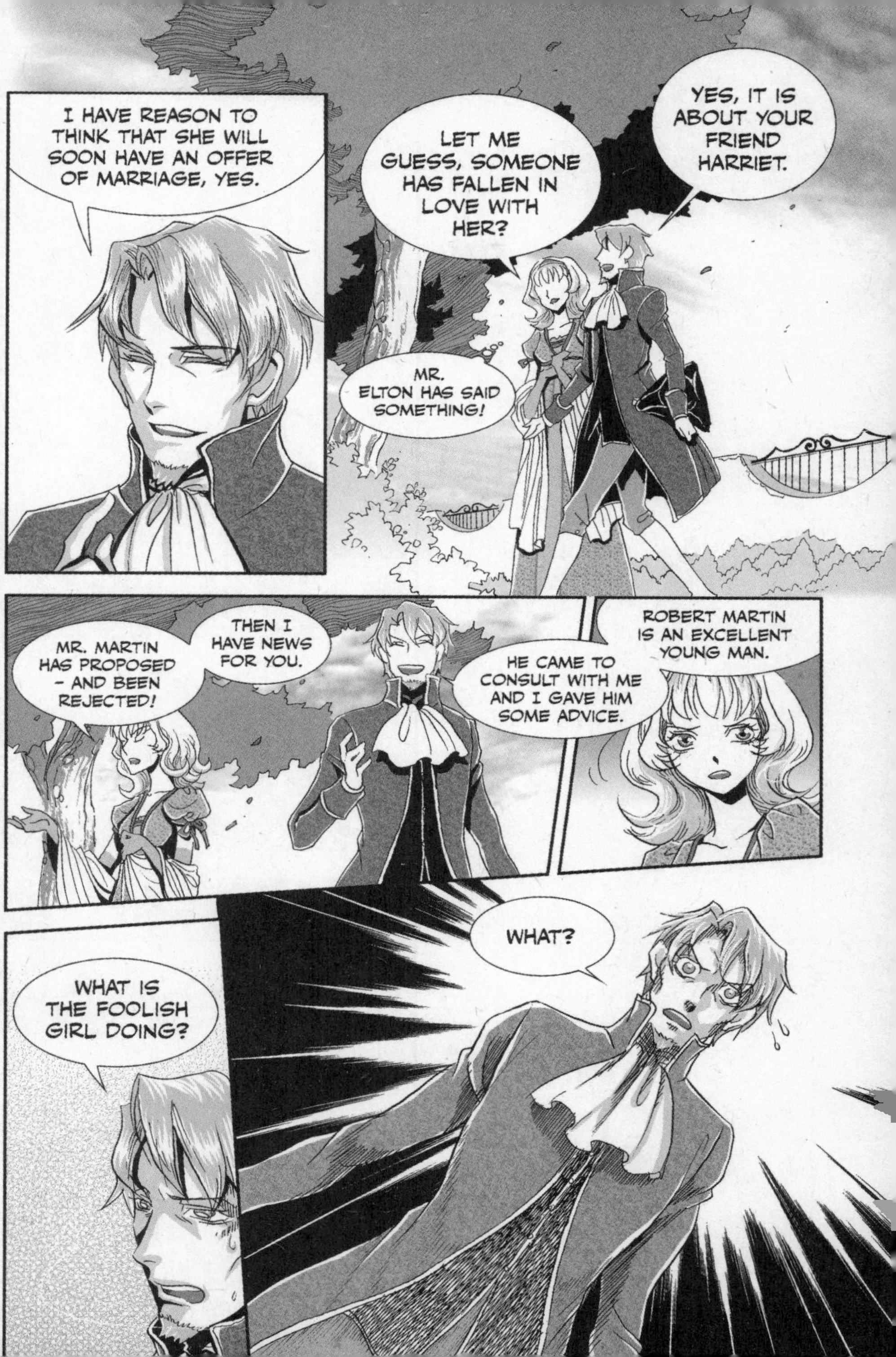
YES, IT IS ABOUT YOUR FRIEND HARRIET.
LET ME GUESS, SOMEONE HAS FALLEN IN LOVE WITH HER?
MR. ELTON HAS SAID SOMETHING!
I HAVE REASON TO THINK THAT SHE WILL SOON HAVE AN OFFER OF MARRIAGE, YES.
ROBERT MARTIN IS AN EXCELLENT YOUNG MAN.
HE CAME TO CONSULT WITH ME AND I GAVE HIM SOME ADVICE.
THEN I HAVE NEWS FOR YOU.
MR. MARTIN HAS PROPOSED - AND BEEN REJECTED!
WHAT?
WHAT IS THE FOOLISH GIRL DOING?

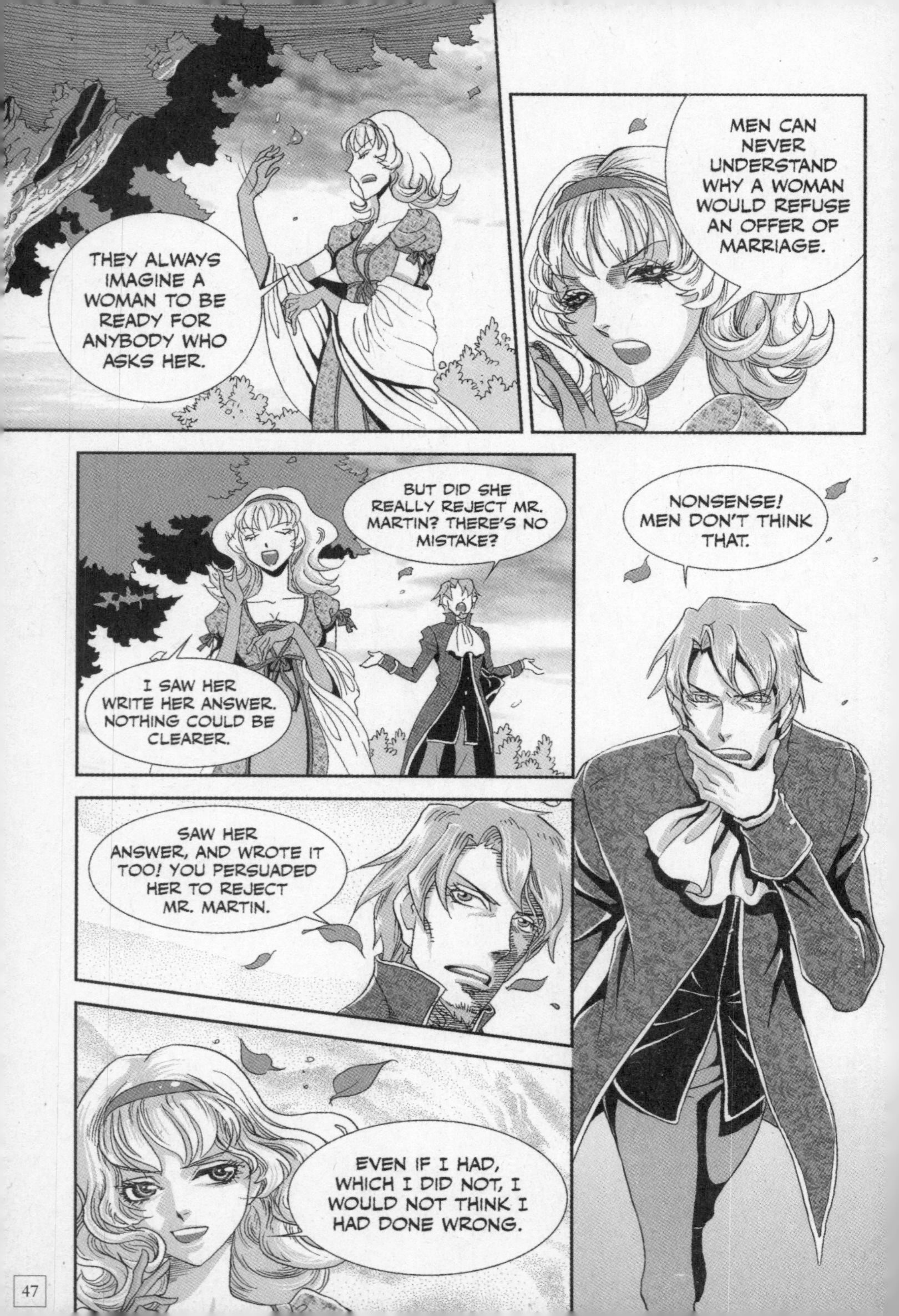
MEN CAN NEVER UNDERSTAND WHY A WOMAN WOULD REFUSE AN OFFER OF MARRIAGE.
THEY ALWAYS IMAGINE A WOMAN TO BE READY FOR ANYBODY WHO ASKS HER.
NONSENSE! MEN DON'T THINK THAT.
BUT DID SHE REALLY REJECT MR. MARTIN? THERE'S NO MISTAKE?
I SAW HER WRITE HER ANSWER. NOTHING COULD BE CLEARER.
SAW HER ANSWER, AND WROTE IT TOO! YOU PERSUADED HER TO REJECT MR. MARTIN.
EVEN IF I HAD, WHICH I DID NOT, I WOULD NOT THINK I HAD DONE WRONG.

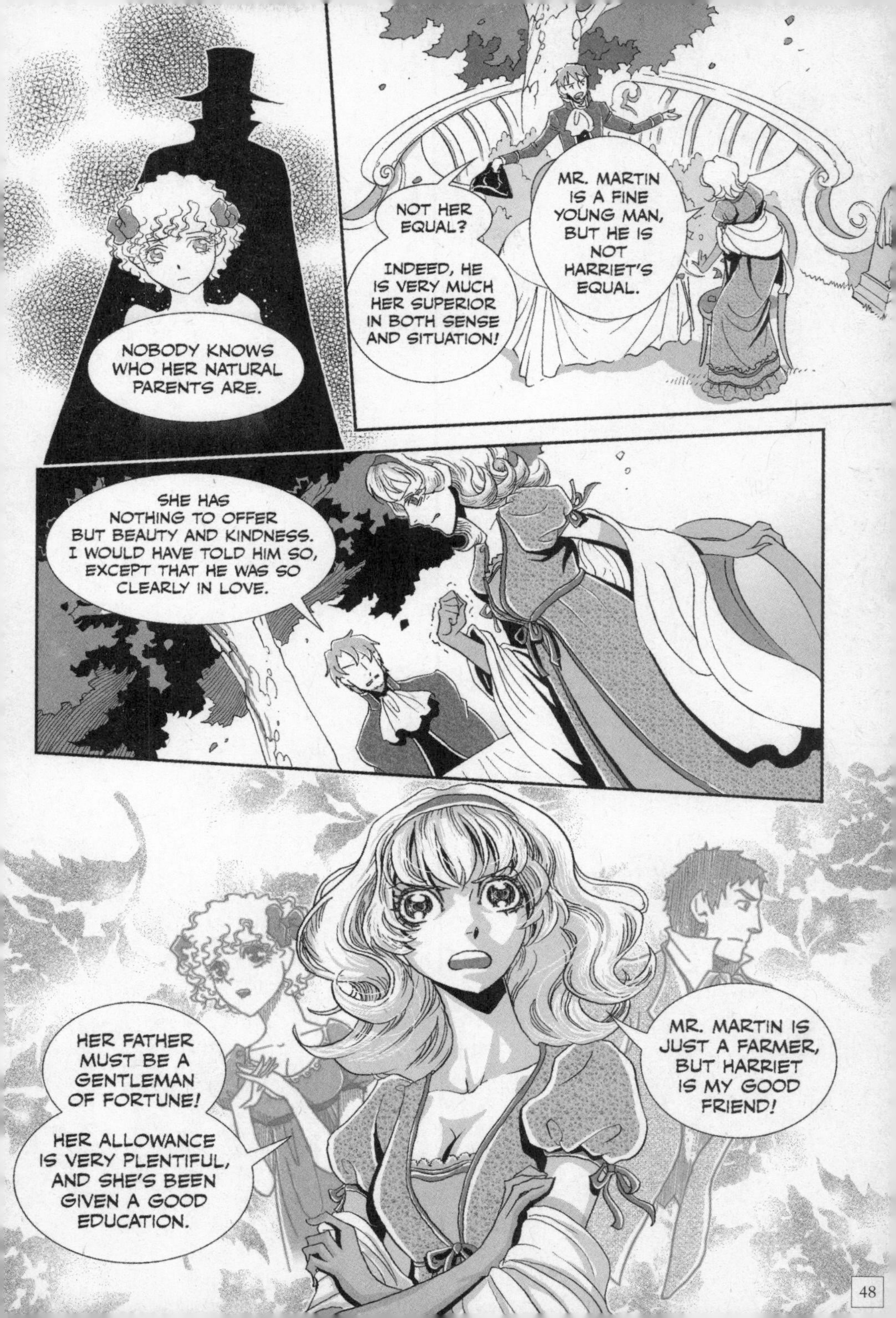
MR. MARTIN IS A FINE YOUNG MAN, BUT HE IS NOT HARRIET'S EQUAL.
NOT HER EQUAL?
INDEED, HE IS VERY MUCH HER SUPERIOR IN BOTH SENSE AND SITUATION!
NOBODY KNOWS WHO HER NATURAL PARENTS ARE.
SHE HAS NOTHING TO OFFER BUT BEAUTY AND KINDNESS. I WOULD HAVE TOLD HIM SO, EXCEPT THAT HE WAS SO CLEARLY IN LOVE.
MR. MARTIN IS JUST A FARMER, BUT HARRIET IS MY GOOD FRIEND!
HER FATHER MUST BE A GENTLEMAN OF FORTUNE!
HER ALLOWANCE IS VERY PLENTIFUL, AND SHE'S BEEN GIVEN A GOOD EDUCATION.

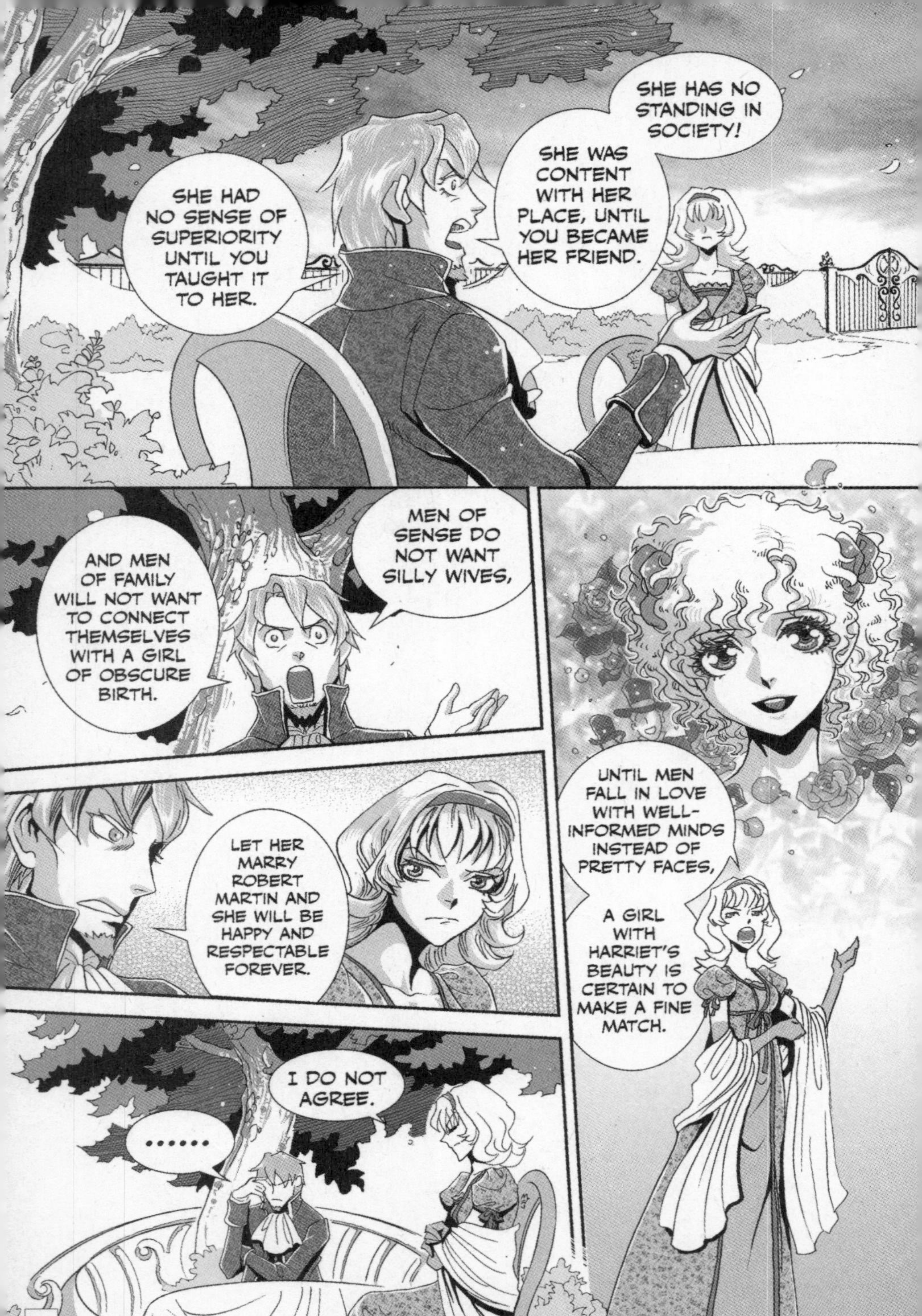
SHE HAS NO STANDING IN SOCIETY!
SHE WAS CONTENT WITH HER PLACE, UNTIL YOU BECAME HER FRIEND.
SHE HAD NO SENSE OF SUPERIORITY UNTIL YOU TAUGHT IT TO HER.
UNTIL MEN FALL IN LOVE WITH WELL-INFORMED MINDS INSTEAD OF PRETTY FACES,
A GIRL WITH HARRIET'S BEAUTY IS CERTAIN TO MAKE A FINE MATCH.
MEN OF SENSE DO NOT WANT SILLY WIVES,
AND MEN OF FAMILY WILL NOT WANT TO CONNECT THEMSELVES WITH A GIRL OF OBSCURE BIRTH.
LET HER MARRY ROBERT MARTIN AND SHE WILL BE HAPPY AND RESPECTABLE FOREVER.
I DO NOT AGREE.
......

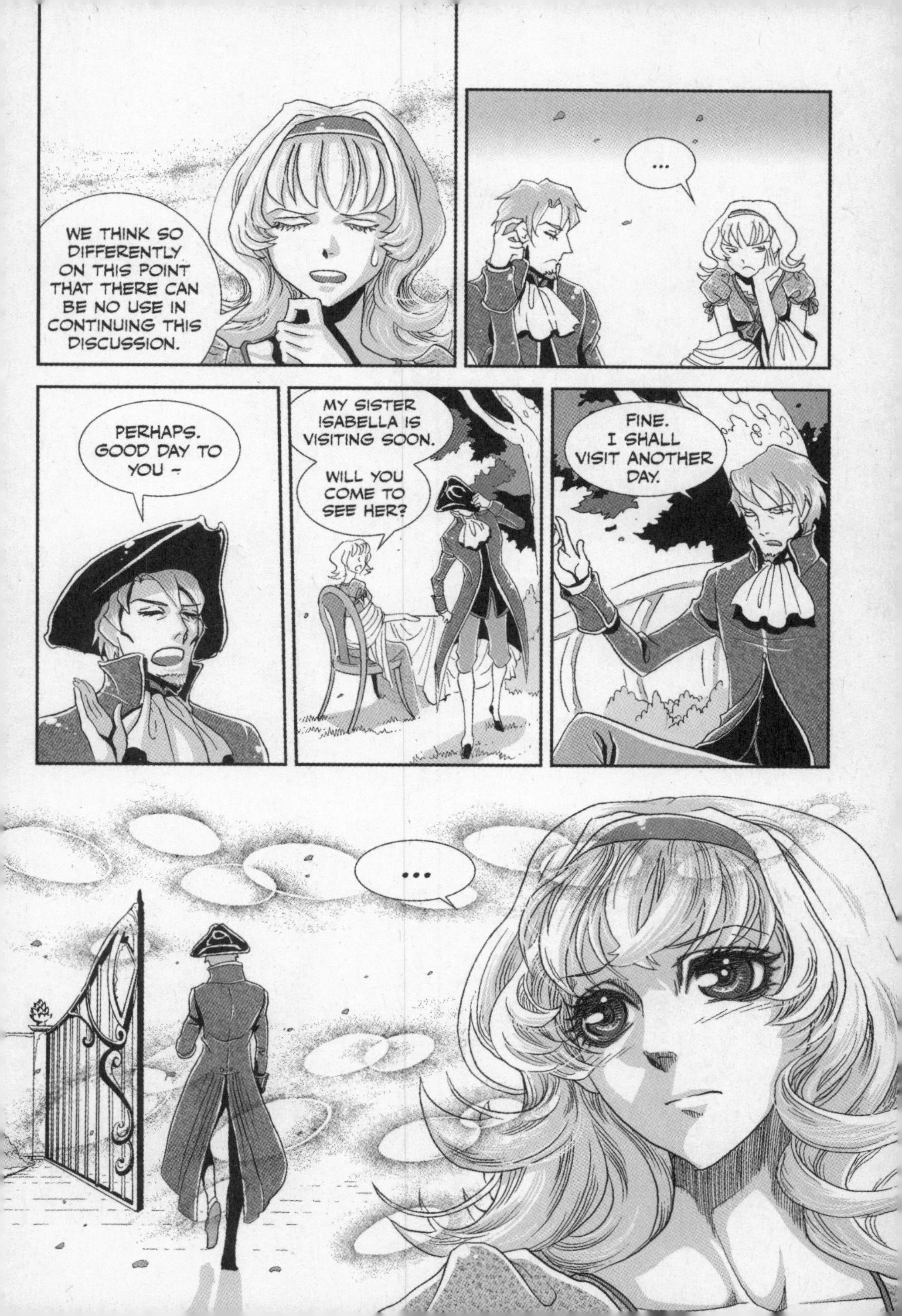
...
WE THINK SO DIFFERENTLY ON THIS POINT THAT THERE CAN BE NO USE IN CONTINUING THIS DISCUSSION.
FINE. I SHALL VISIT ANOTHER DAY.
MY SISTER ISABELLA IS VISITING SOON.
WILL YOU COME TO SEE HER?
PERHAPS. GOOD DAY TO YOU –
...

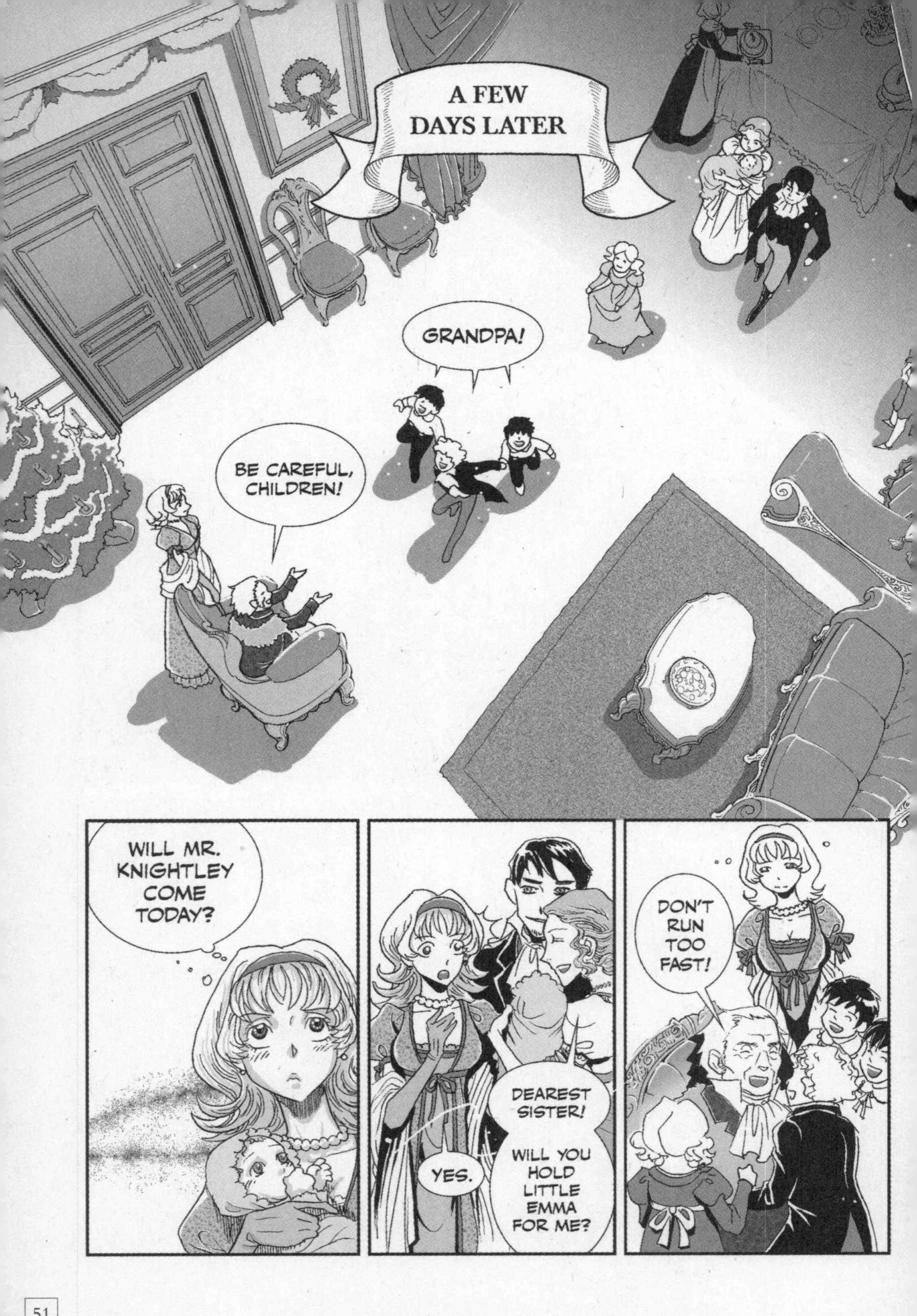
A FEW DAYS LATER
GRANDPA!
BE CAREFUL, CHILDREN!
DON'T RUN TOO FAST!
DEAREST SISTER!
WILL YOU HOLD LITTLE EMMA FOR ME?
YES.
WILL MR. KNIGHTLEY COME TODAY?

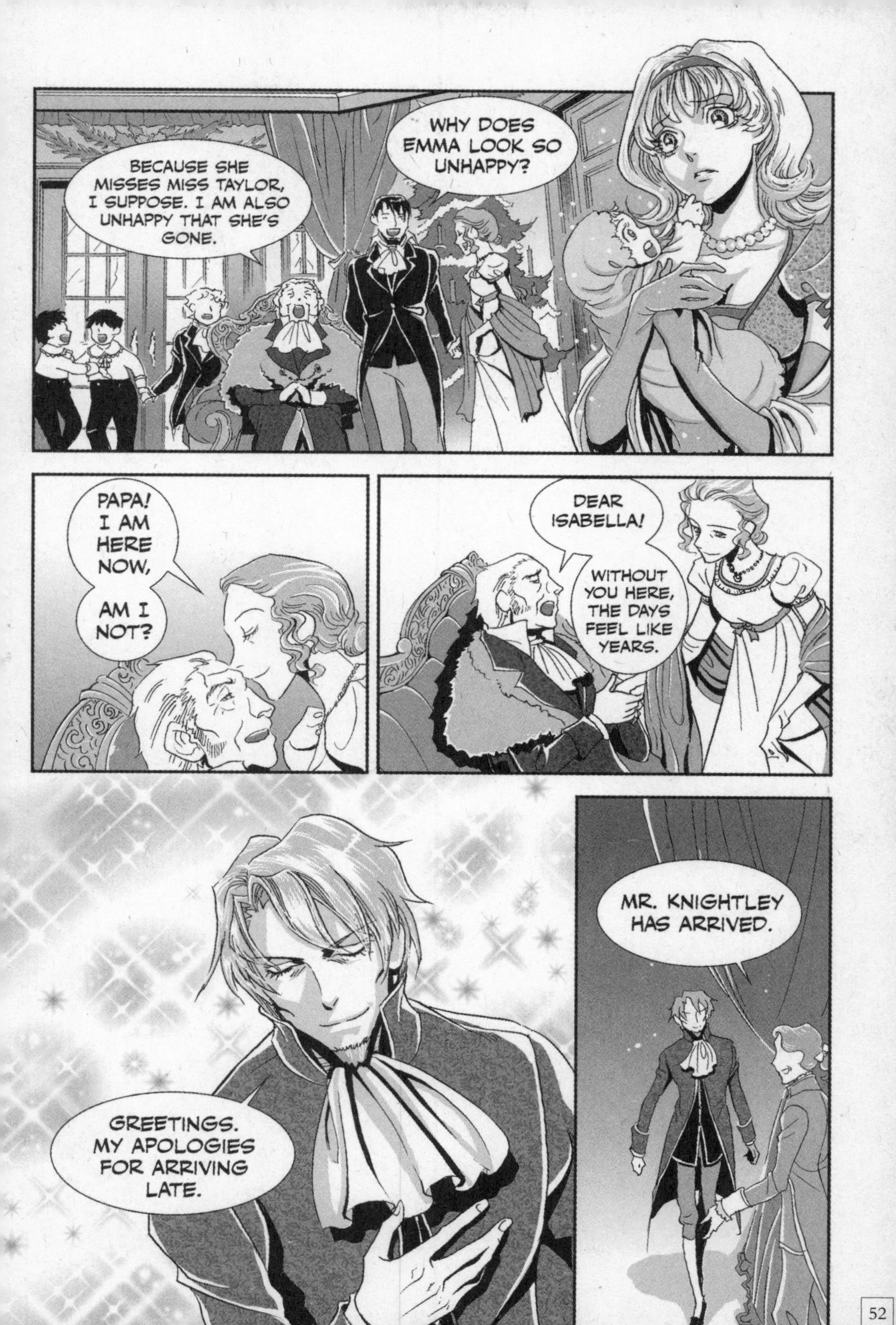
WHY DOES EMMA LOOK SO UNHAPPY?
BECAUSE SHE MISSES MISS TAYLOR, I SUPPOSE. I AM ALSO UNHAPPY THAT SHE'S GONE.
DEAR ISABELLA!
WITHOUT YOU HERE, THE DAYS FEEL LIKE YEARS.
PAPA! I AM HERE NOW,
AM I NOT?
MR. KNIGHTLEY HAS ARRIVED.
GREETINGS. MY APOLOGIES FOR ARRIVING LATE.

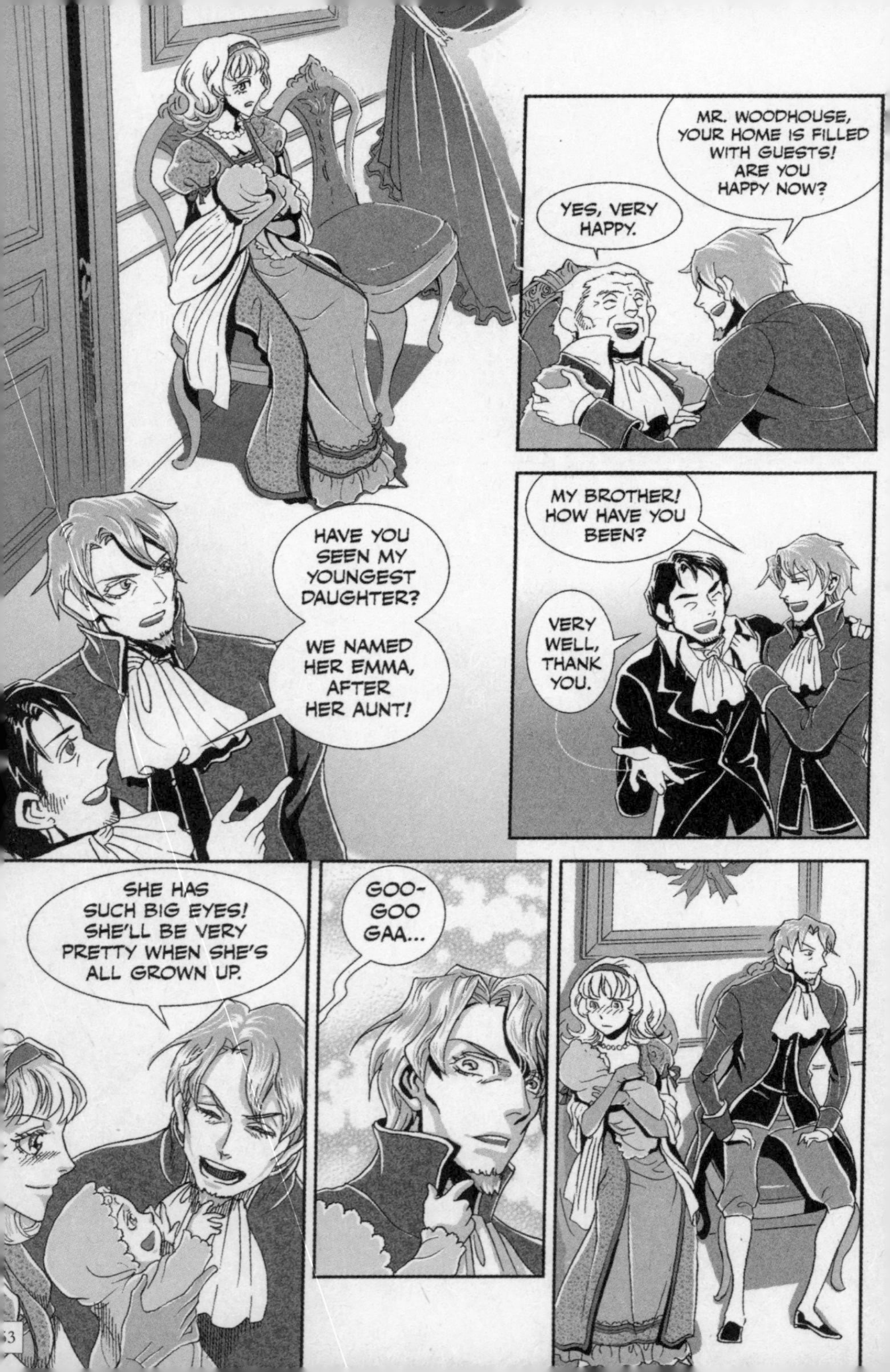
MR. WOODHOUSE, YOUR HOME IS FILLED WITH GUESTS! ARE YOU HAPPY NOW?
YES, VERY HAPPY.
MY BROTHER! HOW HAVE YOU BEEN?
VERY WELL, THANK YOU.
HAVE YOU SEEN MY YOUNGEST DAUGHTER?
WE NAMED HER EMMA, AFTER HER AUNT!
GOO-GOO GAA...
SHE HAS SUCH BIG EYES! SHE'LL BE VERY PRETTY WHEN SHE'S ALL GROWN UP.

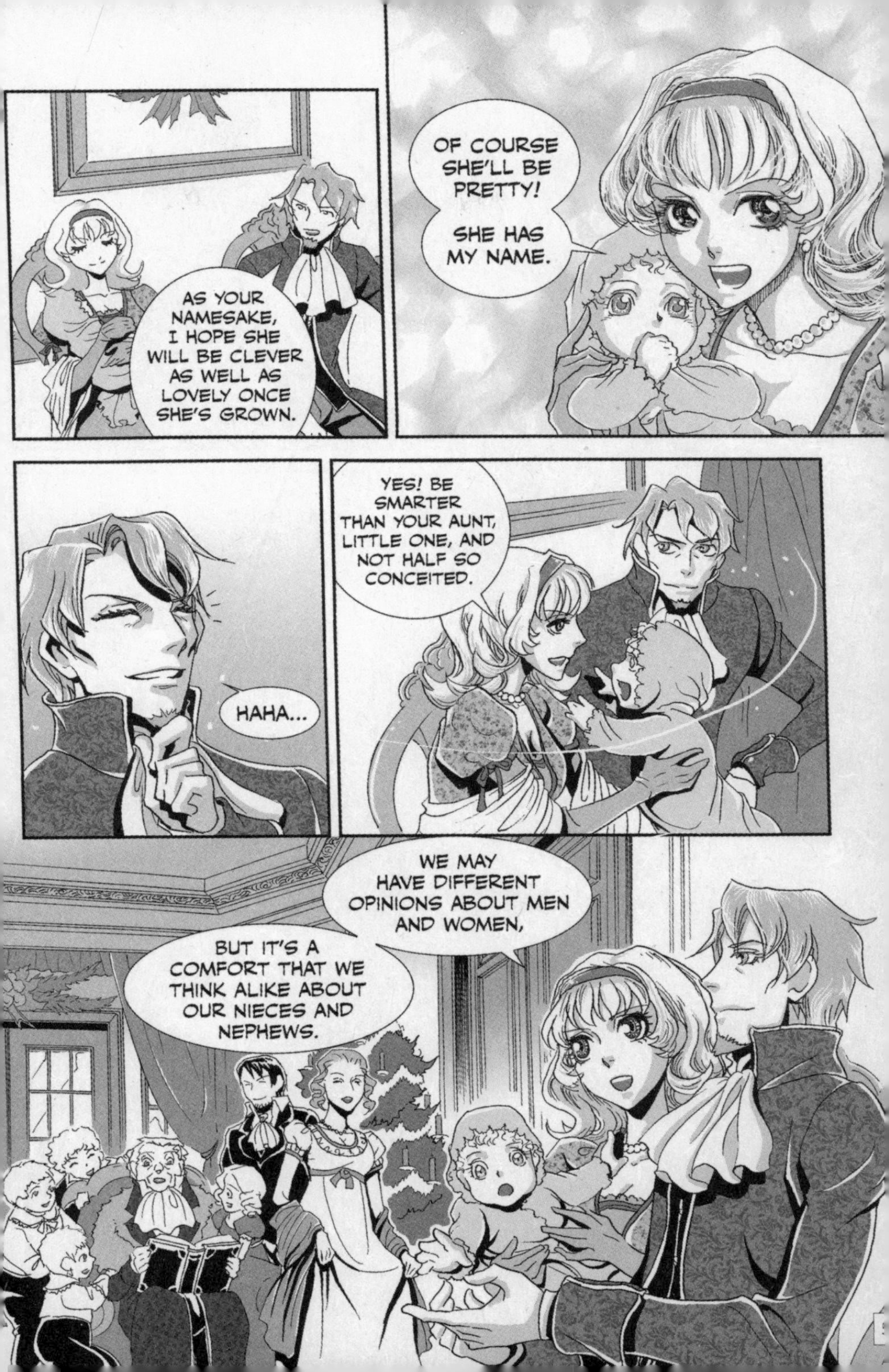
OF COURSE SHE'LL BE PRETTY!
SHE HAS MY NAME.
AS YOUR NAMESAKE, I HOPE SHE WILL BE CLEVER AS WELL AS LOVELY ONCE SHE'S GROWN.
YES! BE SMARTER THAN YOUR AUNT, LITTLE ONE, AND NOT HALF SO CONCEITED.
HAHA...
WE MAY HAVE DIFFERENT OPINIONS ABOUT MEN AND WOMEN,
BUT IT'S A COMFORT THAT WE THINK ALIKE ABOUT OUR NIECES AND NEPHEWS.

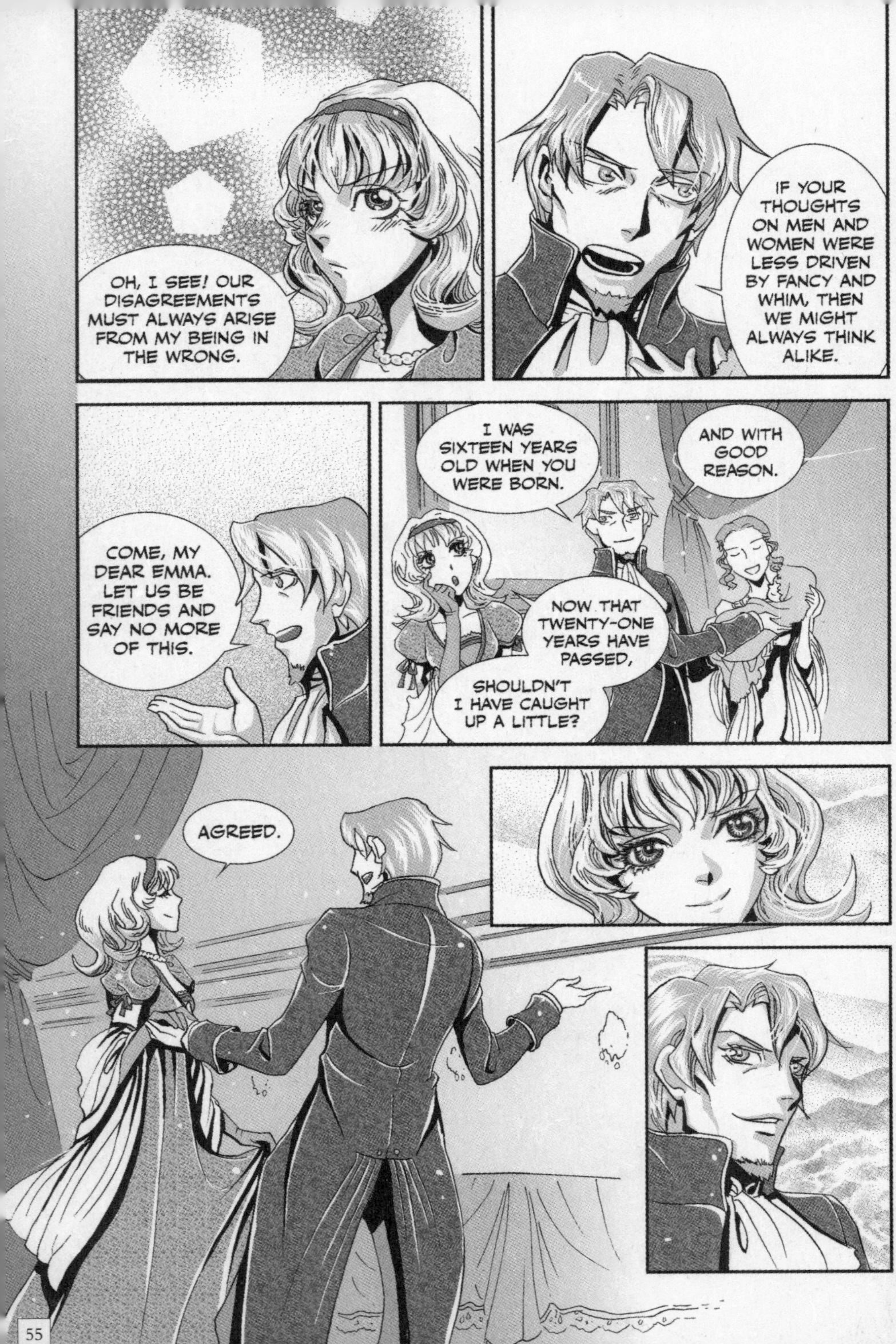
IF YOUR THOUGHTS ON MEN AND WOMEN WERE LESS DRIVEN BY FANCY AND WHIM, THEN WE MIGHT ALWAYS THINK ALIKE.
OH, I SEE! OUR DISAGREEMENTS MUST ALWAYS ARISE FROM MY BEING IN THE WRONG.
AND WITH GOOD REASON.
I WAS SIXTEEN YEARS OLD WHEN YOU WERE BORN.
NOW THAT TWENTY-ONE YEARS HAVE PASSED,
SHOULDN'T I HAVE CAUGHT UP A LITTLE?
COME, MY DEAR EMMA. LET US BE FRIENDS AND SAY NO MORE OF THIS.
AGREED.

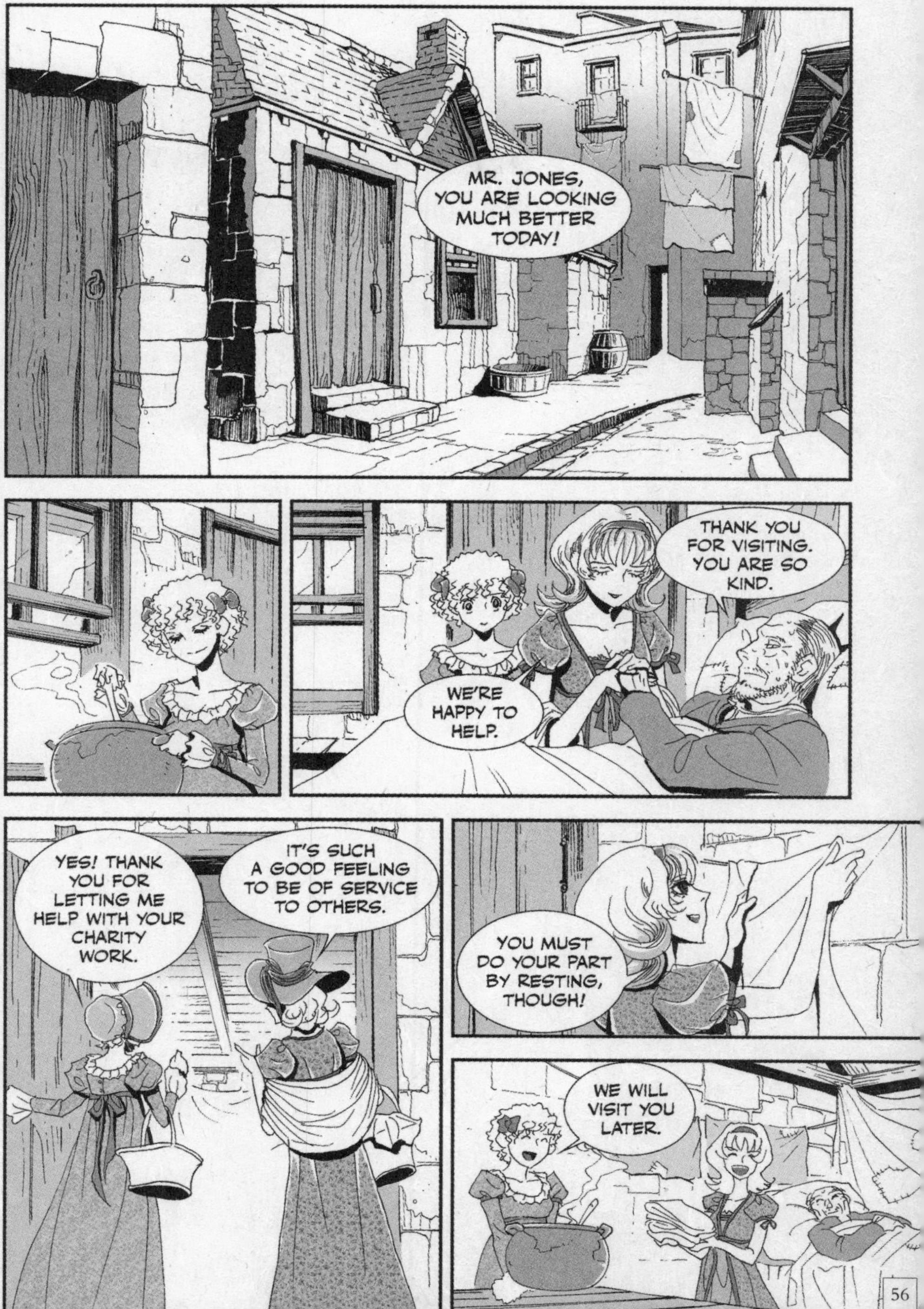
MR. JONES, YOU ARE LOOKING MUCH BETTER TODAY!
THANK YOU FOR VISITING. YOU ARE SO KIND.
WE'RE HAPPY TO HELP.
YOU MUST DO YOUR PART BY RESTING, THOUGH!
WE WILL VISIT YOU LATER.
IT'S SUCH A GOOD FEELING TO BE OF SERVICE TO OTHERS.
YES! THANK YOU FOR LETTING ME HELP WITH YOUR CHARITY WORK.

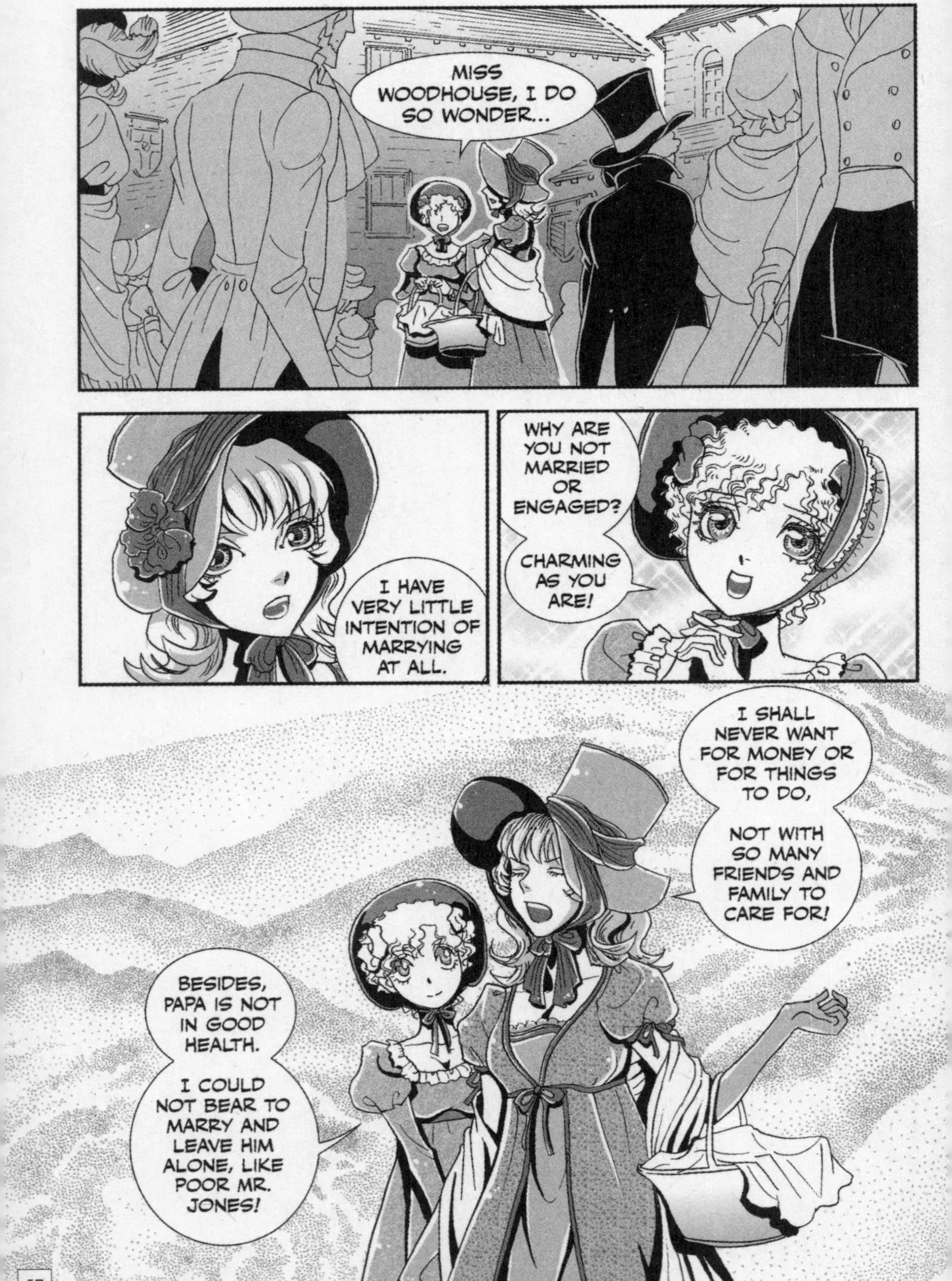
MISS WOODHOUSE, I DO SO WONDER...
WHY ARE YOU NOT MARRIED OR ENGAGED?
CHARMING AS YOU ARE!
I HAVE VERY LITTLE INTENTION OF MARRYING AT ALL.
I SHALL NEVER WANT FOR MONEY OR FOR THINGS TO DO,
NOT WITH SO MANY FRIENDS AND FAMILY TO CARE FOR!
BESIDES, PAPA IS NOT IN GOOD HEALTH.
I COULD NOT BEAR TO MARRY AND LEAVE HIM ALONE, LIKE POOR MR. JONES!

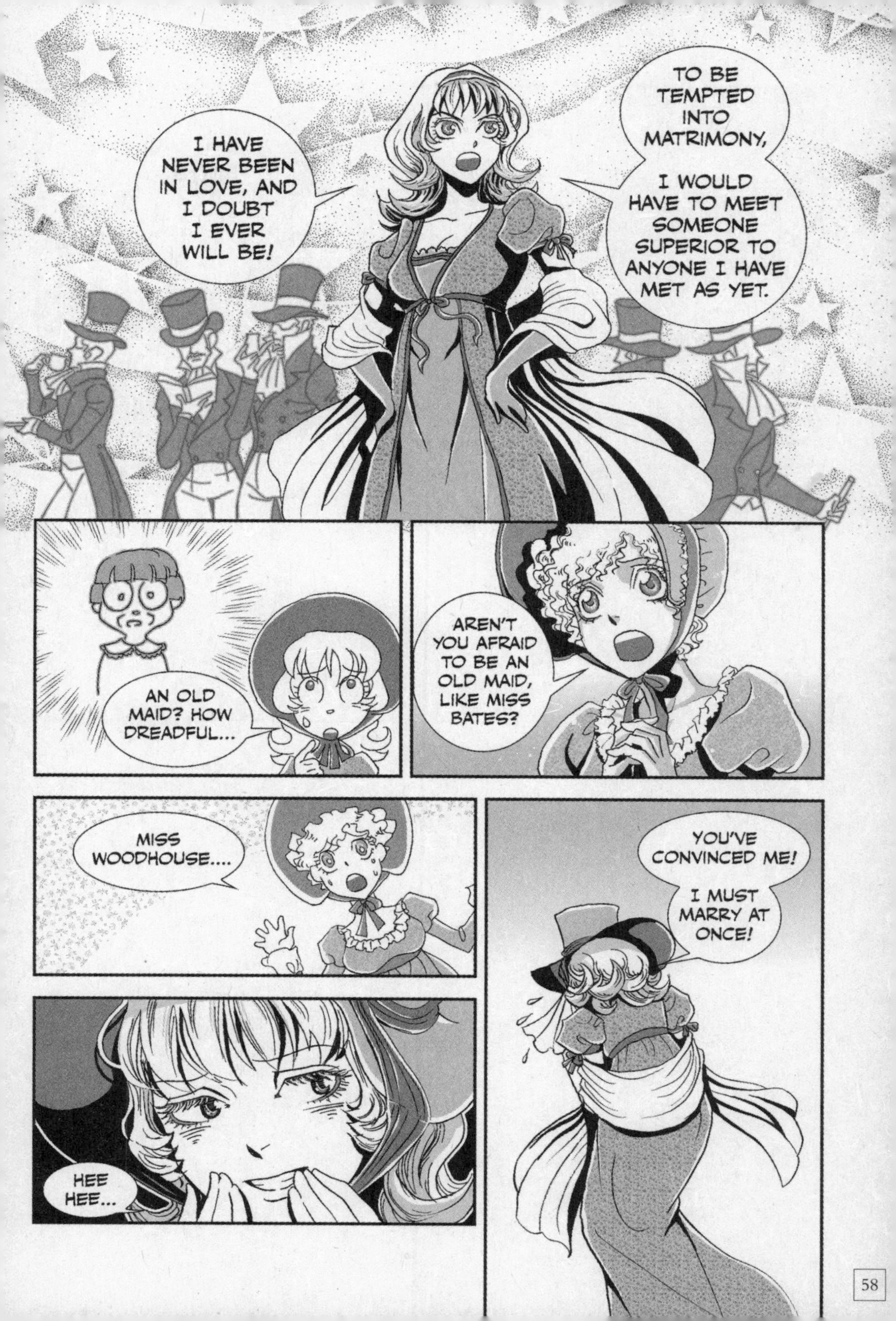
TO BE TEMPTED INTO MATRIMONY,
I WOULD HAVE TO MEET SOMEONE SUPERIOR TO ANYONE I HAVE MET AS YET.
I HAVE NEVER BEEN IN LOVE, AND I DOUBT I EVER WILL BE!
AREN'T YOU AFRAID TO BE AN OLD MAID, LIKE MISS BATES?
AN OLD MAID? HOW DREADFUL...
YOU'VE CONVINCED ME!
I MUST MARRY AT ONCE!
MISS WOODHOUSE....
HEE HEE...

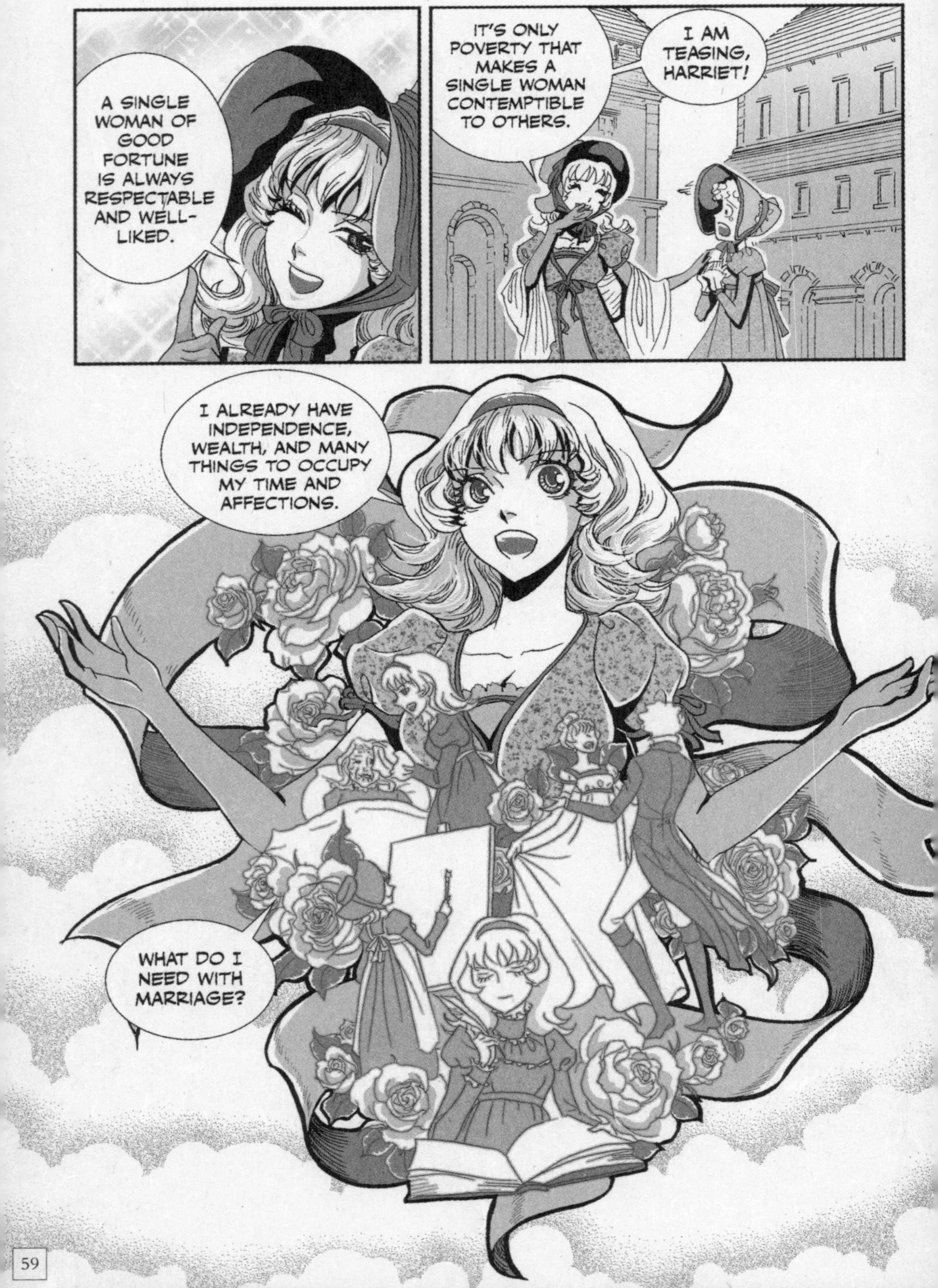
I AM TEASING, HARRIET!
IT'S ONLY POVERTY THAT MAKES A SINGLE WOMAN CONTEMPTIBLE TO OTHERS.
A SINGLE WOMAN OF GOOD FORTUNE IS ALWAYS RESPECTABLE AND WELL-LIKED.
I ALREADY HAVE INDEPENDENCE, WEALTH, AND MANY THINGS TO OCCUPY MY TIME AND AFFECTIONS.
WHAT DO I NEED WITH MARRIAGE?

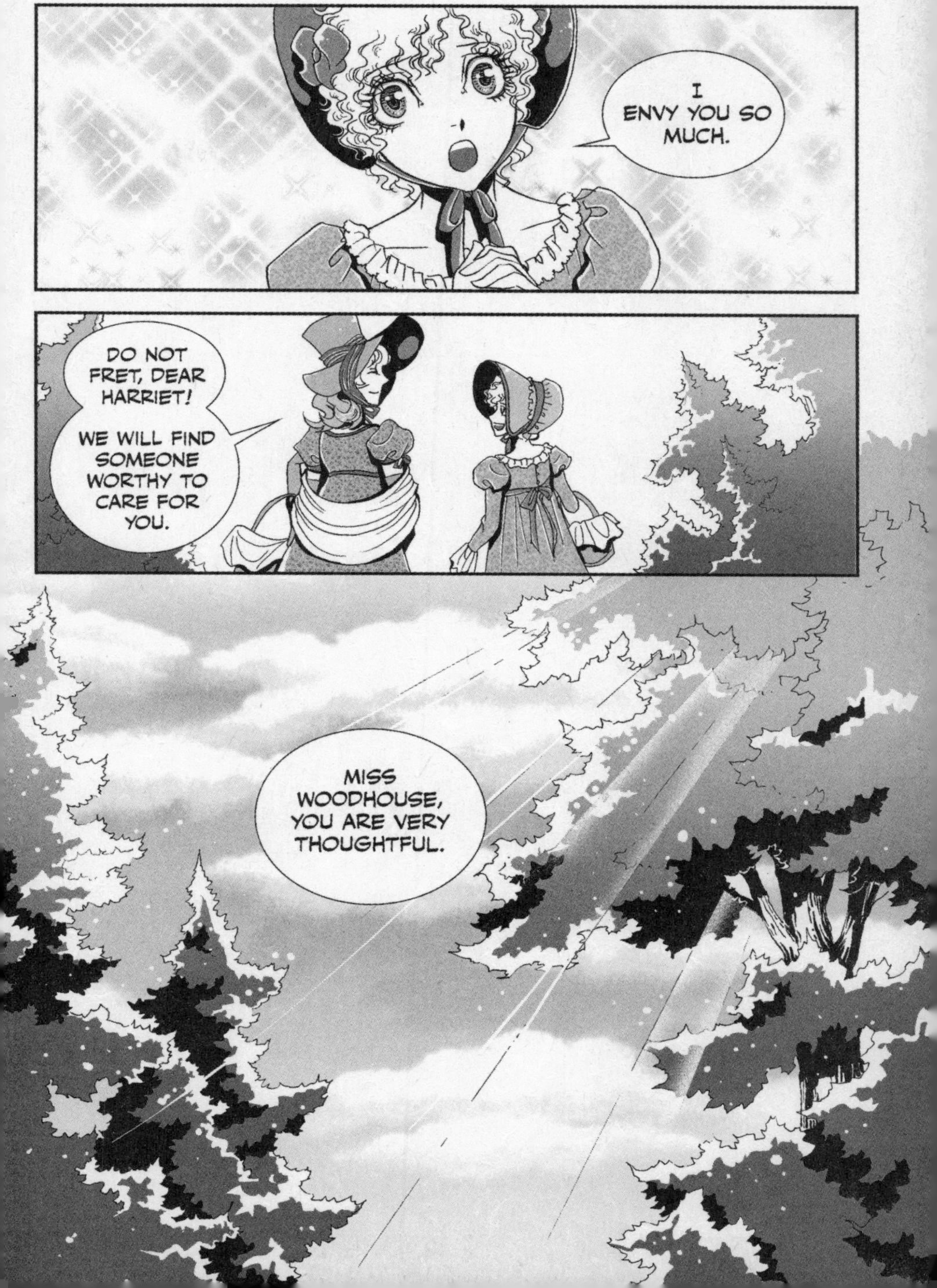
I ENVY YOU SO MUCH.
DO NOT FRET, DEAR HARRIET!
WE WILL FIND SOMEONE WORTHY TO CARE FOR YOU.
MISS WOODHOUSE, YOU ARE VERY THOUGHTFUL.

CHARACTER MODEL SHEET

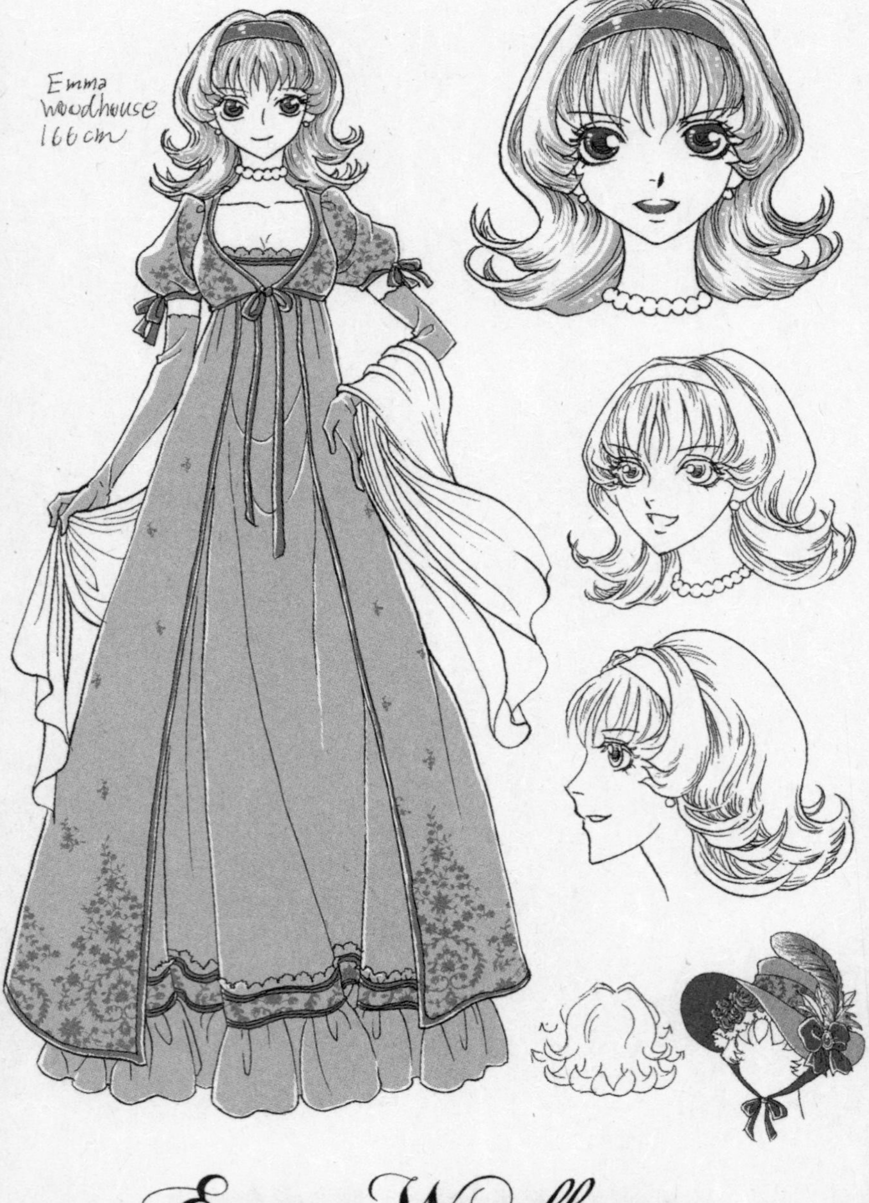
Emma
woodhouse
166cm

Emma Woodhouse

CHARACTER MODEL SHEET

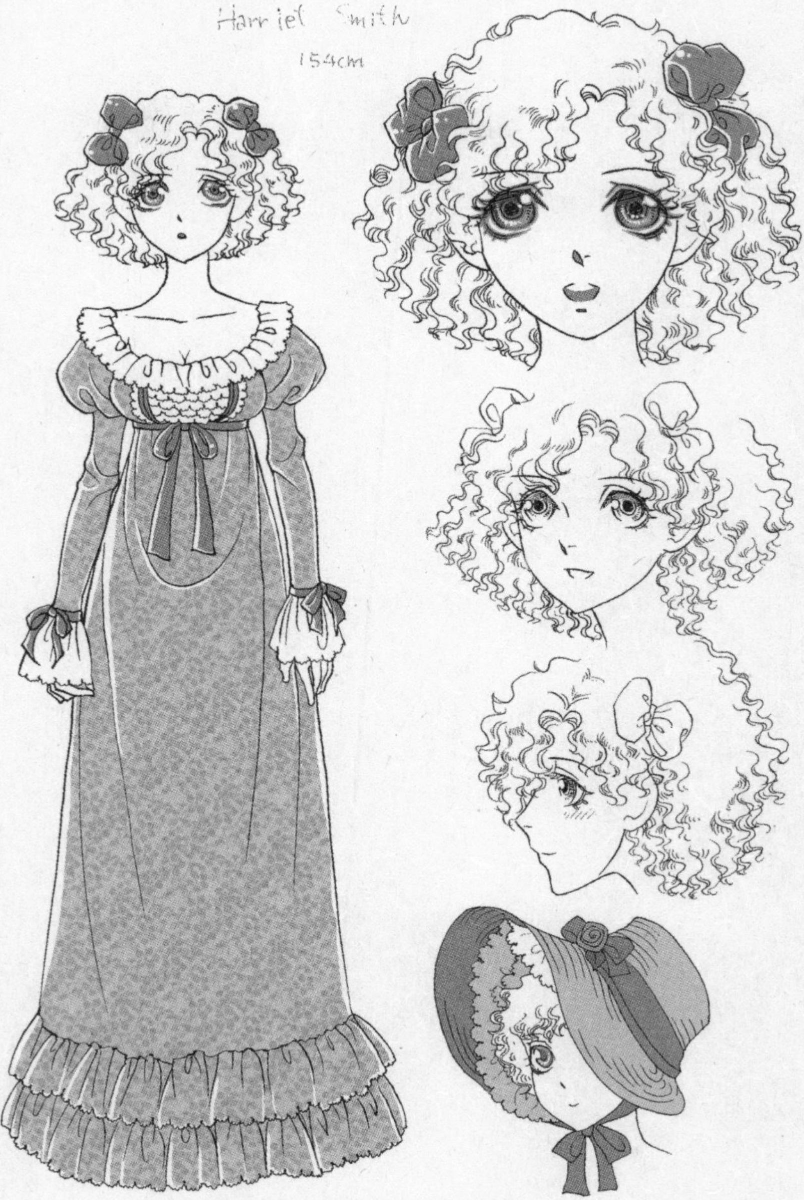
Harriet Smith
154cm

Harriet Smith

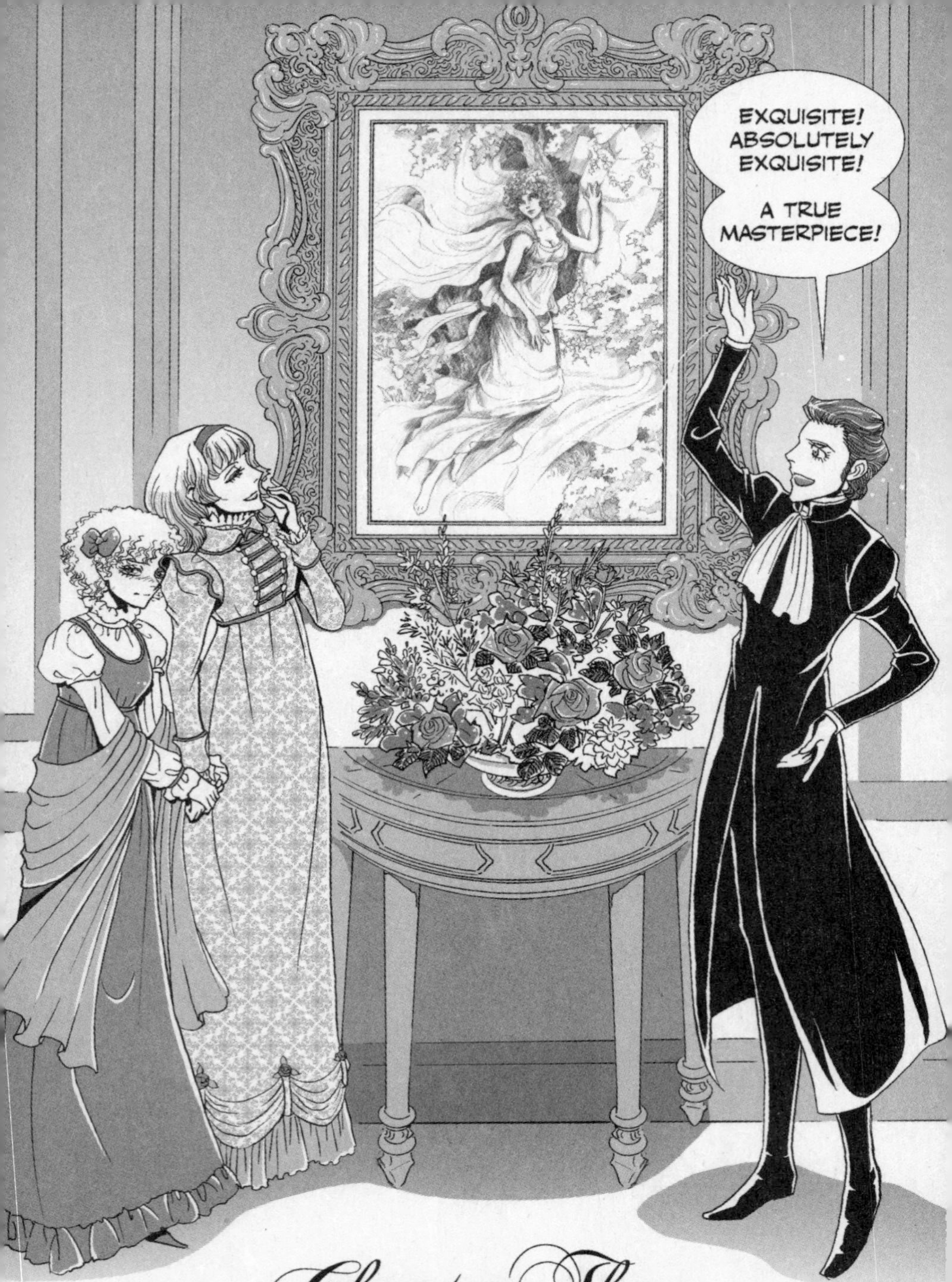
EXQUISITE! ABSOLUTELY EXQUISITE!
A TRUE MASTERPIECE!

Chapter Three

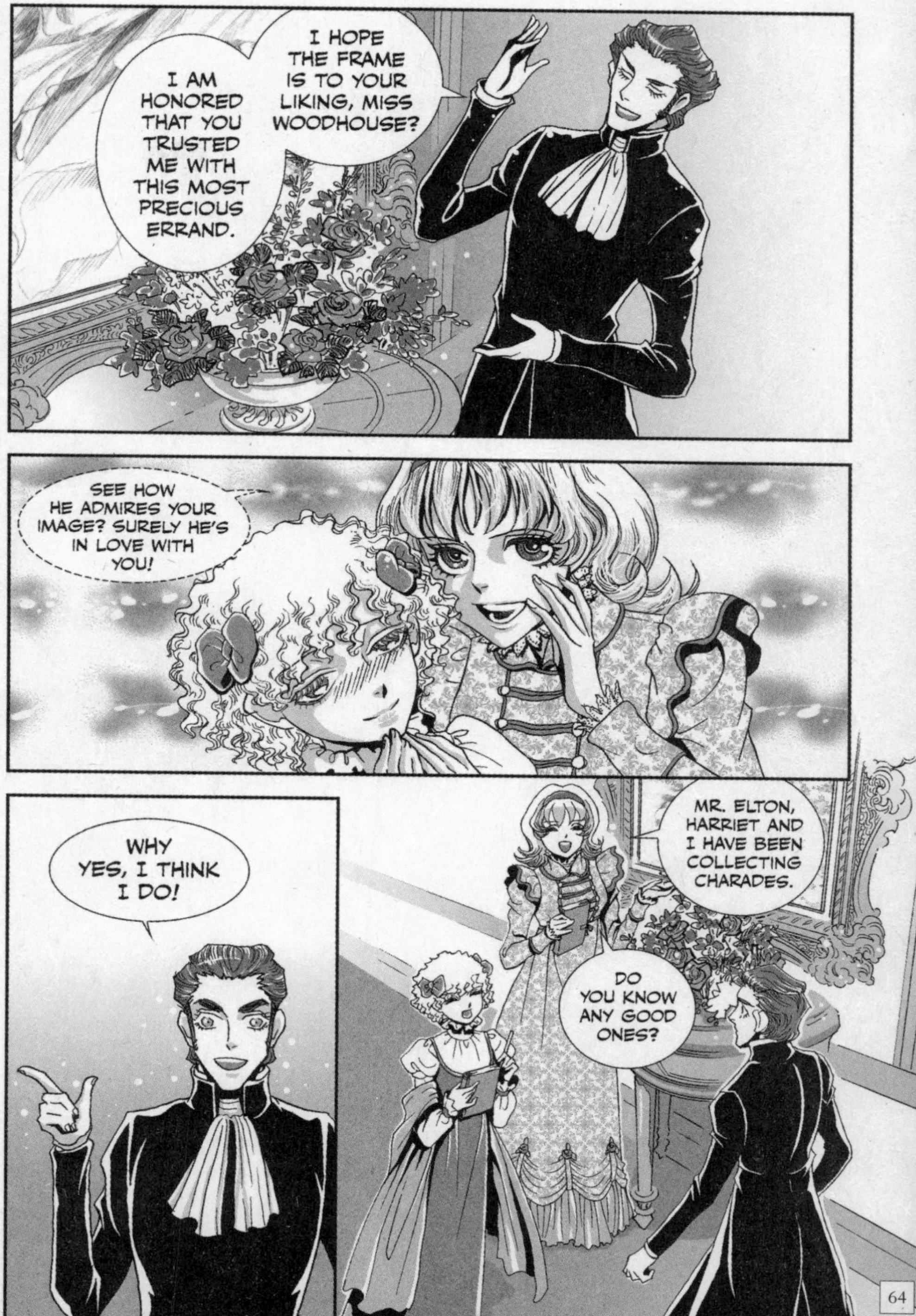
I HOPE THE FRAME IS TO YOUR LIKING, MISS WOODHOUSE?
I AM HONORED THAT YOU TRUSTED ME WITH THIS MOST PRECIOUS ERRAND.
SEE HOW HE ADMIRES YOUR IMAGE? SURELY HE'S IN LOVE WITH YOU!
MR. ELTON, HARRIET AND I HAVE BEEN COLLECTING CHARADES.
DO YOU KNOW ANY GOOD ONES?
WHY YES, I THINK I DO!

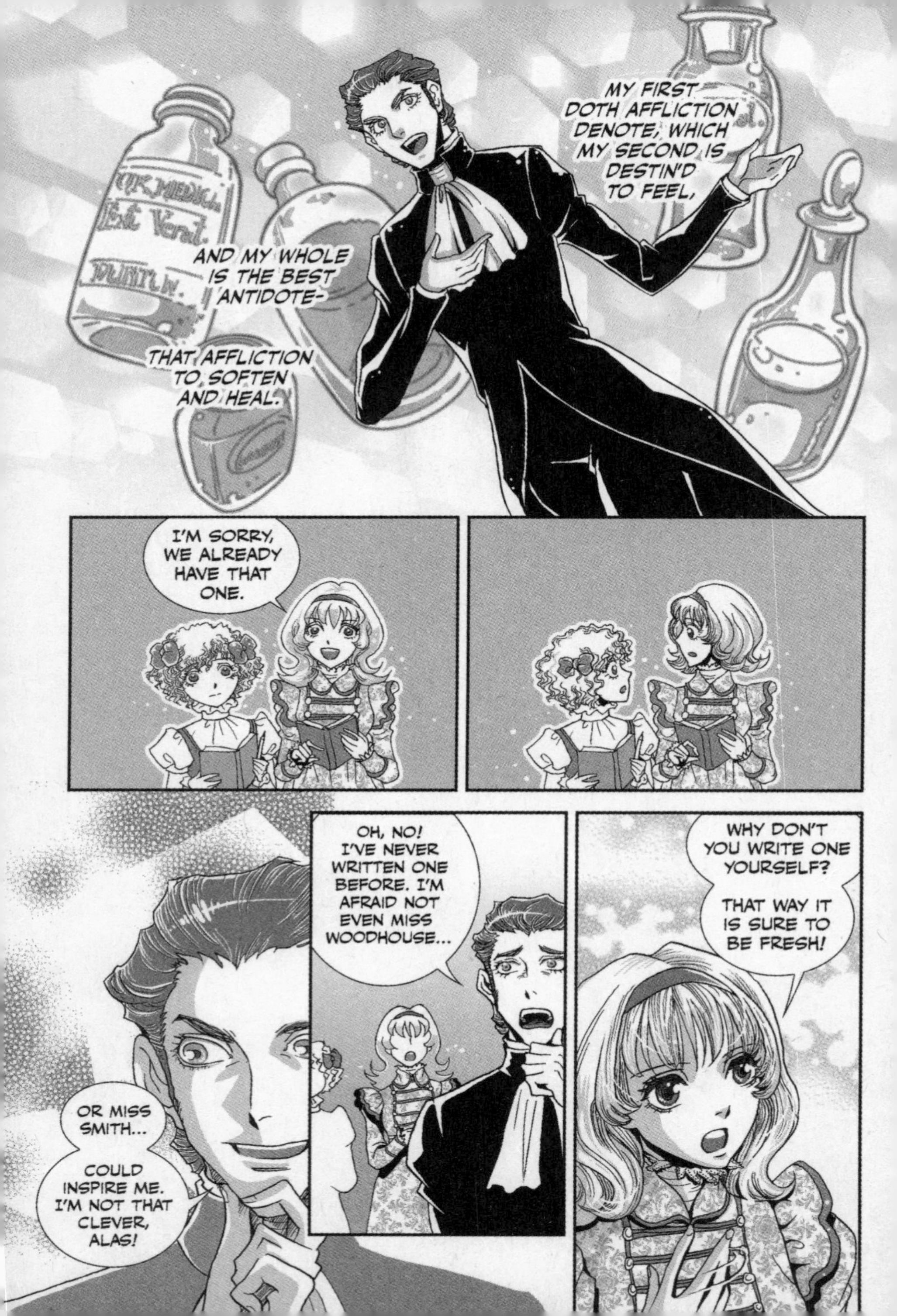
MY FIRST DOTH AFFLICTION DENOTE, WHICH MY SECOND IS DESTIN'D TO FEEL,
AND MY WHOLE IS THE BEST ANTIDOTE-
THAT AFFLICTION TO SOFTEN AND HEAL.
I'M SORRY, WE ALREADY HAVE THAT ONE.
WHY DON'T YOU WRITE ONE YOURSELF?
THAT WAY IT IS SURE TO BE FRESH!
OH, NO! I'VE NEVER WRITTEN ONE BEFORE. I'M AFRAID NOT EVEN MISS WOODHOUSE...
OR MISS SMITH...
COULD INSPIRE ME. I'M NOT THAT CLEVER, ALAS!

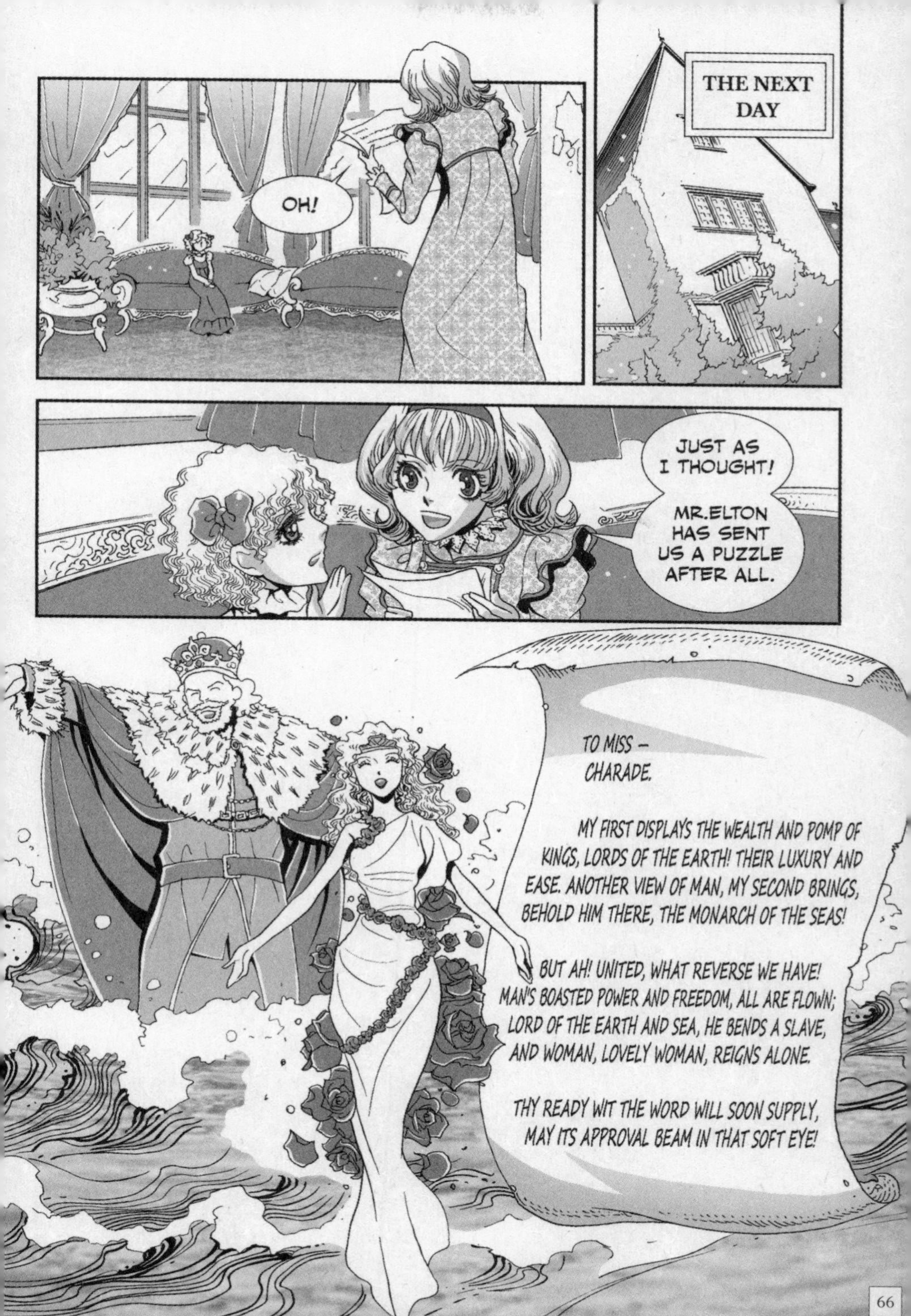
THE NEXT DAY
OH!
JUST AS I THOUGHT!
MR.ELTON HAS SENT US A PUZZLE AFTER ALL.
TO MISS —
CHARADE.
MY FIRST DISPLAYS THE WEALTH AND POMP OF KINGS, LORDS OF THE EARTH! THEIR LUXURY AND EASE. ANOTHER VIEW OF MAN, MY SECOND BRINGS, BEHOLD HIM THERE, THE MONARCH OF THE SEAS!
BUT AH! UNITED, WHAT REVERSE WE HAVE! MAN'S BOASTED POWER AND FREEDOM, ALL ARE FLOWN; LORD OF THE EARTH AND SEA, HE BENDS A SLAVE, AND WOMAN, LOVELY WOMAN, REIGNS ALONE.
THY READY WIT THE WORD WILL SOON SUPPLY, MAY ITS APPROVAL BEAM IN THAT SOFT EYE!

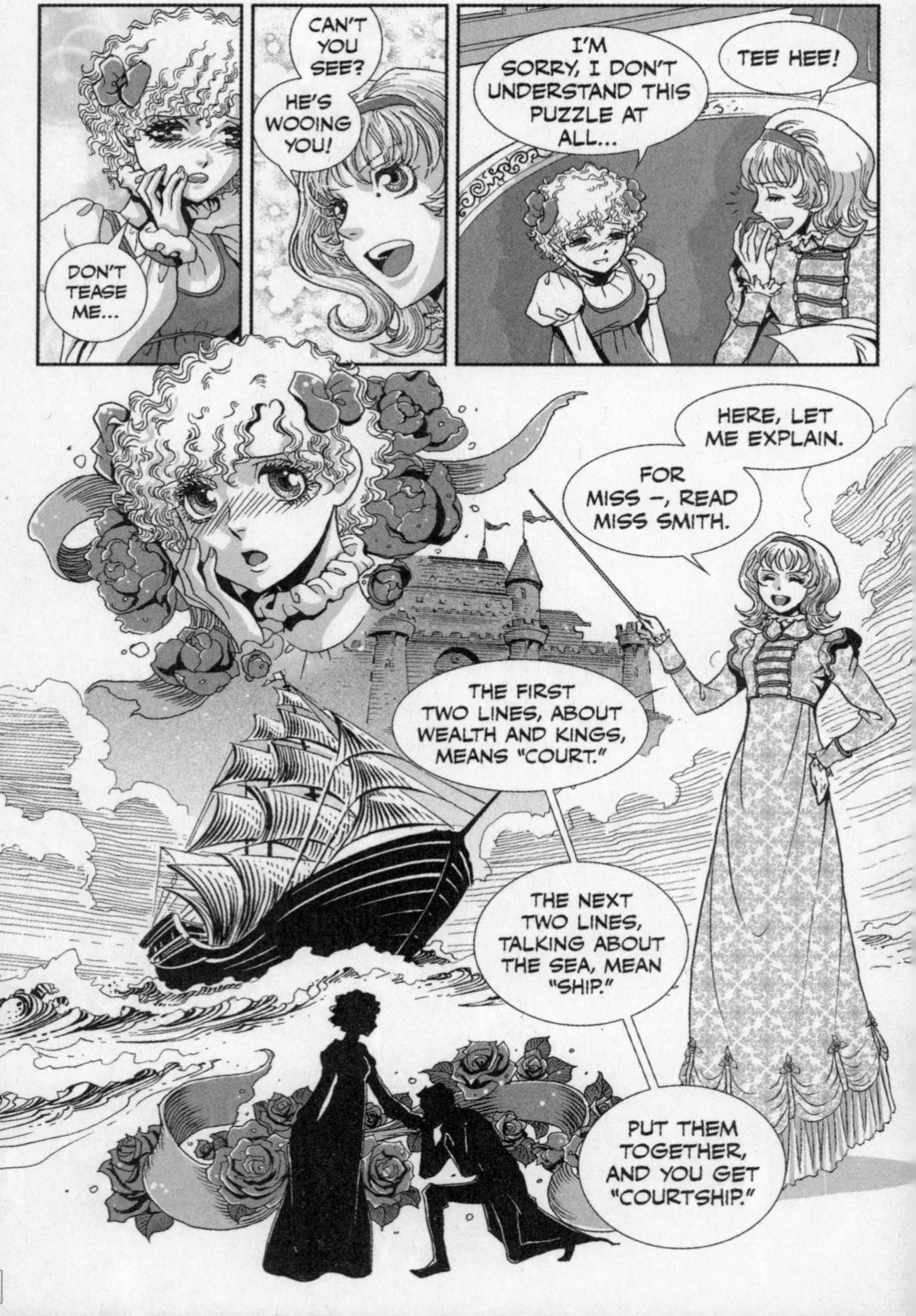
TEE HEE!
I'M SORRY, I DON'T UNDERSTAND THIS PUZZLE AT ALL...
CAN'T YOU SEE?
HE'S WOOING YOU!
DON'T TEASE ME...
HERE, LET ME EXPLAIN.
FOR MISS –, READ MISS SMITH.
THE FIRST TWO LINES, ABOUT WEALTH AND KINGS, MEANS "COURT."
THE NEXT TWO LINES, TALKING ABOUT THE SEA, MEAN "SHIP."
PUT THEM TOGETHER, AND YOU GET "COURTSHIP."

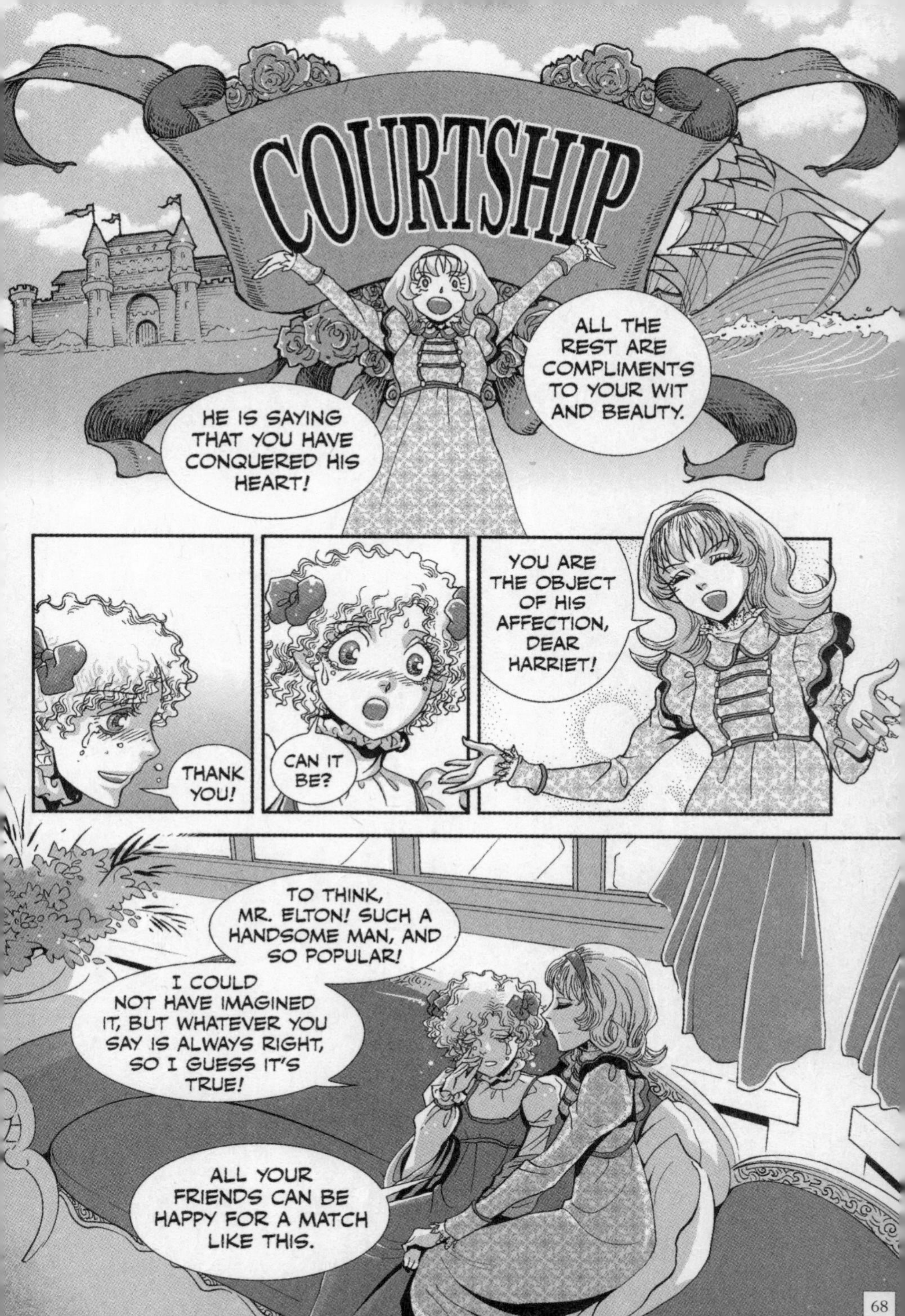
COURTSHIP
ALL THE REST ARE COMPLIMENTS TO YOUR WIT AND BEAUTY.
HE IS SAYING THAT YOU HAVE CONQUERED HIS HEART!
YOU ARE THE OBJECT OF HIS AFFECTION, DEAR HARRIET!
CAN IT BE?
THANK YOU!
TO THINK, MR. ELTON! SUCH A HANDSOME MAN, AND SO POPULAR!
I COULD NOT HAVE IMAGINED IT, BUT WHATEVER YOU SAY IS ALWAYS RIGHT, SO I GUESS IT'S TRUE!
ALL YOUR FRIENDS CAN BE HAPPY FOR A MATCH LIKE THIS.

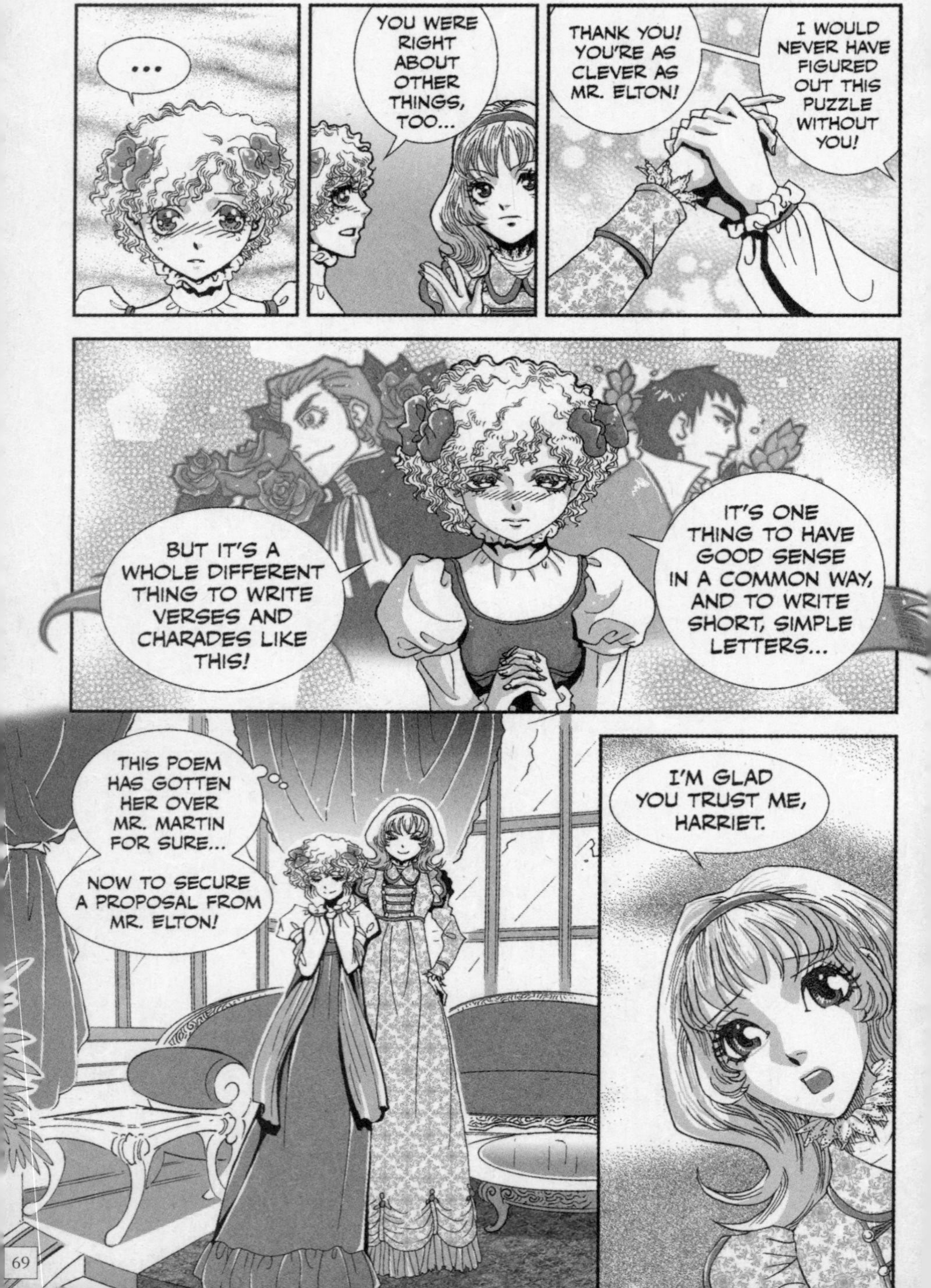
I WOULD NEVER HAVE FIGURED OUT THIS PUZZLE WITHOUT YOU!
THANK YOU! YOU'RE AS CLEVER AS MR. ELTON!
YOU WERE RIGHT ABOUT OTHER THINGS, TOO...
...
IT'S ONE THING TO HAVE GOOD SENSE IN A COMMON WAY, AND TO WRITE SHORT, SIMPLE LETTERS...
BUT IT'S A WHOLE DIFFERENT THING TO WRITE VERSES AND CHARADES LIKE THIS!
I'M GLAD YOU TRUST ME, HARRIET.
THIS POEM HAS GOTTEN HER OVER MR. MARTIN FOR SURE...
NOW TO SECURE A PROPOSAL FROM MR. ELTON!

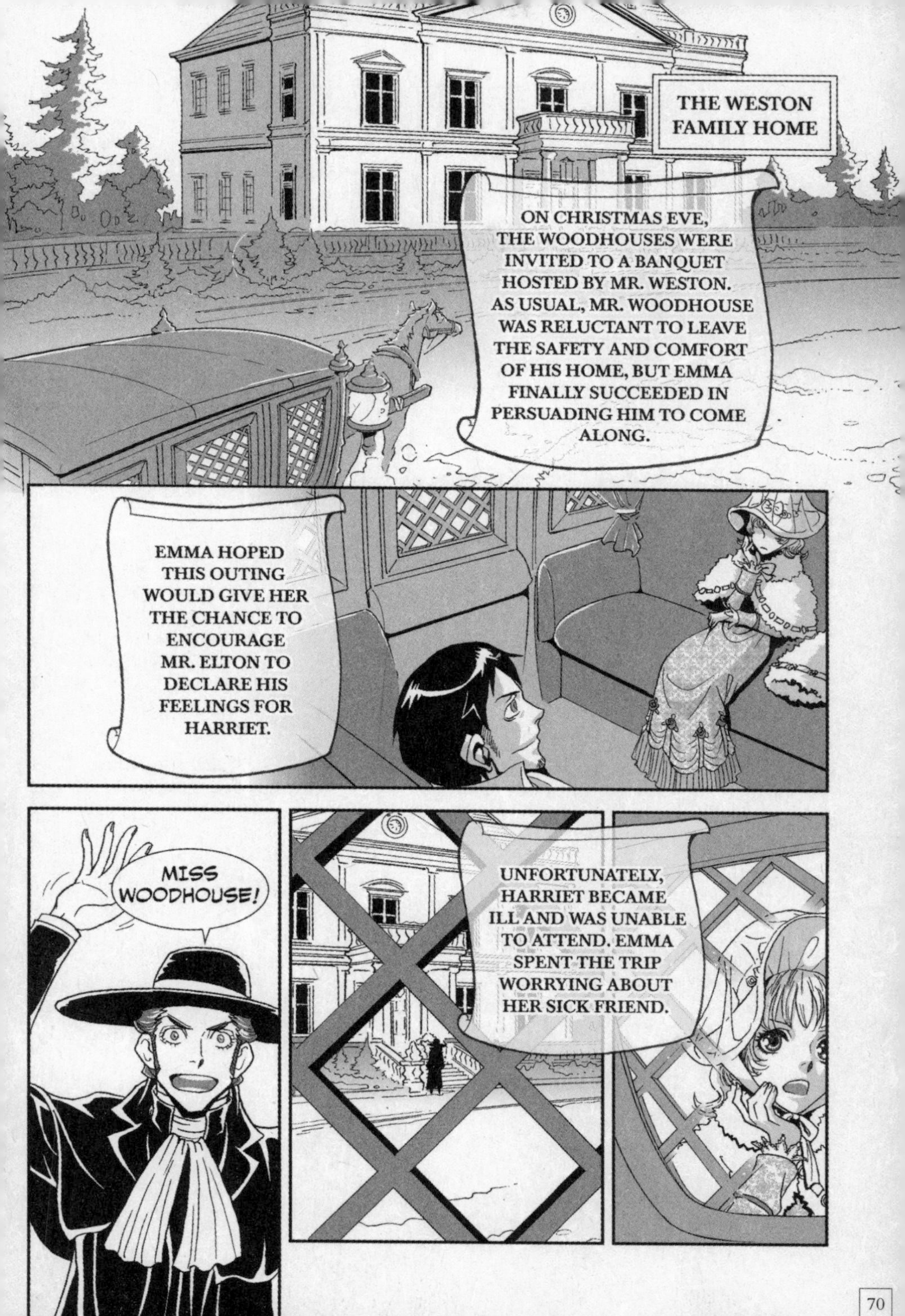
THE WESTON FAMILY HOME
ON CHRISTMAS EVE, THE WOODHOUSES WERE INVITED TO A BANQUET HOSTED BY MR. WESTON. AS USUAL, MR. WOODHOUSE WAS RELUCTANT TO LEAVE THE SAFETY AND COMFORT OF HIS HOME, BUT EMMA FINALLY SUCCEEDED IN PERSUADING HIM TO COME ALONG.
EMMA HOPED THIS OUTING WOULD GIVE HER THE CHANCE TO ENCOURAGE MR. ELTON TO DECLARE HIS FEELINGS FOR HARRIET.
UNFORTUNATELY, HARRIET BECAME ILL AND WAS UNABLE TO ATTEND. EMMA SPENT THE TRIP WORRYING ABOUT HER SICK FRIEND.
MISS WOODHOUSE!

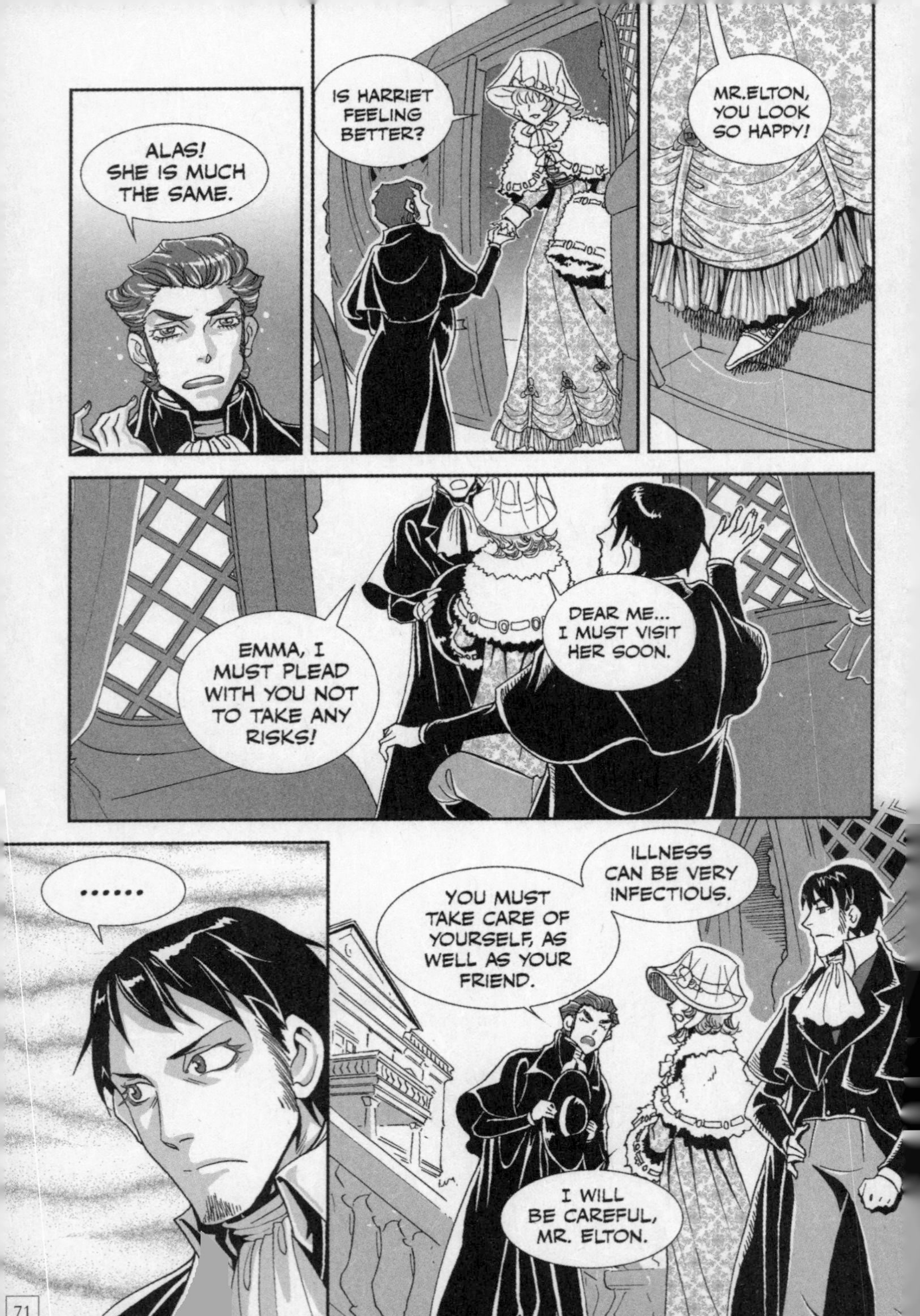
MR.ELTON, YOU LOOK SO HAPPY!
IS HARRIET FEELING BETTER?
ALAS! SHE IS MUCH THE SAME.
DEAR ME... I MUST VISIT HER SOON.
EMMA, I MUST PLEAD WITH YOU NOT TO TAKE ANY RISKS!
ILLNESS CAN BE VERY INFECTIOUS.
YOU MUST TAKE CARE OF YOURSELF, AS WELL AS YOUR FRIEND.
I WILL BE CAREFUL, MR. ELTON.
......

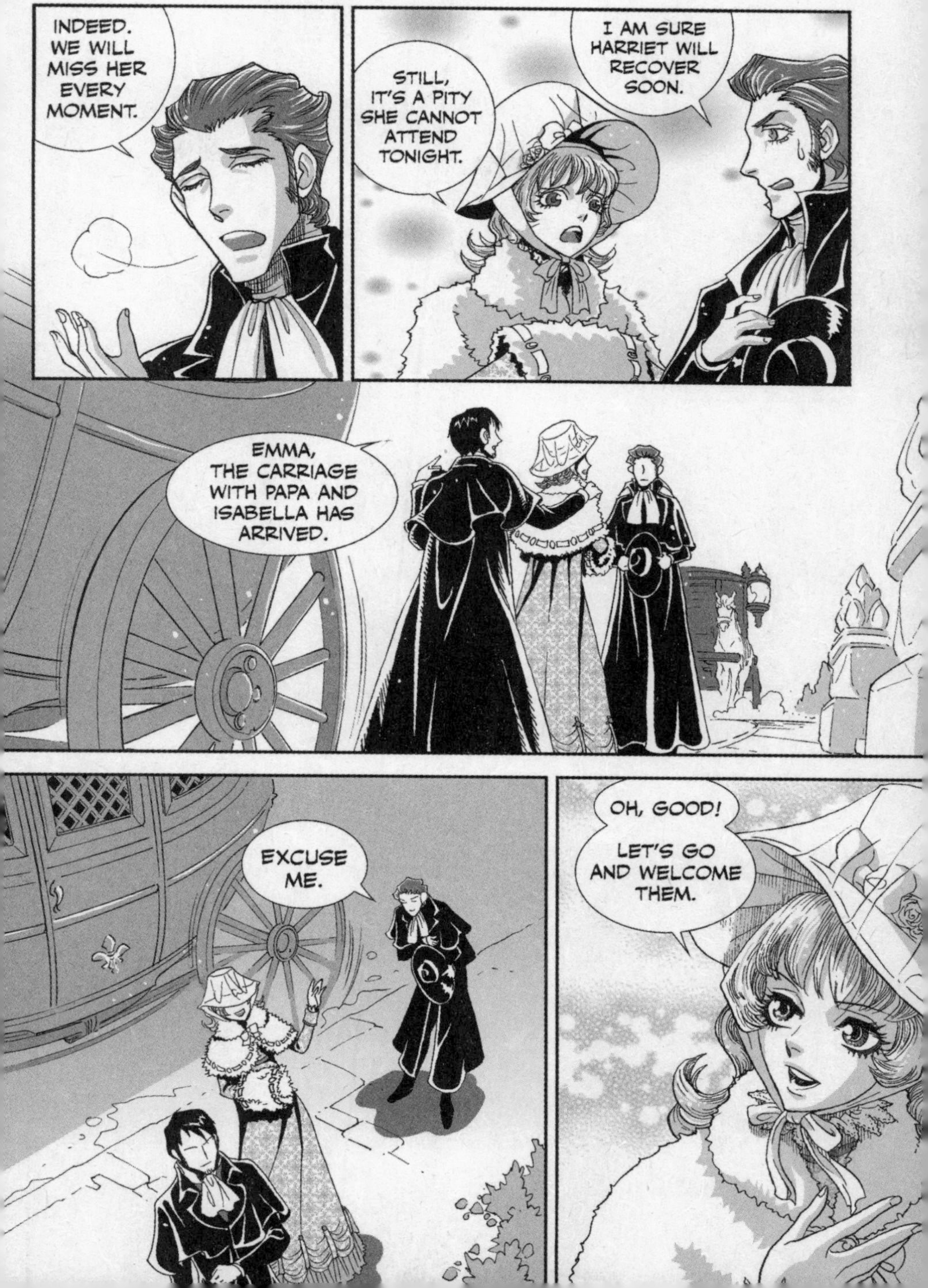
I AM SURE HARRIET WILL RECOVER SOON.
STILL, IT'S A PITY SHE CANNOT ATTEND TONIGHT.
INDEED. WE WILL MISS HER EVERY MOMENT.
EMMA, THE CARRIAGE WITH PAPA AND ISABELLA HAS ARRIVED.
OH, GOOD!
LET'S GO AND WELCOME THEM.
EXCUSE ME.

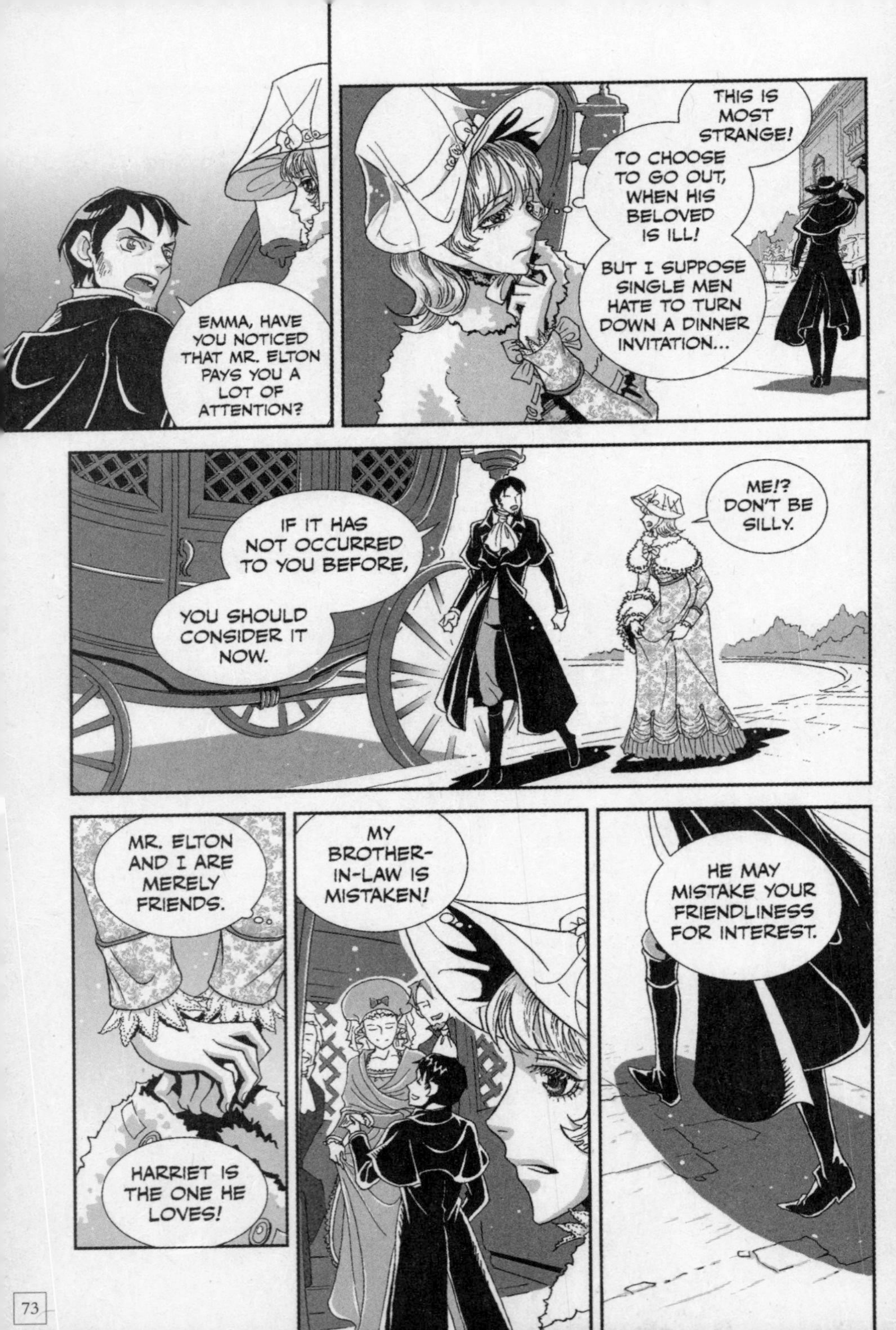
THIS IS MOST STRANGE!
TO CHOOSE TO GO OUT, WHEN HIS BELOVED IS ILL!
BUT I SUPPOSE SINGLE MEN HATE TO TURN DOWN A DINNER INVITATION...
EMMA, HAVE YOU NOTICED THAT MR. ELTON PAYS YOU A LOT OF ATTENTION?
ME!? DON'T BE SILLY.
IF IT HAS NOT OCCURRED TO YOU BEFORE,
YOU SHOULD CONSIDER IT NOW.
HE MAY MISTAKE YOUR FRIENDLINESS FOR INTEREST.
MY BROTHER-IN-LAW IS MISTAKEN!
MR. ELTON AND I ARE MERELY FRIENDS.
HARRIET IS THE ONE HE LOVES!

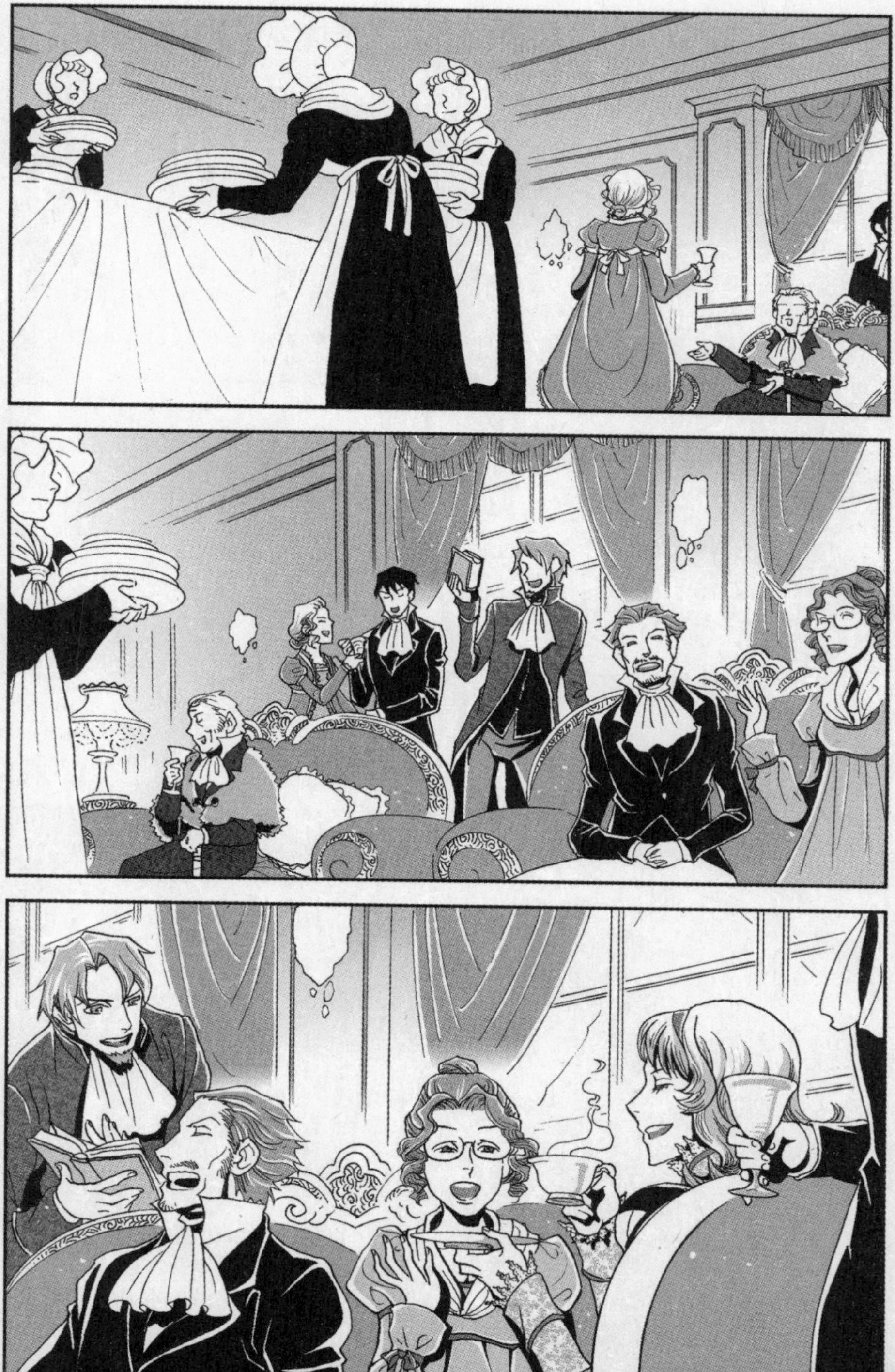

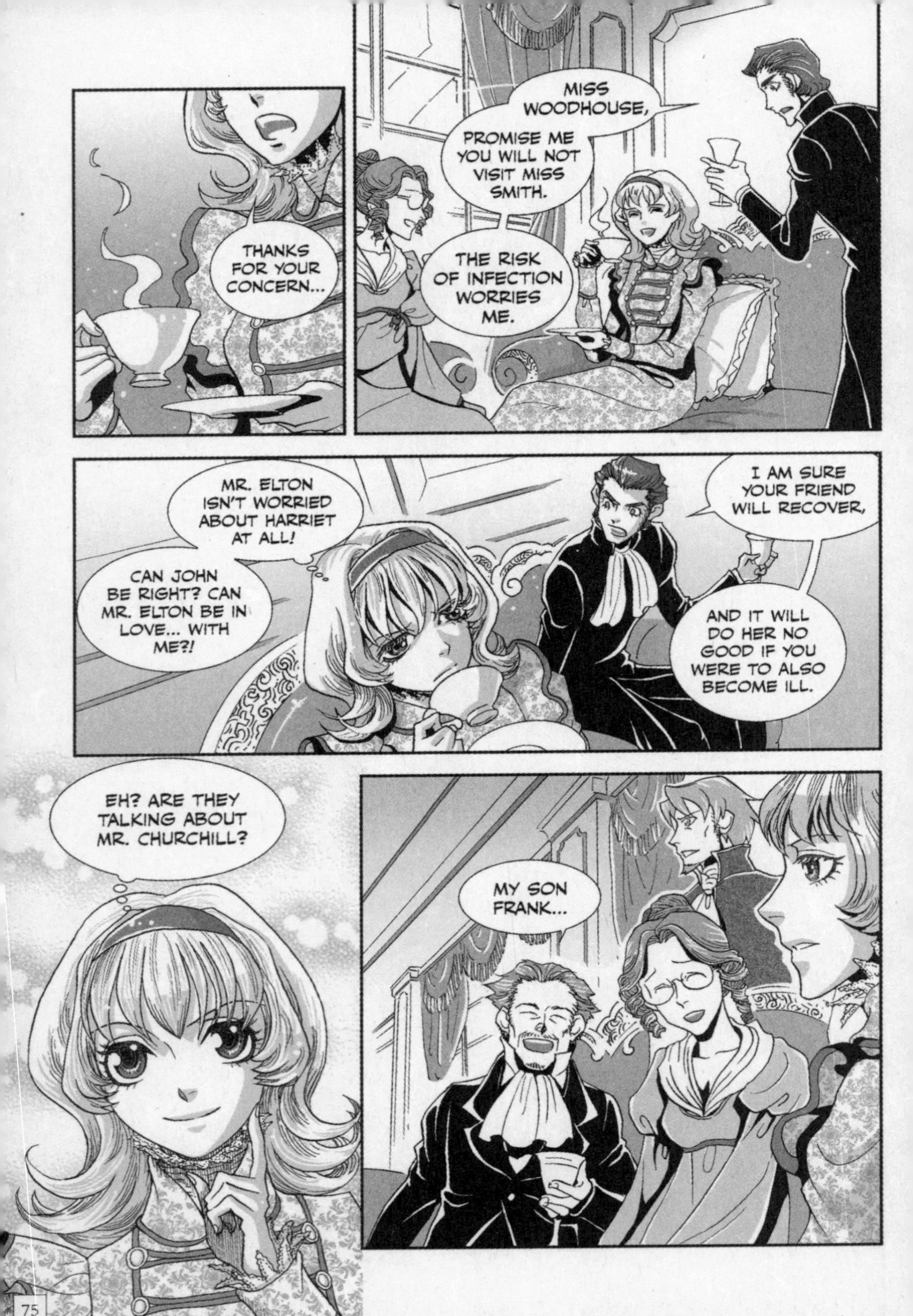
MISS WOODHOUSE, PROMISE ME YOU WILL NOT VISIT MISS SMITH.
THE RISK OF INFECTION WORRIES ME.
THANKS FOR YOUR CONCERN...
I AM SURE YOUR FRIEND WILL RECOVER,
AND IT WILL DO HER NO GOOD IF YOU WERE TO ALSO BECOME ILL.
MR. ELTON ISN'T WORRIED ABOUT HARRIET AT ALL!
CAN JOHN BE RIGHT? CAN MR. ELTON BE IN LOVE... WITH ME?!
MY SON FRANK...
EH? ARE THEY TALKING ABOUT MR. CHURCHILL?

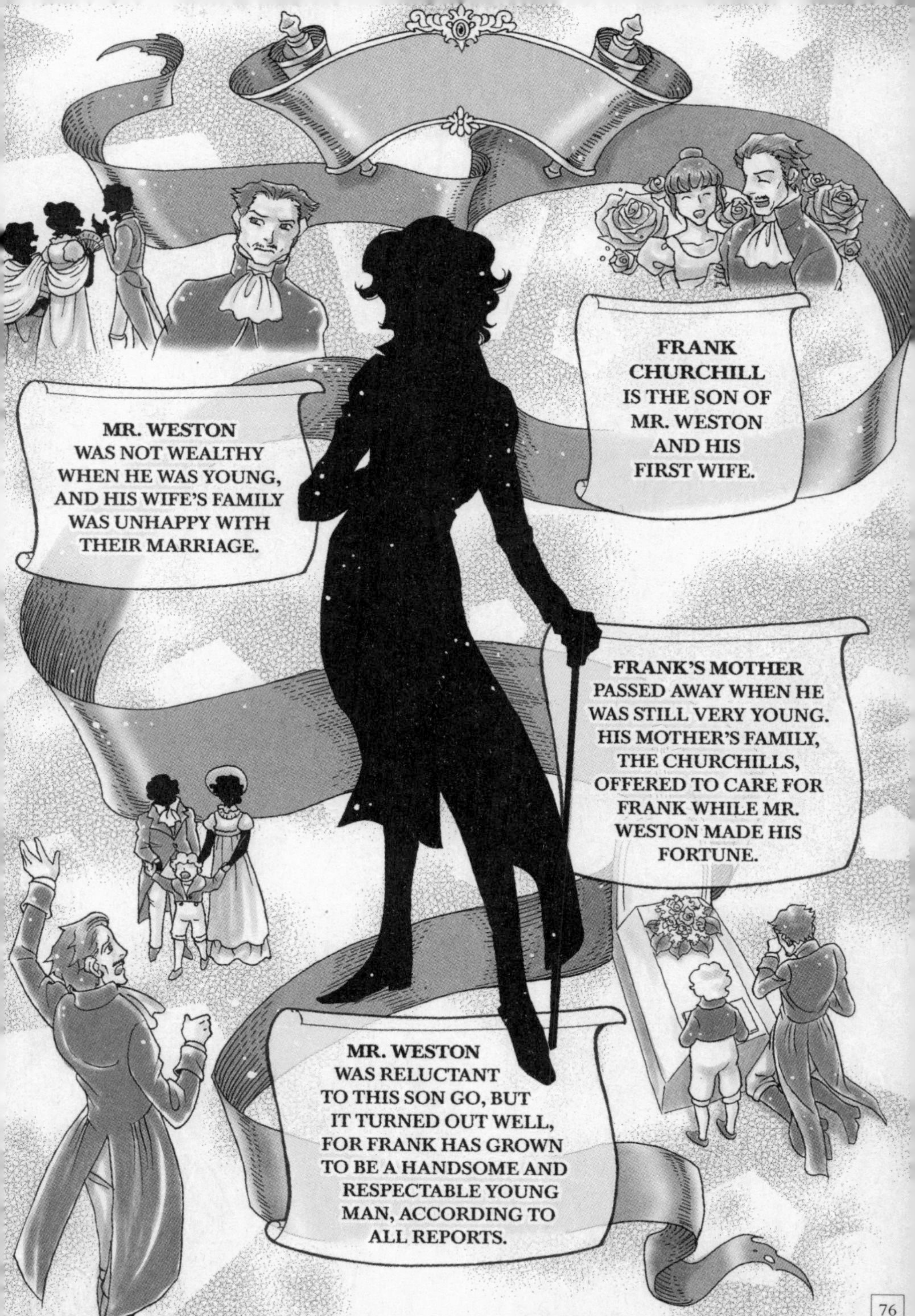
FRANK CHURCHILL IS THE SON OF MR. WESTON AND HIS FIRST WIFE.
MR. WESTON WAS NOT WEALTHY WHEN HE WAS YOUNG, AND HIS WIFE'S FAMILY WAS UNHAPPY WITH THEIR MARRIAGE.
FRANK'S MOTHER PASSED AWAY WHEN HE WAS STILL VERY YOUNG. HIS MOTHER'S FAMILY, THE CHURCHILLS, OFFERED TO CARE FOR FRANK WHILE MR. WESTON MADE HIS FORTUNE.
MR. WESTON WAS RELUCTANT TO THIS SON GO, BUT IT TURNED OUT WELL, FOR FRANK HAS GROWN TO BE A HANDSOME AND RESPECTABLE YOUNG MAN, ACCORDING TO ALL REPORTS.

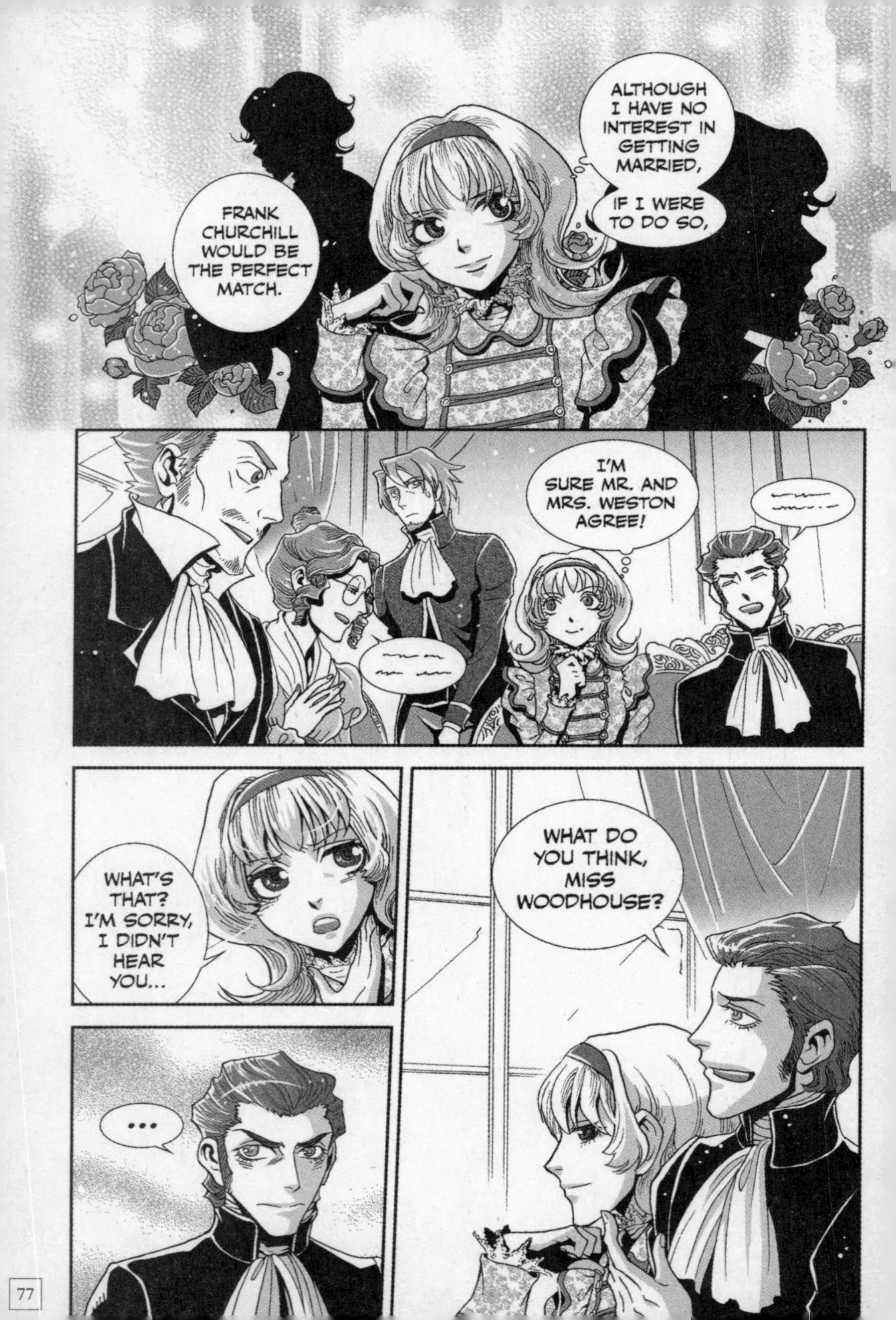
ALTHOUGH I HAVE NO INTEREST IN GETTING MARRIED,
IF I WERE TO DO SO,
FRANK CHURCHILL WOULD BE THE PERFECT MATCH.
I'M SURE MR. AND MRS. WESTON AGREE!
WHAT DO YOU THINK, MISS WOODHOUSE?
WHAT'S THAT? I'M SORRY, I DIDN'T HEAR YOU...
...

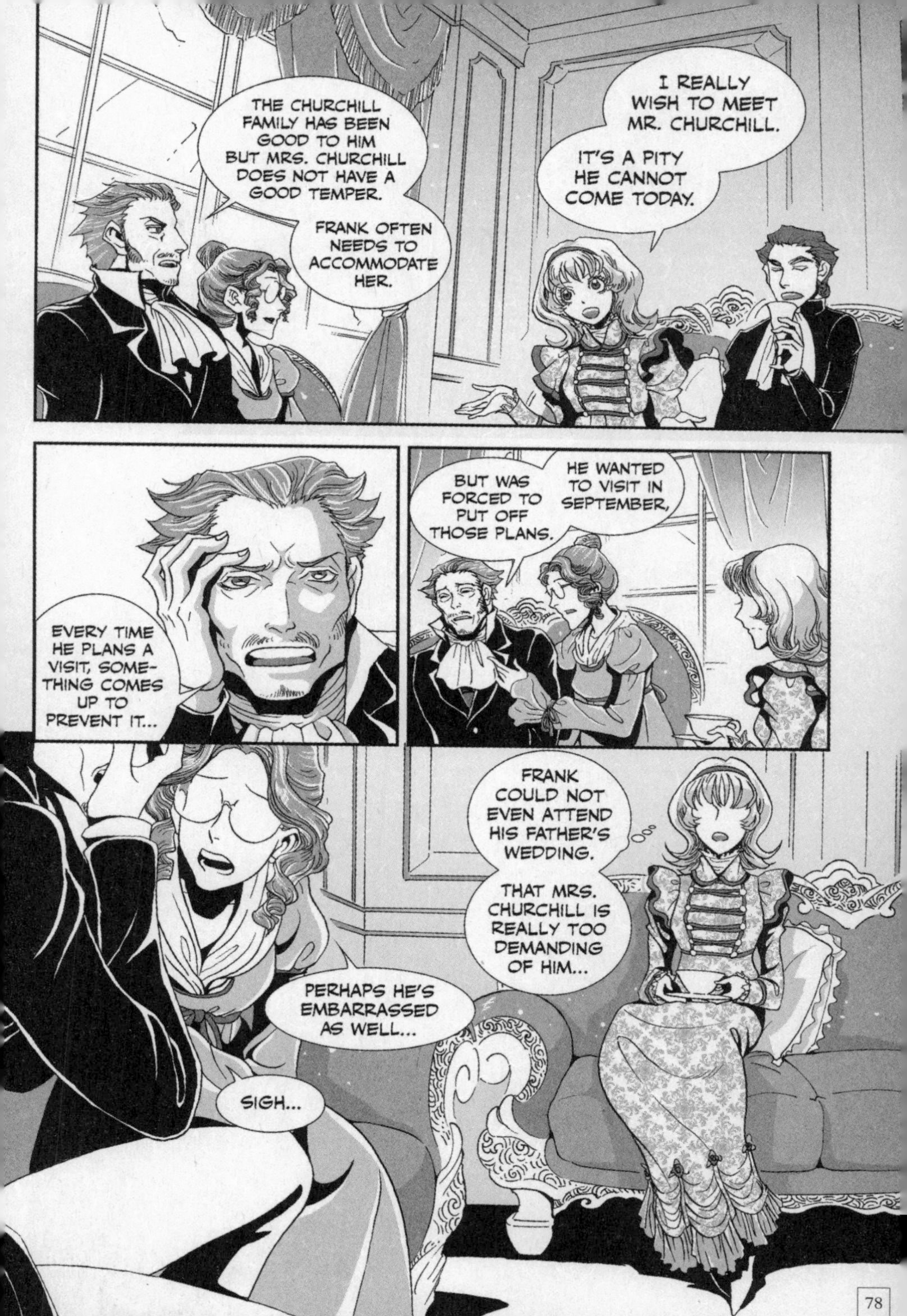
I REALLY WISH TO MEET MR. CHURCHILL.
IT'S A PITY HE CANNOT COME TODAY.
THE CHURCHILL FAMILY HAS BEEN GOOD TO HIM BUT MRS. CHURCHILL DOES NOT HAVE A GOOD TEMPER.
FRANK OFTEN NEEDS TO ACCOMMODATE HER.
HE WANTED TO VISIT IN SEPTEMBER,
BUT WAS FORCED TO PUT OFF THOSE PLANS.
EVERY TIME HE PLANS A VISIT, SOME-THING COMES UP TO PREVENT IT...
FRANK COULD NOT EVEN ATTEND HIS FATHER'S WEDDING.
THAT MRS. CHURCHILL IS REALLY TOO DEMANDING OF HIM...
PERHAPS HE'S EMBARRASSED AS WELL...
SIGH...

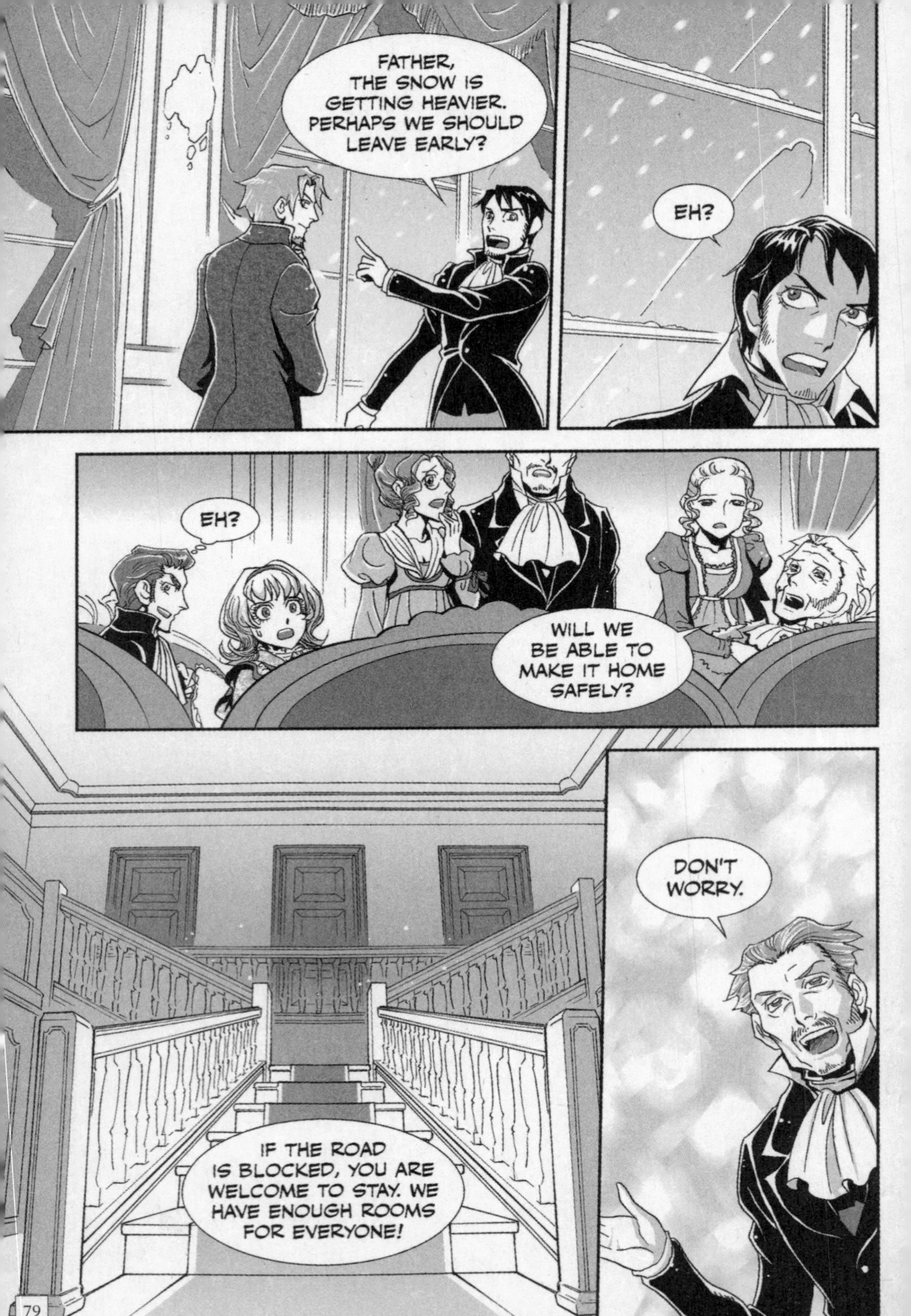
EH?
FATHER, THE SNOW IS GETTING HEAVIER. PERHAPS WE SHOULD LEAVE EARLY?
WILL WE BE ABLE TO MAKE IT HOME SAFELY?
EH?
DON'T WORRY.
IF THE ROAD IS BLOCKED, YOU ARE WELCOME TO STAY. WE HAVE ENOUGH ROOMS FOR EVERYONE!

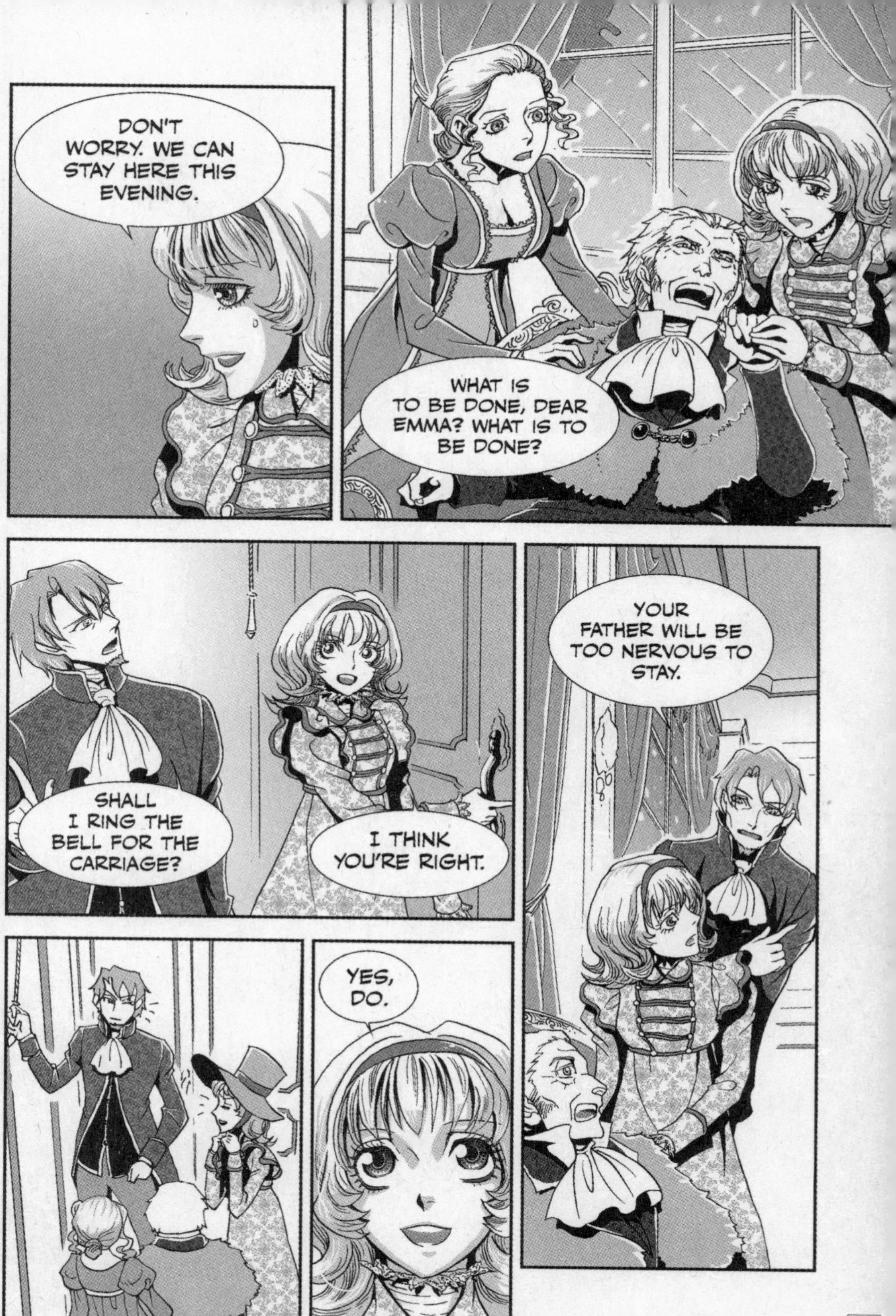
WHAT IS TO BE DONE, DEAR EMMA? WHAT IS TO BE DONE?
DON'T WORRY. WE CAN STAY HERE THIS EVENING.
YOUR FATHER WILL BE TOO NERVOUS TO STAY.
SHALL I RING THE BELL FOR THE CARRIAGE?
I THINK YOU'RE RIGHT.
YES, DO.

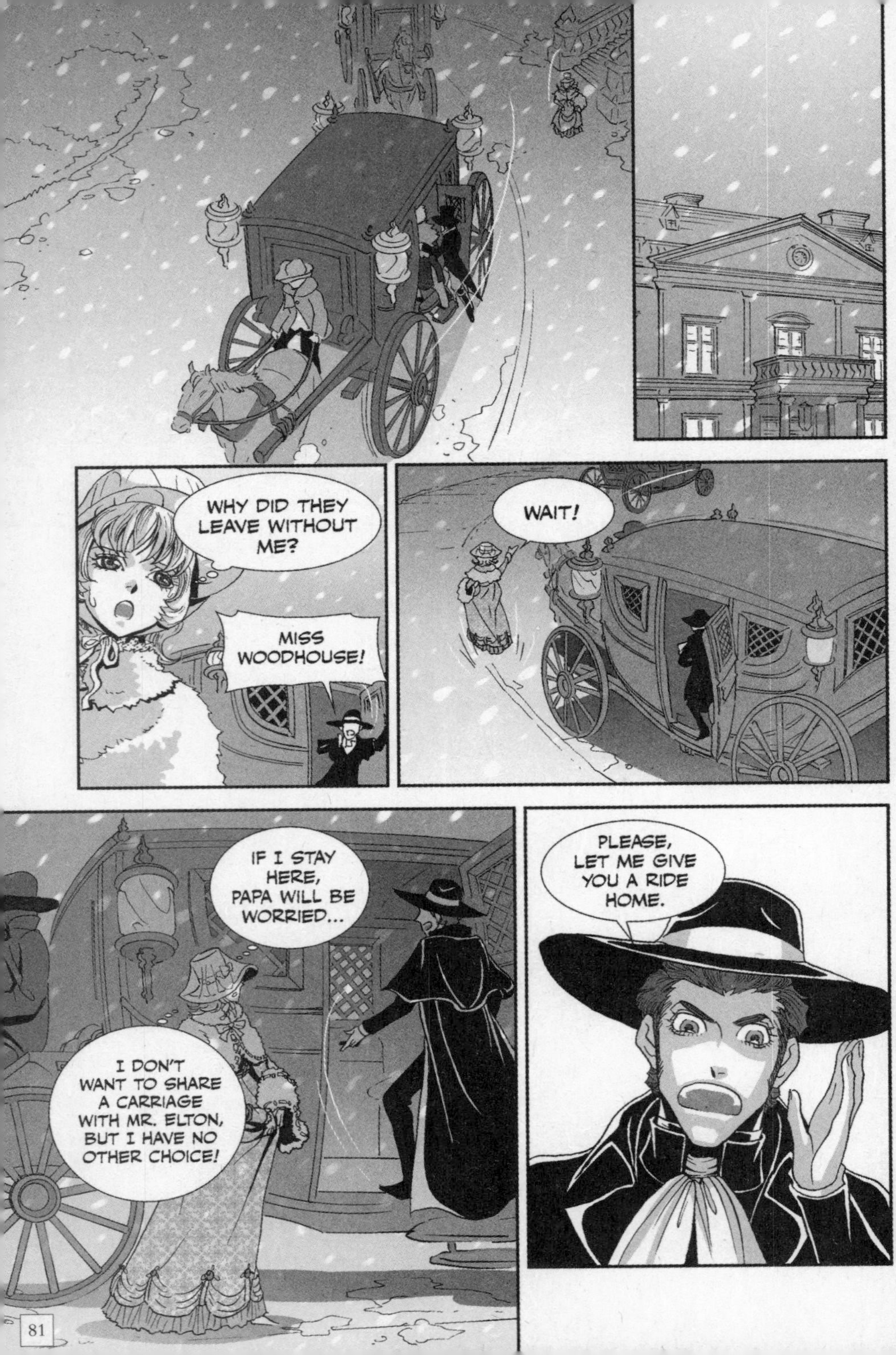
WAIT!
WHY DID THEY LEAVE WITHOUT ME?
MISS WOODHOUSE!
PLEASE, LET ME GIVE YOU A RIDE HOME.
IF I STAY HERE, PAPA WILL BE WORRIED...
I DON'T WANT TO SHARE A CARRIAGE WITH MR. ELTON, BUT I HAVE NO OTHER CHOICE!

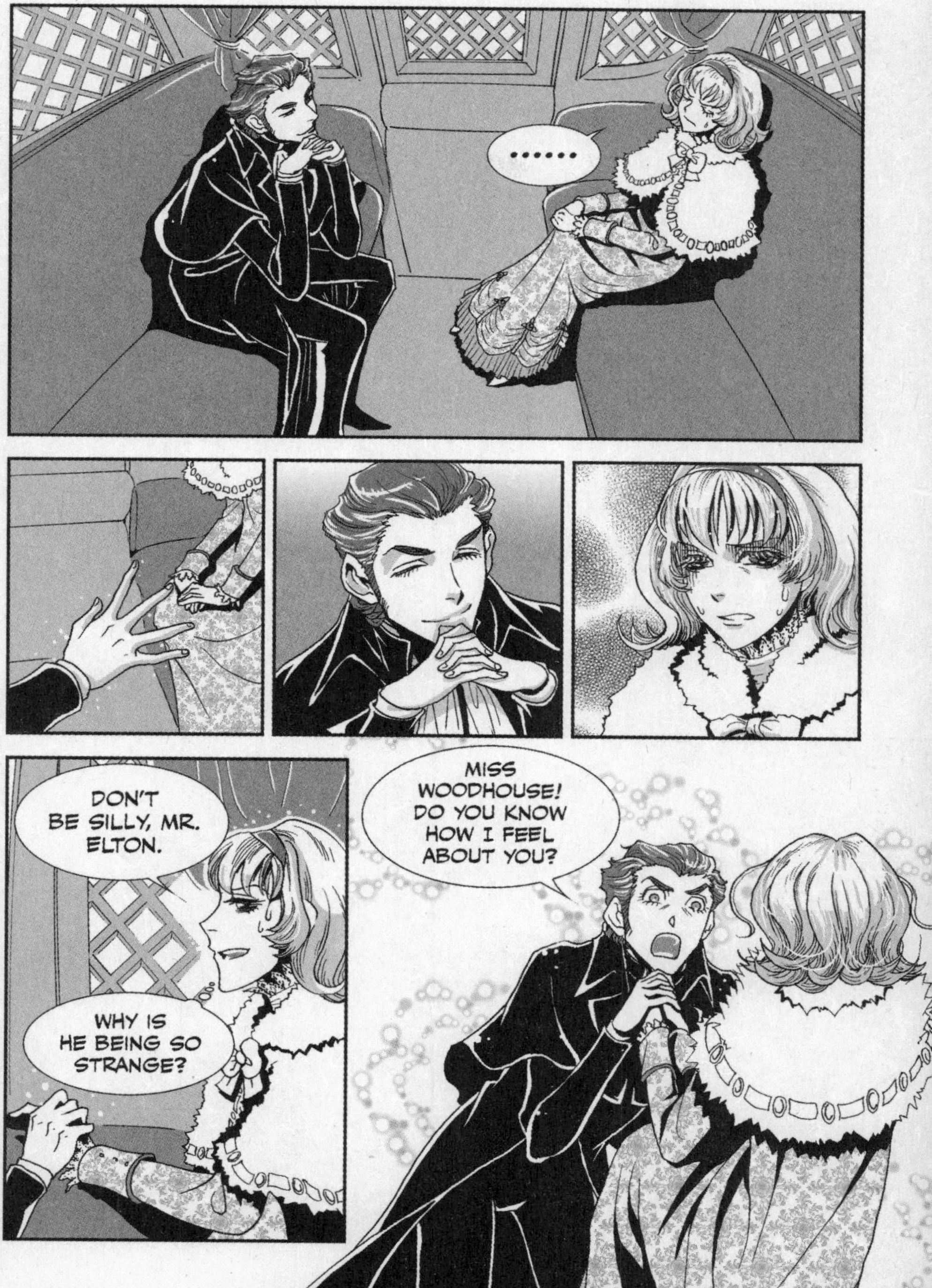
......
MISS WOODHOUSE! DO YOU KNOW HOW I FEEL ABOUT YOU?
DON'T BE SILLY, MR. ELTON.
WHY IS HE BEING SO STRANGE?

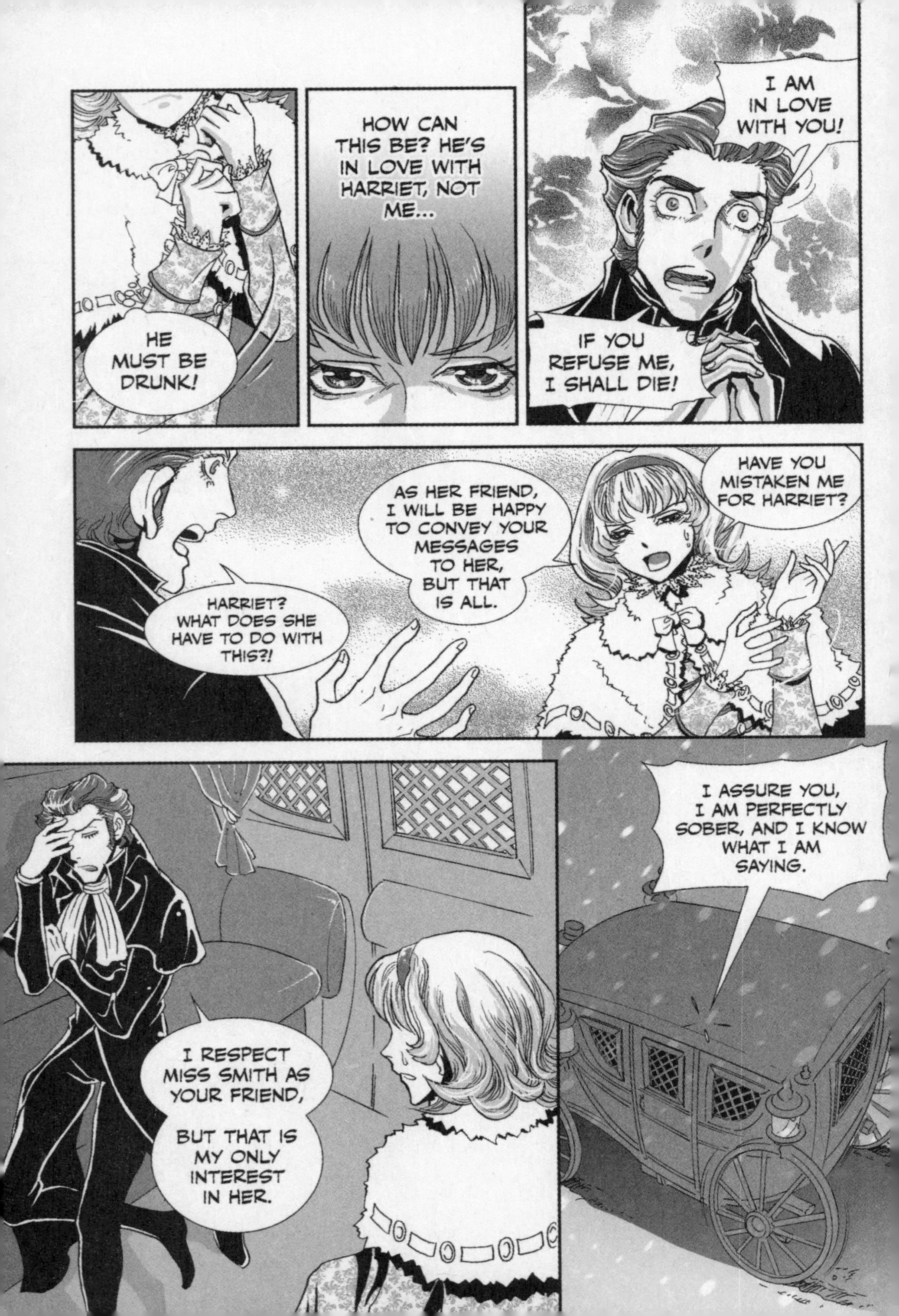
I AM IN LOVE WITH YOU!
IF YOU REFUSE ME, I SHALL DIE!
HOW CAN THIS BE? HE'S IN LOVE WITH HARRIET, NOT ME...
HE MUST BE DRUNK!
HAVE YOU MISTAKEN ME FOR HARRIET?
AS HER FRIEND, I WILL BE HAPPY TO CONVEY YOUR MESSAGES TO HER, BUT THAT IS ALL.
HARRIET? WHAT DOES SHE HAVE TO DO WITH THIS?!
I ASSURE YOU, I AM PERFECTLY SOBER, AND I KNOW WHAT I AM SAYING.
I RESPECT MISS SMITH AS YOUR FRIEND,
BUT THAT IS MY ONLY INTEREST IN HER.

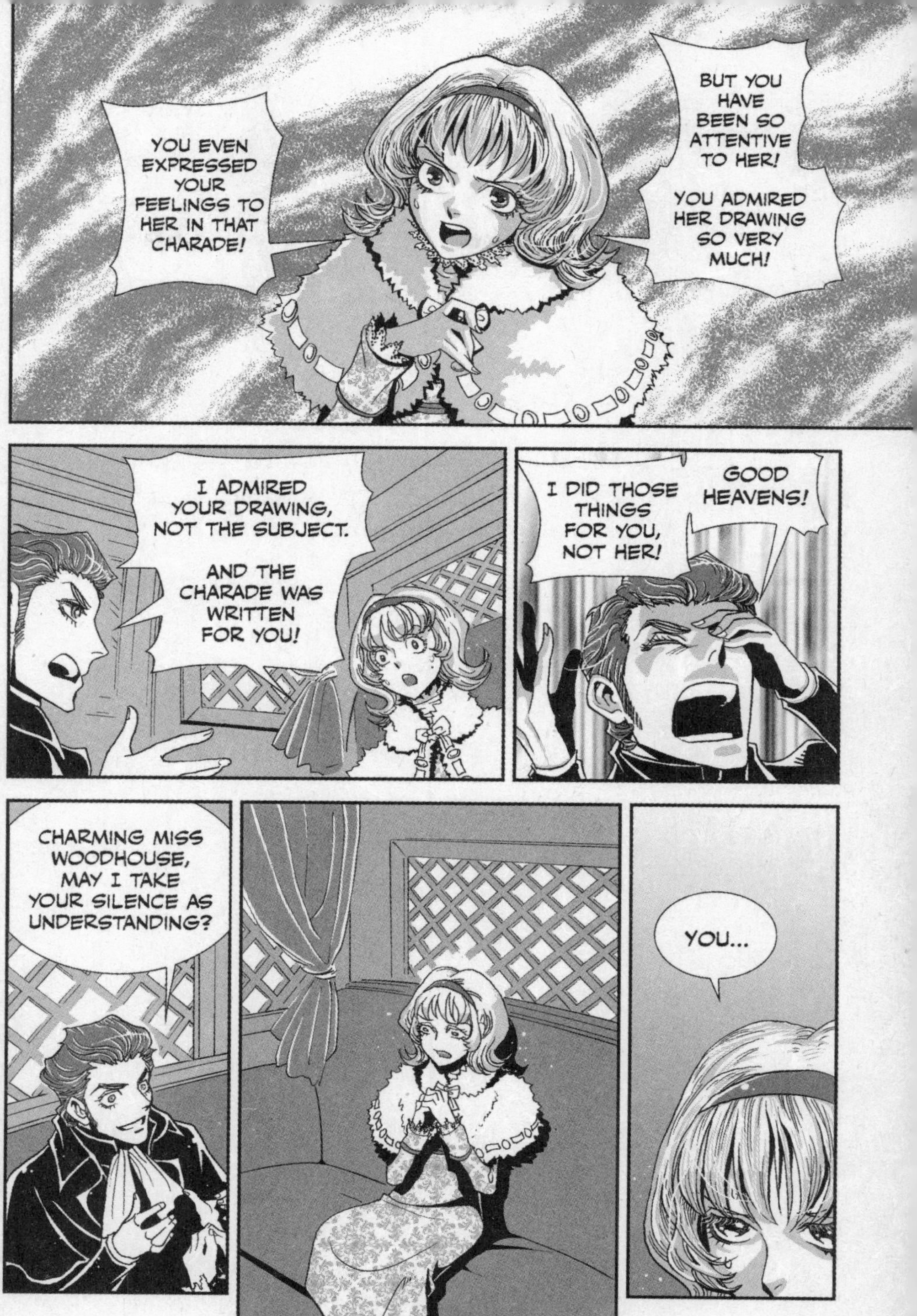
BUT YOU HAVE BEEN SO ATTENTIVE TO HER!
YOU ADMIRED HER DRAWING SO VERY MUCH!
YOU EVEN EXPRESSED YOUR FEELINGS TO HER IN THAT CHARADE!
GOOD HEAVENS!
I DID THOSE THINGS FOR YOU, NOT HER!
I ADMIRED YOUR DRAWING, NOT THE SUBJECT.
AND THE CHARADE WAS WRITTEN FOR YOU!
YOU...
CHARMING MISS WOODHOUSE, MAY I TAKE YOUR SILENCE AS UNDERSTANDING?

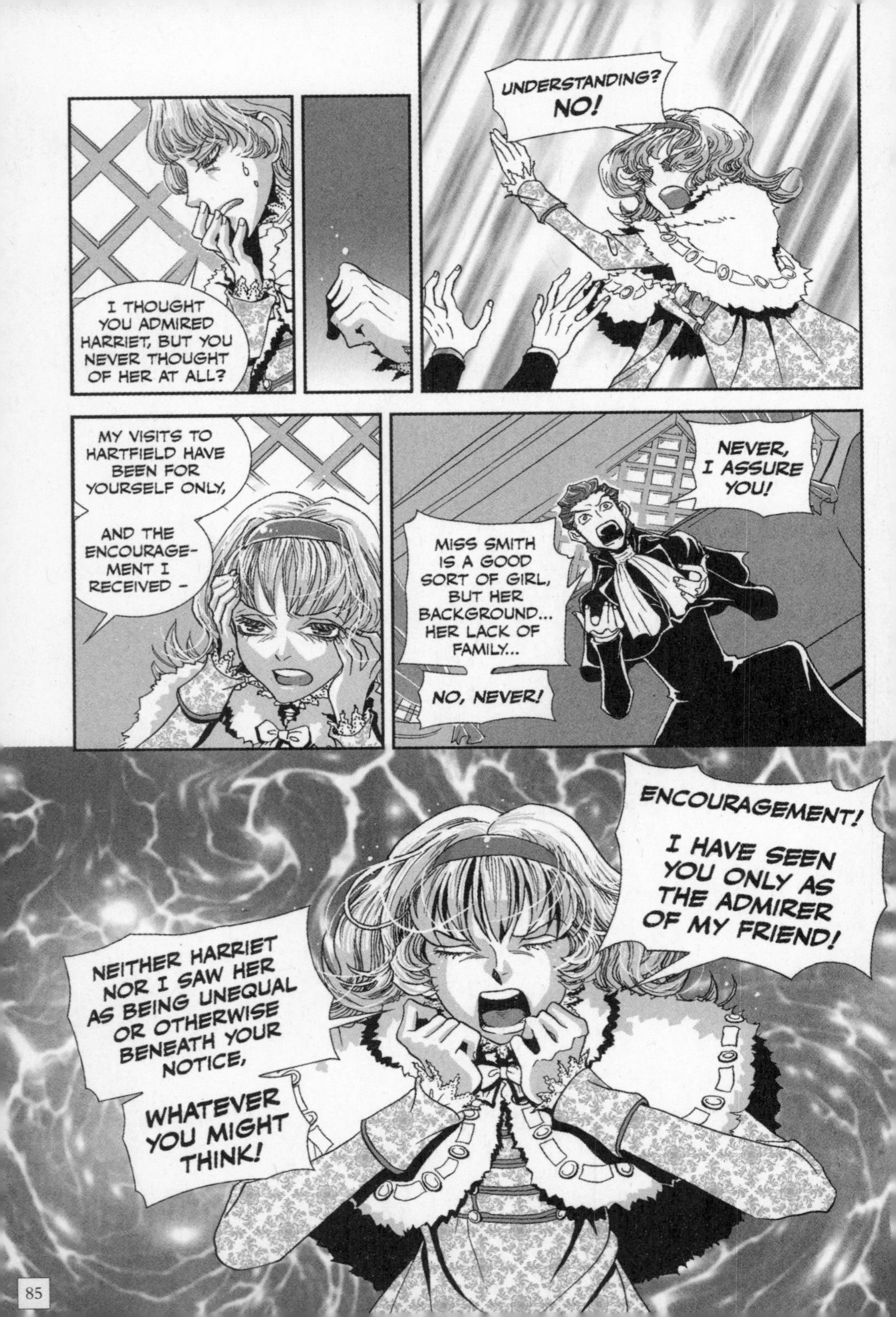
UNDERSTANDING? NO!
I THOUGHT YOU ADMIRED HARRIET, BUT YOU NEVER THOUGHT OF HER AT ALL?
NEVER, I ASSURE YOU!
MISS SMITH IS A GOOD SORT OF GIRL, BUT HER BACKGROUND... HER LACK OF FAMILY...
NO, NEVER!
MY VISITS TO HARTFIELD HAVE BEEN FOR YOURSELF ONLY,
AND THE ENCOURAGEMENT I RECEIVED –
ENCOURAGEMENT!
I HAVE SEEN YOU ONLY AS THE ADMIRER OF MY FRIEND!
NEITHER HARRIET NOR I SAW HER AS BEING UNEQUAL OR OTHERWISE BENEATH YOUR NOTICE,
WHATEVER YOU MIGHT THINK!

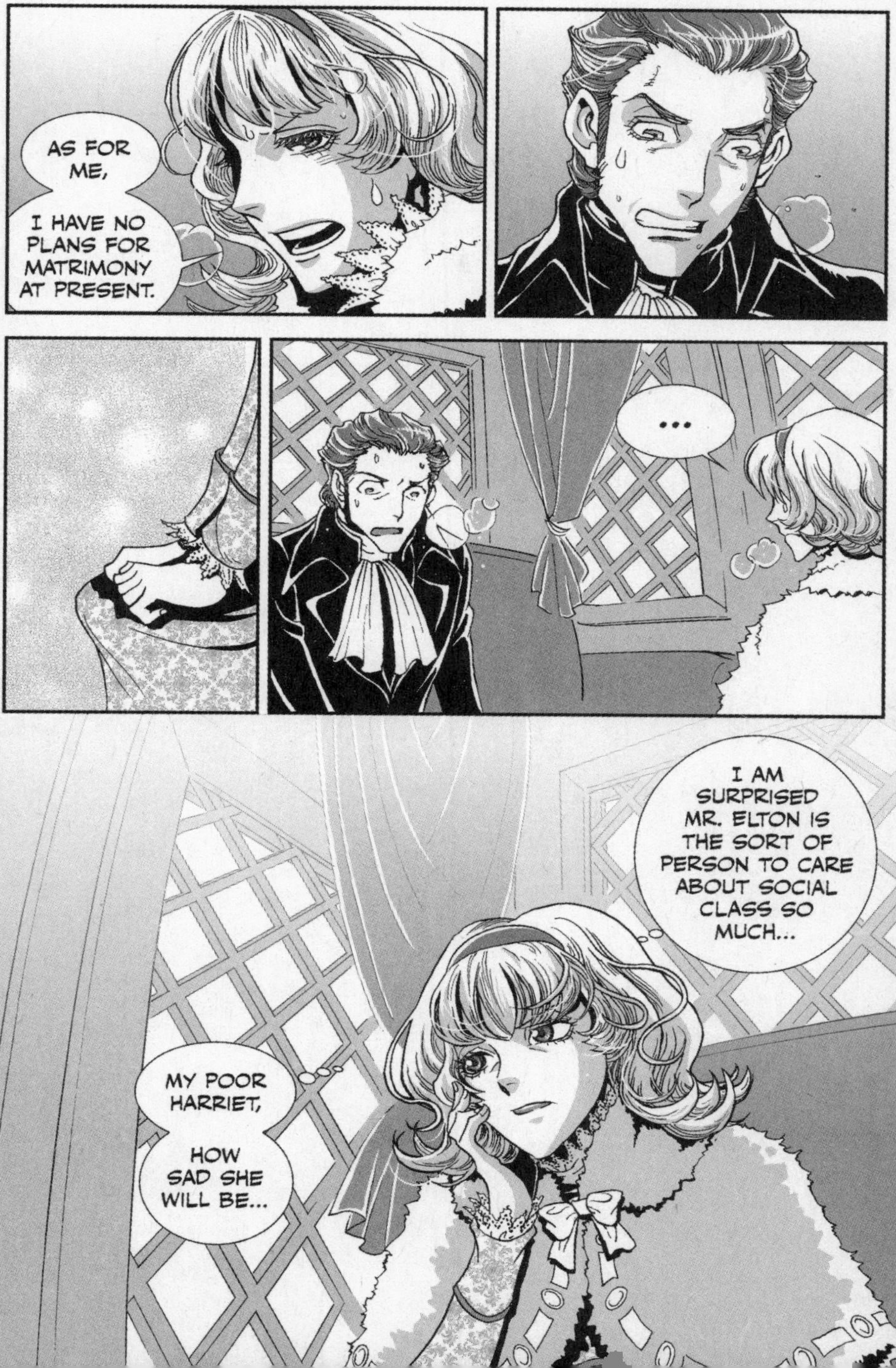
AS FOR ME,
I HAVE NO PLANS FOR MATRIMONY AT PRESENT.
...
I AM SURPRISED MR. ELTON IS THE SORT OF PERSON TO CARE ABOUT SOCIAL CLASS SO MUCH...
MY POOR HARRIET,
HOW SAD SHE WILL BE...

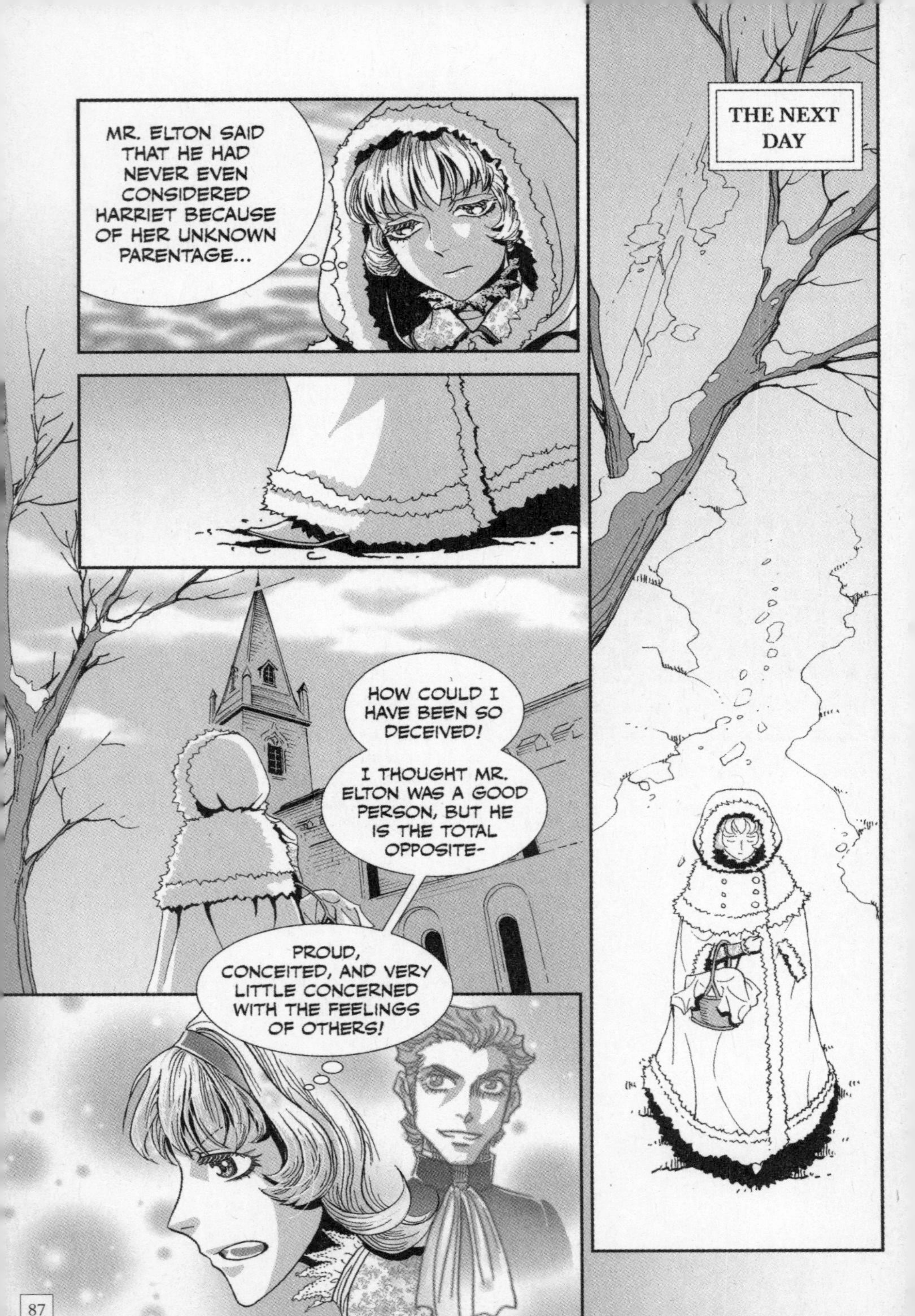
THE NEXT DAY
MR. ELTON SAID THAT HE HAD NEVER EVEN CONSIDERED HARRIET BECAUSE OF HER UNKNOWN PARENTAGE...
HOW COULD I HAVE BEEN SO DECEIVED!
I THOUGHT MR. ELTON WAS A GOOD PERSON, BUT HE IS THE TOTAL OPPOSITE-
PROUD, CONCEITED, AND VERY LITTLE CONCERNED WITH THE FEELINGS OF OTHERS!

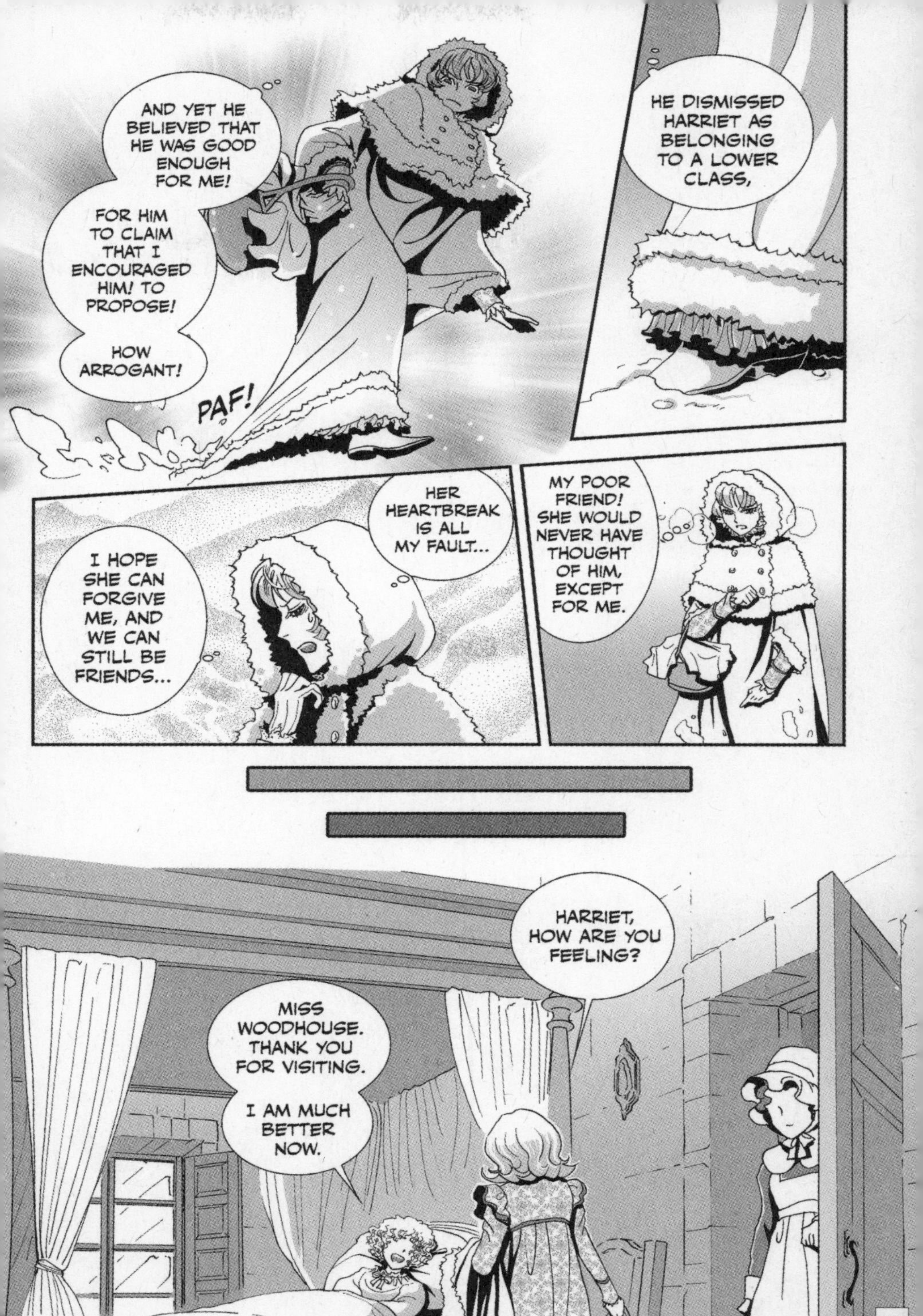
HE DISMISSED HARRIET AS BELONGING TO A LOWER CLASS,
AND YET HE BELIEVED THAT HE WAS GOOD ENOUGH FOR ME!
FOR HIM TO CLAIM THAT I ENCOURAGED HIM! TO PROPOSE!
HOW ARROGANT!
PAF!
MY POOR FRIEND! SHE WOULD NEVER HAVE THOUGHT OF HIM, EXCEPT FOR ME.
HER HEARTBREAK IS ALL MY FAULT...
I HOPE SHE CAN FORGIVE ME, AND WE CAN STILL BE FRIENDS...
HARRIET, HOW ARE YOU FEELING?
MISS WOODHOUSE. THANK YOU FOR VISITING.
I AM MUCH BETTER NOW.

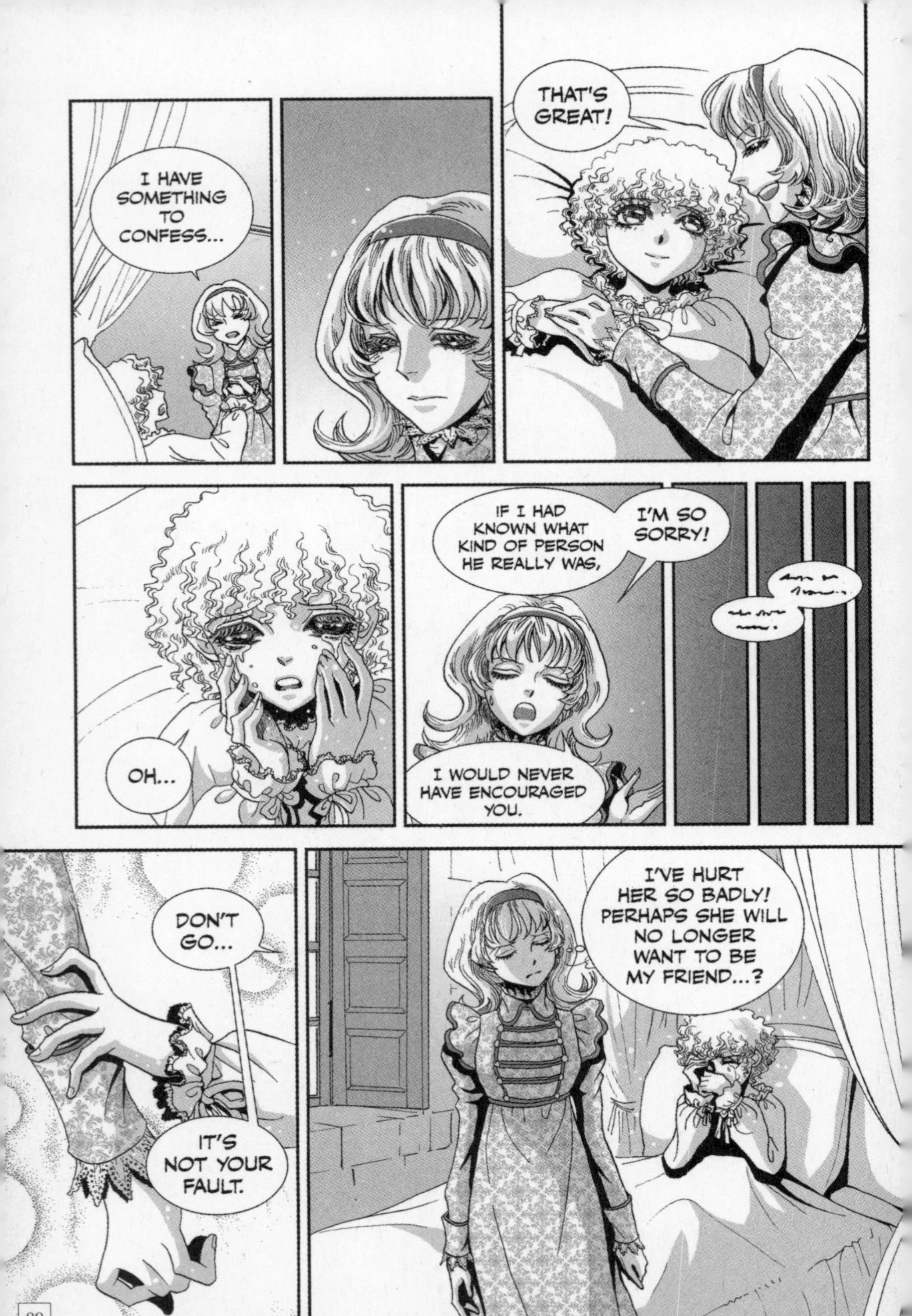
THAT'S GREAT!
I HAVE SOMETHING TO CONFESS...
I'M SO SORRY!
IF I HAD KNOWN WHAT KIND OF PERSON HE REALLY WAS,
I WOULD NEVER HAVE ENCOURAGED YOU.
OH...
I'VE HURT HER SO BADLY! PERHAPS SHE WILL NO LONGER WANT TO BE MY FRIEND...?
DON'T GO...
IT'S NOT YOUR FAULT.

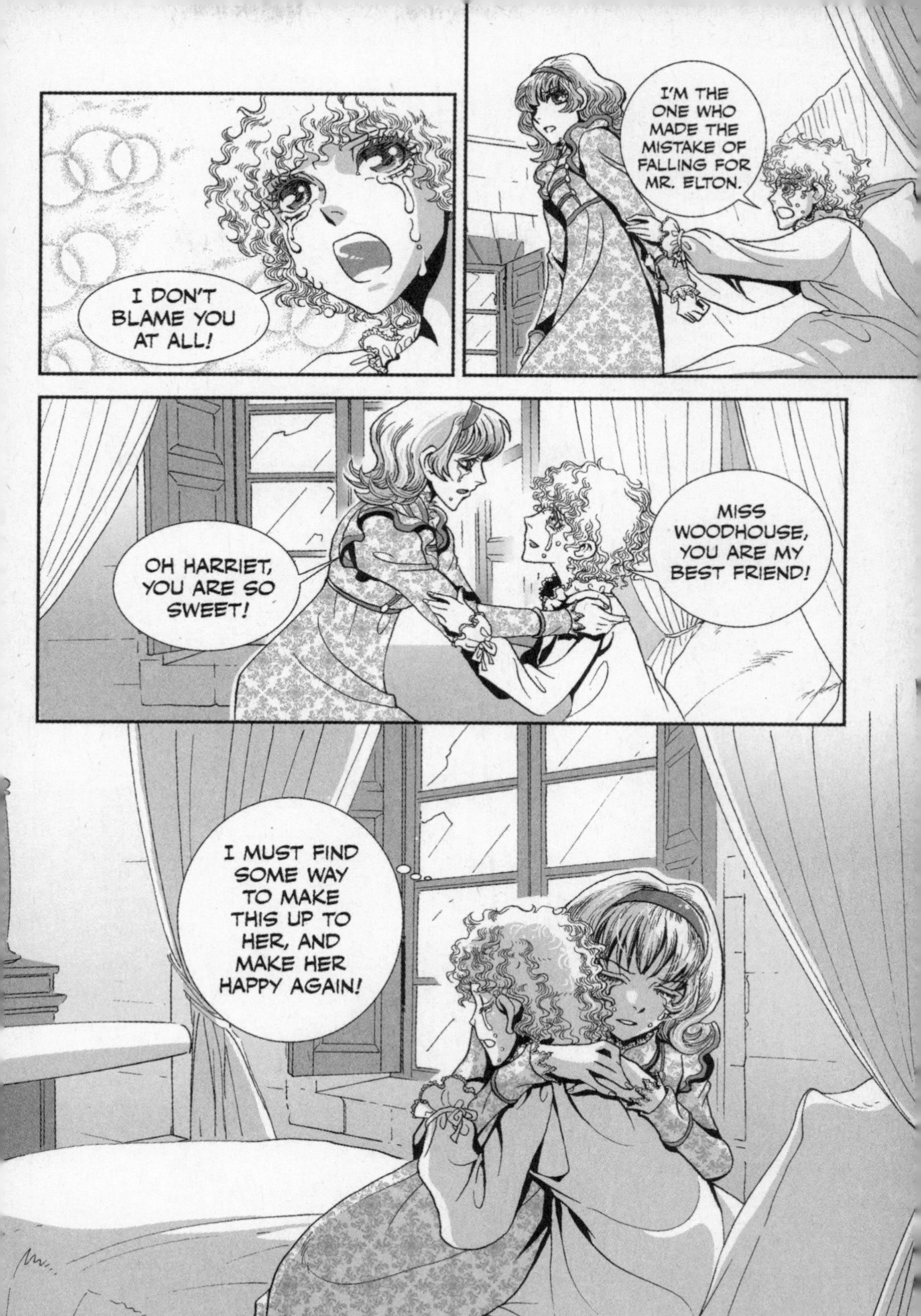
I'M THE ONE WHO MADE THE MISTAKE OF FALLING FOR MR. ELTON.
I DON'T BLAME YOU AT ALL!
MISS WOODHOUSE, YOU ARE MY BEST FRIEND!
OH HARRIET, YOU ARE SO SWEET!
I MUST FIND SOME WAY TO MAKE THIS UP TO HER, AND MAKE HER HAPPY AGAIN!

CHARACTER MODEL SHEET

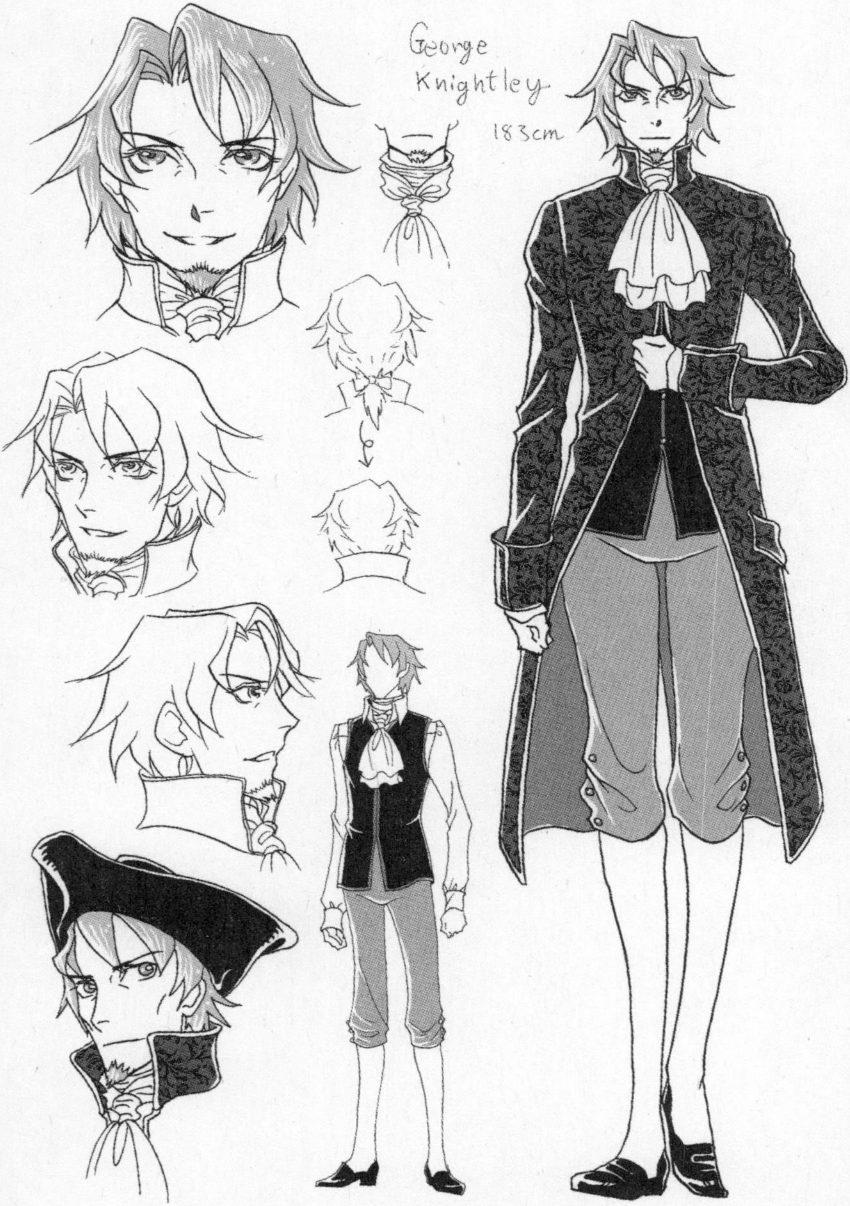
George
Knightley
183cm

George Knightley

CHARACTER MODEL SHEET

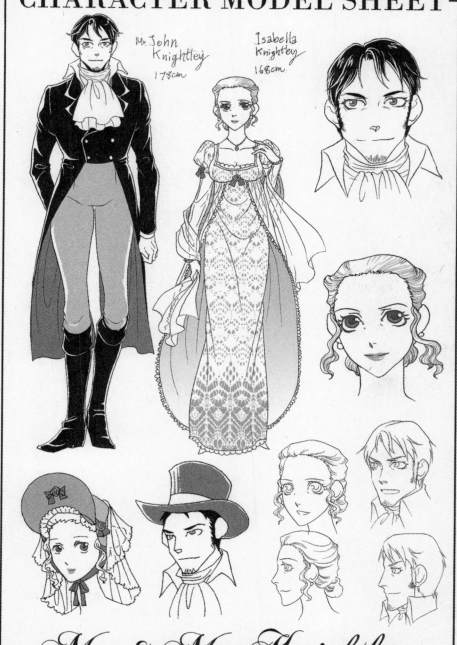

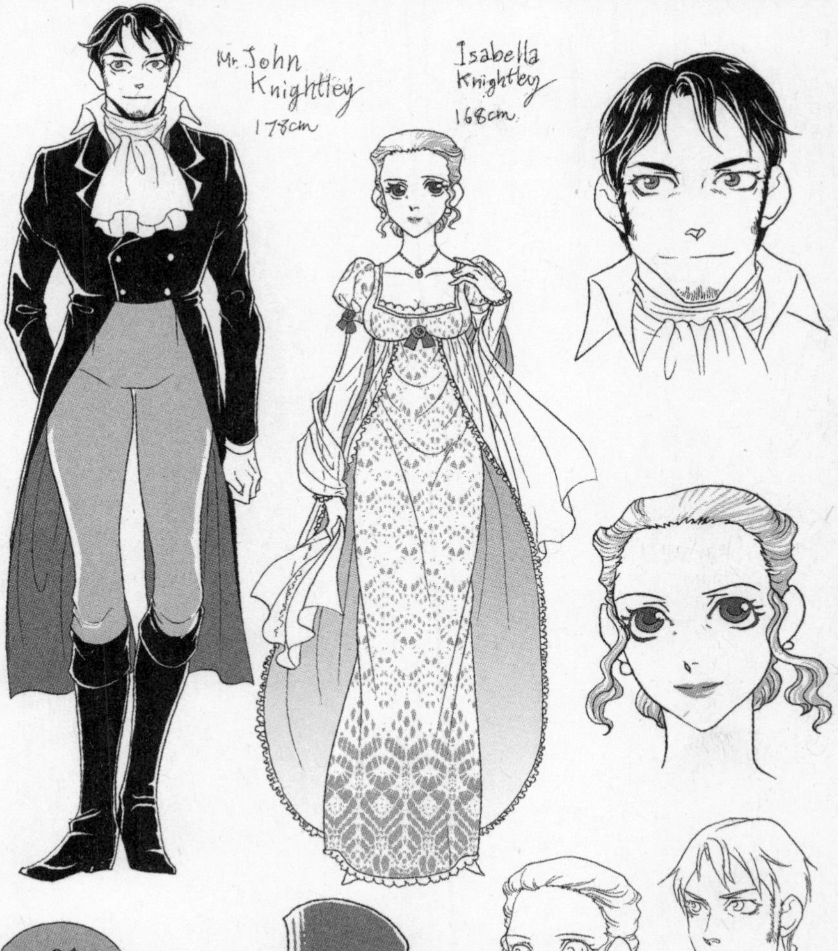
Mr. John Knightley
178cm
Isabella Knightley
168cm

Mr. & Mrs. Knightley

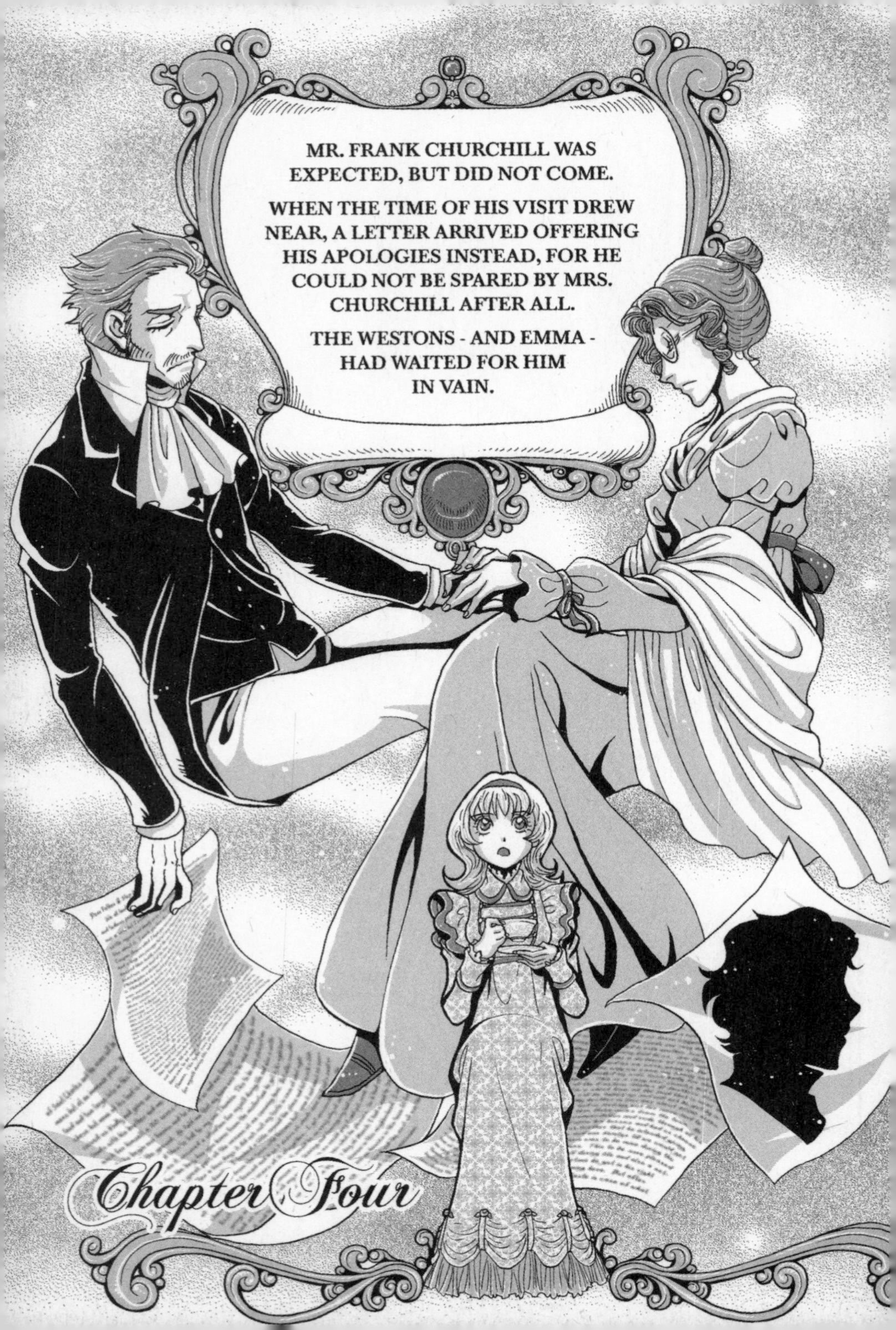
MR. FRANK CHURCHILL WAS EXPECTED, BUT DID NOT COME.
WHEN THE TIME OF HIS VISIT DREW NEAR, A LETTER ARRIVED OFFERING HIS APOLOGIES INSTEAD, FOR HE COULD NOT BE SPARED BY MRS. CHURCHILL AFTER ALL.
THE WESTONS - AND EMMA - HAD WAITED FOR HIM IN VAIN.
Chapter Four

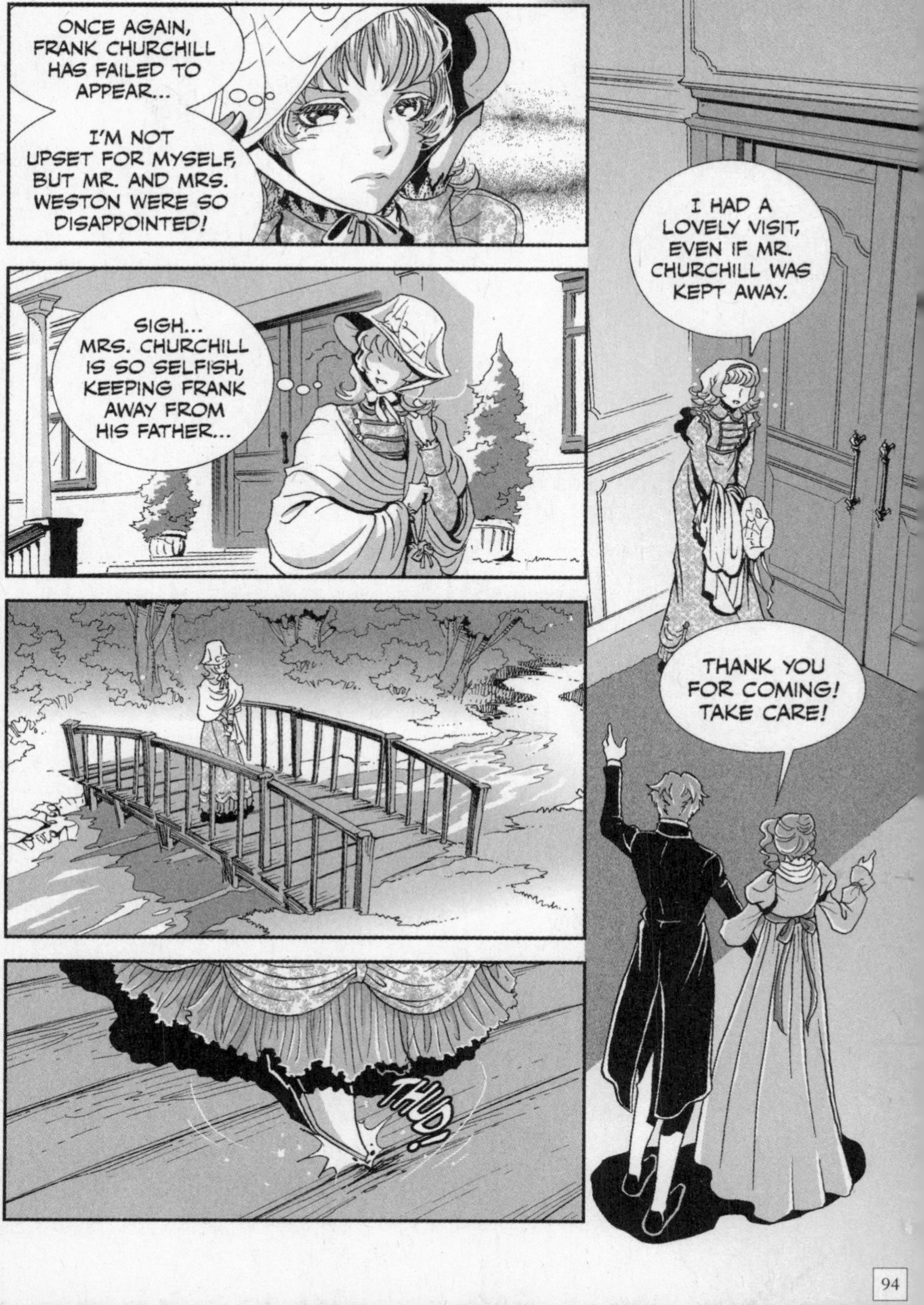
I HAD A LOVELY VISIT, EVEN IF MR. CHURCHILL WAS KEPT AWAY.
THANK YOU FOR COMING! TAKE CARE!
ONCE AGAIN, FRANK CHURCHILL HAS FAILED TO APPEAR...
I'M NOT UPSET FOR MYSELF, BUT MR. AND MRS. WESTON WERE SO DISAPPOINTED!
SIGH... MRS. CHURCHILL IS SO SELFISH, KEEPING FRANK AWAY FROM HIS FATHER...
THUD!

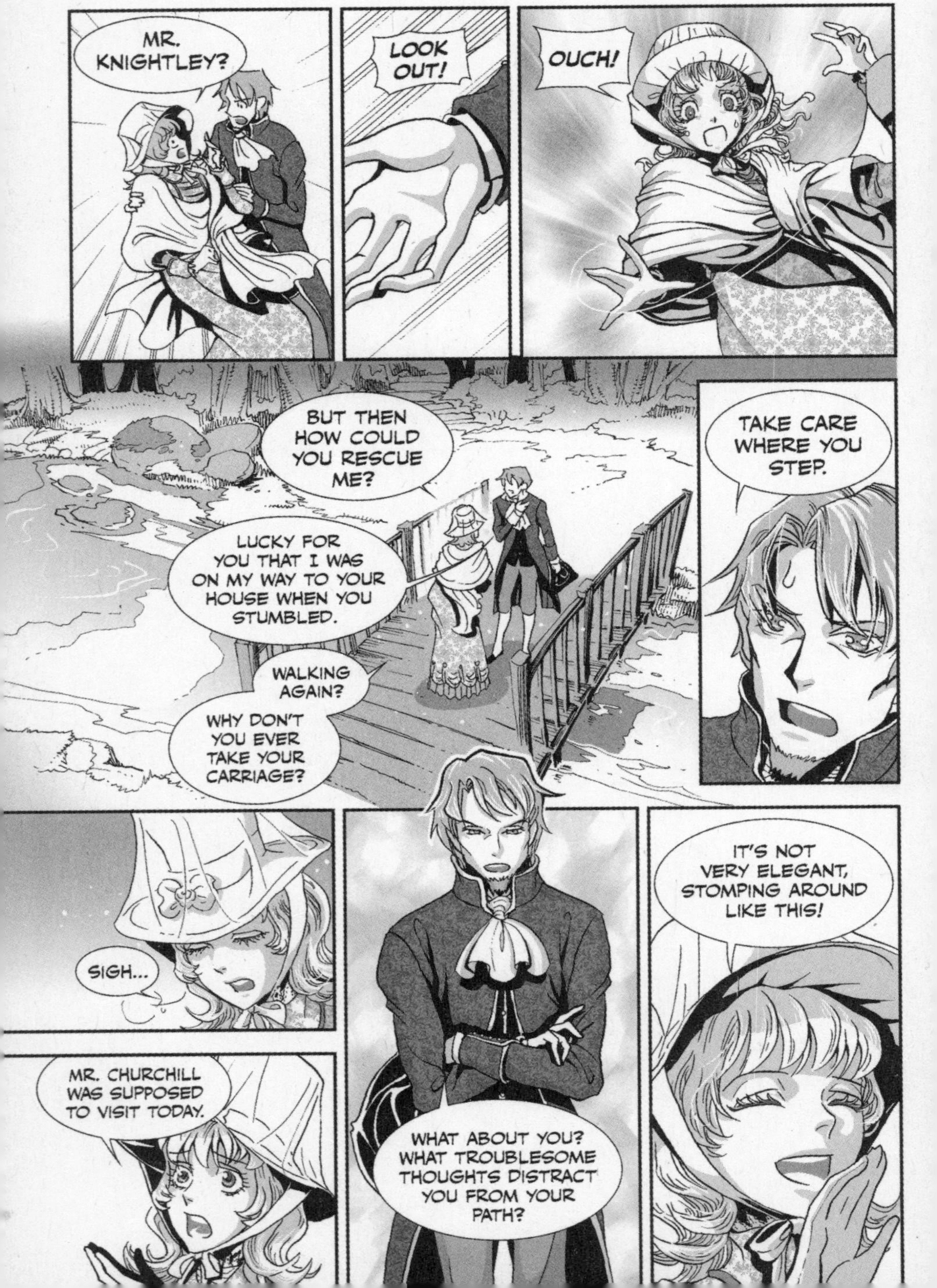
OUCH!
LOOK OUT!
MR. KNIGHTLEY?
TAKE CARE WHERE YOU STEP.
BUT THEN HOW COULD YOU RESCUE ME?
LUCKY FOR YOU THAT I WAS ON MY WAY TO YOUR HOUSE WHEN YOU STUMBLED.
WALKING AGAIN?
WHY DON'T YOU EVER TAKE YOUR CARRIAGE?
IT'S NOT VERY ELEGANT, STOMPING AROUND LIKE THIS!
WHAT ABOUT YOU? WHAT TROUBLESOME THOUGHTS DISTRACT YOU FROM YOUR PATH?
SIGH...
MR. CHURCHILL WAS SUPPOSED TO VISIT TODAY.

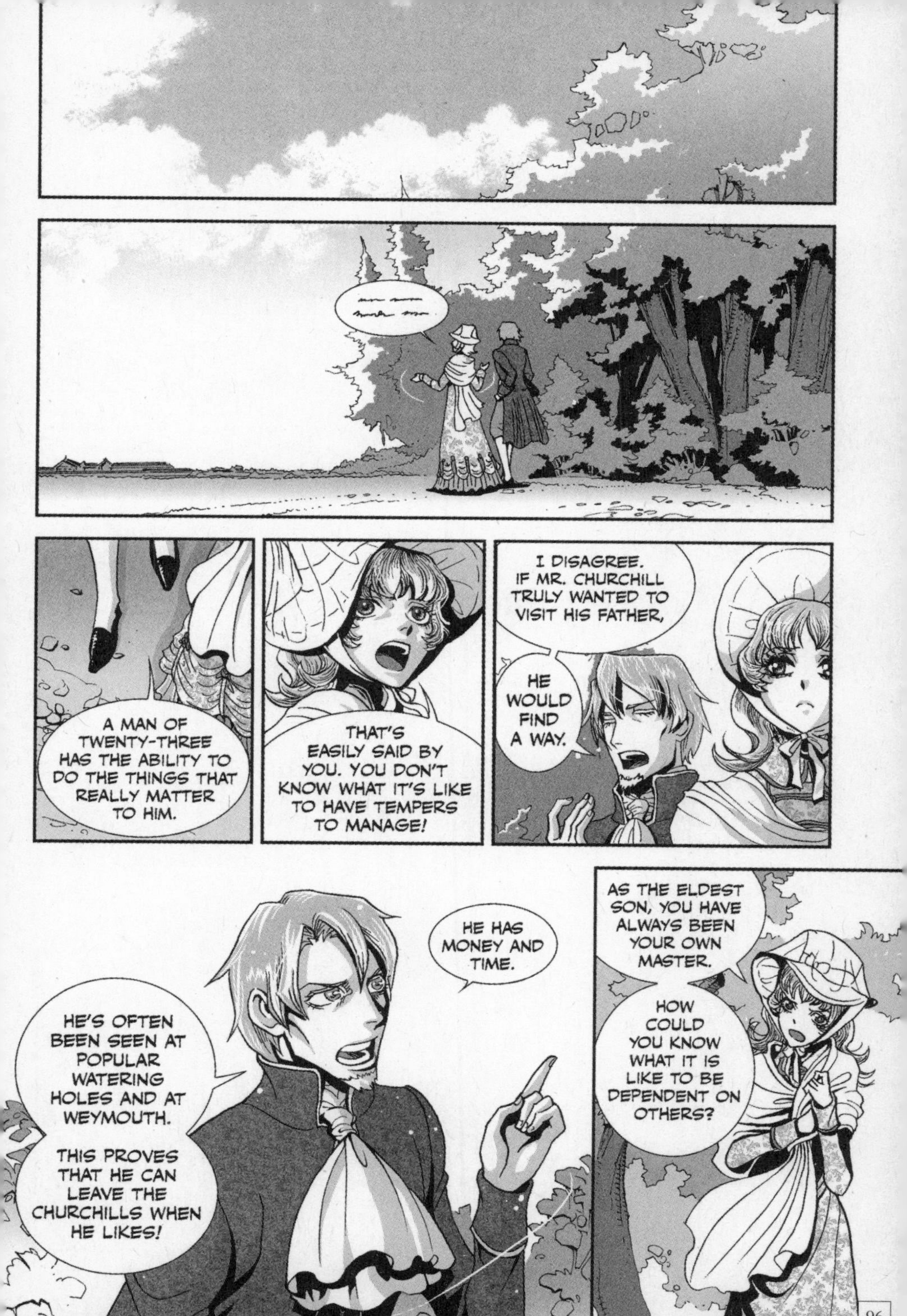
I DISAGREE. IF MR. CHURCHILL TRULY WANTED TO VISIT HIS FATHER,
HE WOULD FIND A WAY.
THAT'S EASILY SAID BY YOU. YOU DON'T KNOW WHAT IT'S LIKE TO HAVE TEMPERS TO MANAGE!
A MAN OF TWENTY-THREE HAS THE ABILITY TO DO THE THINGS THAT REALLY MATTER TO HIM.
AS THE ELDEST SON, YOU HAVE ALWAYS BEEN YOUR OWN MASTER.
HOW COULD YOU KNOW WHAT IT IS LIKE TO BE DEPENDENT ON OTHERS?
HE HAS MONEY AND TIME.
HE'S OFTEN BEEN SEEN AT POPULAR WATERING HOLES AND AT WEYMOUTH.
THIS PROVES THAT HE CAN LEAVE THE CHURCHILLS WHEN HE LIKES!

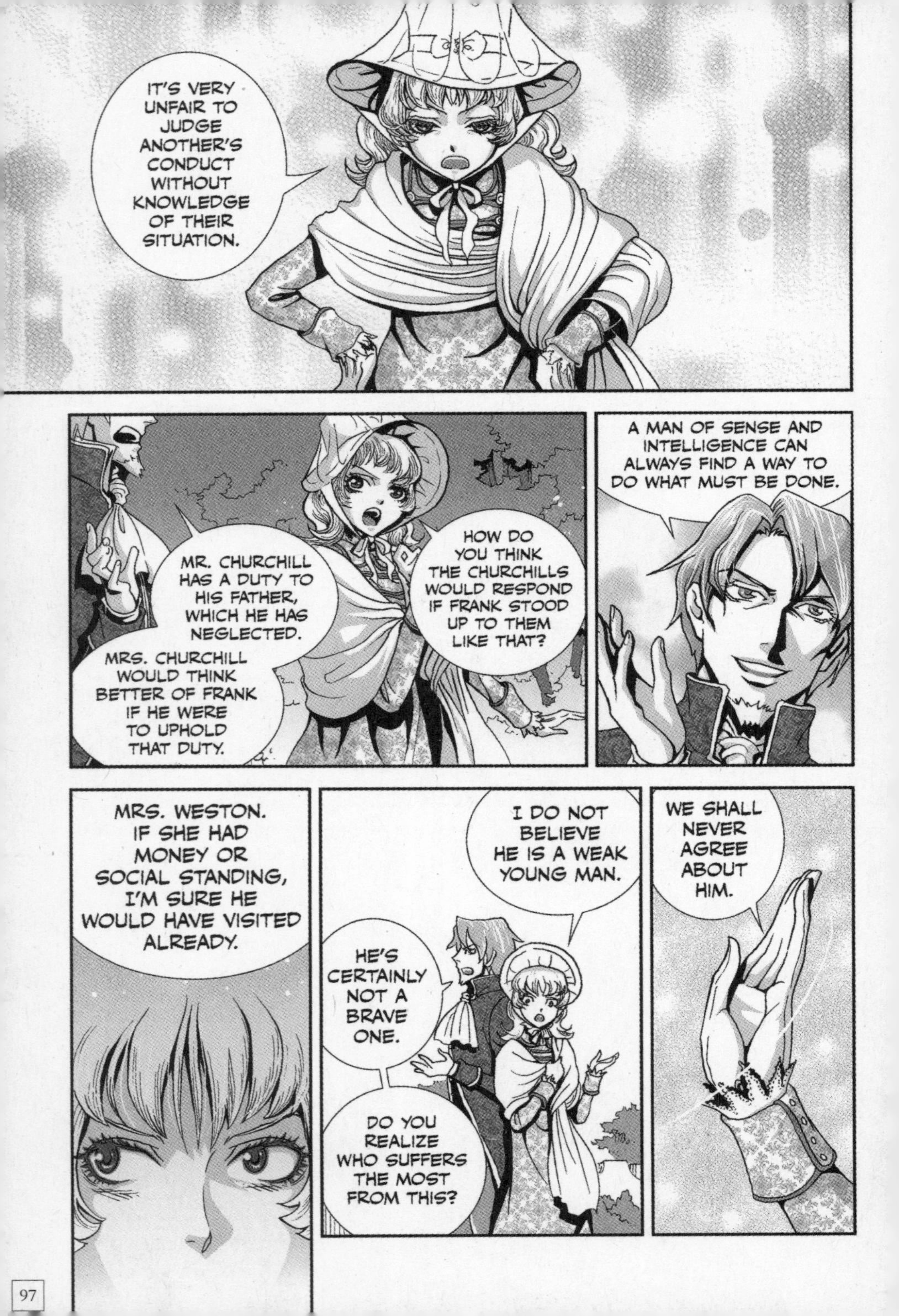
IT'S VERY UNFAIR TO JUDGE ANOTHER'S CONDUCT WITHOUT KNOWLEDGE OF THEIR SITUATION.
A MAN OF SENSE AND INTELLIGENCE CAN ALWAYS FIND A WAY TO DO WHAT MUST BE DONE.
HOW DO YOU THINK THE CHURCHILLS WOULD RESPOND IF FRANK STOOD UP TO THEM LIKE THAT?
MR. CHURCHILL HAS A DUTY TO HIS FATHER, WHICH HE HAS NEGLECTED.
MRS. CHURCHILL WOULD THINK BETTER OF FRANK IF HE WERE TO UPHOLD THAT DUTY.
WE SHALL NEVER AGREE ABOUT HIM.
I DO NOT BELIEVE HE IS A WEAK YOUNG MAN.
HE'S CERTAINLY NOT A BRAVE ONE.
DO YOU REALIZE WHO SUFFERS THE MOST FROM THIS?
MRS. WESTON. IF SHE HAD MONEY OR SOCIAL STANDING, I'M SURE HE WOULD HAVE VISITED ALREADY.

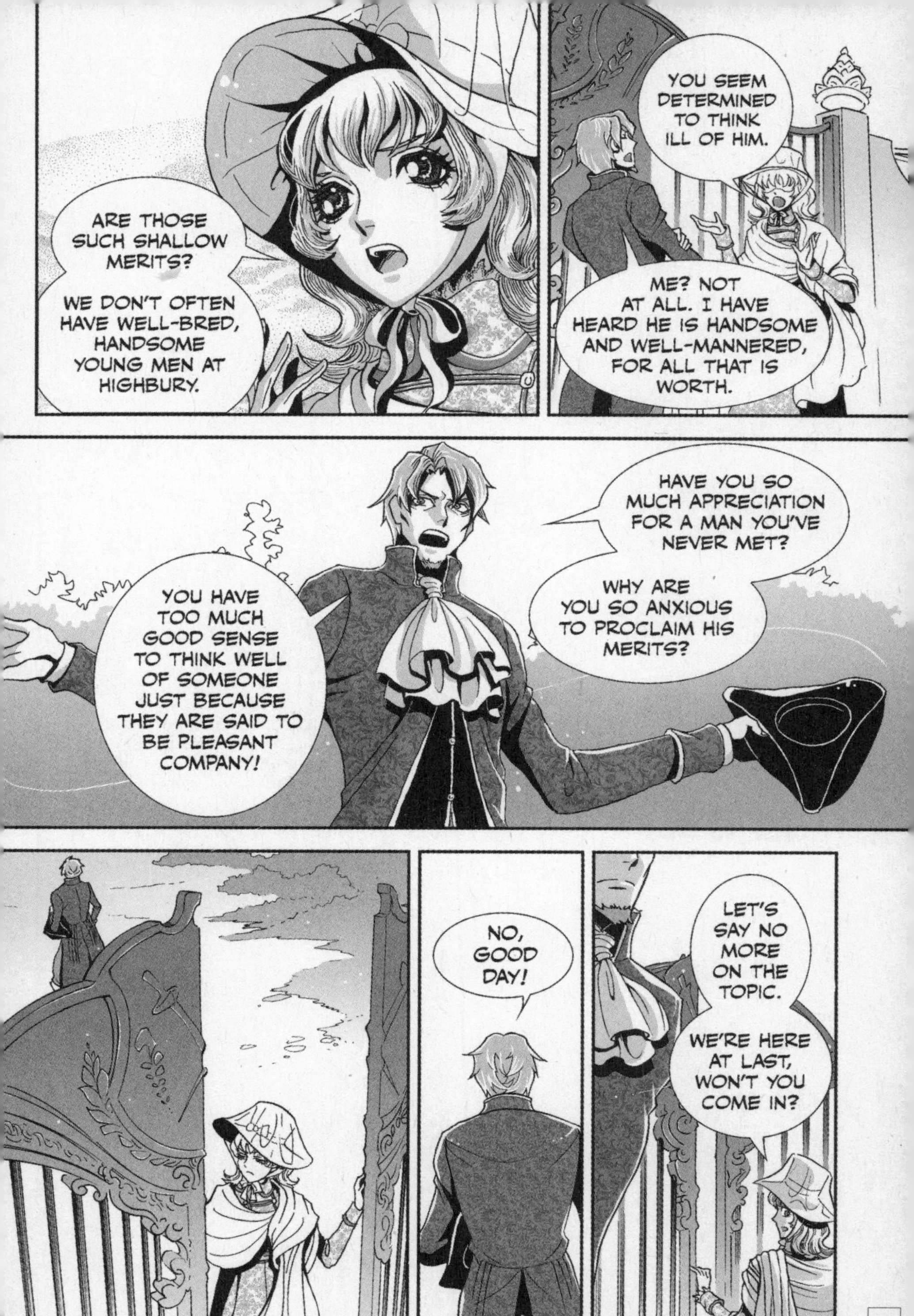

YOU SEEM DETERMINED TO THINK ILL OF HIM.
ME? NOT AT ALL. I HAVE HEARD HE IS HANDSOME AND WELL-MANNERED, FOR ALL THAT IS WORTH.
ARE THOSE SUCH SHALLOW MERITS?
WE DON'T OFTEN HAVE WELL-BRED, HANDSOME YOUNG MEN AT HIGHBURY.
HAVE YOU SO MUCH APPRECIATION FOR A MAN YOU'VE NEVER MET?
WHY ARE YOU SO ANXIOUS TO PROCLAIM HIS MERITS?
YOU HAVE TOO MUCH GOOD SENSE TO THINK WELL OF SOMEONE JUST BECAUSE THEY ARE SAID TO BE PLEASANT COMPANY!
LET'S SAY NO MORE ON THE TOPIC.
WE'RE HERE AT LAST, WON'T YOU COME IN?
NO, GOOD DAY!

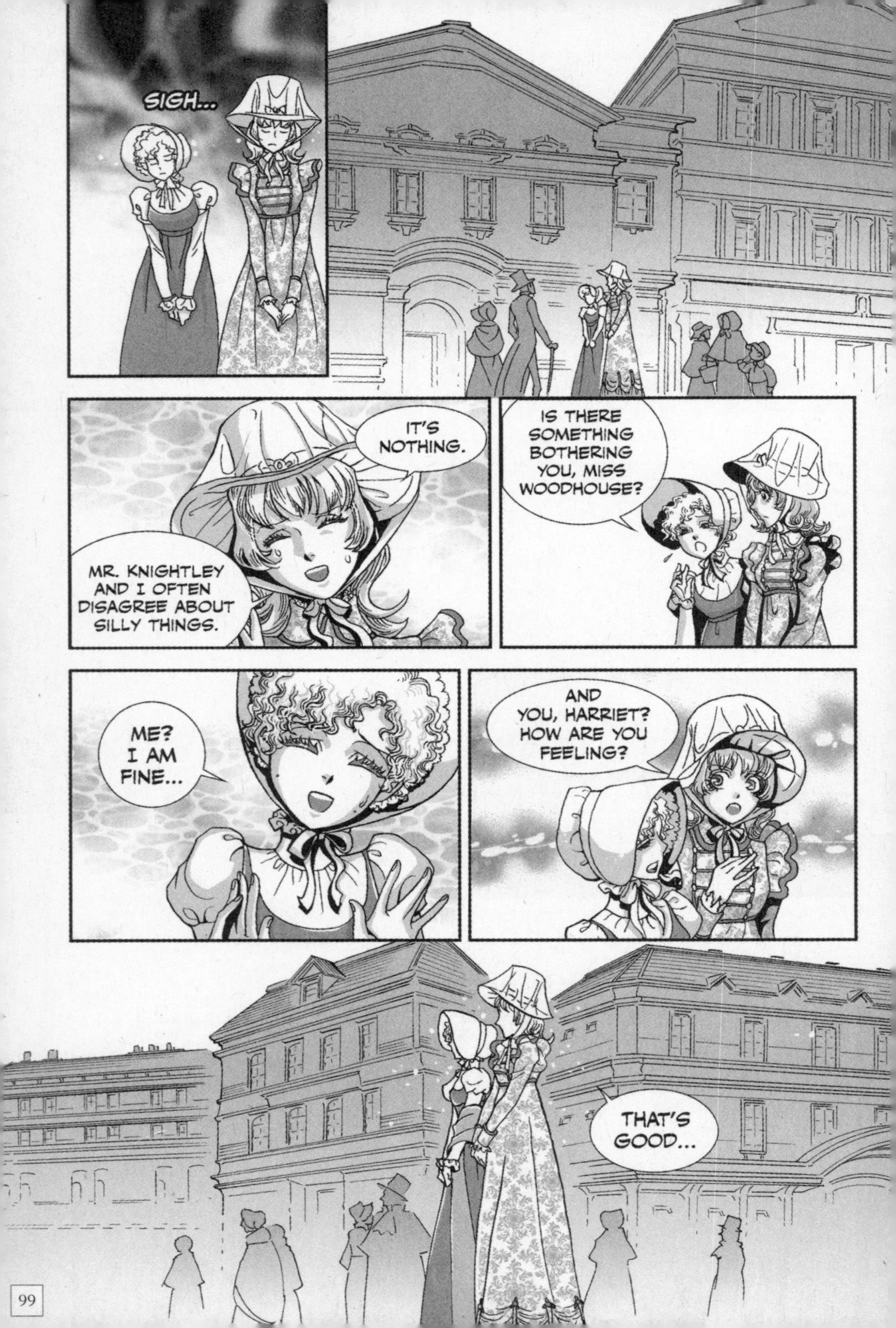
SIGH...
IS THERE SOMETHING BOTHERING YOU, MISS WOODHOUSE?
IT'S NOTHING.
MR. KNIGHTLEY AND I OFTEN DISAGREE ABOUT SILLY THINGS.
AND YOU, HARRIET? HOW ARE YOU FEELING?
ME? I AM FINE...
THAT'S GOOD...

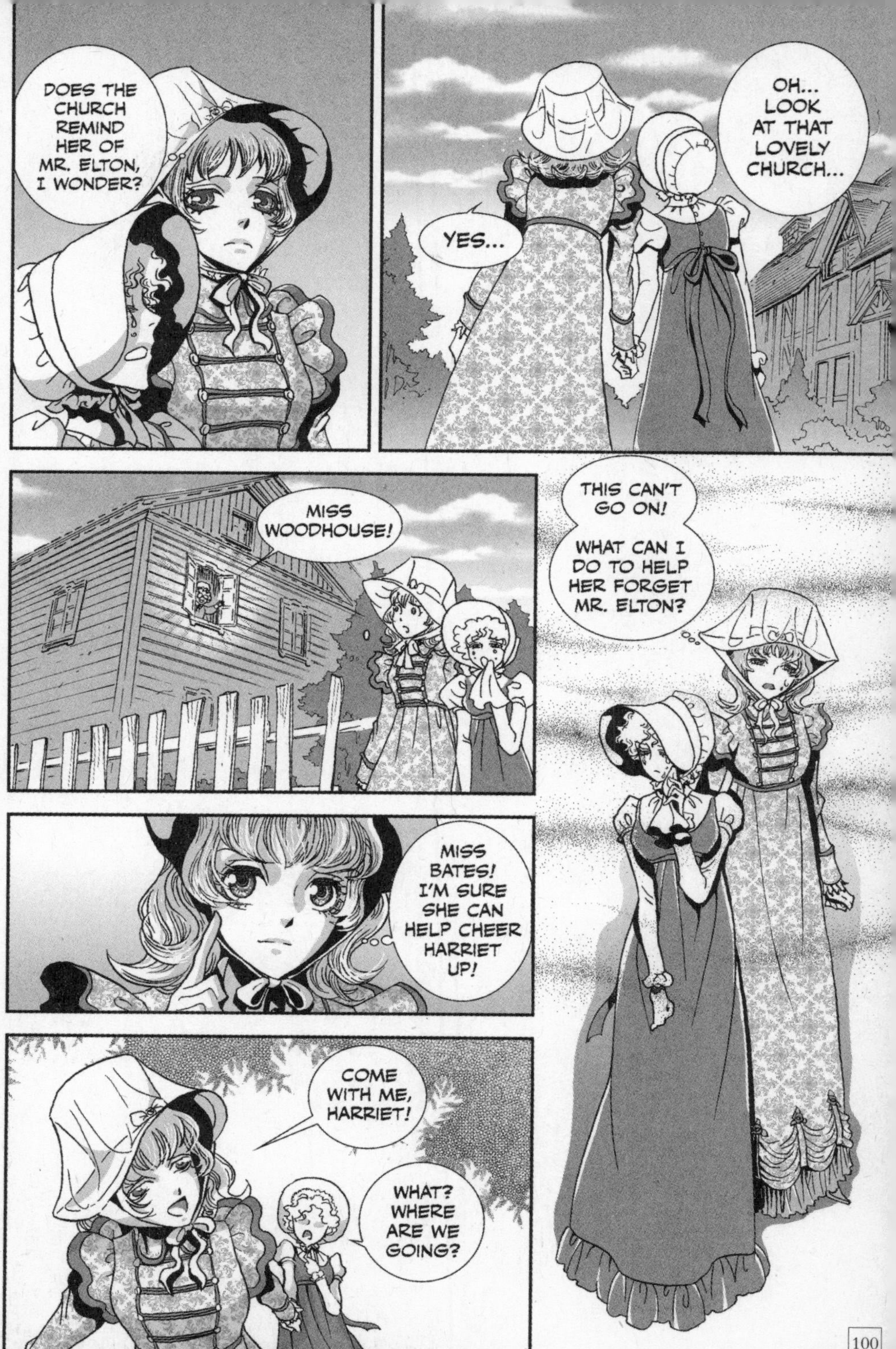
OH... LOOK AT THAT LOVELY CHURCH...
YES...
DOES THE CHURCH REMIND HER OF MR. ELTON, I WONDER?
THIS CAN'T GO ON!
WHAT CAN I DO TO HELP HER FORGET MR. ELTON?
MISS WOODHOUSE!
MISS BATES! I'M SURE SHE CAN HELP CHEER HARRIET UP!
COME WITH ME, HARRIET!
WHAT? WHERE ARE WE GOING?

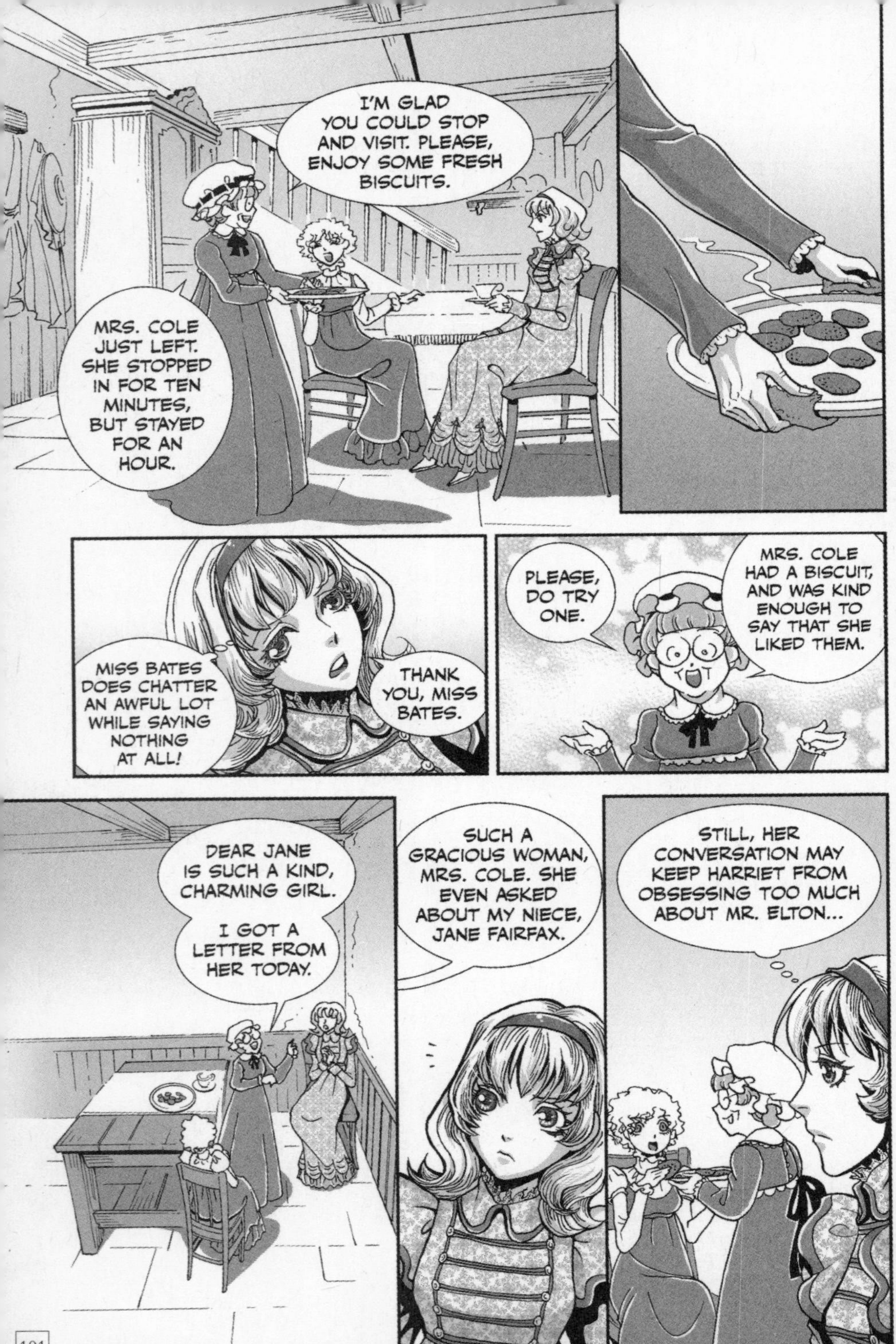
I'M GLAD YOU COULD STOP AND VISIT. PLEASE, ENJOY SOME FRESH BISCUITS.
MRS. COLE JUST LEFT. SHE STOPPED IN FOR TEN MINUTES, BUT STAYED FOR AN HOUR.
MRS. COLE HAD A BISCUIT, AND WAS KIND ENOUGH TO SAY THAT SHE LIKED THEM.
PLEASE, DO TRY ONE.
THANK YOU, MISS BATES.
MISS BATES DOES CHATTER AN AWFUL LOT WHILE SAYING NOTHING AT ALL!
STILL, HER CONVERSATION MAY KEEP HARRIET FROM OBSESSING TOO MUCH ABOUT MR. ELTON...
SUCH A GRACIOUS WOMAN, MRS. COLE. SHE EVEN ASKED ABOUT MY NIECE, JANE FAIRFAX.
DEAR JANE IS SUCH A KIND, CHARMING GIRL.
I GOT A LETTER FROM HER TODAY.

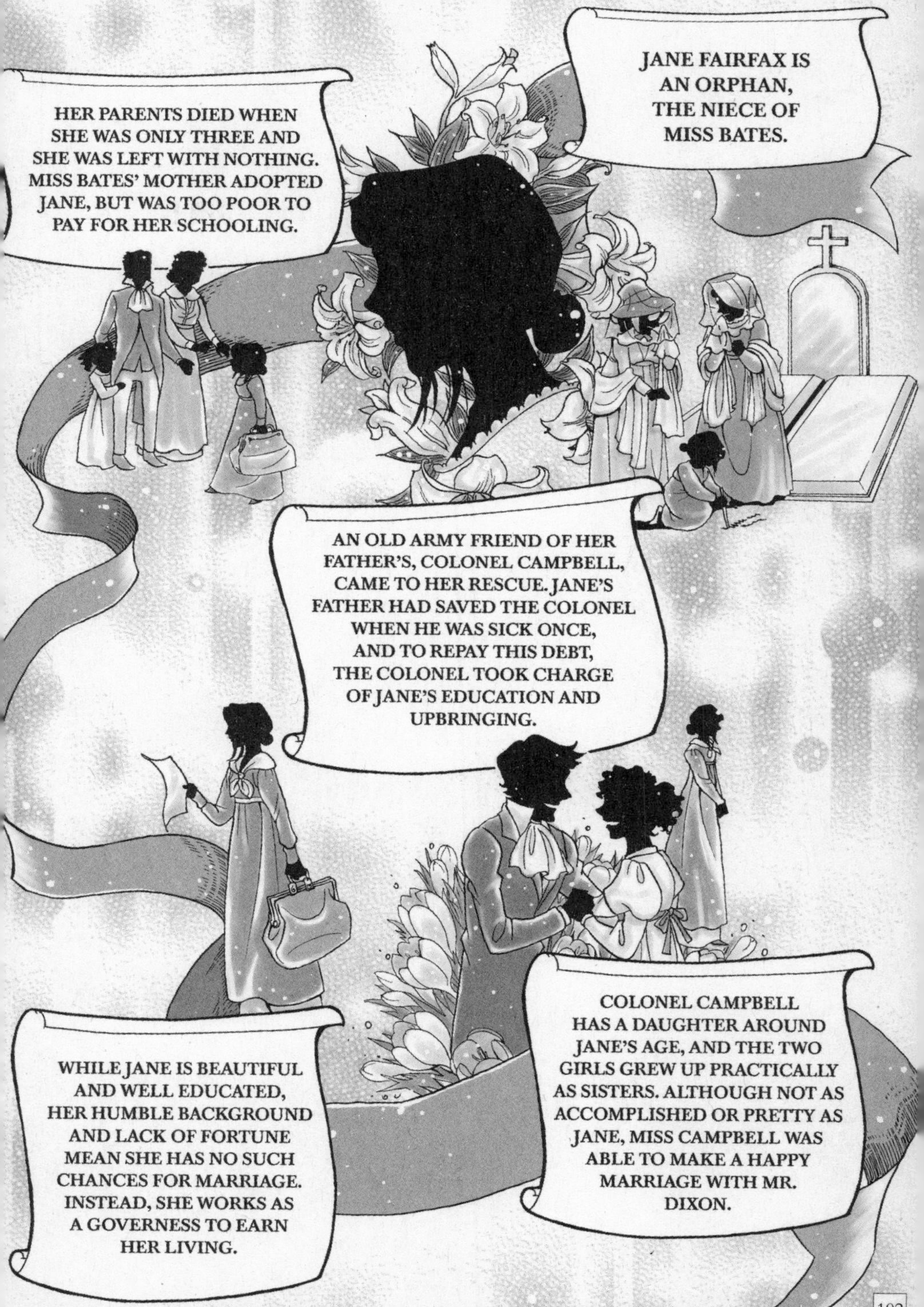
JANE FAIRFAX IS AN ORPHAN, THE NIECE OF MISS BATES.
HER PARENTS DIED WHEN SHE WAS ONLY THREE AND SHE WAS LEFT WITH NOTHING. MISS BATES' MOTHER ADOPTED JANE, BUT WAS TOO POOR TO PAY FOR HER SCHOOLING.
AN OLD ARMY FRIEND OF HER FATHER'S, COLONEL CAMPBELL, CAME TO HER RESCUE. JANE'S FATHER HAD SAVED THE COLONEL WHEN HE WAS SICK ONCE, AND TO REPAY THIS DEBT, THE COLONEL TOOK CHARGE OF JANE'S EDUCATION AND UPBRINGING.
COLONEL CAMPBELL HAS A DAUGHTER AROUND JANE'S AGE, AND THE TWO GIRLS GREW UP PRACTICALLY AS SISTERS. ALTHOUGH NOT AS ACCOMPLISHED OR PRETTY AS JANE, MISS CAMPBELL WAS ABLE TO MAKE A HAPPY MARRIAGE WITH MR. DIXON.
WHILE JANE IS BEAUTIFUL AND WELL EDUCATED, HER HUMBLE BACKGROUND AND LACK OF FORTUNE MEAN SHE HAS NO SUCH CHANCES FOR MARRIAGE. INSTEAD, SHE WORKS AS A GOVERNESS TO EARN HER LIVING.

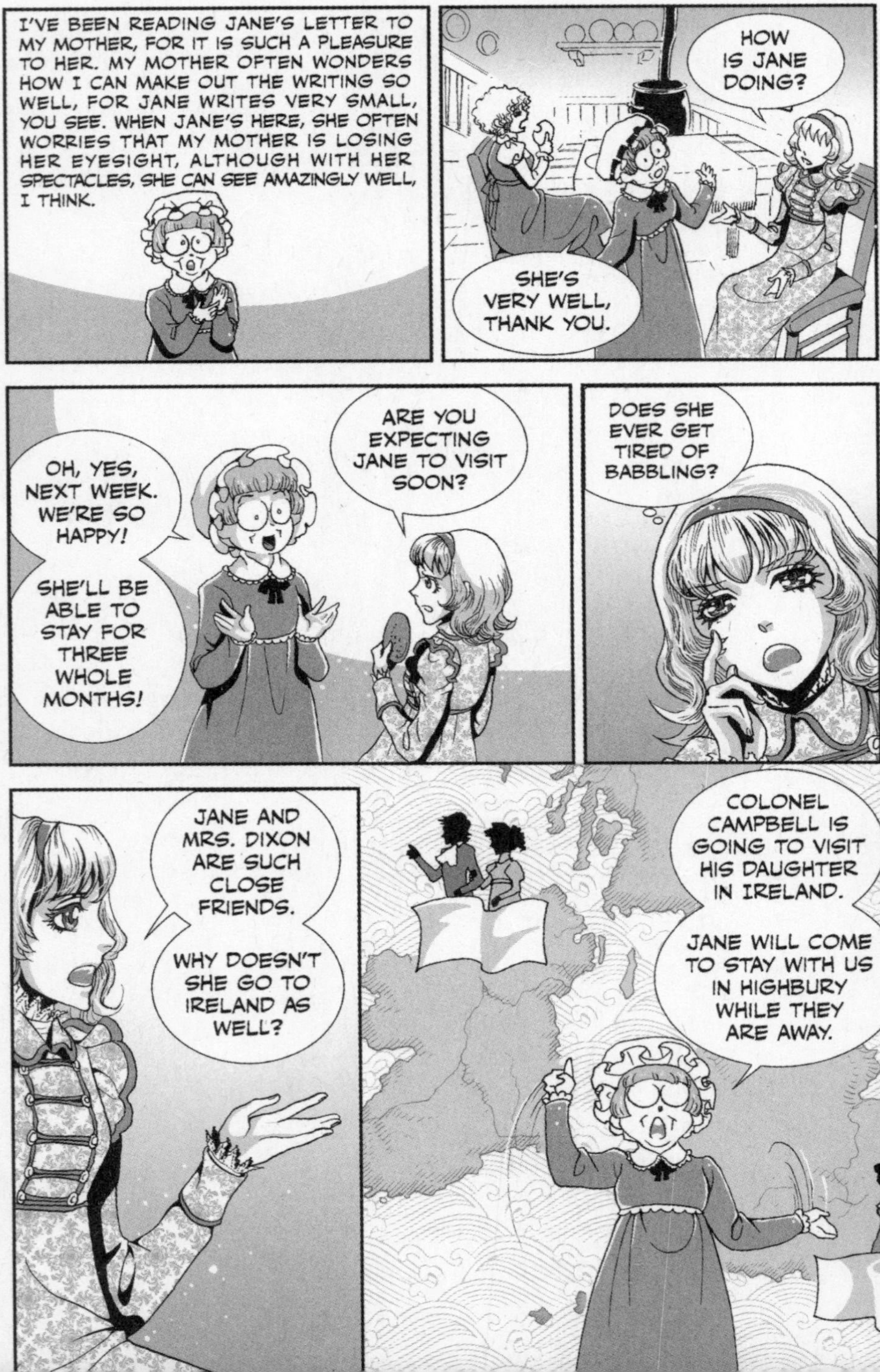
HOW IS JANE DOING?
SHE'S VERY WELL, THANK YOU.
I'VE BEEN READING JANE'S LETTER TO MY MOTHER, FOR IT IS SUCH A PLEASURE TO HER. MY MOTHER OFTEN WONDERS HOW I CAN MAKE OUT THE WRITING SO WELL, FOR JANE WRITES VERY SMALL, YOU SEE. WHEN JANE'S HERE, SHE OFTEN WORRIES THAT MY MOTHER IS LOSING HER EYESIGHT, ALTHOUGH WITH HER SPECTACLES, SHE CAN SEE AMAZINGLY WELL, I THINK.
DOES SHE EVER GET TIRED OF BABBLING?
ARE YOU EXPECTING JANE TO VISIT SOON?
OH, YES, NEXT WEEK. WE'RE SO HAPPY!
SHE'LL BE ABLE TO STAY FOR THREE WHOLE MONTHS!
COLONEL CAMPBELL IS GOING TO VISIT HIS DAUGHTER IN IRELAND.
JANE WILL COME TO STAY WITH US IN HIGHBURY WHILE THEY ARE AWAY.
JANE AND MRS. DIXON ARE SUCH CLOSE FRIENDS.
WHY DOESN'T SHE GO TO IRELAND AS WELL?

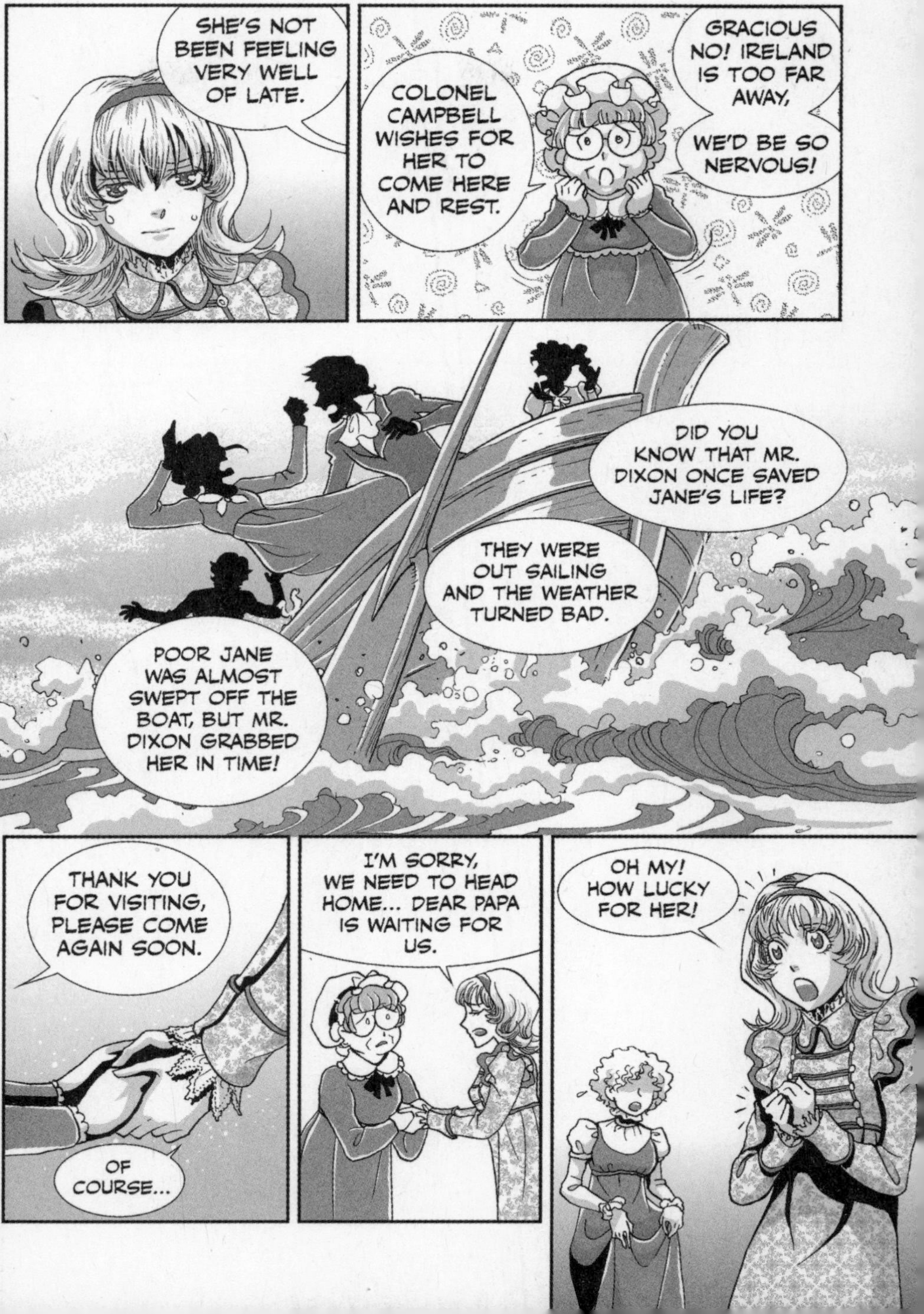
GRACIOUS NO! IRELAND IS TOO FAR AWAY,
WE'D BE SO NERVOUS!
COLONEL CAMPBELL WISHES FOR HER TO COME HERE AND REST.
SHE'S NOT BEEN FEELING VERY WELL OF LATE.
DID YOU KNOW THAT MR. DIXON ONCE SAVED JANE'S LIFE?
THEY WERE OUT SAILING AND THE WEATHER TURNED BAD.
POOR JANE WAS ALMOST SWEPT OFF THE BOAT, BUT MR. DIXON GRABBED HER IN TIME!
OH MY! HOW LUCKY FOR HER!
I'M SORRY, WE NEED TO HEAD HOME... DEAR PAPA IS WAITING FOR US.
THANK YOU FOR VISITING, PLEASE COME AGAIN SOON.
OF COURSE...

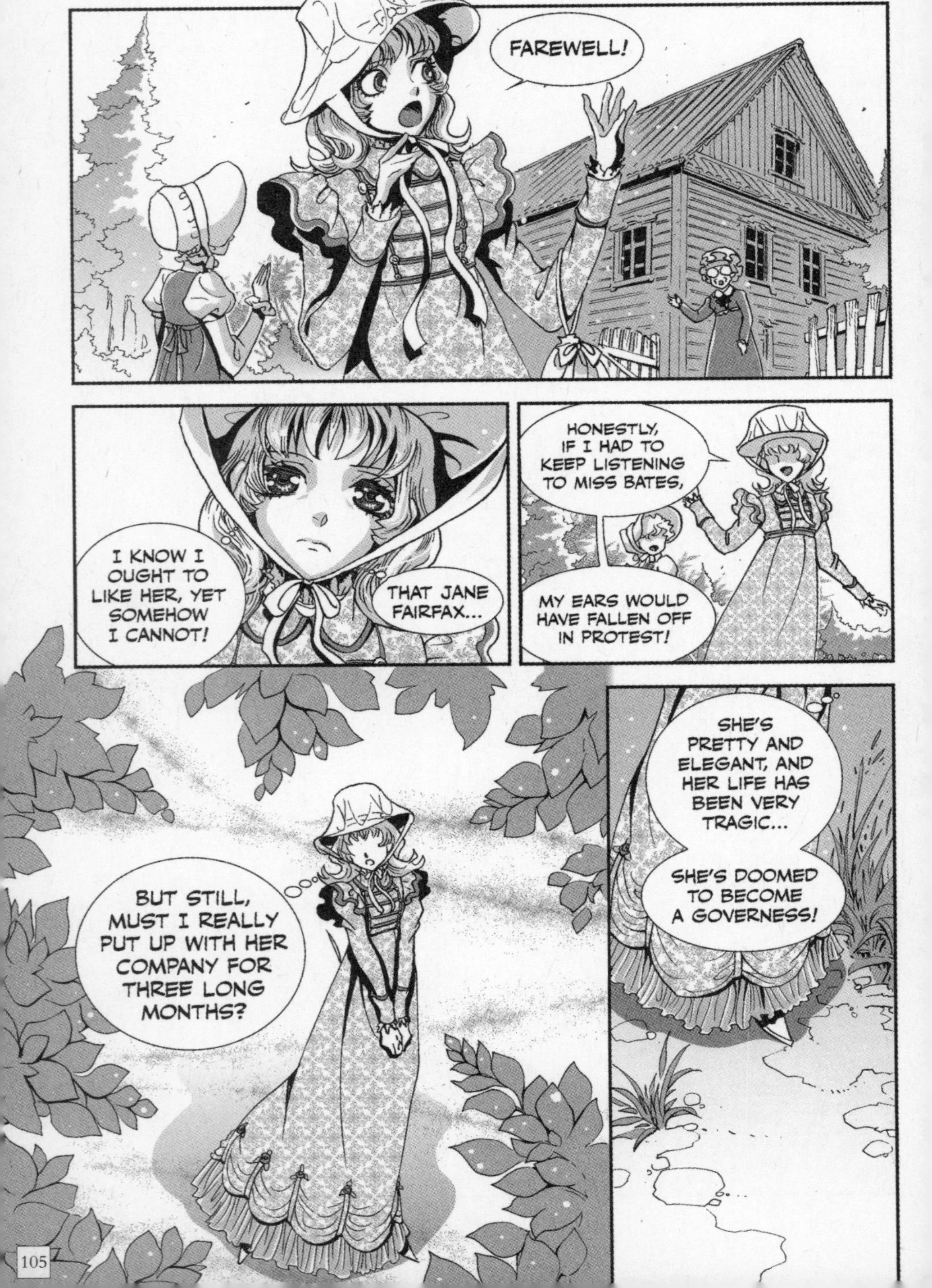
FAREWELL!
HONESTLY, IF I HAD TO KEEP LISTENING TO MISS BATES,
MY EARS WOULD HAVE FALLEN OFF IN PROTEST!
THAT JANE FAIRFAX...
I KNOW I OUGHT TO LIKE HER, YET SOMEHOW I CANNOT!
SHE'S PRETTY AND ELEGANT, AND HER LIFE HAS BEEN VERY TRAGIC...
SHE'S DOOMED TO BECOME A GOVERNESS!
BUT STILL, MUST I REALLY PUT UP WITH HER COMPANY FOR THREE LONG MONTHS?

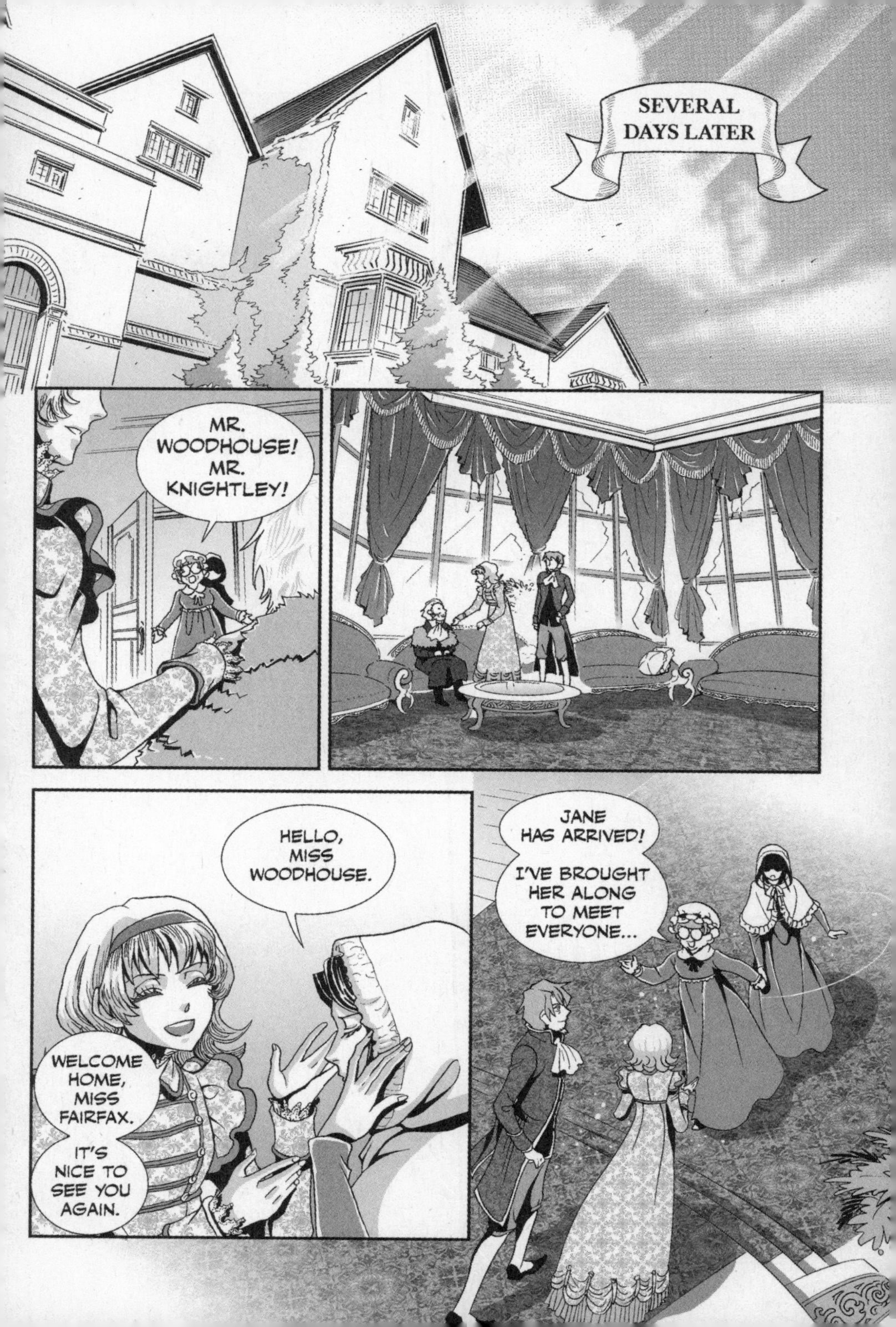
SEVERAL DAYS LATER
MR. WOODHOUSE! MR. KNIGHTLEY!
JANE HAS ARRIVED!
I'VE BROUGHT HER ALONG TO MEET EVERYONE...
HELLO, MISS WOODHOUSE.
WELCOME HOME, MISS FAIRFAX.
IT'S NICE TO SEE YOU AGAIN.

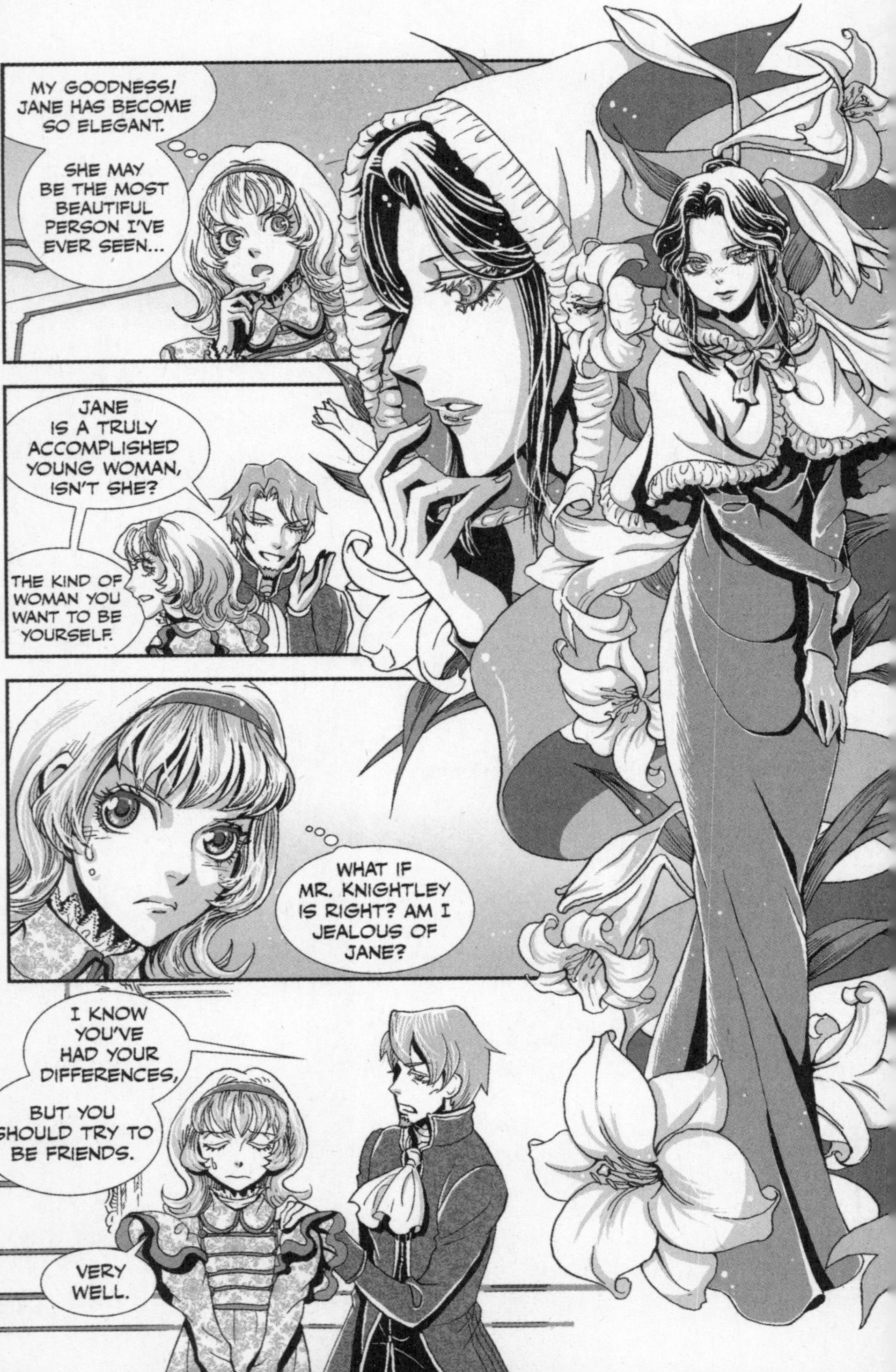
MY GOODNESS! JANE HAS BECOME SO ELEGANT.
SHE MAY BE THE MOST BEAUTIFUL PERSON I'VE EVER SEEN...
JANE IS A TRULY ACCOMPLISHED YOUNG WOMAN, ISN'T SHE?
THE KIND OF WOMAN YOU WANT TO BE YOURSELF.
WHAT IF MR. KNIGHTLEY IS RIGHT? AM I JEALOUS OF JANE?
I KNOW YOU'VE HAD YOUR DIFFERENCES,
BUT YOU SHOULD TRY TO BE FRIENDS.
VERY WELL.

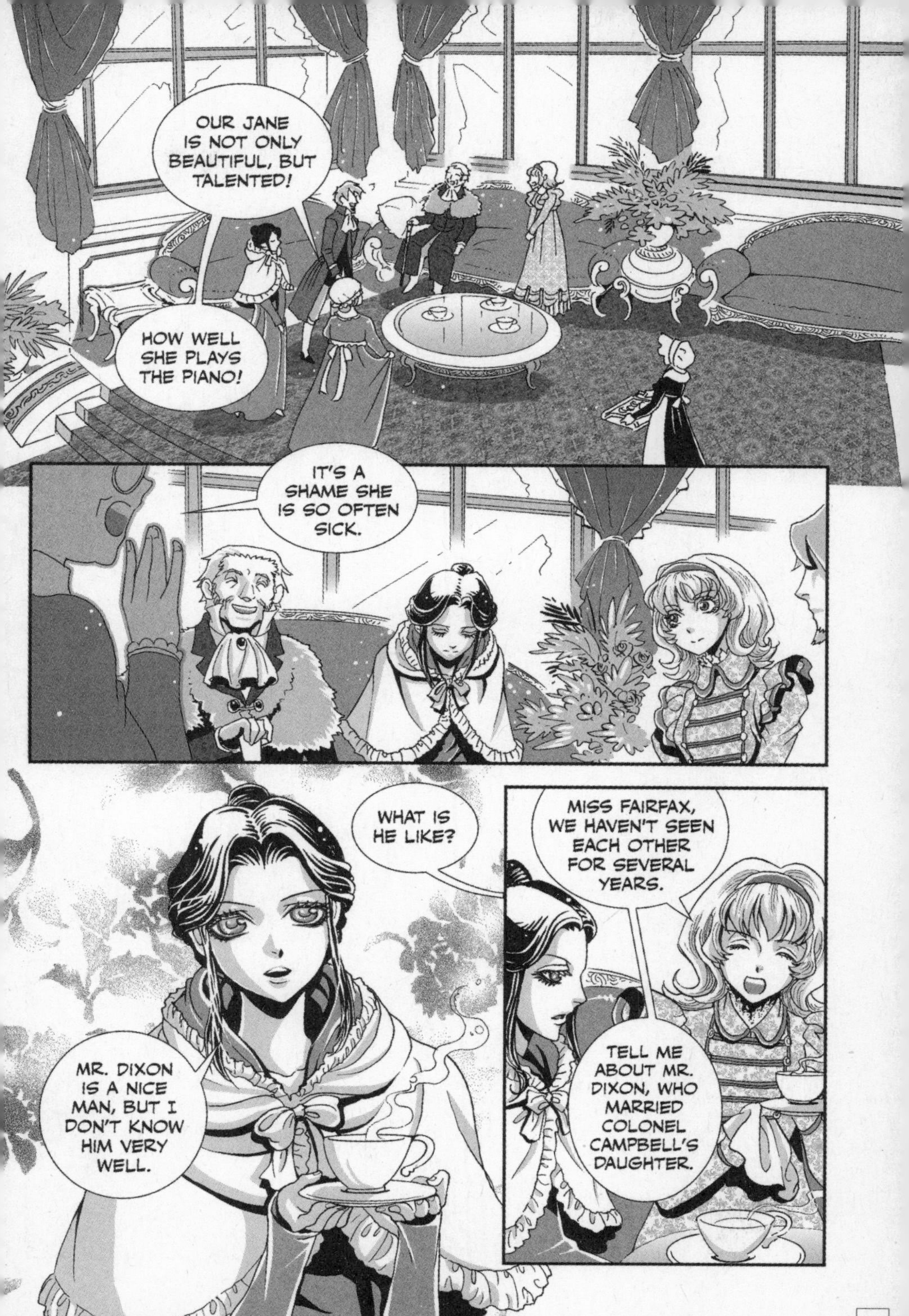
OUR JANE IS NOT ONLY BEAUTIFUL, BUT TALENTED!
HOW WELL SHE PLAYS THE PIANO!
IT'S A SHAME SHE IS SO OFTEN SICK.
MISS FAIRFAX, WE HAVEN'T SEEN EACH OTHER FOR SEVERAL YEARS.
TELL ME ABOUT MR. DIXON, WHO MARRIED COLONEL CAMPBELL'S DAUGHTER.
WHAT IS HE LIKE?
MR. DIXON IS A NICE MAN, BUT I DON'T KNOW HIM VERY WELL.

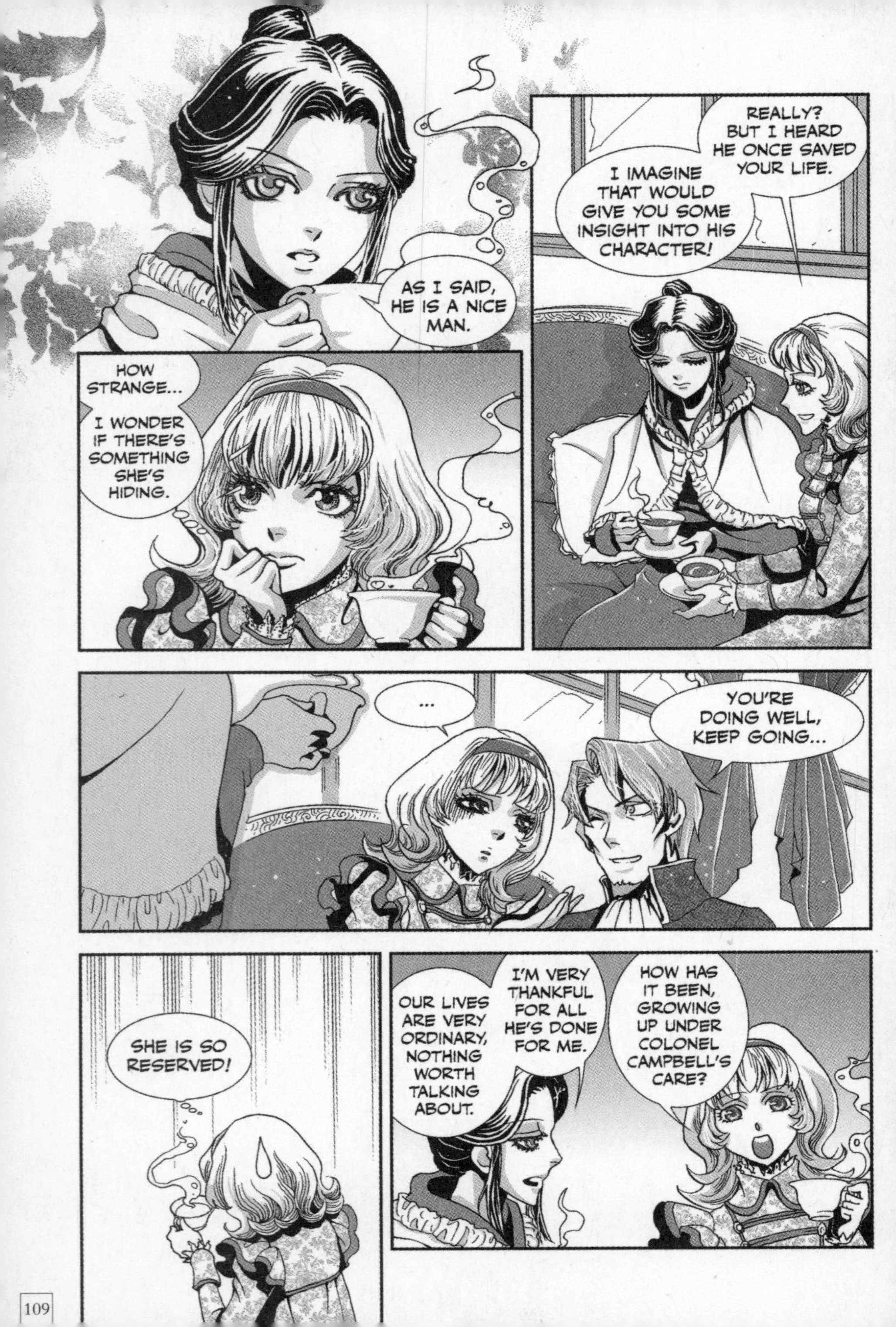
REALLY? BUT I HEARD HE ONCE SAVED YOUR LIFE.
I IMAGINE THAT WOULD GIVE YOU SOME INSIGHT INTO HIS CHARACTER!
AS I SAID, HE IS A NICE MAN.
HOW STRANGE...
I WONDER IF THERE'S SOMETHING SHE'S HIDING.
YOU'RE DOING WELL, KEEP GOING...
...
HOW HAS IT BEEN, GROWING UP UNDER COLONEL CAMPBELL'S CARE?
I'M VERY THANKFUL FOR ALL HE'S DONE FOR ME.
OUR LIVES ARE VERY ORDINARY, NOTHING WORTH TALKING ABOUT.
SHE IS SO RESERVED!

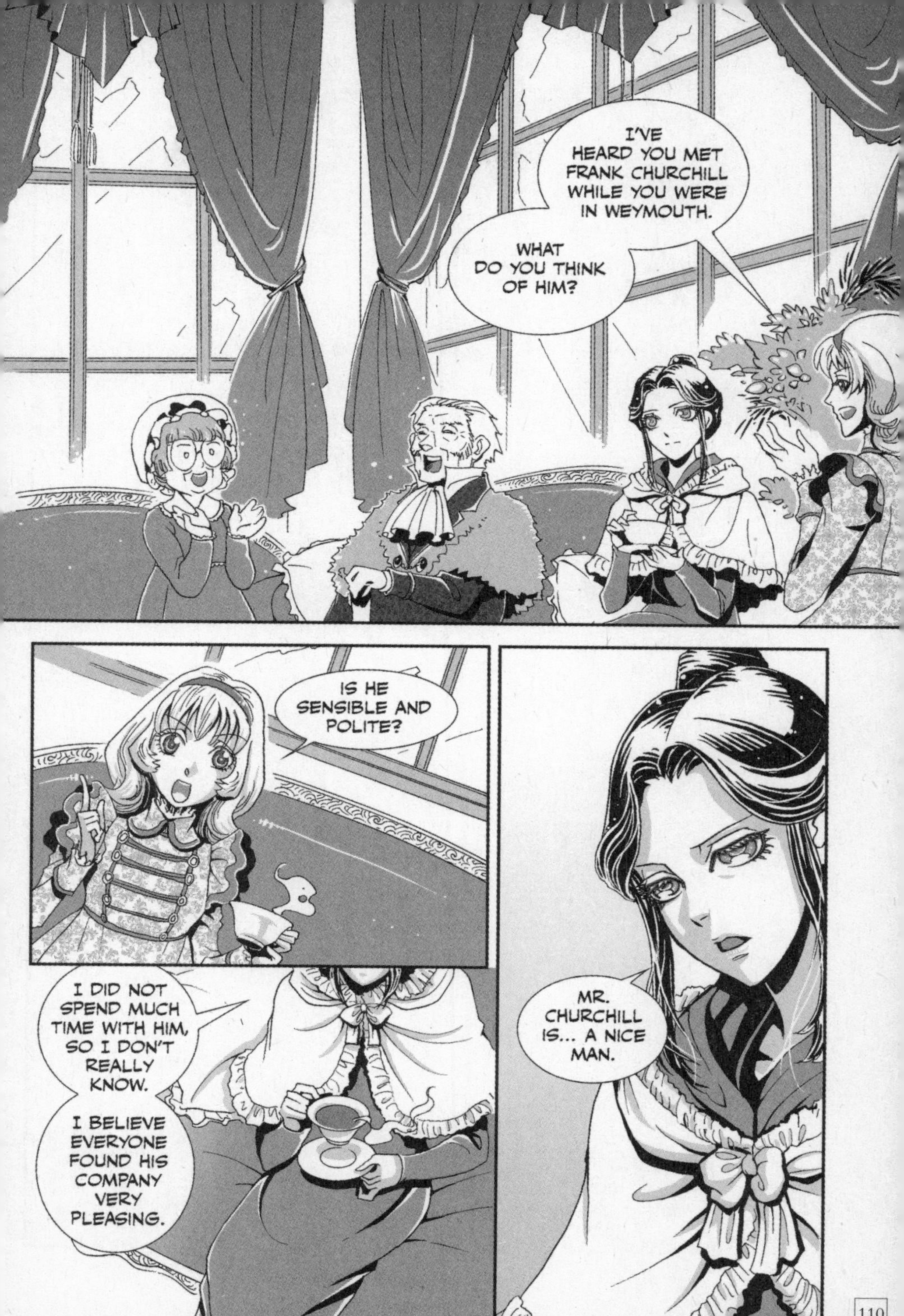
I'VE HEARD YOU MET FRANK CHURCHILL WHILE YOU WERE IN WEYMOUTH.
WHAT DO YOU THINK OF HIM?
MR. CHURCHILL IS... A NICE MAN.
IS HE SENSIBLE AND POLITE?
I DID NOT SPEND MUCH TIME WITH HIM, SO I DON'T REALLY KNOW.
I BELIEVE EVERYONE FOUND HIS COMPANY VERY PLEASING.

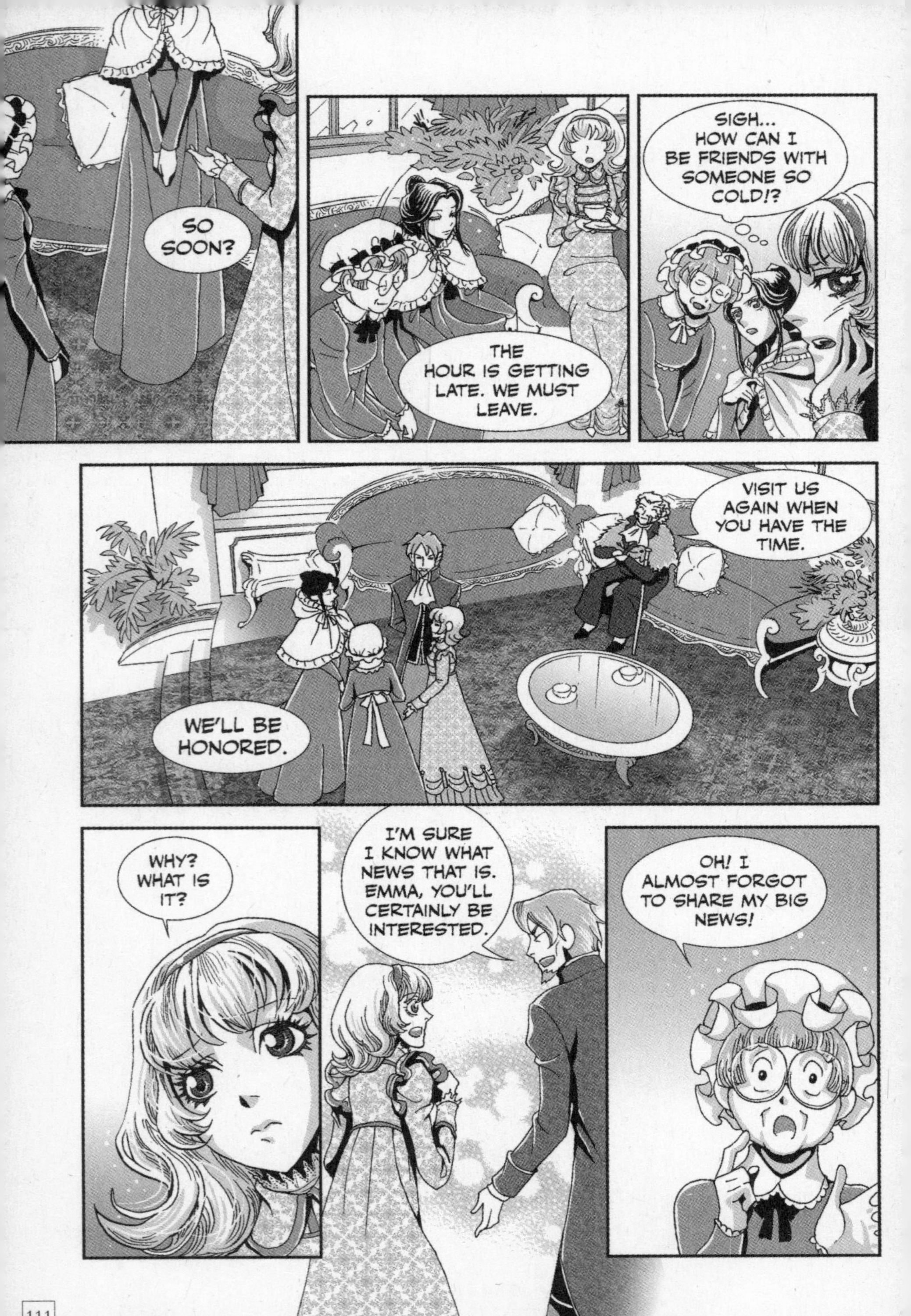
SIGH... HOW CAN I BE FRIENDS WITH SOMEONE SO COLD!?
THE HOUR IS GETTING LATE. WE MUST LEAVE.
SO SOON?
VISIT US AGAIN WHEN YOU HAVE THE TIME.
WE'LL BE HONORED.
OH! I ALMOST FORGOT TO SHARE MY BIG NEWS!
I'M SURE I KNOW WHAT NEWS THAT IS. EMMA, YOU'LL CERTAINLY BE INTERESTED.
WHY? WHAT IS IT?

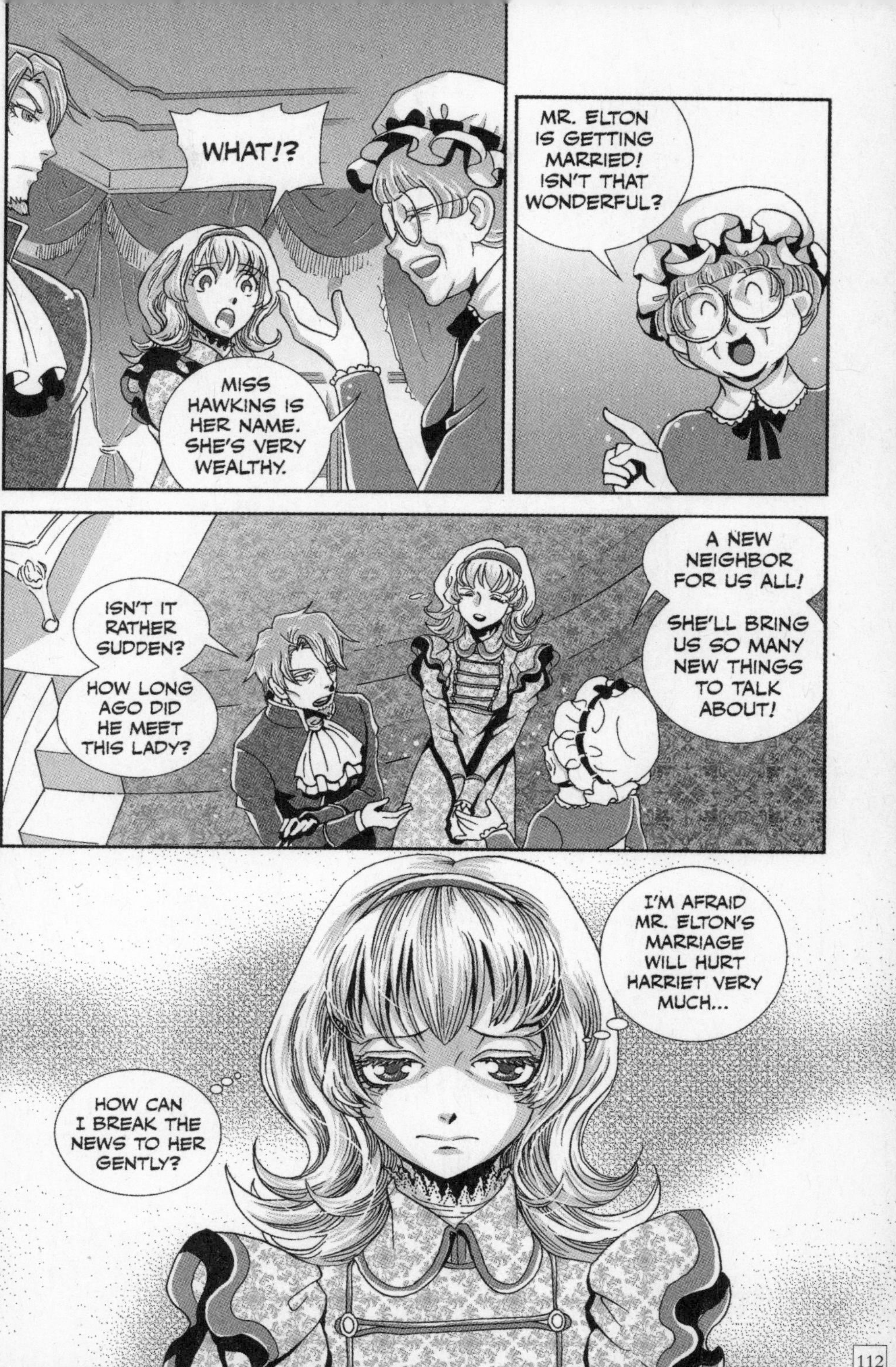
MR. ELTON IS GETTING MARRIED! ISN'T THAT WONDERFUL?
WHAT!?
MISS HAWKINS IS HER NAME. SHE'S VERY WEALTHY.
A NEW NEIGHBOR FOR US ALL!
SHE'LL BRING US SO MANY NEW THINGS TO TALK ABOUT!
ISN'T IT RATHER SUDDEN?
HOW LONG AGO DID HE MEET THIS LADY?
I'M AFRAID MR. ELTON'S MARRIAGE WILL HURT HARRIET VERY MUCH...
HOW CAN I BREAK THE NEWS TO HER GENTLY?

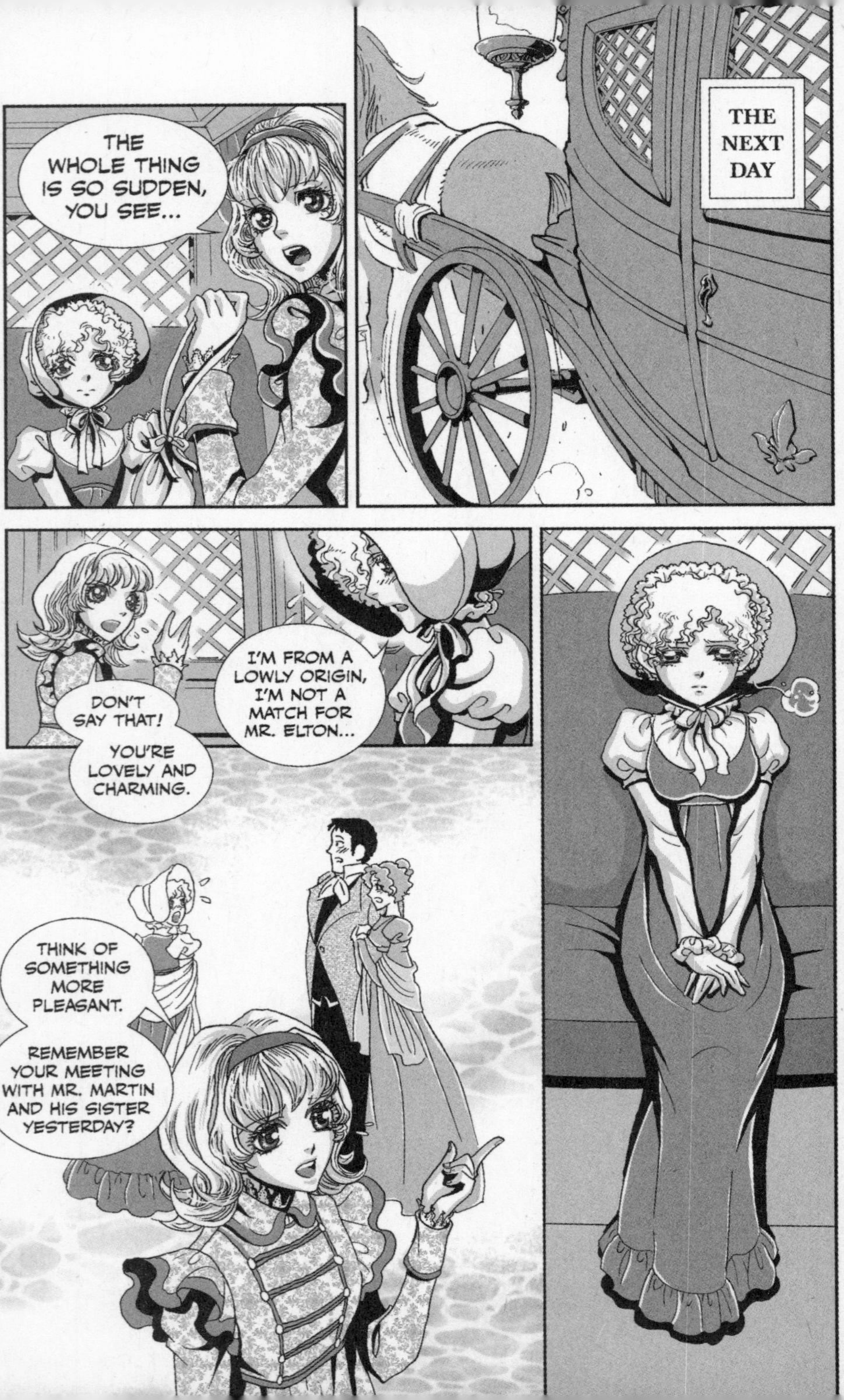
THE NEXT DAY
THE WHOLE THING IS SO SUDDEN, YOU SEE...
I'M FROM A LOWLY ORIGIN, I'M NOT A MATCH FOR MR. ELTON...
DON'T SAY THAT!
YOU'RE LOVELY AND CHARMING.
THINK OF SOMETHING MORE PLEASANT.
REMEMBER YOUR MEETING WITH MR. MARTIN AND HIS SISTER YESTERDAY?

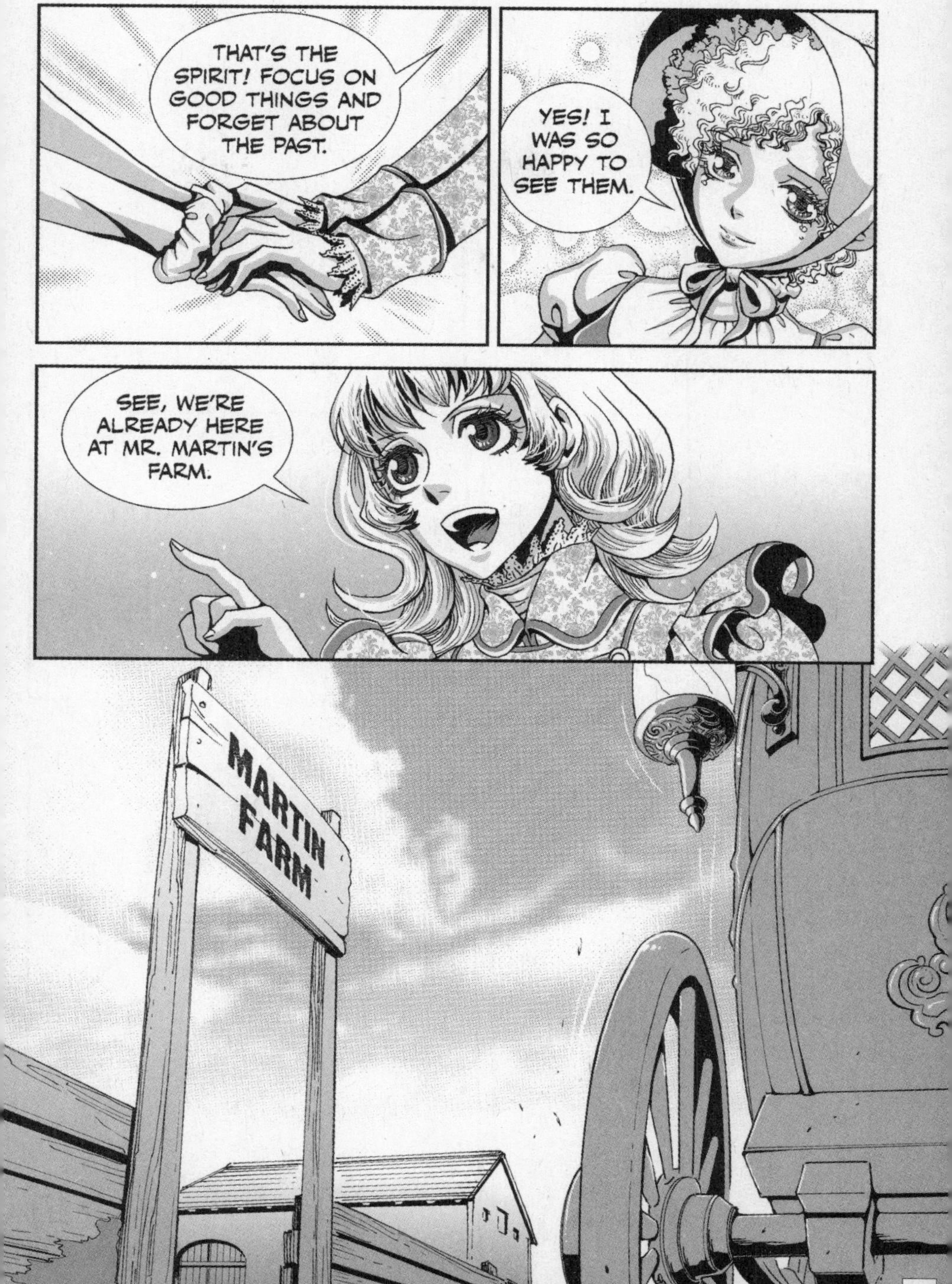
YES! I WAS SO HAPPY TO SEE THEM.
THAT'S THE SPIRIT! FOCUS ON GOOD THINGS AND FORGET ABOUT THE PAST.
SEE, WE'RE ALREADY HERE AT MR. MARTIN'S FARM.
MARTIN FARM

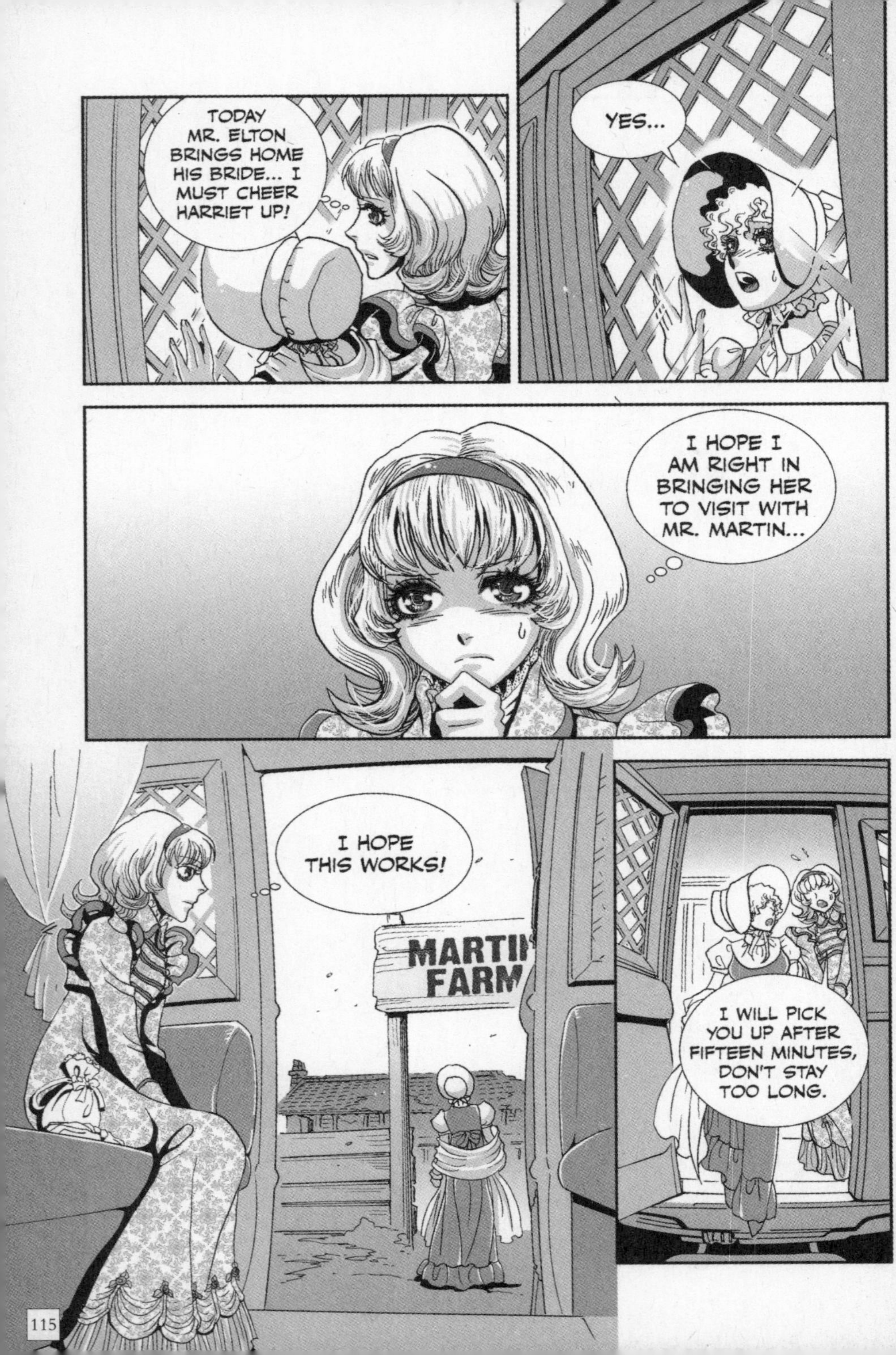
YES...
TODAY MR. ELTON BRINGS HOME HIS BRIDE... I MUST CHEER HARRIET UP!
I HOPE I AM RIGHT IN BRINGING HER TO VISIT WITH MR. MARTIN...
I WILL PICK YOU UP AFTER FIFTEEN MINUTES, DON'T STAY TOO LONG.
I HOPE THIS WORKS!
MARTI
FARM

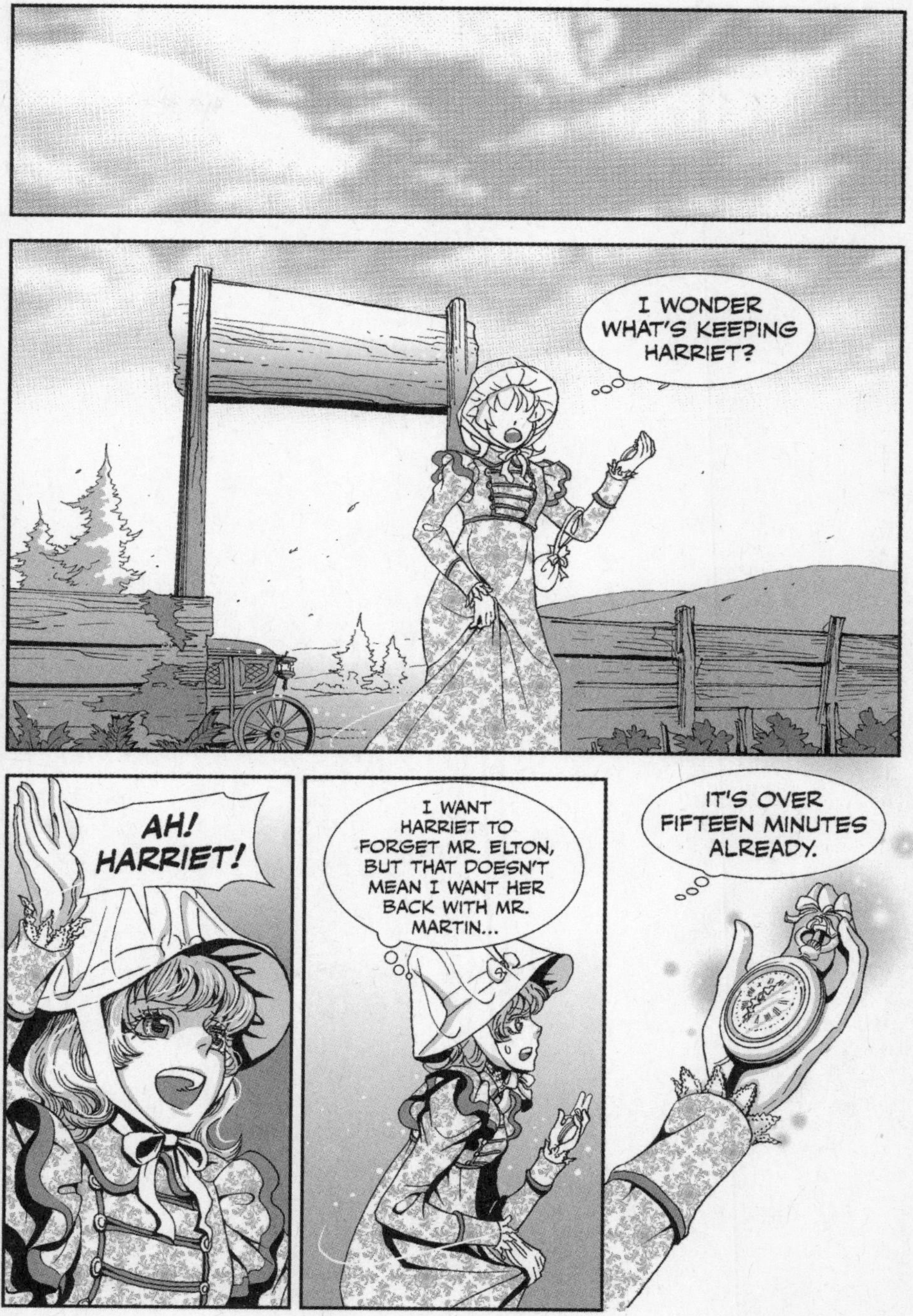
I WONDER WHAT'S KEEPING HARRIET?
IT'S OVER FIFTEEN MINUTES ALREADY.
I WANT HARRIET TO FORGET MR. ELTON, BUT THAT DOESN'T MEAN I WANT HER BACK WITH MR. MARTIN...
AH! HARRIET!

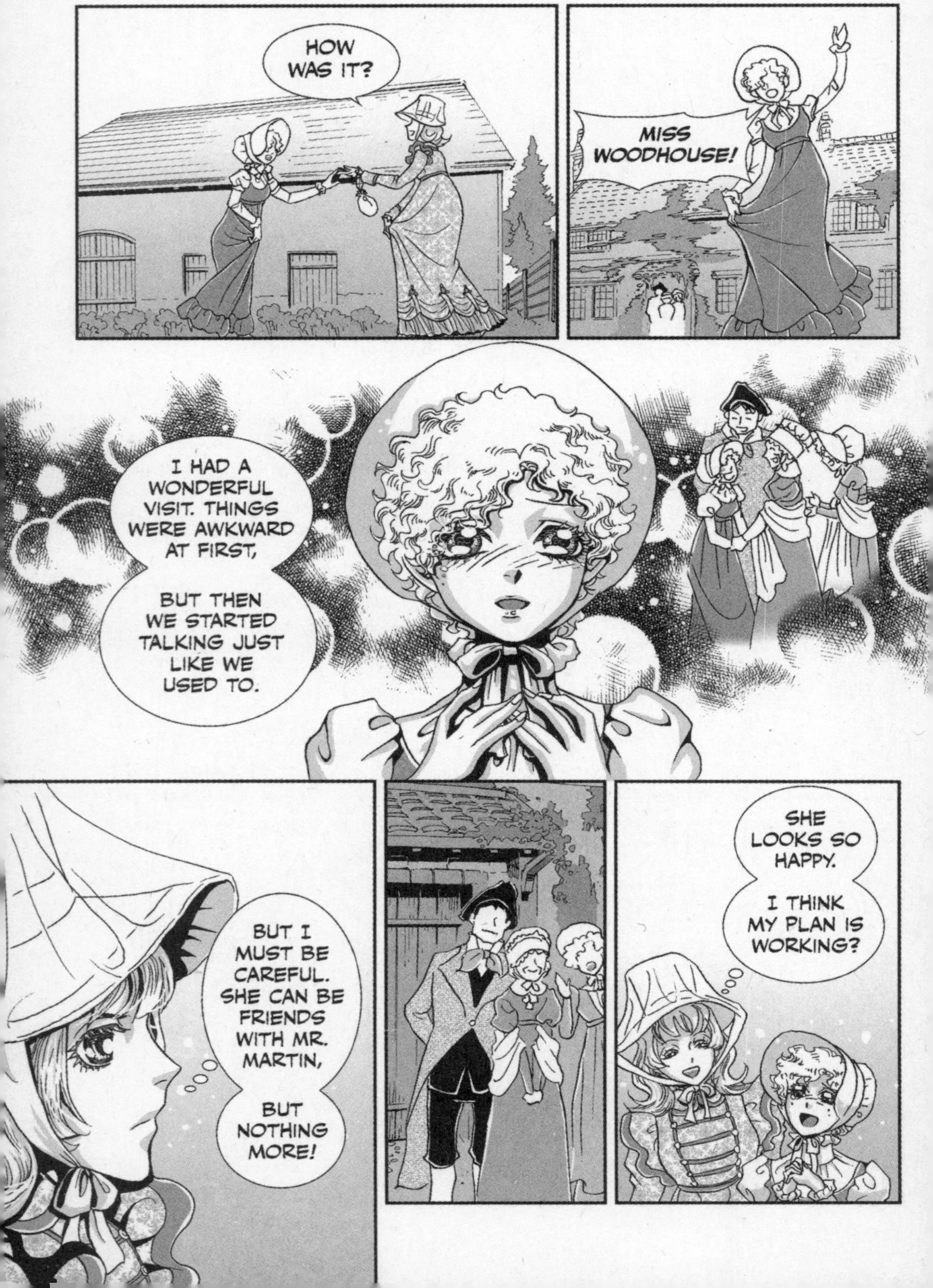
MISS WOODHOUSE!
HOW WAS IT?
I HAD A WONDERFUL VISIT. THINGS WERE AWKWARD AT FIRST,
BUT THEN WE STARTED TALKING JUST LIKE WE USED TO.
SHE LOOKS SO HAPPY.
I THINK MY PLAN IS WORKING?
BUT I MUST BE CAREFUL. SHE CAN BE FRIENDS WITH MR. MARTIN,
BUT NOTHING MORE!

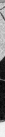

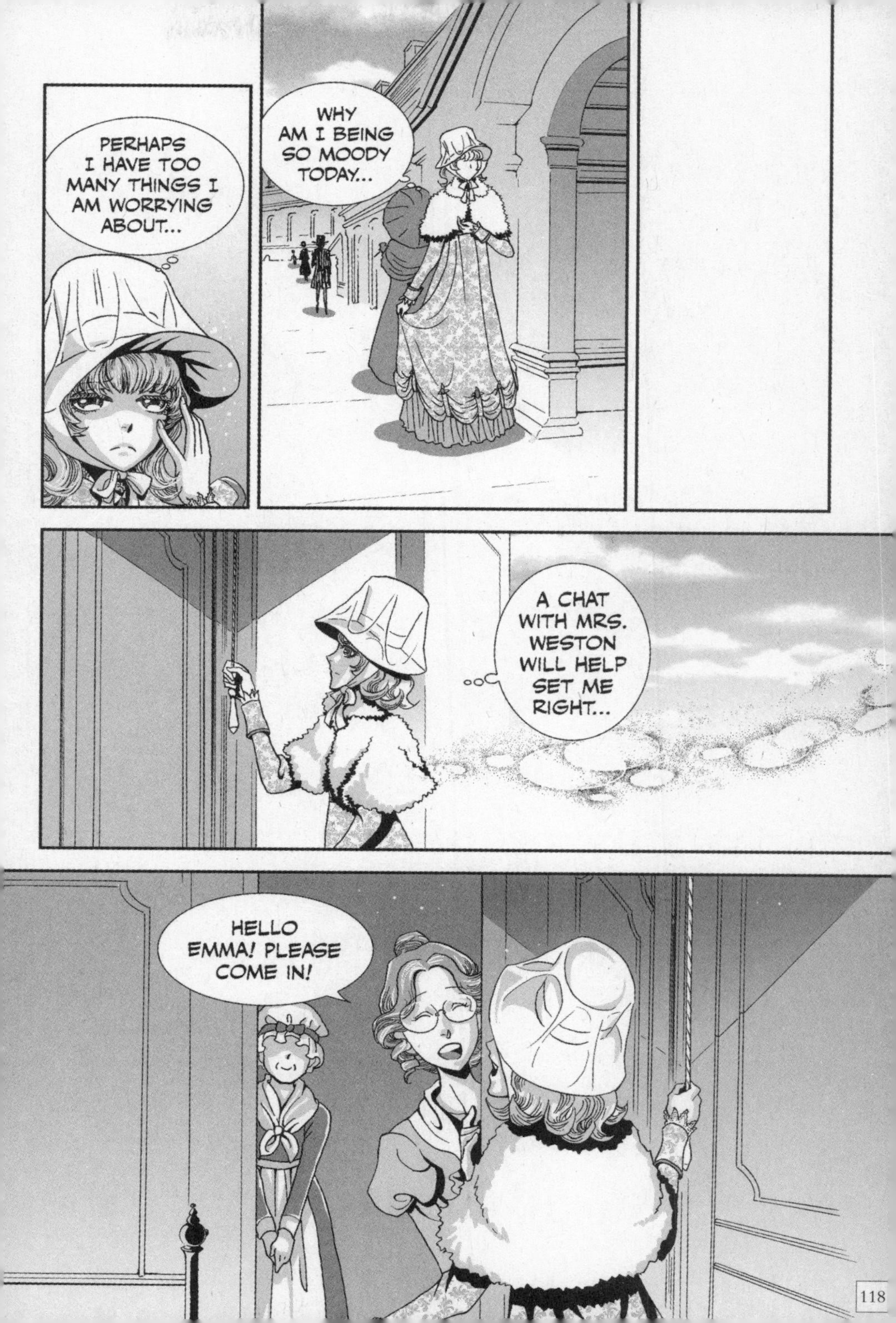
WHY AM I BEING SO MOODY TODAY...
PERHAPS I HAVE TOO MANY THINGS I AM WORRYING ABOUT...
A CHAT WITH MRS. WESTON WILL HELP SET ME RIGHT...
HELLO EMMA! PLEASE COME IN!

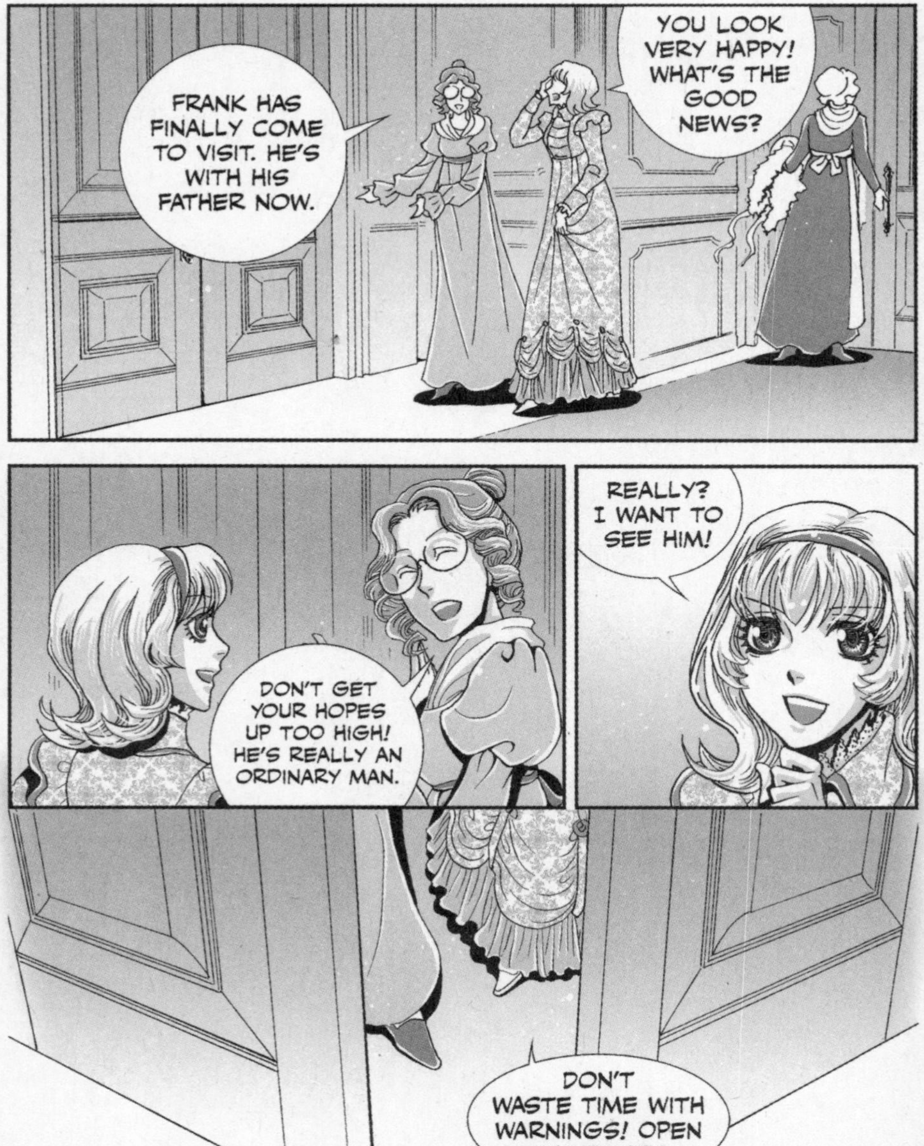
YOU LOOK VERY HAPPY! WHAT'S THE GOOD NEWS?
FRANK HAS FINALLY COME TO VISIT. HE'S WITH HIS FATHER NOW.
REALLY? I WANT TO SEE HIM!
DON'T GET YOUR HOPES UP TOO HIGH! HE'S REALLY AN ORDINARY MAN.
DON'T WASTE TIME WITH WARNINGS! OPEN THE DOOR!

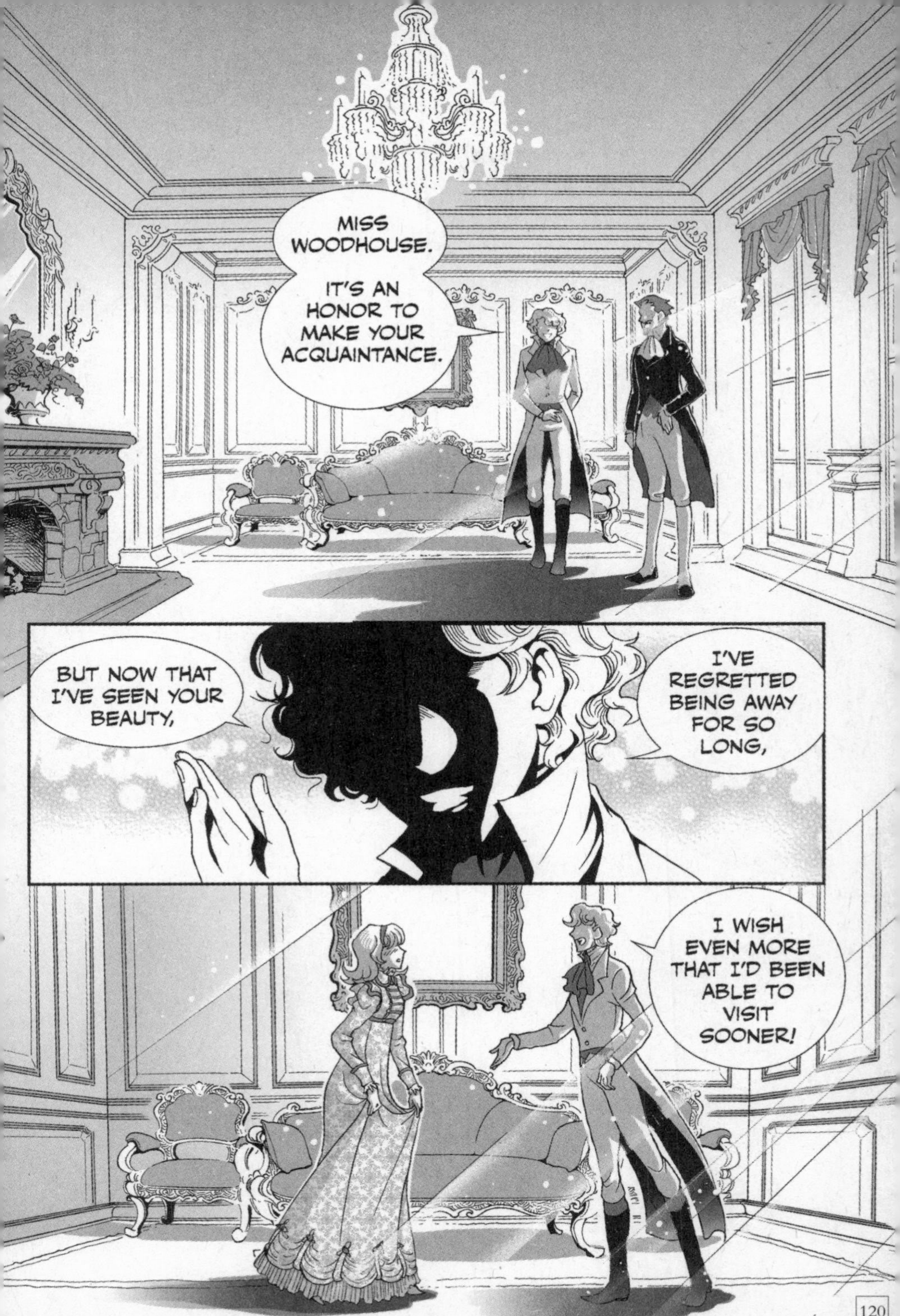
MISS WOODHOUSE.
IT'S AN HONOR TO MAKE YOUR ACQUAINTANCE.
I'VE REGRETTED BEING AWAY FOR SO LONG,
BUT NOW THAT I'VE SEEN YOUR BEAUTY,
I WISH EVEN MORE THAT I'D BEEN ABLE TO VISIT SOONER!

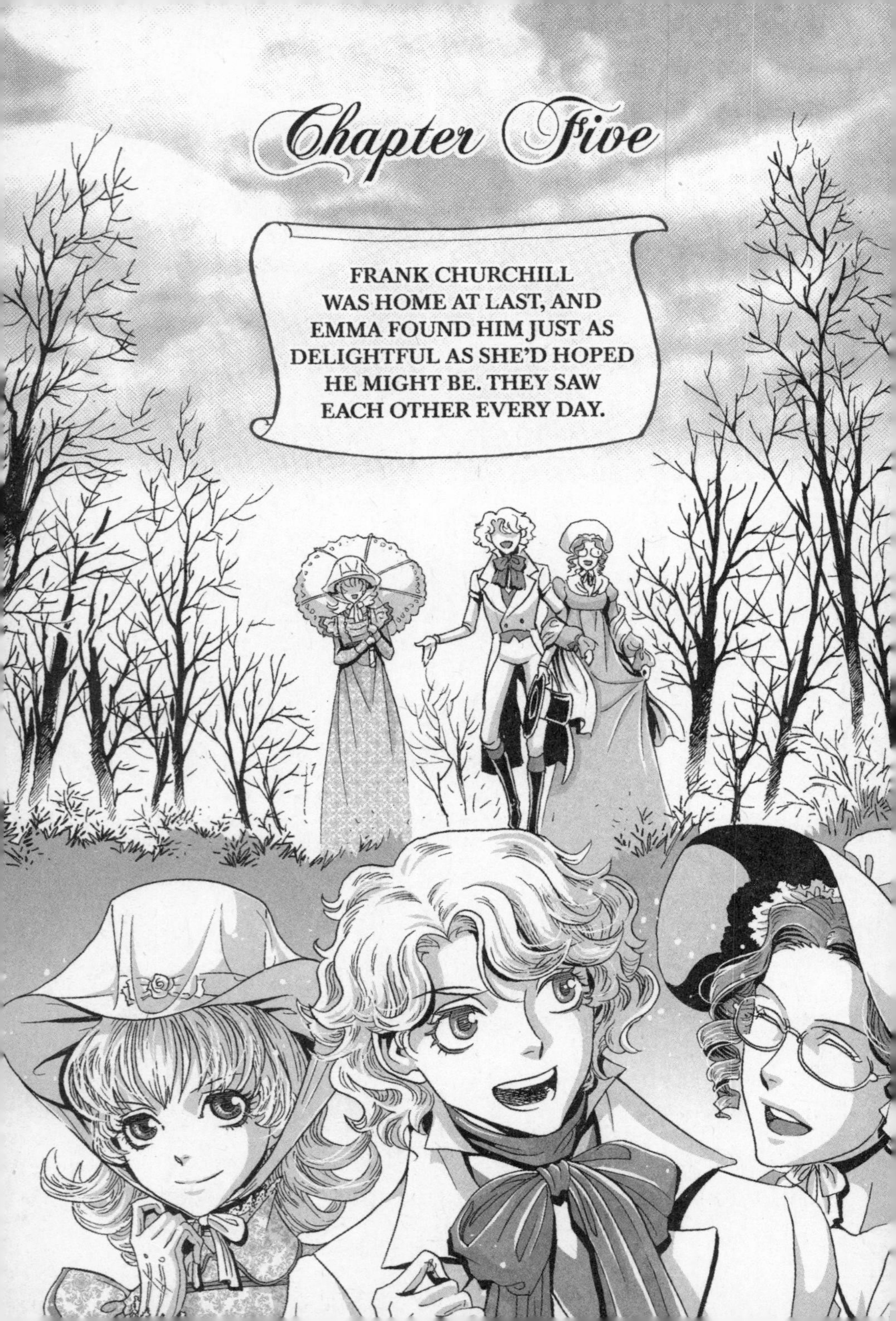
Chapter Five
FRANK CHURCHILL WAS HOME AT LAST, AND EMMA FOUND HIM JUST AS DELIGHTFUL AS SHE'D HOPED HE MIGHT BE. THEY SAW EACH OTHER EVERY DAY.

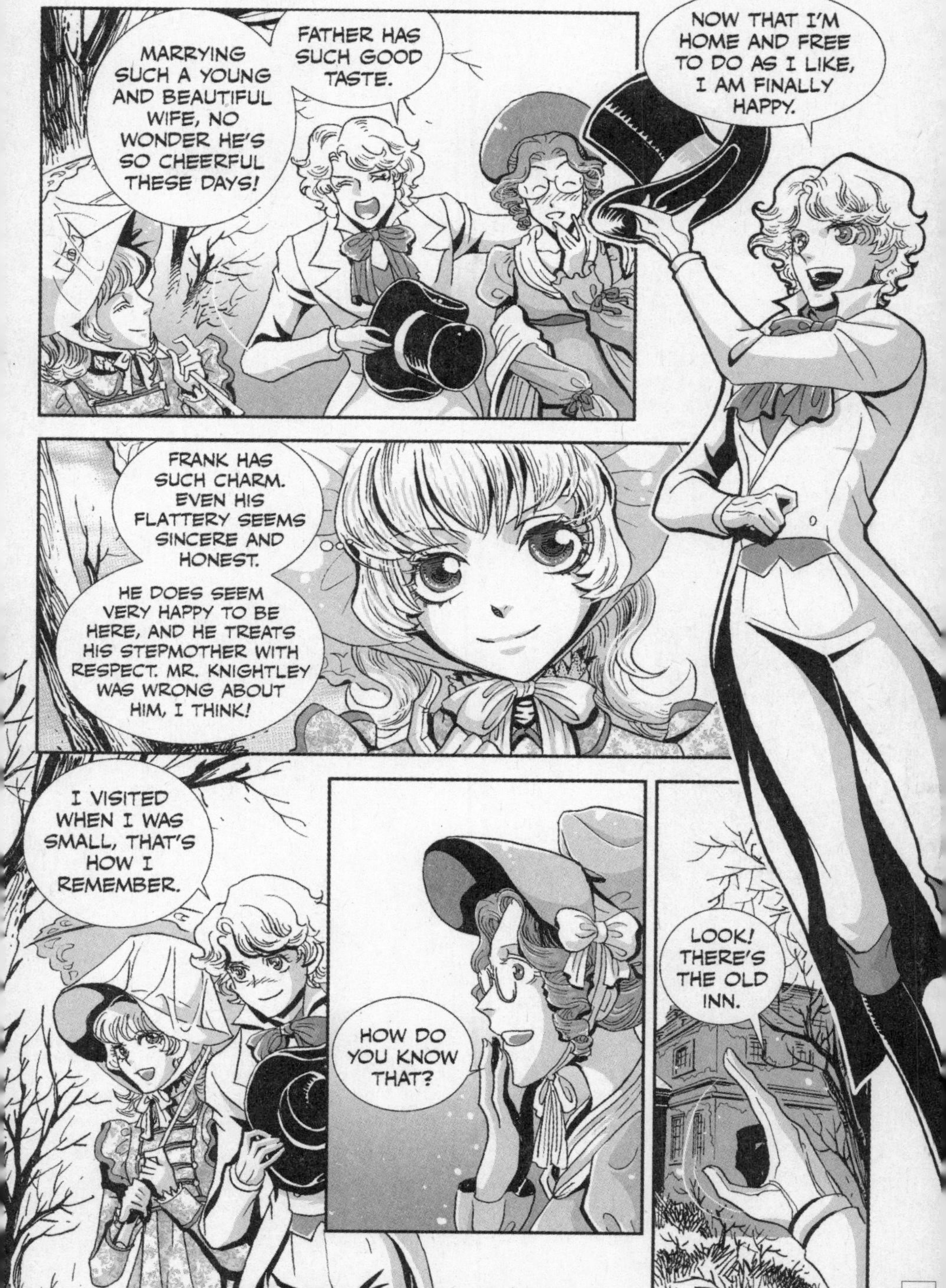
NOW THAT I'M HOME AND FREE TO DO AS I LIKE, I AM FINALLY HAPPY.
FATHER HAS SUCH GOOD TASTE.
MARRYING SUCH A YOUNG AND BEAUTIFUL WIFE, NO WONDER HE'S SO CHEERFUL THESE DAYS!
FRANK HAS SUCH CHARM. EVEN HIS FLATTERY SEEMS SINCERE AND HONEST.
HE DOES SEEM VERY HAPPY TO BE HERE, AND HE TREATS HIS STEPMOTHER WITH RESPECT. MR. KNIGHTLEY WAS WRONG ABOUT HIM, I THINK!
LOOK! THERE'S THE OLD INN.
HOW DO YOU KNOW THAT?
I VISITED WHEN I WAS SMALL, THAT'S HOW I REMEMBER.

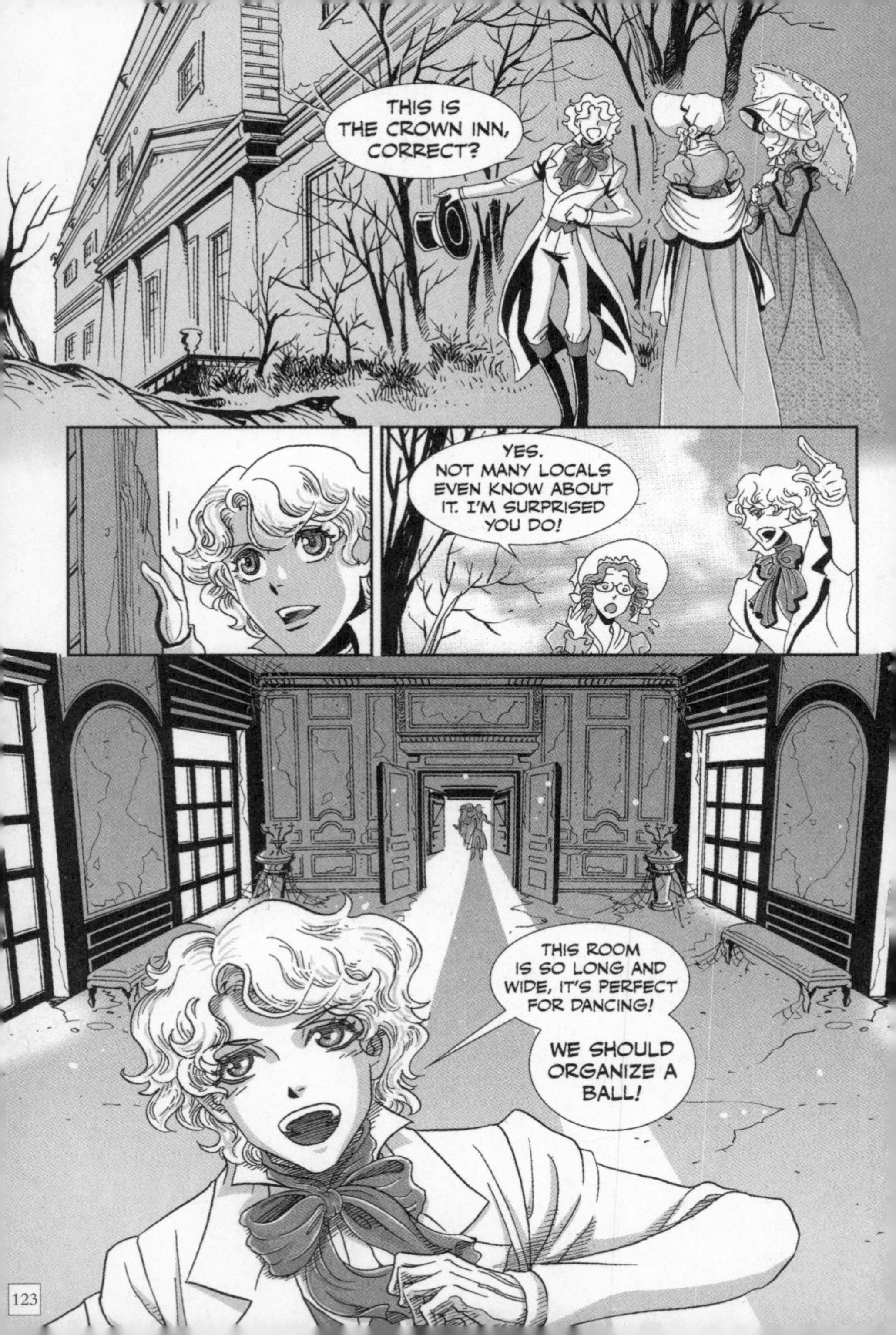
THIS IS THE CROWN INN, CORRECT?
YES. NOT MANY LOCALS EVEN KNOW ABOUT IT. I'M SURPRISED YOU DO!
THIS ROOM IS SO LONG AND WIDE, IT'S PERFECT FOR DANCING!
WE SHOULD ORGANIZE A BALL!

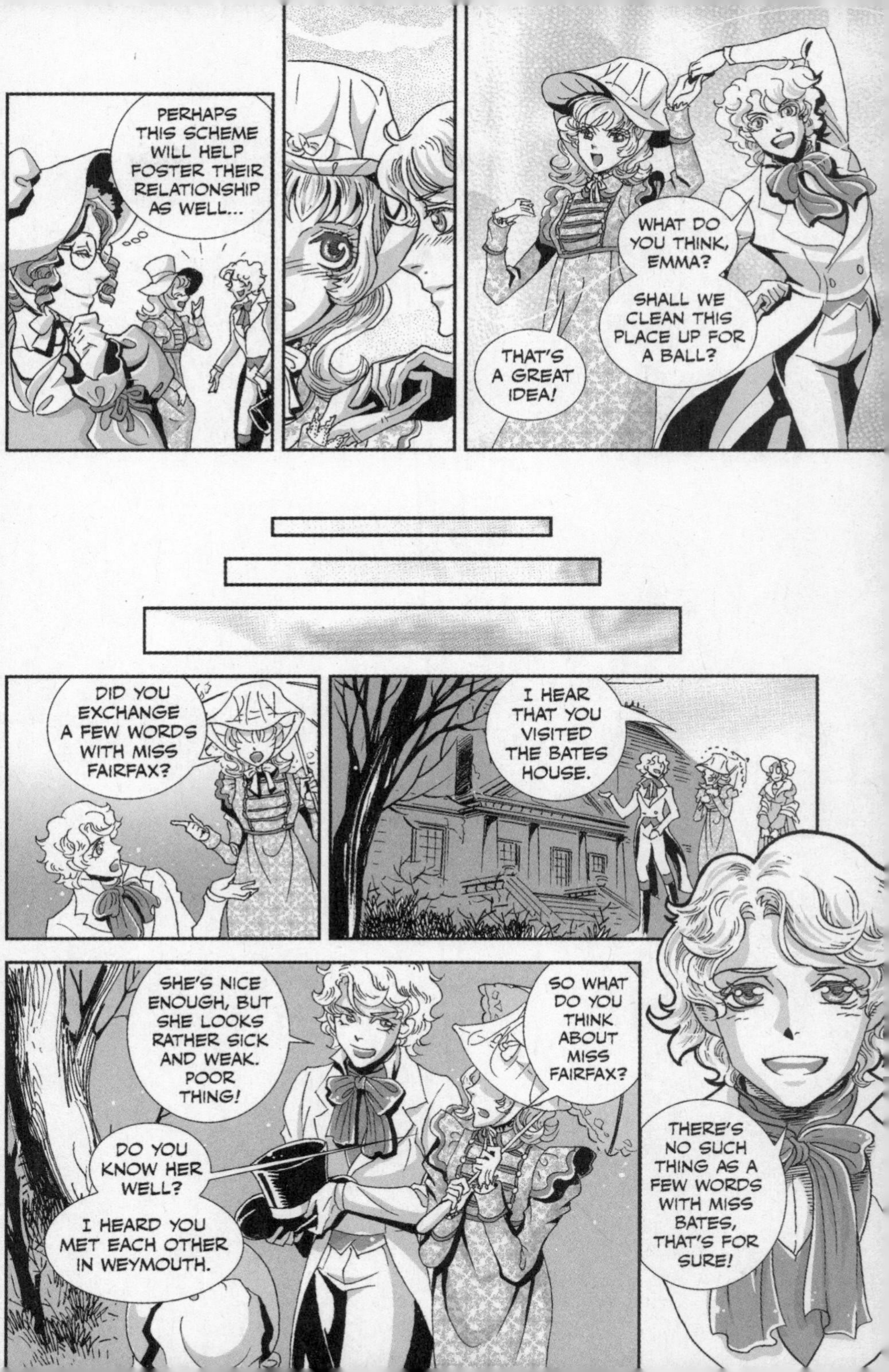
WHAT DO YOU THINK, EMMA?
SHALL WE CLEAN THIS PLACE UP FOR A BALL?
THAT'S A GREAT IDEA!
PERHAPS THIS SCHEME WILL HELP FOSTER THEIR RELATIONSHIP AS WELL...
I HEAR THAT YOU VISITED THE BATES HOUSE.
DID YOU EXCHANGE A FEW WORDS WITH MISS FAIRFAX?
THERE'S NO SUCH THING AS A FEW WORDS WITH MISS BATES, THAT'S FOR SURE!
SO WHAT DO YOU THINK ABOUT MISS FAIRFAX?
SHE'S NICE ENOUGH, BUT SHE LOOKS RATHER SICK AND WEAK. POOR THING!
DO YOU KNOW HER WELL?
I HEARD YOU MET EACH OTHER IN WEYMOUTH.

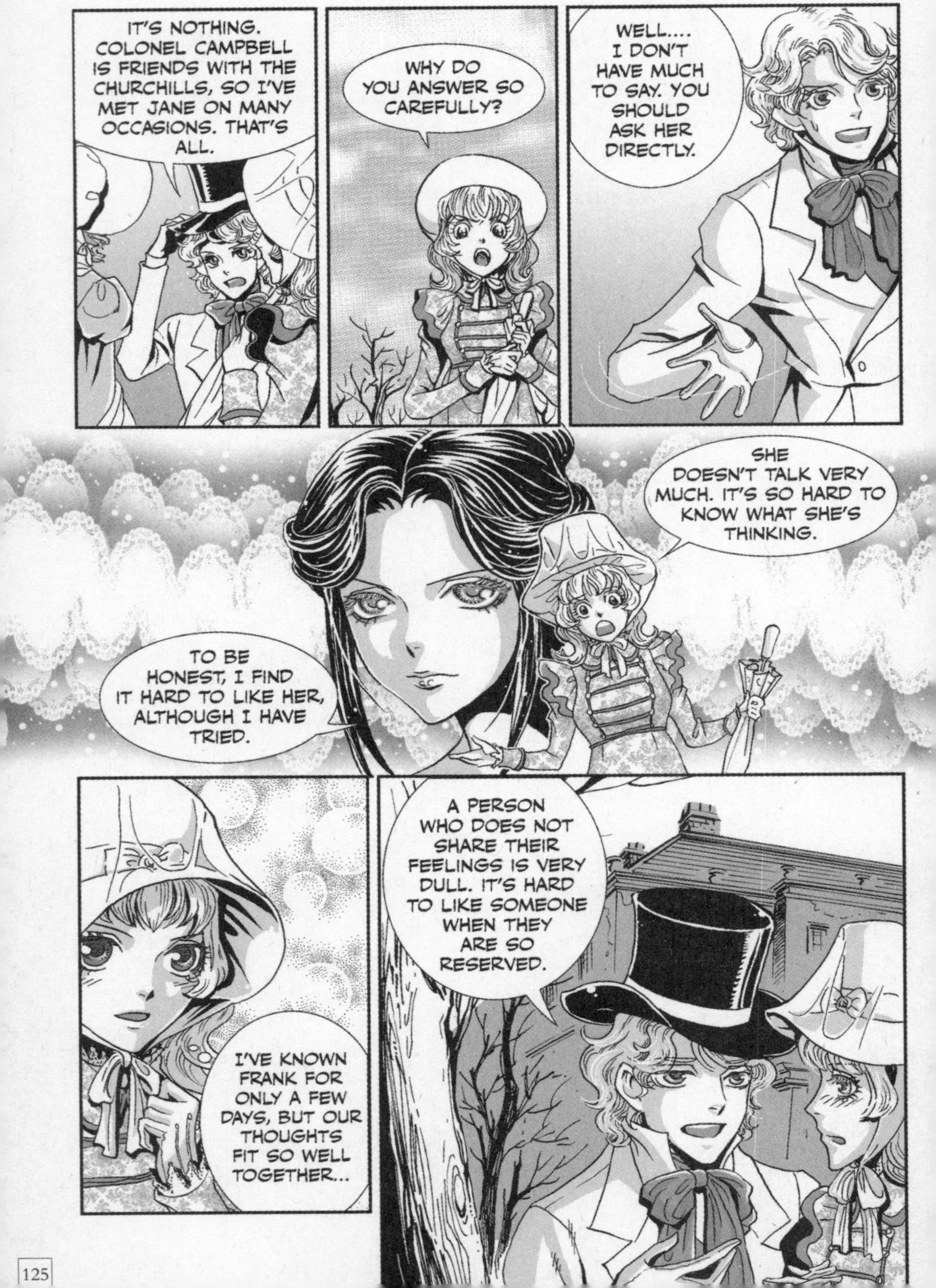
WELL.... I DON'T HAVE MUCH TO SAY. YOU SHOULD ASK HER DIRECTLY.
WHY DO YOU ANSWER SO CAREFULLY?
IT'S NOTHING. COLONEL CAMPBELL IS FRIENDS WITH THE CHURCHILLS, SO I'VE MET JANE ON MANY OCCASIONS. THAT'S ALL.
SHE DOESN'T TALK VERY MUCH. IT'S SO HARD TO KNOW WHAT SHE'S THINKING.
TO BE HONEST, I FIND IT HARD TO LIKE HER, ALTHOUGH I HAVE TRIED.
A PERSON WHO DOES NOT SHARE THEIR FEELINGS IS VERY DULL. IT'S HARD TO LIKE SOMEONE WHEN THEY ARE SO RESERVED.
I'VE KNOWN FRANK FOR ONLY A FEW DAYS, BUT OUR THOUGHTS FIT SO WELL TOGETHER...

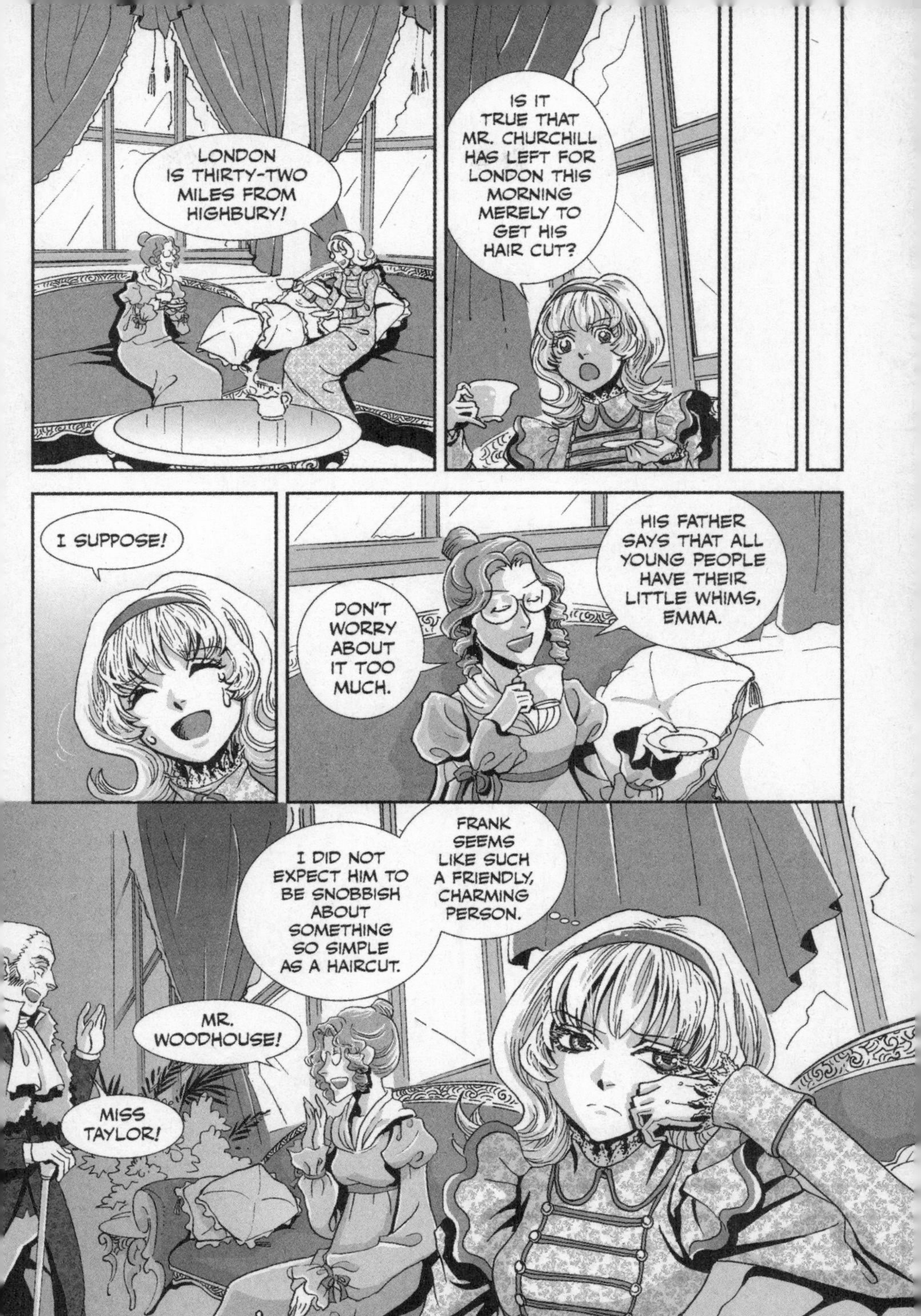

IS IT TRUE THAT MR. CHURCHILL HAS LEFT FOR LONDON THIS MORNING MERELY TO GET HIS HAIR CUT?
LONDON IS THIRTY-TWO MILES FROM HIGHBURY!
HIS FATHER SAYS THAT ALL YOUNG PEOPLE HAVE THEIR LITTLE WHIMS, EMMA.
DON'T WORRY ABOUT IT TOO MUCH.
I SUPPOSE!
FRANK SEEMS LIKE SUCH A FRIENDLY, CHARMING PERSON.
I DID NOT EXPECT HIM TO BE SNOBBISH ABOUT SOMETHING SO SIMPLE AS A HAIRCUT.
MR. WOODHOUSE!
MISS TAYLOR!

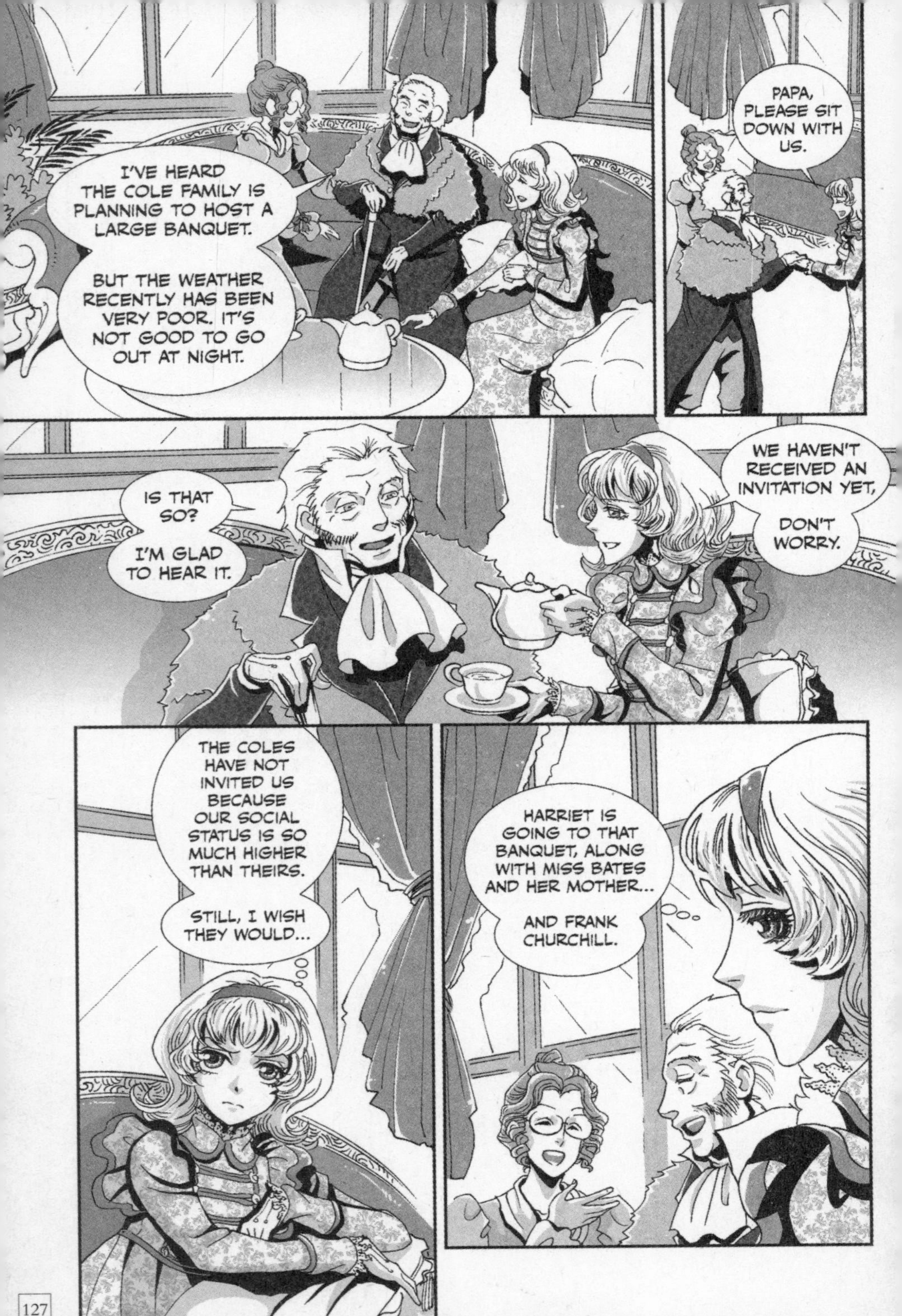
PAPA, PLEASE SIT DOWN WITH US.
I'VE HEARD THE COLE FAMILY IS PLANNING TO HOST A LARGE BANQUET.
BUT THE WEATHER RECENTLY HAS BEEN VERY POOR. IT'S NOT GOOD TO GO OUT AT NIGHT.
WE HAVEN'T RECEIVED AN INVITATION YET,
DON'T WORRY.
IS THAT SO?
I'M GLAD TO HEAR IT.
HARRIET IS GOING TO THAT BANQUET, ALONG WITH MISS BATES AND HER MOTHER...
AND FRANK CHURCHILL.
THE COLES HAVE NOT INVITED US BECAUSE OUR SOCIAL STATUS IS SO MUCH HIGHER THAN THEIRS.
STILL, I WISH THEY WOULD...

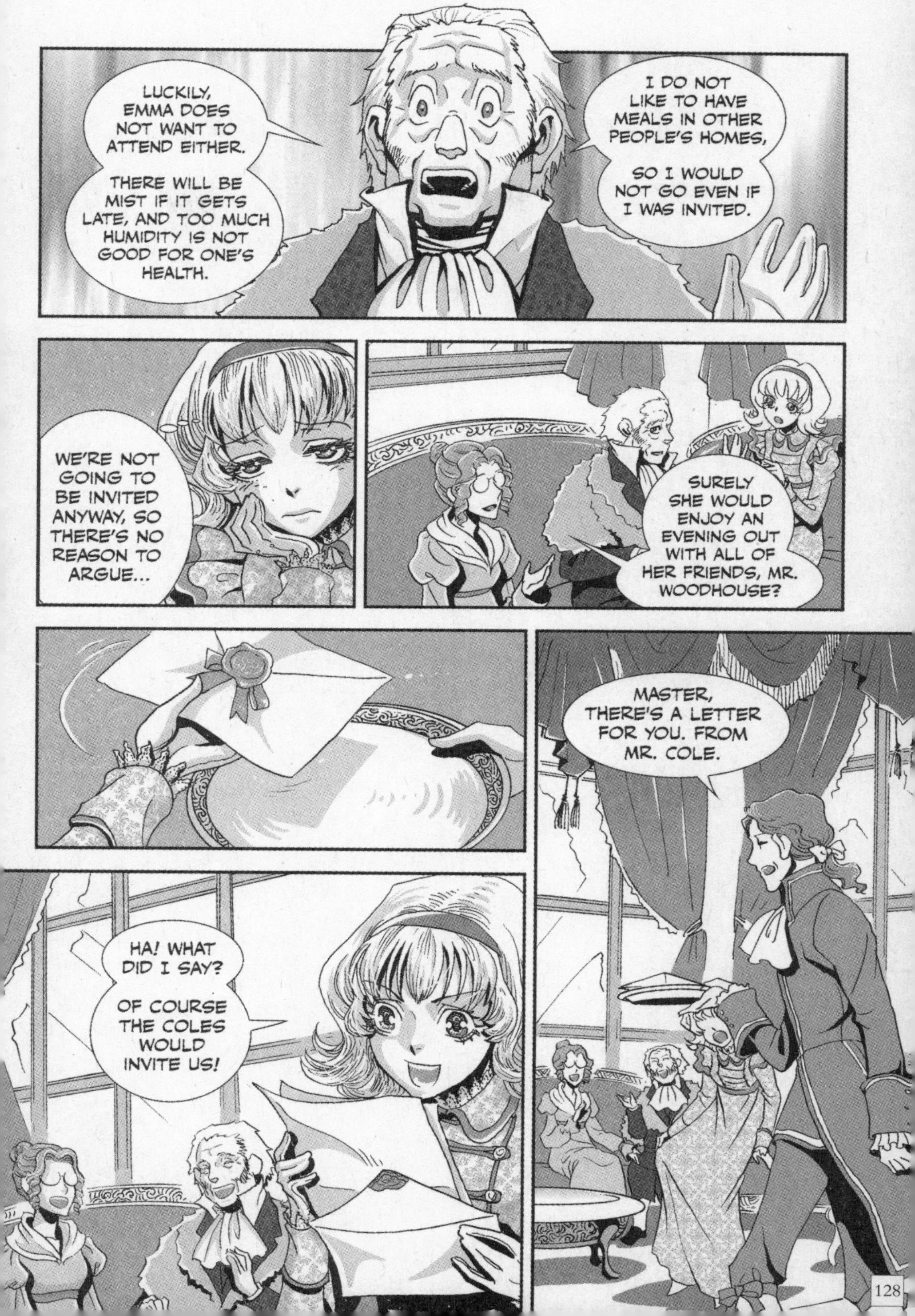
I DO NOT LIKE TO HAVE MEALS IN OTHER PEOPLE'S HOMES,
SO I WOULD NOT GO EVEN IF I WAS INVITED.
LUCKILY, EMMA DOES NOT WANT TO ATTEND EITHER.
THERE WILL BE MIST IF IT GETS LATE, AND TOO MUCH HUMIDITY IS NOT GOOD FOR ONE'S HEALTH.
SURELY SHE WOULD ENJOY AN EVENING OUT WITH ALL OF HER FRIENDS, MR. WOODHOUSE?
WE'RE NOT GOING TO BE INVITED ANYWAY, SO THERE'S NO REASON TO ARGUE...
MASTER, THERE'S A LETTER FOR YOU. FROM MR. COLE.
HA! WHAT DID I SAY?
OF COURSE THE COLES WOULD INVITE US!

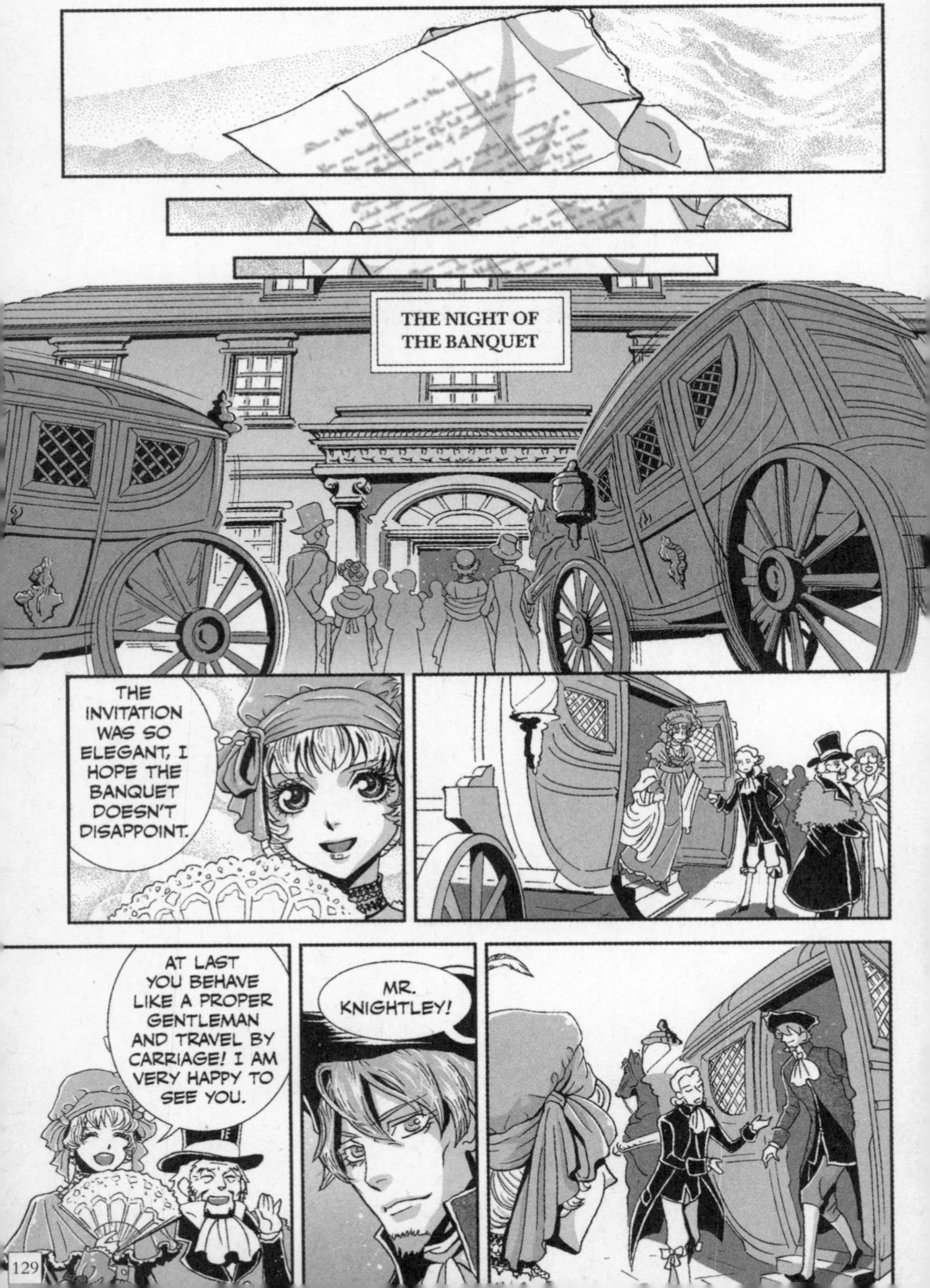
THE NIGHT OF THE BANQUET
THE INVITATION WAS SO ELEGANT, I HOPE THE BANQUET DOESN'T DISAPPOINT.
MR. KNIGHTLEY!
AT LAST YOU BEHAVE LIKE A PROPER GENTLEMAN AND TRAVEL BY CARRIAGE! I AM VERY HAPPY TO SEE YOU.

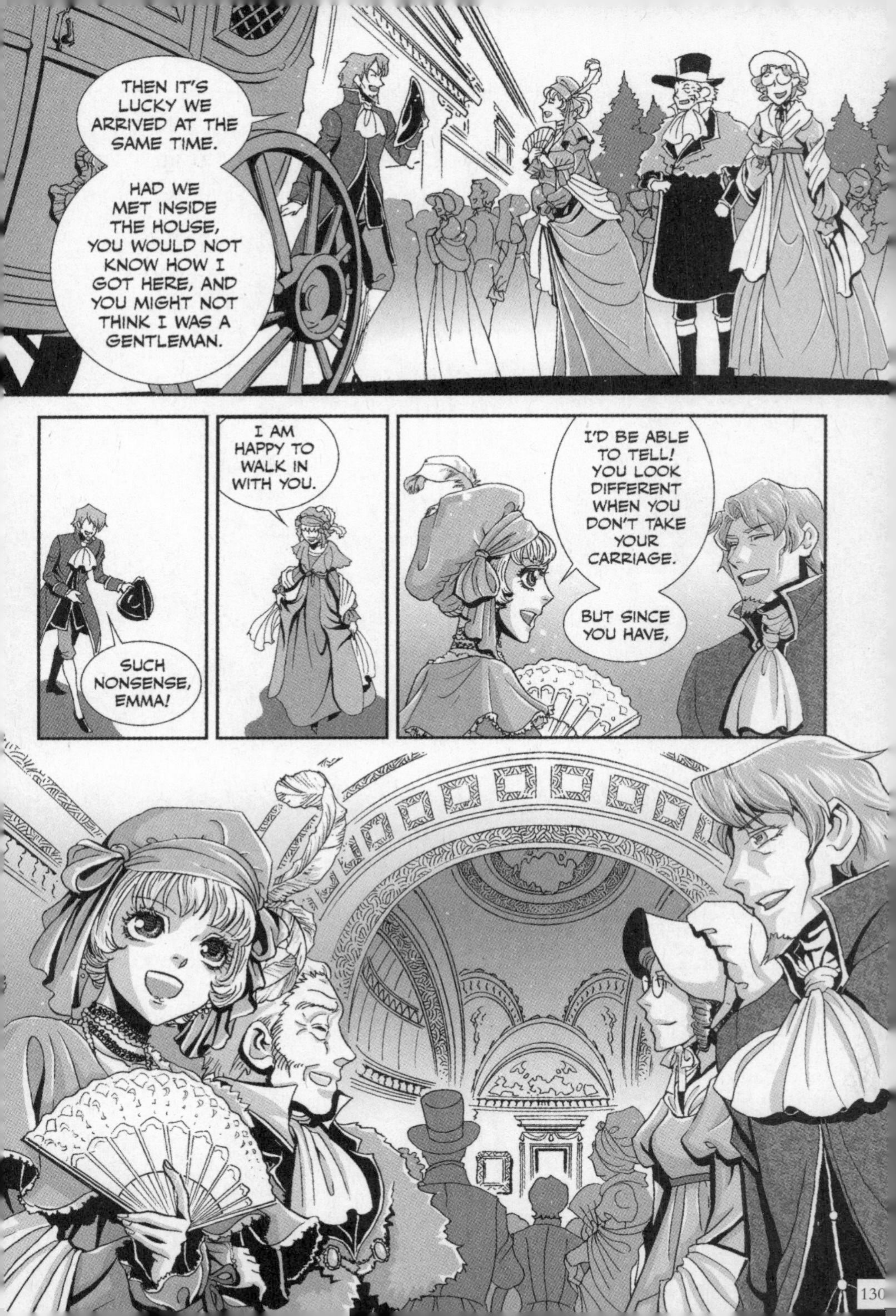
THEN IT'S LUCKY WE ARRIVED AT THE SAME TIME.
HAD WE MET INSIDE THE HOUSE, YOU WOULD NOT KNOW HOW I GOT HERE, AND YOU MIGHT NOT THINK I WAS A GENTLEMAN.
I'D BE ABLE TO TELL! YOU LOOK DIFFERENT WHEN YOU DON'T TAKE YOUR CARRIAGE.
BUT SINCE YOU HAVE,
I AM HAPPY TO WALK IN WITH YOU.
SUCH NONSENSE, EMMA!

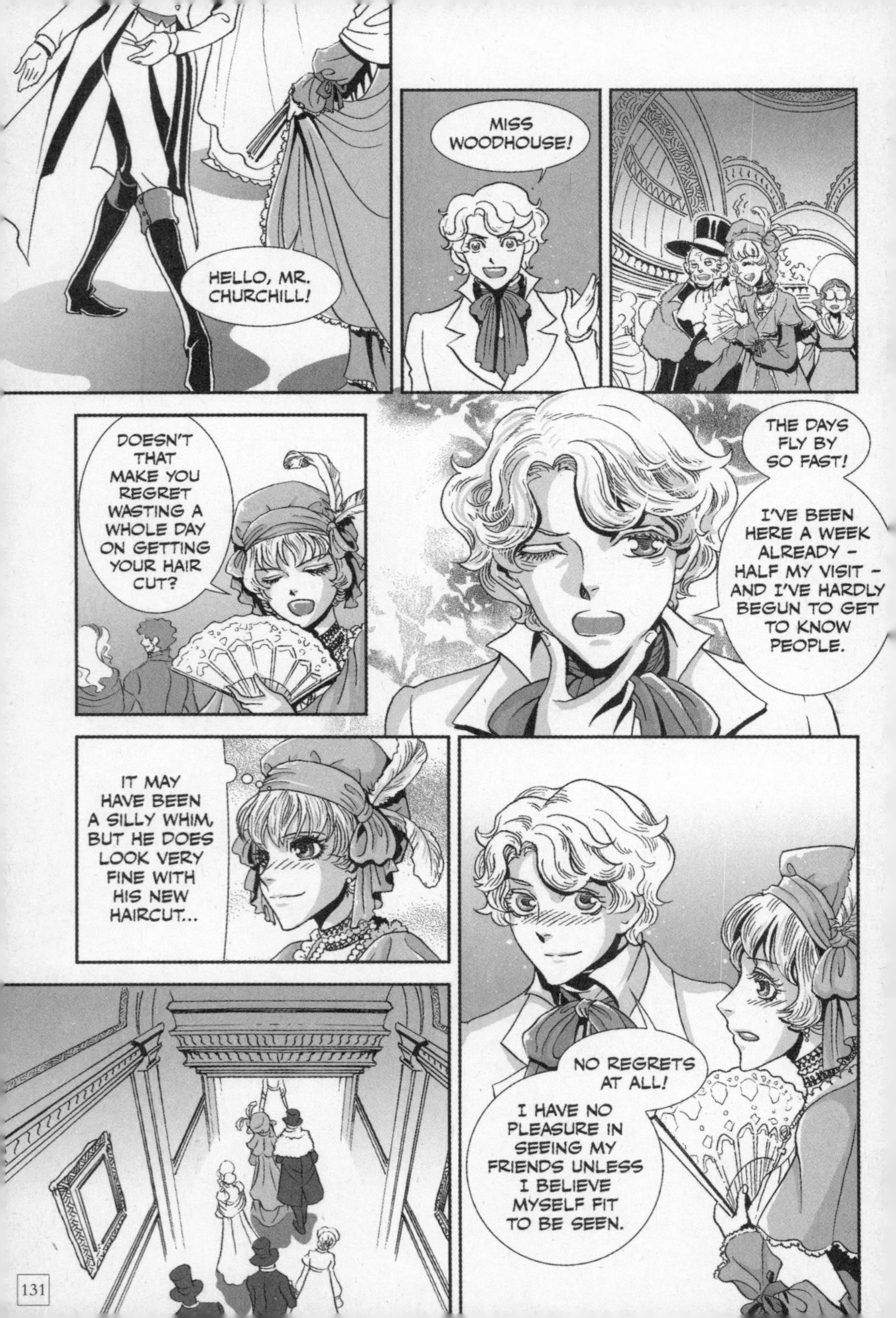
MISS WOODHOUSE!
HELLO, MR. CHURCHILL!
THE DAYS FLY BY SO FAST!
I'VE BEEN HERE A WEEK ALREADY - HALF MY VISIT - AND I'VE HARDLY BEGUN TO GET TO KNOW PEOPLE.
DOESN'T THAT MAKE YOU REGRET WASTING A WHOLE DAY ON GETTING YOUR HAIR CUT?
NO REGRETS AT ALL!
I HAVE NO PLEASURE IN SEEING MY FRIENDS UNLESS I BELIEVE MYSELF FIT TO BE SEEN.
IT MAY HAVE BEEN A SILLY WHIM, BUT HE DOES LOOK VERY FINE WITH HIS NEW HAIRCUT...

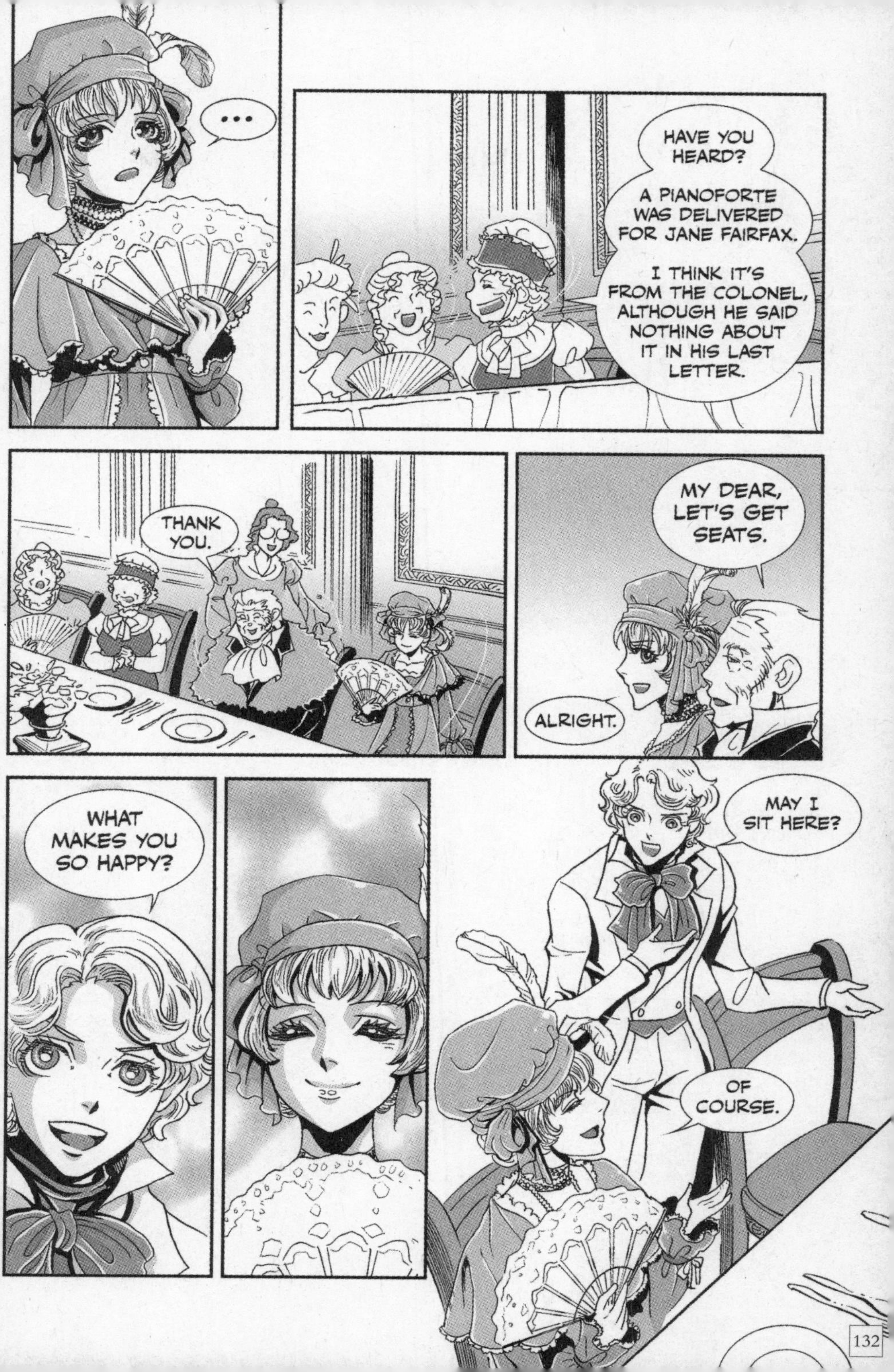
HAVE YOU HEARD?
A PIANOFORTE WAS DELIVERED FOR JANE FAIRFAX.
I THINK IT'S FROM THE COLONEL, ALTHOUGH HE SAID NOTHING ABOUT IT IN HIS LAST LETTER.
...
MY DEAR, LET'S GET SEATS.
ALRIGHT.
THANK YOU.
MAY I SIT HERE?
OF COURSE.
WHAT MAKES YOU SO HAPPY?

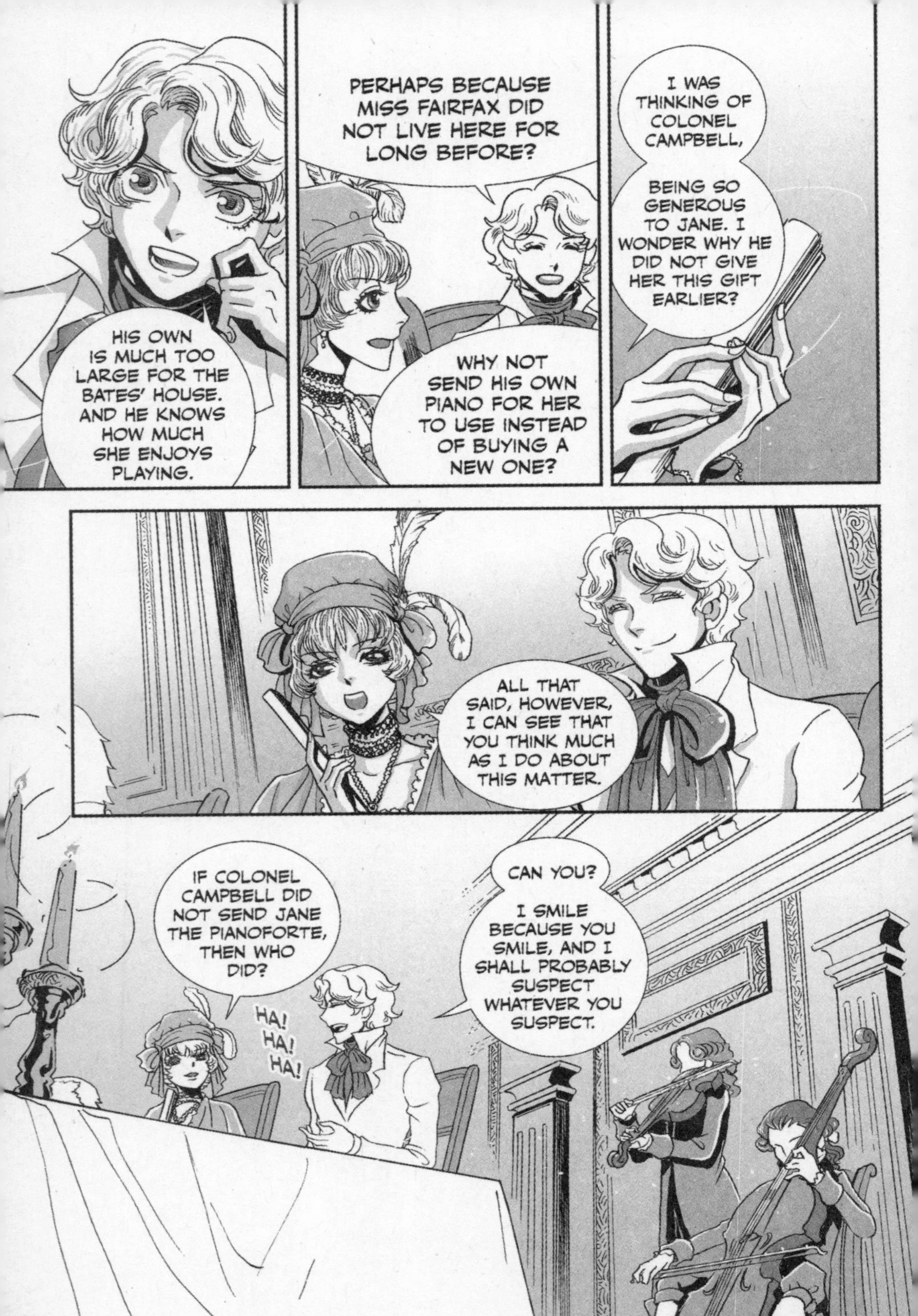
I WAS THINKING OF COLONEL CAMPBELL,
BEING SO GENEROUS TO JANE. I WONDER WHY HE DID NOT GIVE HER THIS GIFT EARLIER?
PERHAPS BECAUSE MISS FAIRFAX DID NOT LIVE HERE FOR LONG BEFORE?
WHY NOT SEND HIS OWN PIANO FOR HER TO USE INSTEAD OF BUYING A NEW ONE?
HIS OWN IS MUCH TOO LARGE FOR THE BATES' HOUSE. AND HE KNOWS HOW MUCH SHE ENJOYS PLAYING.
ALL THAT SAID, HOWEVER, I CAN SEE THAT YOU THINK MUCH AS I DO ABOUT THIS MATTER.
CAN YOU?
I SMILE BECAUSE YOU SMILE, AND I SHALL PROBABLY SUSPECT WHATEVER YOU SUSPECT.
IF COLONEL CAMPBELL DID NOT SEND JANE THE PIANOFORTE, THEN WHO DID?
HA! HA! HA!

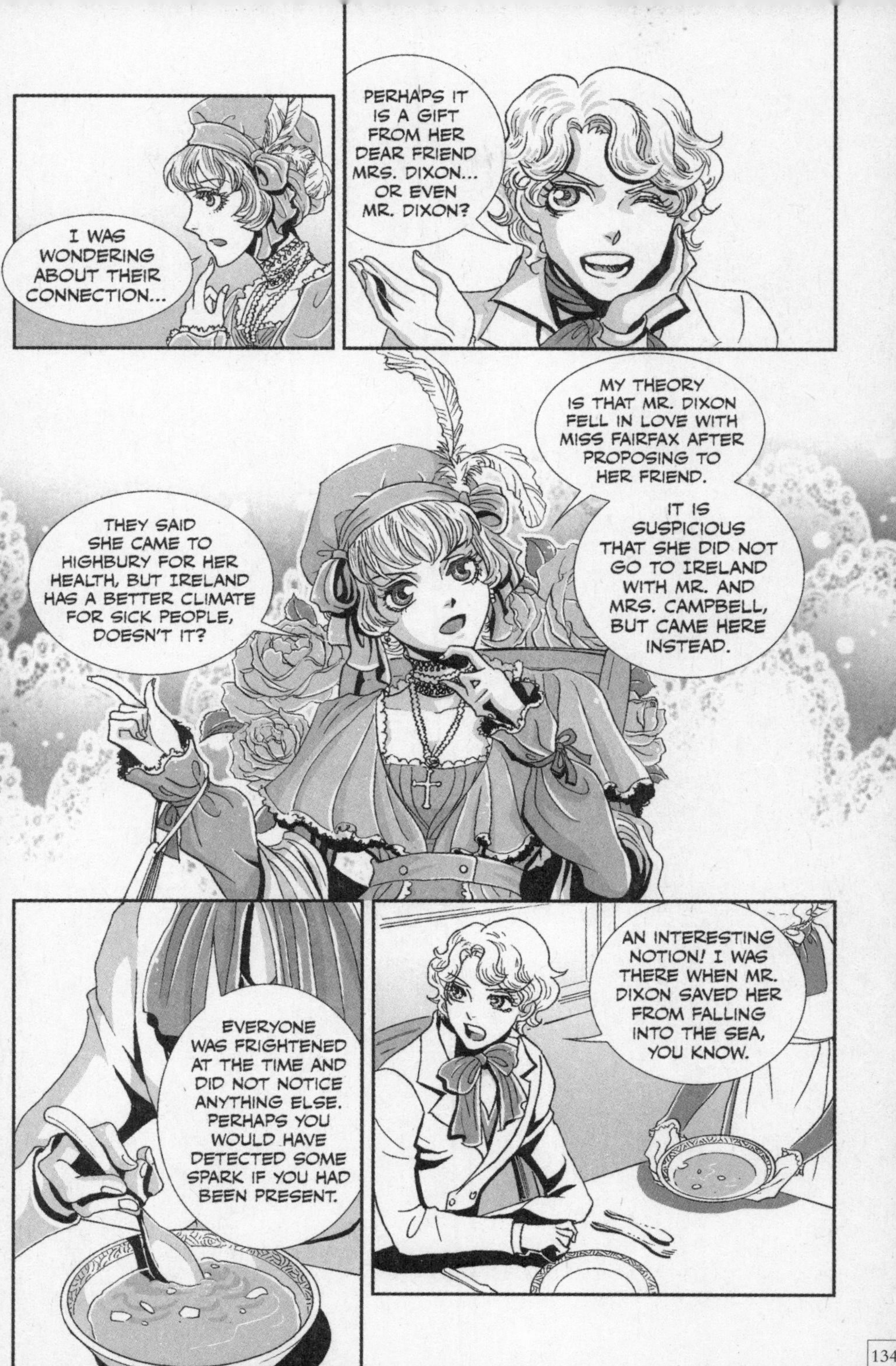
PERHAPS IT IS A GIFT FROM HER DEAR FRIEND MRS. DIXON... OR EVEN MR. DIXON?
I WAS WONDERING ABOUT THEIR CONNECTION...
MY THEORY IS THAT MR. DIXON FELL IN LOVE WITH MISS FAIRFAX AFTER PROPOSING TO HER FRIEND.
IT IS SUSPICIOUS THAT SHE DID NOT GO TO IRELAND WITH MR. AND MRS. CAMPBELL, BUT CAME HERE INSTEAD.
THEY SAID SHE CAME TO HIGHBURY FOR HER HEALTH, BUT IRELAND HAS A BETTER CLIMATE FOR SICK PEOPLE, DOESN'T IT?
AN INTERESTING NOTION! I WAS THERE WHEN MR. DIXON SAVED HER FROM FALLING INTO THE SEA, YOU KNOW.
EVERYONE WAS FRIGHTENED AT THE TIME AND DID NOT NOTICE ANYTHING ELSE. PERHAPS YOU WOULD HAVE DETECTED SOME SPARK IF YOU HAD BEEN PRESENT.

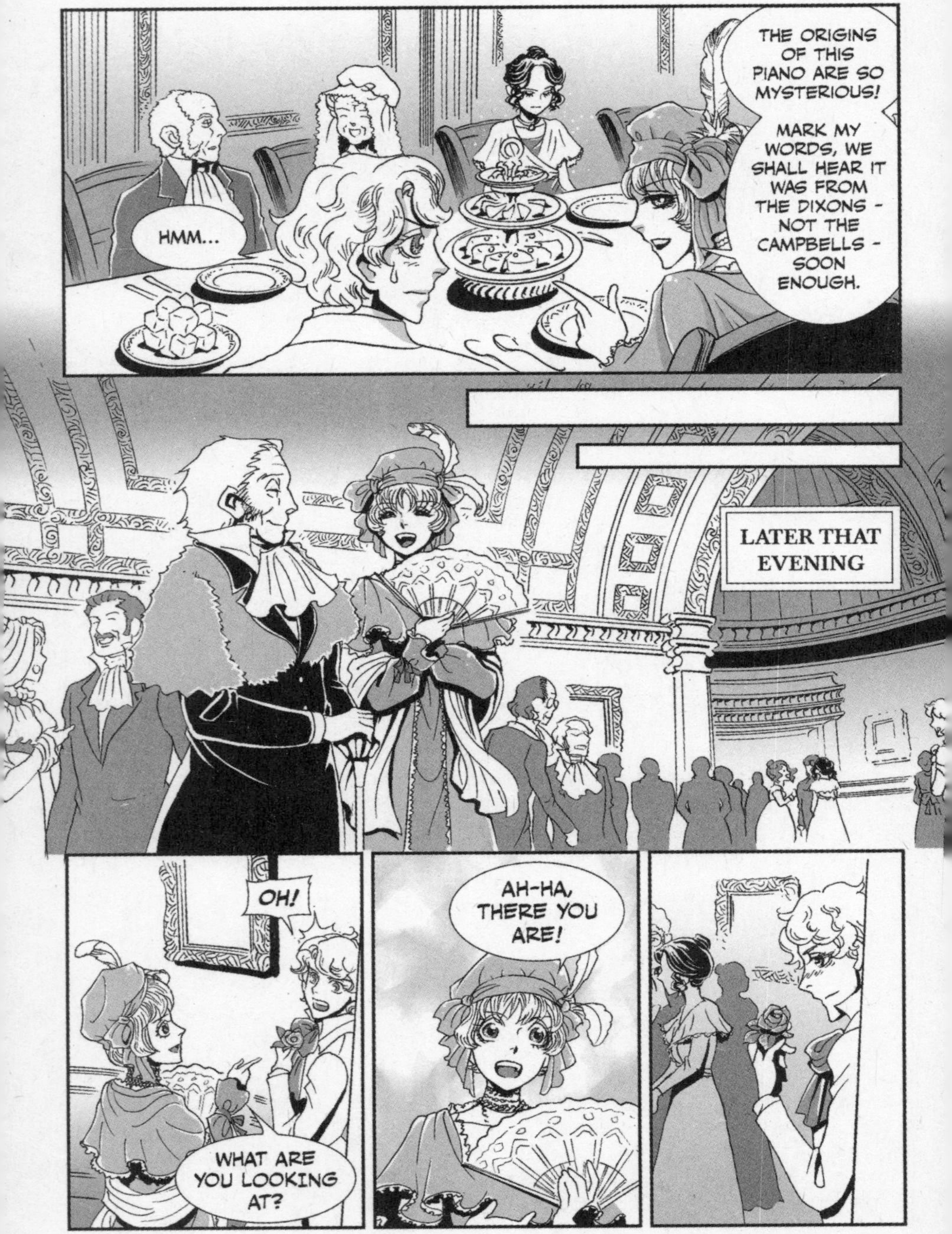
THE ORIGINS OF THIS PIANO ARE SO MYSTERIOUS!
MARK MY WORDS, WE SHALL HEAR IT WAS FROM THE DIXONS - NOT THE CAMPBELLS - SOON ENOUGH.
HMM...
LATER THAT EVENING
AH-HA, THERE YOU ARE!
OH!
WHAT ARE YOU LOOKING AT?

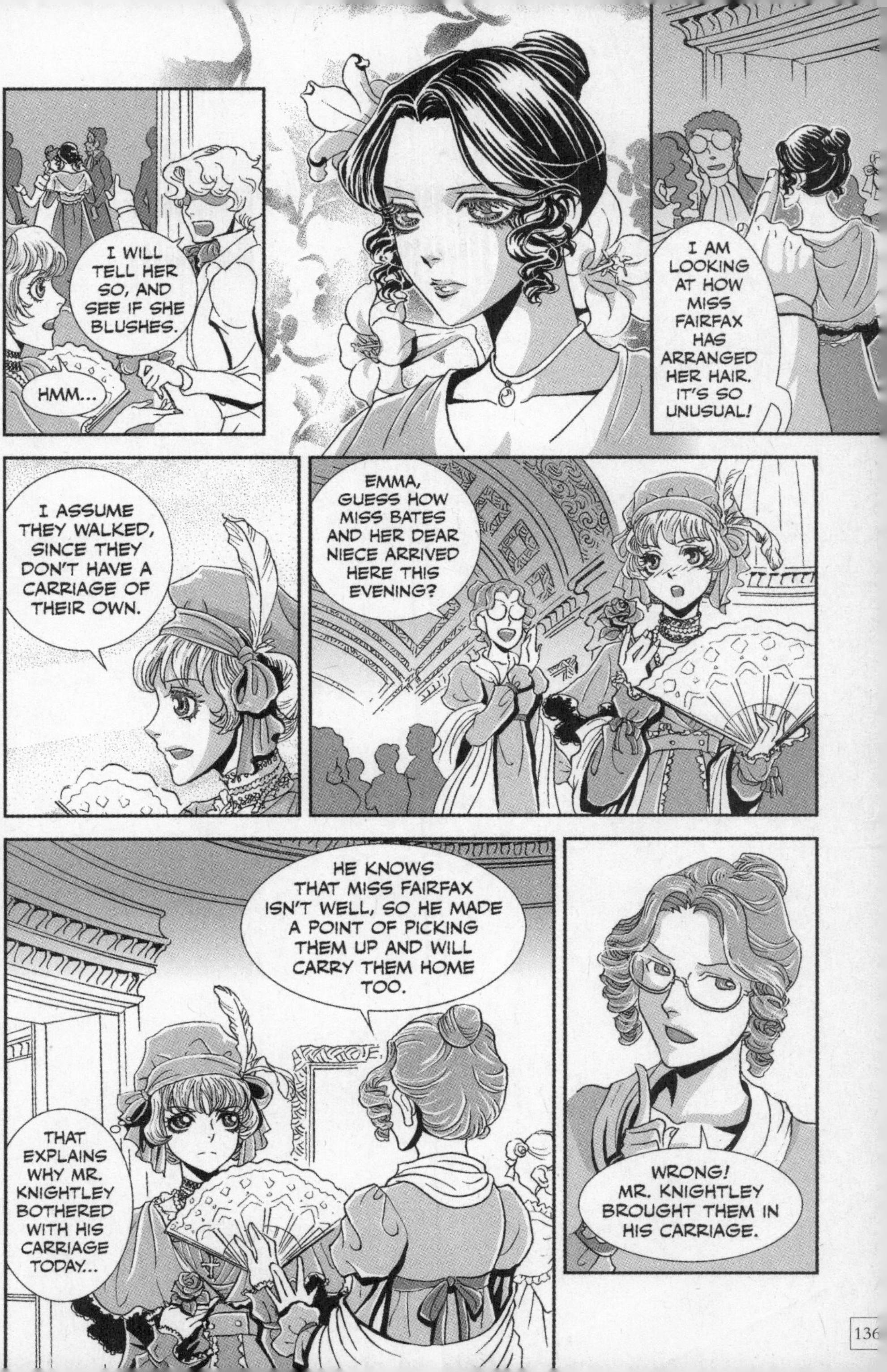
I AM LOOKING AT HOW MISS FAIRFAX HAS ARRANGED HER HAIR. IT'S SO UNUSUAL!
I WILL TELL HER SO, AND SEE IF SHE BLUSHES.
HMM...
EMMA, GUESS HOW MISS BATES AND HER DEAR NIECE ARRIVED HERE THIS EVENING?
I ASSUME THEY WALKED, SINCE THEY DON'T HAVE A CARRIAGE OF THEIR OWN.
WRONG! MR. KNIGHTLEY BROUGHT THEM IN HIS CARRIAGE.
HE KNOWS THAT MISS FAIRFAX ISN'T WELL, SO HE MADE A POINT OF PICKING THEM UP AND WILL CARRY THEM HOME TOO.
THAT EXPLAINS WHY MR. KNIGHTLEY BOTHERED WITH HIS CARRIAGE TODAY...

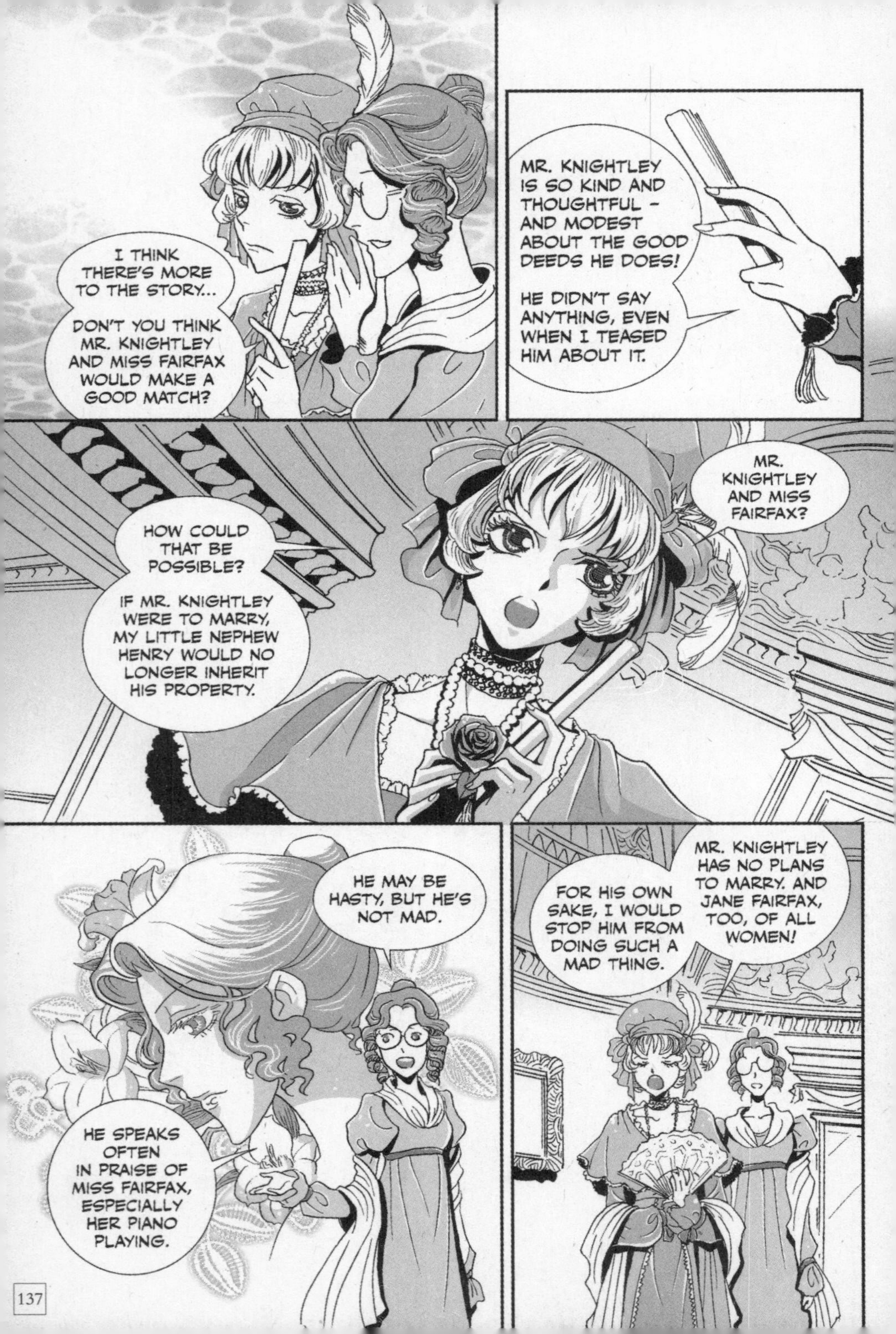
MR. KNIGHTLEY IS SO KIND AND THOUGHTFUL – AND MODEST ABOUT THE GOOD DEEDS HE DOES!
HE DIDN'T SAY ANYTHING, EVEN WHEN I TEASED HIM ABOUT IT.
I THINK THERE'S MORE TO THE STORY...
DON'T YOU THINK MR. KNIGHTLEY AND MISS FAIRFAX WOULD MAKE A GOOD MATCH?
MR. KNIGHTLEY AND MISS FAIRFAX?
HOW COULD THAT BE POSSIBLE?
IF MR. KNIGHTLEY WERE TO MARRY, MY LITTLE NEPHEW HENRY WOULD NO LONGER INHERIT HIS PROPERTY.
MR. KNIGHTLEY HAS NO PLANS TO MARRY. AND JANE FAIRFAX, TOO, OF ALL WOMEN!
FOR HIS OWN SAKE, I WOULD STOP HIM FROM DOING SUCH A MAD THING.
HE MAY BE HASTY, BUT HE'S NOT MAD.
HE SPEAKS OFTEN IN PRAISE OF MISS FAIRFAX, ESPECIALLY HER PIANO PLAYING.

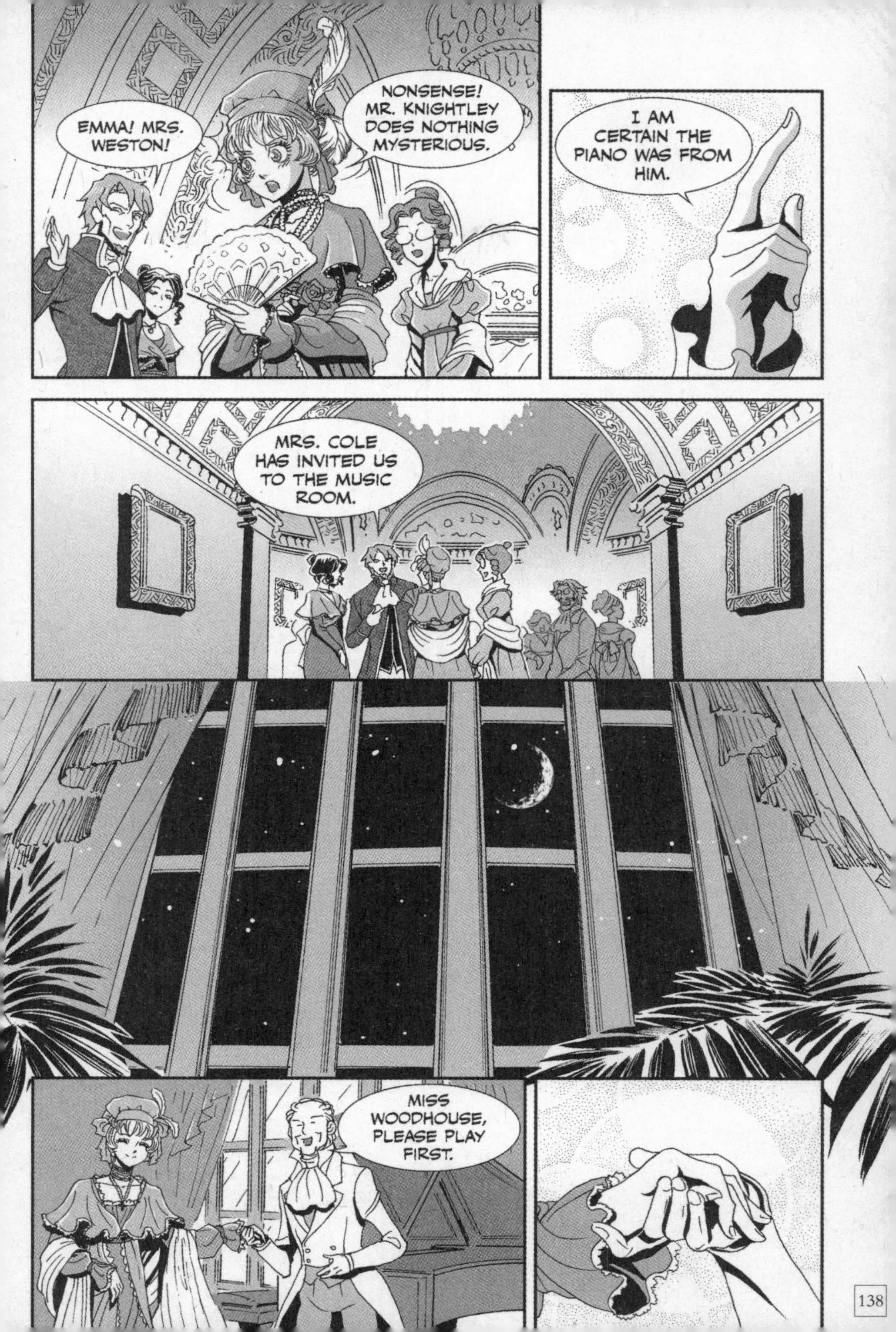
I AM CERTAIN THE PIANO WAS FROM HIM.
NONSENSE! MR. KNIGHTLEY DOES NOTHING MYSTERIOUS.
EMMA! MRS. WESTON!
MRS. COLE HAS INVITED US TO THE MUSIC ROOM.
MISS WOODHOUSE, PLEASE PLAY FIRST.

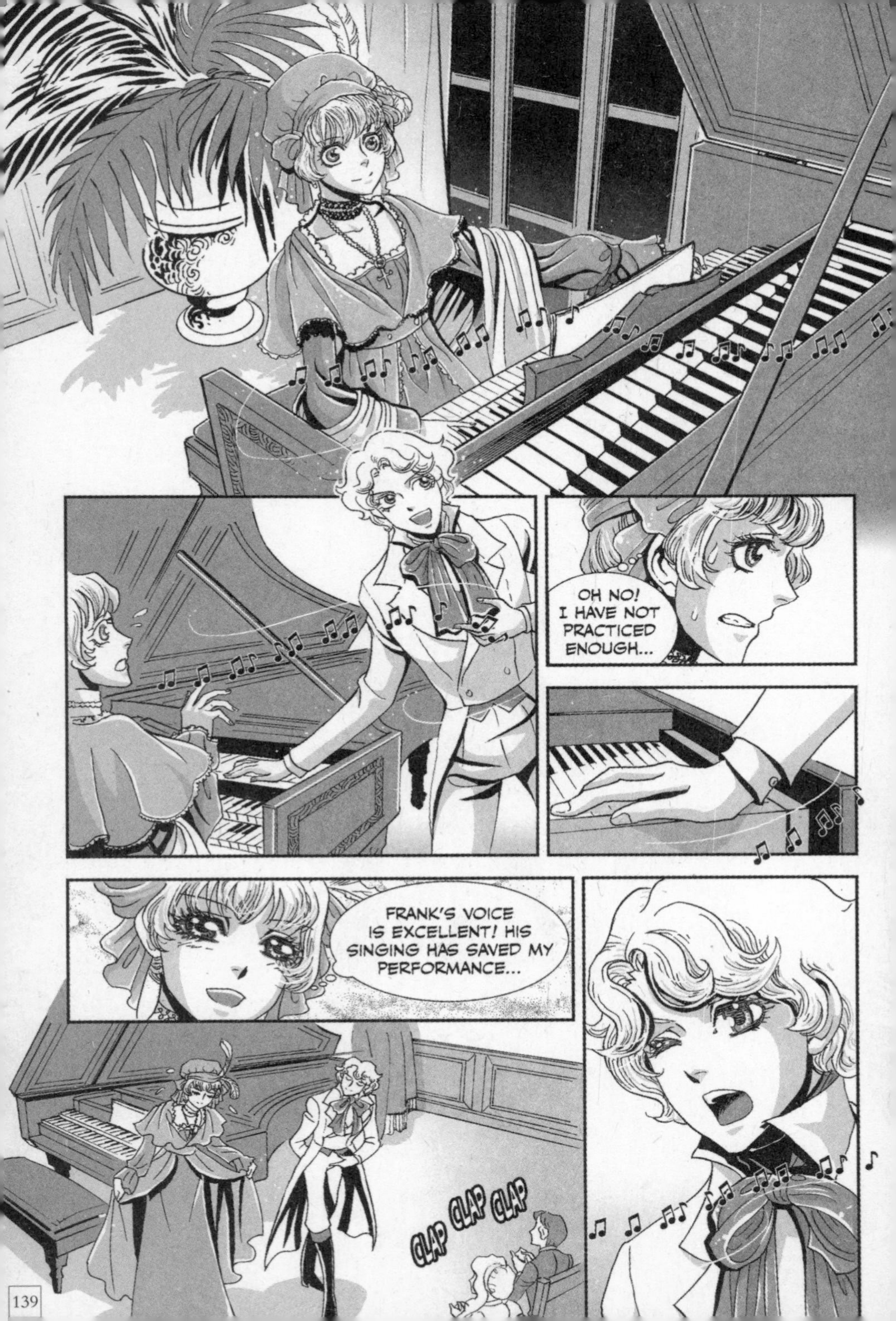
OH NO! I HAVE NOT PRACTICED ENOUGH...
FRANK'S VOICE IS EXCELLENT! HIS SINGING HAS SAVED MY PERFORMANCE...
CLAP CLAP CLAP

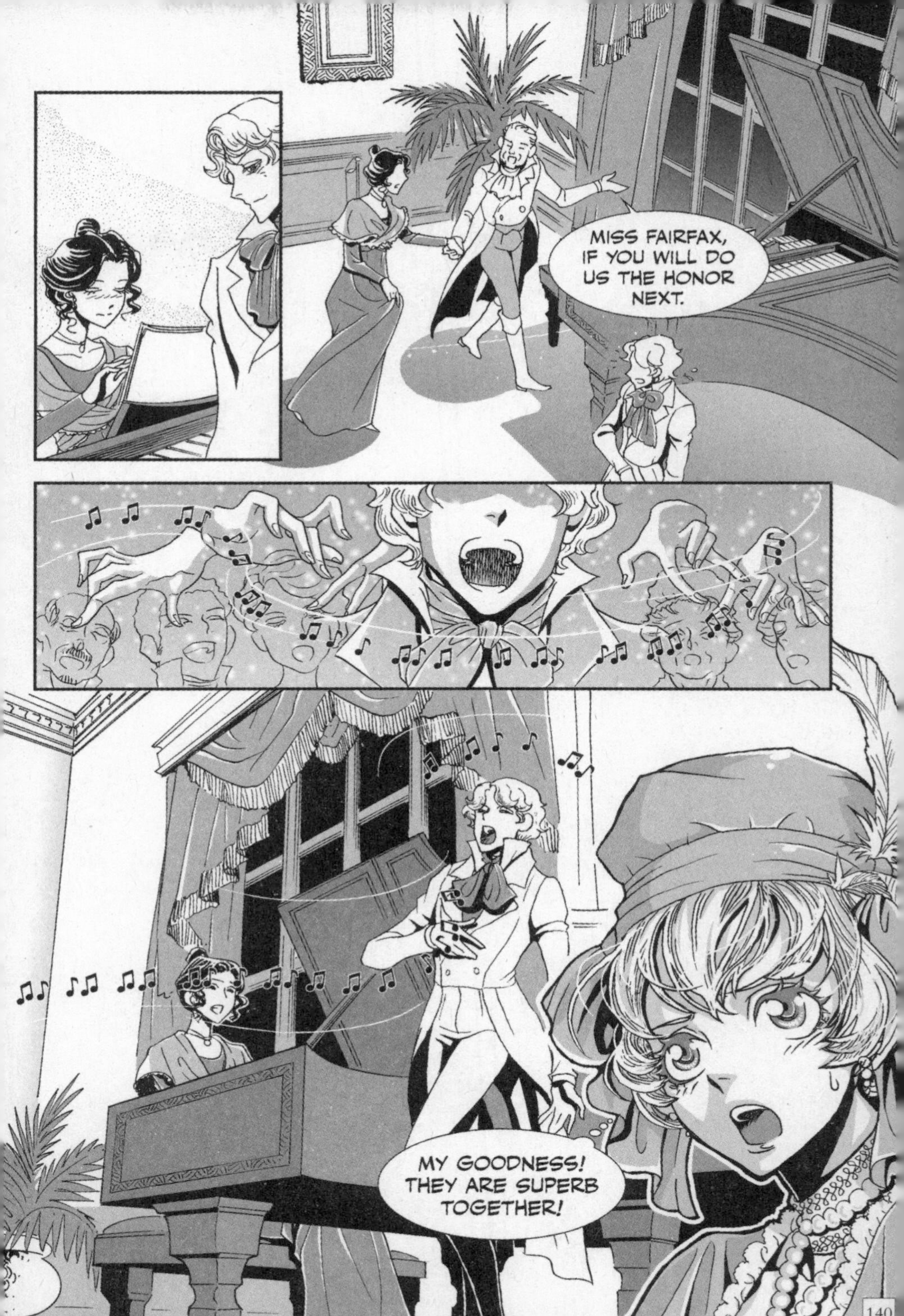
MISS FAIRFAX, IF YOU WILL DO US THE HONOR NEXT.
MY GOODNESS! THEY ARE SUPERB TOGETHER!

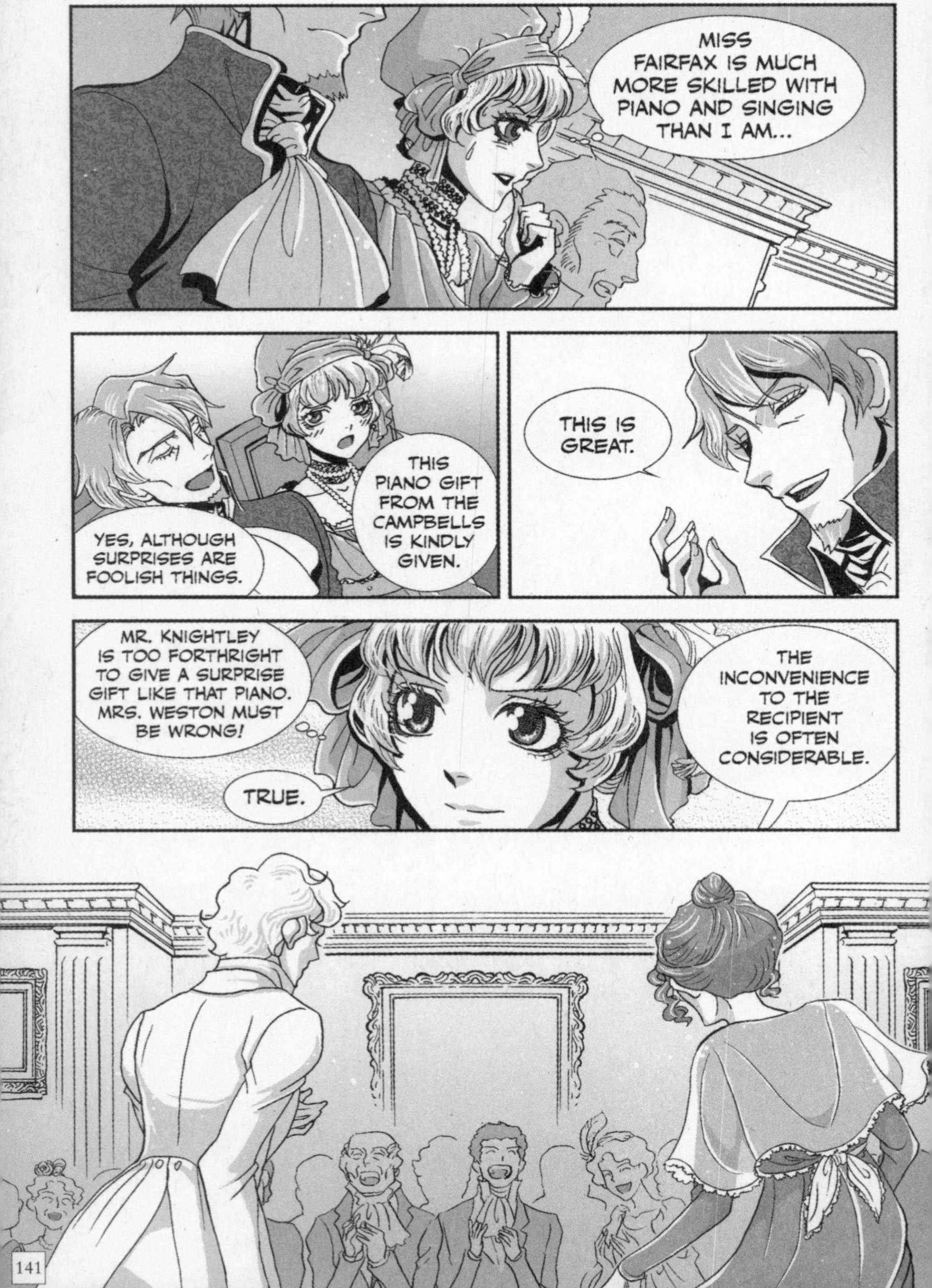
MISS FAIRFAX IS MUCH MORE SKILLED WITH PIANO AND SINGING THAN I AM...
THIS IS GREAT.
THIS PIANO GIFT FROM THE CAMPBELLS IS KINDLY GIVEN.
YES, ALTHOUGH SURPRISES ARE FOOLISH THINGS.
THE INCONVENIENCE TO THE RECIPIENT IS OFTEN CONSIDERABLE.
MR. KNIGHTLEY IS TOO FORTHRIGHT TO GIVE A SURPRISE GIFT LIKE THAT PIANO. MRS. WESTON MUST BE WRONG!
TRUE.

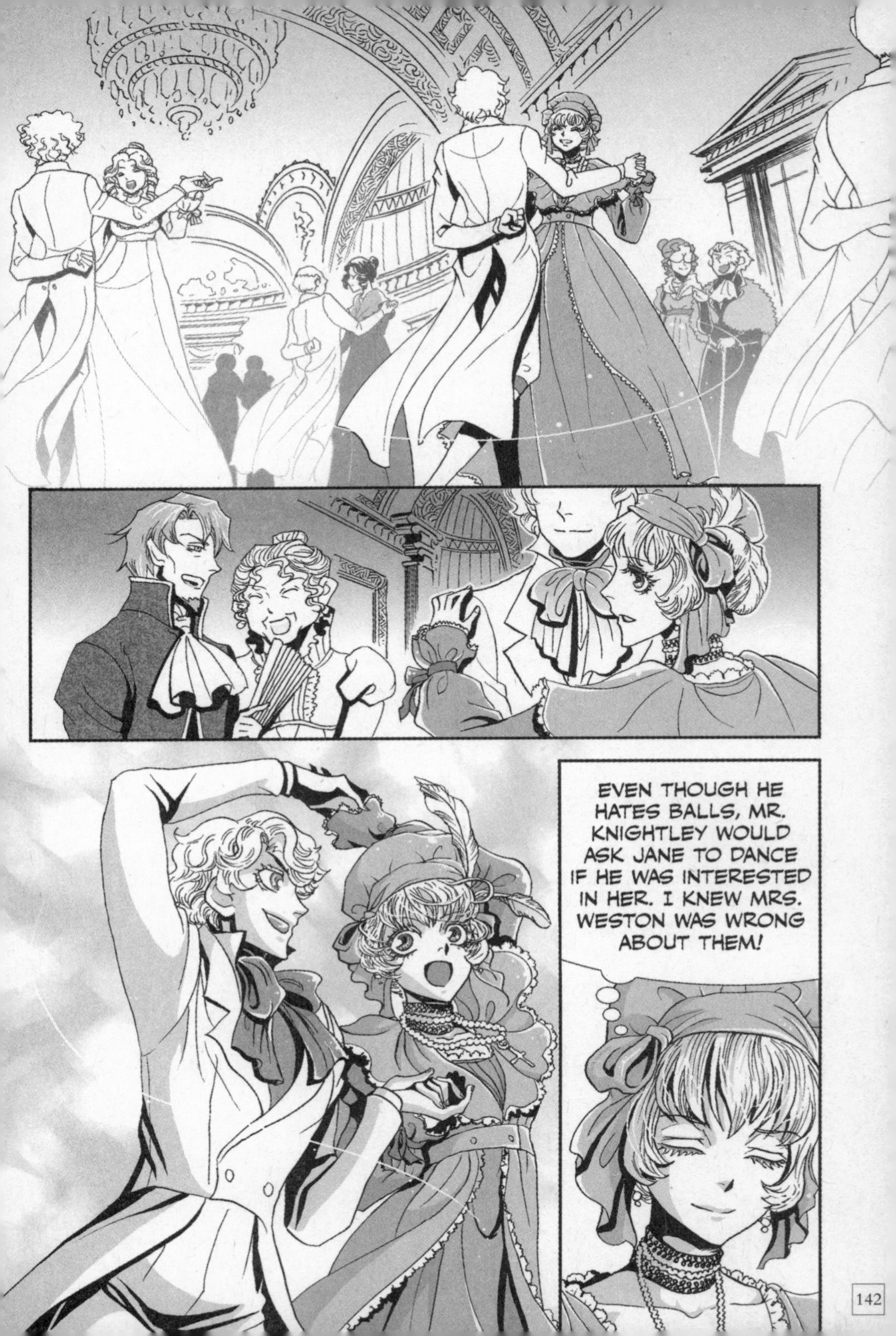
EVEN THOUGH HE HATES BALLS, MR. KNIGHTLEY WOULD ASK JANE TO DANCE IF HE WAS INTERESTED IN HER. I KNEW MRS. WESTON WAS WRONG ABOUT THEM!

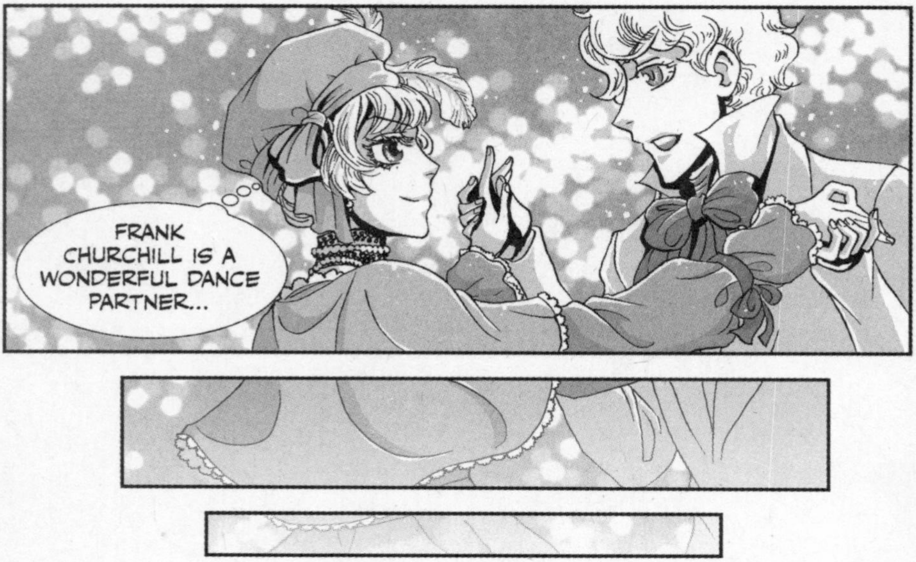
FRANK CHURCHILL IS A WONDERFUL DANCE PARTNER...

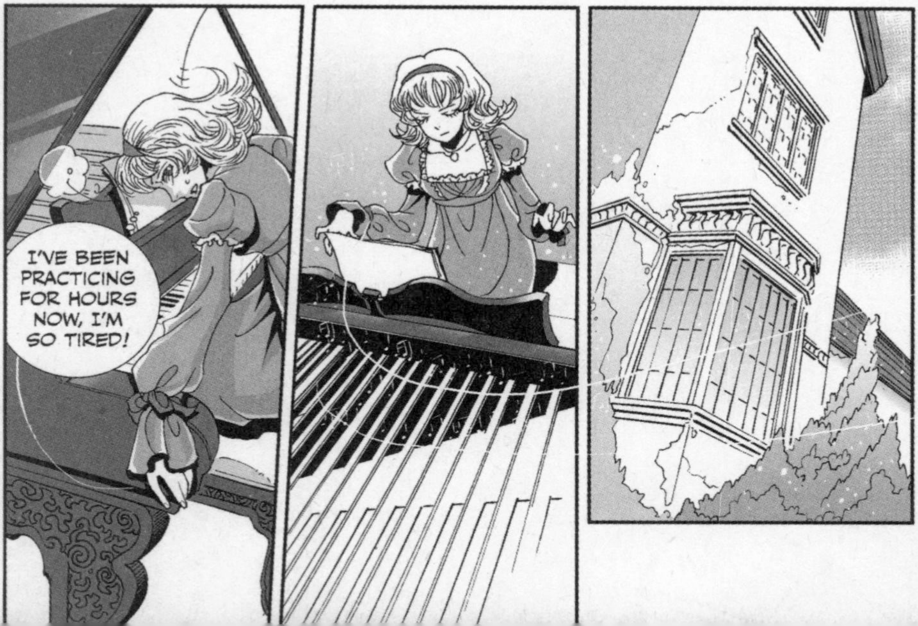
I'VE BEEN PRACTICING FOR HOURS NOW, I'M SO TIRED!

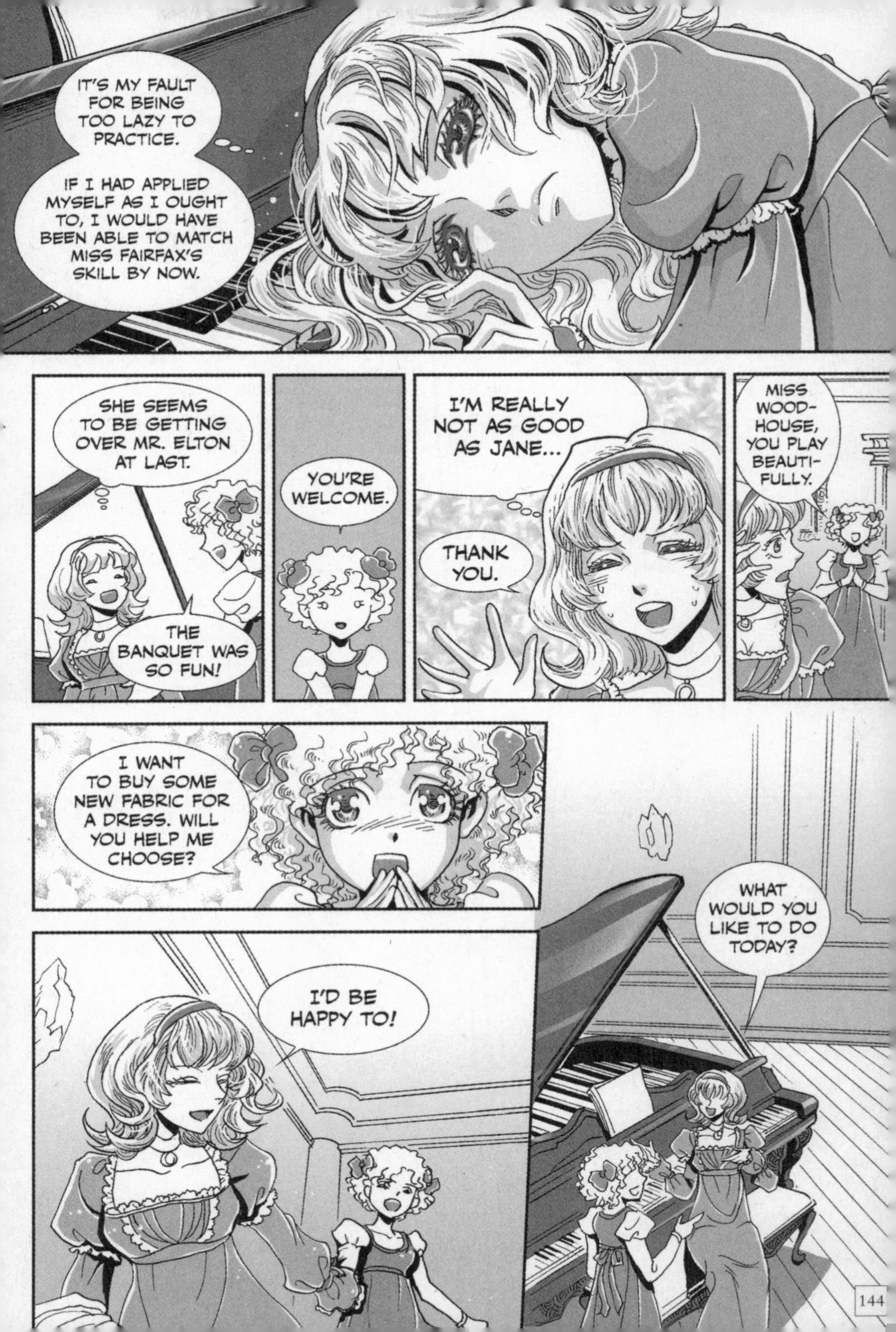
IT'S MY FAULT FOR BEING TOO LAZY TO PRACTICE.
IF I HAD APPLIED MYSELF AS I OUGHT TO, I WOULD HAVE BEEN ABLE TO MATCH MISS FAIRFAX'S SKILL BY NOW.
MISS WOOD-HOUSE, YOU PLAY BEAUTI-FULLY.
I'M REALLY NOT AS GOOD AS JANE...
THANK YOU.
YOU'RE WELCOME.
SHE SEEMS TO BE GETTING OVER MR. ELTON AT LAST.
THE BANQUET WAS SO FUN!
WHAT WOULD YOU LIKE TO DO TODAY?
I WANT TO BUY SOME NEW FABRIC FOR A DRESS. WILL YOU HELP ME CHOOSE?
I'D BE HAPPY TO!

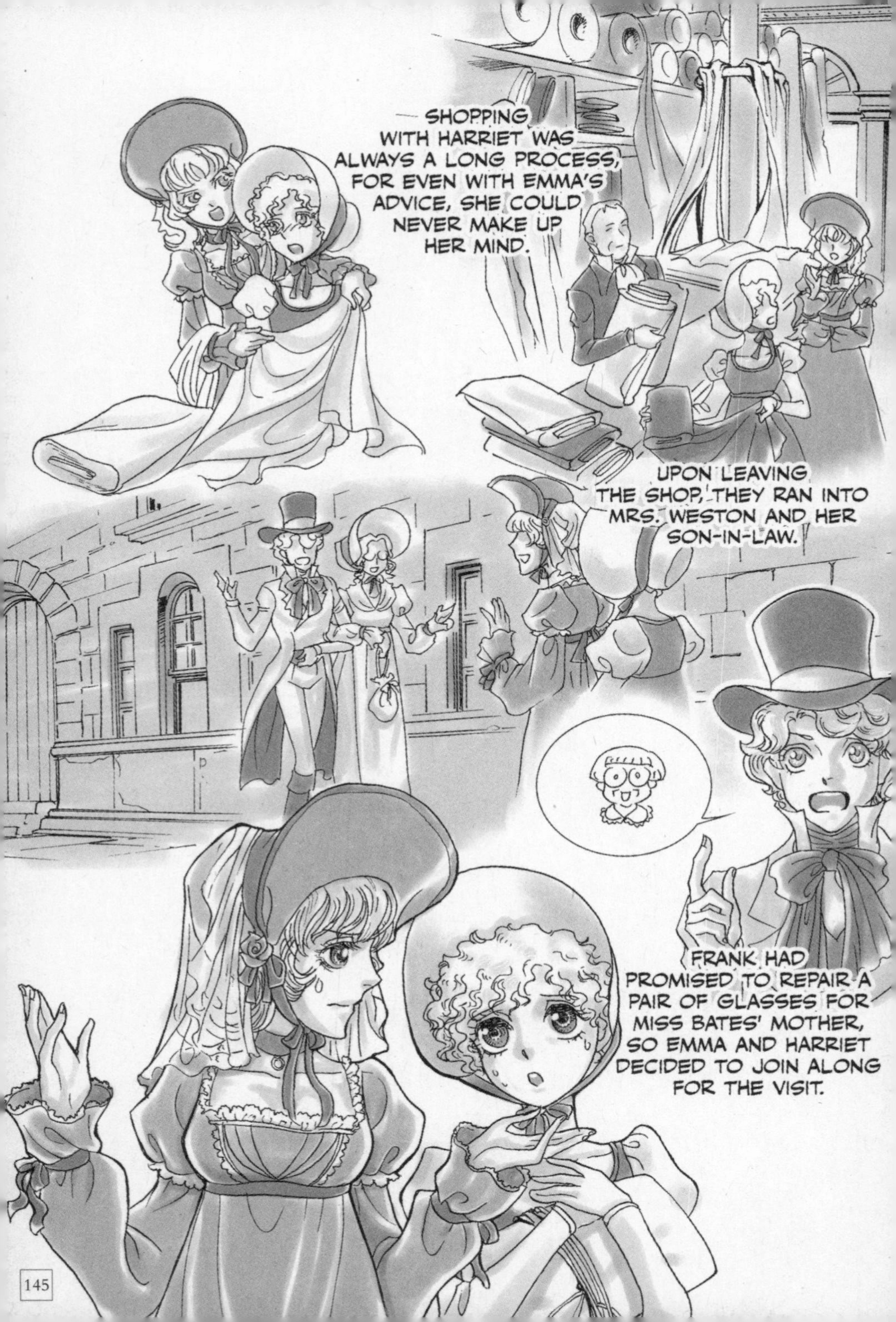
SHOPPING WITH HARRIET WAS ALWAYS A LONG PROCESS, FOR EVEN WITH EMMA'S ADVICE, SHE COULD NEVER MAKE UP HER MIND.
UPON LEAVING THE SHOP, THEY RAN INTO MRS. WESTON AND HER SON-IN-LAW.
FRANK HAD PROMISED TO REPAIR A PAIR OF GLASSES FOR MISS BATES' MOTHER, SO EMMA AND HARRIET DECIDED TO JOIN ALONG FOR THE VISIT.

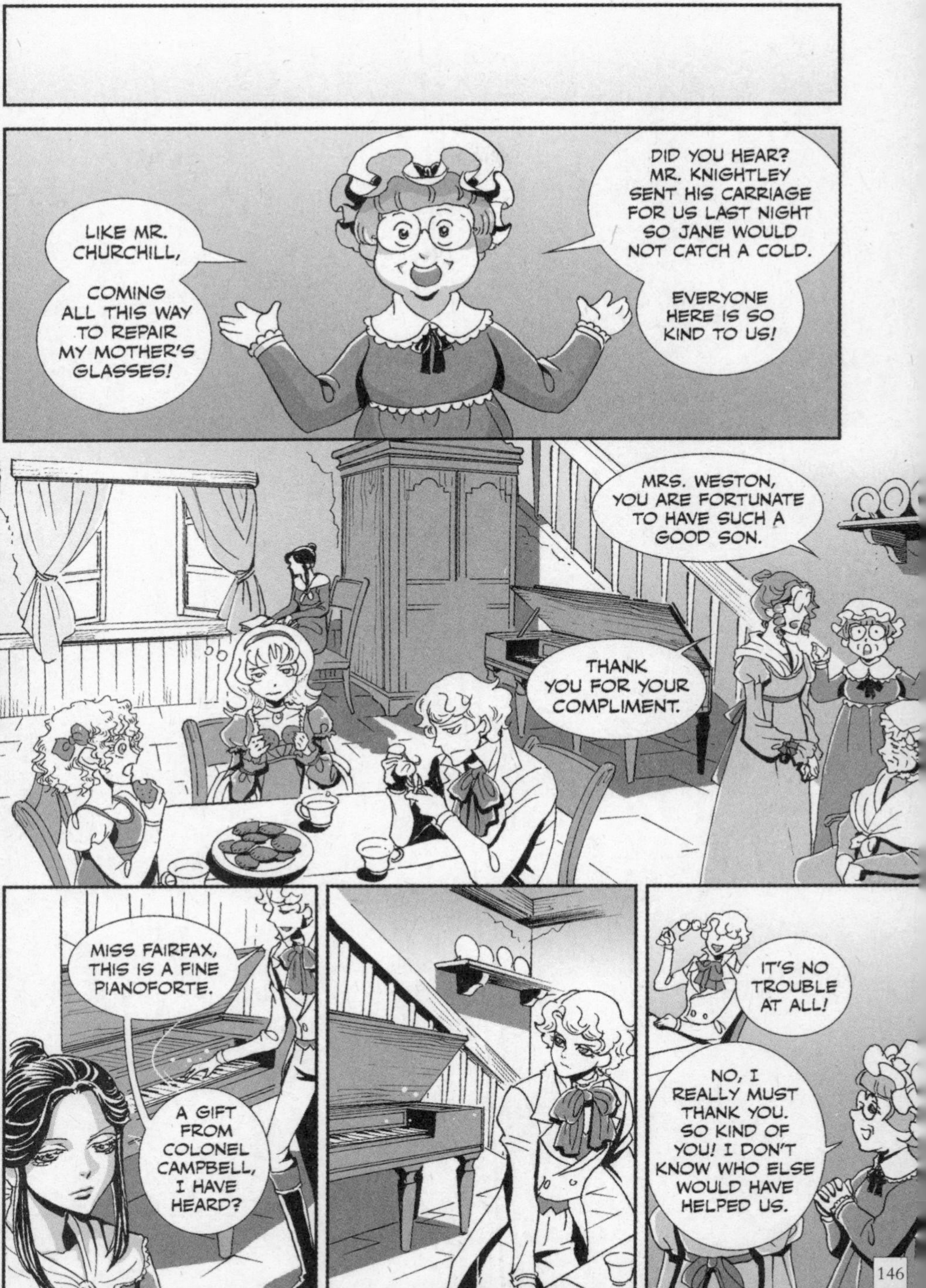

DID YOU HEAR? MR. KNIGHTLEY SENT HIS CARRIAGE FOR US LAST NIGHT SO JANE WOULD NOT CATCH A COLD.
EVERYONE HERE IS SO KIND TO US!
LIKE MR. CHURCHILL,
COMING ALL THIS WAY TO REPAIR MY MOTHER'S GLASSES!
MRS. WESTON, YOU ARE FORTUNATE TO HAVE SUCH A GOOD SON.
THANK YOU FOR YOUR COMPLIMENT.
IT'S NO TROUBLE AT ALL!
NO, I REALLY MUST THANK YOU. SO KIND OF YOU! I DON'T KNOW WHO ELSE WOULD HAVE HELPED US.
MISS FAIRFAX, THIS IS A FINE PIANOFORTE.
A GIFT FROM COLONEL CAMPBELL, I HAVE HEARD?

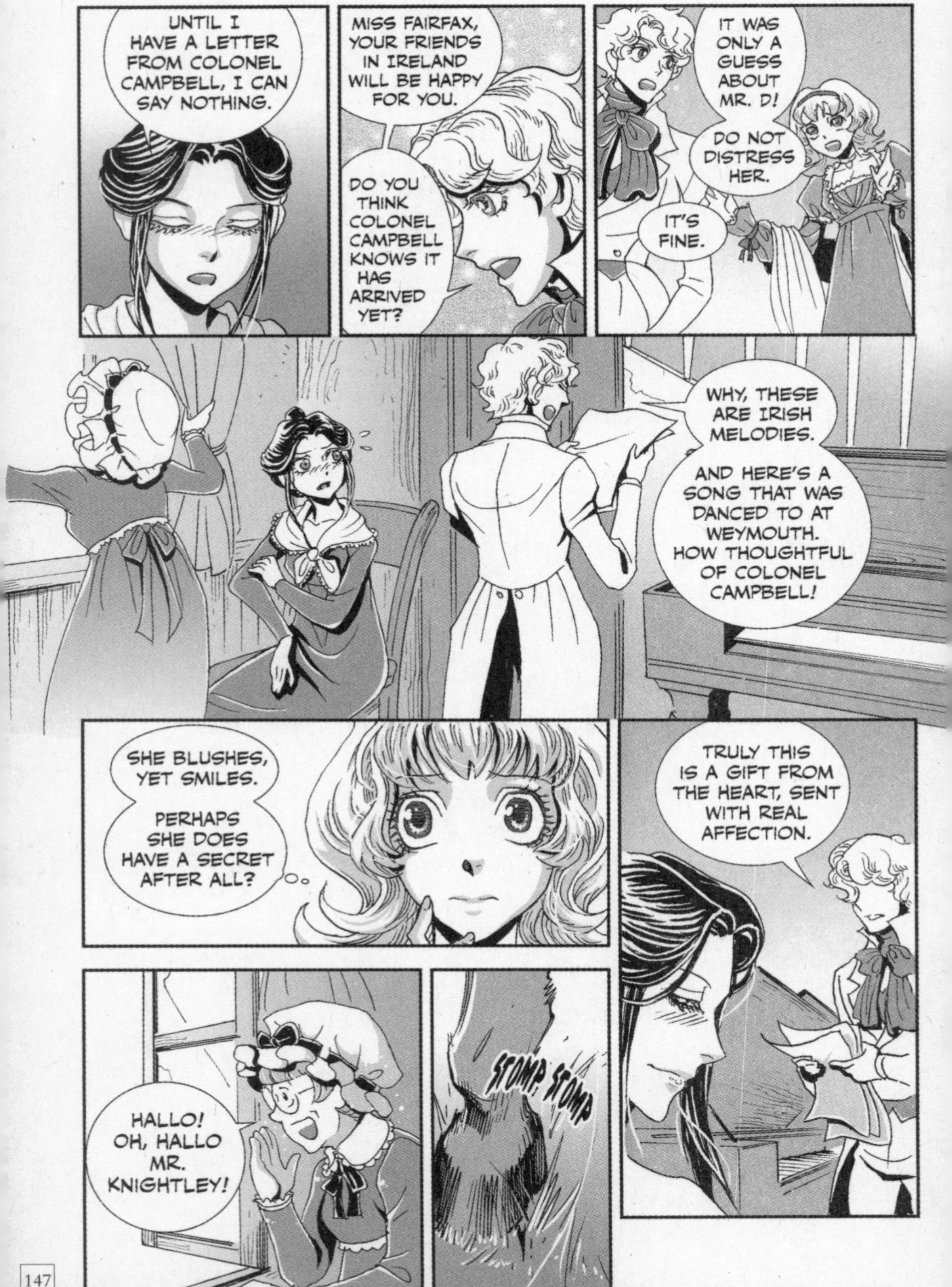
IT WAS ONLY A GUESS ABOUT MR. D!
DO NOT DISTRESS HER.
IT'S FINE.
MISS FAIRFAX, YOUR FRIENDS IN IRELAND WILL BE HAPPY FOR YOU.
DO YOU THINK COLONEL CAMPBELL KNOWS IT HAS ARRIVED YET?
UNTIL I HAVE A LETTER FROM COLONEL CAMPBELL, I CAN SAY NOTHING.
WHY, THESE ARE IRISH MELODIES.
AND HERE'S A SONG THAT WAS DANCED TO AT WEYMOUTH. HOW THOUGHTFUL OF COLONEL CAMPBELL!
TRULY THIS IS A GIFT FROM THE HEART, SENT WITH REAL AFFECTION.
SHE BLUSHES, YET SMILES.
PERHAPS SHE DOES HAVE A SECRET AFTER ALL?
STOMP STOMP
HALLO! OH, HALLO MR. KNIGHTLEY!

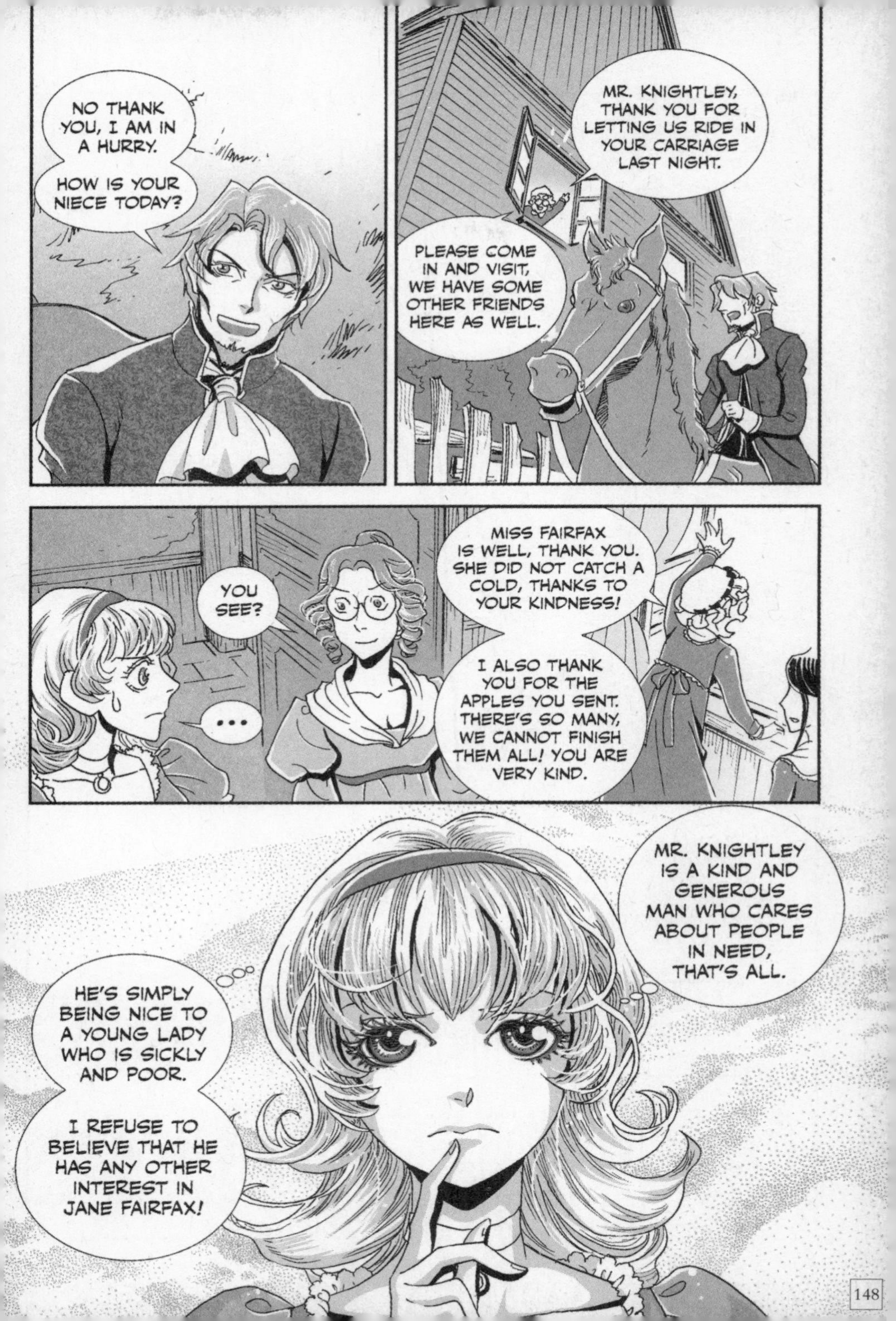
MR. KNIGHTLEY, THANK YOU FOR LETTING US RIDE IN YOUR CARRIAGE LAST NIGHT.
PLEASE COME IN AND VISIT, WE HAVE SOME OTHER FRIENDS HERE AS WELL.
NO THANK YOU, I AM IN A HURRY.
HOW IS YOUR NIECE TODAY?
MISS FAIRFAX IS WELL, THANK YOU. SHE DID NOT CATCH A COLD, THANKS TO YOUR KINDNESS!
I ALSO THANK YOU FOR THE APPLES YOU SENT. THERE'S SO MANY, WE CANNOT FINISH THEM ALL! YOU ARE VERY KIND.
YOU SEE?
...
MR. KNIGHTLEY IS A KIND AND GENEROUS MAN WHO CARES ABOUT PEOPLE IN NEED, THAT'S ALL.
HE'S SIMPLY BEING NICE TO A YOUNG LADY WHO IS SICKLY AND POOR.
I REFUSE TO BELIEVE THAT HE HAS ANY OTHER INTEREST IN JANE FAIRFAX!

CHARACTER MODEL SHEET

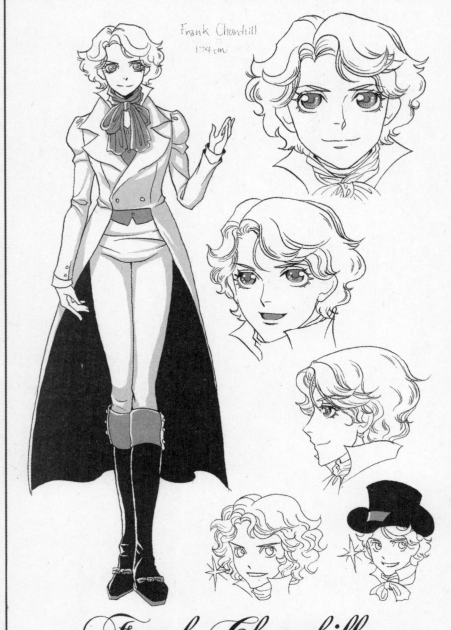

Frank Churchill
174 cm

Frank Churchill

CHARACTER MODEL SHEET

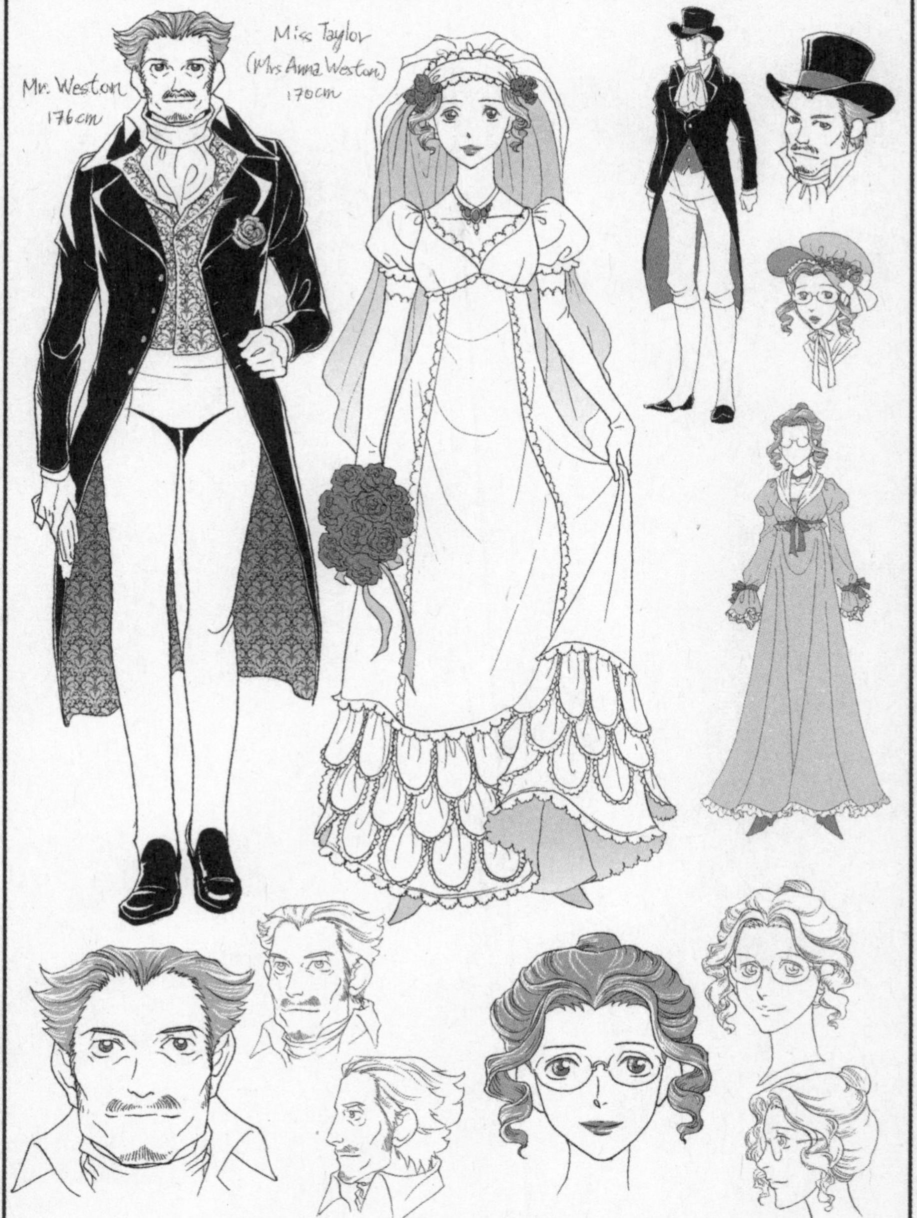
Mr. Weston
176cm
Miss Taylor
(Mrs Anna Weston)
170cm

Mr. & Mrs. Weston

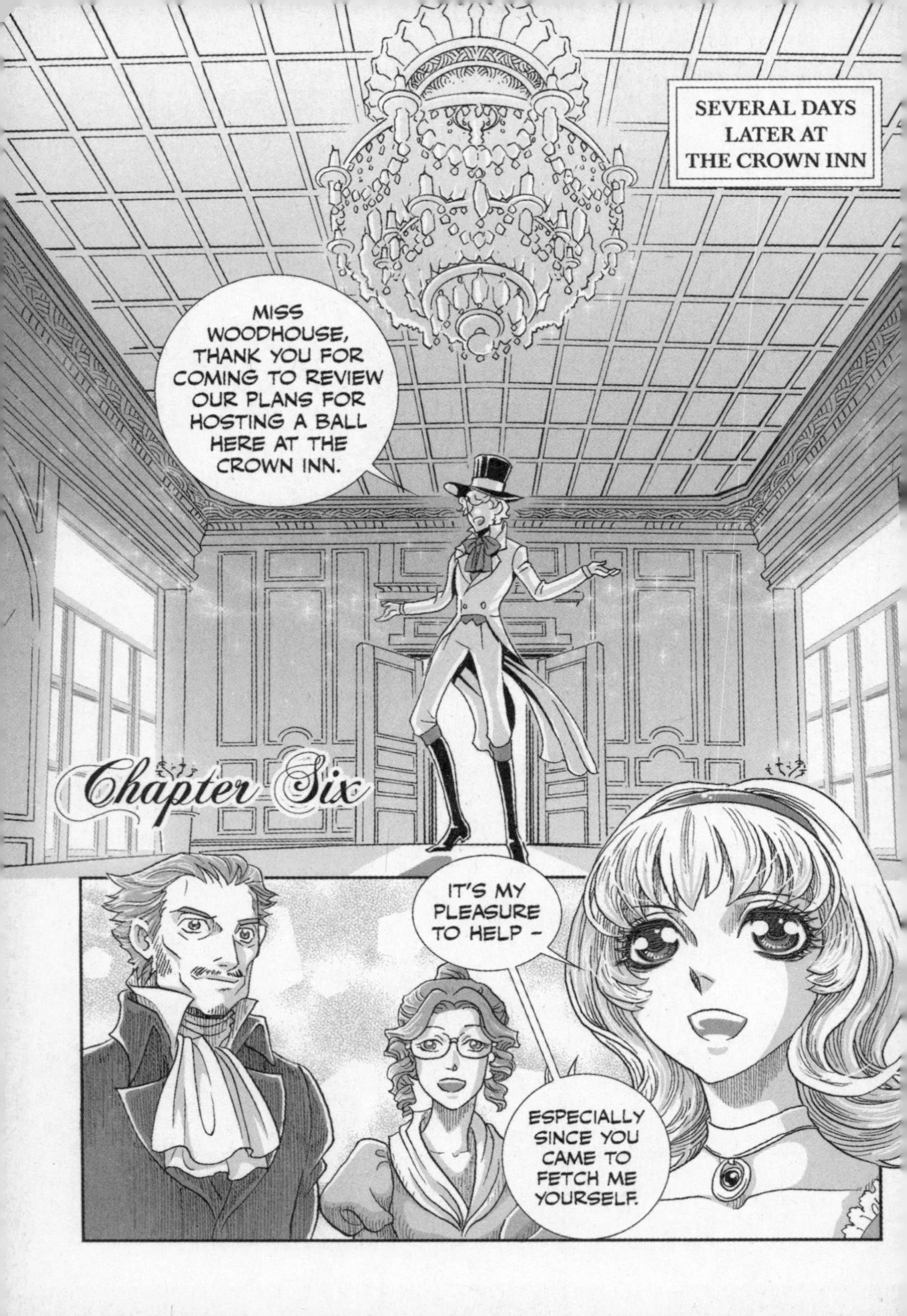
SEVERAL DAYS LATER AT THE CROWN INN
MISS WOODHOUSE, THANK YOU FOR COMING TO REVIEW OUR PLANS FOR HOSTING A BALL HERE AT THE CROWN INN.
Chapter Six
IT'S MY PLEASURE TO HELP -
ESPECIALLY SINCE YOU CAME TO FETCH ME YOURSELF.

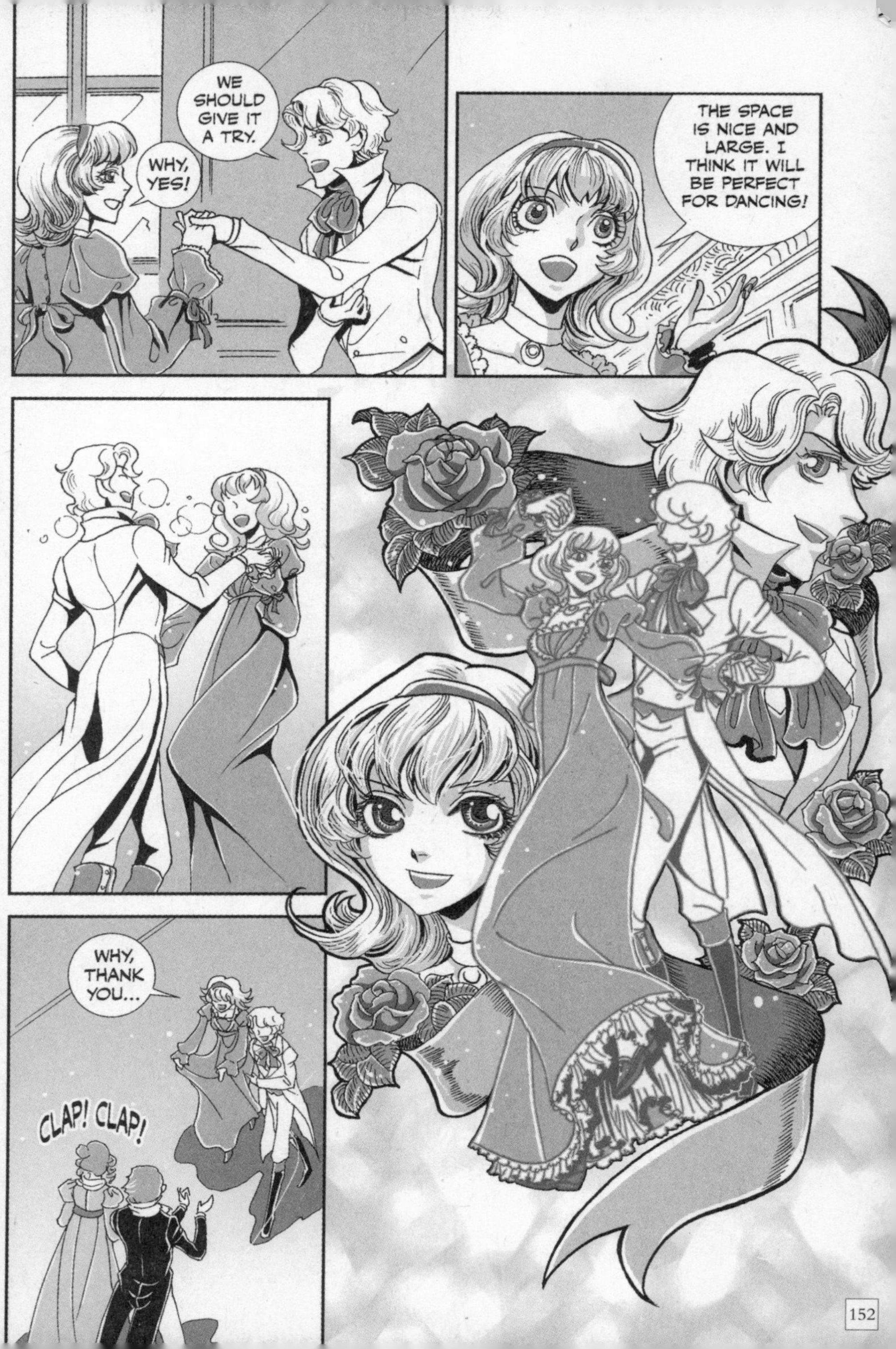
THE SPACE IS NICE AND LARGE. I THINK IT WILL BE PERFECT FOR DANCING!
WE SHOULD GIVE IT A TRY.
WHY, YES!
WHY, THANK YOU...
CLAP! CLAP!

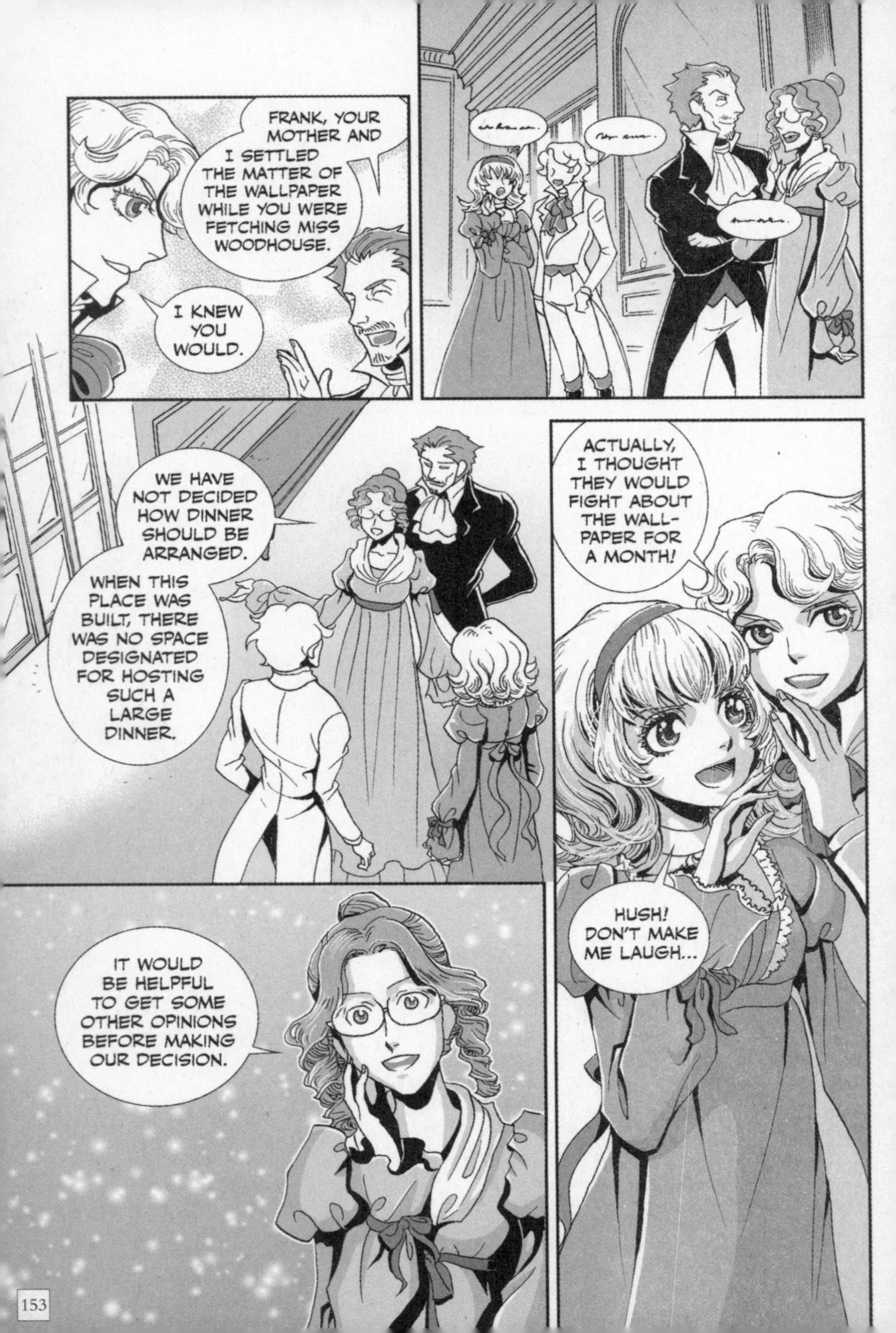
FRANK, YOUR MOTHER AND I SETTLED THE MATTER OF THE WALLPAPER WHILE YOU WERE FETCHING MISS WOODHOUSE.
I KNEW YOU WOULD.
ACTUALLY, I THOUGHT THEY WOULD FIGHT ABOUT THE WALL-PAPER FOR A MONTH!
HUSH! DON'T MAKE ME LAUGH...
WE HAVE NOT DECIDED HOW DINNER SHOULD BE ARRANGED.
WHEN THIS PLACE WAS BUILT, THERE WAS NO SPACE DESIGNATED FOR HOSTING SUCH A LARGE DINNER.
IT WOULD BE HELPFUL TO GET SOME OTHER OPINIONS BEFORE MAKING OUR DECISION.

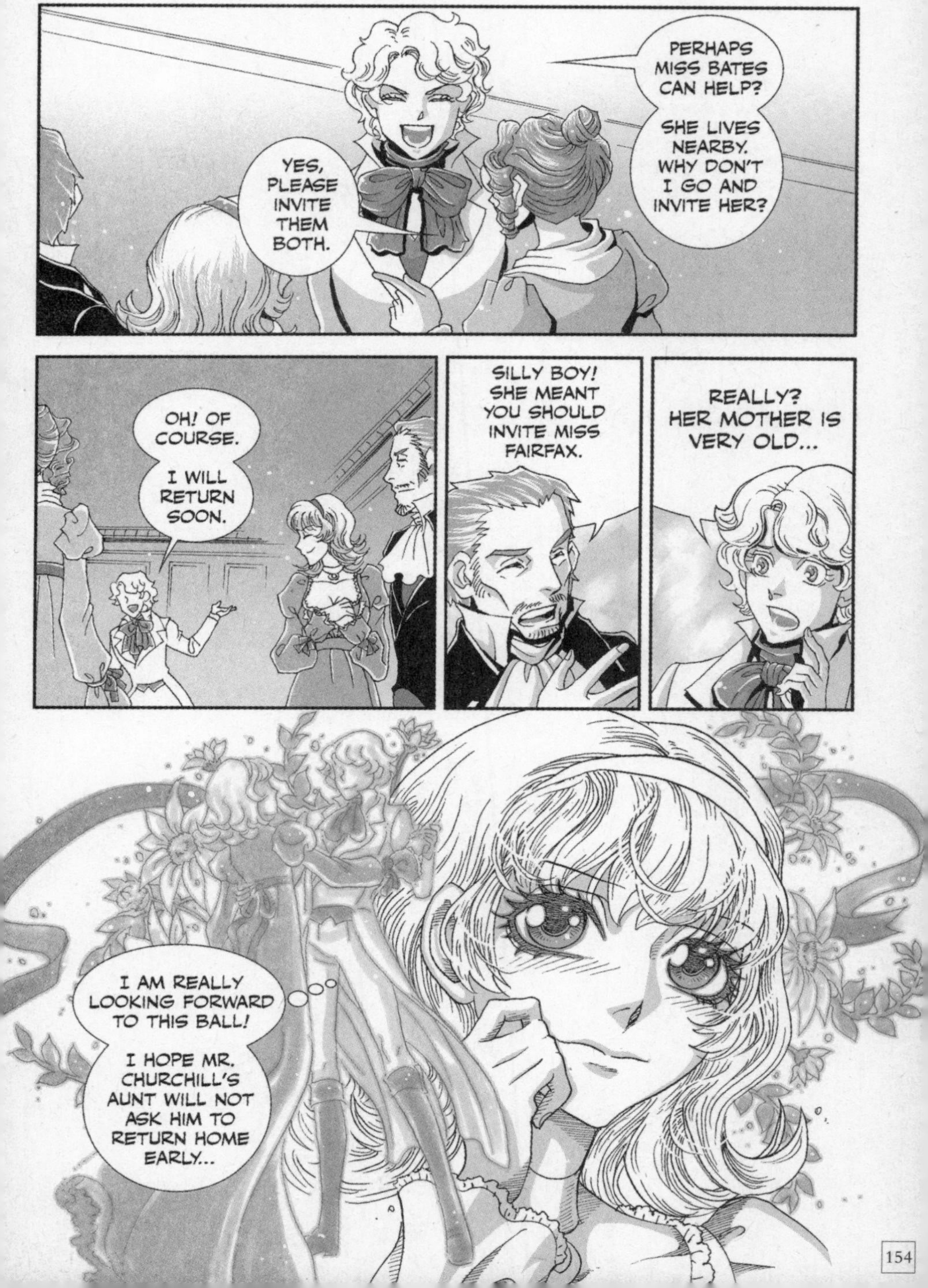
PERHAPS MISS BATES CAN HELP?
SHE LIVES NEARBY. WHY DON'T I GO AND INVITE HER?
YES, PLEASE INVITE THEM BOTH.
REALLY? HER MOTHER IS VERY OLD...
SILLY BOY! SHE MEANT YOU SHOULD INVITE MISS FAIRFAX.
OH! OF COURSE.
I WILL RETURN SOON.
I AM REALLY LOOKING FORWARD TO THIS BALL!
I HOPE MR. CHURCHILL'S AUNT WILL NOT ASK HIM TO RETURN HOME EARLY...

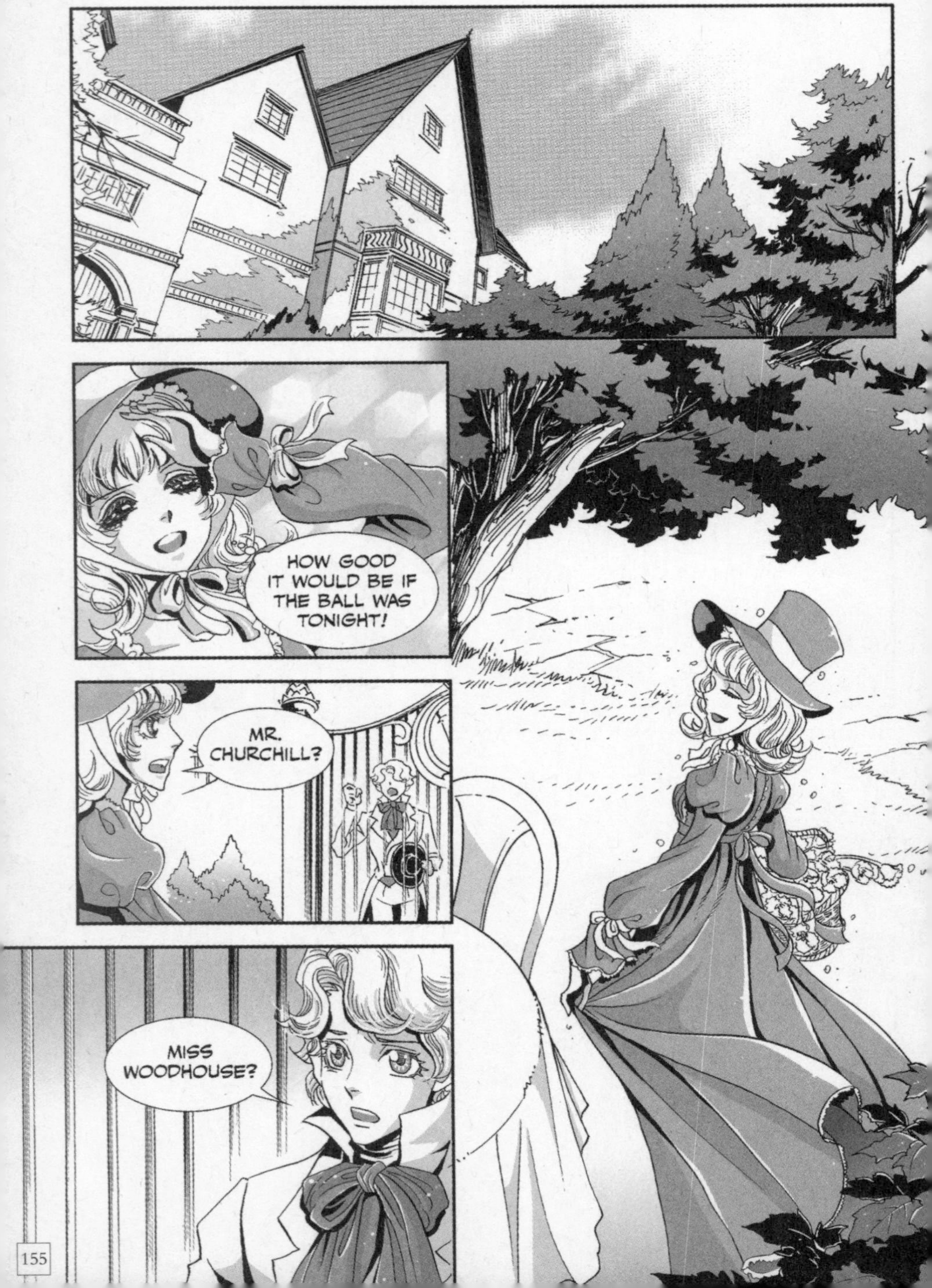
HOW GOOD IT WOULD BE IF THE BALL WAS TONIGHT!
MR. CHURCHILL?
MISS WOODHOUSE?

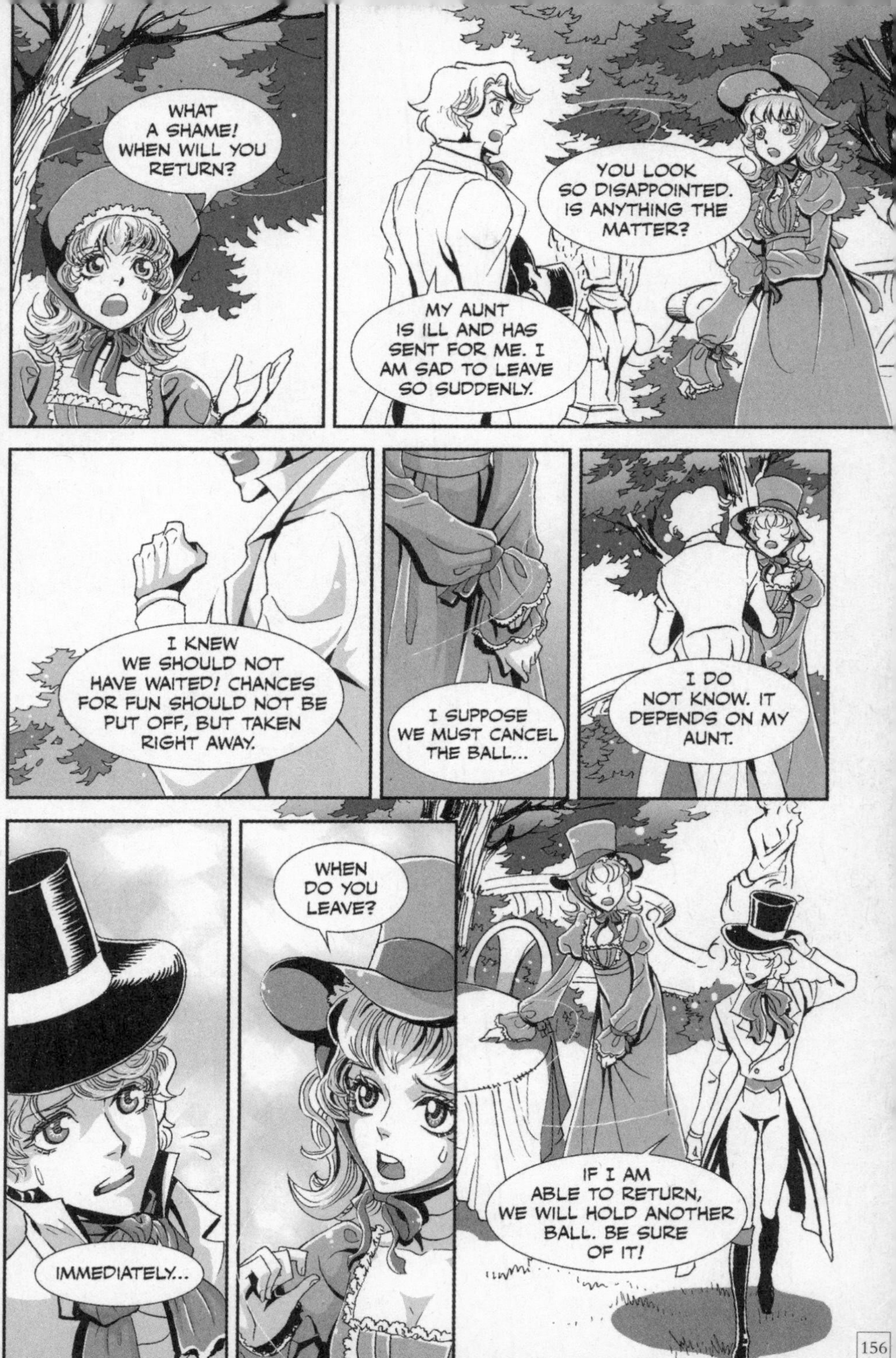
YOU LOOK SO DISAPPOINTED. IS ANYTHING THE MATTER?
MY AUNT IS ILL AND HAS SENT FOR ME. I AM SAD TO LEAVE SO SUDDENLY.
WHAT A SHAME! WHEN WILL YOU RETURN?
I DO NOT KNOW. IT DEPENDS ON MY AUNT.
I SUPPOSE WE MUST CANCEL THE BALL...
I KNEW WE SHOULD NOT HAVE WAITED! CHANCES FOR FUN SHOULD NOT BE PUT OFF, BUT TAKEN RIGHT AWAY.
IF I AM ABLE TO RETURN, WE WILL HOLD ANOTHER BALL. BE SURE OF IT!
WHEN DO YOU LEAVE?
IMMEDIATELY...

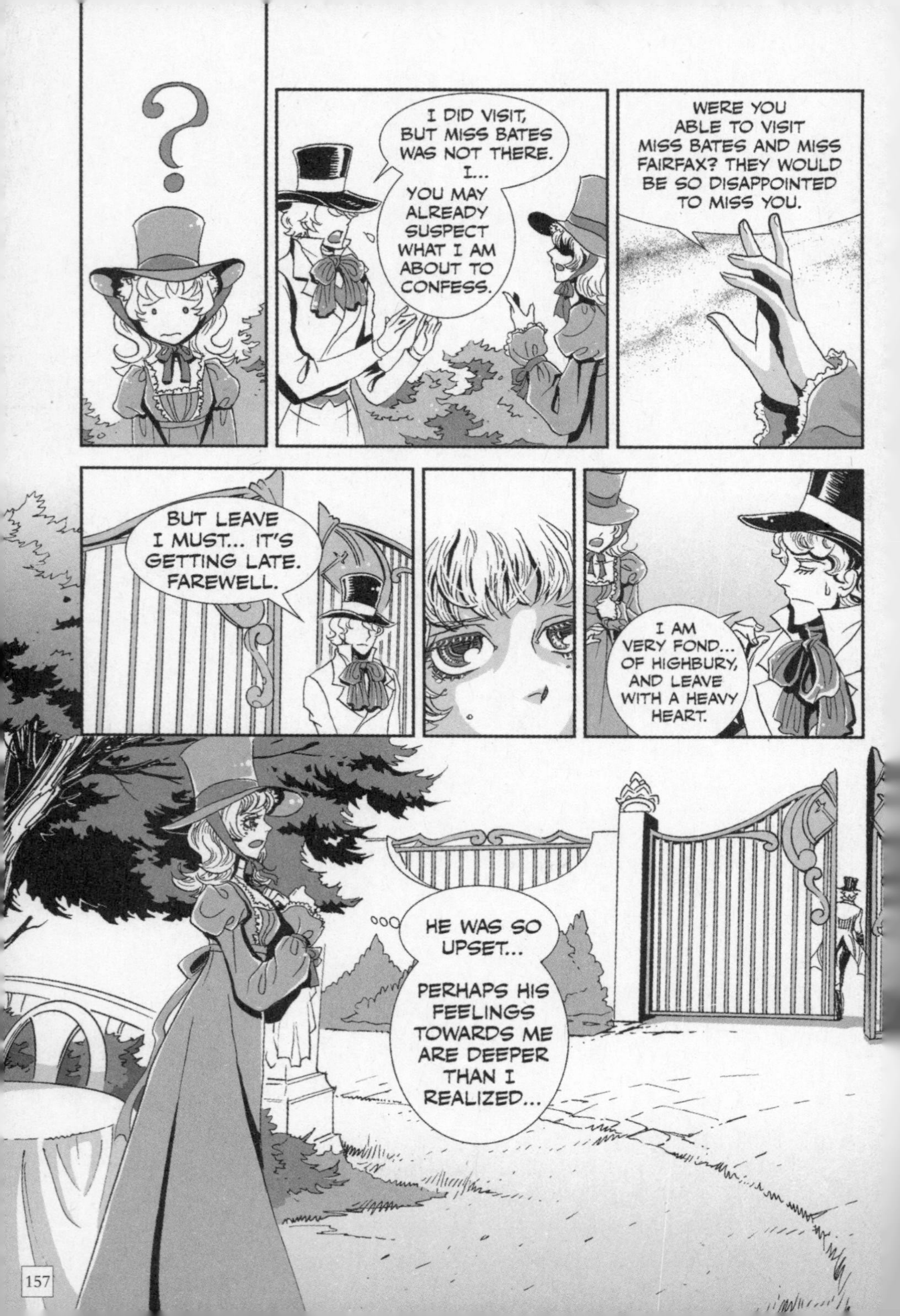
WERE YOU ABLE TO VISIT MISS BATES AND MISS FAIRFAX? THEY WOULD BE SO DISAPPOINTED TO MISS YOU.
I DID VISIT, BUT MISS BATES WAS NOT THERE. I... YOU MAY ALREADY SUSPECT WHAT I AM ABOUT TO CONFESS.
I AM VERY FOND... OF HIGHBURY, AND LEAVE WITH A HEAVY HEART.
BUT LEAVE I MUST... IT'S GETTING LATE. FAREWELL.
HE WAS SO UPSET...
PERHAPS HIS FEELINGS TOWARDS ME ARE DEEPER THAN I REALIZED...

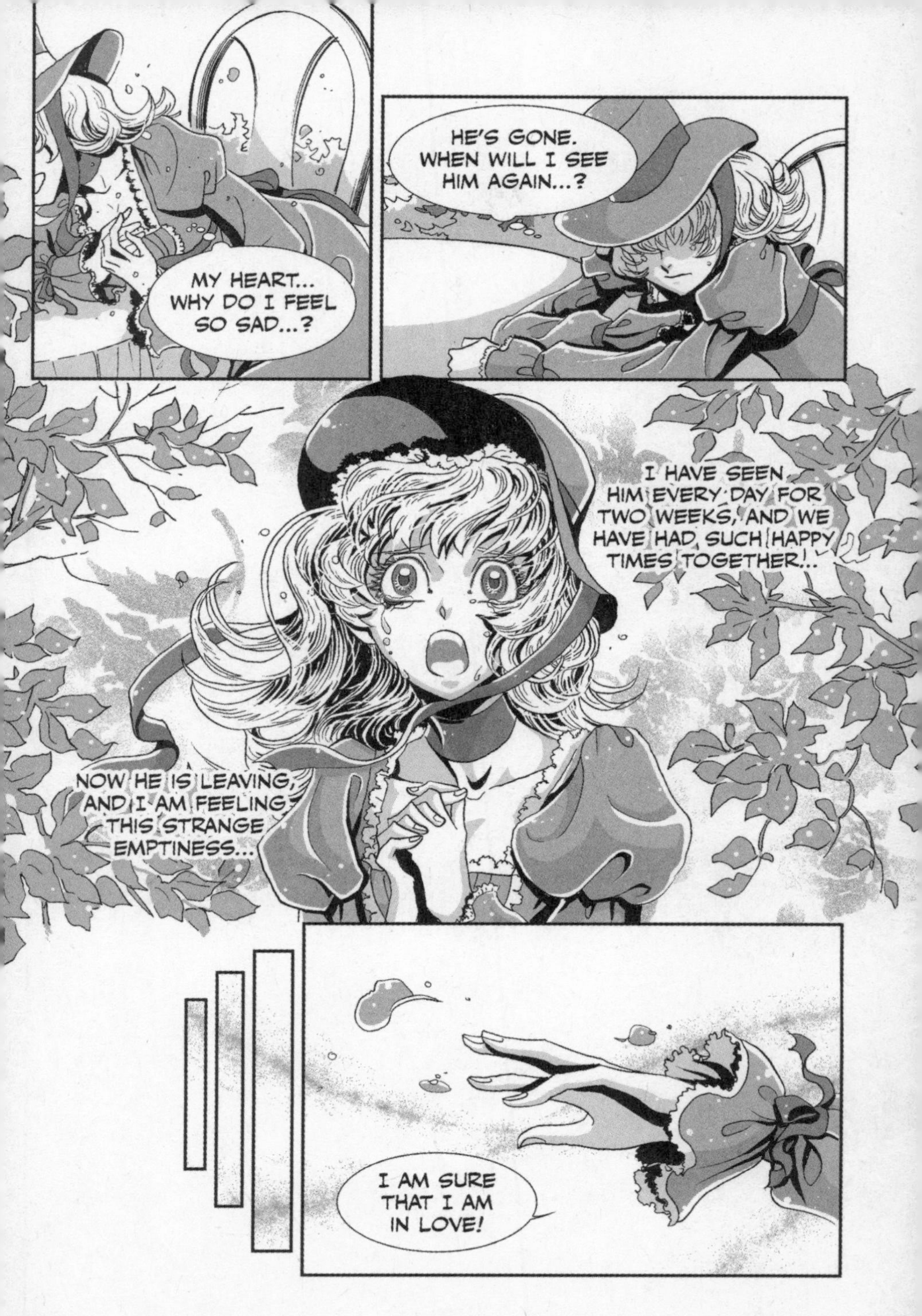
HE'S GONE. WHEN WILL I SEE HIM AGAIN...?
MY HEART... WHY DO I FEEL SO SAD...?
I HAVE SEEN HIM EVERY DAY FOR TWO WEEKS, AND WE HAVE HAD SUCH HAPPY TIMES TOGETHER!..
NOW HE IS LEAVING, AND I AM FEELING THIS STRANGE EMPTINESS...
I AM SURE THAT I AM IN LOVE!

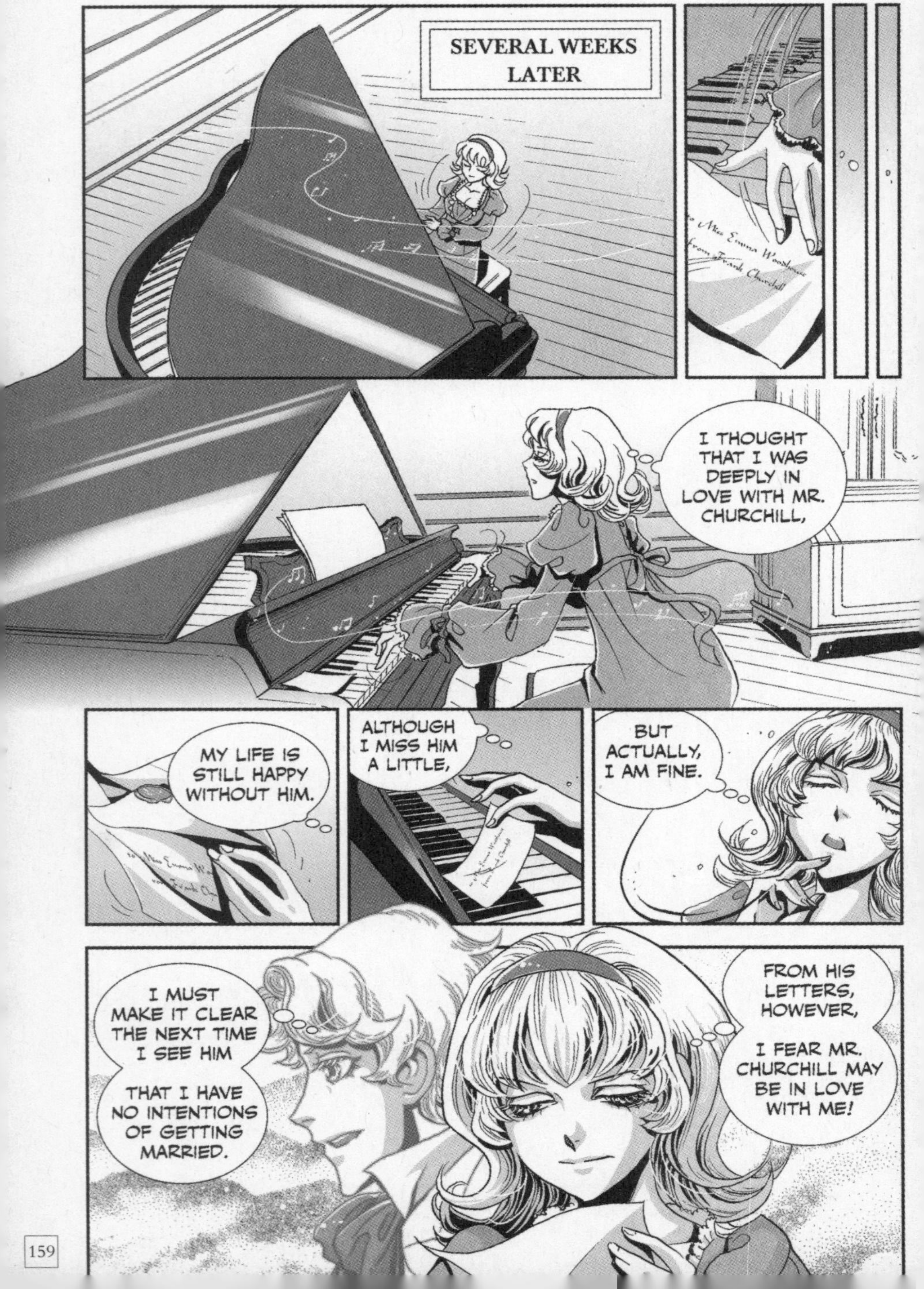
to Miss Emma Woodhouse
from Frank Churchill
SEVERAL WEEKS LATER
I THOUGHT THAT I WAS DEEPLY IN LOVE WITH MR. CHURCHILL,
BUT ACTUALLY, I AM FINE.
ALTHOUGH I MISS HIM A LITTLE,
MY LIFE IS STILL HAPPY WITHOUT HIM.
FROM HIS LETTERS, HOWEVER,
I FEAR MR. CHURCHILL MAY BE IN LOVE WITH ME!
I MUST MAKE IT CLEAR THE NEXT TIME I SEE HIM
THAT I HAVE NO INTENTIONS OF GETTING MARRIED.

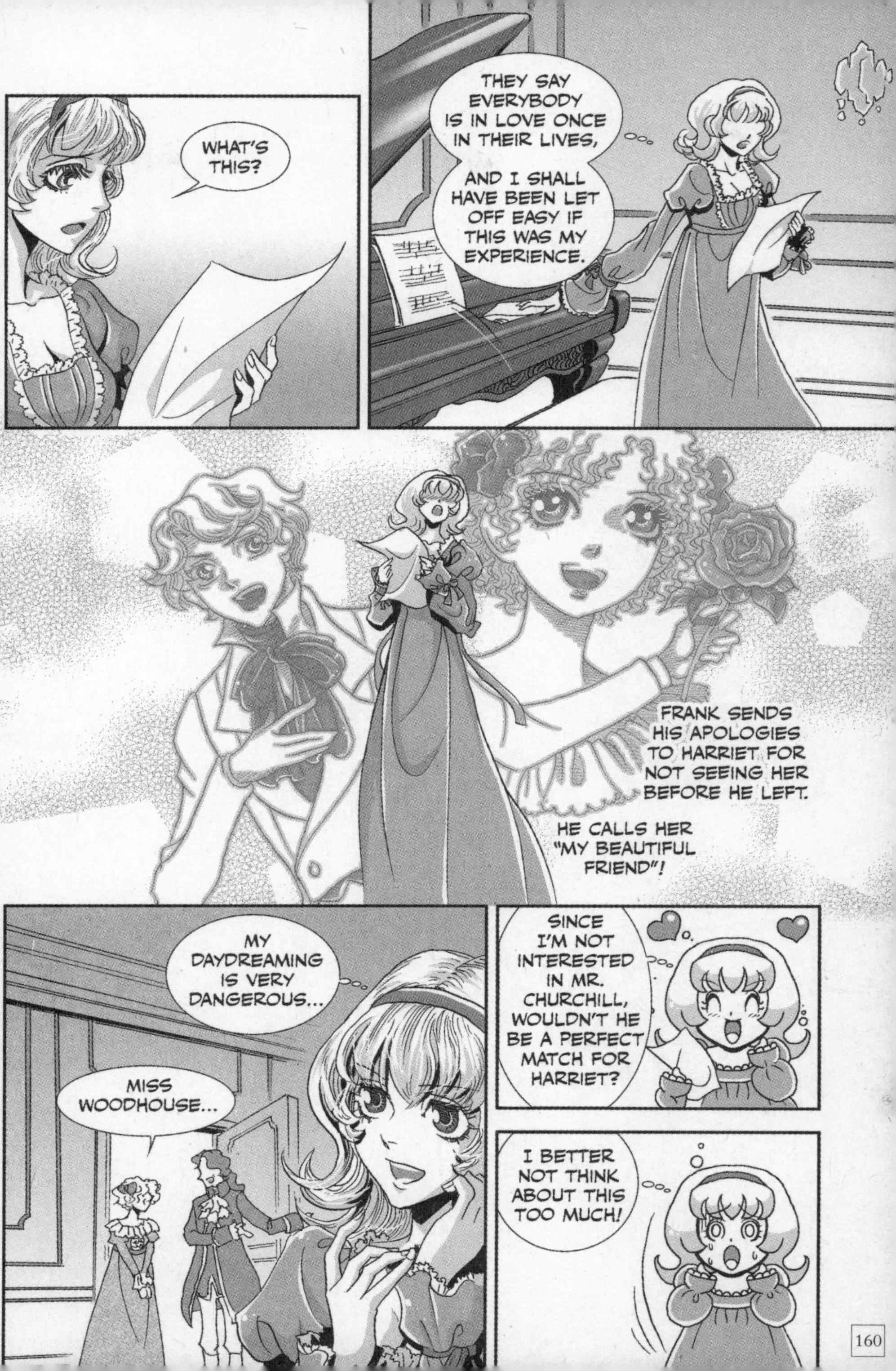
THEY SAY EVERYBODY IS IN LOVE ONCE IN THEIR LIVES,
AND I SHALL HAVE BEEN LET OFF EASY IF THIS WAS MY EXPERIENCE.
WHAT'S THIS?
FRANK SENDS HIS APOLOGIES TO HARRIET FOR NOT SEEING HER BEFORE HE LEFT.
HE CALLS HER "MY BEAUTIFUL FRIEND"!
SINCE I'M NOT INTERESTED IN MR. CHURCHILL, WOULDN'T HE BE A PERFECT MATCH FOR HARRIET?
I BETTER NOT THINK ABOUT THIS TOO MUCH!
MY DAYDREAMING IS VERY DANGEROUS...
MISS WOODHOUSE...

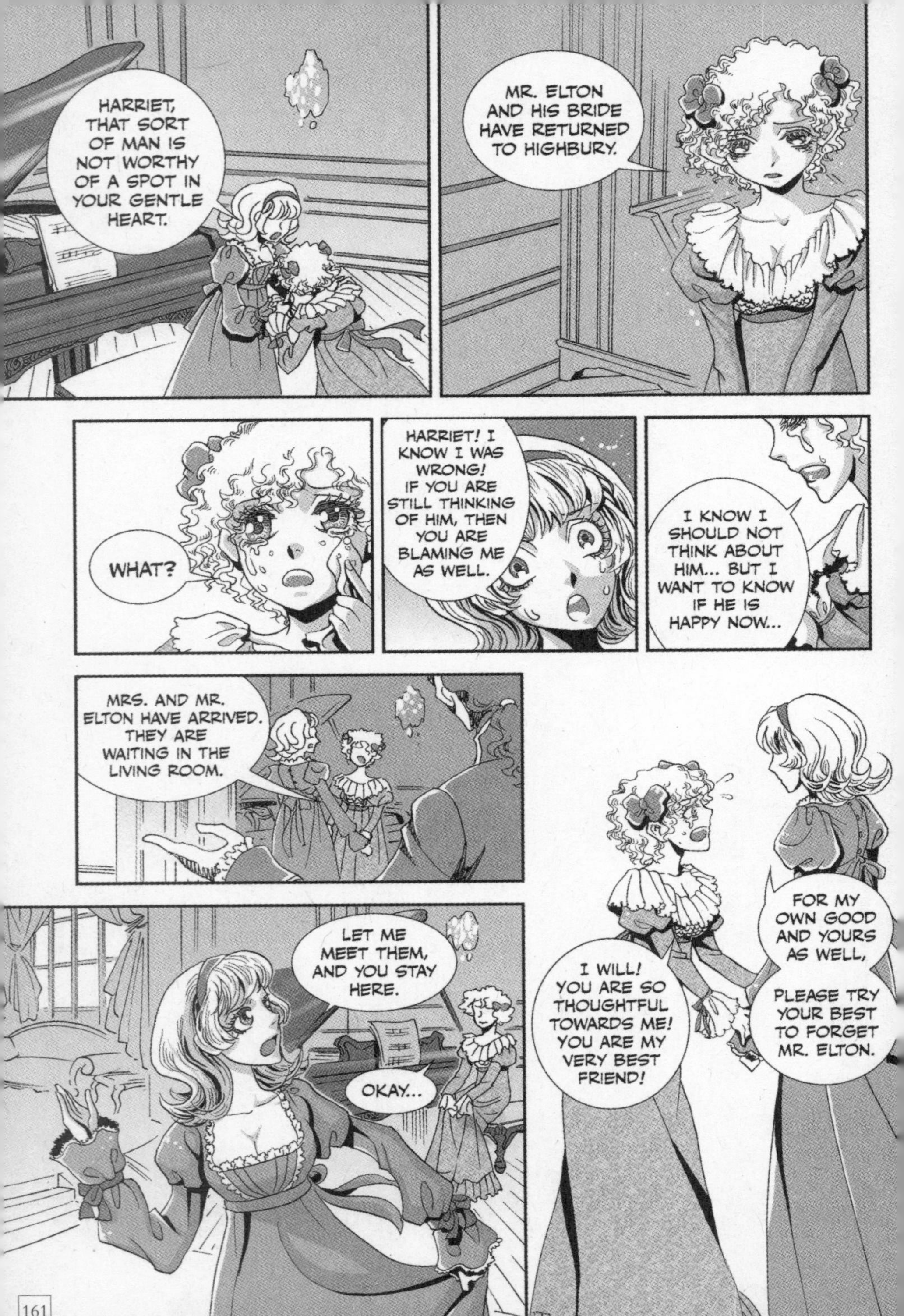
MR. ELTON AND HIS BRIDE HAVE RETURNED TO HIGHBURY.
HARRIET, THAT SORT OF MAN IS NOT WORTHY OF A SPOT IN YOUR GENTLE HEART.
I KNOW I SHOULD NOT THINK ABOUT HIM... BUT I WANT TO KNOW IF HE IS HAPPY NOW...
HARRIET! I KNOW I WAS WRONG! IF YOU ARE STILL THINKING OF HIM, THEN YOU ARE BLAMING ME AS WELL.
WHAT?
FOR MY OWN GOOD AND YOURS AS WELL,
PLEASE TRY YOUR BEST TO FORGET MR. ELTON.
I WILL! YOU ARE SO THOUGHTFUL TOWARDS ME! YOU ARE MY VERY BEST FRIEND!
MRS. AND MR. ELTON HAVE ARRIVED. THEY ARE WAITING IN THE LIVING ROOM.
LET ME MEET THEM, AND YOU STAY HERE.
OKAY...

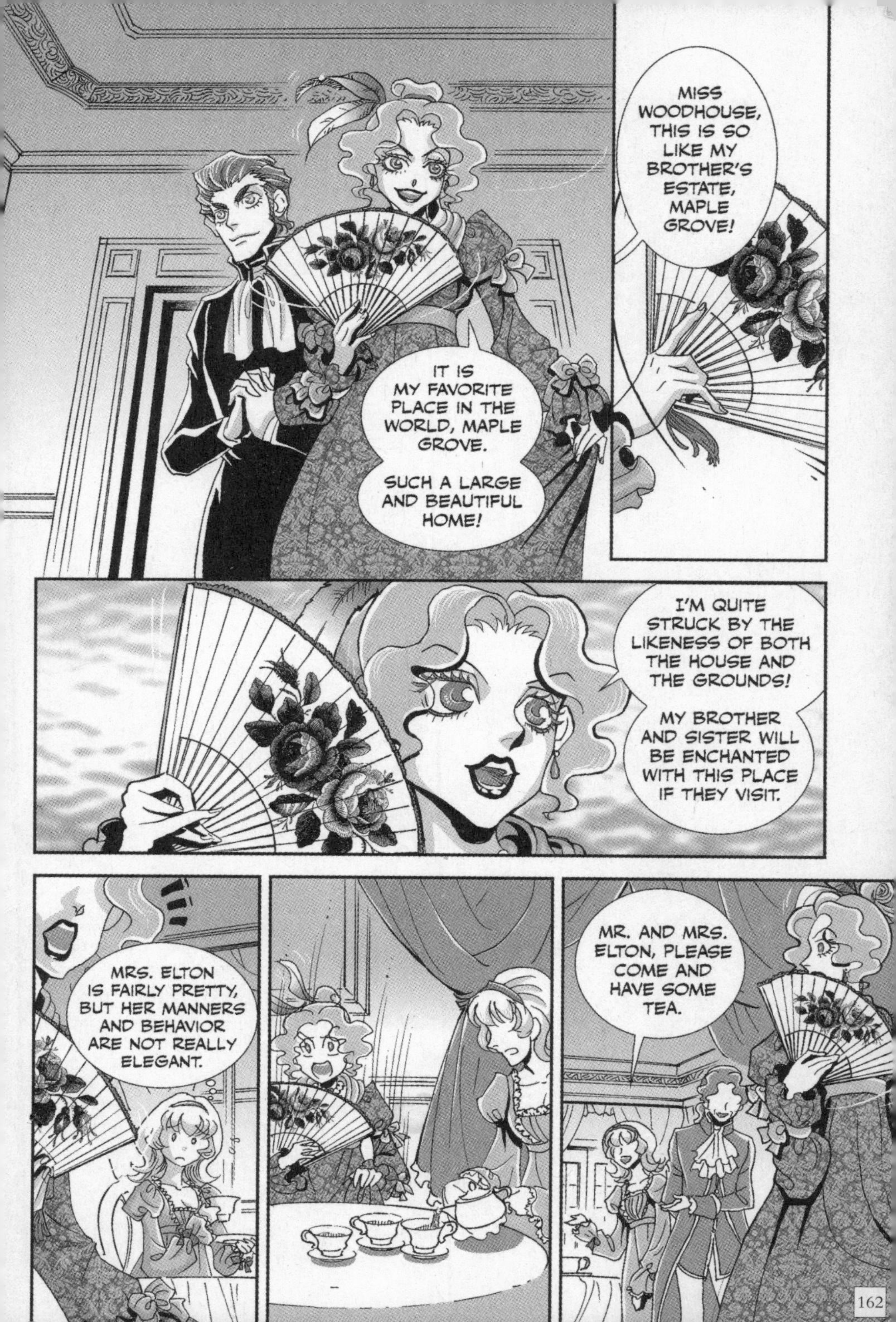
MISS WOODHOUSE, THIS IS SO LIKE MY BROTHER'S ESTATE, MAPLE GROVE!
IT IS MY FAVORITE PLACE IN THE WORLD, MAPLE GROVE.
SUCH A LARGE AND BEAUTIFUL HOME!
I'M QUITE STRUCK BY THE LIKENESS OF BOTH THE HOUSE AND THE GROUNDS!
MY BROTHER AND SISTER WILL BE ENCHANTED WITH THIS PLACE IF THEY VISIT.
MR. AND MRS. ELTON, PLEASE COME AND HAVE SOME TEA.
MRS. ELTON IS FAIRLY PRETTY, BUT HER MANNERS AND BEHAVIOR ARE NOT REALLY ELEGANT.

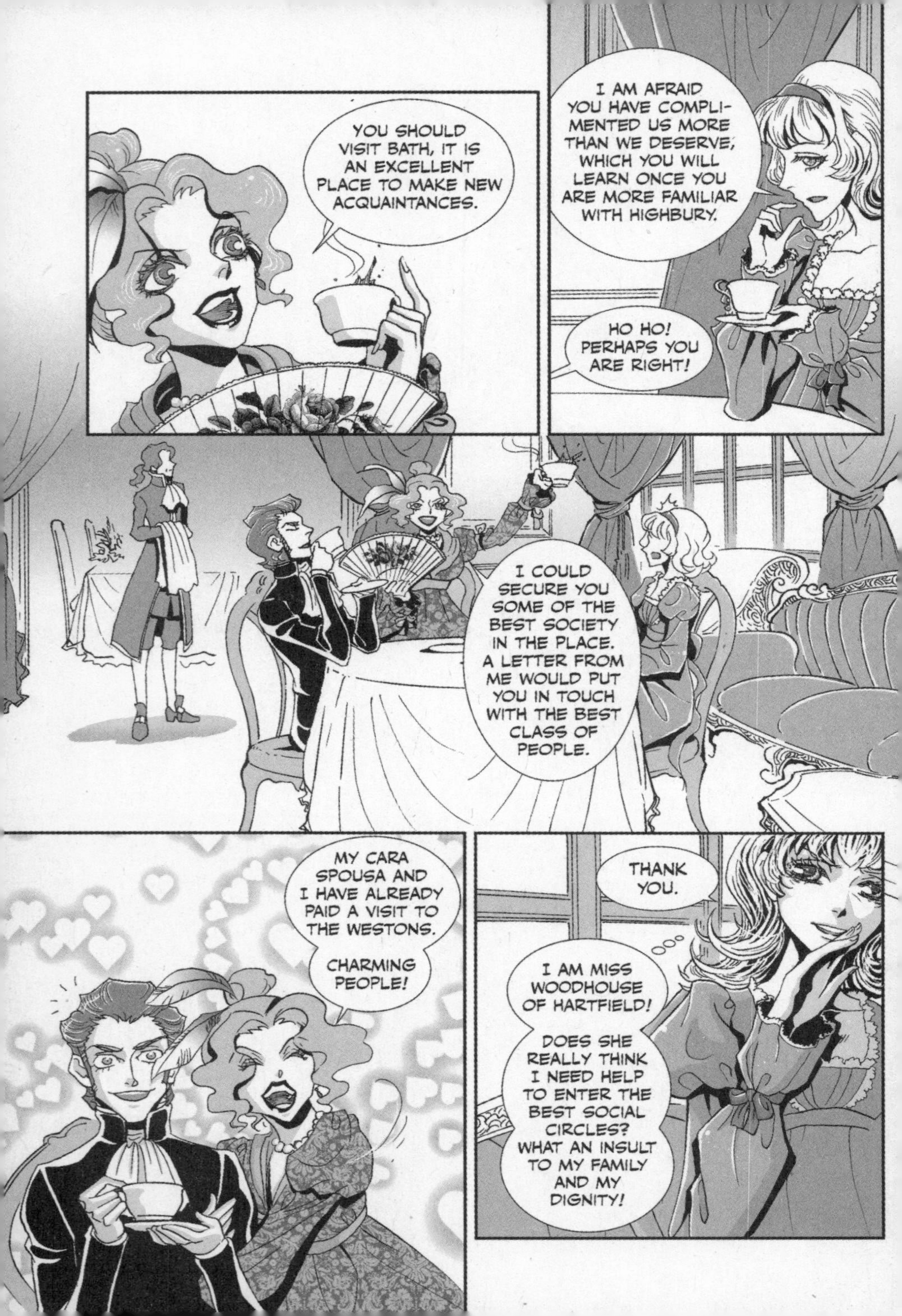

I AM AFRAID YOU HAVE COMPLIMENTED US MORE THAN WE DESERVE, WHICH YOU WILL LEARN ONCE YOU ARE MORE FAMILIAR WITH HIGHBURY.
HO HO! PERHAPS YOU ARE RIGHT!
YOU SHOULD VISIT BATH, IT IS AN EXCELLENT PLACE TO MAKE NEW ACQUAINTANCES.
I COULD SECURE YOU SOME OF THE BEST SOCIETY IN THE PLACE. A LETTER FROM ME WOULD PUT YOU IN TOUCH WITH THE BEST CLASS OF PEOPLE.
THANK YOU.
I AM MISS WOODHOUSE OF HARTFIELD!
DOES SHE REALLY THINK I NEED HELP TO ENTER THE BEST SOCIAL CIRCLES? WHAT AN INSULT TO MY FAMILY AND MY DIGNITY!
MY CARA SPOUSA AND I HAVE ALREADY PAID A VISIT TO THE WESTONS.
CHARMING PEOPLE!

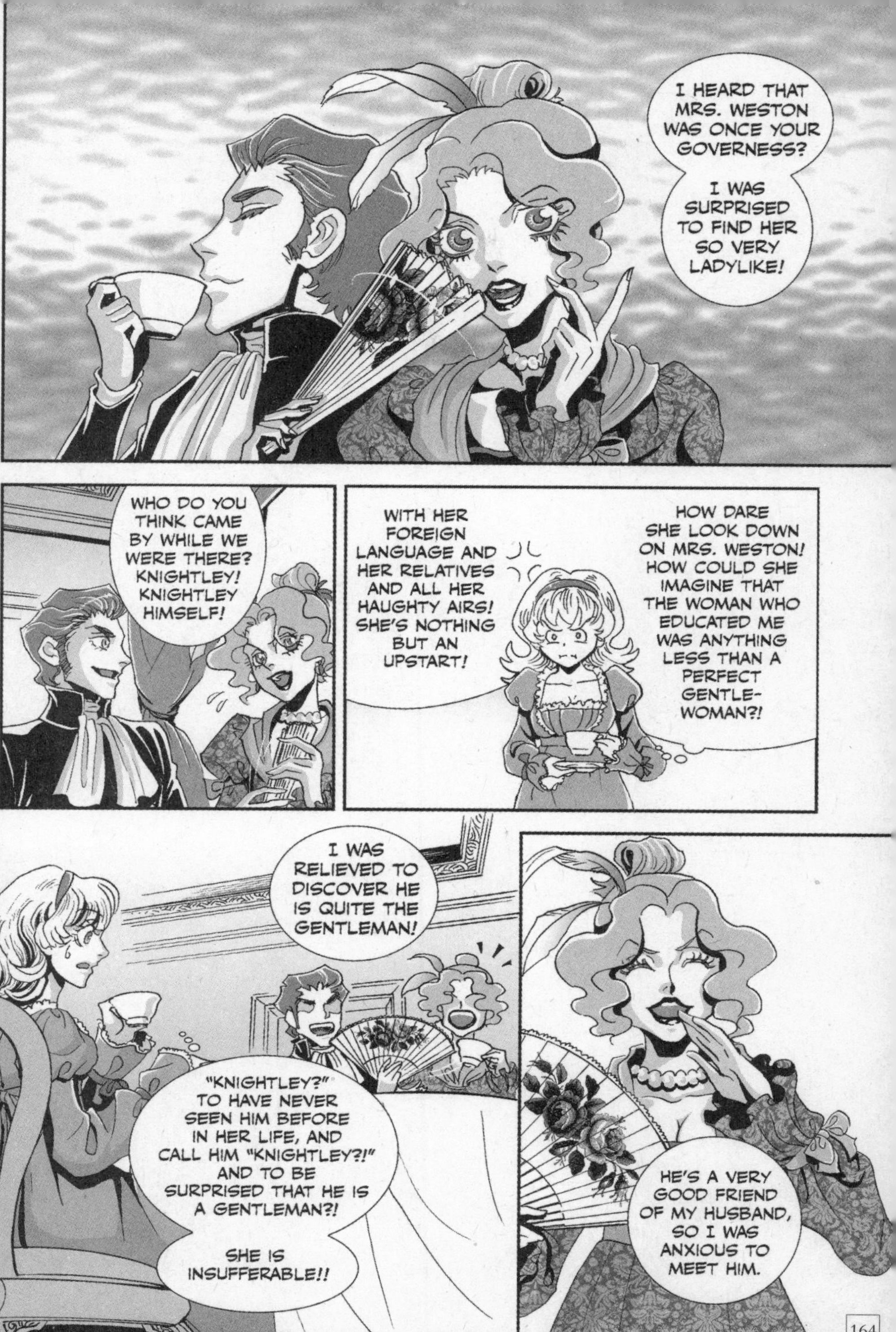
I HEARD THAT MRS. WESTON WAS ONCE YOUR GOVERNESS?
I WAS SURPRISED TO FIND HER SO VERY LADYLIKE!
HOW DARE SHE LOOK DOWN ON MRS. WESTON! HOW COULD SHE IMAGINE THAT THE WOMAN WHO EDUCATED ME WAS ANYTHING LESS THAN A PERFECT GENTLE-WOMAN?!
WITH HER FOREIGN LANGUAGE AND HER RELATIVES AND ALL HER HAUGHTY AIRS! SHE'S NOTHING BUT AN UPSTART!
WHO DO YOU THINK CAME BY WHILE WE WERE THERE? KNIGHTLEY! KNIGHTLEY HIMSELF!
HE'S A VERY GOOD FRIEND OF MY HUSBAND, SO I WAS ANXIOUS TO MEET HIM.
I WAS RELIEVED TO DISCOVER HE IS QUITE THE GENTLEMAN!
"KNIGHTLEY?" TO HAVE NEVER SEEN HIM BEFORE IN HER LIFE, AND CALL HIM "KNIGHTLEY?!" AND TO BE SURPRISED THAT HE IS A GENTLEMAN?!
SHE IS INSUFFERABLE!!

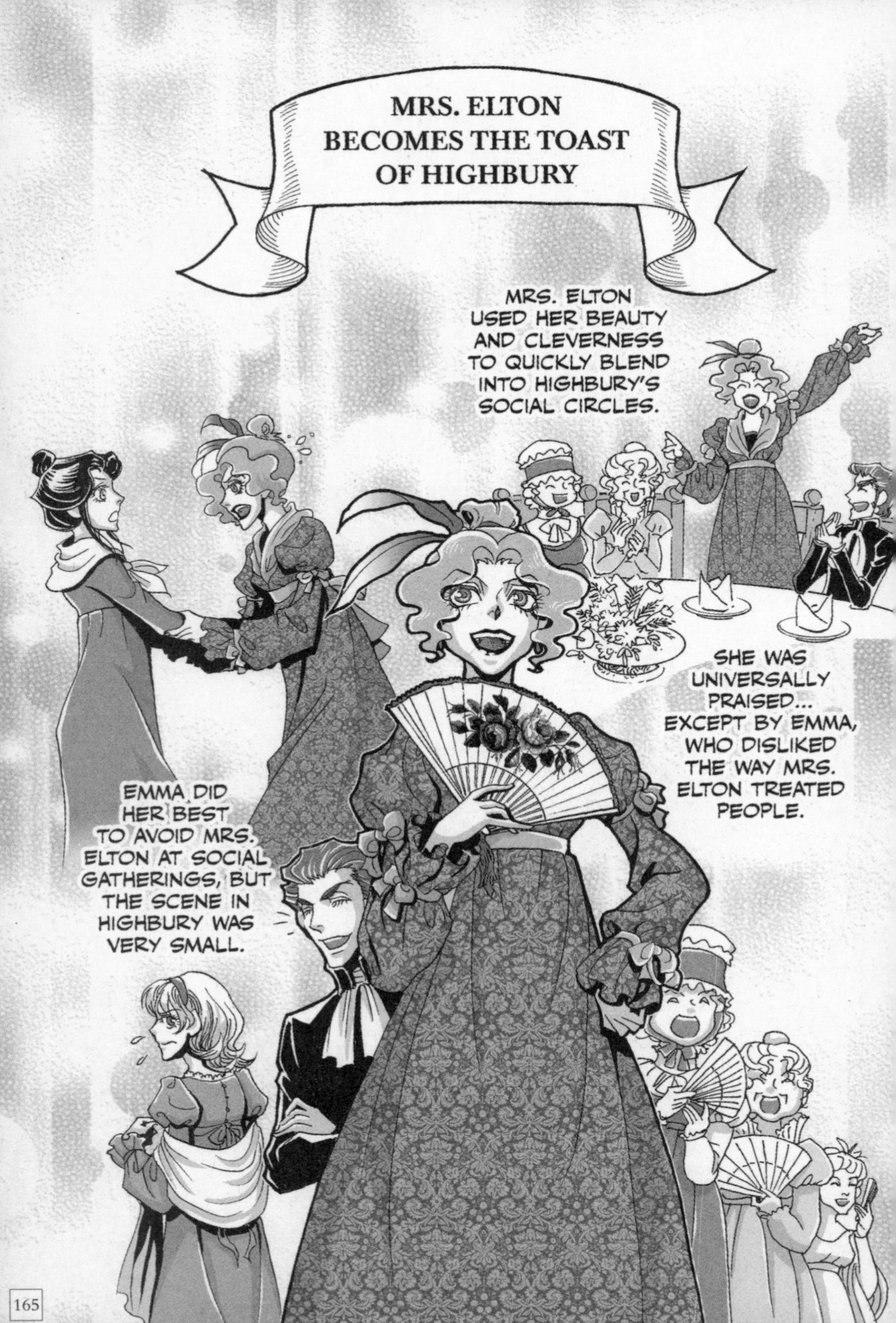
MRS. ELTON BECOMES THE TOAST OF HIGHBURY
MRS. ELTON USED HER BEAUTY AND CLEVERNESS TO QUICKLY BLEND INTO HIGHBURY'S SOCIAL CIRCLES.
SHE WAS UNIVERSALLY PRAISED... EXCEPT BY EMMA, WHO DISLIKED THE WAY MRS. ELTON TREATED PEOPLE.
EMMA DID HER BEST TO AVOID MRS. ELTON AT SOCIAL GATHERINGS, BUT THE SCENE IN HIGHBURY WAS VERY SMALL.

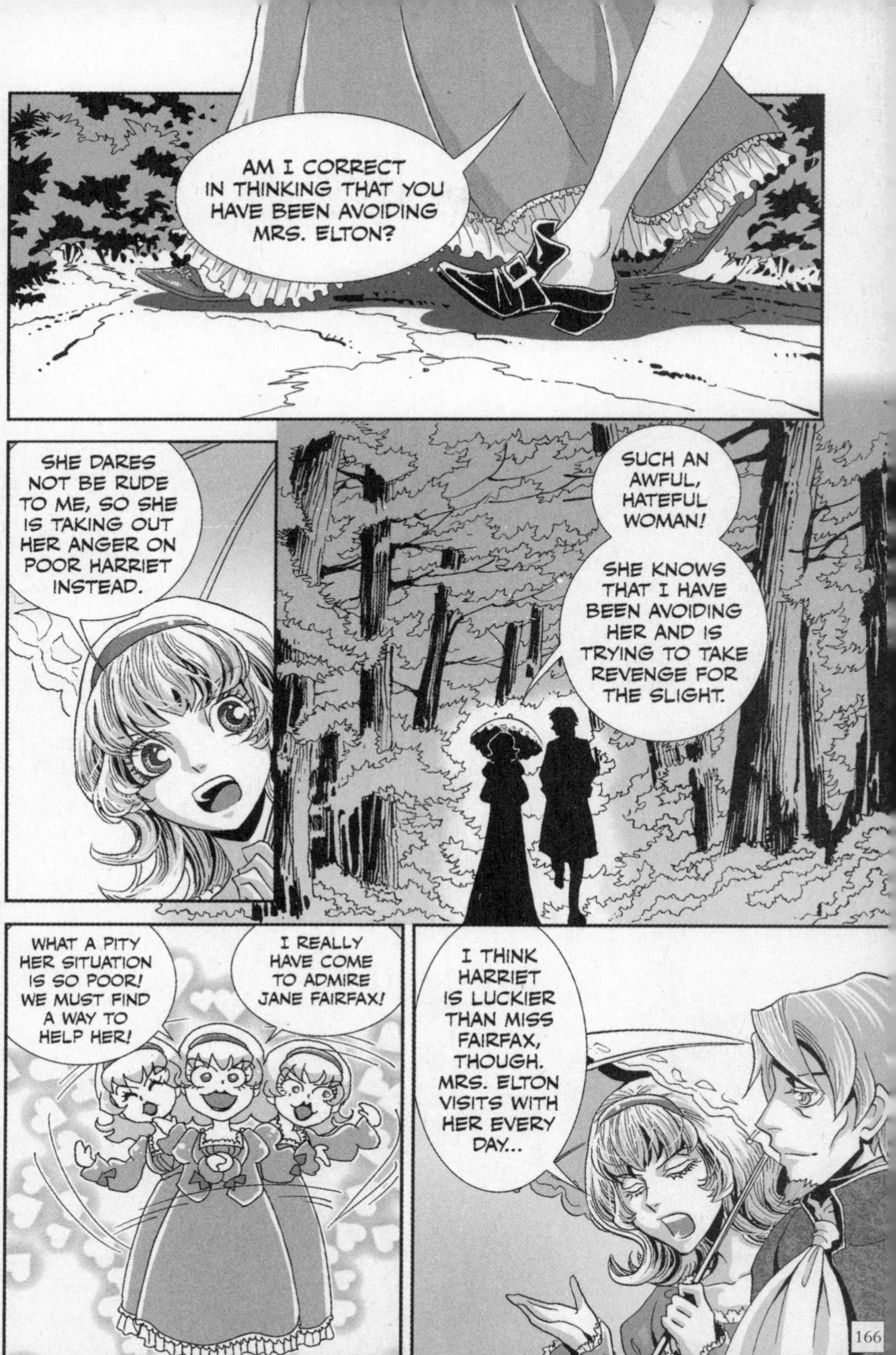
AM I CORRECT IN THINKING THAT YOU HAVE BEEN AVOIDING MRS. ELTON?
SUCH AN AWFUL, HATEFUL WOMAN!
SHE KNOWS THAT I HAVE BEEN AVOIDING HER AND IS TRYING TO TAKE REVENGE FOR THE SLIGHT.
SHE DARES NOT BE RUDE TO ME, SO SHE IS TAKING OUT HER ANGER ON POOR HARRIET INSTEAD.
I THINK HARRIET IS LUCKIER THAN MISS FAIRFAX, THOUGH. MRS. ELTON VISITS WITH HER EVERY DAY...
I REALLY HAVE COME TO ADMIRE JANE FAIRFAX!
WHAT A PITY HER SITUATION IS SO POOR! WE MUST FIND A WAY TO HELP HER!

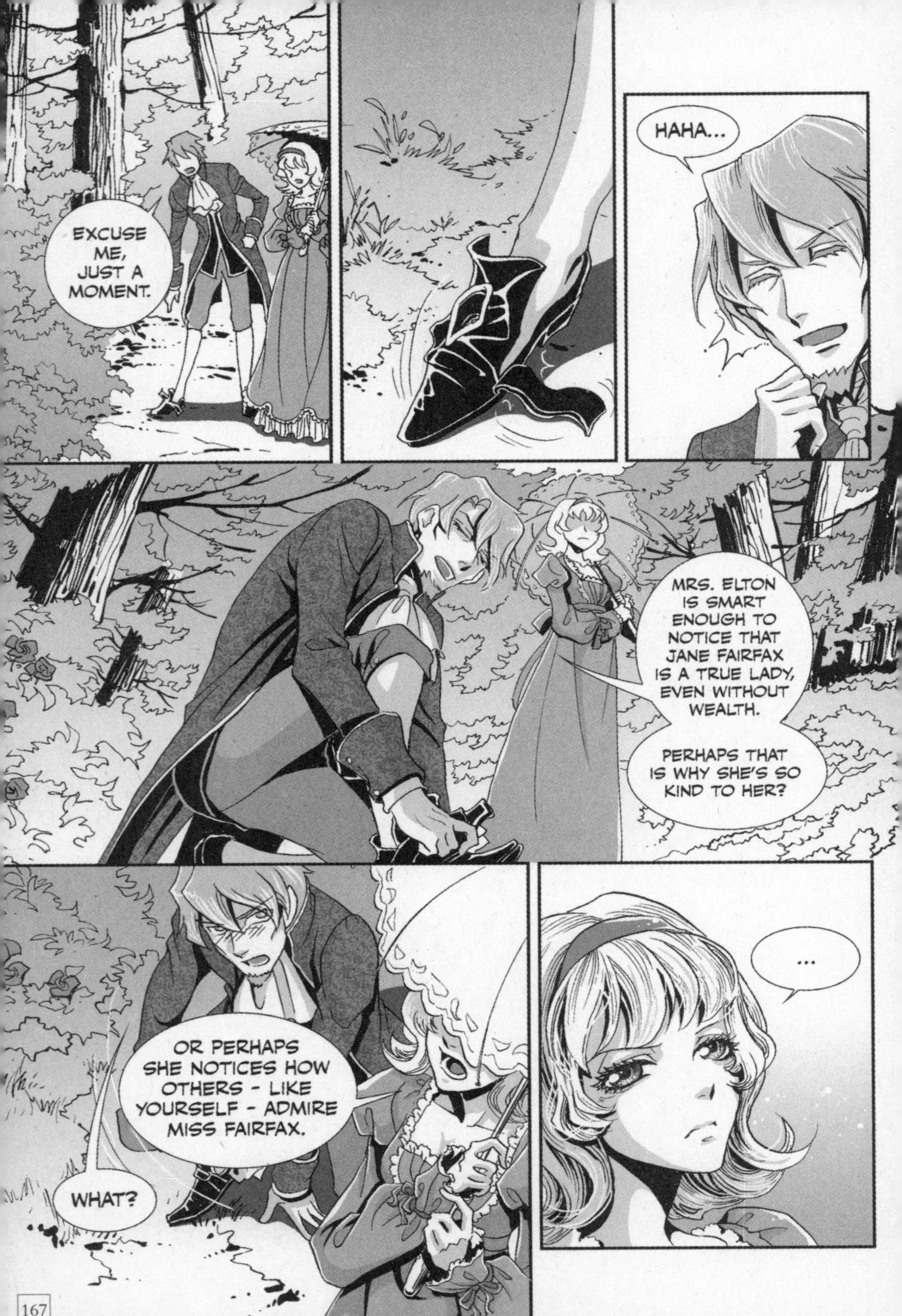
HAHA...
EXCUSE ME, JUST A MOMENT.
MRS. ELTON IS SMART ENOUGH TO NOTICE THAT JANE FAIRFAX IS A TRUE LADY, EVEN WITHOUT WEALTH.
PERHAPS THAT IS WHY SHE'S SO KIND TO HER?
...
OR PERHAPS SHE NOTICES HOW OTHERS - LIKE YOURSELF - ADMIRE MISS FAIRFAX.
WHAT?

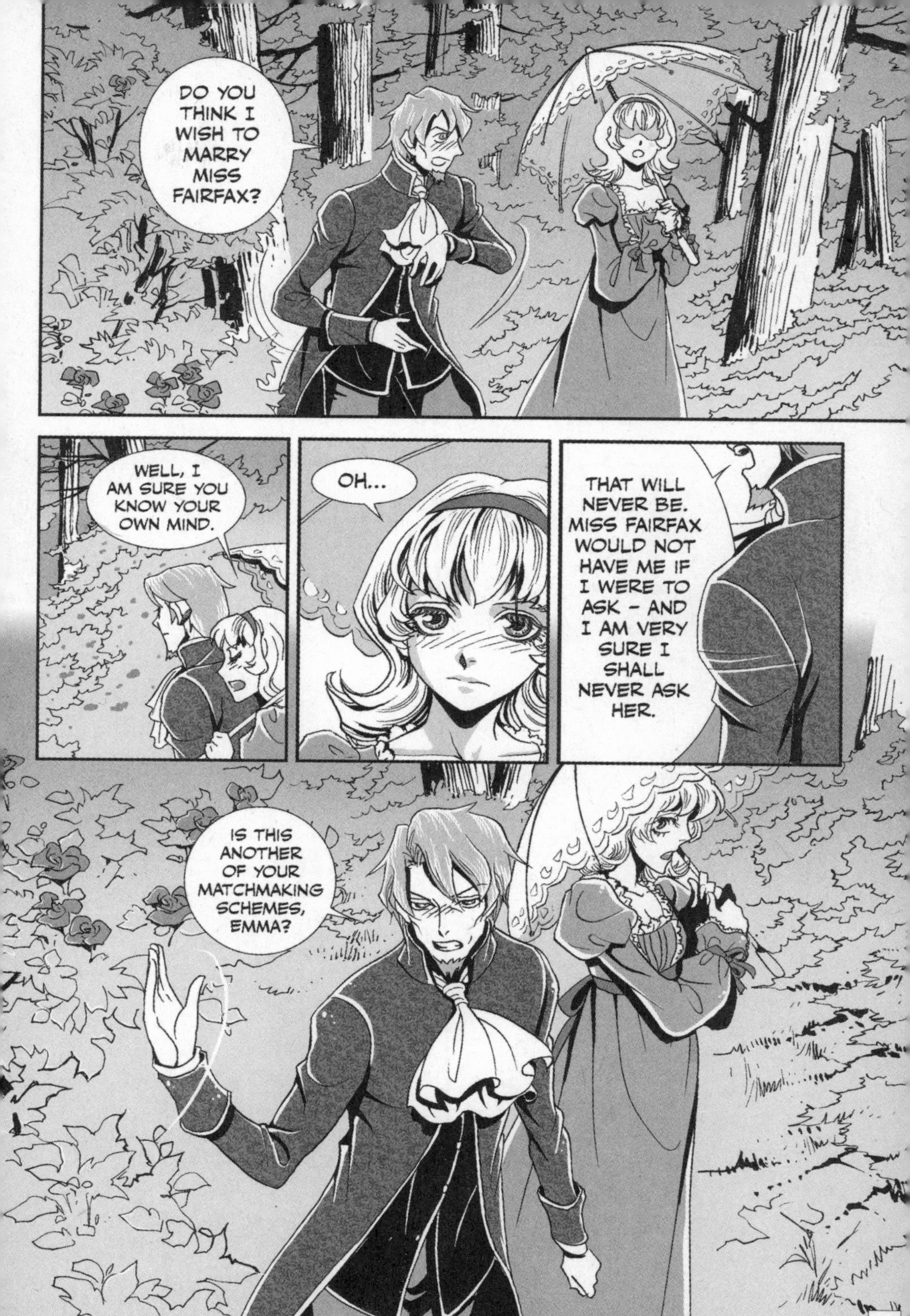
DO YOU THINK I WISH TO MARRY MISS FAIRFAX?
THAT WILL NEVER BE. MISS FAIRFAX WOULD NOT HAVE ME IF I WERE TO ASK - AND I AM VERY SURE I SHALL NEVER ASK HER.
OH...
WELL, I AM SURE YOU KNOW YOUR OWN MIND.
IS THIS ANOTHER OF YOUR MATCHMAKING SCHEMES, EMMA?

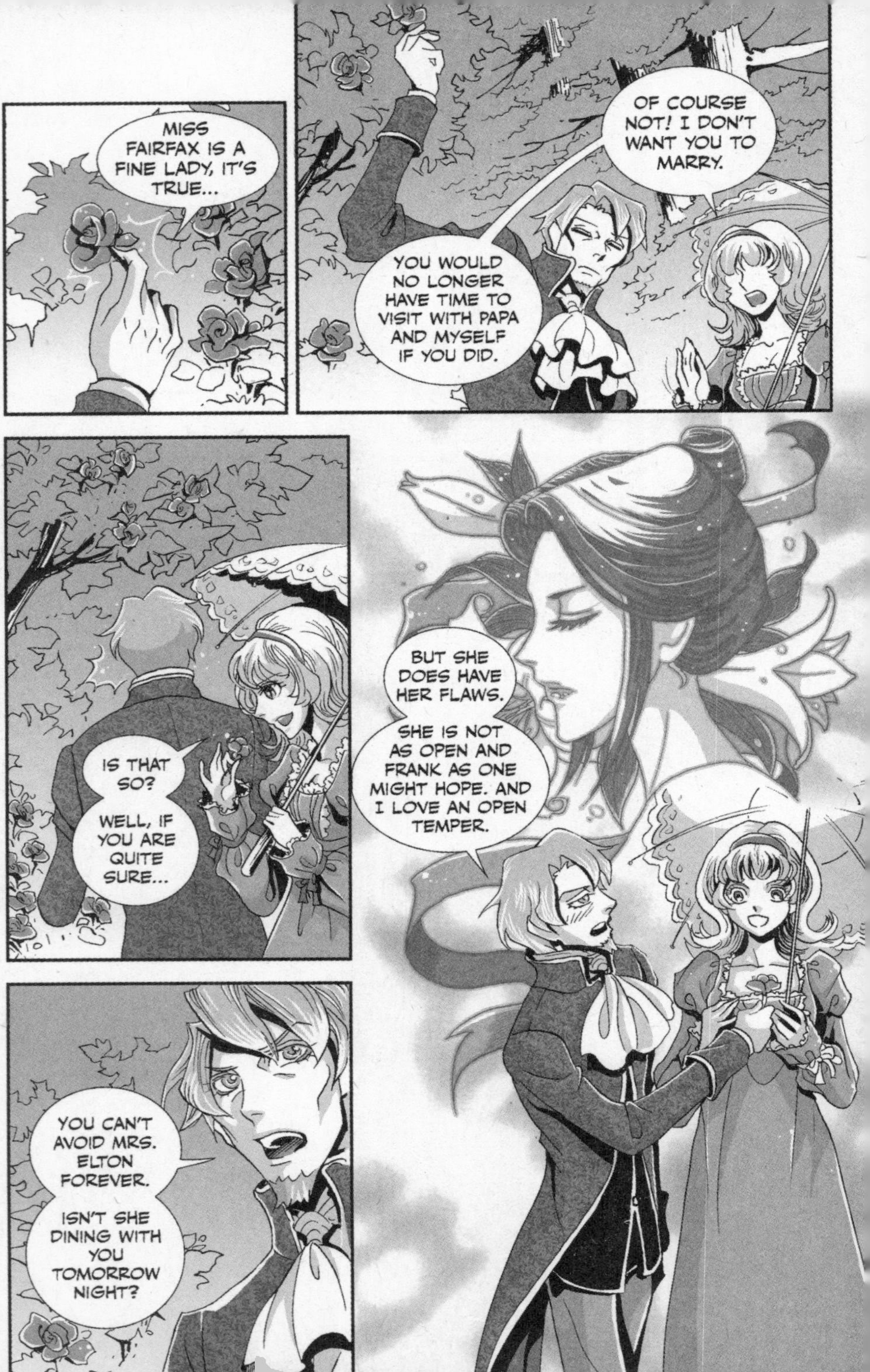
OF COURSE NOT! I DON'T WANT YOU TO MARRY.
YOU WOULD NO LONGER HAVE TIME TO VISIT WITH PAPA AND MYSELF IF YOU DID.
MISS FAIRFAX IS A FINE LADY, IT'S TRUE...
BUT SHE DOES HAVE HER FLAWS.
SHE IS NOT AS OPEN AND FRANK AS ONE MIGHT HOPE. AND I LOVE AN OPEN TEMPER.
IS THAT SO?
WELL, IF YOU ARE QUITE SURE...
YOU CAN'T AVOID MRS. ELTON FOREVER.
ISN'T SHE DINING WITH YOU TOMORROW NIGHT?

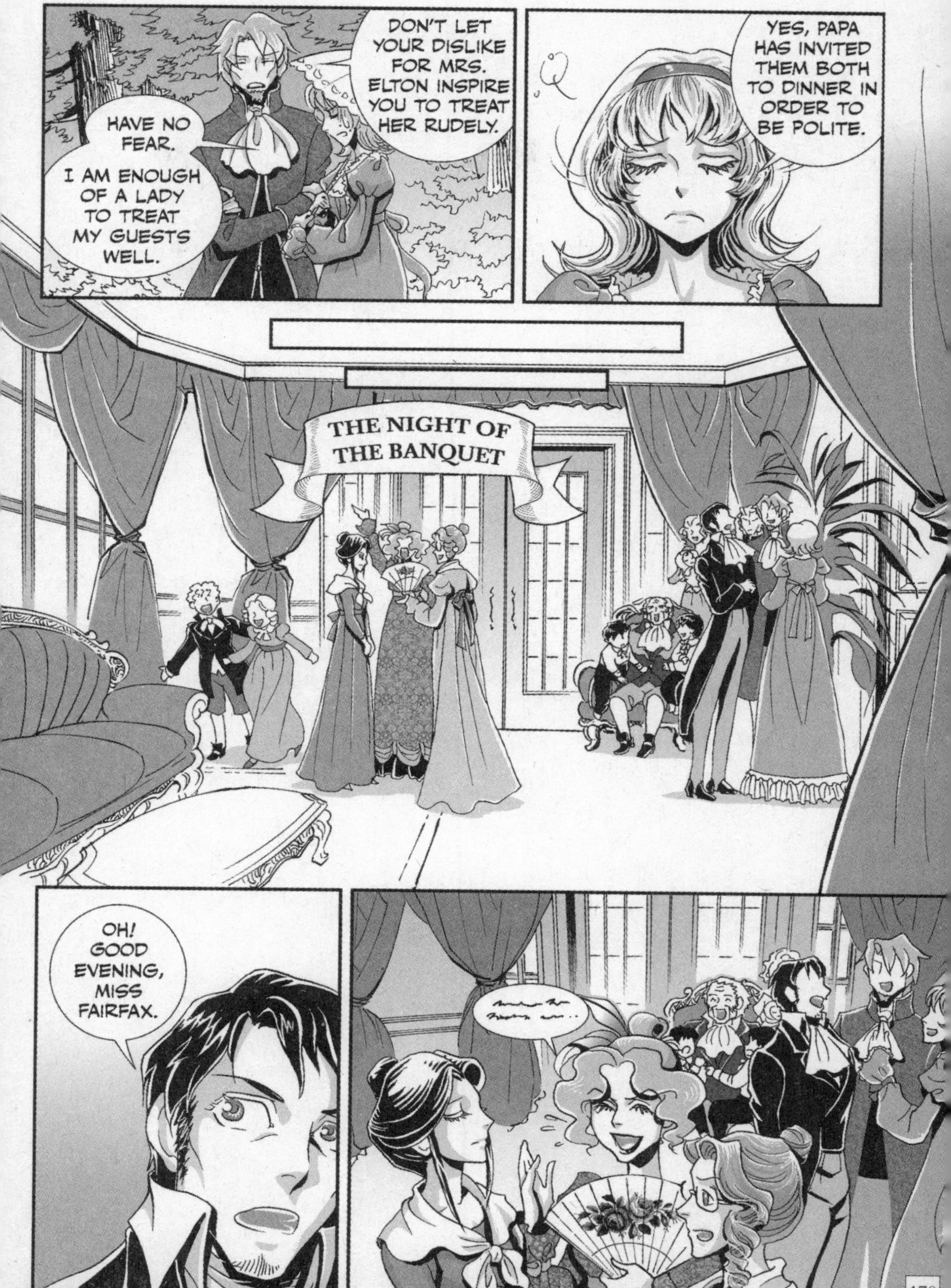
YES, PAPA HAS INVITED THEM BOTH TO DINNER IN ORDER TO BE POLITE.
DON'T LET YOUR DISLIKE FOR MRS. ELTON INSPIRE YOU TO TREAT HER RUDELY.
HAVE NO FEAR.
I AM ENOUGH OF A LADY TO TREAT MY GUESTS WELL.
THE NIGHT OF THE BANQUET
OH! GOOD EVENING, MISS FAIRFAX.

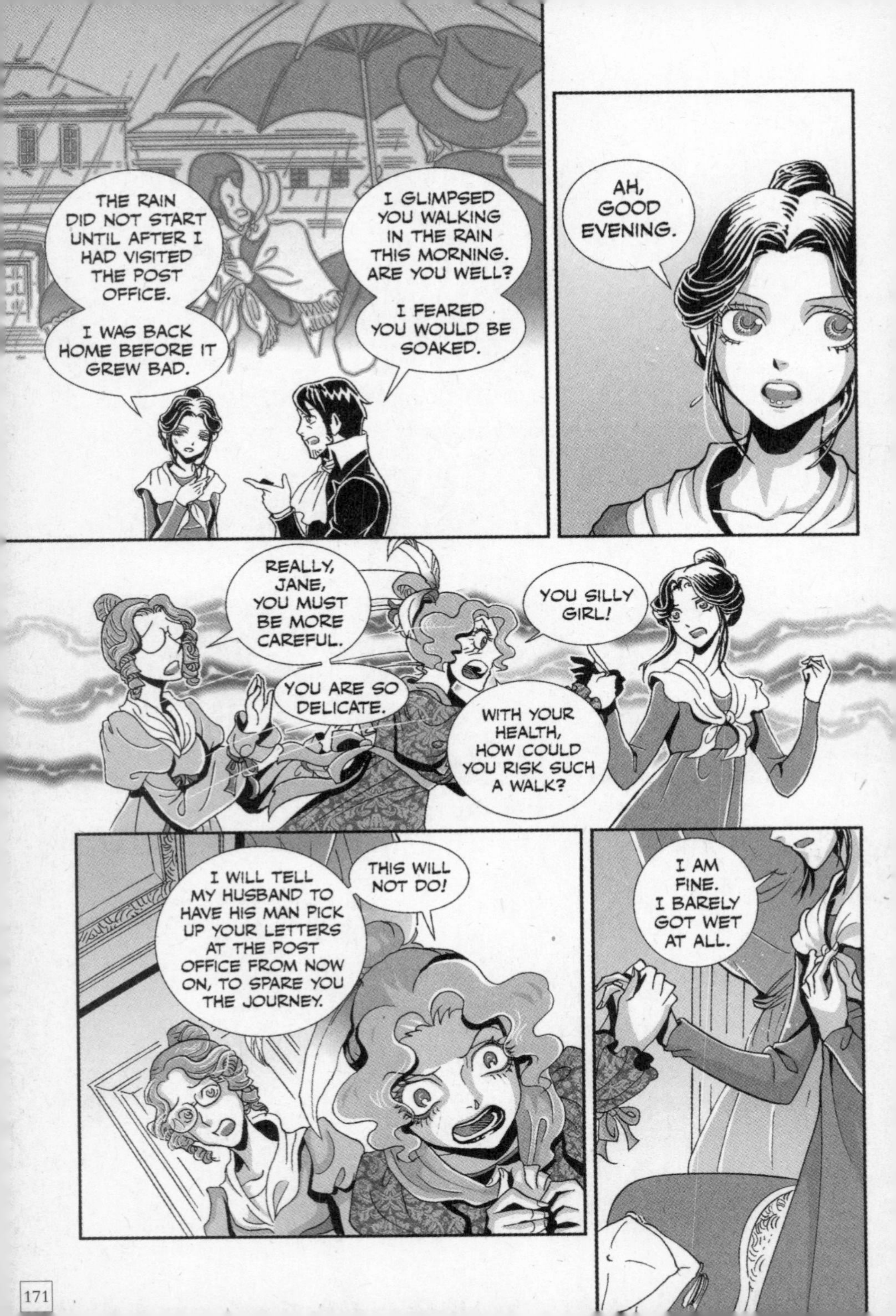
AH, GOOD EVENING.
I GLIMPSED YOU WALKING IN THE RAIN THIS MORNING. ARE YOU WELL?
I FEARED YOU WOULD BE SOAKED.
THE RAIN DID NOT START UNTIL AFTER I HAD VISITED THE POST OFFICE.
I WAS BACK HOME BEFORE IT GREW BAD.
YOU SILLY GIRL!
REALLY, JANE, YOU MUST BE MORE CAREFUL.
WITH YOUR HEALTH, HOW COULD YOU RISK SUCH A WALK?
YOU ARE SO DELICATE.
I AM FINE. I BARELY GOT WET AT ALL.
THIS WILL NOT DO!
I WILL TELL MY HUSBAND TO HAVE HIS MAN PICK UP YOUR LETTERS AT THE POST OFFICE FROM NOW ON, TO SPARE YOU THE JOURNEY.

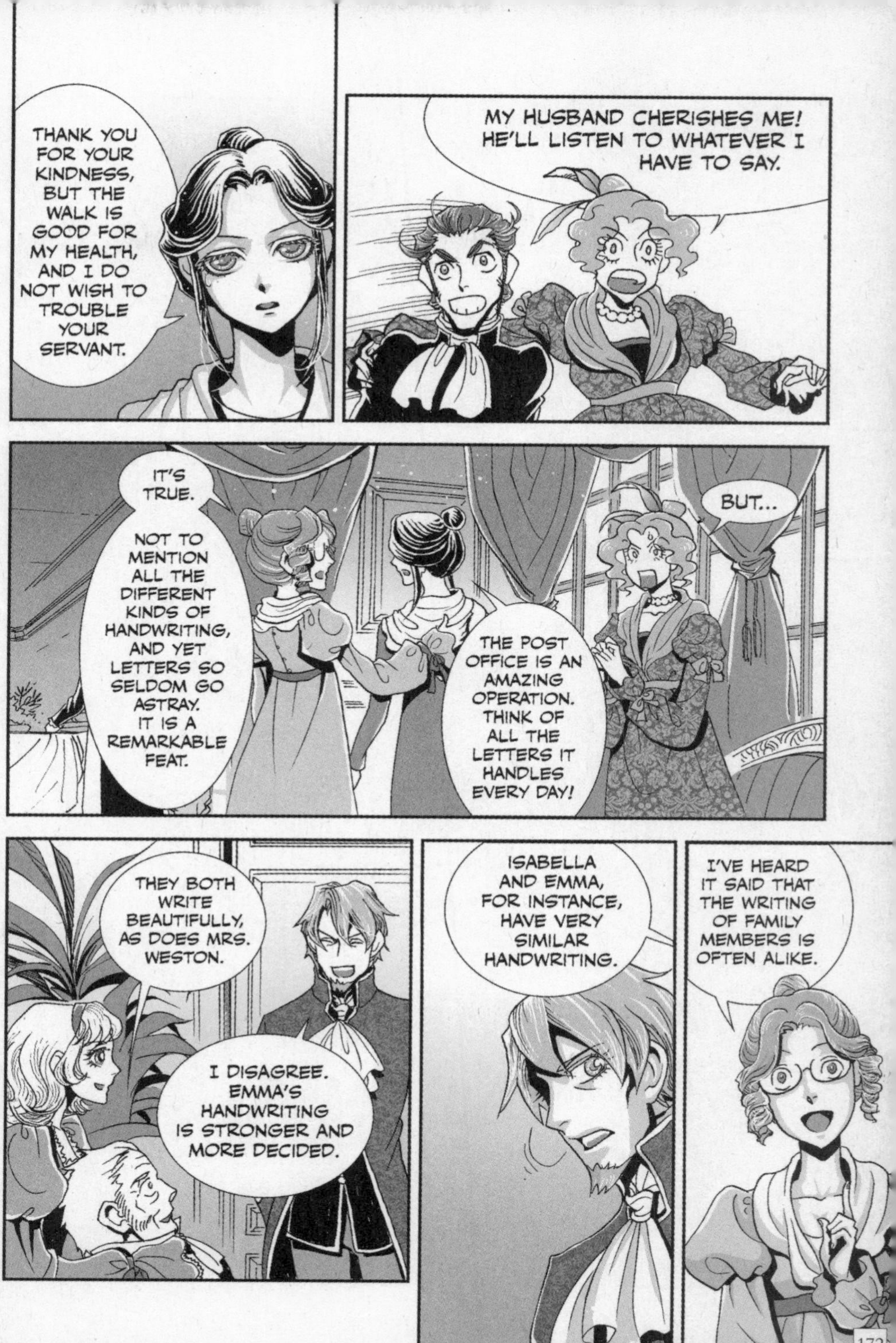
MY HUSBAND CHERISHES ME! HE'LL LISTEN TO WHATEVER I HAVE TO SAY.
THANK YOU FOR YOUR KINDNESS, BUT THE WALK IS GOOD FOR MY HEALTH, AND I DO NOT WISH TO TROUBLE YOUR SERVANT.
BUT...
THE POST OFFICE IS AN AMAZING OPERATION. THINK OF ALL THE LETTERS IT HANDLES EVERY DAY!
IT'S TRUE.
NOT TO MENTION ALL THE DIFFERENT KINDS OF HANDWRITING, AND YET LETTERS SO SELDOM GO ASTRAY. IT IS A REMARKABLE FEAT.
I'VE HEARD IT SAID THAT THE WRITING OF FAMILY MEMBERS IS OFTEN ALIKE.
ISABELLA AND EMMA, FOR INSTANCE, HAVE VERY SIMILAR HANDWRITING.
THEY BOTH WRITE BEAUTIFULLY, AS DOES MRS. WESTON.
I DISAGREE. EMMA'S HANDWRITING IS STRONGER AND MORE DECIDED.

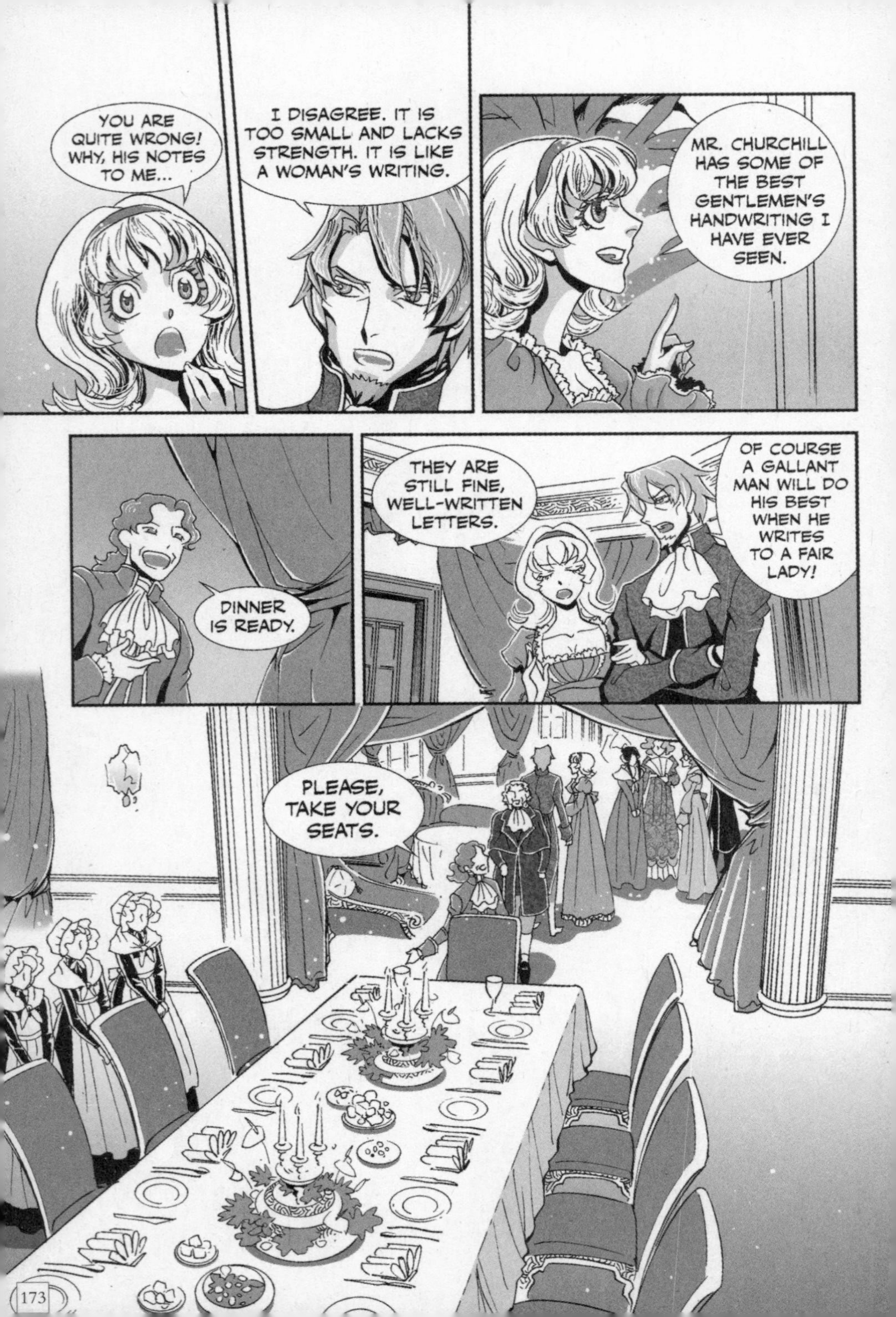
MR. CHURCHILL HAS SOME OF THE BEST GENTLEMEN'S HANDWRITING I HAVE EVER SEEN.
I DISAGREE. IT IS TOO SMALL AND LACKS STRENGTH. IT IS LIKE A WOMAN'S WRITING.
YOU ARE QUITE WRONG! WHY, HIS NOTES TO ME...
OF COURSE A GALLANT MAN WILL DO HIS BEST WHEN HE WRITES TO A FAIR LADY!
THEY ARE STILL FINE, WELL-WRITTEN LETTERS.
DINNER IS READY.
PLEASE, TAKE YOUR SEATS.

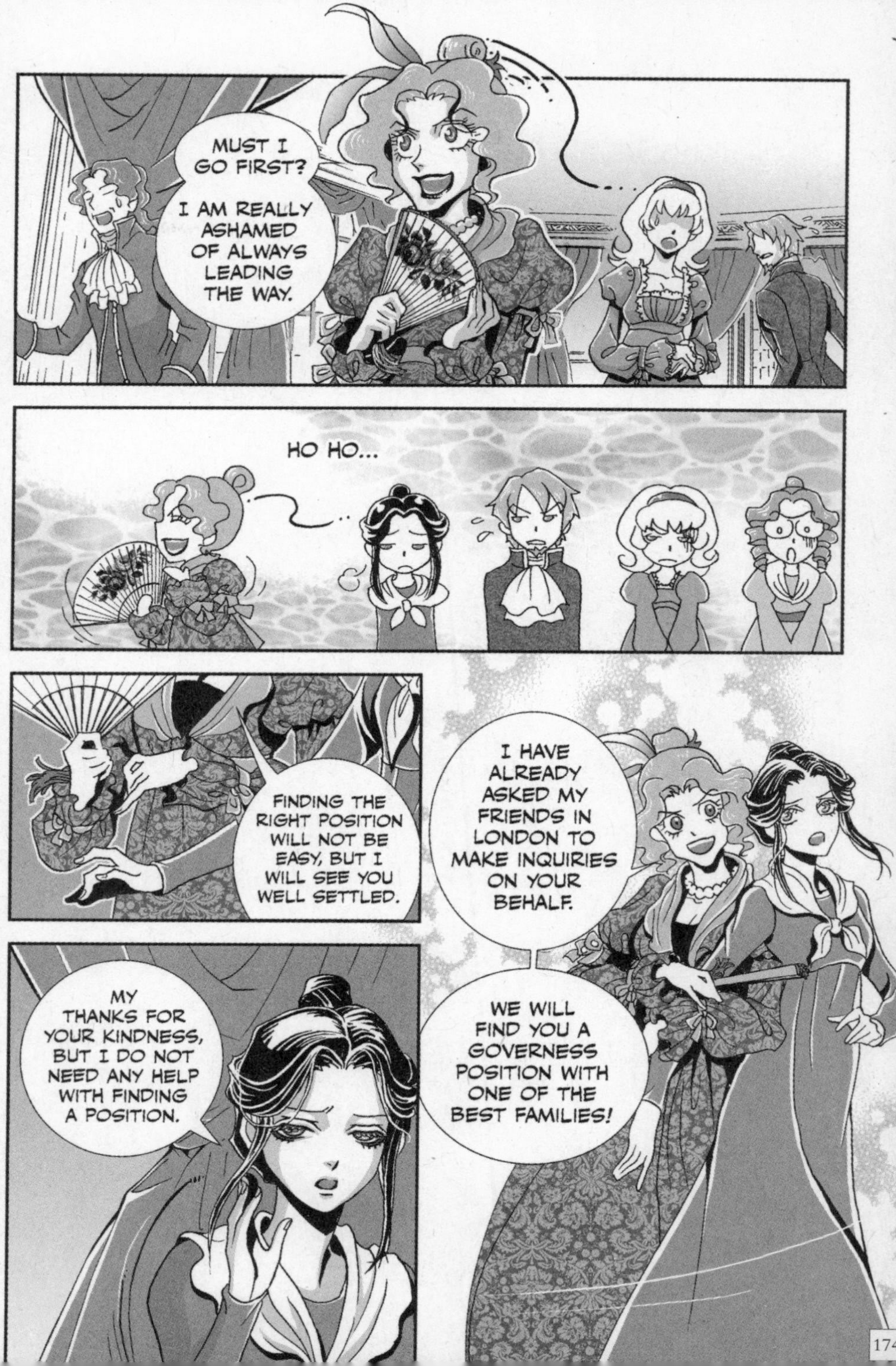
MUST I GO FIRST?
I AM REALLY ASHAMED OF ALWAYS LEADING THE WAY.
HO HO...
I HAVE ALREADY ASKED MY FRIENDS IN LONDON TO MAKE INQUIRIES ON YOUR BEHALF.
WE WILL FIND YOU A GOVERNESS POSITION WITH ONE OF THE BEST FAMILIES!
FINDING THE RIGHT POSITION WILL NOT BE EASY, BUT I WILL SEE YOU WELL SETTLED.
MY THANKS FOR YOUR KINDNESS, BUT I DO NOT NEED ANY HELP WITH FINDING A POSITION.

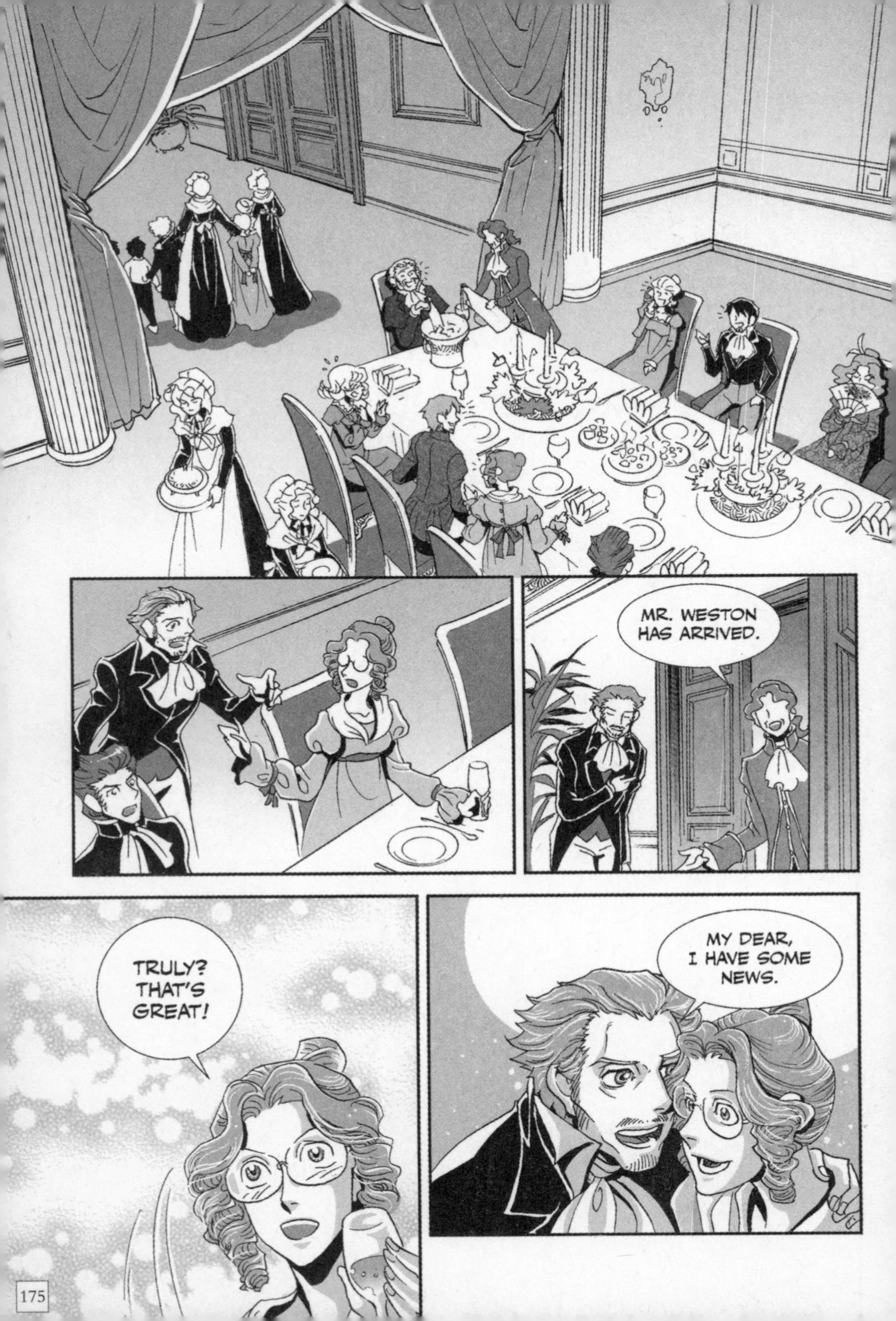
MR. WESTON HAS ARRIVED.
MY DEAR, I HAVE SOME NEWS.
TRULY? THAT'S GREAT!

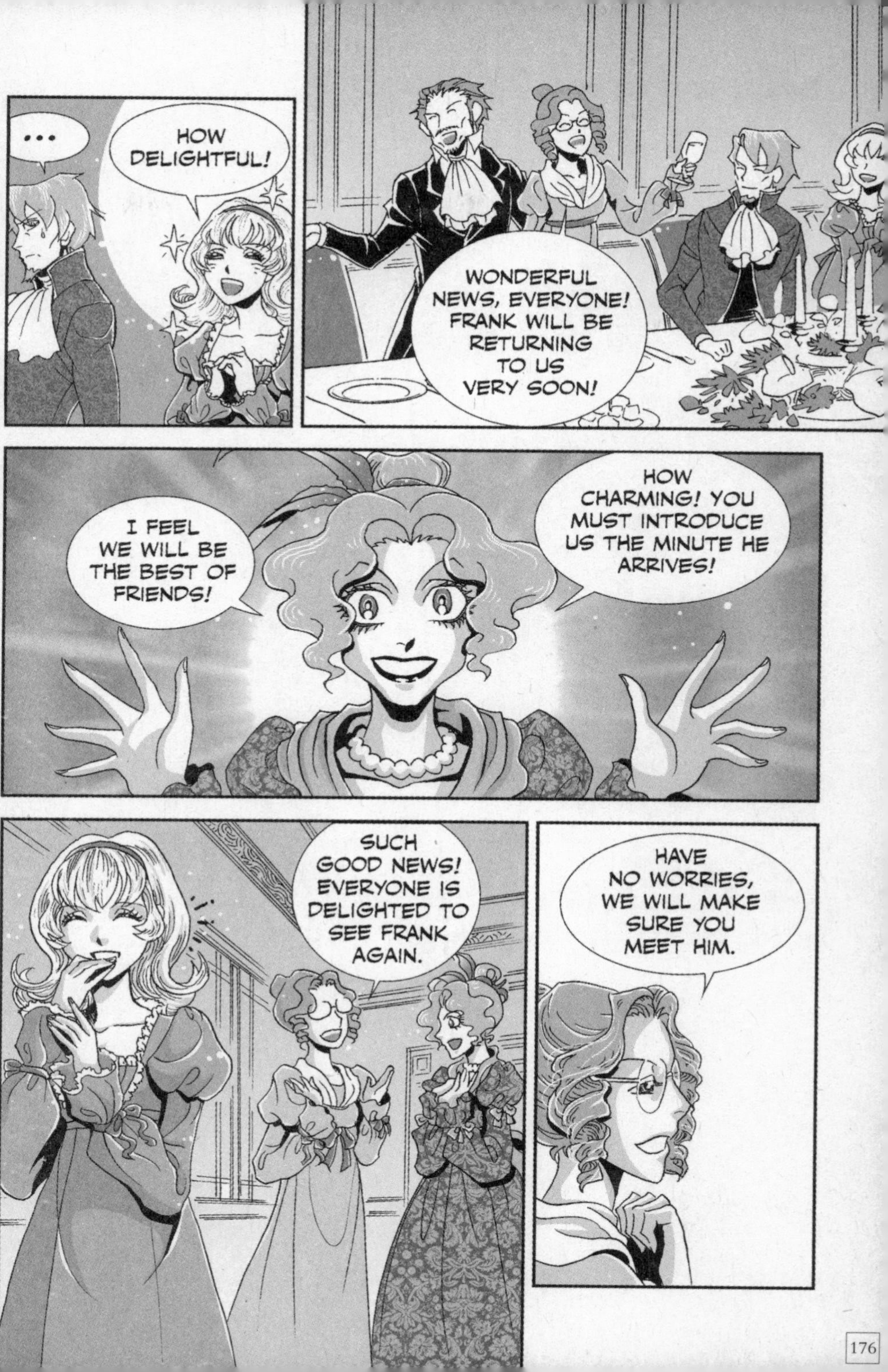

WONDERFUL NEWS, EVERYONE! FRANK WILL BE RETURNING TO US VERY SOON!
HOW DELIGHTFUL!
...
HOW CHARMING! YOU MUST INTRODUCE US THE MINUTE HE ARRIVES!
I FEEL WE WILL BE THE BEST OF FRIENDS!
HAVE NO WORRIES, WE WILL MAKE SURE YOU MEET HIM.
SUCH GOOD NEWS! EVERYONE IS DELIGHTED TO SEE FRANK AGAIN.

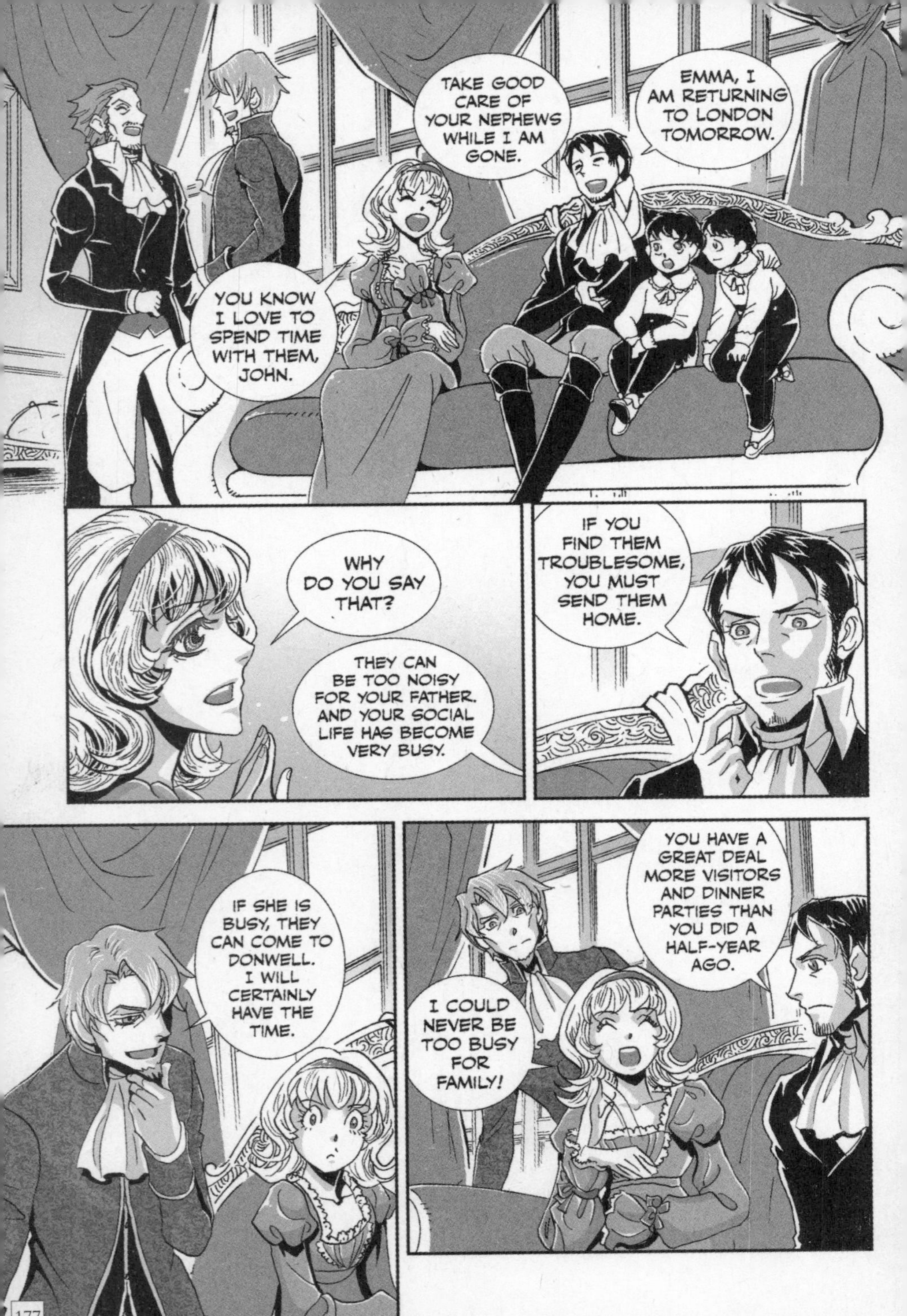
EMMA, I AM RETURNING TO LONDON TOMORROW.
TAKE GOOD CARE OF YOUR NEPHEWS WHILE I AM GONE.
YOU KNOW I LOVE TO SPEND TIME WITH THEM, JOHN.
IF YOU FIND THEM TROUBLESOME, YOU MUST SEND THEM HOME.
WHY DO YOU SAY THAT?
THEY CAN BE TOO NOISY FOR YOUR FATHER. AND YOUR SOCIAL LIFE HAS BECOME VERY BUSY.
YOU HAVE A GREAT DEAL MORE VISITORS AND DINNER PARTIES THAN YOU DID A HALF-YEAR AGO.
I COULD NEVER BE TOO BUSY FOR FAMILY!
IF SHE IS BUSY, THEY CAN COME TO DONWELL. I WILL CERTAINLY HAVE THE TIME.

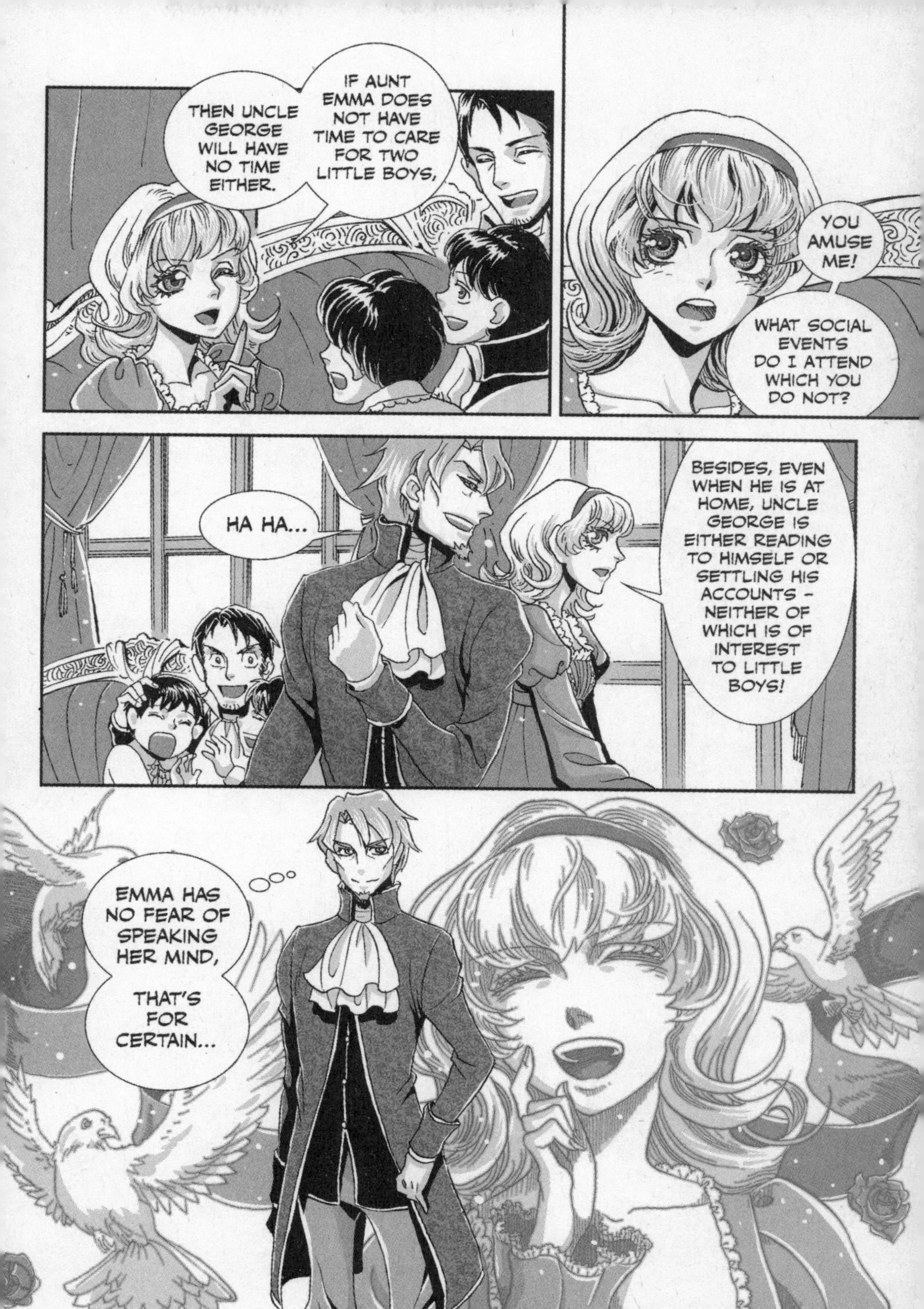
YOU AMUSE ME!
WHAT SOCIAL EVENTS DO I ATTEND WHICH YOU DO NOT?
IF AUNT EMMA DOES NOT HAVE TIME TO CARE FOR TWO LITTLE BOYS,
THEN UNCLE GEORGE WILL HAVE NO TIME EITHER.
BESIDES, EVEN WHEN HE IS AT HOME, UNCLE GEORGE IS EITHER READING TO HIMSELF OR SETTLING HIS ACCOUNTS - NEITHER OF WHICH IS OF INTEREST TO LITTLE BOYS!
HA HA...
EMMA HAS NO FEAR OF SPEAKING HER MIND,
THAT'S FOR CERTAIN...

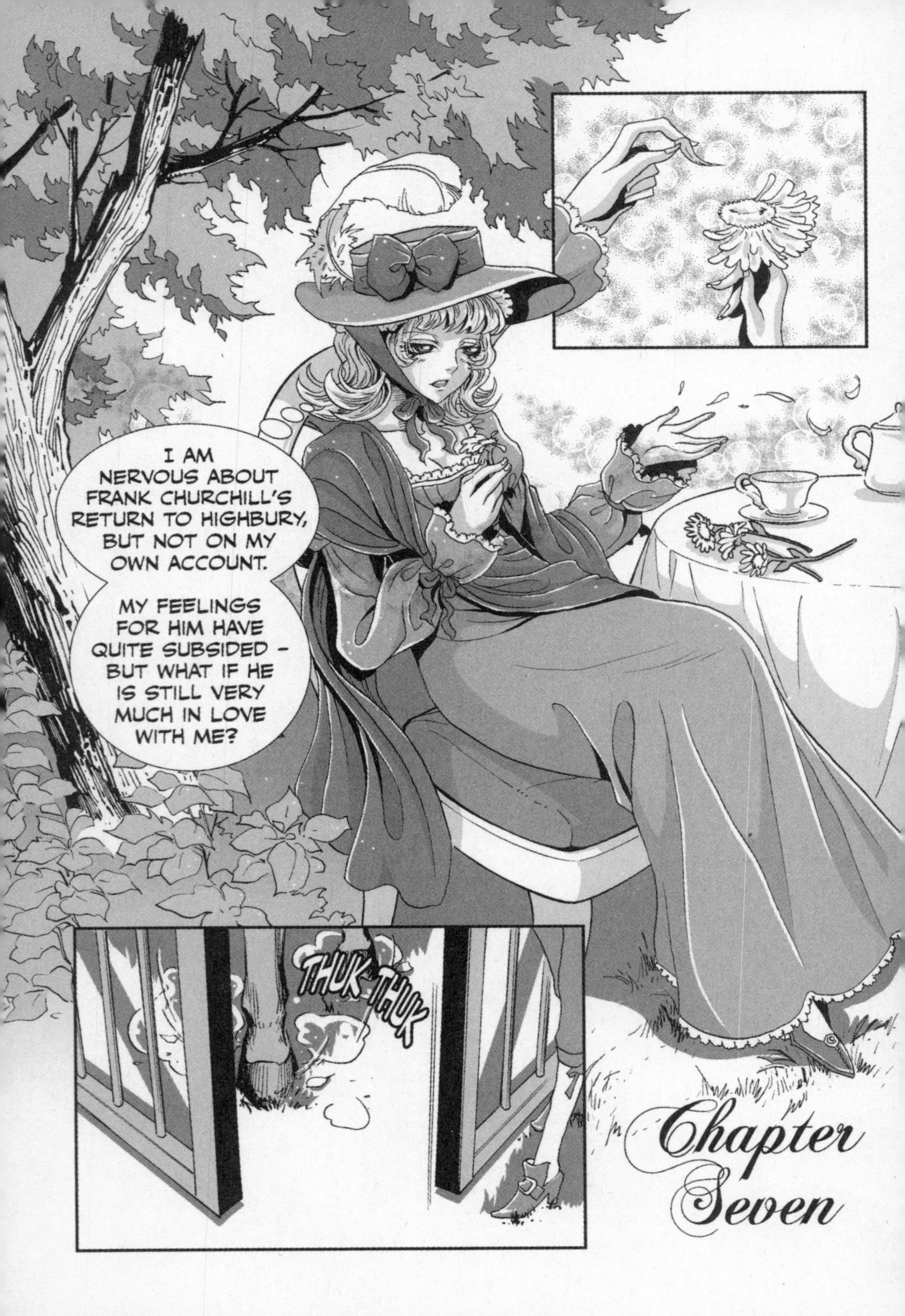
I AM NERVOUS ABOUT FRANK CHURCHILL'S RETURN TO HIGHBURY, BUT NOT ON MY OWN ACCOUNT.
MY FEELINGS FOR HIM HAVE QUITE SUBSIDED - BUT WHAT IF HE IS STILL VERY MUCH IN LOVE WITH ME?
THUK THUK
Chapter Seven

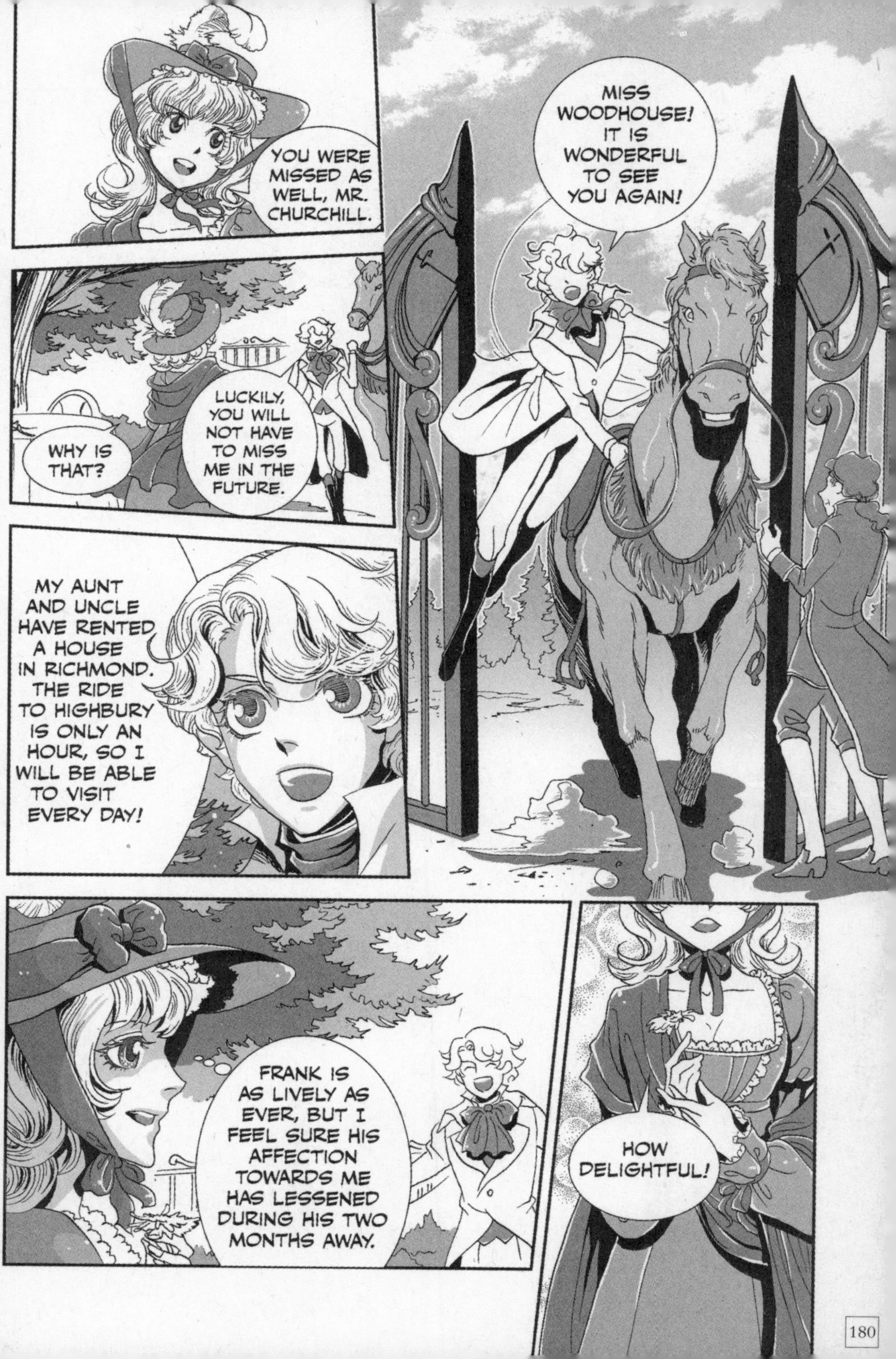
MISS WOODHOUSE! IT IS WONDERFUL TO SEE YOU AGAIN!
YOU WERE MISSED AS WELL, MR. CHURCHILL.
LUCKILY, YOU WILL NOT HAVE TO MISS ME IN THE FUTURE.
WHY IS THAT?
MY AUNT AND UNCLE HAVE RENTED A HOUSE IN RICHMOND. THE RIDE TO HIGHBURY IS ONLY AN HOUR, SO I WILL BE ABLE TO VISIT EVERY DAY!
HOW DELIGHTFUL!
FRANK IS AS LIVELY AS EVER, BUT I FEEL SURE HIS AFFECTION TOWARDS ME HAS LESSENED DURING HIS TWO MONTHS AWAY.

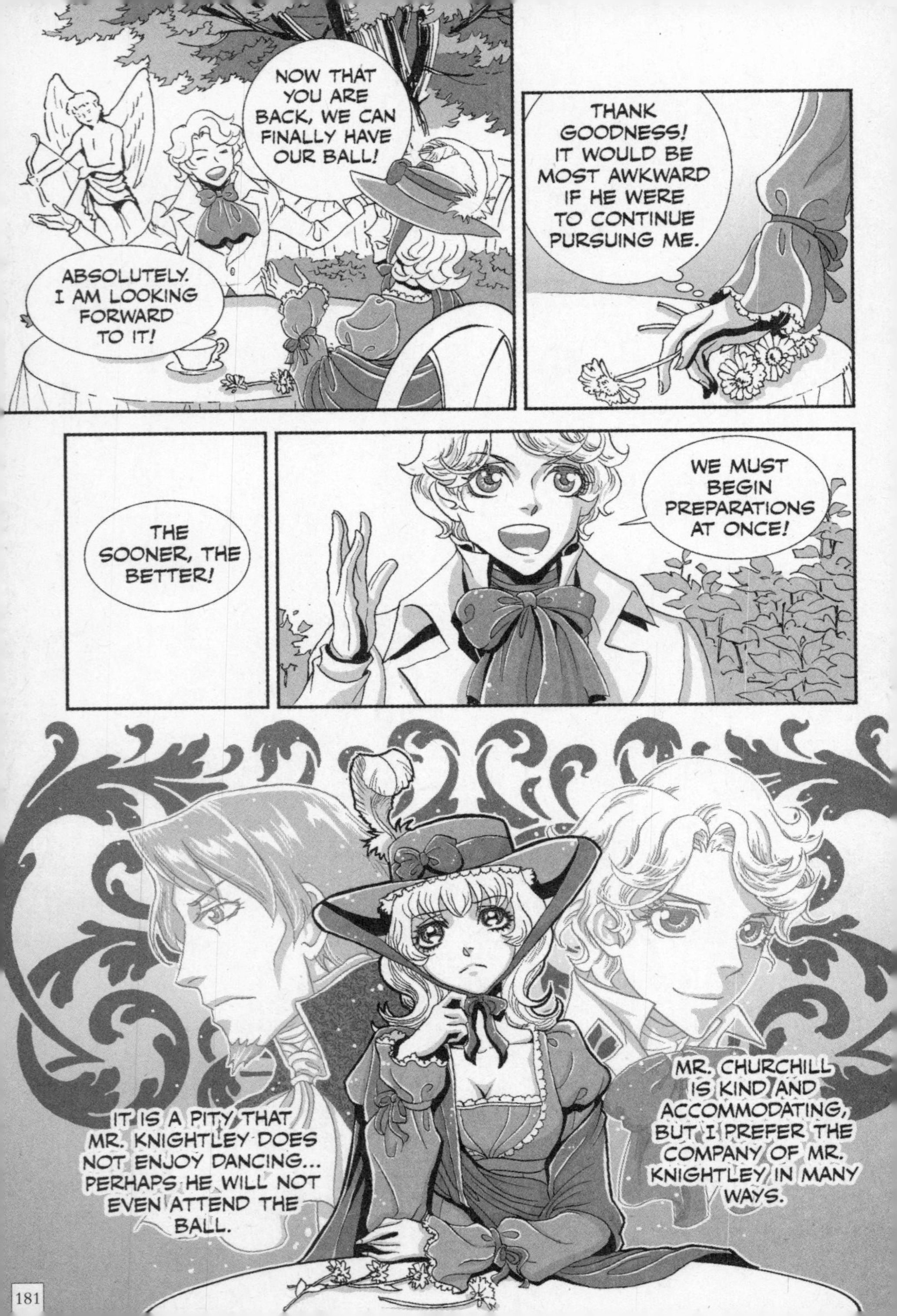
THANK GOODNESS! IT WOULD BE MOST AWKWARD IF HE WERE TO CONTINUE PURSUING ME.
NOW THAT YOU ARE BACK, WE CAN FINALLY HAVE OUR BALL!
ABSOLUTELY. I AM LOOKING FORWARD TO IT!
WE MUST BEGIN PREPARATIONS AT ONCE!
THE SOONER, THE BETTER!
MR. CHURCHILL IS KIND AND ACCOMMODATING, BUT I PREFER THE COMPANY OF MR. KNIGHTLEY IN MANY WAYS.
IT IS A PITY THAT MR. KNIGHTLEY DOES NOT ENJOY DANCING... PERHAPS HE WILL NOT EVEN ATTEND THE BALL.

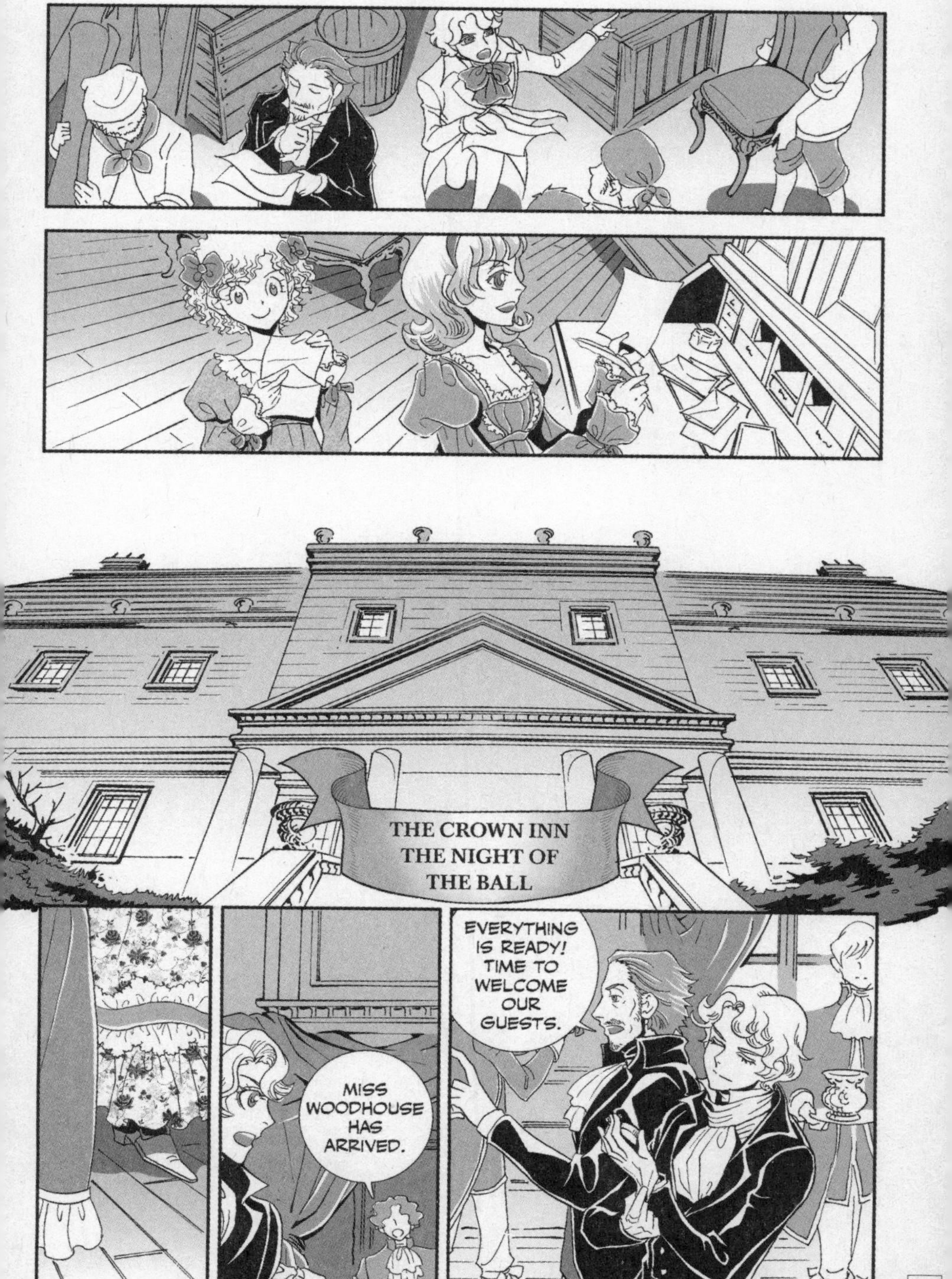
THE CROWN INN
THE NIGHT OF
THE BALL
EVERYTHING IS READY! TIME TO WELCOME OUR GUESTS.
MISS WOODHOUSE HAS ARRIVED.

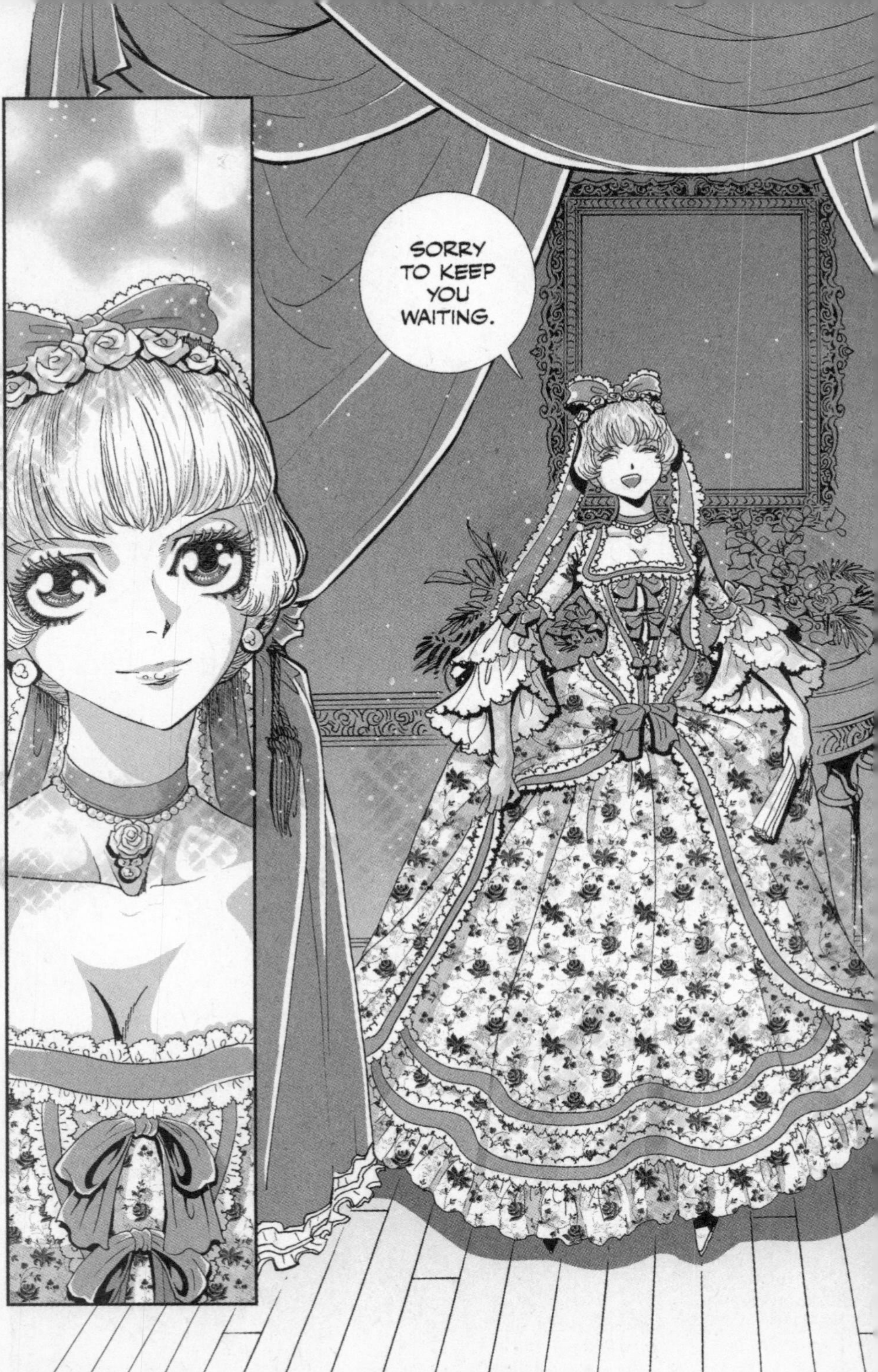
SORRY TO KEEP YOU WAITING.

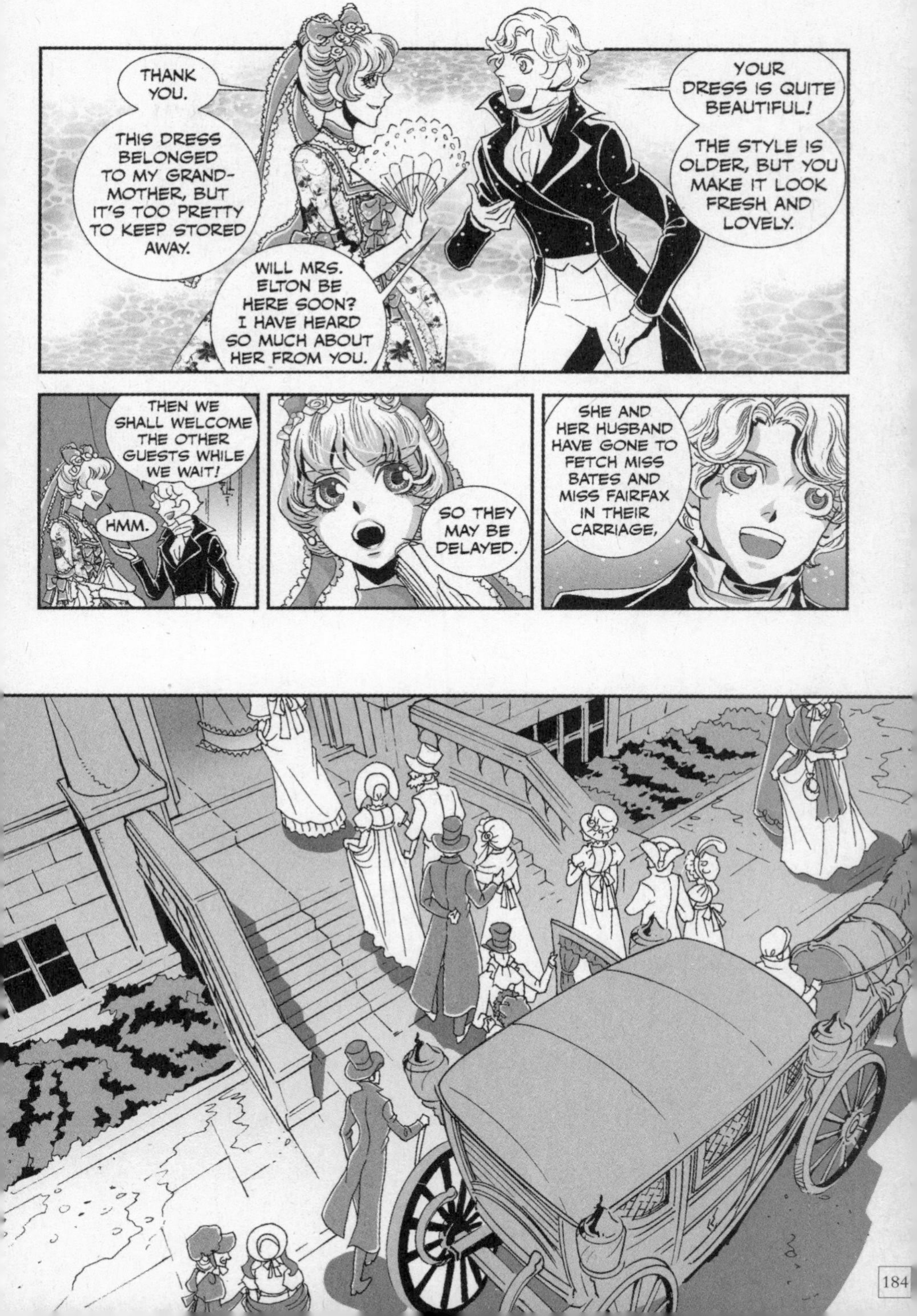
YOUR DRESS IS QUITE BEAUTIFUL!
THE STYLE IS OLDER, BUT YOU MAKE IT LOOK FRESH AND LOVELY.
THANK YOU.
THIS DRESS BELONGED TO MY GRAND-MOTHER, BUT IT'S TOO PRETTY TO KEEP STORED AWAY.
WILL MRS. ELTON BE HERE SOON? I HAVE HEARD SO MUCH ABOUT HER FROM YOU.
SHE AND HER HUSBAND HAVE GONE TO FETCH MISS BATES AND MISS FAIRFAX IN THEIR CARRIAGE,
SO THEY MAY BE DELAYED.
THEN WE SHALL WELCOME THE OTHER GUESTS WHILE WE WAIT!
HMM.

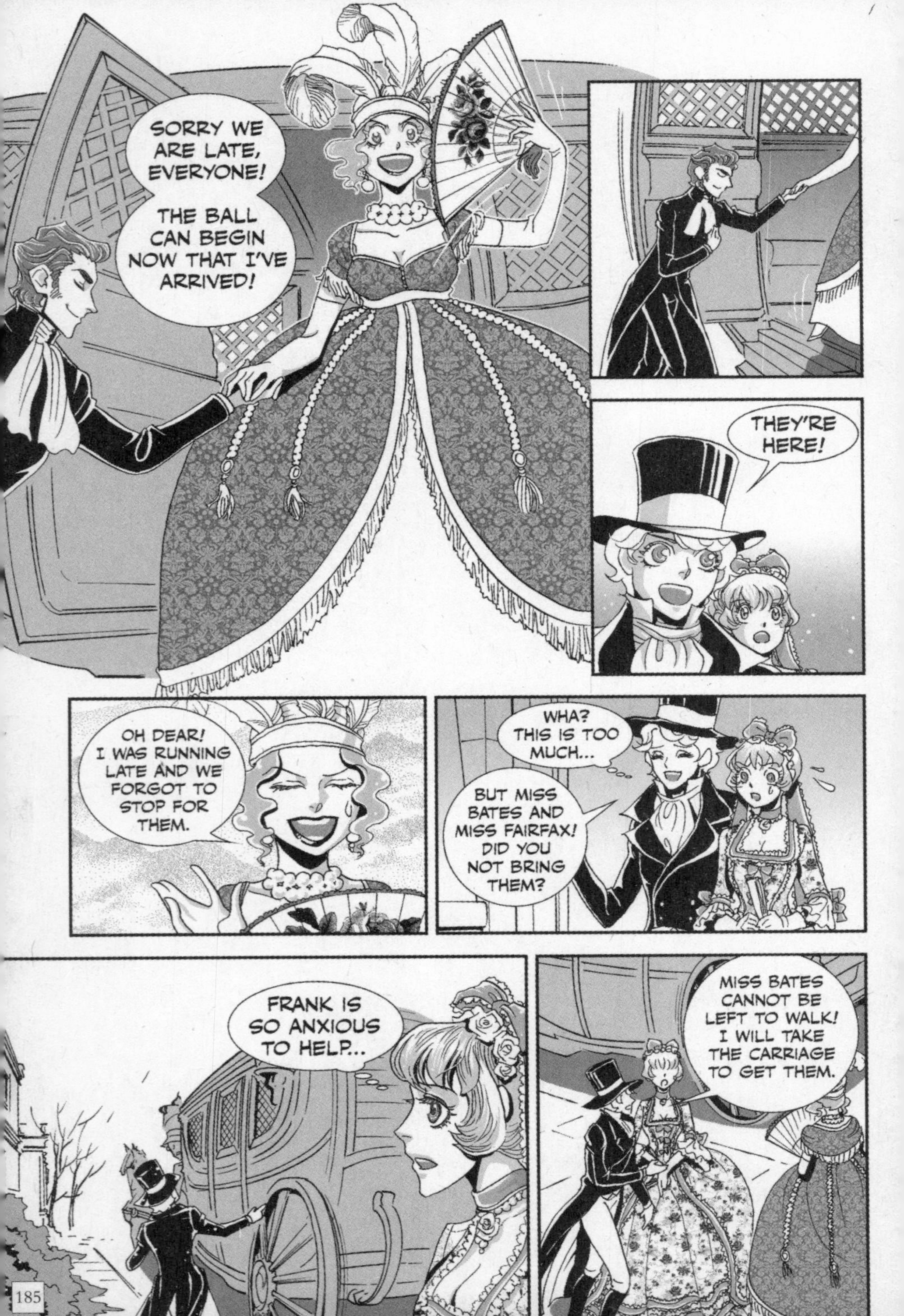
THEY'RE HERE!
SORRY WE ARE LATE, EVERYONE!
THE BALL CAN BEGIN NOW THAT I'VE ARRIVED!
WHA? THIS IS TOO MUCH...
BUT MISS BATES AND MISS FAIRFAX! DID YOU NOT BRING THEM?
OH DEAR! I WAS RUNNING LATE AND WE FORGOT TO STOP FOR THEM.
MISS BATES CANNOT BE LEFT TO WALK! I WILL TAKE THE CARRIAGE TO GET THEM.
FRANK IS SO ANXIOUS TO HELP...

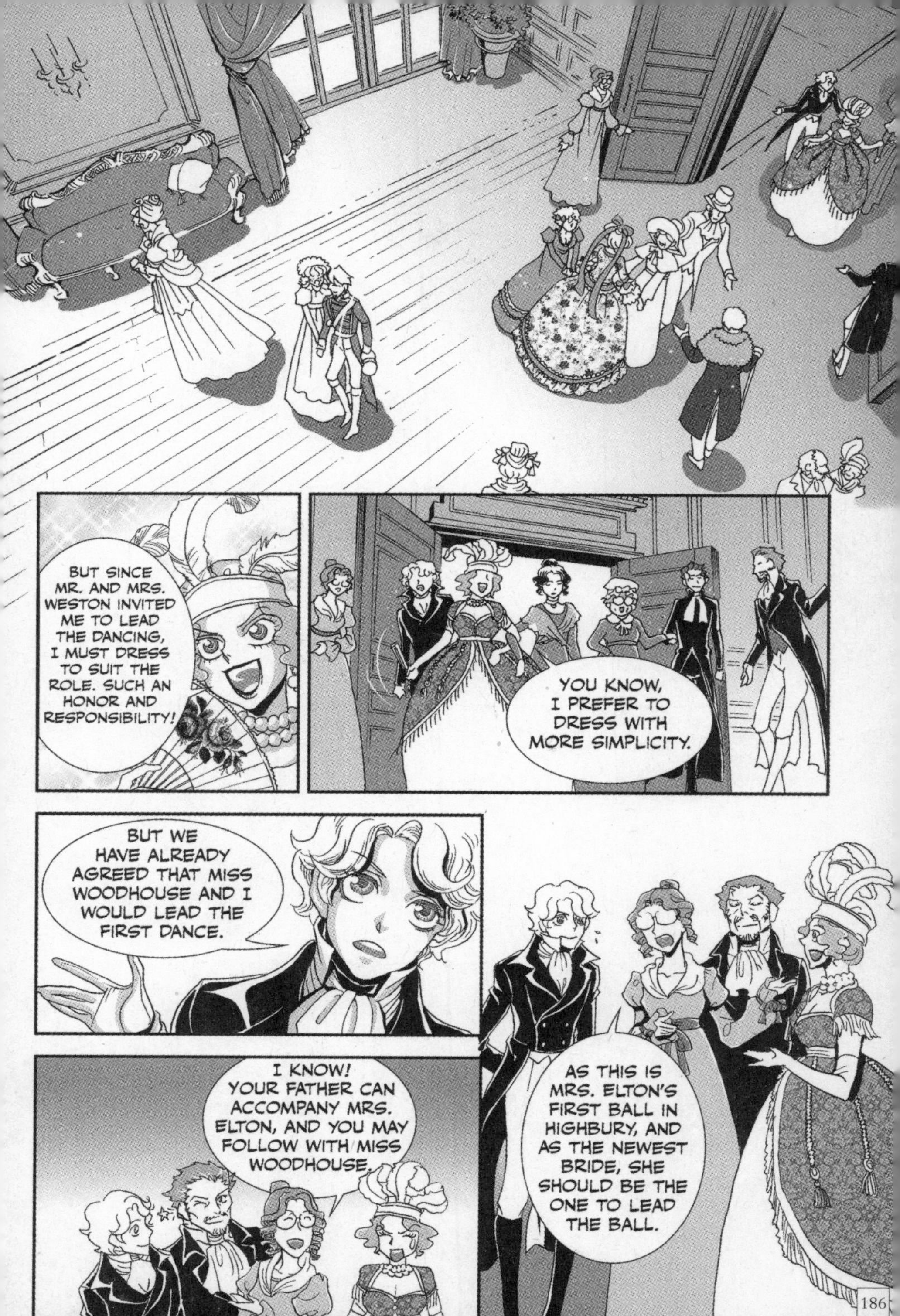
YOU KNOW, I PREFER TO DRESS WITH MORE SIMPLICITY.
BUT SINCE MR. AND MRS. WESTON INVITED ME TO LEAD THE DANCING, I MUST DRESS TO SUIT THE ROLE. SUCH AN HONOR AND RESPONSIBILITY!
AS THIS IS MRS. ELTON'S FIRST BALL IN HIGHBURY, AND AS THE NEWEST BRIDE, SHE SHOULD BE THE ONE TO LEAD THE BALL.
BUT WE HAVE ALREADY AGREED THAT MISS WOODHOUSE AND I WOULD LEAD THE FIRST DANCE.
I KNOW! YOUR FATHER CAN ACCOMPANY MRS. ELTON, AND YOU MAY FOLLOW WITH MISS WOODHOUSE.

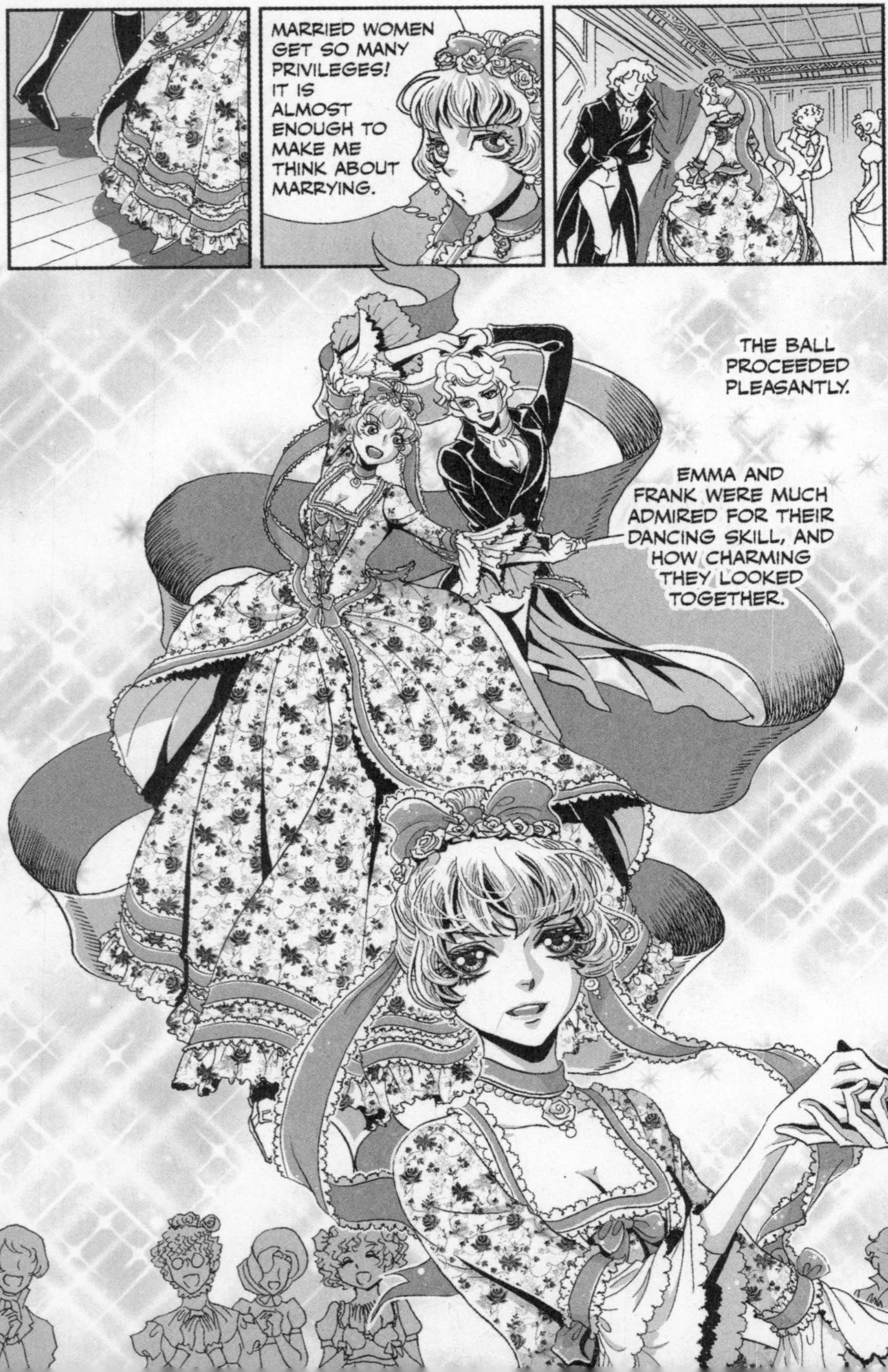
MARRIED WOMEN GET SO MANY PRIVILEGES! IT IS ALMOST ENOUGH TO MAKE ME THINK ABOUT MARRYING.
THE BALL PROCEEDED PLEASANTLY.
EMMA AND FRANK WERE MUCH ADMIRED FOR THEIR DANCING SKILL, AND HOW CHARMING THEY LOOKED TOGETHER.

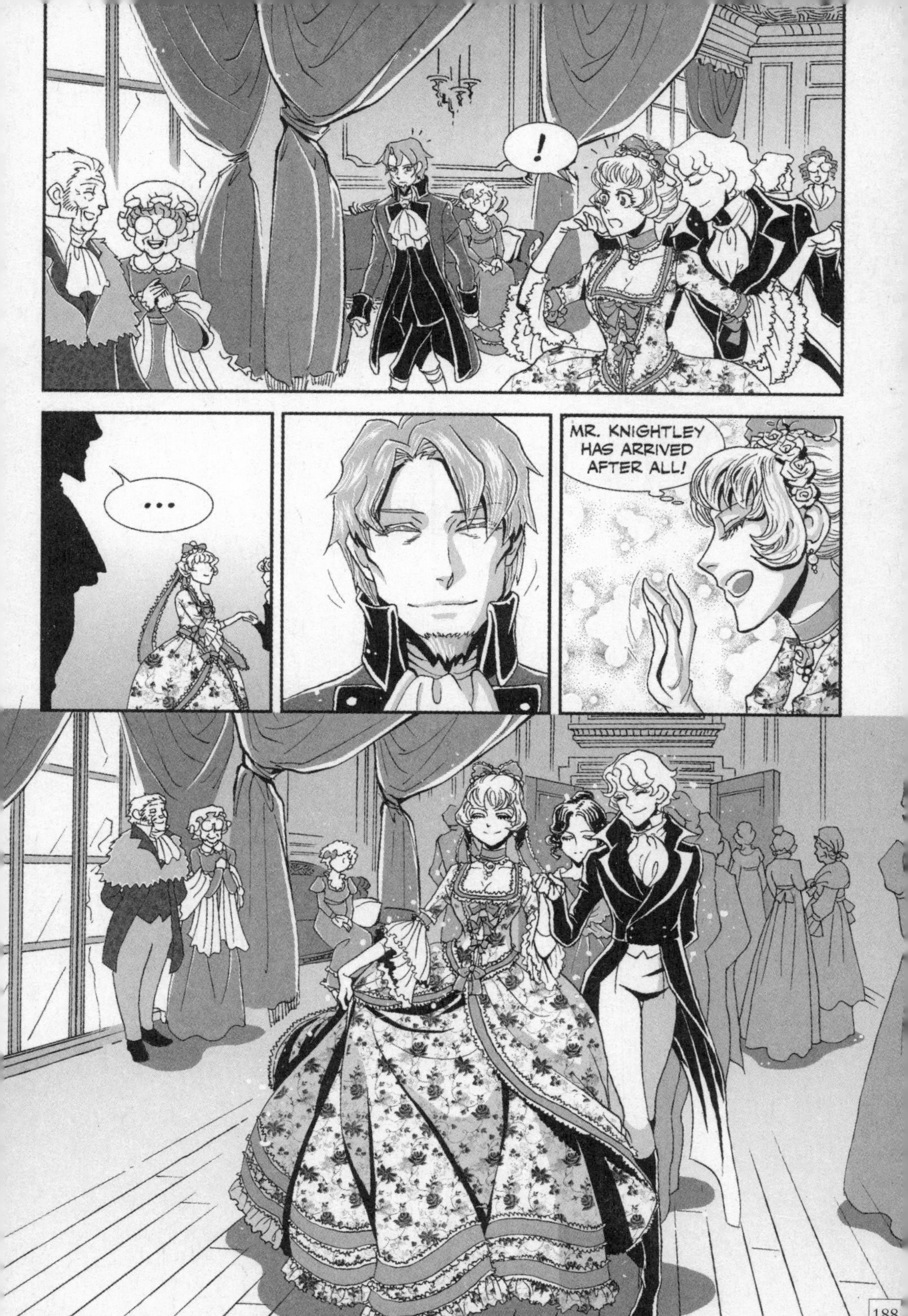
!
MR. KNIGHTLEY HAS ARRIVED AFTER ALL!
...

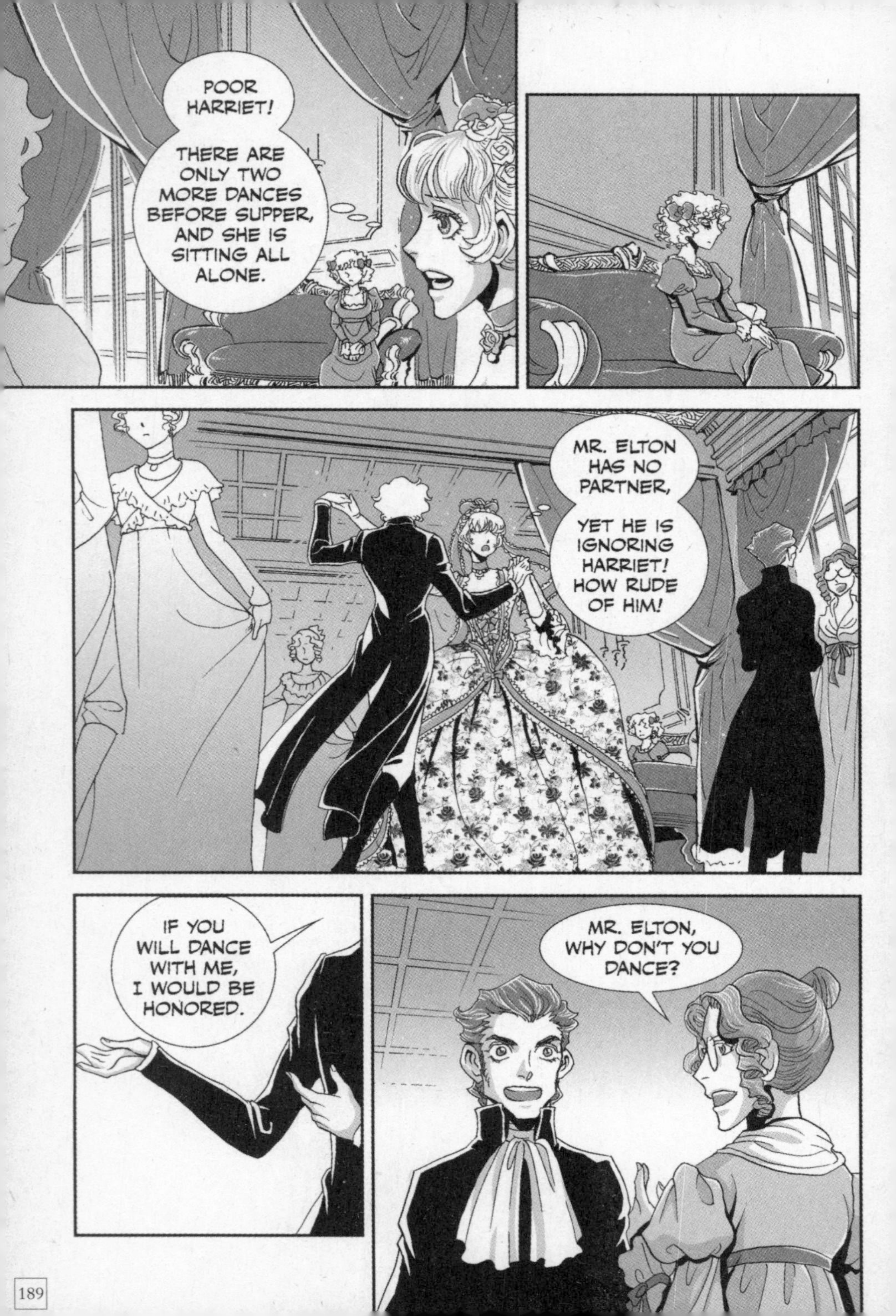
POOR HARRIET!
THERE ARE ONLY TWO MORE DANCES BEFORE SUPPER, AND SHE IS SITTING ALL ALONE.
MR. ELTON HAS NO PARTNER,
YET HE IS IGNORING HARRIET! HOW RUDE OF HIM!
MR. ELTON, WHY DON'T YOU DANCE?
IF YOU WILL DANCE WITH ME, I WOULD BE HONORED.

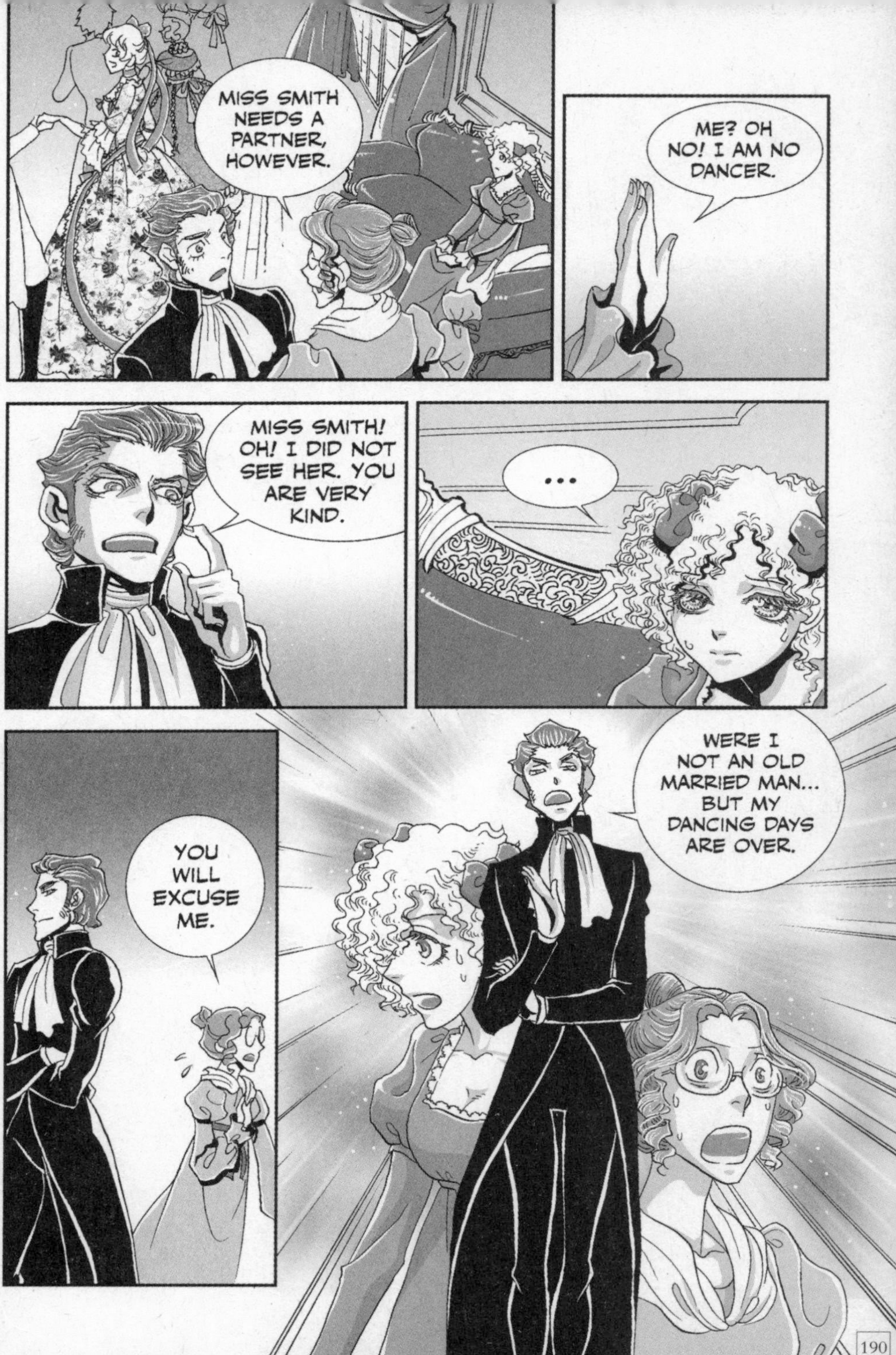
ME? OH NO! I AM NO DANCER.
MISS SMITH NEEDS A PARTNER, HOWEVER.
...
MISS SMITH! OH! I DID NOT SEE HER. YOU ARE VERY KIND.
WERE I NOT AN OLD MARRIED MAN... BUT MY DANCING DAYS ARE OVER.
YOU WILL EXCUSE ME.

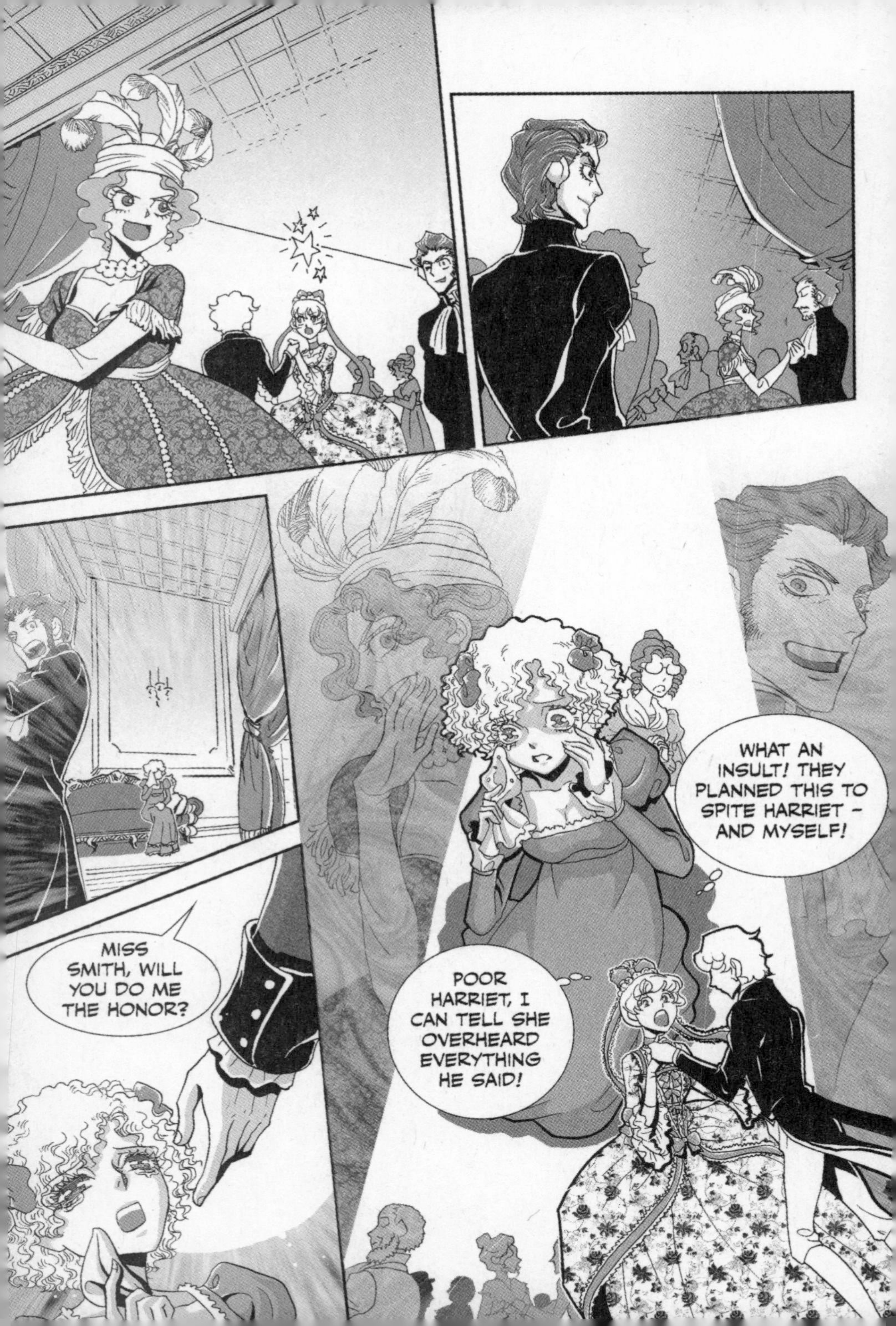
WHAT AN INSULT! THEY PLANNED THIS TO SPITE HARRIET - AND MYSELF!
POOR HARRIET, I CAN TELL SHE OVERHEARD EVERYTHING HE SAID!
MISS SMITH, WILL YOU DO ME THE HONOR?

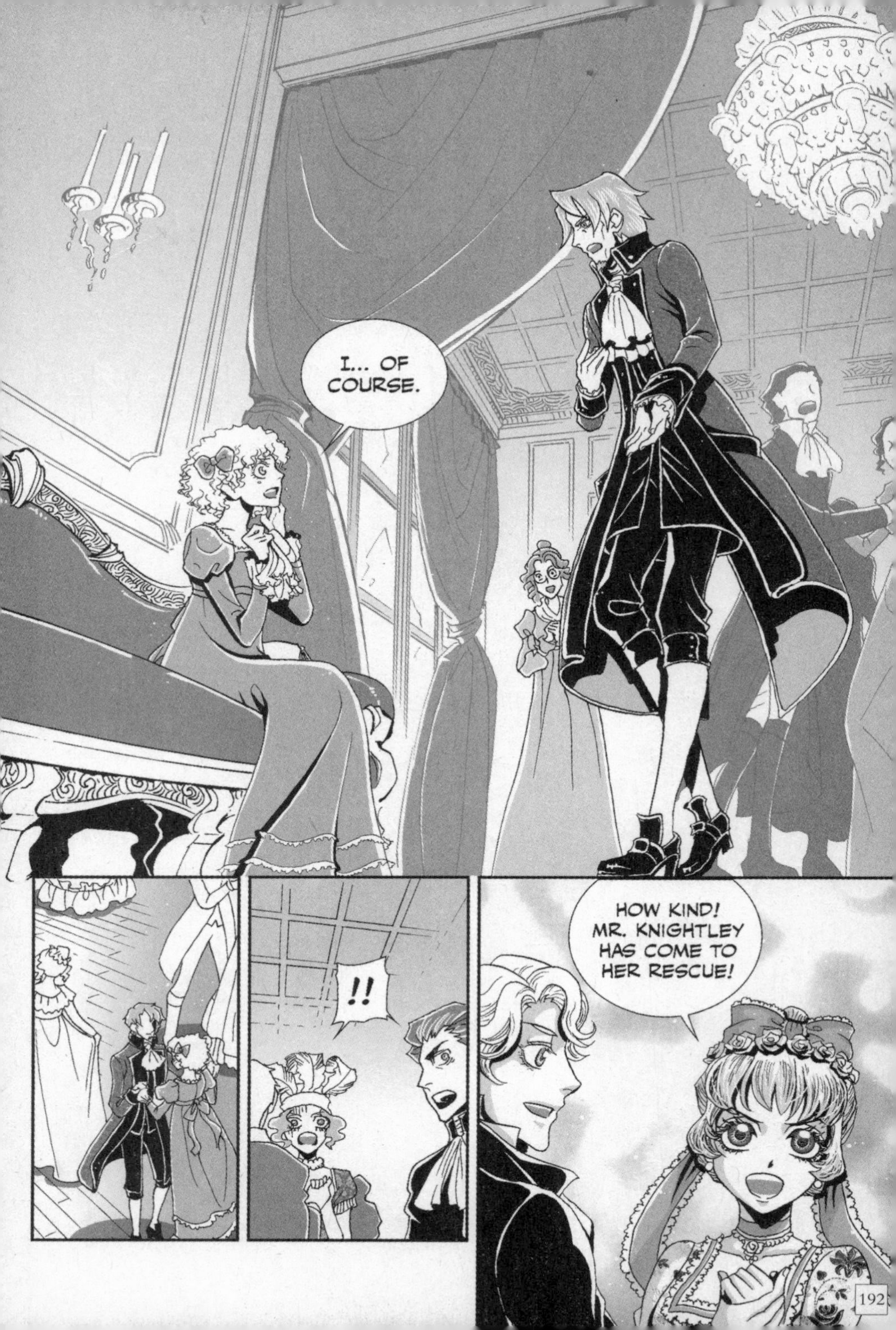
I... OF COURSE.
HOW KIND! MR. KNIGHTLEY HAS COME TO HER RESCUE!
!!

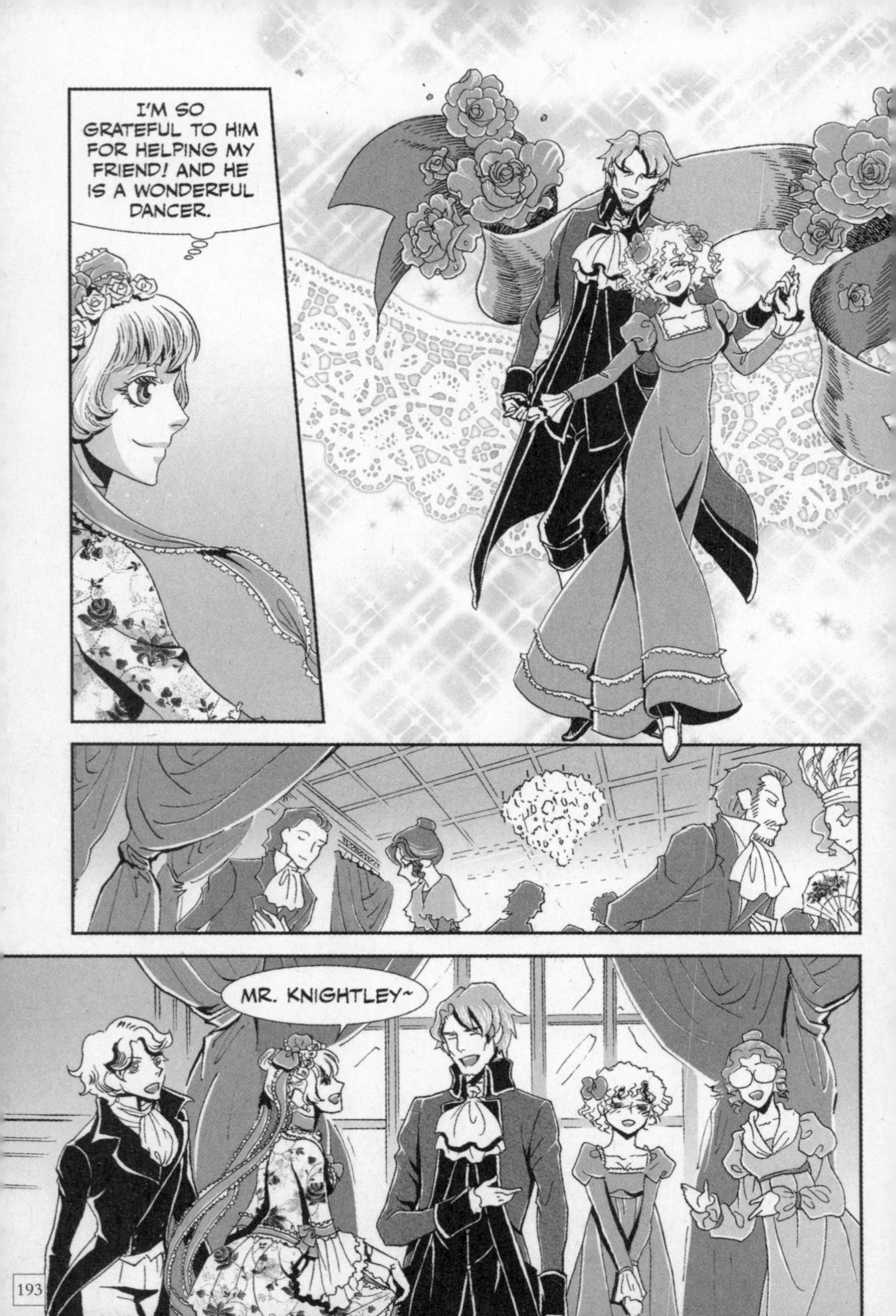
I'M SO GRATEFUL TO HIM FOR HELPING MY FRIEND! AND HE IS A WONDERFUL DANCER.
MR. KNIGHTLEY~

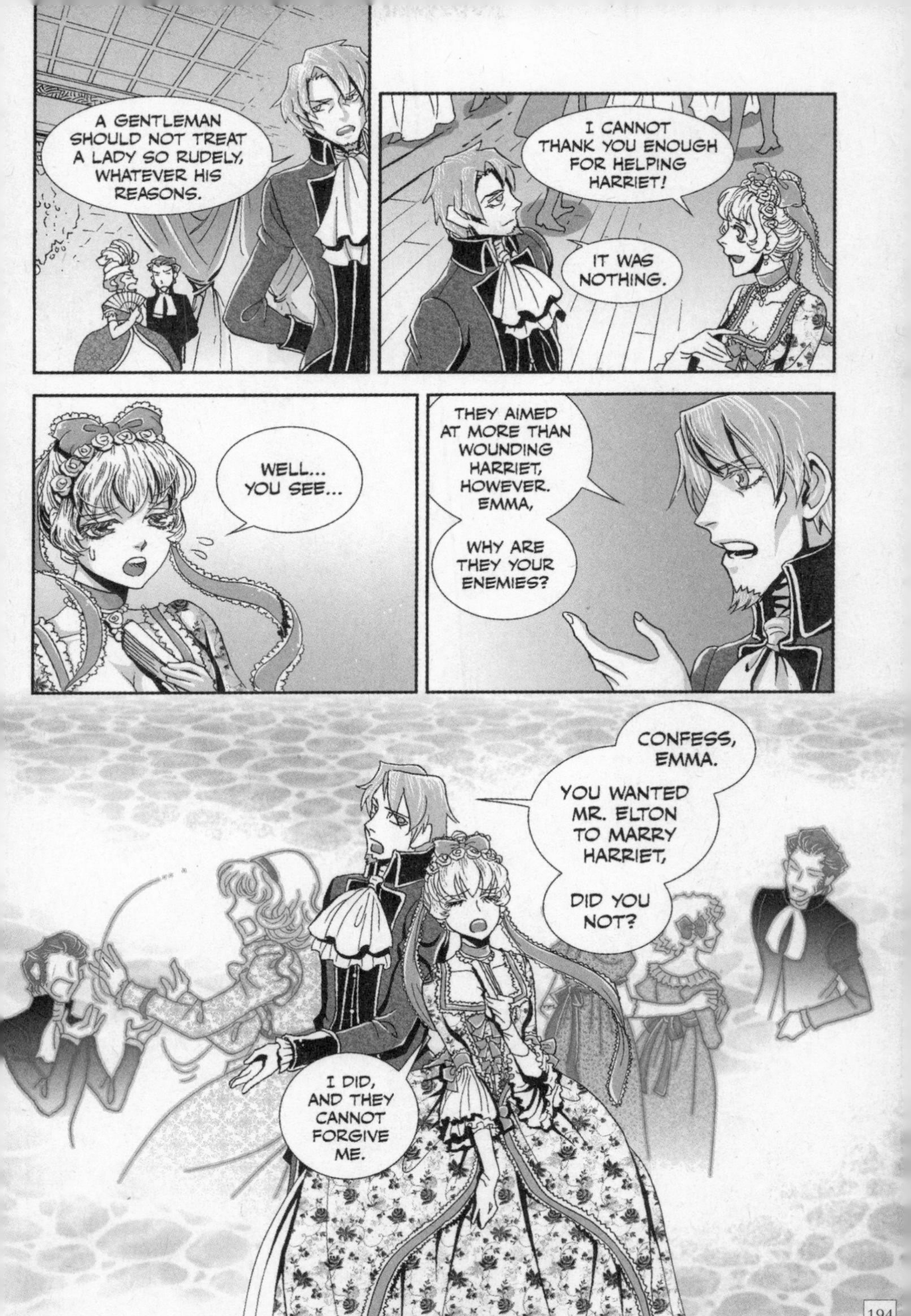
I CANNOT THANK YOU ENOUGH FOR HELPING HARRIET!
IT WAS NOTHING.
A GENTLEMAN SHOULD NOT TREAT A LADY SO RUDELY, WHATEVER HIS REASONS.
THEY AIMED AT MORE THAN WOUNDING HARRIET, HOWEVER. EMMA,
WHY ARE THEY YOUR ENEMIES?
WELL... YOU SEE...
CONFESS, EMMA.
YOU WANTED MR. ELTON TO MARRY HARRIET,
DID YOU NOT?
I DID, AND THEY CANNOT FORGIVE ME.

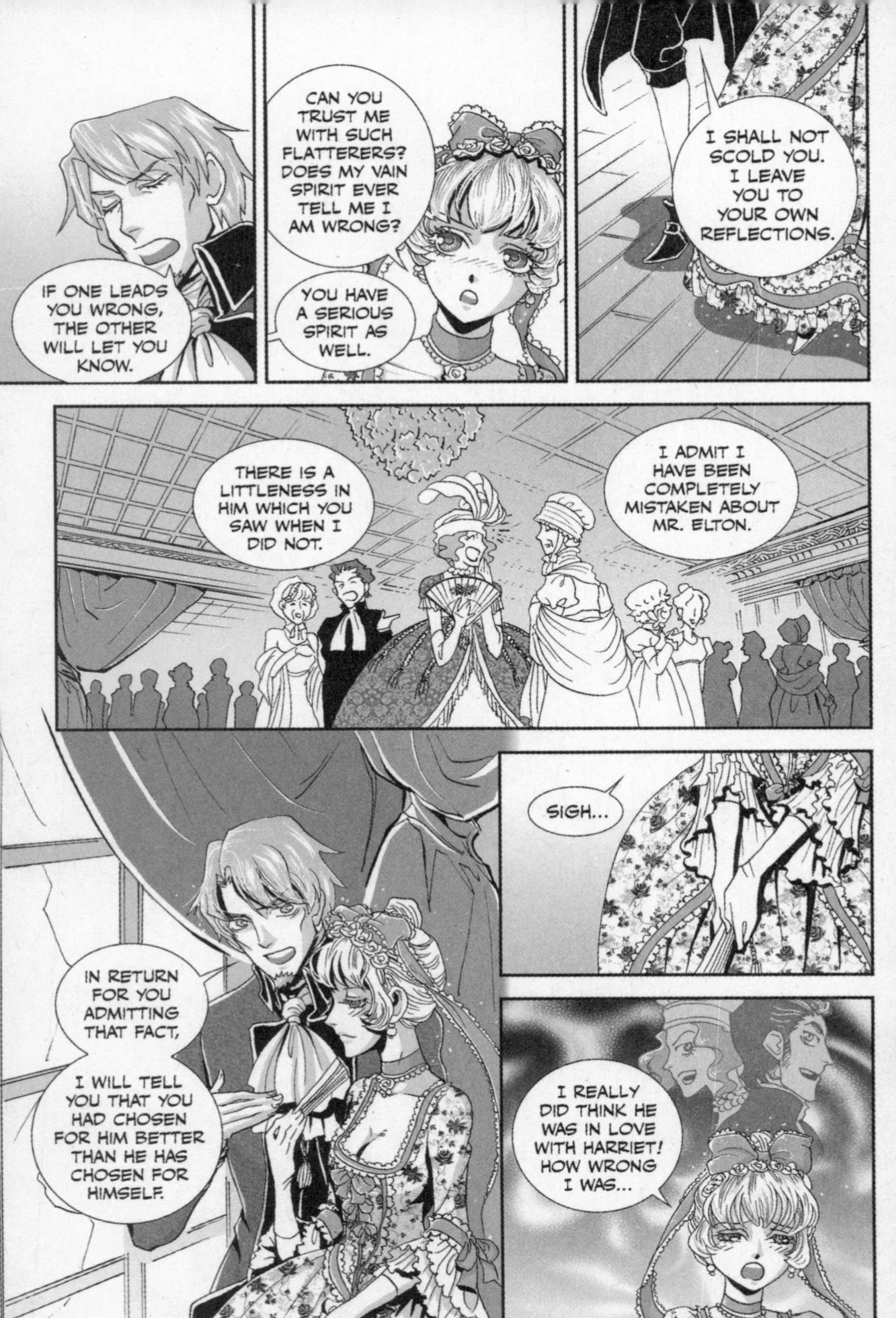
I SHALL NOT SCOLD YOU. I LEAVE YOU TO YOUR OWN REFLECTIONS.
CAN YOU TRUST ME WITH SUCH FLATTERERS? DOES MY VAIN SPIRIT EVER TELL ME I AM WRONG?
YOU HAVE A SERIOUS SPIRIT AS WELL.
IF ONE LEADS YOU WRONG, THE OTHER WILL LET YOU KNOW.
I ADMIT I HAVE BEEN COMPLETELY MISTAKEN ABOUT MR. ELTON.
THERE IS A LITTLENESS IN HIM WHICH YOU SAW WHEN I DID NOT.
SIGH...
I REALLY DID THINK HE WAS IN LOVE WITH HARRIET! HOW WRONG I WAS...
IN RETURN FOR YOU ADMITTING THAT FACT,
I WILL TELL YOU THAT YOU HAD CHOSEN FOR HIM BETTER THAN HE HAS CHOSEN FOR HIMSELF.

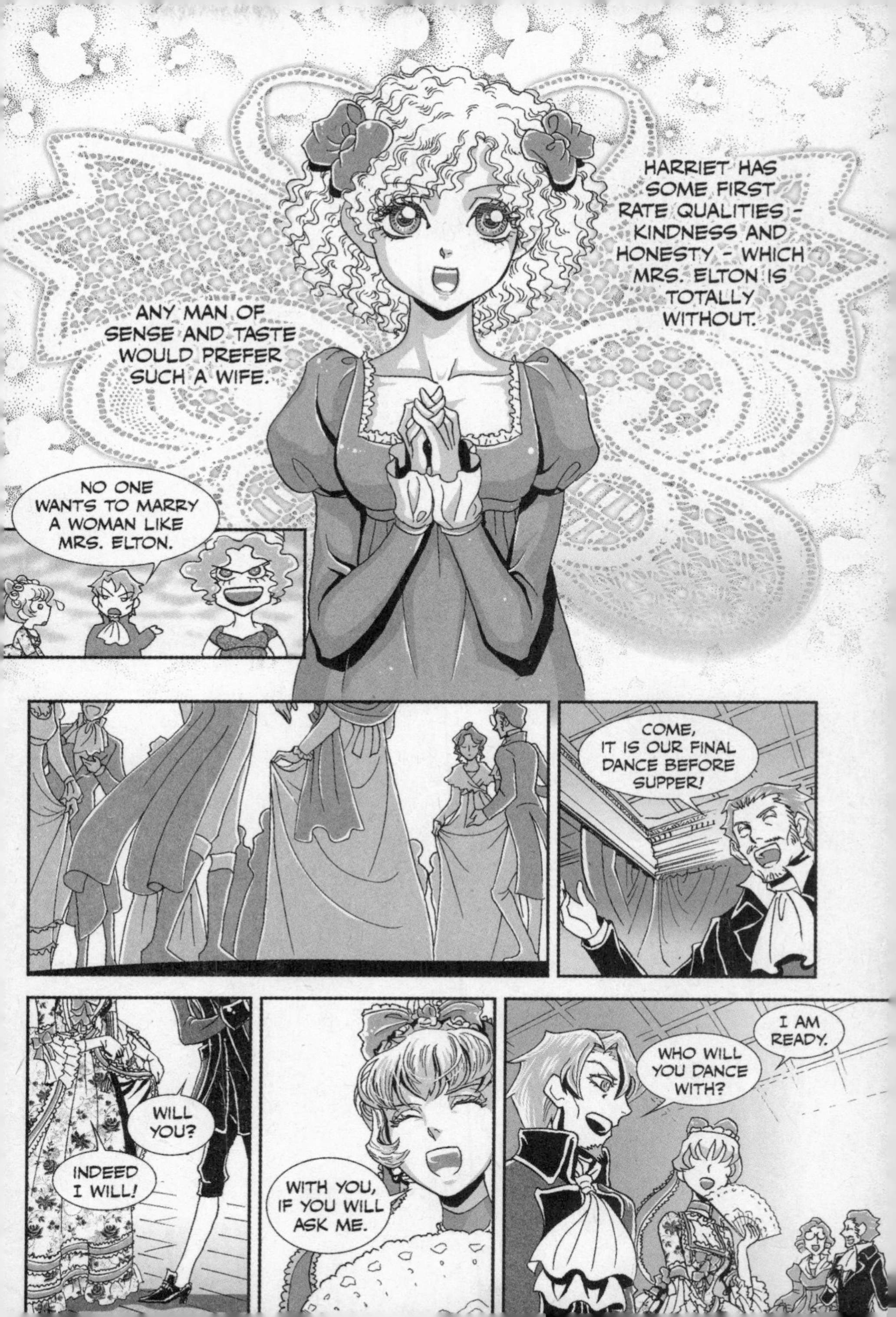
HARRIET HAS SOME FIRST RATE QUALITIES - KINDNESS AND HONESTY - WHICH MRS. ELTON IS TOTALLY WITHOUT.
ANY MAN OF SENSE AND TASTE WOULD PREFER SUCH A WIFE.
NO ONE WANTS TO MARRY A WOMAN LIKE MRS. ELTON.
COME, IT IS OUR FINAL DANCE BEFORE SUPPER!
I AM READY.
WHO WILL YOU DANCE WITH?
WITH YOU, IF YOU WILL ASK ME.
WILL YOU?
INDEED I WILL!

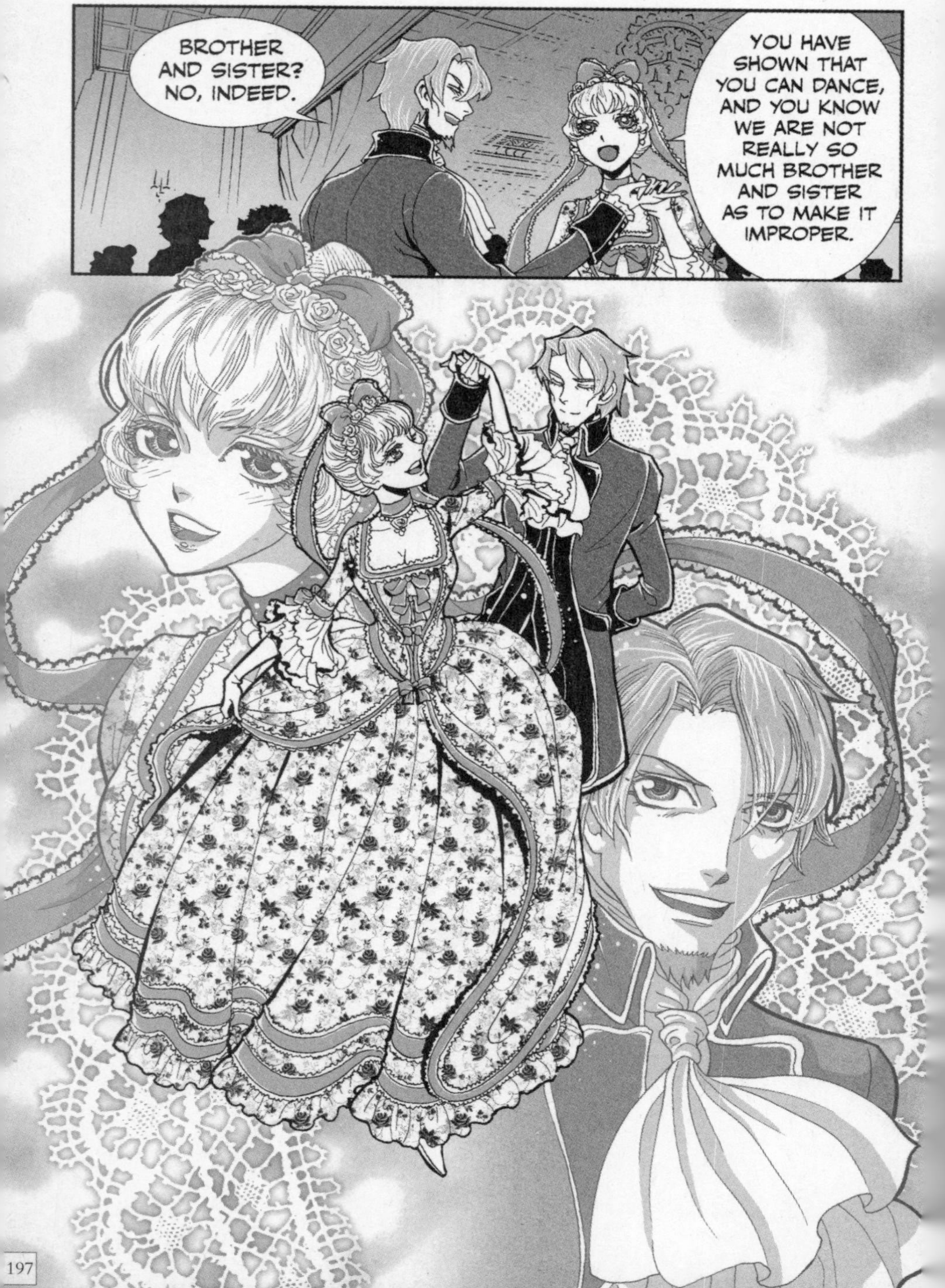
YOU HAVE SHOWN THAT YOU CAN DANCE, AND YOU KNOW WE ARE NOT REALLY SO MUCH BROTHER AND SISTER AS TO MAKE IT IMPROPER.
BROTHER AND SISTER? NO, INDEED.

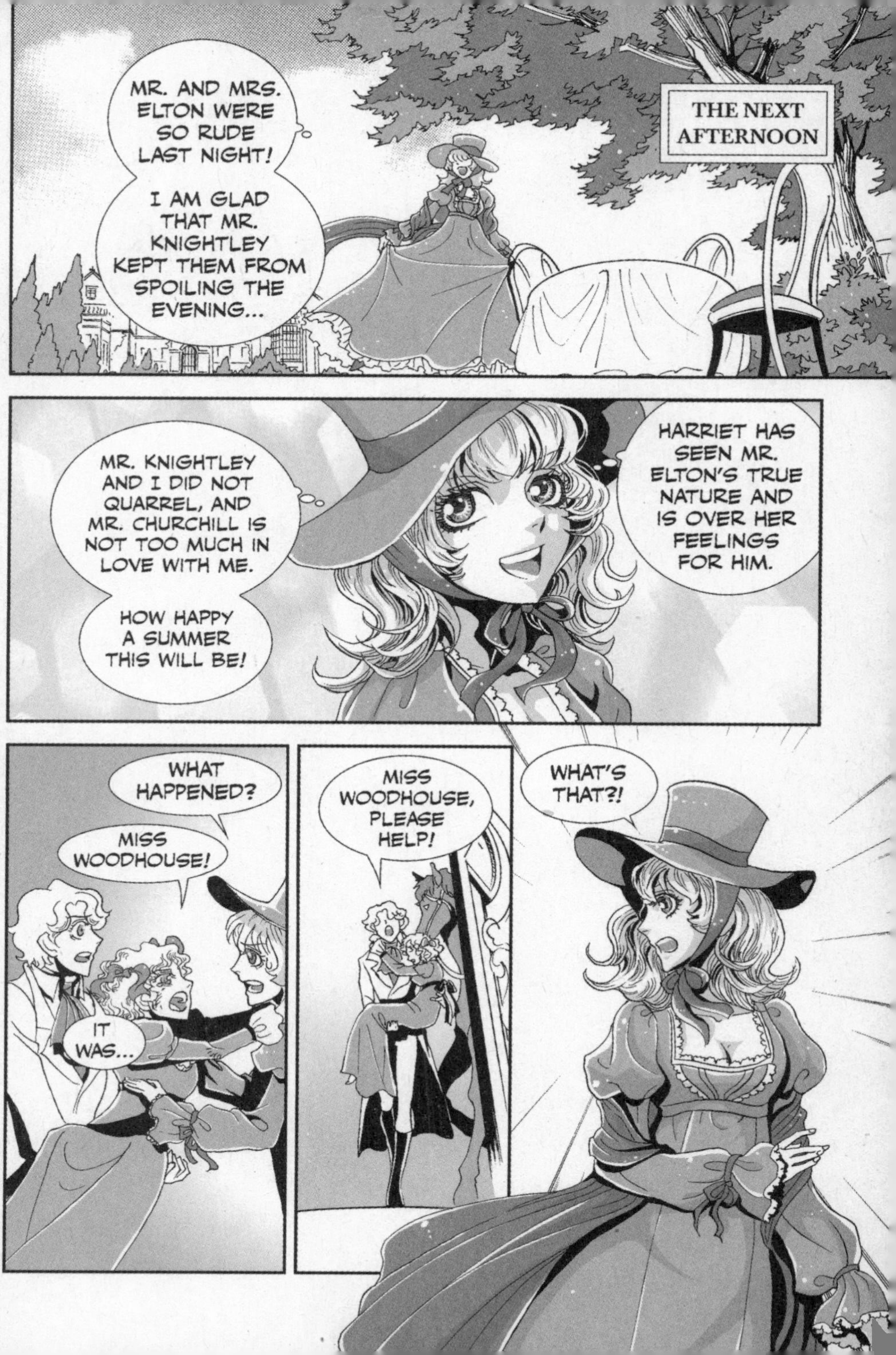
THE NEXT AFTERNOON
MR. AND MRS. ELTON WERE SO RUDE LAST NIGHT!
I AM GLAD THAT MR. KNIGHTLEY KEPT THEM FROM SPOILING THE EVENING...
HARRIET HAS SEEN MR. ELTON'S TRUE NATURE AND IS OVER HER FEELINGS FOR HIM.
MR. KNIGHTLEY AND I DID NOT QUARREL, AND MR. CHURCHILL IS NOT TOO MUCH IN LOVE WITH ME.
HOW HAPPY A SUMMER THIS WILL BE!
WHAT'S THAT?!
MISS WOODHOUSE, PLEASE HELP!
WHAT HAPPENED?
MISS WOODHOUSE!
IT WAS...

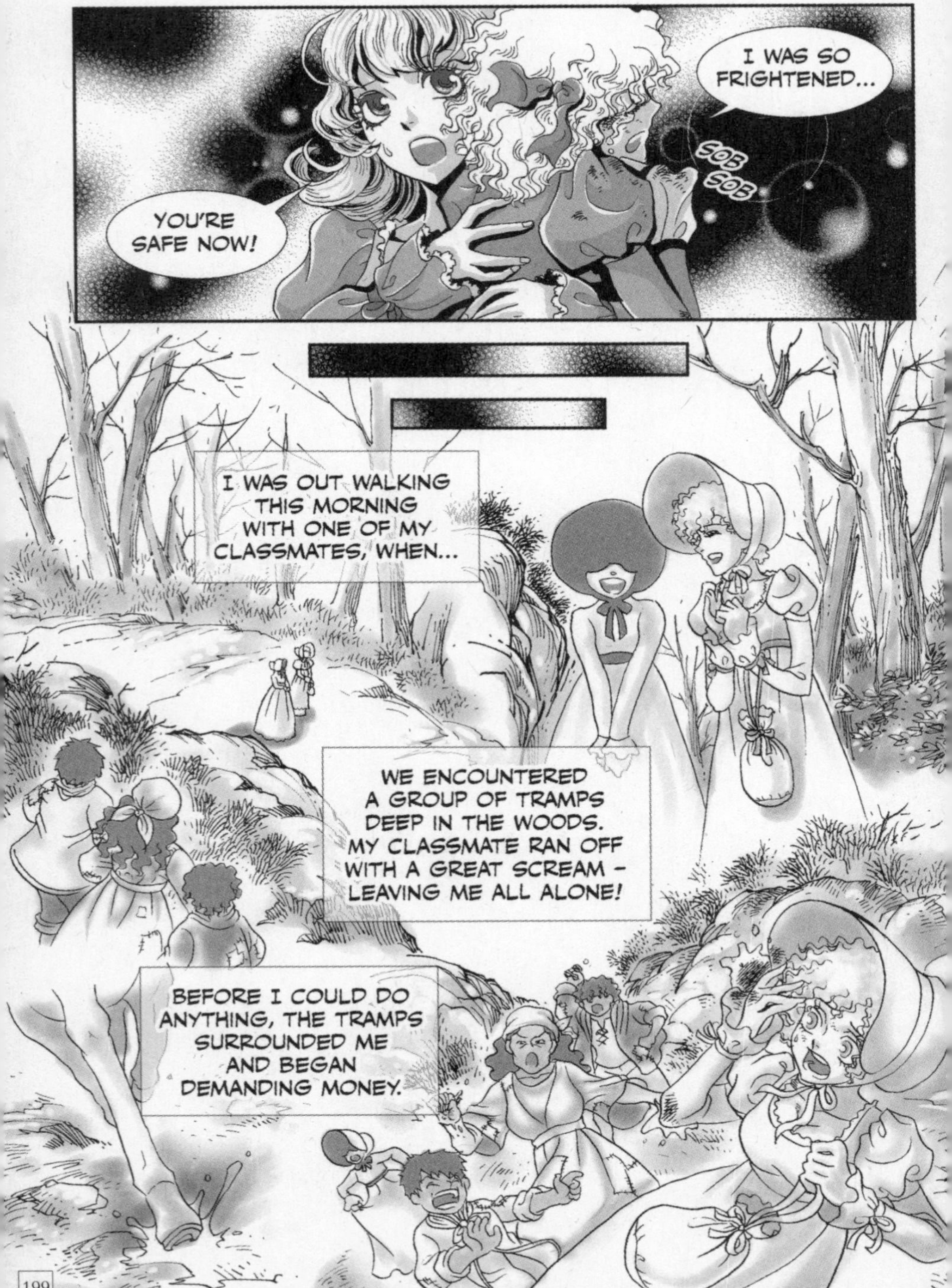
I WAS SO FRIGHTENED...
SOB SOB
YOU'RE SAFE NOW!
I WAS OUT WALKING THIS MORNING WITH ONE OF MY CLASSMATES, WHEN...
WE ENCOUNTERED A GROUP OF TRAMPS DEEP IN THE WOODS. MY CLASSMATE RAN OFF WITH A GREAT SCREAM - LEAVING ME ALL ALONE!
BEFORE I COULD DO ANYTHING, THE TRAMPS SURROUNDED ME AND BEGAN DEMANDING MONEY.

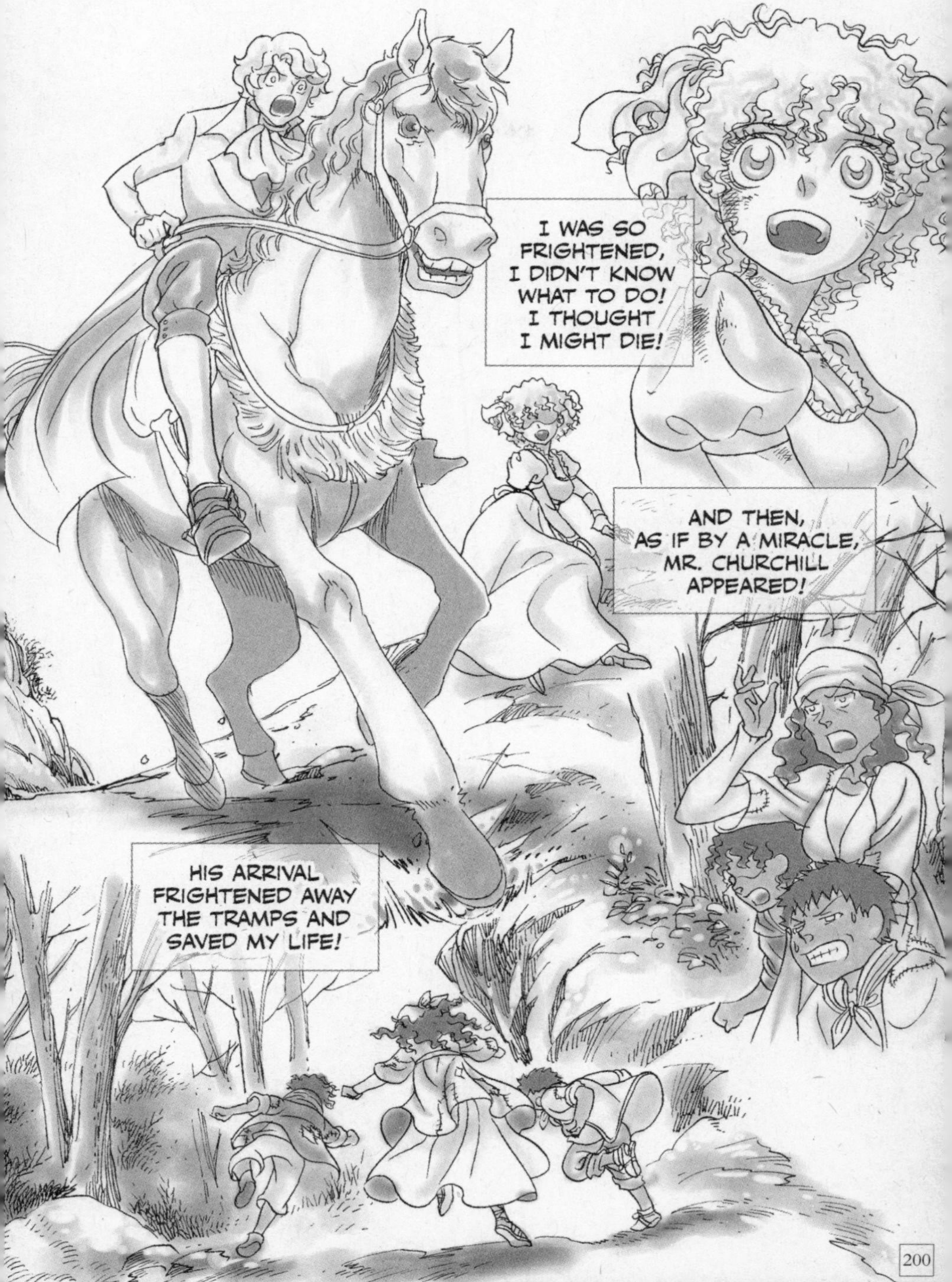
I WAS SO FRIGHTENED, I DIDN'T KNOW WHAT TO DO! I THOUGHT I MIGHT DIE!
AND THEN, AS IF BY A MIRACLE, MR. CHURCHILL APPEARED!
HIS ARRIVAL FRIGHTENED AWAY THE TRAMPS AND SAVED MY LIFE!

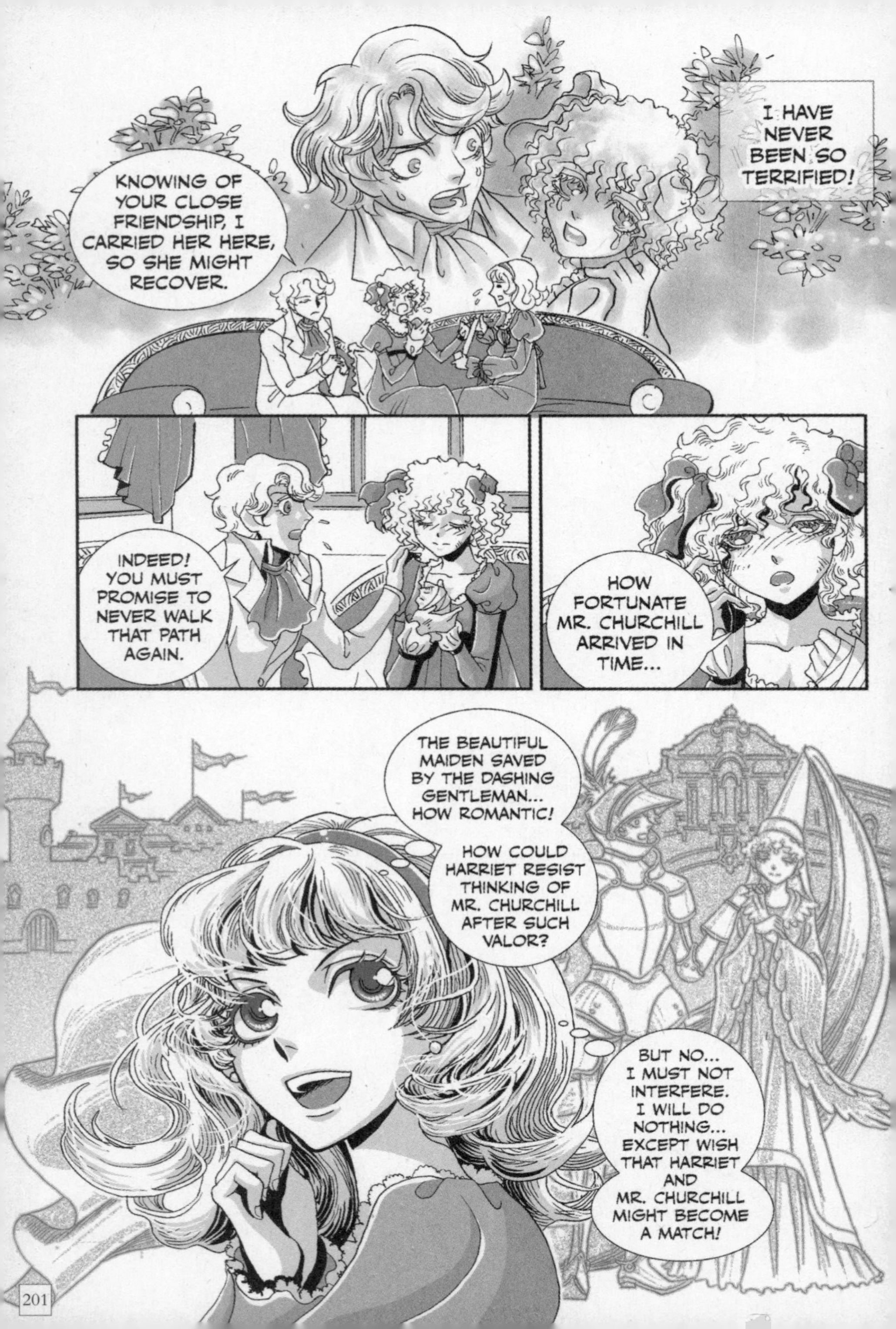
I HAVE NEVER BEEN SO TERRIFIED!
KNOWING OF YOUR CLOSE FRIENDSHIP, I CARRIED HER HERE, SO SHE MIGHT RECOVER.
HOW FORTUNATE MR. CHURCHILL ARRIVED IN TIME...
INDEED! YOU MUST PROMISE TO NEVER WALK THAT PATH AGAIN.
THE BEAUTIFUL MAIDEN SAVED BY THE DASHING GENTLEMAN... HOW ROMANTIC!
HOW COULD HARRIET RESIST THINKING OF MR. CHURCHILL AFTER SUCH VALOR?
BUT NO... I MUST NOT INTERFERE. I WILL DO NOTHING... EXCEPT WISH THAT HARRIET AND MR. CHURCHILL MIGHT BECOME A MATCH!

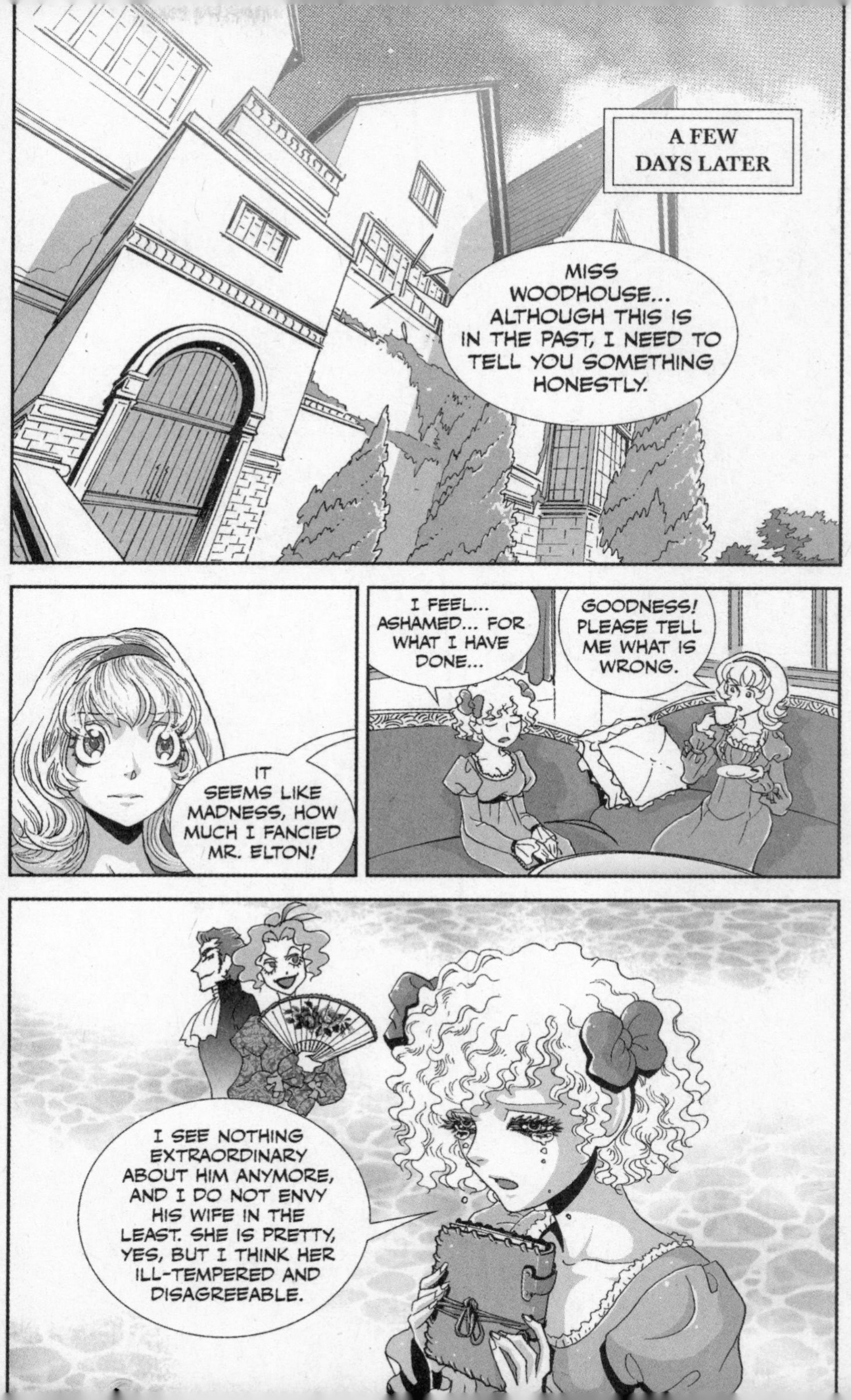

A FEW DAYS LATER
MISS WOODHOUSE... ALTHOUGH THIS IS IN THE PAST, I NEED TO TELL YOU SOMETHING HONESTLY.
GOODNESS! PLEASE TELL ME WHAT IS WRONG.
I FEEL... ASHAMED... FOR WHAT I HAVE DONE...
IT SEEMS LIKE MADNESS, HOW MUCH I FANCIED MR. ELTON!
I SEE NOTHING EXTRAORDINARY ABOUT HIM ANYMORE, AND I DO NOT ENVY HIS WIFE IN THE LEAST. SHE IS PRETTY, YES, BUT I THINK HER ILL-TEMPERED AND DISAGREEABLE.

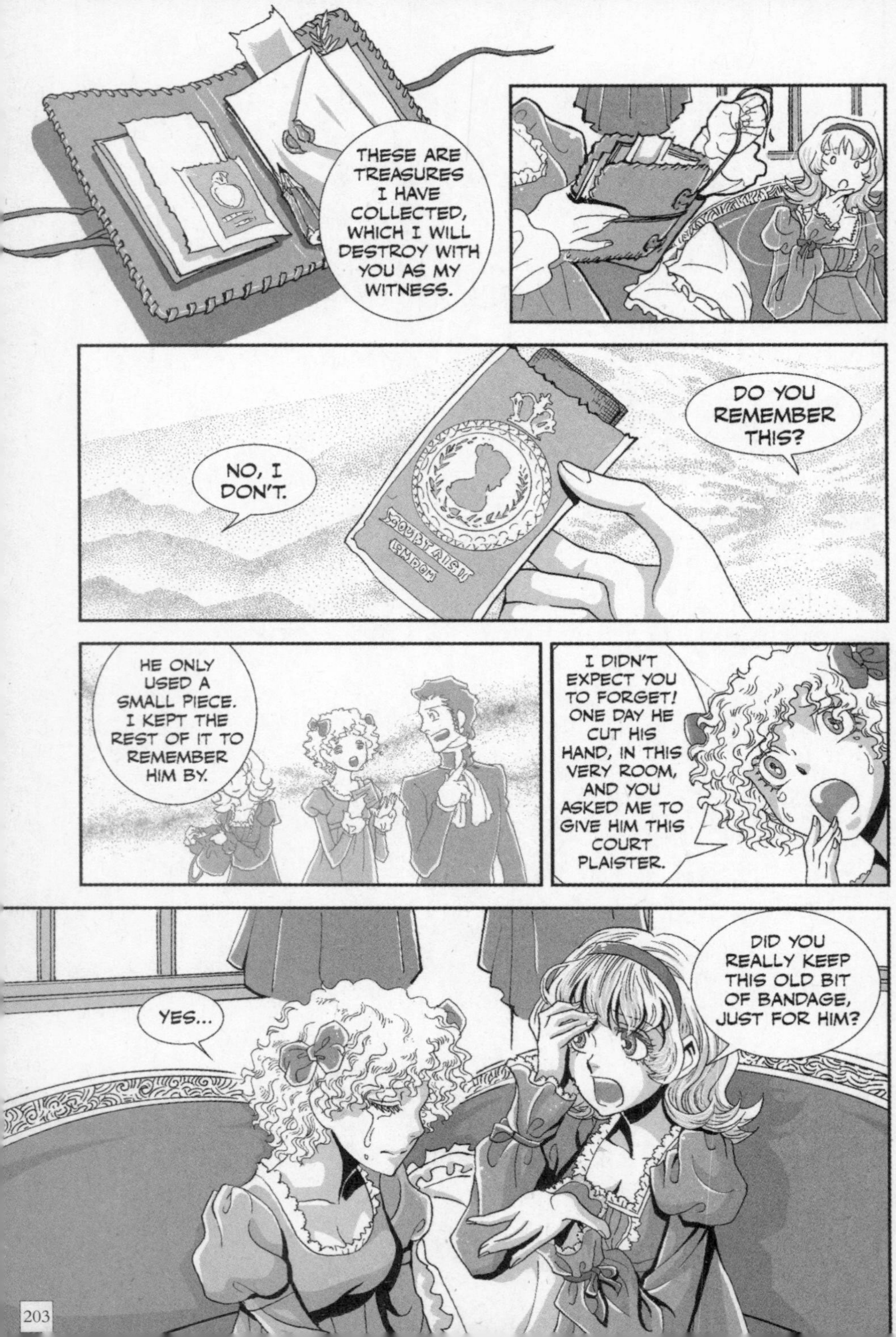
THESE ARE TREASURES I HAVE COLLECTED, WHICH I WILL DESTROY WITH YOU AS MY WITNESS.
DO YOU REMEMBER THIS?
NO, I DON'T.
I DIDN'T EXPECT YOU TO FORGET! ONE DAY HE CUT HIS HAND, IN THIS VERY ROOM, AND YOU ASKED ME TO GIVE HIM THIS COURT PLAISTER.
HE ONLY USED A SMALL PIECE. I KEPT THE REST OF IT TO REMEMBER HIM BY.
DID YOU REALLY KEEP THIS OLD BIT OF BANDAGE, JUST FOR HIM?
YES...

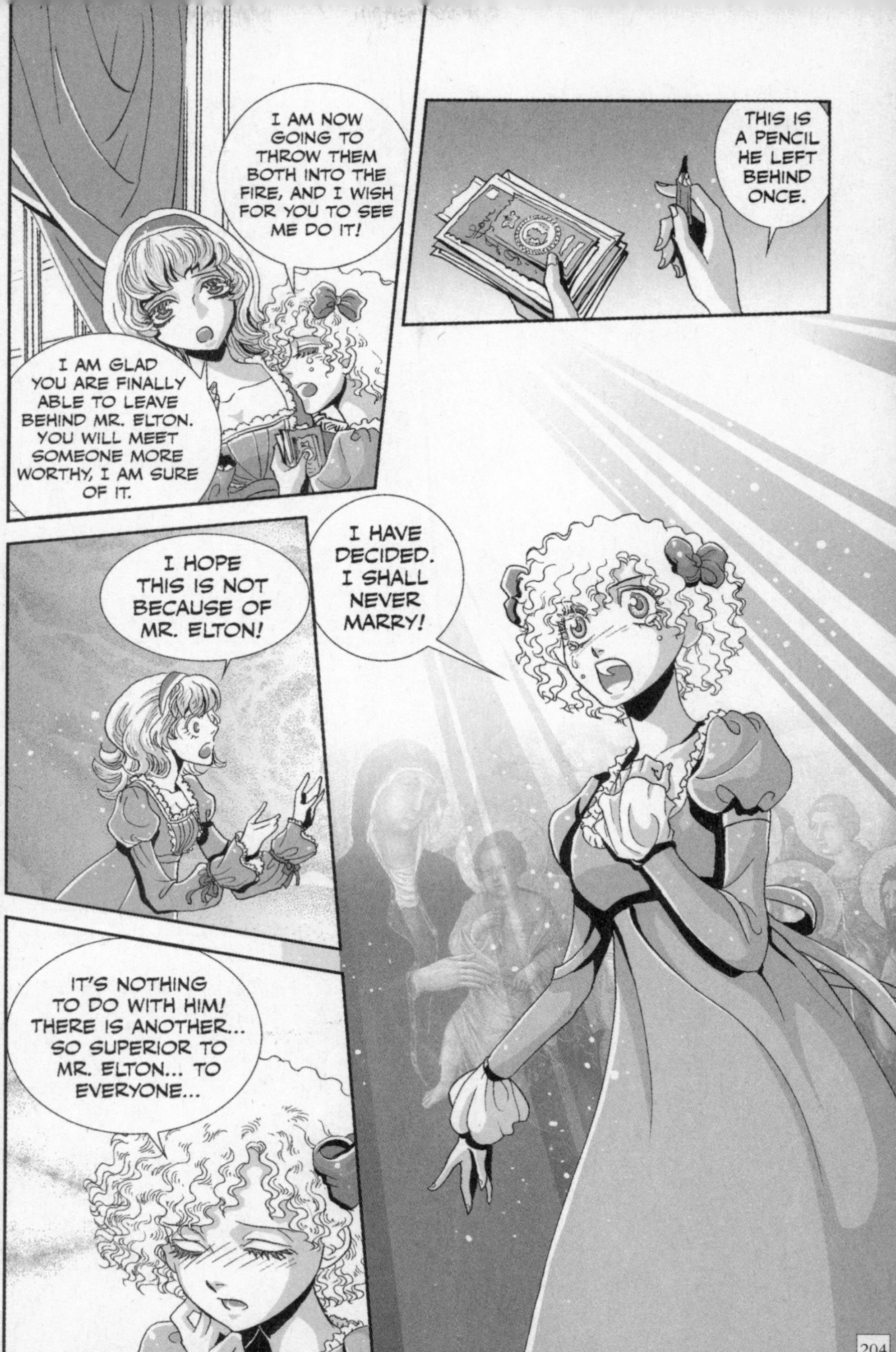
THIS IS A PENCIL HE LEFT BEHIND ONCE.
I AM NOW GOING TO THROW THEM BOTH INTO THE FIRE, AND I WISH FOR YOU TO SEE ME DO IT!
I AM GLAD YOU ARE FINALLY ABLE TO LEAVE BEHIND MR. ELTON. YOU WILL MEET SOMEONE MORE WORTHY, I AM SURE OF IT.
I HAVE DECIDED. I SHALL NEVER MARRY!
I HOPE THIS IS NOT BECAUSE OF MR. ELTON!
IT'S NOTHING TO DO WITH HIM! THERE IS ANOTHER... SO SUPERIOR TO MR. ELTON... TO EVERYONE...

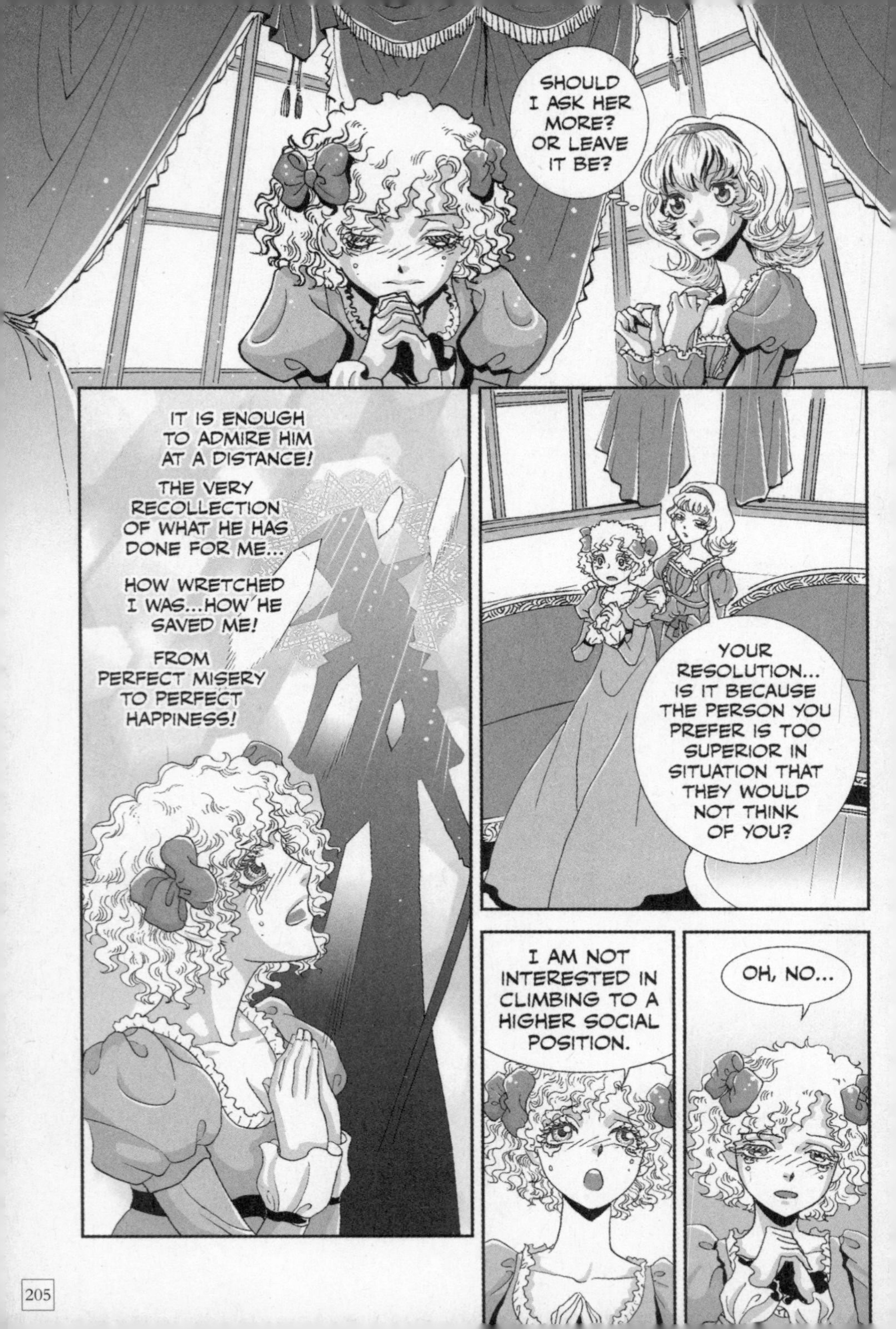
SHOULD I ASK HER MORE? OR LEAVE IT BE?
YOUR RESOLUTION... IS IT BECAUSE THE PERSON YOU PREFER IS TOO SUPERIOR IN SITUATION THAT THEY WOULD NOT THINK OF YOU?
OH, NO...
I AM NOT INTERESTED IN CLIMBING TO A HIGHER SOCIAL POSITION.
IT IS ENOUGH TO ADMIRE HIM AT A DISTANCE!
THE VERY RECOLLECTION OF WHAT HE HAS DONE FOR ME...
HOW WRETCHED I WAS...HOW HE SAVED ME!
FROM PERFECT MISERY TO PERFECT HAPPINESS!

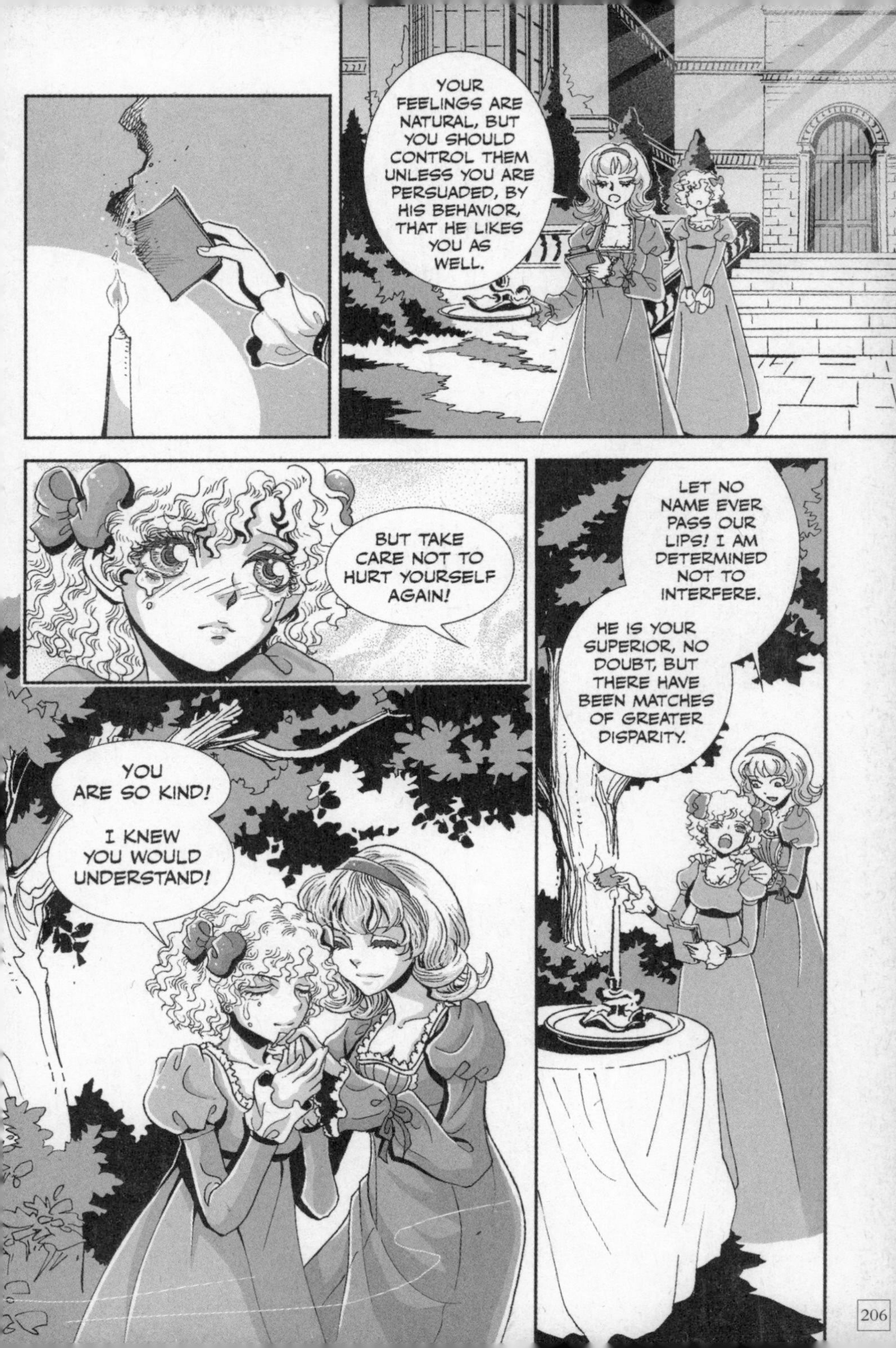

YOUR FEELINGS ARE NATURAL, BUT YOU SHOULD CONTROL THEM UNLESS YOU ARE PERSUADED, BY HIS BEHAVIOR, THAT HE LIKES YOU AS WELL.
LET NO NAME EVER PASS OUR LIPS! I AM DETERMINED NOT TO INTERFERE.
HE IS YOUR SUPERIOR, NO DOUBT, BUT THERE HAVE BEEN MATCHES OF GREATER DISPARITY.
BUT TAKE CARE NOT TO HURT YOURSELF AGAIN!
YOU ARE SO KIND!
I KNEW YOU WOULD UNDERSTAND!

CHARACTER MODEL SHEET

Jane Fairfax
164cm

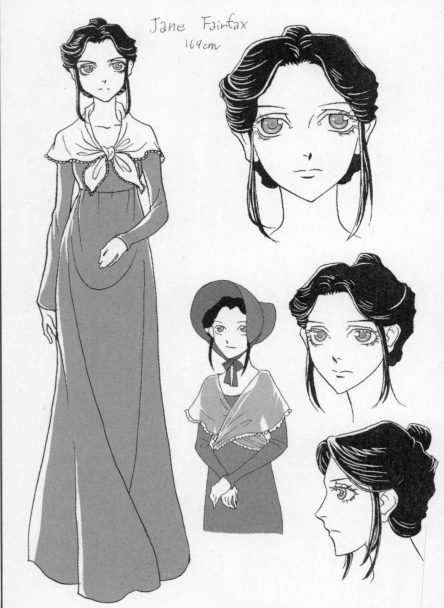

Jane Fairfax

CHARACTER MODEL SHEET

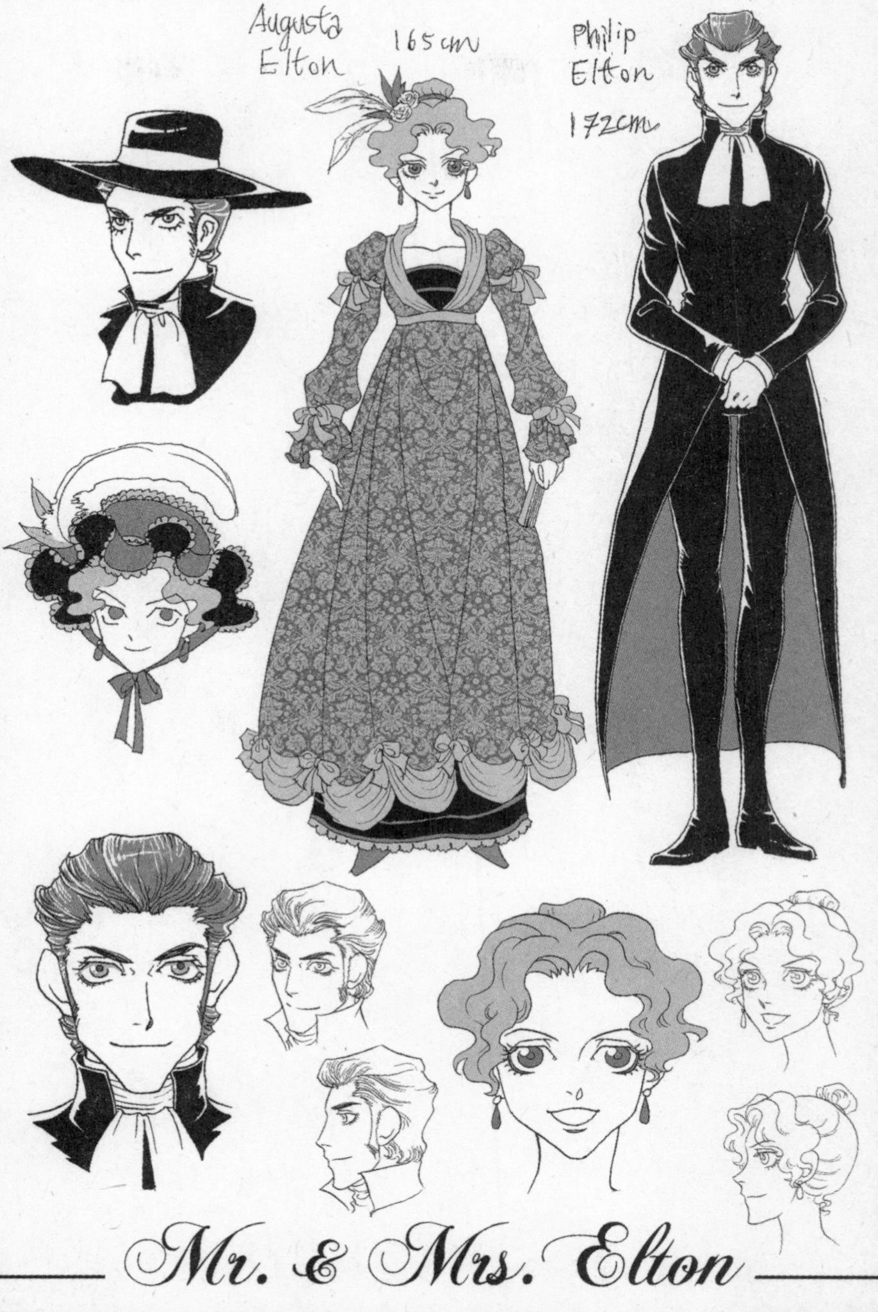
Augusta Elton
165cm
Philip Elton
172cm

Mr. & Mrs. Elton

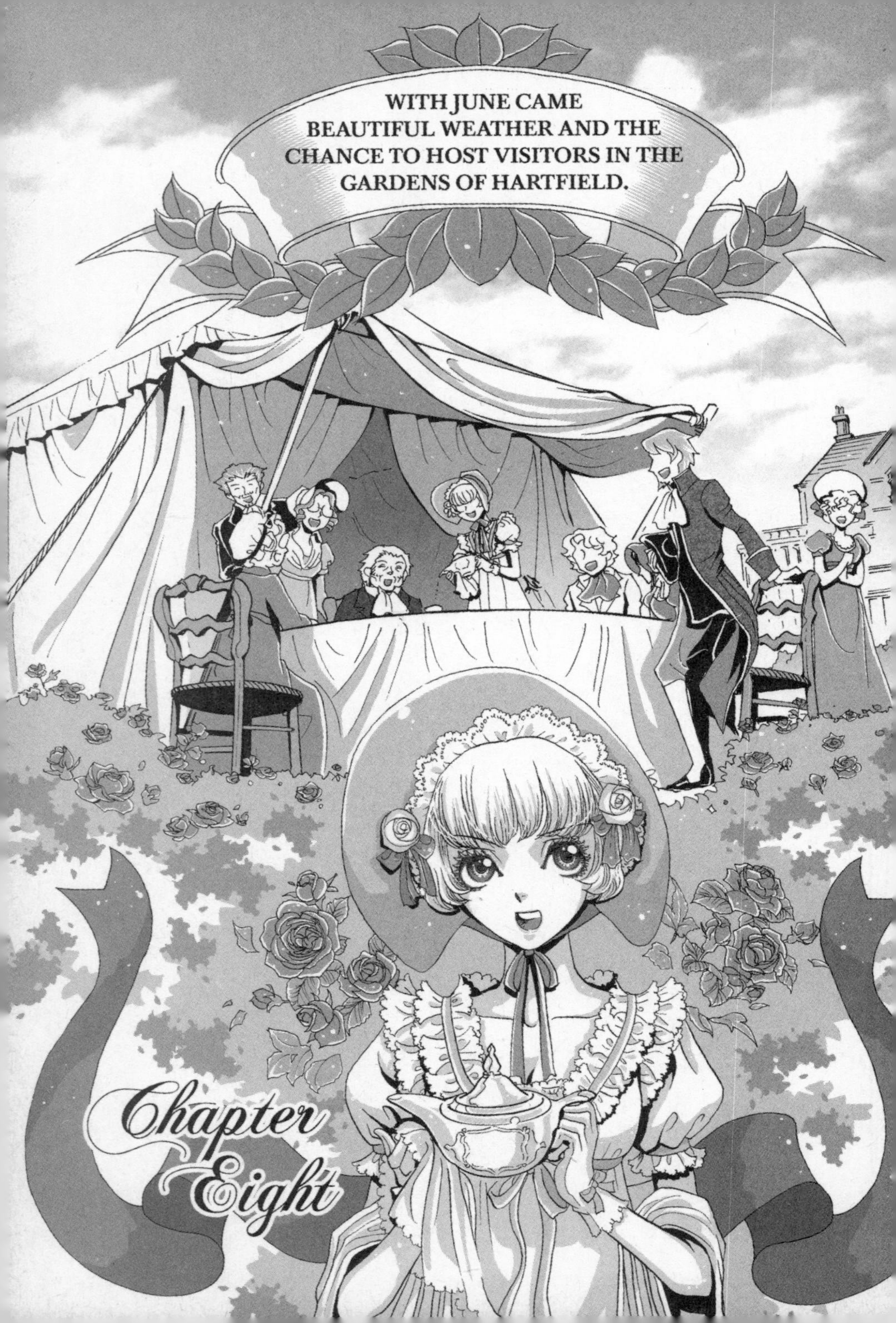
WITH JUNE CAME BEAUTIFUL WEATHER AND THE CHANCE TO HOST VISITORS IN THE GARDENS OF HARTFIELD.
Chapter Eight

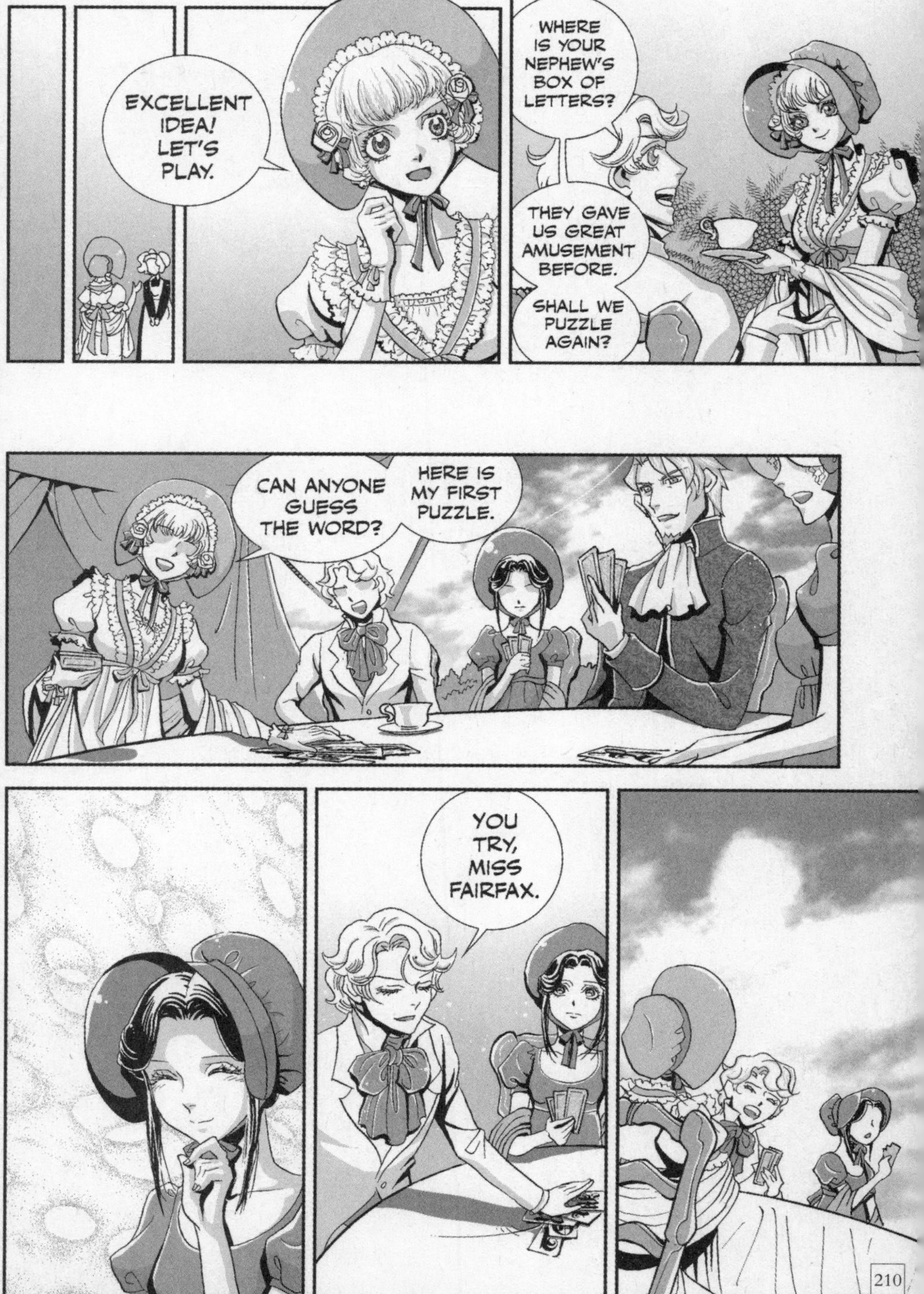
WHERE IS YOUR NEPHEW'S BOX OF LETTERS?
THEY GAVE US GREAT AMUSEMENT BEFORE.
SHALL WE PUZZLE AGAIN?
EXCELLENT IDEA! LET'S PLAY.
HERE IS MY FIRST PUZZLE.
CAN ANYONE GUESS THE WORD?
YOU TRY, MISS FAIRFAX.

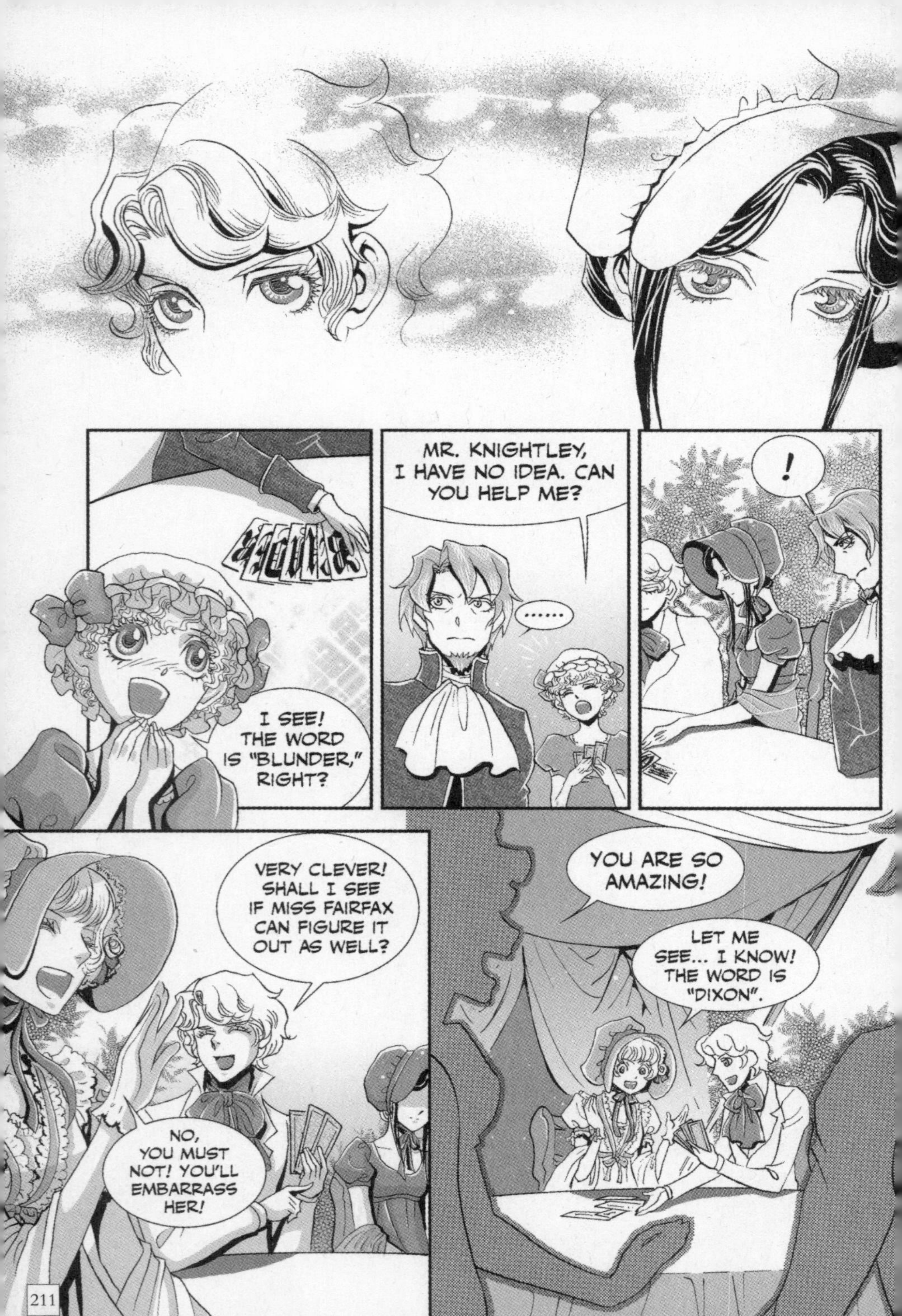
!
MR. KNIGHTLEY, I HAVE NO IDEA. CAN YOU HELP ME?
......
I SEE! THE WORD IS "BLUNDER," RIGHT?
YOU ARE SO AMAZING!
LET ME SEE... I KNOW! THE WORD IS "DIXON".
VERY CLEVER! SHALL I SEE IF MISS FAIRFAX CAN FIGURE IT OUT AS WELL?
NO, YOU MUST NOT! YOU'LL EMBARRASS HER!

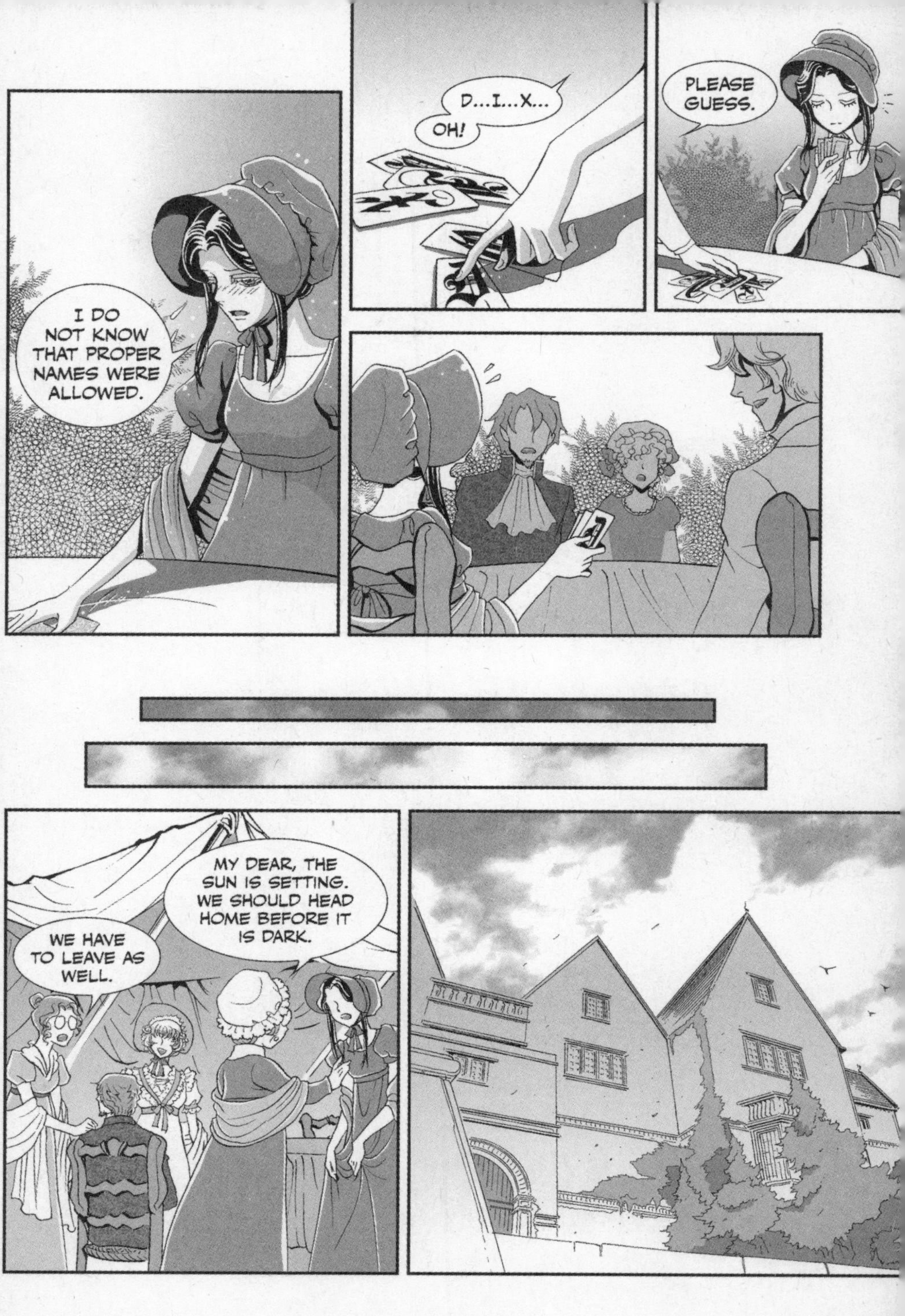
PLEASE GUESS.
D...I...X...
OH!
I DO NOT KNOW THAT PROPER NAMES WERE ALLOWED.
MY DEAR, THE SUN IS SETTING. WE SHOULD HEAD HOME BEFORE IT IS DARK.
WE HAVE TO LEAVE AS WELL.

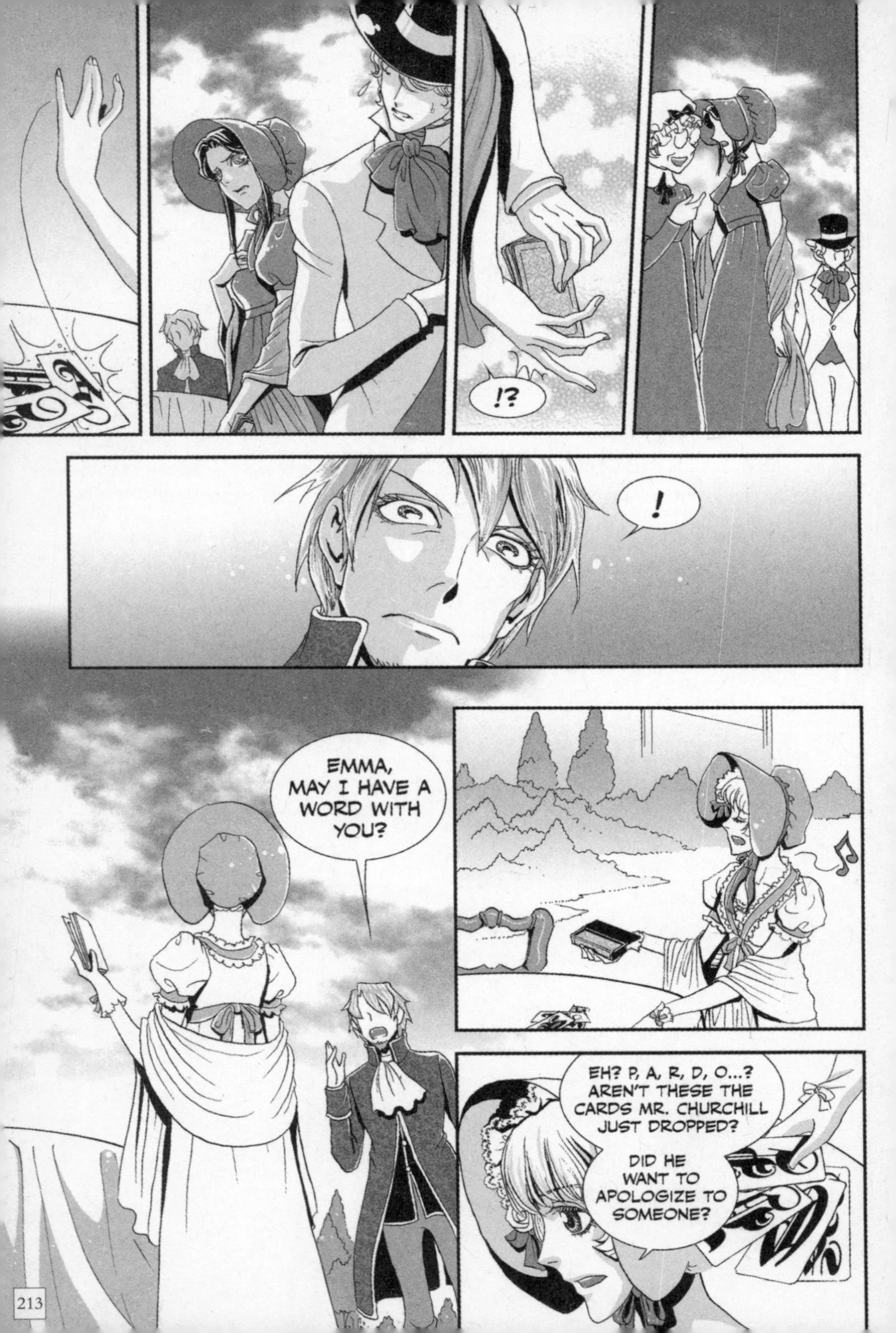
!?
!
EH? P, A, R, D, O...? AREN'T THESE THE CARDS MR. CHURCHILL JUST DROPPED?
DID HE WANT TO APOLOGIZE TO SOMEONE?
EMMA, MAY I HAVE A WORD WITH YOU?

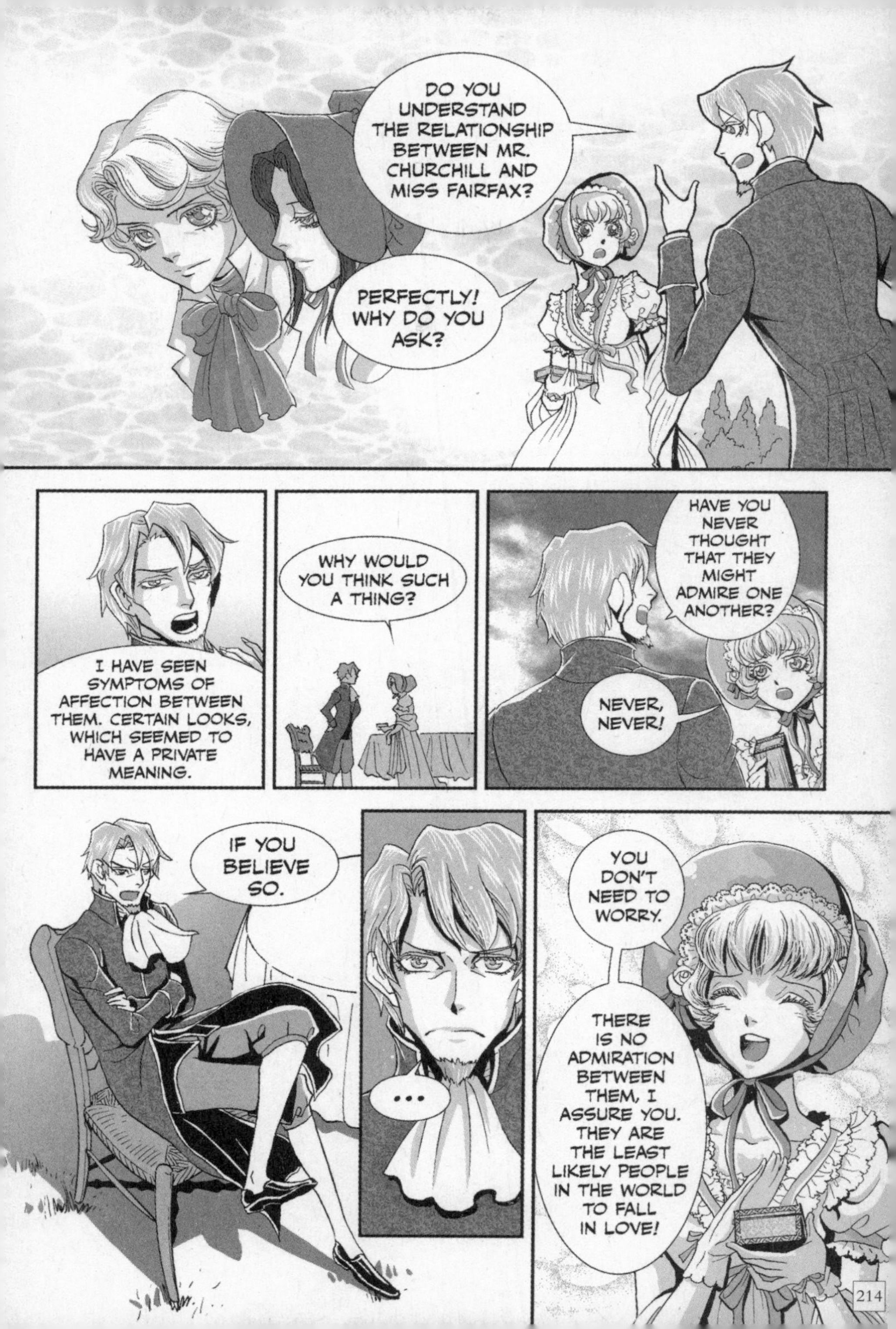
DO YOU UNDERSTAND THE RELATIONSHIP BETWEEN MR. CHURCHILL AND MISS FAIRFAX?
PERFECTLY! WHY DO YOU ASK?
HAVE YOU NEVER THOUGHT THAT THEY MIGHT ADMIRE ONE ANOTHER?
NEVER, NEVER!
WHY WOULD YOU THINK SUCH A THING?
I HAVE SEEN SYMPTOMS OF AFFECTION BETWEEN THEM. CERTAIN LOOKS, WHICH SEEMED TO HAVE A PRIVATE MEANING.
YOU DON'T NEED TO WORRY.
THERE IS NO ADMIRATION BETWEEN THEM, I ASSURE YOU. THEY ARE THE LEAST LIKELY PEOPLE IN THE WORLD TO FALL IN LOVE!
...
IF YOU BELIEVE SO.

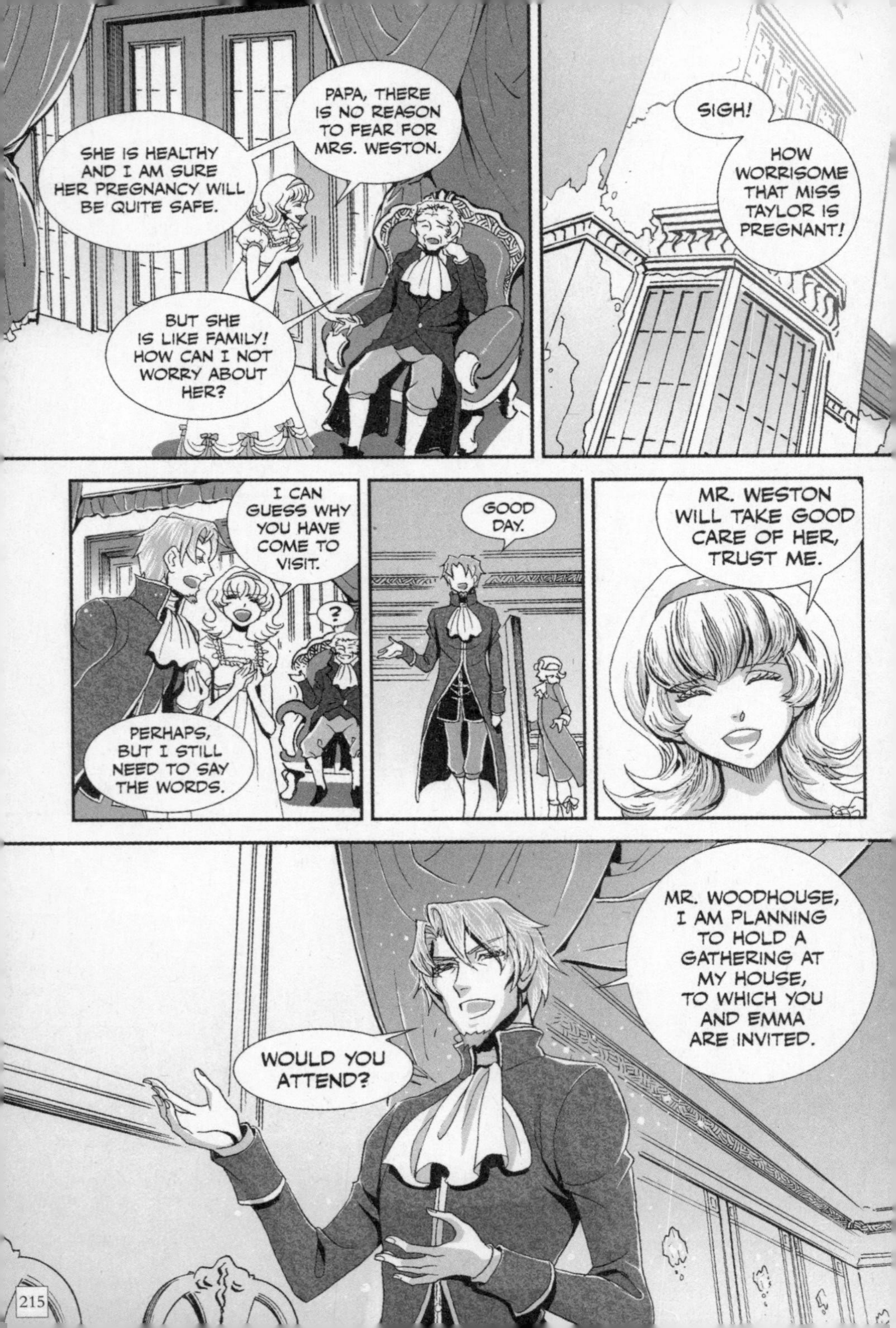
SIGH!
HOW WORRISOME THAT MISS TAYLOR IS PREGNANT!
PAPA, THERE IS NO REASON TO FEAR FOR MRS. WESTON.
SHE IS HEALTHY AND I AM SURE HER PREGNANCY WILL BE QUITE SAFE.
BUT SHE IS LIKE FAMILY! HOW CAN I NOT WORRY ABOUT HER?
MR. WESTON WILL TAKE GOOD CARE OF HER, TRUST ME.
GOOD DAY.
I CAN GUESS WHY YOU HAVE COME TO VISIT.
?
PERHAPS, BUT I STILL NEED TO SAY THE WORDS.
MR. WOODHOUSE, I AM PLANNING TO HOLD A GATHERING AT MY HOUSE, TO WHICH YOU AND EMMA ARE INVITED.
WOULD YOU ATTEND?

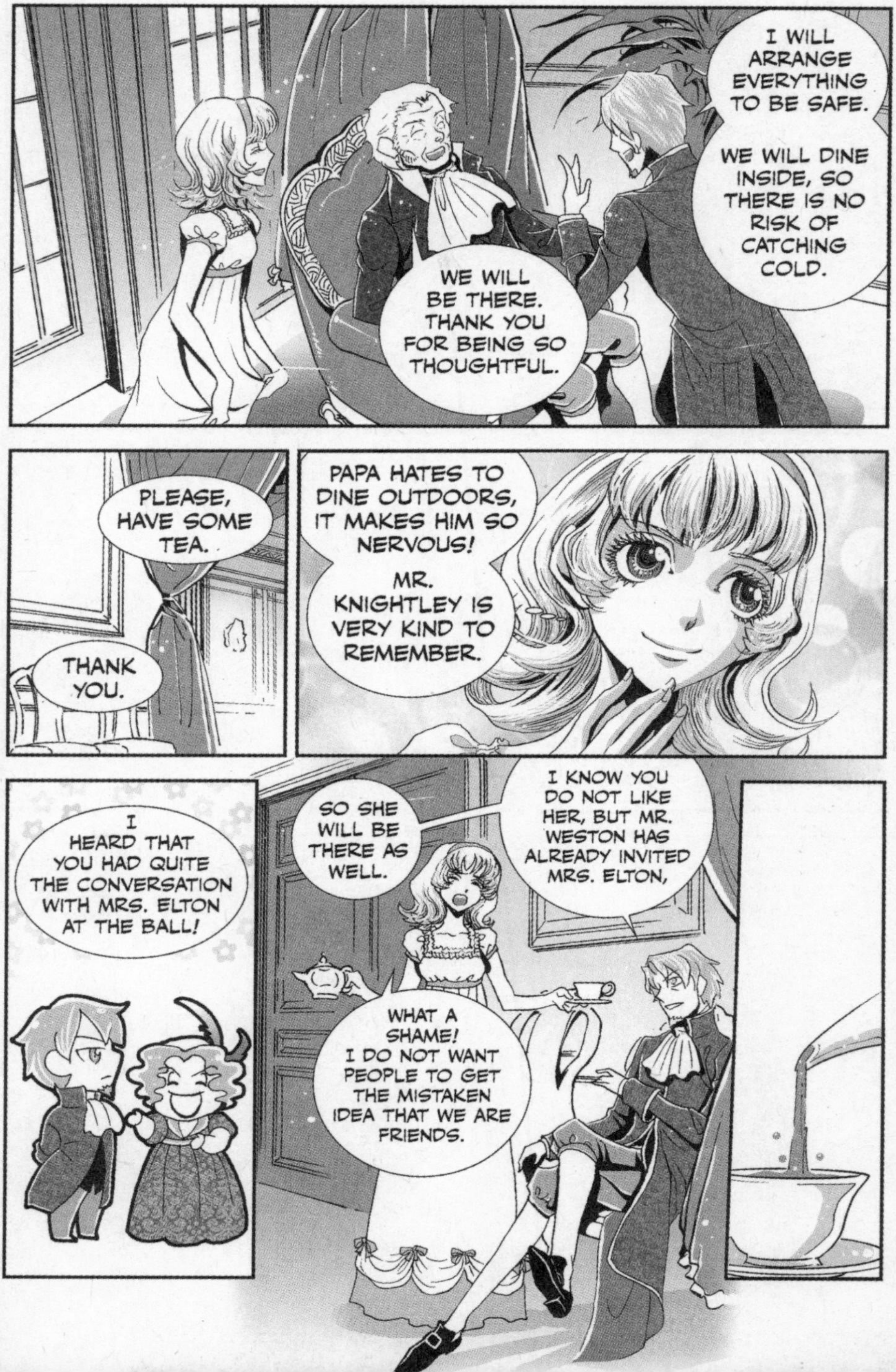
I WILL ARRANGE EVERYTHING TO BE SAFE.
WE WILL DINE INSIDE, SO THERE IS NO RISK OF CATCHING COLD.
WE WILL BE THERE. THANK YOU FOR BEING SO THOUGHTFUL.
PAPA HATES TO DINE OUTDOORS, IT MAKES HIM SO NERVOUS!
MR. KNIGHTLEY IS VERY KIND TO REMEMBER.
PLEASE, HAVE SOME TEA.
THANK YOU.
I KNOW YOU DO NOT LIKE HER, BUT MR. WESTON HAS ALREADY INVITED MRS. ELTON,
SO SHE WILL BE THERE AS WELL.
WHAT A SHAME! I DO NOT WANT PEOPLE TO GET THE MISTAKEN IDEA THAT WE ARE FRIENDS.
I HEARD THAT YOU HAD QUITE THE CONVERSATION WITH MRS. ELTON AT THE BALL!

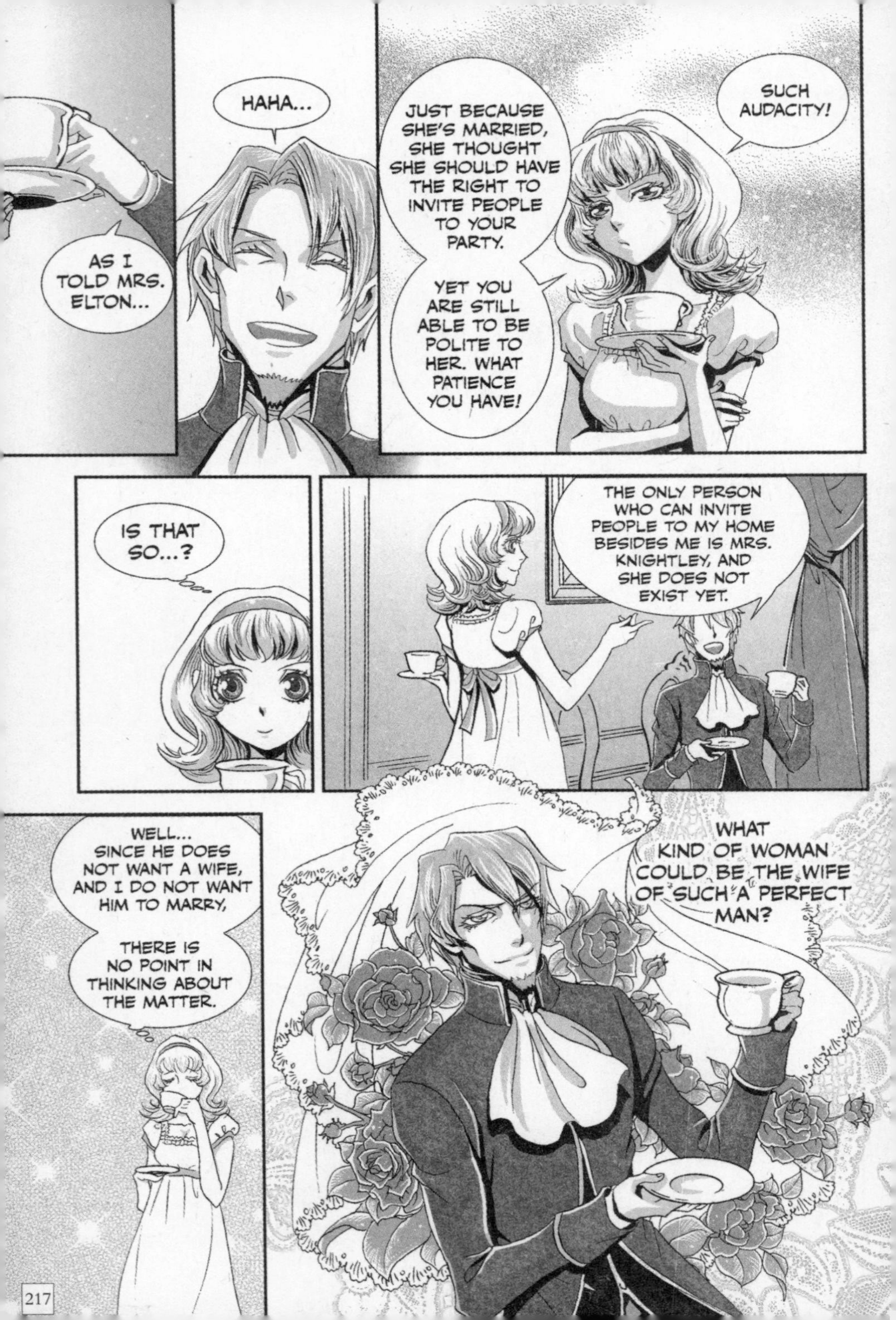
SUCH AUDACITY!
JUST BECAUSE SHE'S MARRIED, SHE THOUGHT SHE SHOULD HAVE THE RIGHT TO INVITE PEOPLE TO YOUR PARTY.
YET YOU ARE STILL ABLE TO BE POLITE TO HER. WHAT PATIENCE YOU HAVE!
HAHA...
AS I TOLD MRS. ELTON...
THE ONLY PERSON WHO CAN INVITE PEOPLE TO MY HOME BESIDES ME IS MRS. KNIGHTLEY, AND SHE DOES NOT EXIST YET.
IS THAT SO...?
WHAT KIND OF WOMAN COULD BE THE WIFE OF SUCH A PERFECT MAN?
WELL... SINCE HE DOES NOT WANT A WIFE, AND I DO NOT WANT HIM TO MARRY,
THERE IS NO POINT IN THINKING ABOUT THE MATTER.

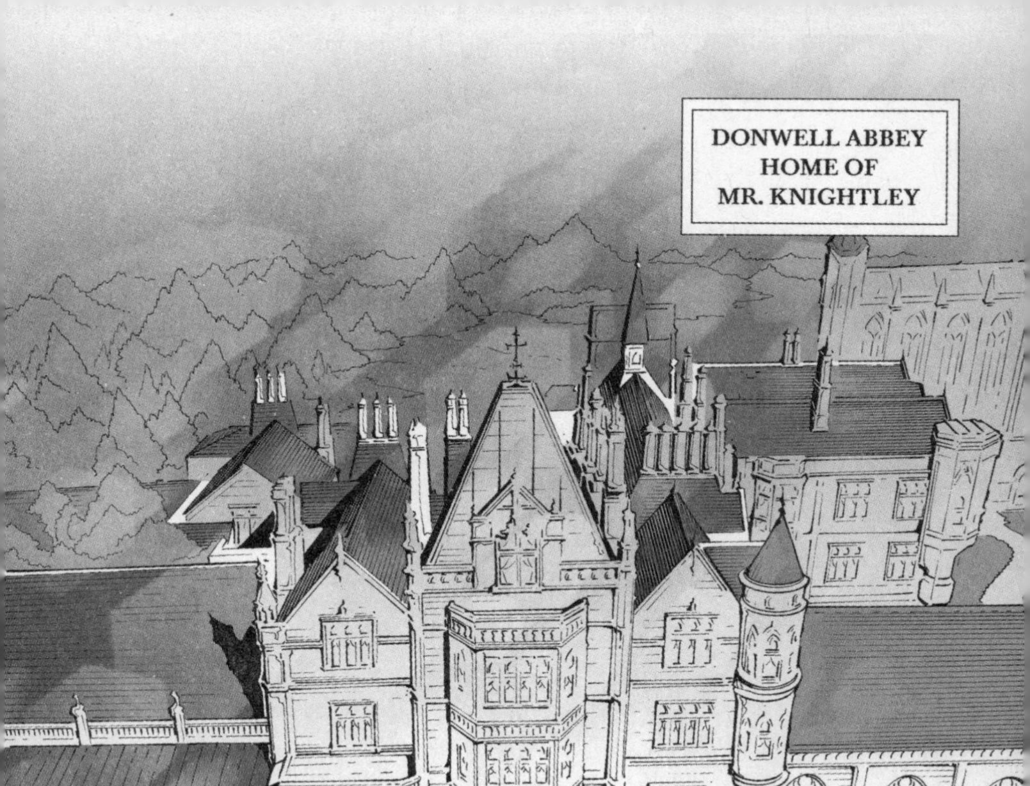
DONWELL ABBEY
HOME OF
MR. KNIGHTLEY

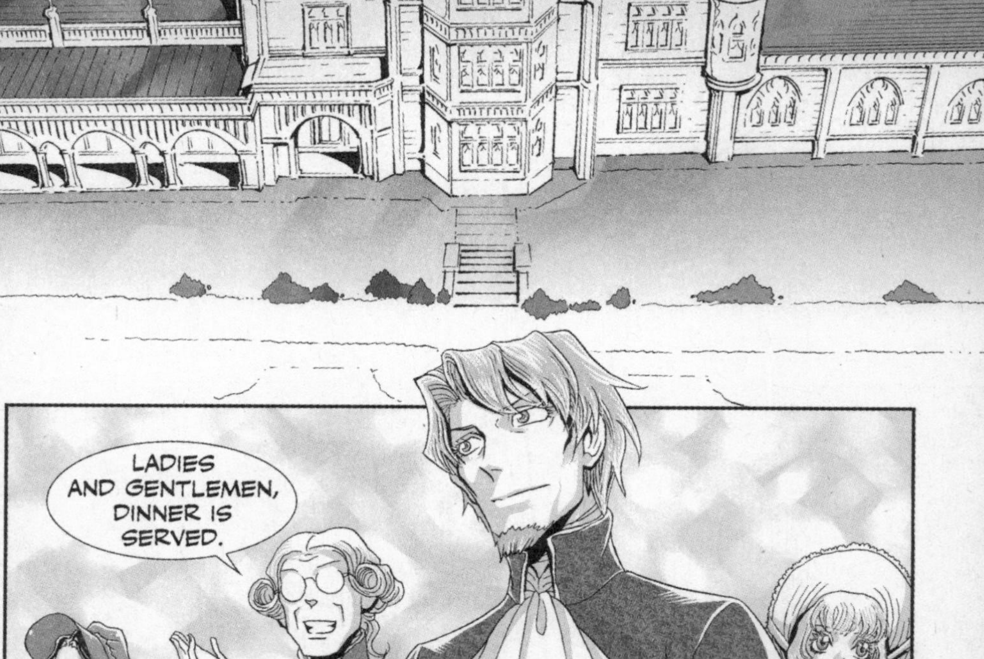
LADIES AND GENTLEMEN, DINNER IS SERVED.

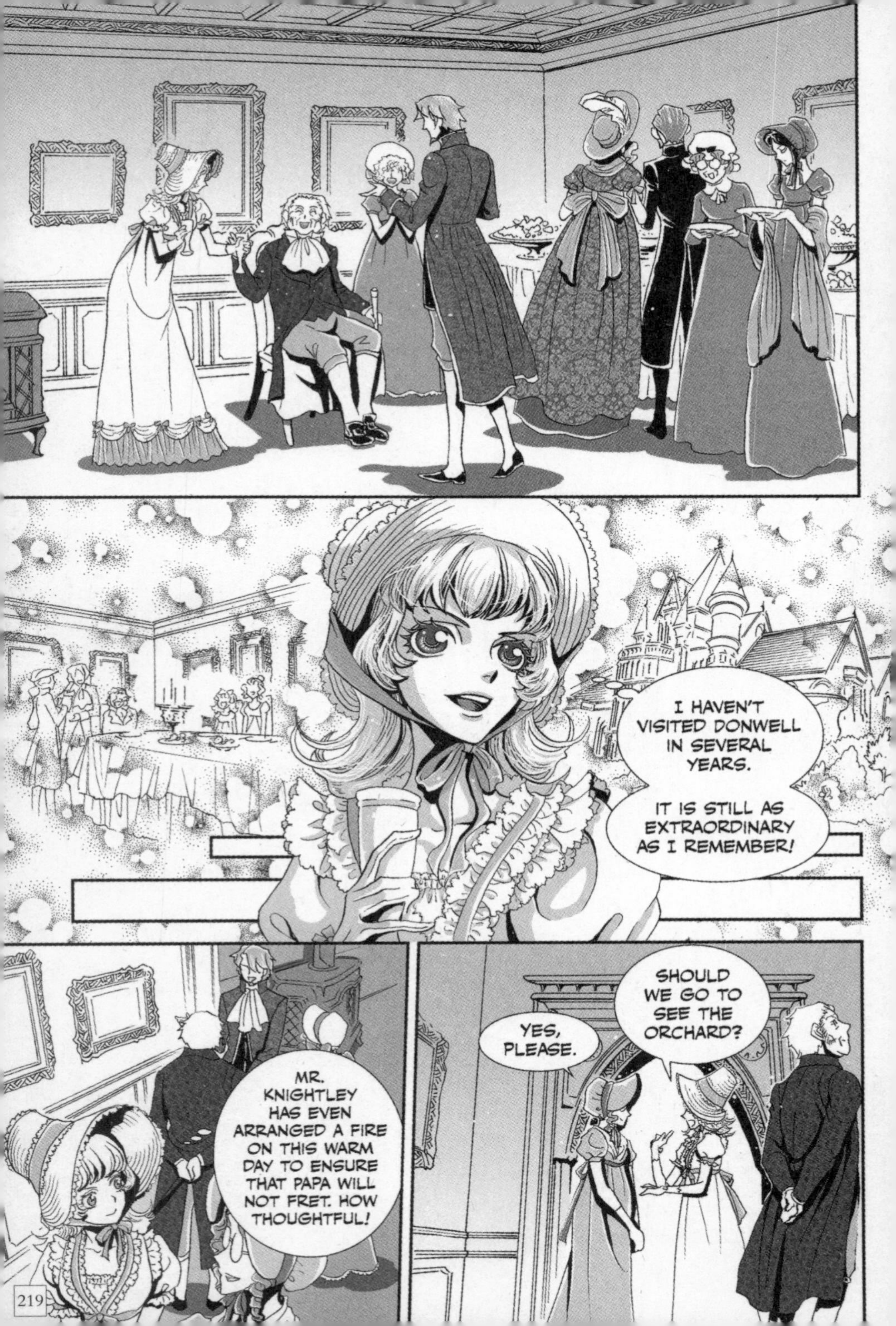
I HAVEN'T VISITED DONWELL IN SEVERAL YEARS.
IT IS STILL AS EXTRAORDINARY AS I REMEMBER!
MR. KNIGHTLEY HAS EVEN ARRANGED A FIRE ON THIS WARM DAY TO ENSURE THAT PAPA WILL NOT FRET. HOW THOUGHTFUL!
SHOULD WE GO TO SEE THE ORCHARD?
YES, PLEASE.

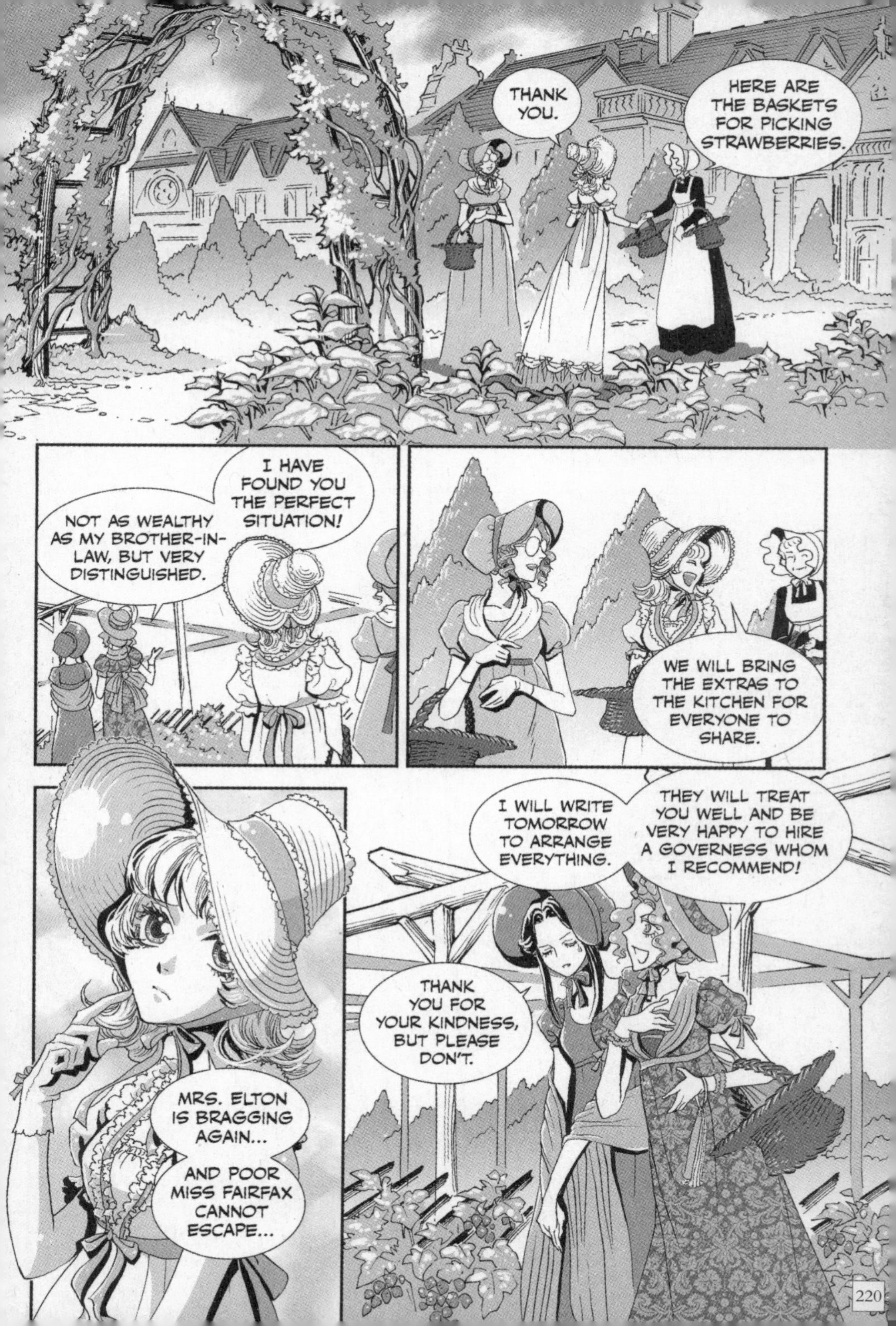
HERE ARE THE BASKETS FOR PICKING STRAWBERRIES.
THANK YOU.
WE WILL BRING THE EXTRAS TO THE KITCHEN FOR EVERYONE TO SHARE.
I HAVE FOUND YOU THE PERFECT SITUATION!
NOT AS WEALTHY AS MY BROTHER-IN-LAW, BUT VERY DISTINGUISHED.
THEY WILL TREAT YOU WELL AND BE VERY HAPPY TO HIRE A GOVERNESS WHOM I RECOMMEND!
I WILL WRITE TOMORROW TO ARRANGE EVERYTHING.
THANK YOU FOR YOUR KINDNESS, BUT PLEASE DON'T.
MRS. ELTON IS BRAGGING AGAIN...
AND POOR MISS FAIRFAX CANNOT ESCAPE...

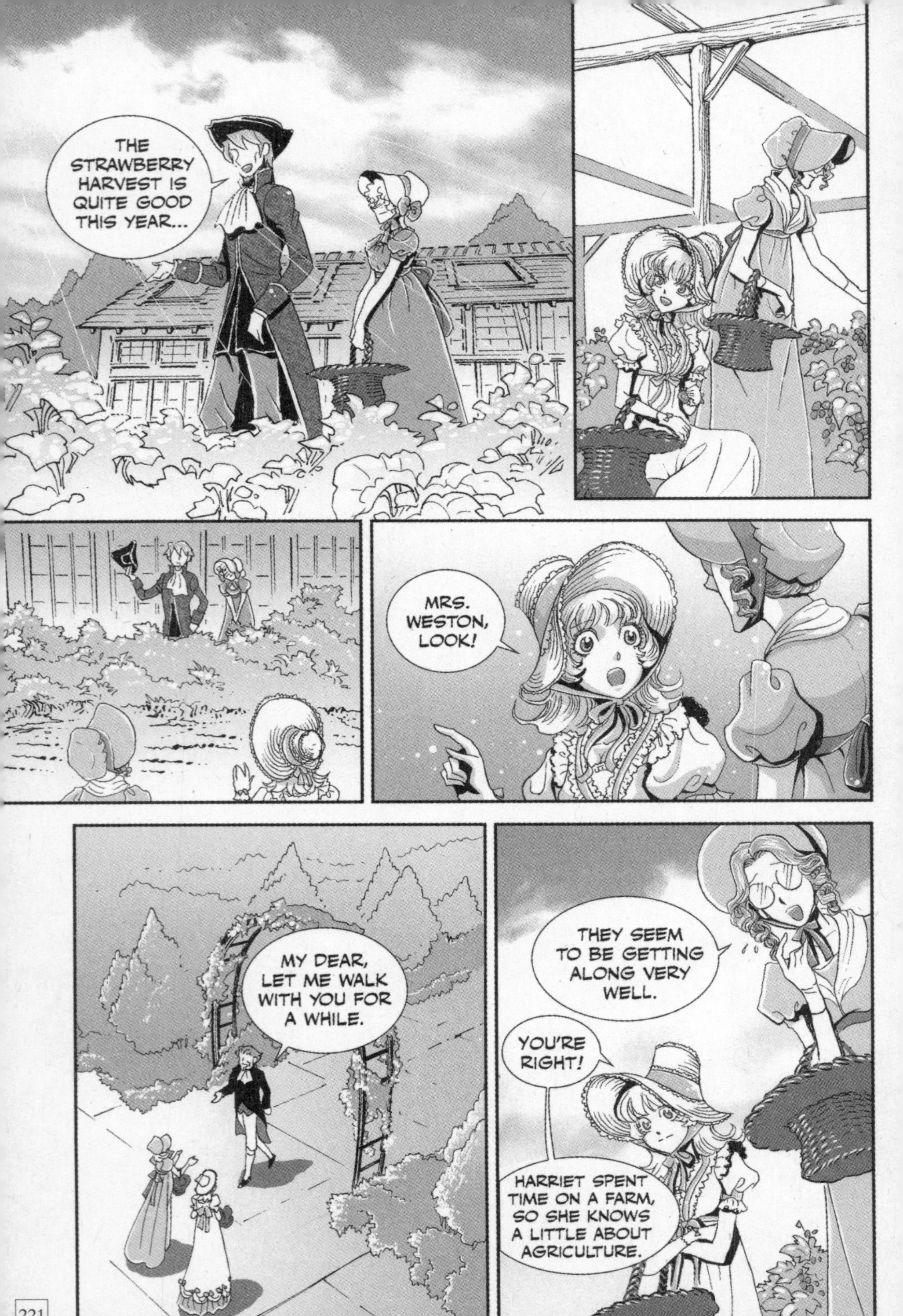
THE STRAWBERRY HARVEST IS QUITE GOOD THIS YEAR...
MRS. WESTON, LOOK!
THEY SEEM TO BE GETTING ALONG VERY WELL.
YOU'RE RIGHT!
HARRIET SPENT TIME ON A FARM, SO SHE KNOWS A LITTLE ABOUT AGRICULTURE.
MY DEAR, LET ME WALK WITH YOU FOR A WHILE.

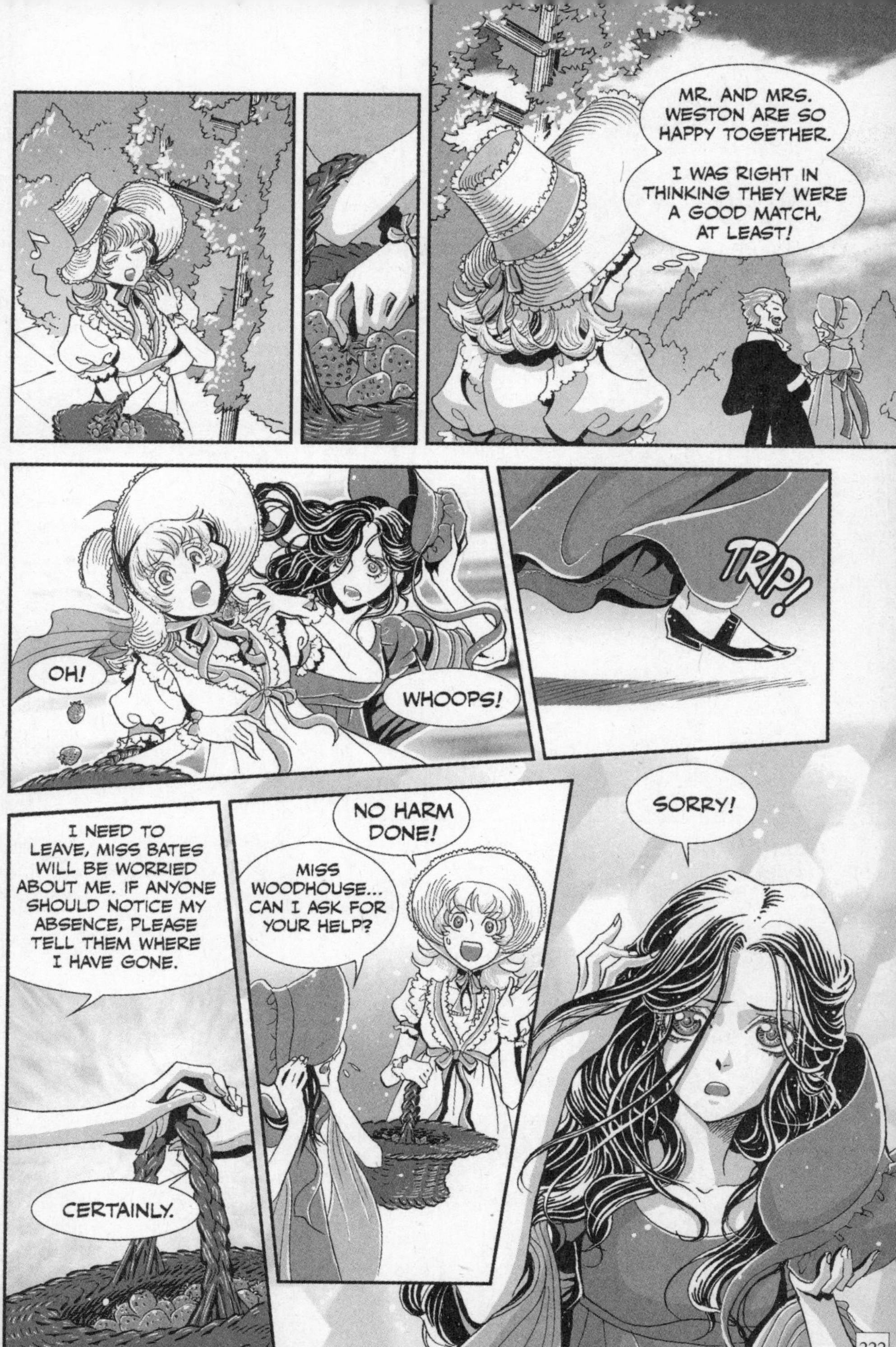
MR. AND MRS. WESTON ARE SO HAPPY TOGETHER.
I WAS RIGHT IN THINKING THEY WERE A GOOD MATCH, AT LEAST!
TRIP!
WHOOPS!
OH!
SORRY!
NO HARM DONE!
MISS WOODHOUSE... CAN I ASK FOR YOUR HELP?
I NEED TO LEAVE, MISS BATES WILL BE WORRIED ABOUT ME. IF ANYONE SHOULD NOTICE MY ABSENCE, PLEASE TELL THEM WHERE I HAVE GONE.
CERTAINLY.

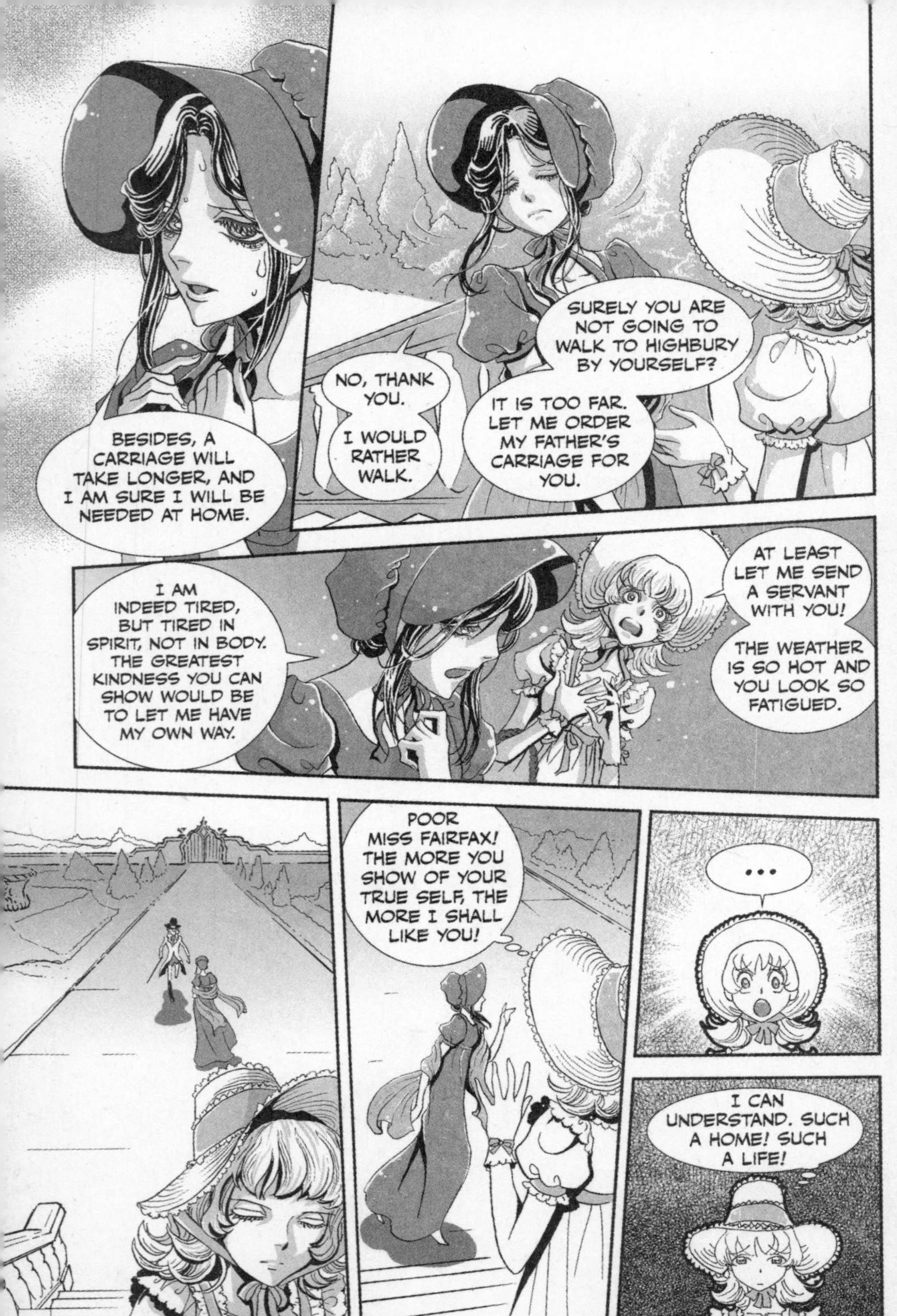
SURELY YOU ARE NOT GOING TO WALK TO HIGHBURY BY YOURSELF?
IT IS TOO FAR. LET ME ORDER MY FATHER'S CARRIAGE FOR YOU.
NO, THANK YOU.
I WOULD RATHER WALK.
BESIDES, A CARRIAGE WILL TAKE LONGER, AND I AM SURE I WILL BE NEEDED AT HOME.
AT LEAST LET ME SEND A SERVANT WITH YOU!
THE WEATHER IS SO HOT AND YOU LOOK SO FATIGUED.
I AM INDEED TIRED, BUT TIRED IN SPIRIT, NOT IN BODY. THE GREATEST KINDNESS YOU CAN SHOW WOULD BE TO LET ME HAVE MY OWN WAY.
...
I CAN UNDERSTAND. SUCH A HOME! SUCH A LIFE!
POOR MISS FAIRFAX! THE MORE YOU SHOW OF YOUR TRUE SELF, THE MORE I SHALL LIKE YOU!

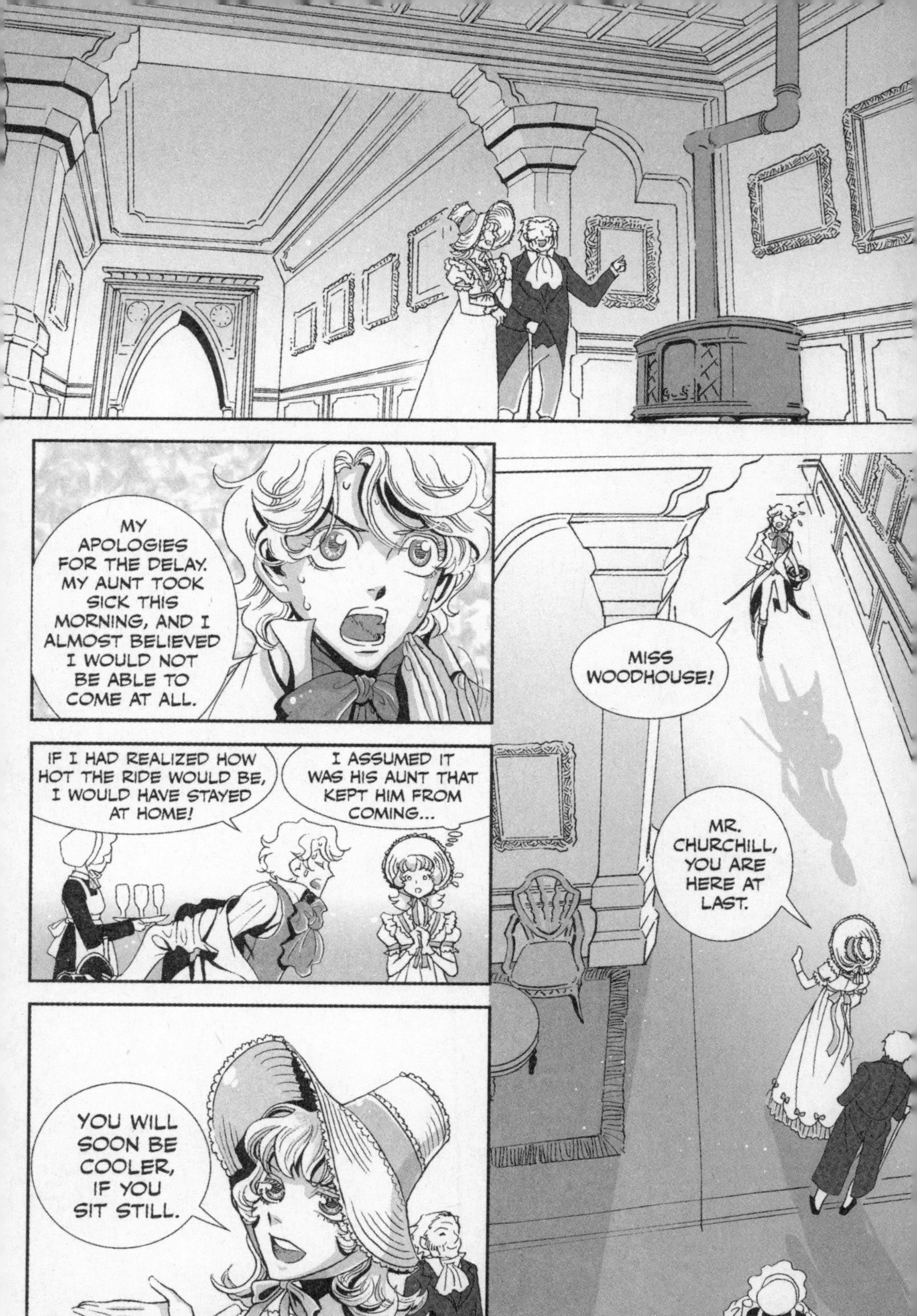
MISS WOODHOUSE!
MR. CHURCHILL, YOU ARE HERE AT LAST.
MY APOLOGIES FOR THE DELAY. MY AUNT TOOK SICK THIS MORNING, AND I ALMOST BELIEVED I WOULD NOT BE ABLE TO COME AT ALL.
I ASSUMED IT WAS HIS AUNT THAT KEPT HIM FROM COMING...
IF I HAD REALIZED HOW HOT THE RIDE WOULD BE, I WOULD HAVE STAYED AT HOME!
YOU WILL SOON BE COOLER, IF YOU SIT STILL.

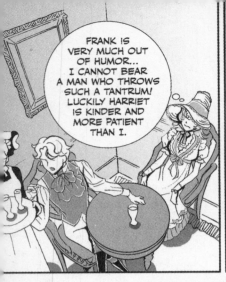

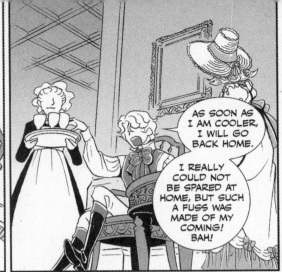

AS SOON AS I AM COOLER, I WILL GO BACK HOME.
I REALLY COULD NOT BE SPARED AT HOME, BUT SUCH A FUSS WAS MADE OF MY COMING! BAH!
FRANK IS VERY MUCH OUT OF HUMOR... I CANNOT BEAR A MAN WHO THROWS SUCH A TANTRUM! LUCKILY HARRIET IS KINDER AND MORE PATIENT THAN I.
AS SOON AS MY AUNT GETS WELL, I SHALL GO ABROAD. I HAVE HAD ENOUGH OF ENGLAND!
YOU ARE SICK OF PROSPERITY AND INDULGENCE? WHY NOT INVENT A FEW HARDSHIPS FOR YOURSELF AND BE CONTENTED TO STAY?
YOU ARE QUITE MISTAKEN. I DO NOT LOOK UPON MYSELF AS EITHER PROSPEROUS OR INDULGED. I AM THWARTED IN EVERYTHING MATERIAL.
I SHALL NOT STIR. I SHALL SIT BY YOU, FOR YOU ARE MY BEST CURE.
YOU ARE ONLY MISERABLE BECAUSE OF THE WEATHER. SIT, HAVE SOME FOOD AND YOU WILL FEEL BETTER SOON.
WE ARE GOING TO BOX HILL TOMORROW. WILL YOU JOIN US?

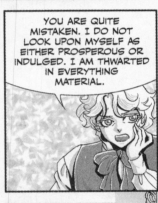

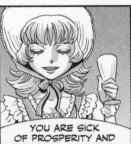

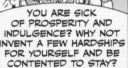

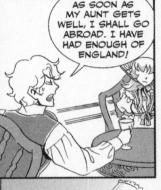

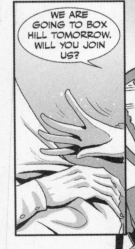

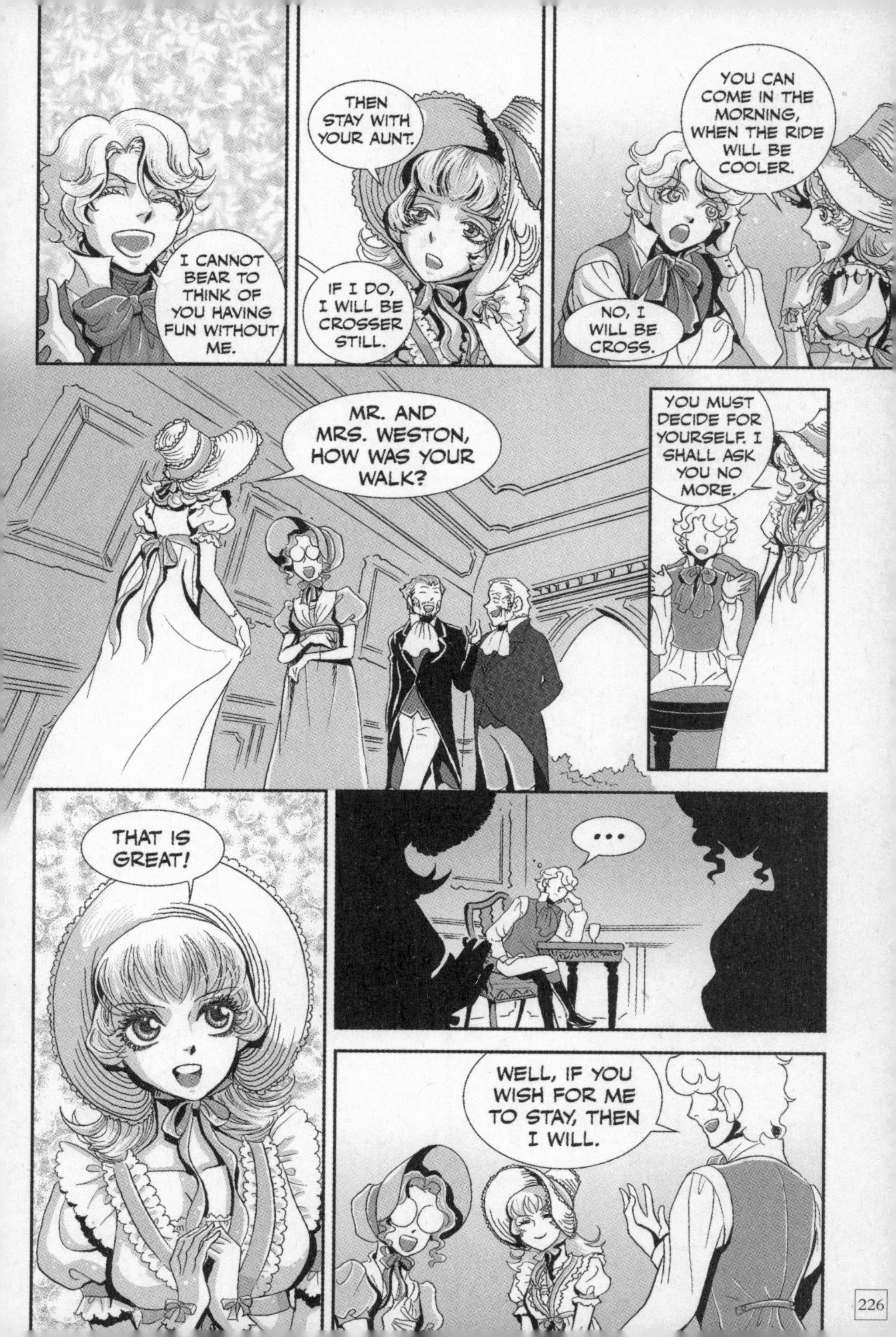
YOU CAN COME IN THE MORNING, WHEN THE RIDE WILL BE COOLER.
NO, I WILL BE CROSS.
THEN STAY WITH YOUR AUNT.
IF I DO, I WILL BE CROSSER STILL.
I CANNOT BEAR TO THINK OF YOU HAVING FUN WITHOUT ME.
YOU MUST DECIDE FOR YOURSELF. I SHALL ASK YOU NO MORE.
MR. AND MRS. WESTON, HOW WAS YOUR WALK?
...
WELL, IF YOU WISH FOR ME TO STAY, THEN I WILL.
THAT IS GREAT!

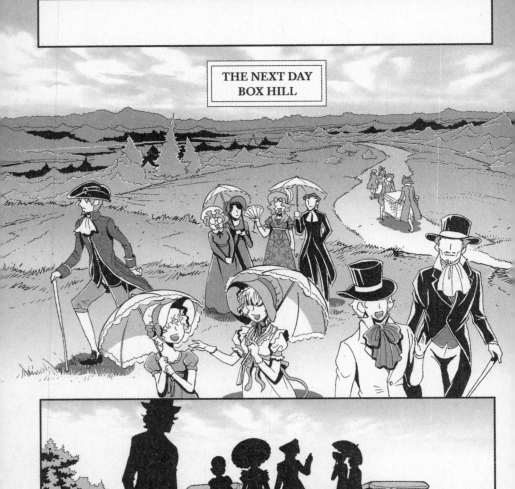

THE NEXT DAY
BOX HILL

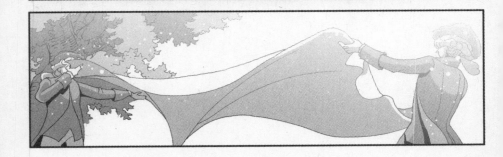

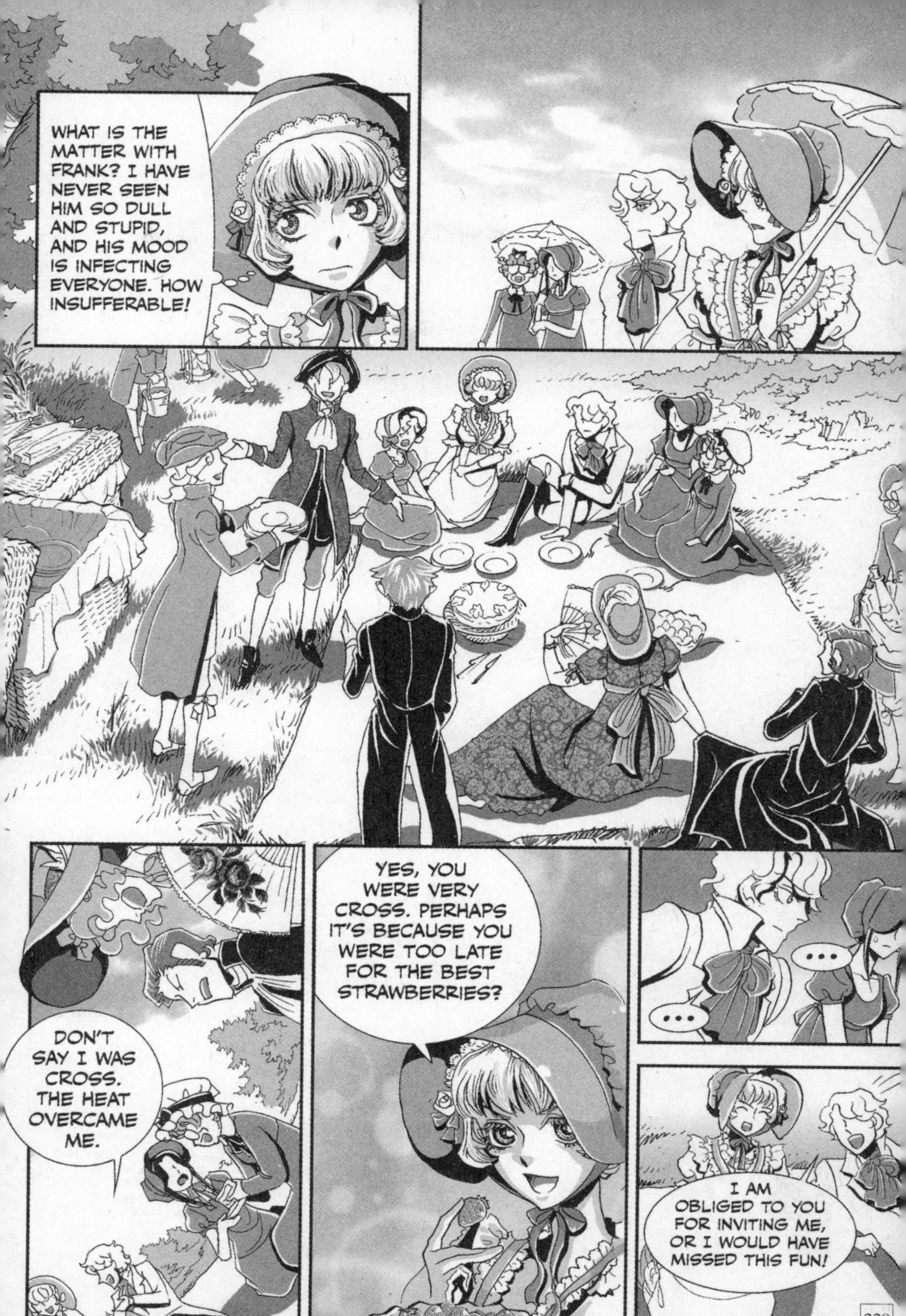
WHAT IS THE MATTER WITH FRANK? I HAVE NEVER SEEN HIM SO DULL AND STUPID, AND HIS MOOD IS INFECTING EVERYONE. HOW INSUFFERABLE!
...
...
I AM OBLIGED TO YOU FOR INVITING ME, OR I WOULD HAVE MISSED THIS FUN!
YES, YOU WERE VERY CROSS. PERHAPS IT'S BECAUSE YOU WERE TOO LATE FOR THE BEST STRAWBERRIES?
DON'T SAY I WAS CROSS. THE HEAT OVERCAME ME.

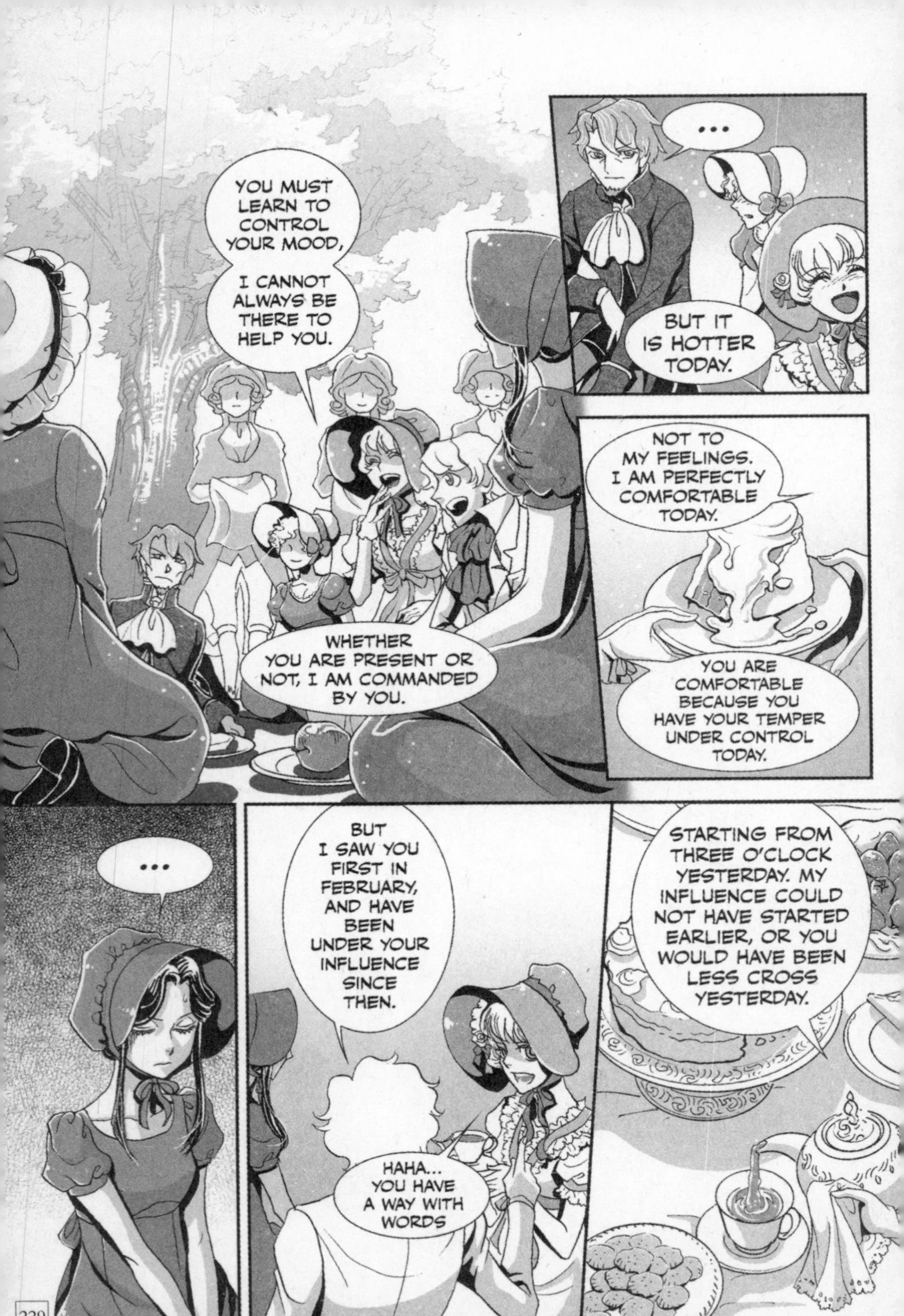
...
BUT IT IS HOTTER TODAY.
NOT TO MY FEELINGS. I AM PERFECTLY COMFORTABLE TODAY.
YOU ARE COMFORTABLE BECAUSE YOU HAVE YOUR TEMPER UNDER CONTROL TODAY.
YOU MUST LEARN TO CONTROL YOUR MOOD,
I CANNOT ALWAYS BE THERE TO HELP YOU.
WHETHER YOU ARE PRESENT OR NOT, I AM COMMANDED BY YOU.
STARTING FROM THREE O'CLOCK YESTERDAY. MY INFLUENCE COULD NOT HAVE STARTED EARLIER, OR YOU WOULD HAVE BEEN LESS CROSS YESTERDAY.
BUT I SAW YOU FIRST IN FEBRUARY, AND HAVE BEEN UNDER YOUR INFLUENCE SINCE THEN.
HAHA... YOU HAVE A WAY WITH WORDS
...

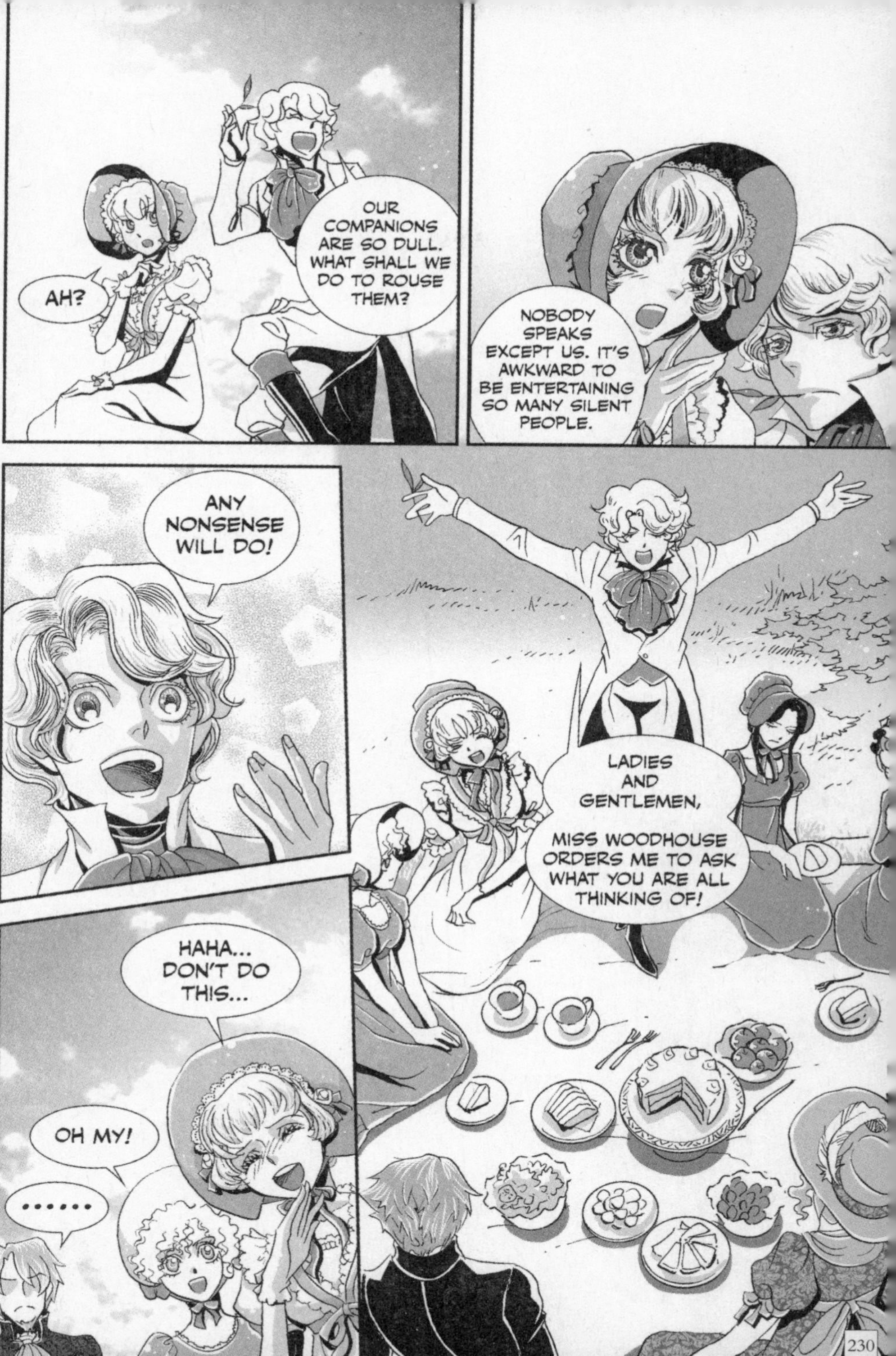
NOBODY SPEAKS EXCEPT US. IT'S AWKWARD TO BE ENTERTAINING SO MANY SILENT PEOPLE.
OUR COMPANIONS ARE SO DULL. WHAT SHALL WE DO TO ROUSE THEM?
AH?
LADIES AND GENTLEMEN,
MISS WOODHOUSE ORDERS ME TO ASK WHAT YOU ARE ALL THINKING OF!
ANY NONSENSE WILL DO!
HAHA... DON'T DO THIS...
OH MY!
......

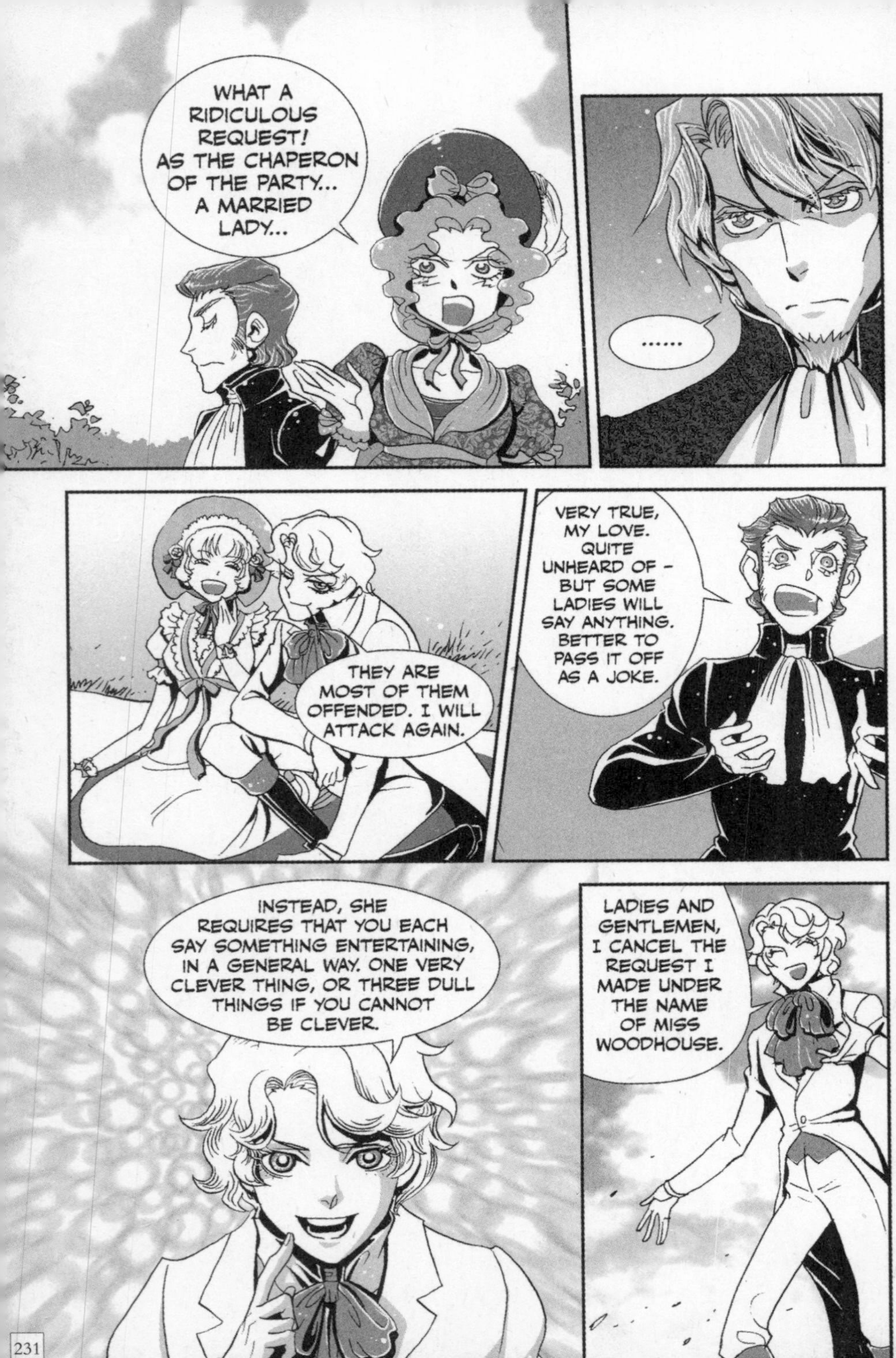

......
WHAT A RIDICULOUS REQUEST! AS THE CHAPERON OF THE PARTY... A MARRIED LADY...
VERY TRUE, MY LOVE. QUITE UNHEARD OF – BUT SOME LADIES WILL SAY ANYTHING. BETTER TO PASS IT OFF AS A JOKE.
THEY ARE MOST OF THEM OFFENDED. I WILL ATTACK AGAIN.
LADIES AND GENTLEMEN, I CANCEL THE REQUEST I MADE UNDER THE NAME OF MISS WOODHOUSE.
INSTEAD, SHE REQUIRES THAT YOU EACH SAY SOMETHING ENTERTAINING, IN A GENERAL WAY. ONE VERY CLEVER THING, OR THREE DULL THINGS IF YOU CANNOT BE CLEVER.

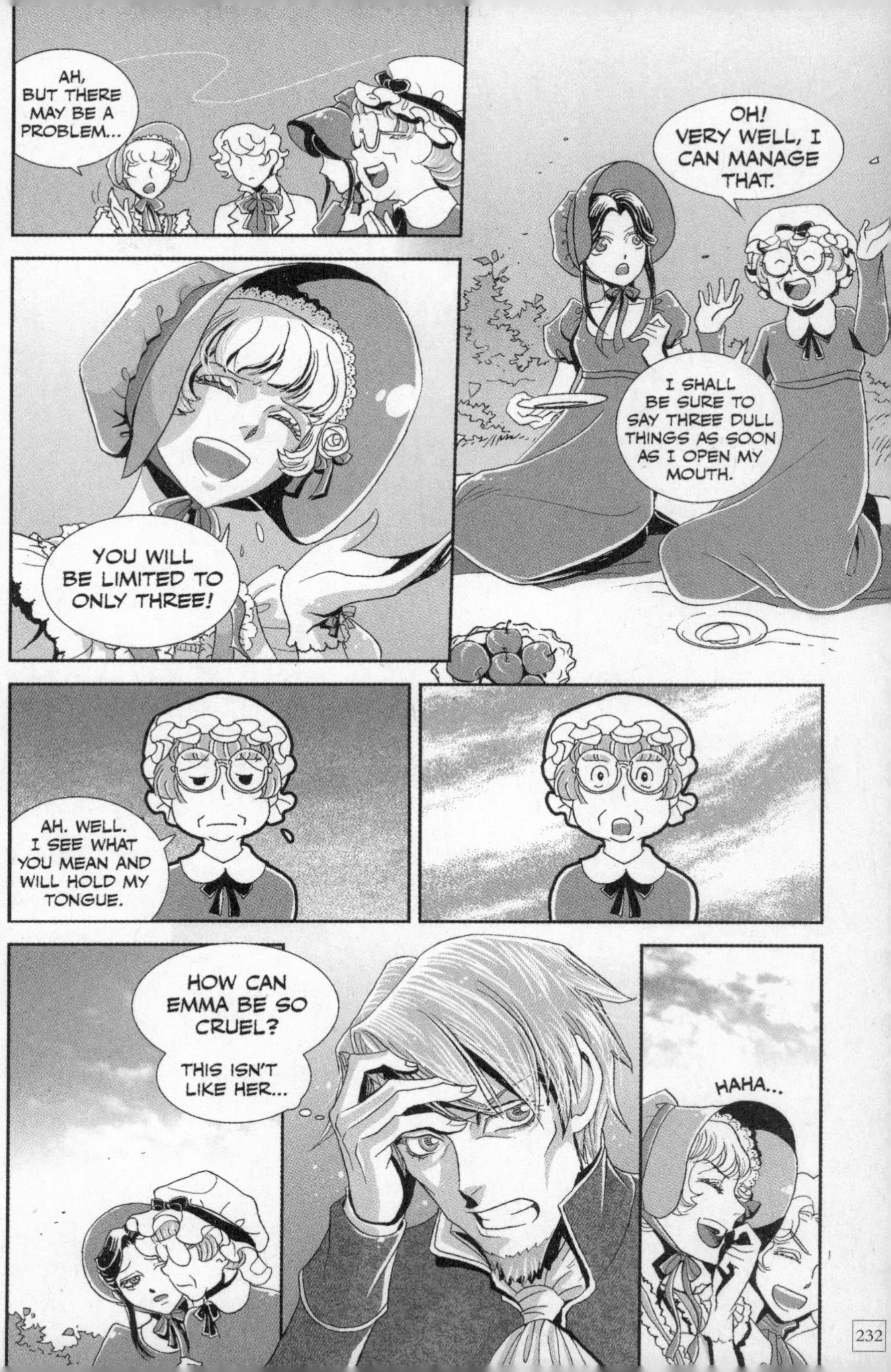
OH! VERY WELL, I CAN MANAGE THAT.
I SHALL BE SURE TO SAY THREE DULL THINGS AS SOON AS I OPEN MY MOUTH.
AH, BUT THERE MAY BE A PROBLEM...
YOU WILL BE LIMITED TO ONLY THREE!
AH. WELL. I SEE WHAT YOU MEAN AND WILL HOLD MY TONGUE.
HAHA...
HOW CAN EMMA BE SO CRUEL?
THIS ISN'T LIKE HER...

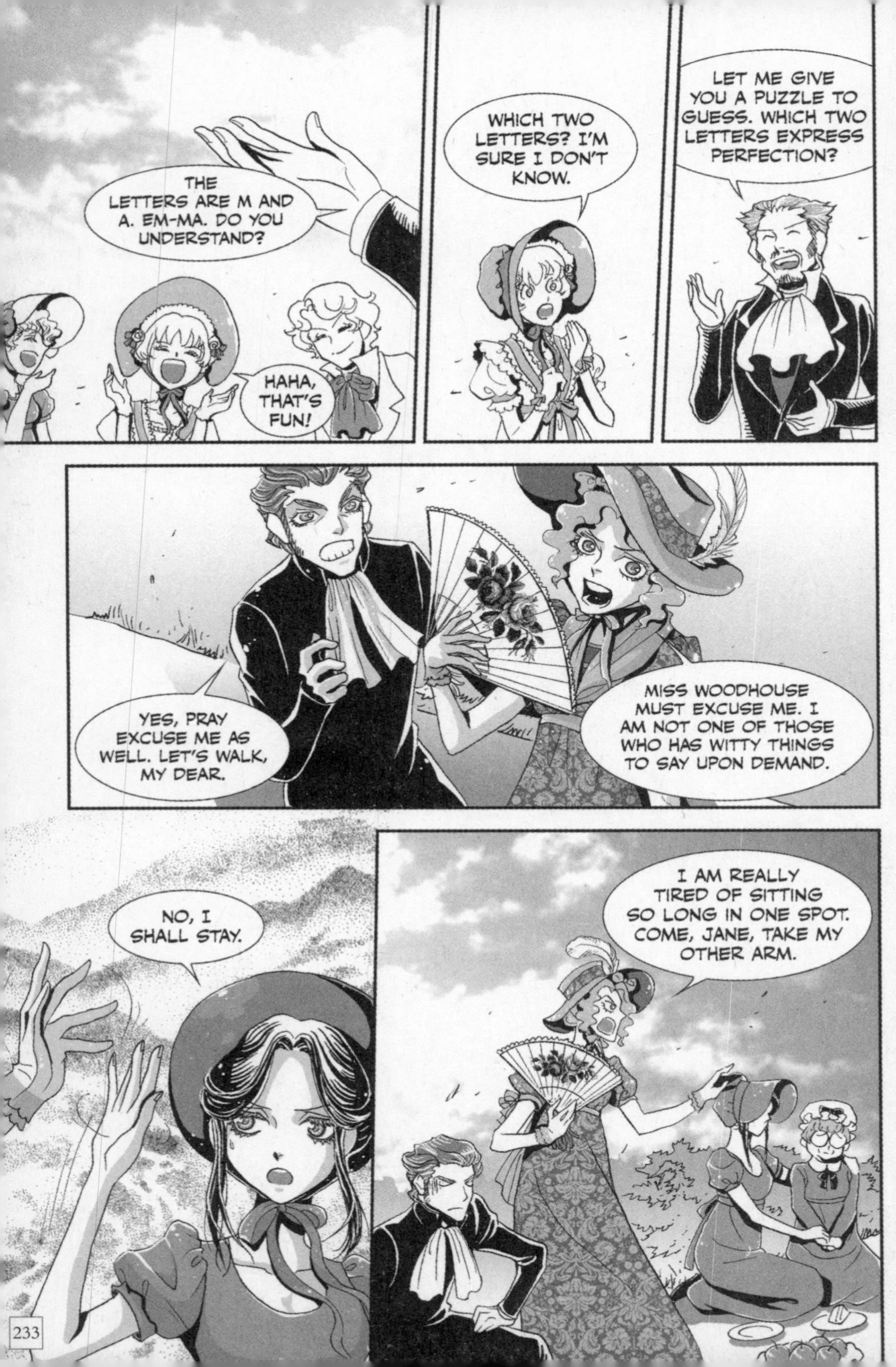
LET ME GIVE YOU A PUZZLE TO GUESS. WHICH TWO LETTERS EXPRESS PERFECTION?
WHICH TWO LETTERS? I'M SURE I DON'T KNOW.
THE LETTERS ARE M AND A. EM-MA. DO YOU UNDERSTAND?
HAHA, THAT'S FUN!
MISS WOODHOUSE MUST EXCUSE ME. I AM NOT ONE OF THOSE WHO HAS WITTY THINGS TO SAY UPON DEMAND.
YES, PRAY EXCUSE ME AS WELL. LET'S WALK, MY DEAR.
I AM REALLY TIRED OF SITTING SO LONG IN ONE SPOT. COME, JANE, TAKE MY OTHER ARM.
NO, I SHALL STAY.

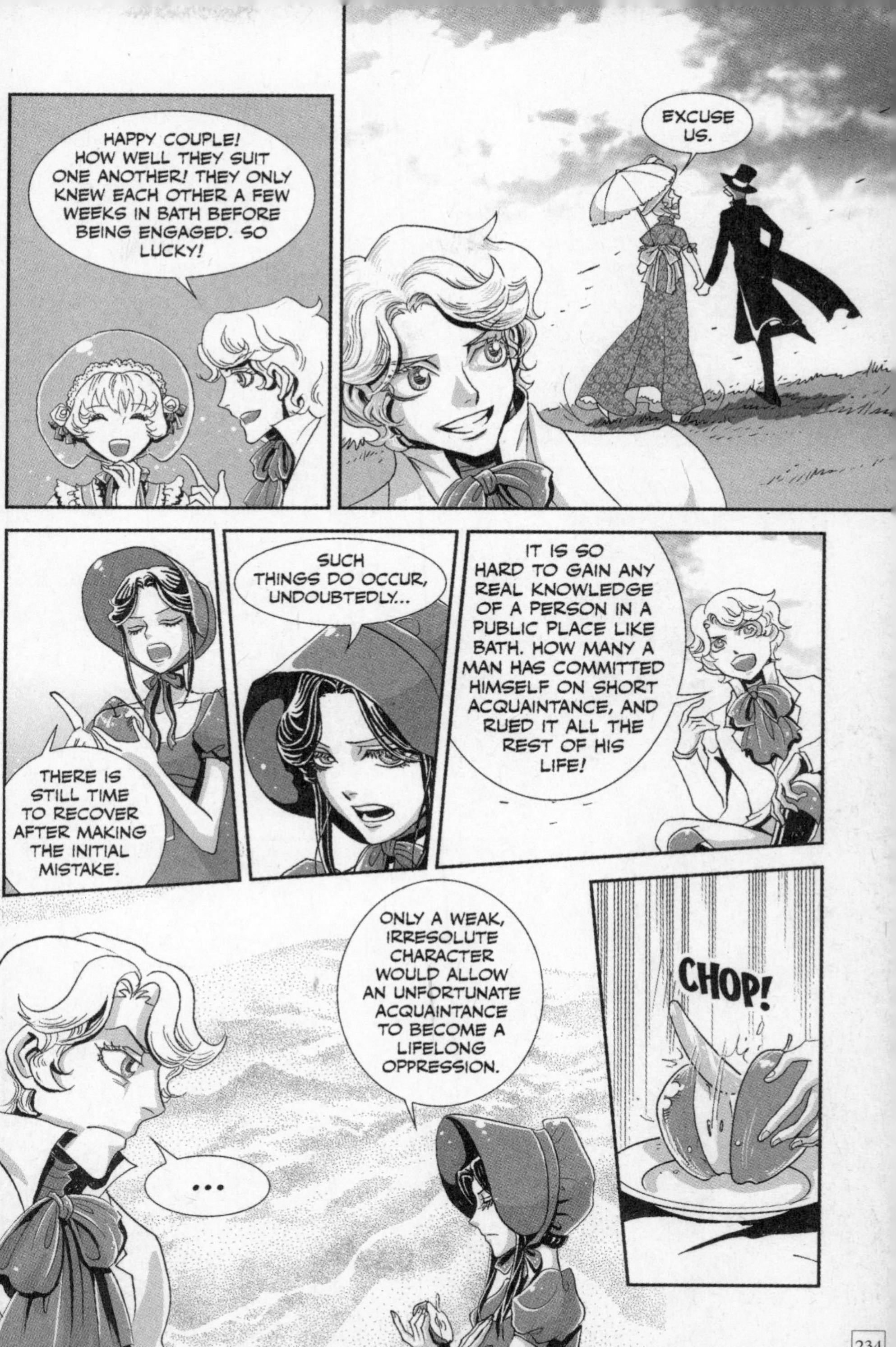
EXCUSE US.
HAPPY COUPLE! HOW WELL THEY SUIT ONE ANOTHER! THEY ONLY KNEW EACH OTHER A FEW WEEKS IN BATH BEFORE BEING ENGAGED. SO LUCKY!
IT IS SO HARD TO GAIN ANY REAL KNOWLEDGE OF A PERSON IN A PUBLIC PLACE LIKE BATH. HOW MANY A MAN HAS COMMITTED HIMSELF ON SHORT ACQUAINTANCE, AND RUED IT ALL THE REST OF HIS LIFE!
SUCH THINGS DO OCCUR, UNDOUBTEDLY...
THERE IS STILL TIME TO RECOVER AFTER MAKING THE INITIAL MISTAKE.
CHOP!
ONLY A WEAK, IRRESOLUTE CHARACTER WOULD ALLOW AN UNFORTUNATE ACQUAINTANCE TO BECOME A LIFELONG OPPRESSION.
...

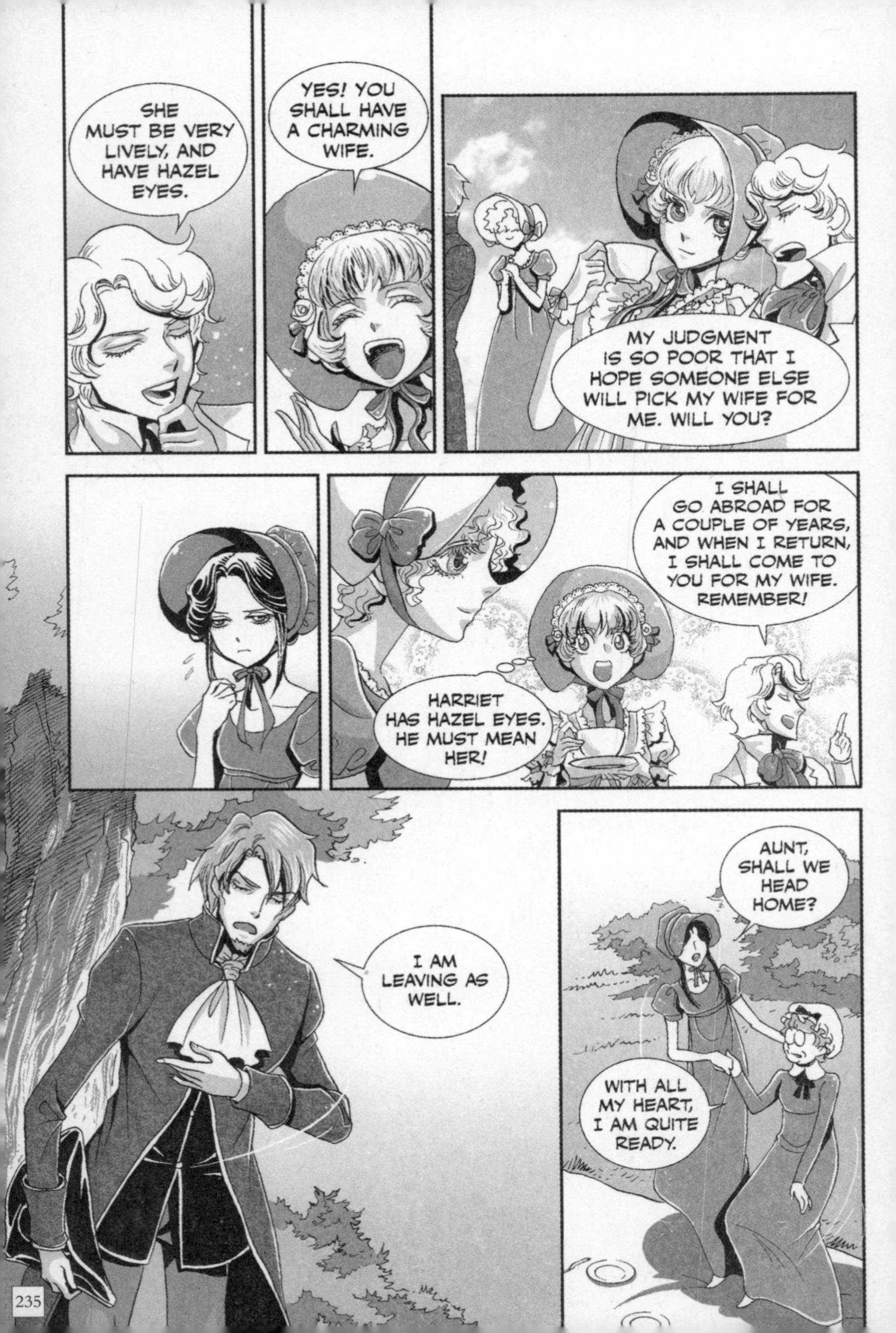
MY JUDGMENT IS SO POOR THAT I HOPE SOMEONE ELSE WILL PICK MY WIFE FOR ME. WILL YOU?
YES! YOU SHALL HAVE A CHARMING WIFE.
SHE MUST BE VERY LIVELY, AND HAVE HAZEL EYES.
I SHALL GO ABROAD FOR A COUPLE OF YEARS, AND WHEN I RETURN, I SHALL COME TO YOU FOR MY WIFE. REMEMBER!
HARRIET HAS HAZEL EYES. HE MUST MEAN HER!
AUNT, SHALL WE HEAD HOME?
WITH ALL MY HEART, I AM QUITE READY.
I AM LEAVING AS WELL.

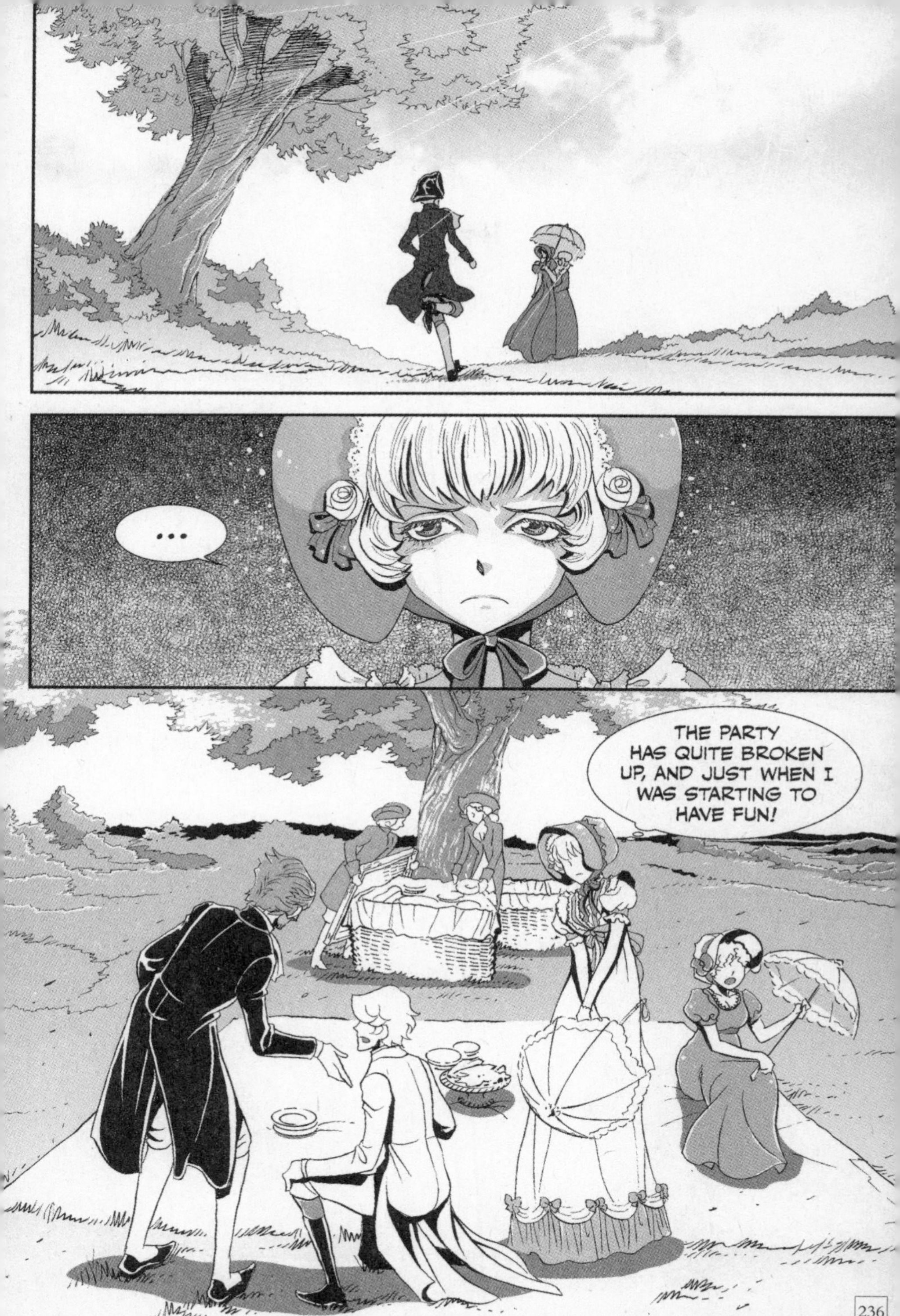
...
THE PARTY HAS QUITE BROKEN UP, AND JUST WHEN I WAS STARTING TO HAVE FUN!

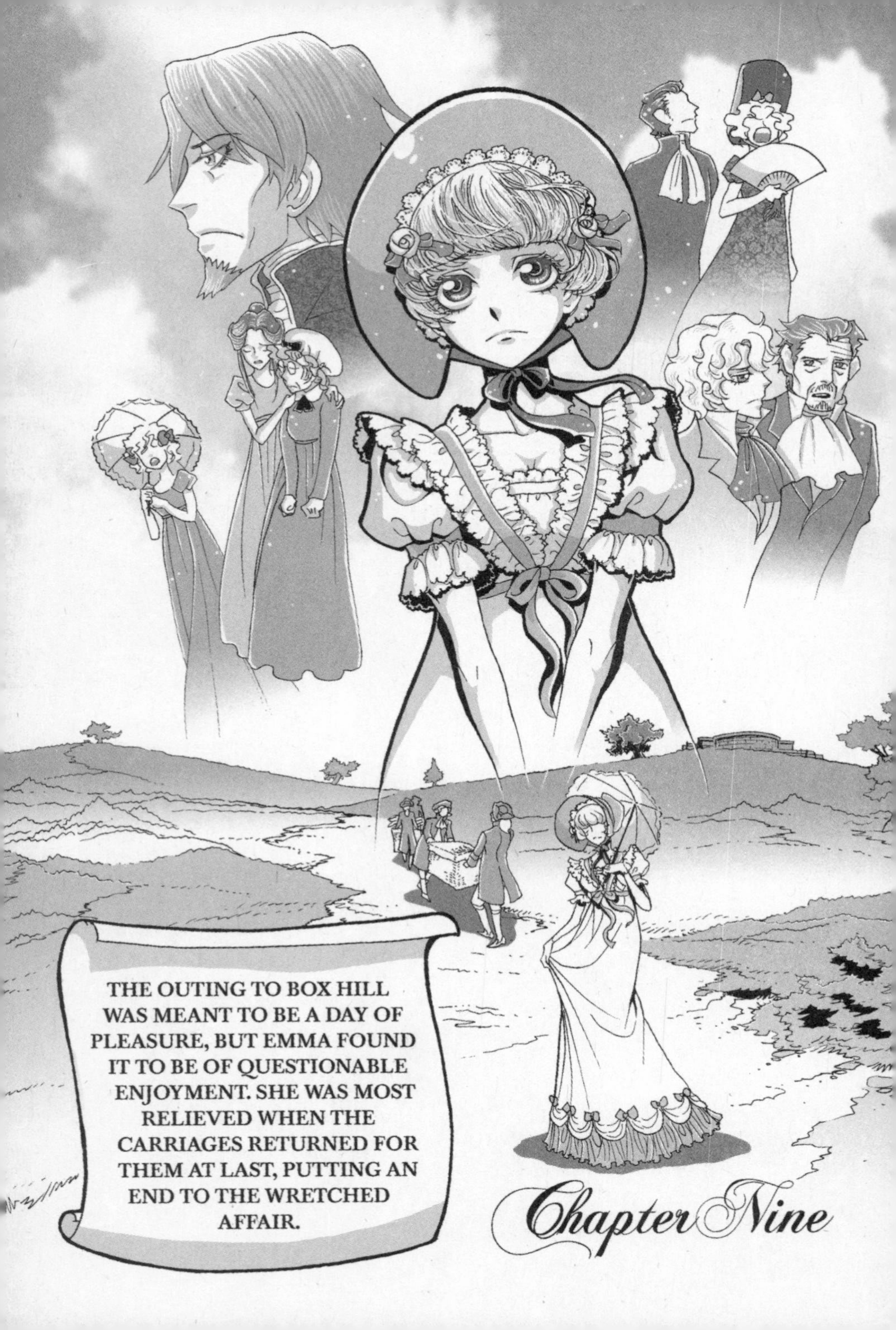
THE OUTING TO BOX HILL WAS MEANT TO BE A DAY OF PLEASURE, BUT EMMA FOUND IT TO BE OF QUESTIONABLE ENJOYMENT. SHE WAS MOST RELIEVED WHEN THE CARRIAGES RETURNED FOR THEM AT LAST, PUTTING AN END TO THE WRETCHED AFFAIR.
Chapter Nine

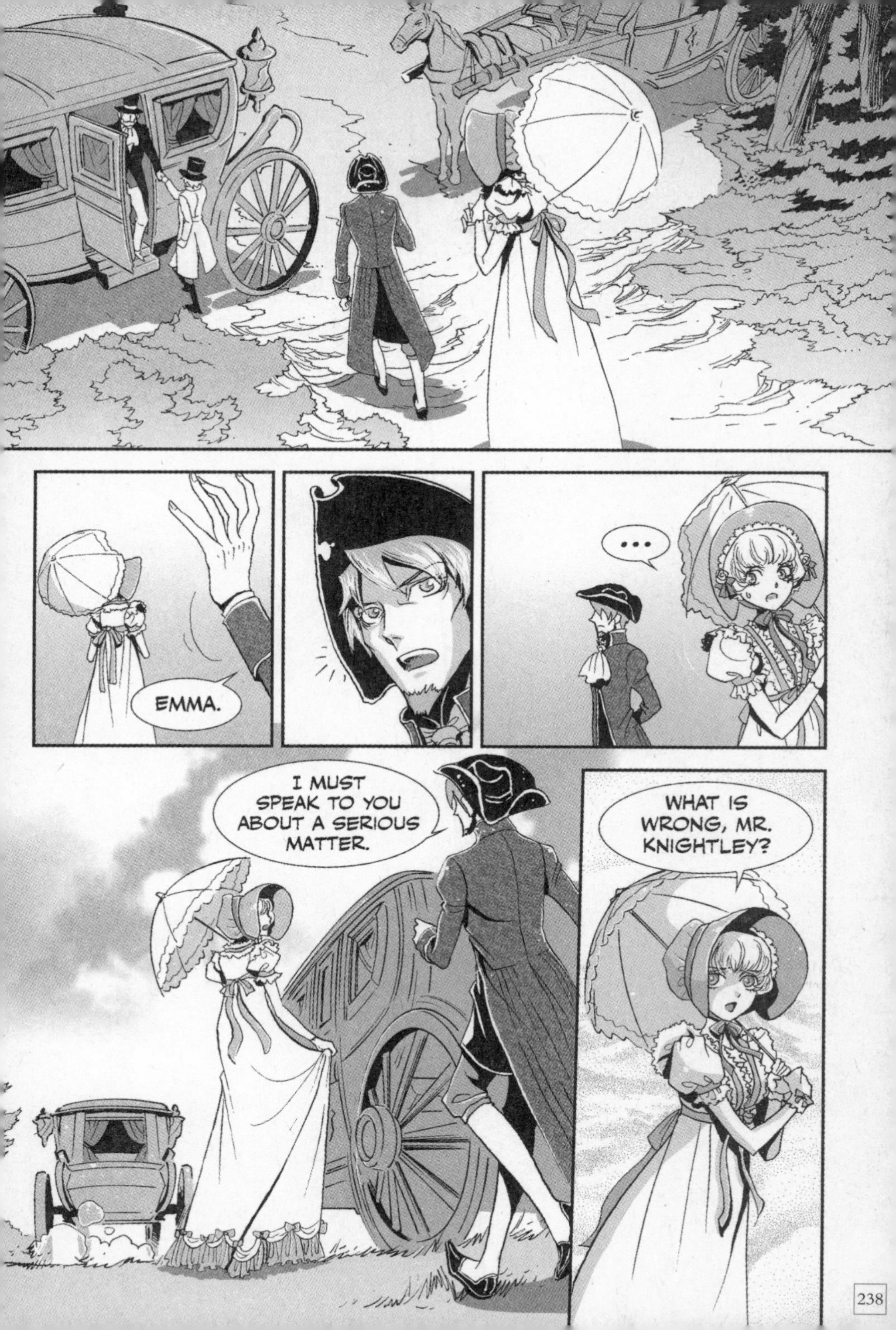
...
EMMA.
WHAT IS WRONG, MR. KNIGHTLEY?
I MUST SPEAK TO YOU ABOUT A SERIOUS MATTER.

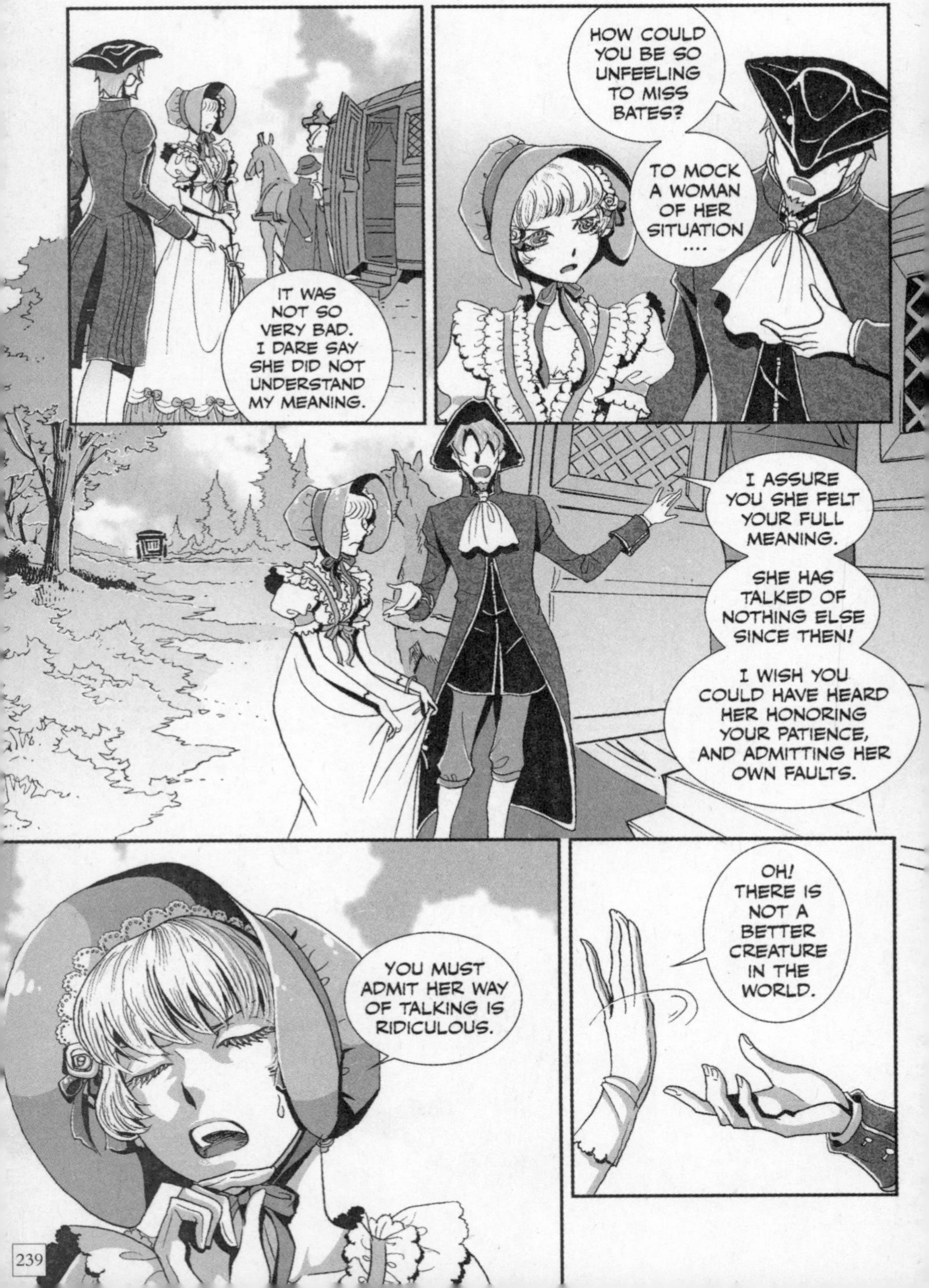
HOW COULD YOU BE SO UNFEELING TO MISS BATES?
TO MOCK A WOMAN OF HER SITUATION ....
IT WAS NOT SO VERY BAD. I DARE SAY SHE DID NOT UNDERSTAND MY MEANING.
I ASSURE YOU SHE FELT YOUR FULL MEANING.
SHE HAS TALKED OF NOTHING ELSE SINCE THEN!
I WISH YOU COULD HAVE HEARD HER HONORING YOUR PATIENCE, AND ADMITTING HER OWN FAULTS.
OH! THERE IS NOT A BETTER CREATURE IN THE WORLD.
YOU MUST ADMIT HER WAY OF TALKING IS RIDICULOUS.

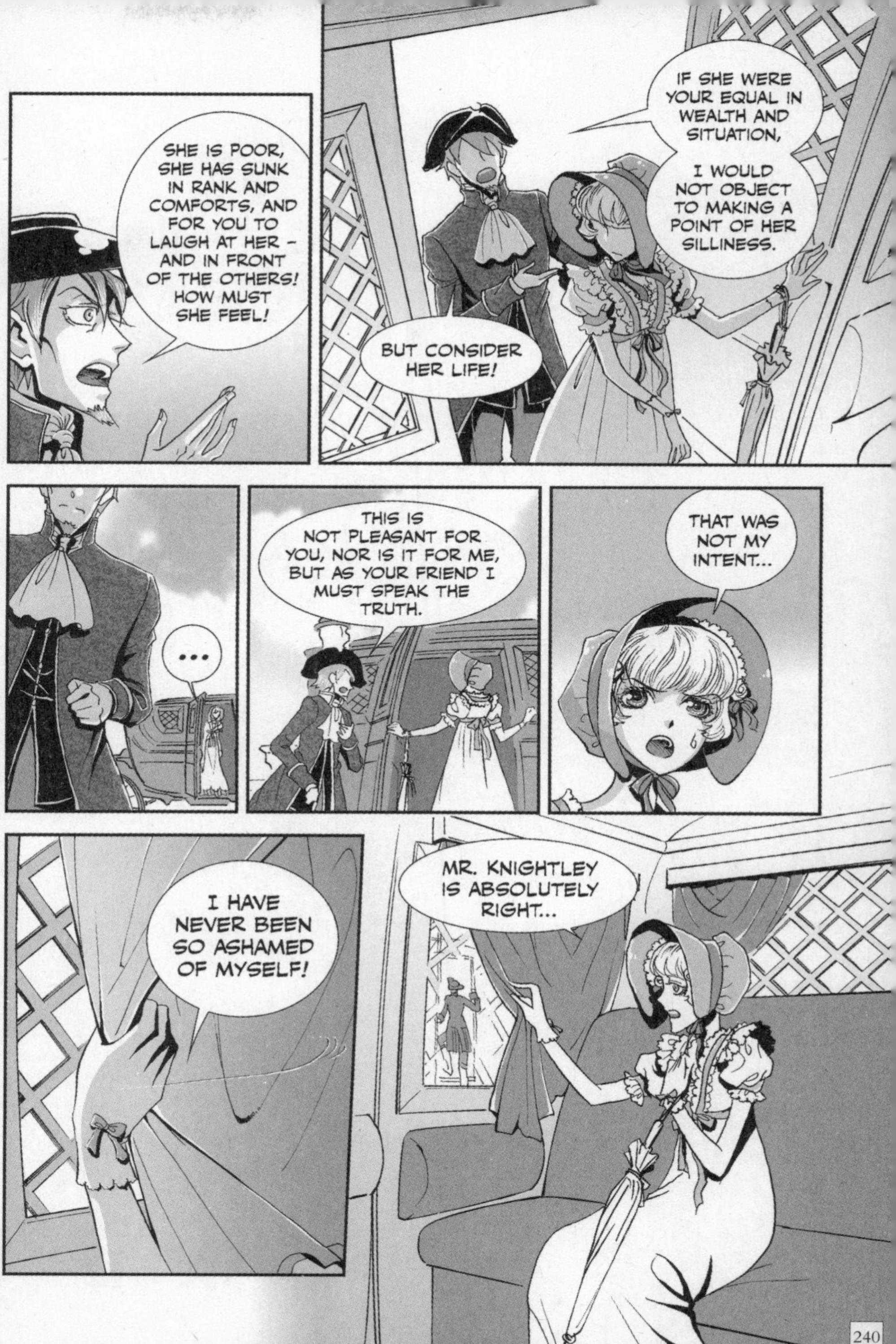
IF SHE WERE YOUR EQUAL IN WEALTH AND SITUATION,
I WOULD NOT OBJECT TO MAKING A POINT OF HER SILLINESS.
BUT CONSIDER HER LIFE!
SHE IS POOR, SHE HAS SUNK IN RANK AND COMFORTS, AND FOR YOU TO LAUGH AT HER - AND IN FRONT OF THE OTHERS! HOW MUST SHE FEEL!
THAT WAS NOT MY INTENT...
THIS IS NOT PLEASANT FOR YOU, NOR IS IT FOR ME, BUT AS YOUR FRIEND I MUST SPEAK THE TRUTH.
...
MR. KNIGHTLEY IS ABSOLUTELY RIGHT...
I HAVE NEVER BEEN SO ASHAMED OF MYSELF!

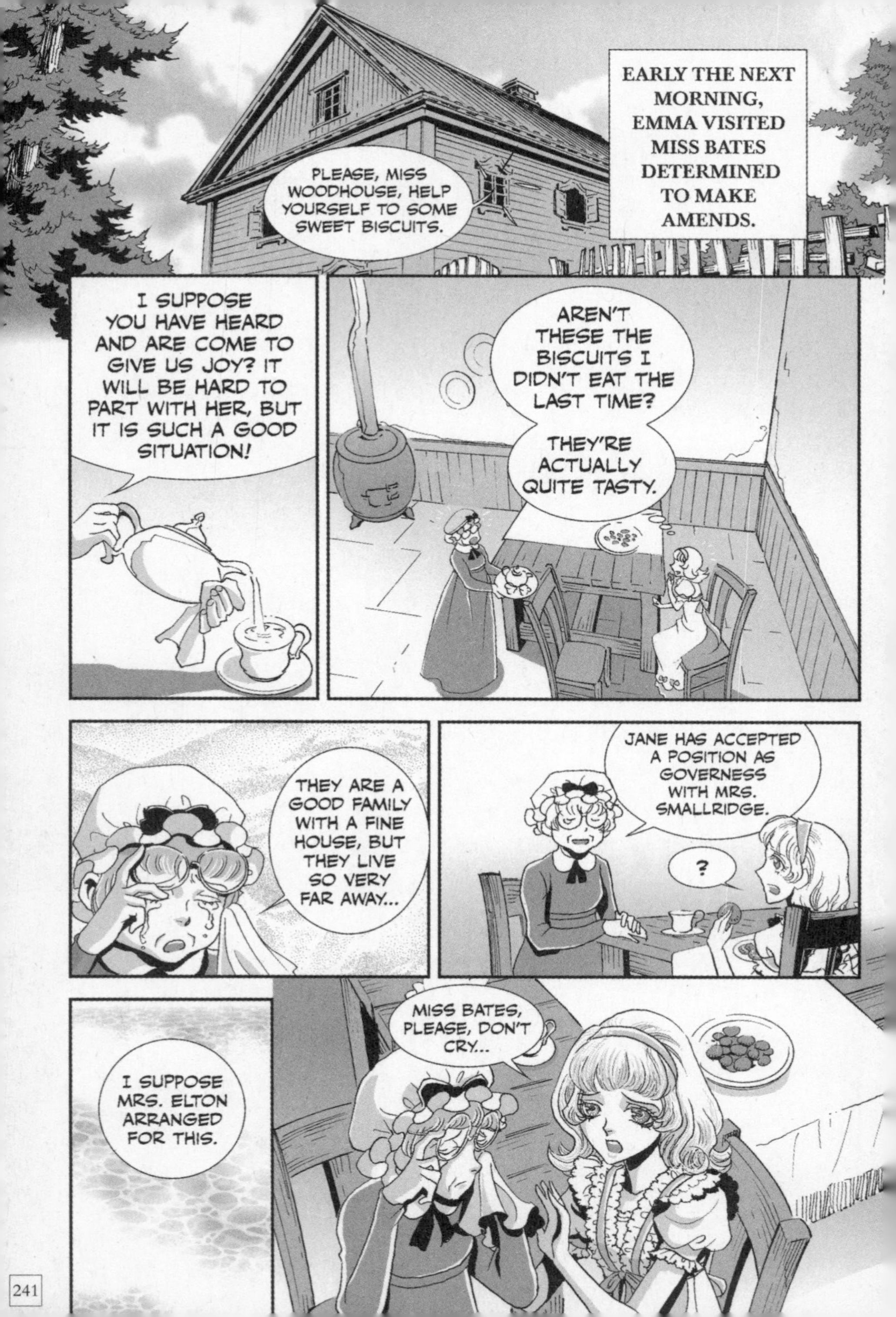
EARLY THE NEXT MORNING, EMMA VISITED MISS BATES DETERMINED TO MAKE AMENDS.
PLEASE, MISS WOODHOUSE, HELP YOURSELF TO SOME SWEET BISCUITS.
AREN'T THESE THE BISCUITS I DIDN'T EAT THE LAST TIME?
THEY'RE ACTUALLY QUITE TASTY.
I SUPPOSE YOU HAVE HEARD AND ARE COME TO GIVE US JOY? IT WILL BE HARD TO PART WITH HER, BUT IT IS SUCH A GOOD SITUATION!
JANE HAS ACCEPTED A POSITION AS GOVERNESS WITH MRS. SMALLRIDGE.
?
THEY ARE A GOOD FAMILY WITH A FINE HOUSE, BUT THEY LIVE SO VERY FAR AWAY...
MISS BATES, PLEASE, DON'T CRY...
I SUPPOSE MRS. ELTON ARRANGED FOR THIS.

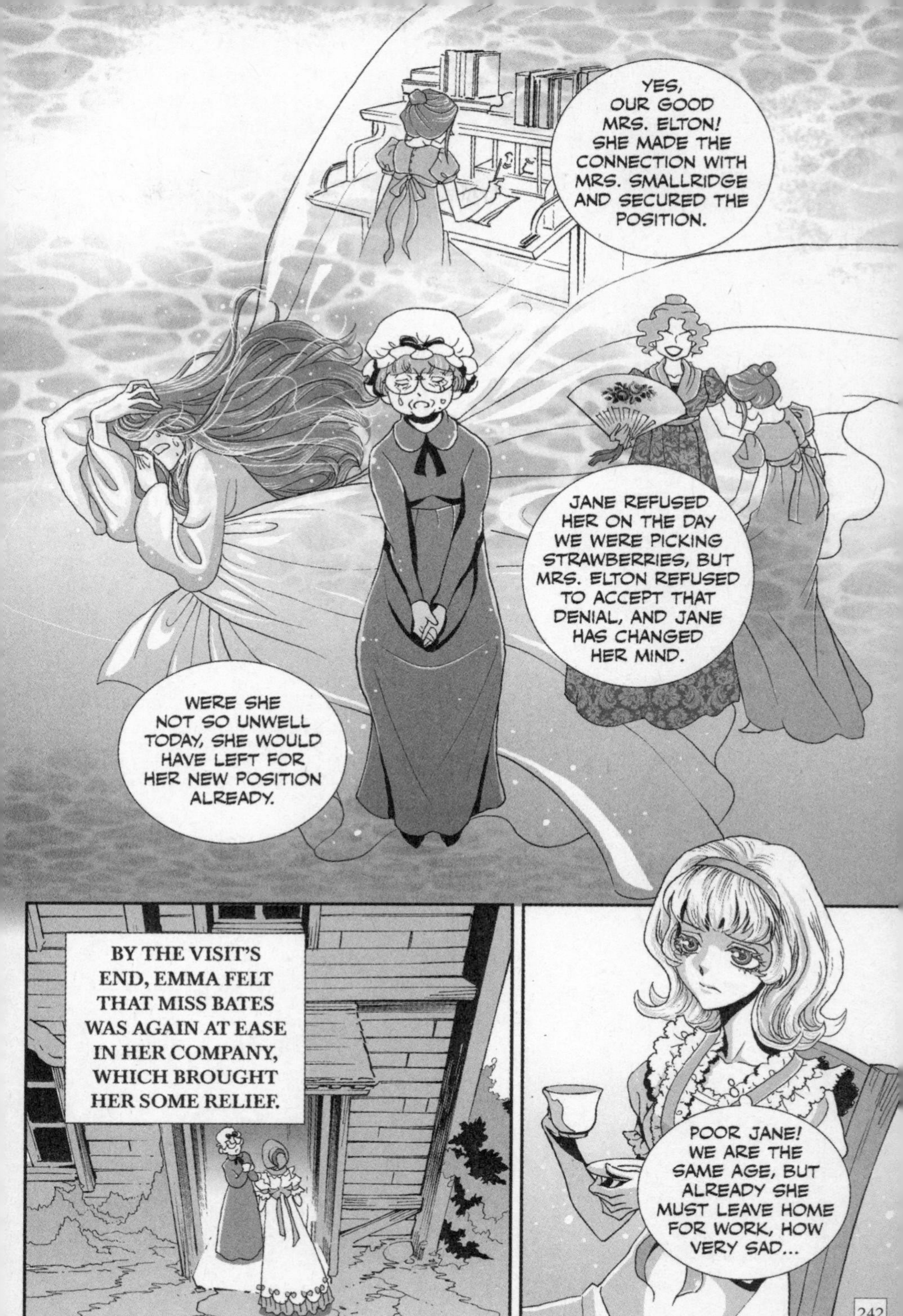

YES, OUR GOOD MRS. ELTON! SHE MADE THE CONNECTION WITH MRS. SMALLRIDGE AND SECURED THE POSITION.
JANE REFUSED HER ON THE DAY WE WERE PICKING STRAWBERRIES, BUT MRS. ELTON REFUSED TO ACCEPT THAT DENIAL, AND JANE HAS CHANGED HER MIND.
WERE SHE NOT SO UNWELL TODAY, SHE WOULD HAVE LEFT FOR HER NEW POSITION ALREADY.
POOR JANE! WE ARE THE SAME AGE, BUT ALREADY SHE MUST LEAVE HOME FOR WORK, HOW VERY SAD...
BY THE VISIT'S END, EMMA FELT THAT MISS BATES WAS AGAIN AT EASE IN HER COMPANY, WHICH BROUGHT HER SOME RELIEF.

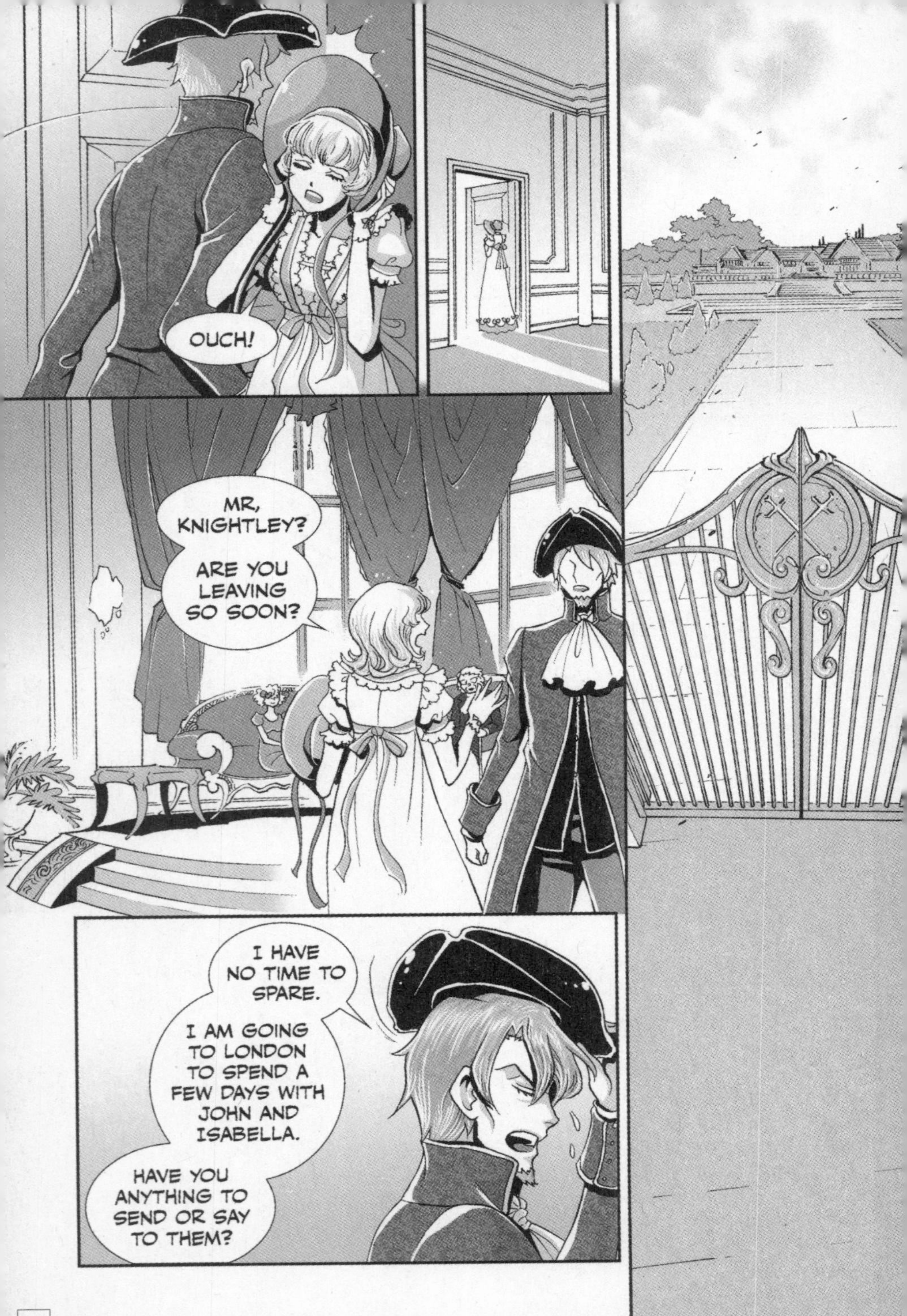
OUCH!
MR, KNIGHTLEY?
ARE YOU LEAVING SO SOON?
I HAVE NO TIME TO SPARE.
I AM GOING TO LONDON TO SPEND A FEW DAYS WITH JOHN AND ISABELLA.
HAVE YOU ANYTHING TO SEND OR SAY TO THEM?

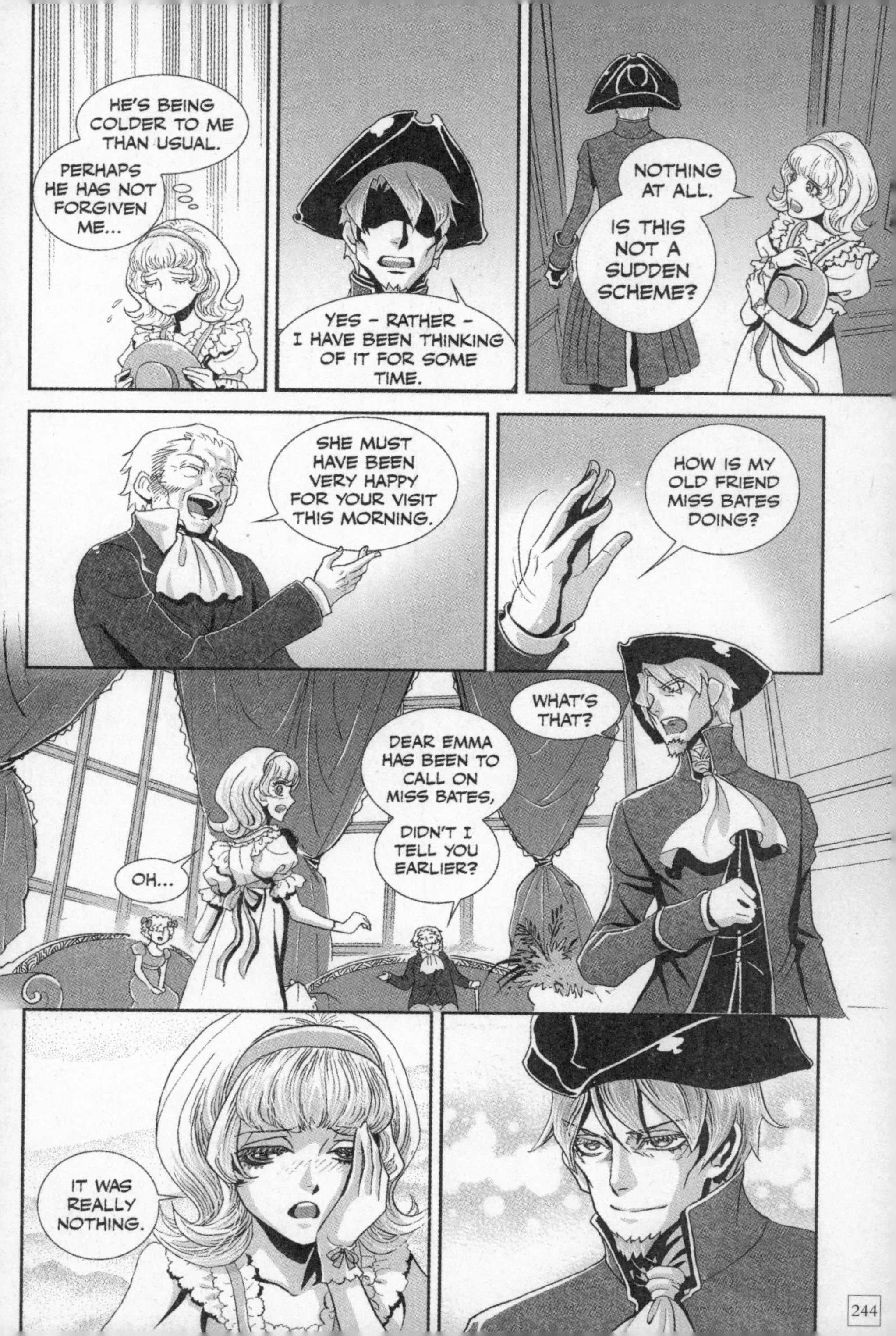
NOTHING AT ALL.
IS THIS NOT A SUDDEN SCHEME?
YES - RATHER - I HAVE BEEN THINKING OF IT FOR SOME TIME.
HE'S BEING COLDER TO ME THAN USUAL.
PERHAPS HE HAS NOT FORGIVEN ME...
HOW IS MY OLD FRIEND MISS BATES DOING?
SHE MUST HAVE BEEN VERY HAPPY FOR YOUR VISIT THIS MORNING.
WHAT'S THAT?
DEAR EMMA HAS BEEN TO CALL ON MISS BATES,
DIDN'T I TELL YOU EARLIER?
OH...
IT WAS REALLY NOTHING.

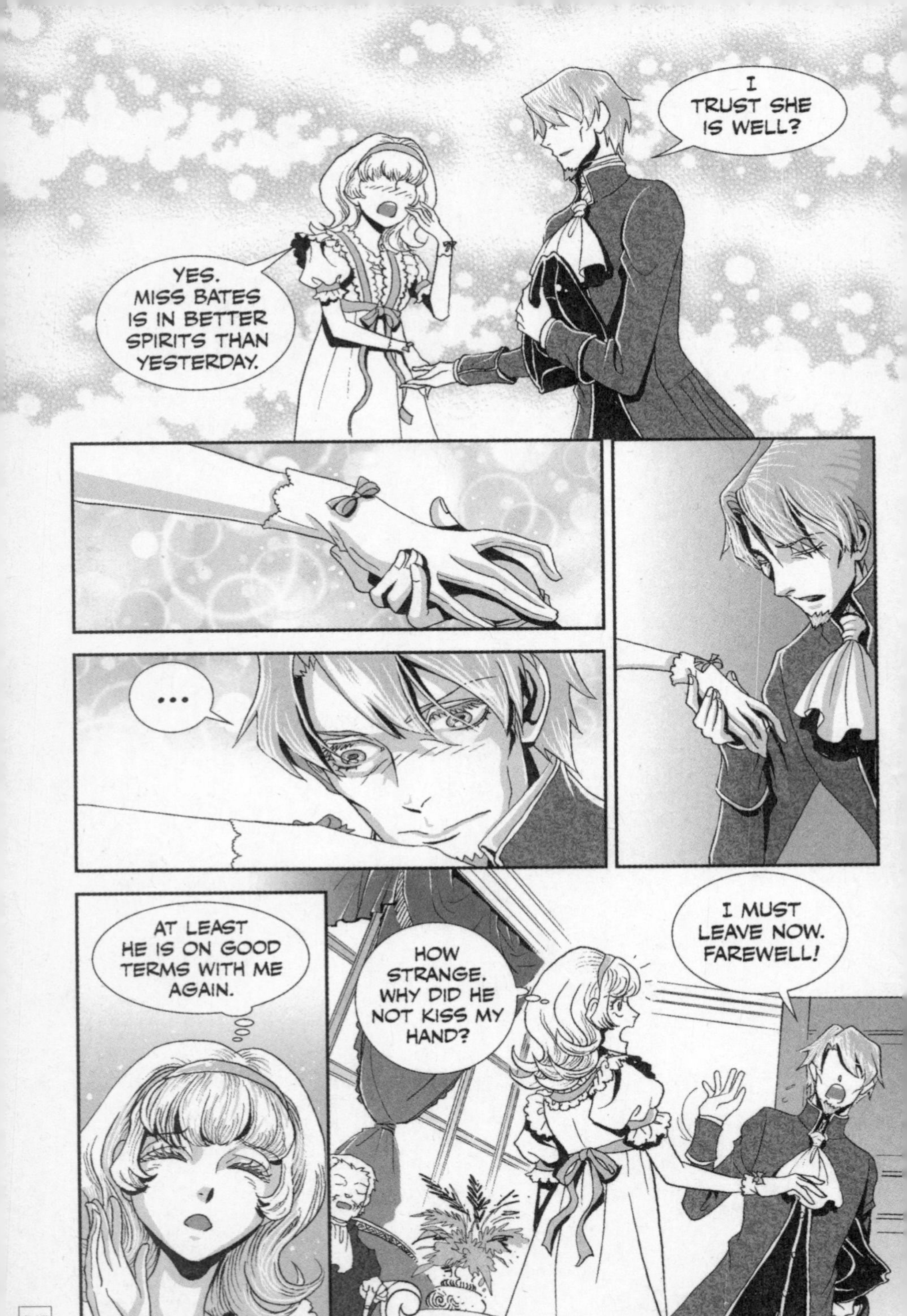
I TRUST SHE IS WELL?
YES. MISS BATES IS IN BETTER SPIRITS THAN YESTERDAY.
...
I MUST LEAVE NOW. FAREWELL!
HOW STRANGE. WHY DID HE NOT KISS MY HAND?
AT LEAST HE IS ON GOOD TERMS WITH ME AGAIN.

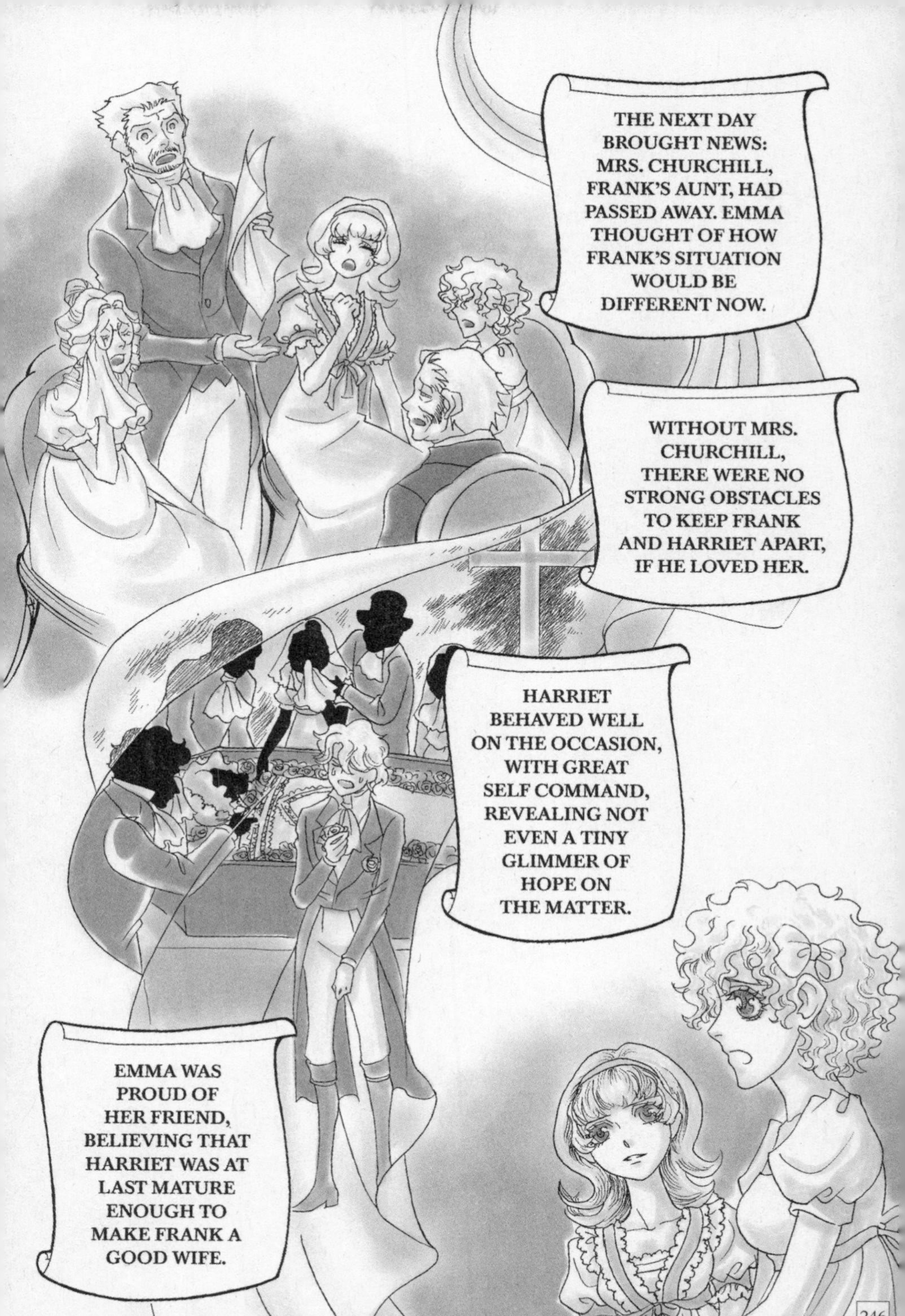
THE NEXT DAY BROUGHT NEWS: MRS. CHURCHILL, FRANK'S AUNT, HAD PASSED AWAY. EMMA THOUGHT OF HOW FRANK'S SITUATION WOULD BE DIFFERENT NOW.
WITHOUT MRS. CHURCHILL, THERE WERE NO STRONG OBSTACLES TO KEEP FRANK AND HARRIET APART, IF HE LOVED HER.
HARRIET BEHAVED WELL ON THE OCCASION, WITH GREAT SELF COMMAND, REVEALING NOT EVEN A TINY GLIMMER OF HOPE ON THE MATTER.
EMMA WAS PROUD OF HER FRIEND, BELIEVING THAT HARRIET WAS AT LAST MATURE ENOUGH TO MAKE FRANK A GOOD WIFE.

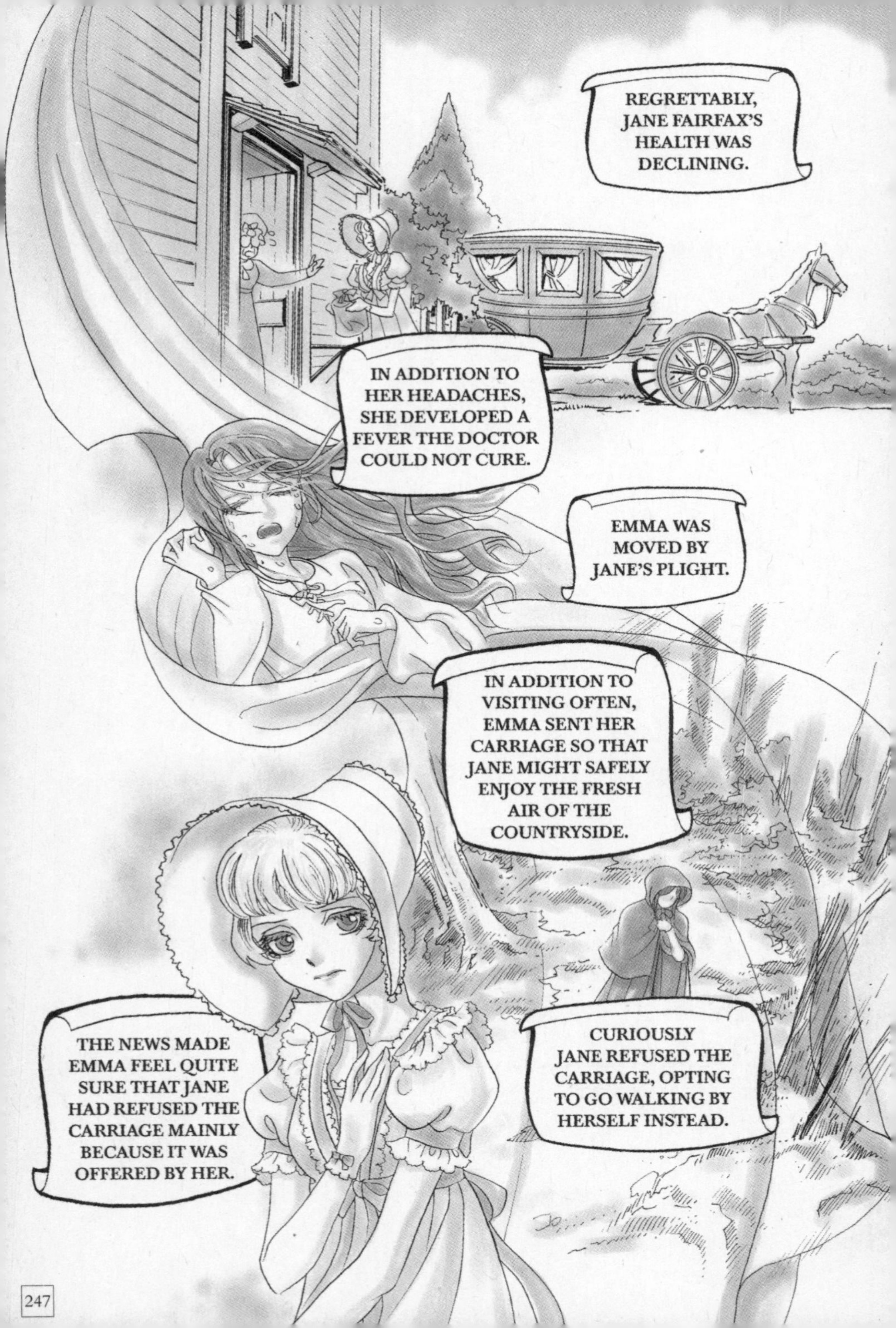
REGRETTABLY, JANE FAIRFAX'S HEALTH WAS DECLINING.
IN ADDITION TO HER HEADACHES, SHE DEVELOPED A FEVER THE DOCTOR COULD NOT CURE.
EMMA WAS MOVED BY JANE'S PLIGHT.
IN ADDITION TO VISITING OFTEN, EMMA SENT HER CARRIAGE SO THAT JANE MIGHT SAFELY ENJOY THE FRESH AIR OF THE COUNTRYSIDE.
CURIOUSLY JANE REFUSED THE CARRIAGE, OPTING TO GO WALKING BY HERSELF INSTEAD.
THE NEWS MADE EMMA FEEL QUITE SURE THAT JANE HAD REFUSED THE CARRIAGE MAINLY BECAUSE IT WAS OFFERED BY HER.

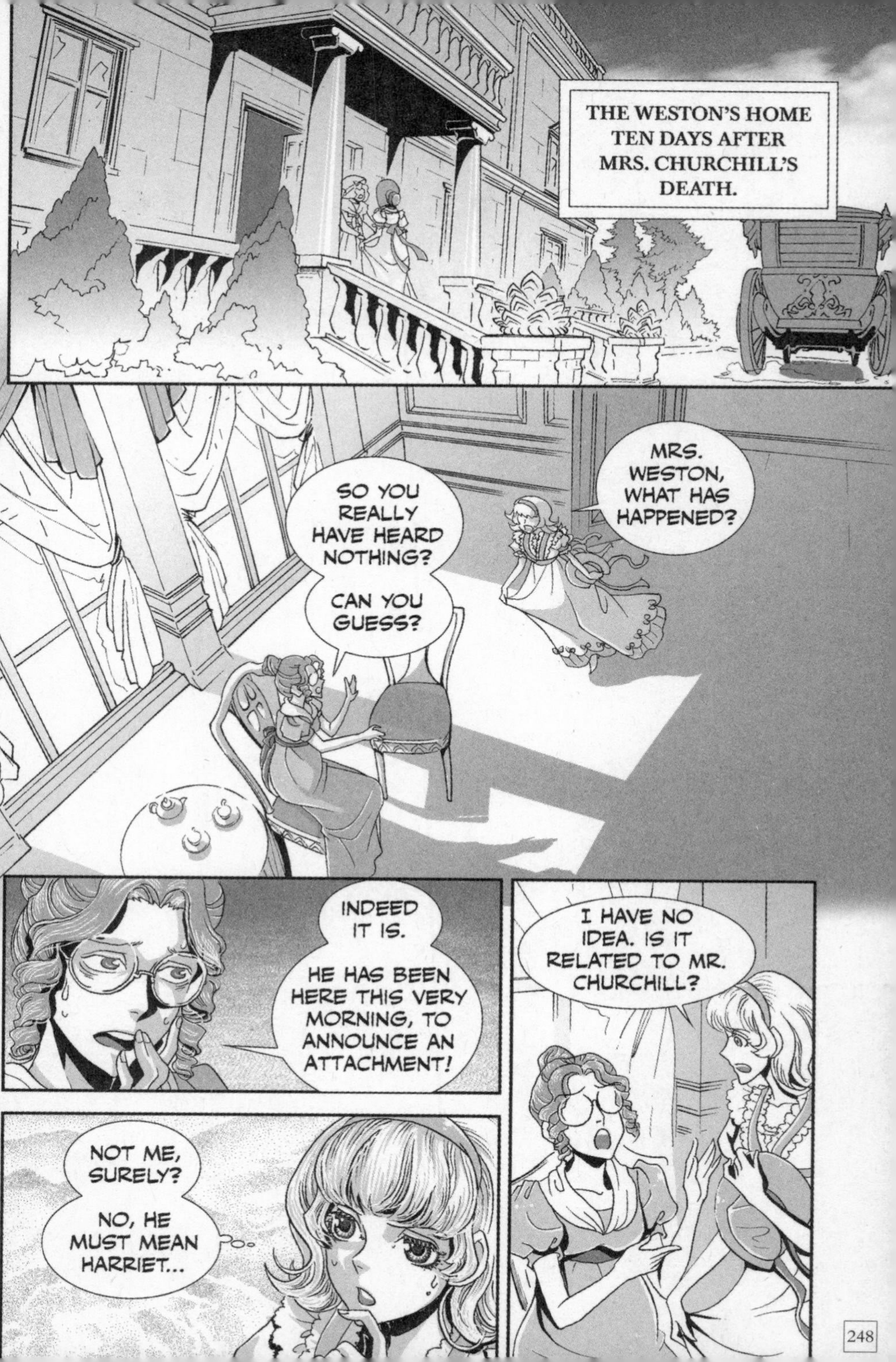
THE WESTON'S HOME TEN DAYS AFTER MRS. CHURCHILL'S DEATH.
MRS. WESTON, WHAT HAS HAPPENED?
SO YOU REALLY HAVE HEARD NOTHING?
CAN YOU GUESS?
I HAVE NO IDEA. IS IT RELATED TO MR. CHURCHILL?
INDEED IT IS.
HE HAS BEEN HERE THIS VERY MORNING, TO ANNOUNCE AN ATTACHMENT!
NOT ME, SURELY?
NO, HE MUST MEAN HARRIET...

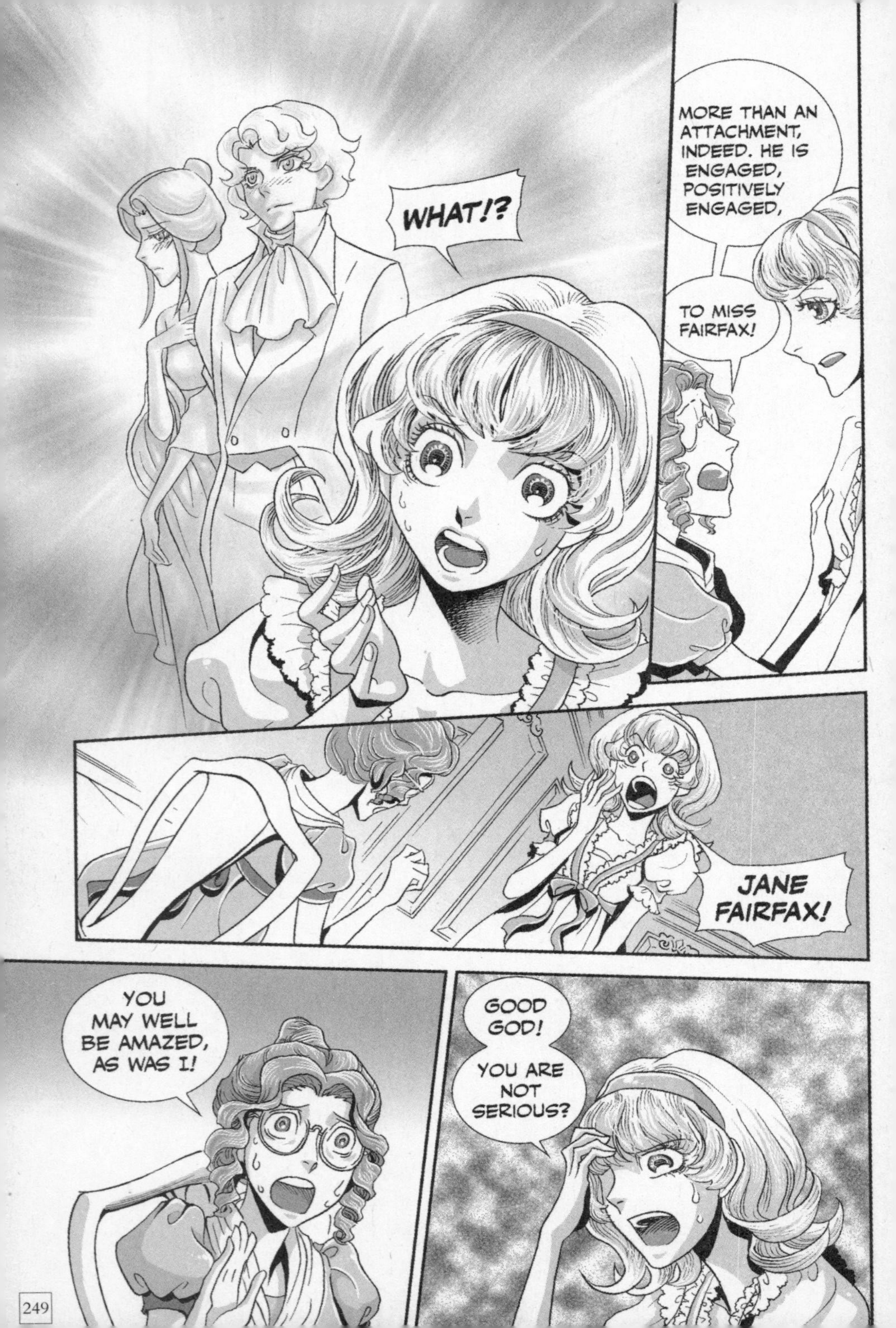
MORE THAN AN ATTACHMENT, INDEED. HE IS ENGAGED, POSITIVELY ENGAGED,
TO MISS FAIRFAX!
WHAT!?
JANE FAIRFAX!
GOOD GOD!
YOU ARE NOT SERIOUS?
YOU MAY WELL BE AMAZED, AS WAS I!

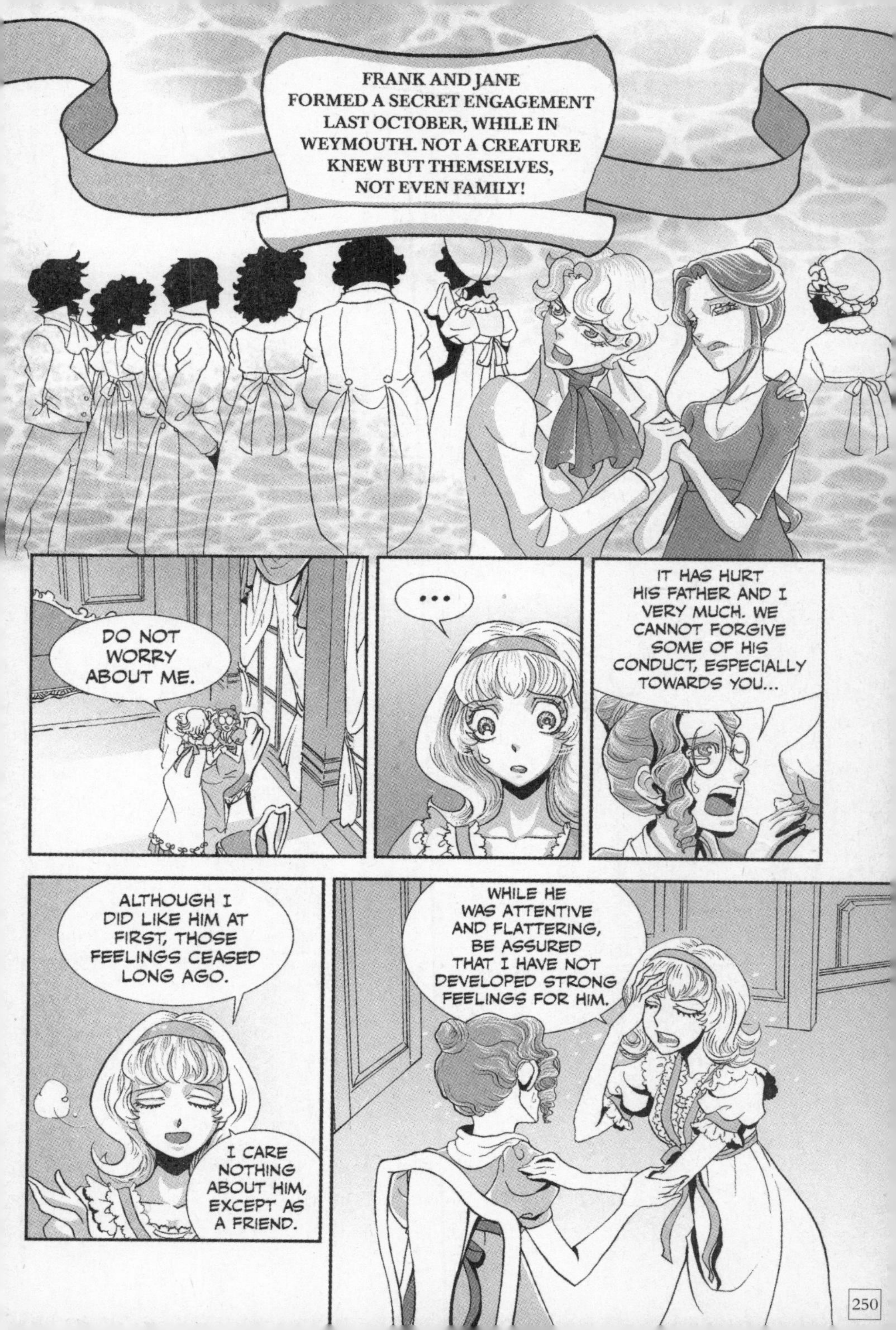
FRANK AND JANE FORMED A SECRET ENGAGEMENT LAST OCTOBER, WHILE IN WEYMOUTH. NOT A CREATURE KNEW BUT THEMSELVES, NOT EVEN FAMILY!
IT HAS HURT HIS FATHER AND I VERY MUCH. WE CANNOT FORGIVE SOME OF HIS CONDUCT, ESPECIALLY TOWARDS YOU...
...
DO NOT WORRY ABOUT ME.
WHILE HE WAS ATTENTIVE AND FLATTERING, BE ASSURED THAT I HAVE NOT DEVELOPED STRONG FEELINGS FOR HIM.
ALTHOUGH I DID LIKE HIM AT FIRST, THOSE FEELINGS CEASED LONG AGO.
I CARE NOTHING ABOUT HIM, EXCEPT AS A FRIEND.

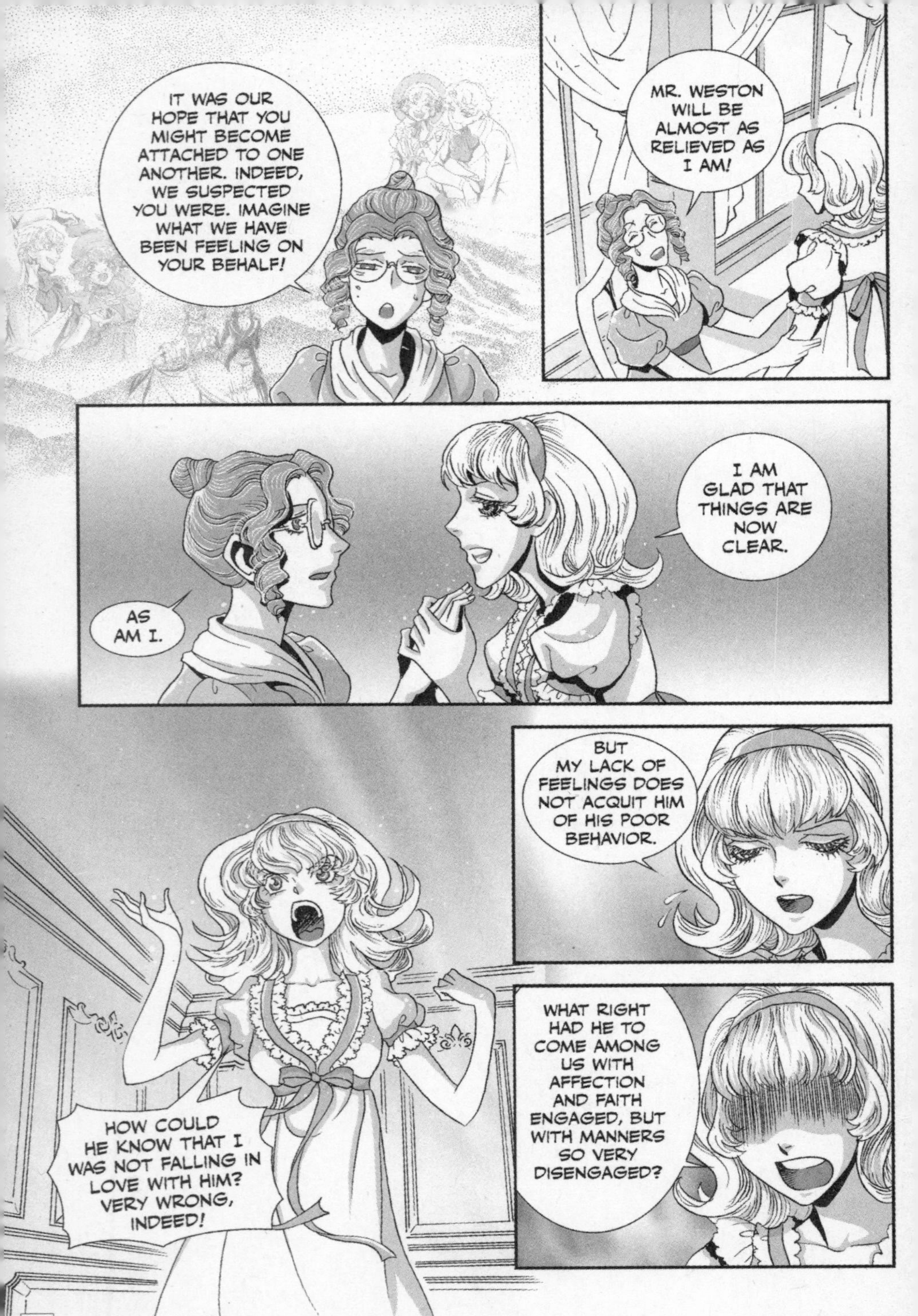
MR. WESTON WILL BE ALMOST AS RELIEVED AS I AM!
IT WAS OUR HOPE THAT YOU MIGHT BECOME ATTACHED TO ONE ANOTHER. INDEED, WE SUSPECTED YOU WERE. IMAGINE WHAT WE HAVE BEEN FEELING ON YOUR BEHALF!
I AM GLAD THAT THINGS ARE NOW CLEAR.
AS AM I.
BUT MY LACK OF FEELINGS DOES NOT ACQUIT HIM OF HIS POOR BEHAVIOR.
WHAT RIGHT HAD HE TO COME AMONG US WITH AFFECTION AND FAITH ENGAGED, BUT WITH MANNERS SO VERY DISENGAGED?
HOW COULD HE KNOW THAT I WAS NOT FALLING IN LOVE WITH HIM? VERY WRONG, INDEED!

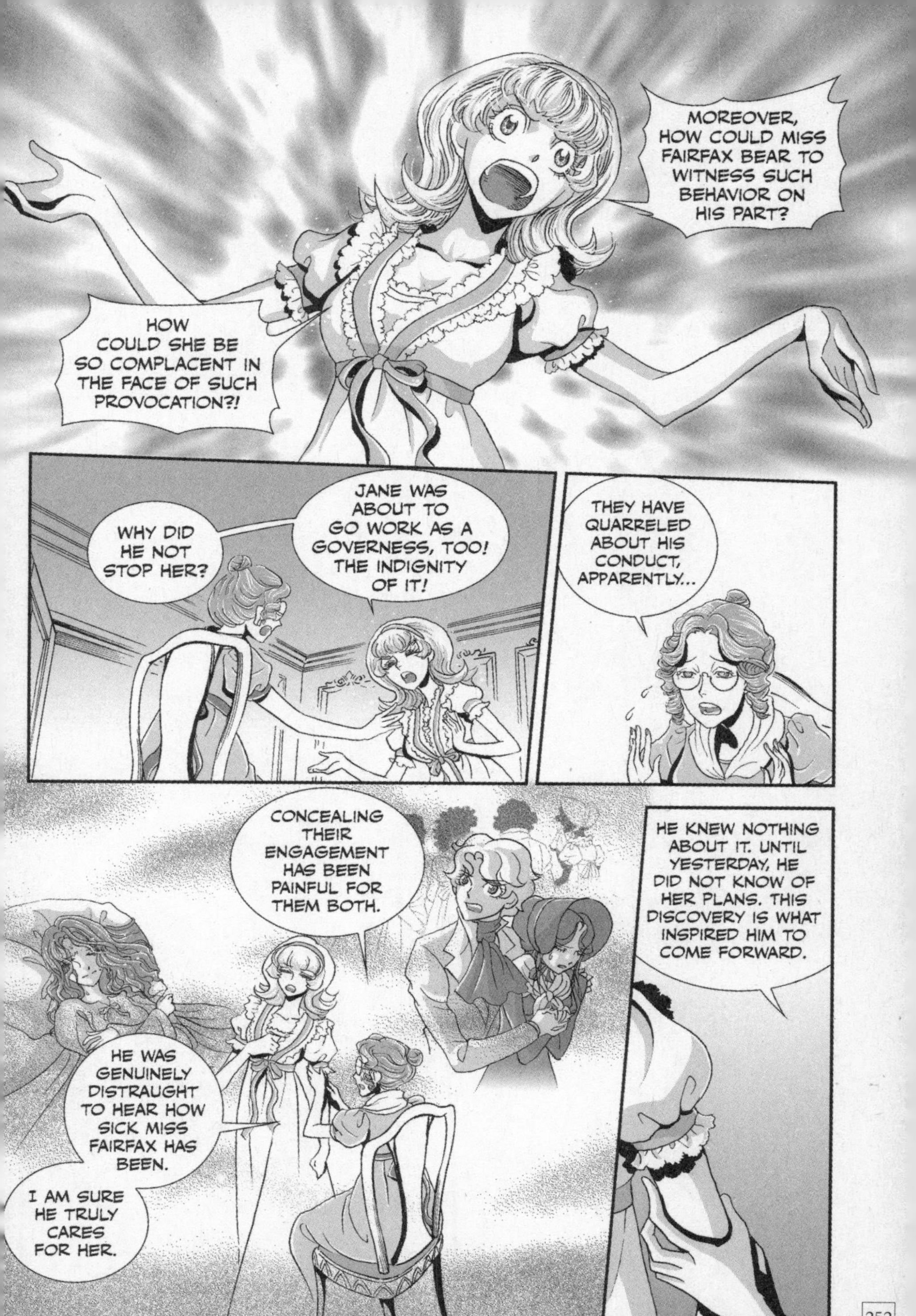
MOREOVER, HOW COULD MISS FAIRFAX BEAR TO WITNESS SUCH BEHAVIOR ON HIS PART?
HOW COULD SHE BE SO COMPLACENT IN THE FACE OF SUCH PROVOCATION?!
THEY HAVE QUARRELED ABOUT HIS CONDUCT, APPARENTLY...
JANE WAS ABOUT TO GO WORK AS A GOVERNESS, TOO! THE INDIGNITY OF IT!
WHY DID HE NOT STOP HER?
HE KNEW NOTHING ABOUT IT. UNTIL YESTERDAY, HE DID NOT KNOW OF HER PLANS. THIS DISCOVERY IS WHAT INSPIRED HIM TO COME FORWARD.
CONCEALING THEIR ENGAGEMENT HAS BEEN PAINFUL FOR THEM BOTH.
HE WAS GENUINELY DISTRAUGHT TO HEAR HOW SICK MISS FAIRFAX HAS BEEN.
I AM SURE HE TRULY CARES FOR HER.

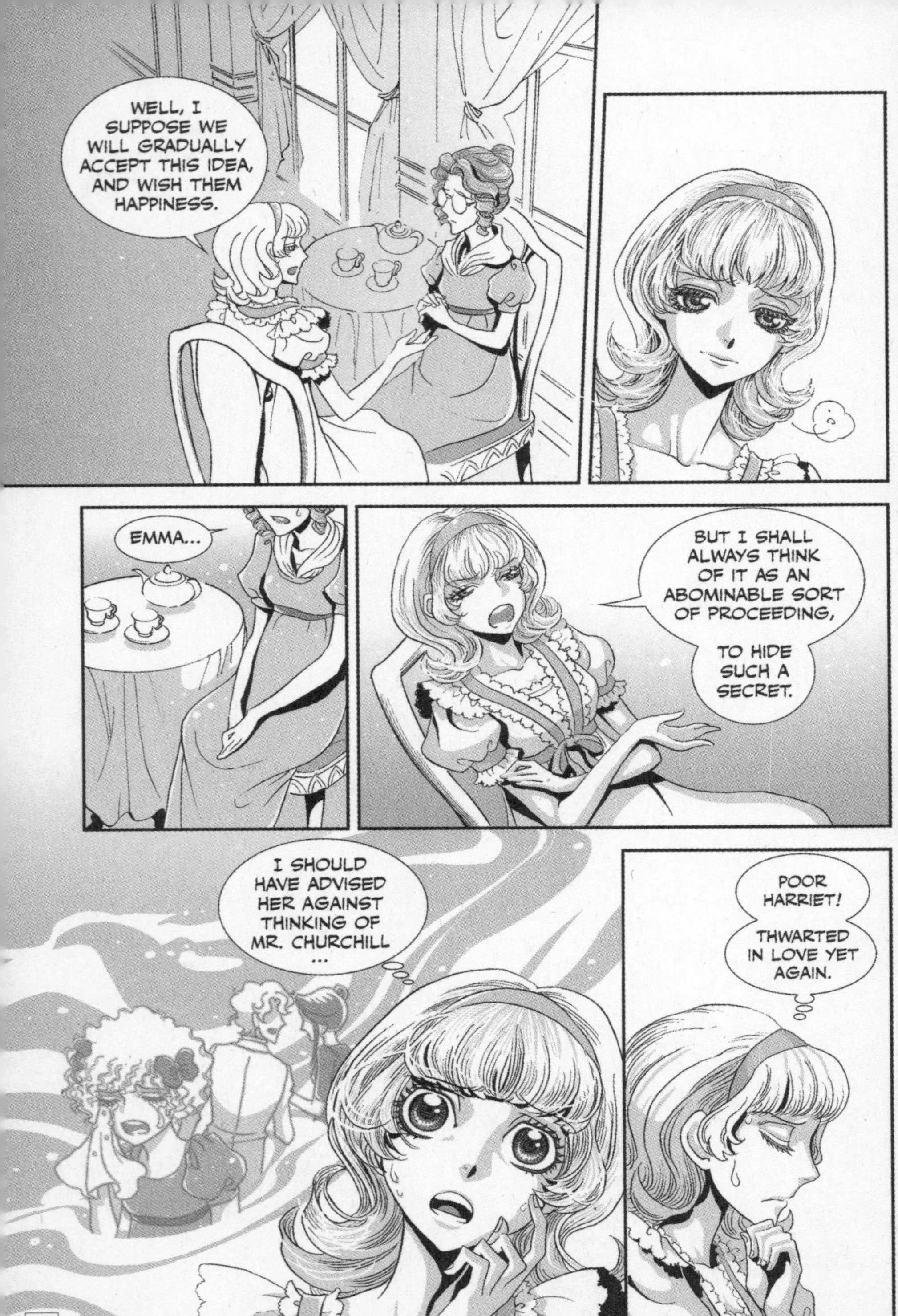
WELL, I SUPPOSE WE WILL GRADUALLY ACCEPT THIS IDEA, AND WISH THEM HAPPINESS.
BUT I SHALL ALWAYS THINK OF IT AS AN ABOMINABLE SORT OF PROCEEDING,
TO HIDE SUCH A SECRET.
EMMA...
POOR HARRIET!
THWARTED IN LOVE YET AGAIN.
I SHOULD HAVE ADVISED HER AGAINST THINKING OF MR. CHURCHILL ...

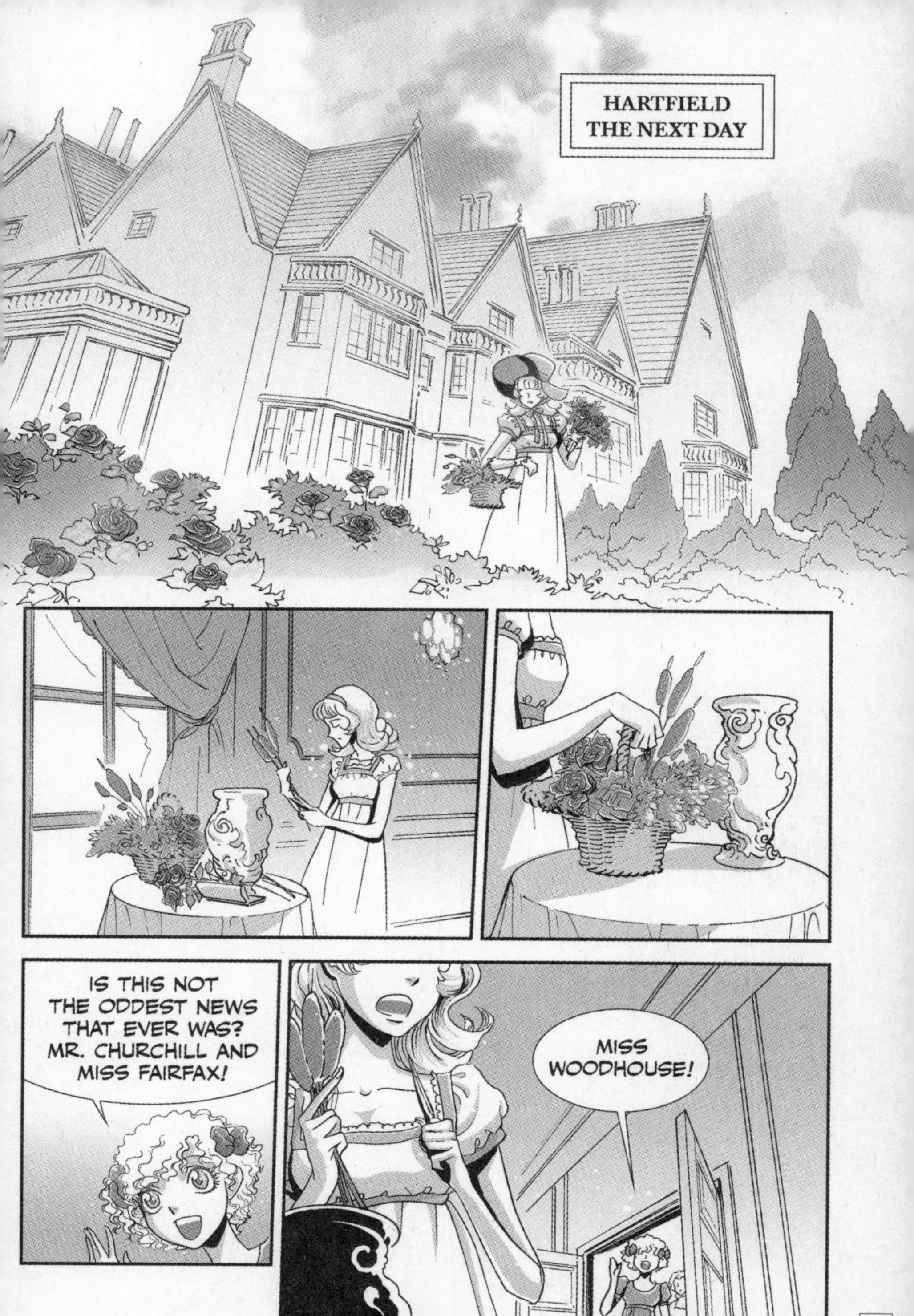
HARTFIELD
THE NEXT DAY
MISS WOODHOUSE!
IS THIS NOT THE ODDEST NEWS THAT EVER WAS? MR. CHURCHILL AND MISS FAIRFAX!

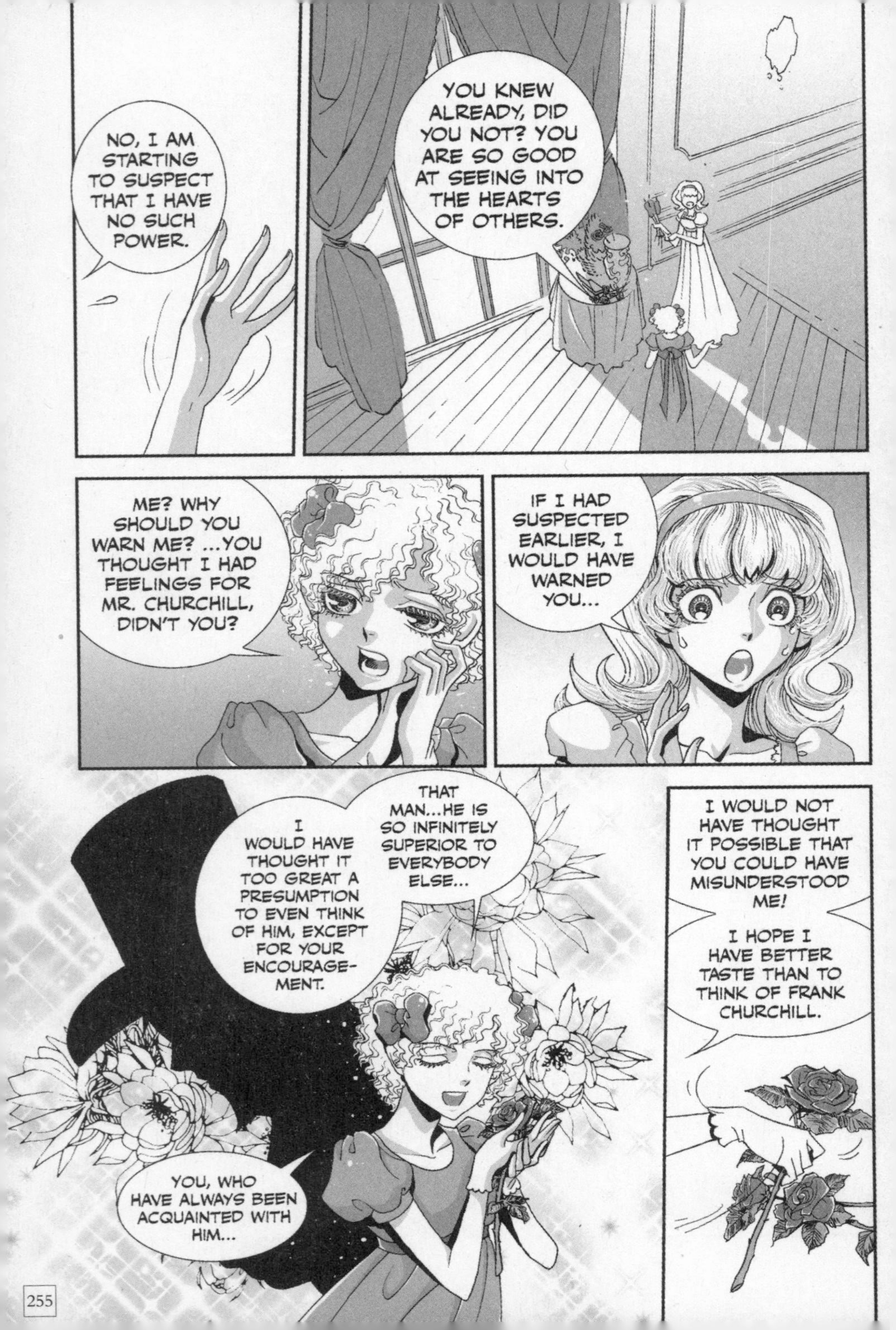
YOU KNEW ALREADY, DID YOU NOT? YOU ARE SO GOOD AT SEEING INTO THE HEARTS OF OTHERS.
NO, I AM STARTING TO SUSPECT THAT I HAVE NO SUCH POWER.
IF I HAD SUSPECTED EARLIER, I WOULD HAVE WARNED YOU...
ME? WHY SHOULD YOU WARN ME? ...YOU THOUGHT I HAD FEELINGS FOR MR. CHURCHILL, DIDN'T YOU?
I WOULD NOT HAVE THOUGHT IT POSSIBLE THAT YOU COULD HAVE MISUNDERSTOOD ME!
I HOPE I HAVE BETTER TASTE THAN TO THINK OF FRANK CHURCHILL.
THAT MAN...HE IS SO INFINITELY SUPERIOR TO EVERYBODY ELSE...
I WOULD HAVE THOUGHT IT TOO GREAT A PRESUMPTION TO EVEN THINK OF HIM, EXCEPT FOR YOUR ENCOURAGE-MENT.
YOU, WHO HAVE ALWAYS BEEN ACQUAINTED WITH HIM...

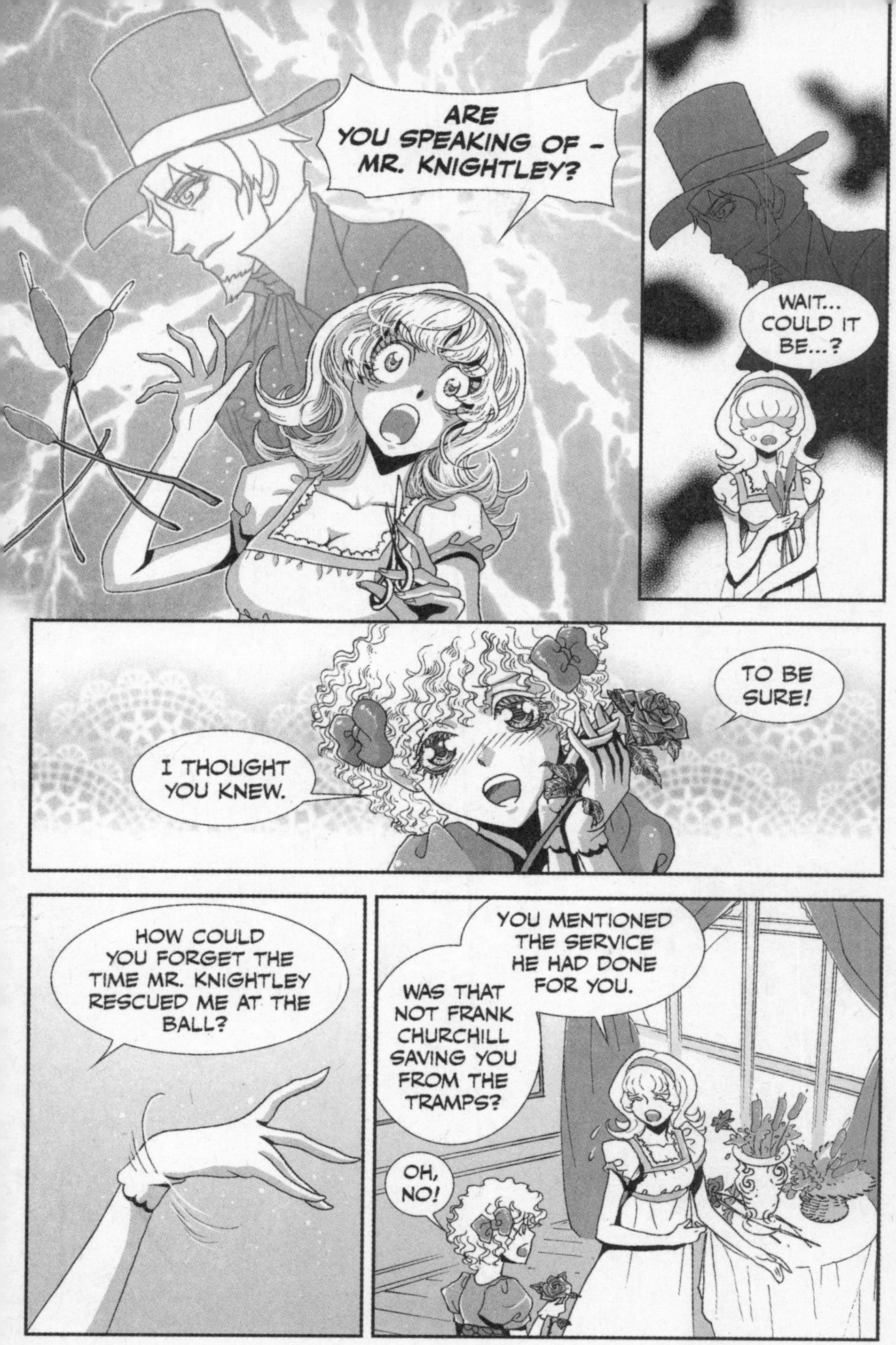
WAIT... COULD IT BE...?
ARE YOU SPEAKING OF - MR. KNIGHTLEY?
TO BE SURE!
I THOUGHT YOU KNEW.
YOU MENTIONED THE SERVICE HE HAD DONE FOR YOU.
WAS THAT NOT FRANK CHURCHILL SAVING YOU FROM THE TRAMPS?
OH, NO!
HOW COULD YOU FORGET THE TIME MR. KNIGHTLEY RESCUED ME AT THE BALL?

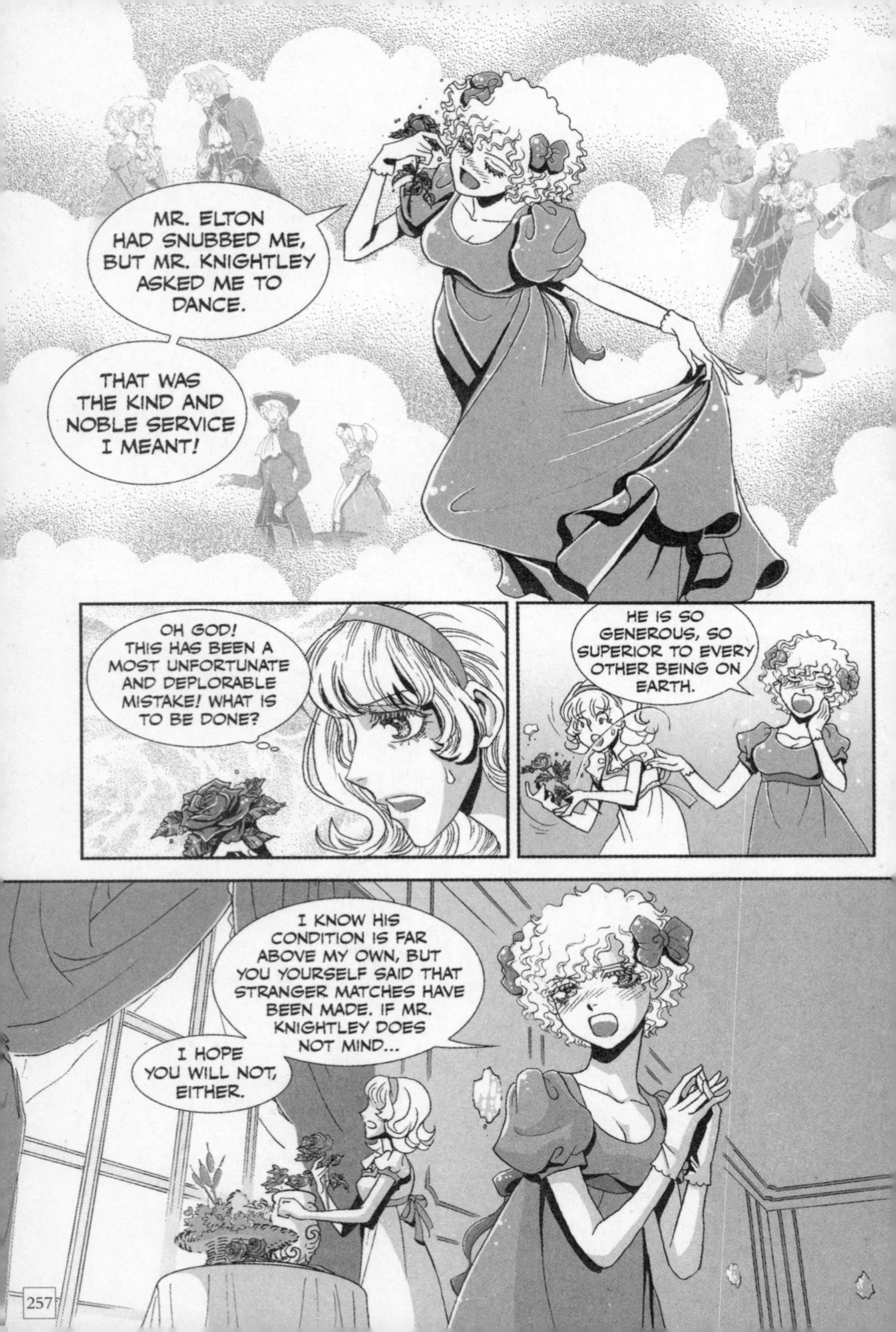
MR. ELTON HAD SNUBBED ME, BUT MR. KNIGHTLEY ASKED ME TO DANCE.
THAT WAS THE KIND AND NOBLE SERVICE I MEANT!
HE IS SO GENEROUS, SO SUPERIOR TO EVERY OTHER BEING ON EARTH.
OH GOD! THIS HAS BEEN A MOST UNFORTUNATE AND DEPLORABLE MISTAKE! WHAT IS TO BE DONE?
I KNOW HIS CONDITION IS FAR ABOVE MY OWN, BUT YOU YOURSELF SAID THAT STRANGER MATCHES HAVE BEEN MADE. IF MR. KNIGHTLEY DOES NOT MIND...
I HOPE YOU WILL NOT, EITHER.

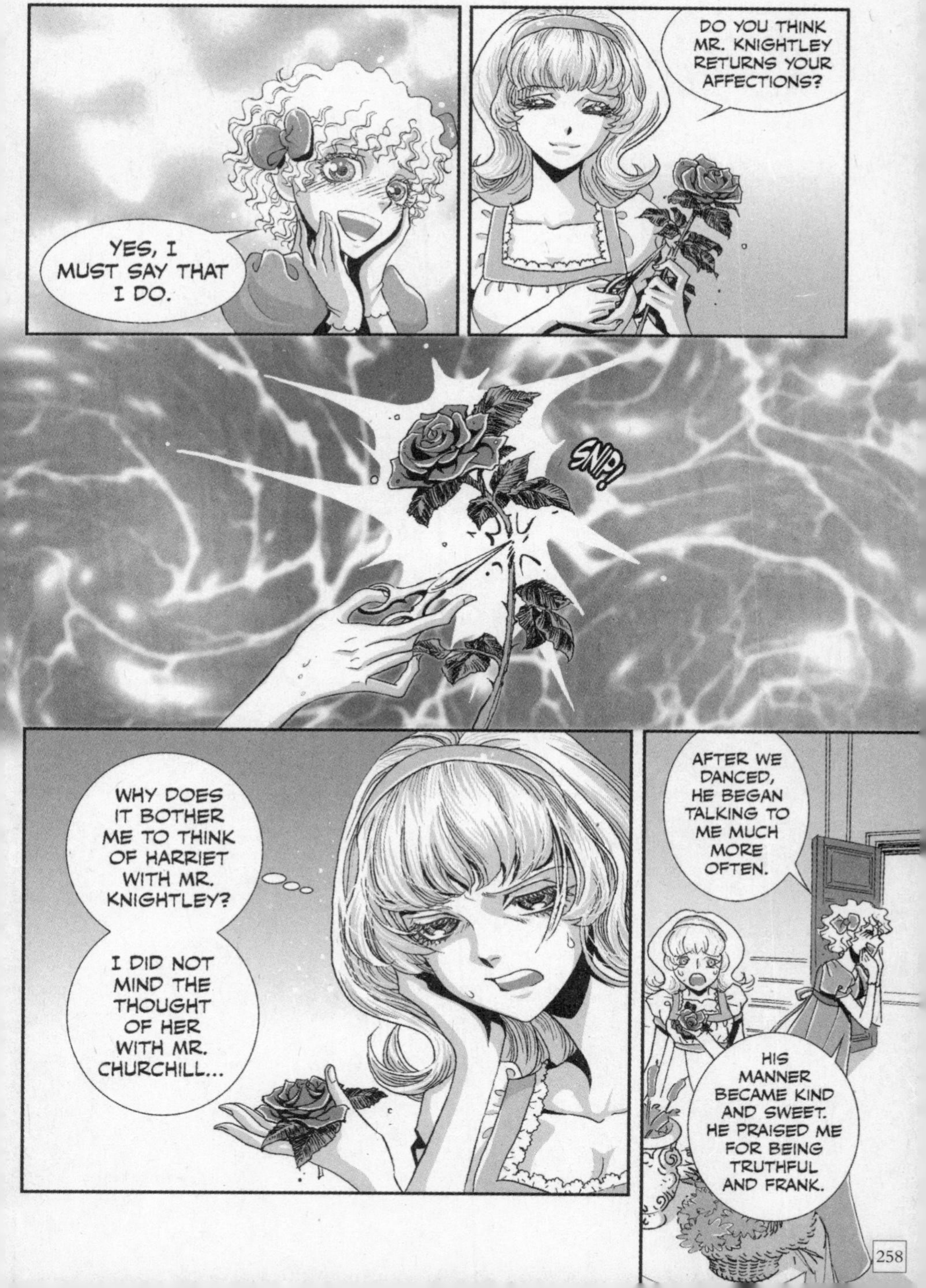
DO YOU THINK MR. KNIGHTLEY RETURNS YOUR AFFECTIONS?
YES, I MUST SAY THAT I DO.
SNIP!
AFTER WE DANCED, HE BEGAN TALKING TO ME MUCH MORE OFTEN.
HIS MANNER BECAME KIND AND SWEET. HE PRAISED ME FOR BEING TRUTHFUL AND FRANK.
WHY DOES IT BOTHER ME TO THINK OF HARRIET WITH MR. KNIGHTLEY?
I DID NOT MIND THE THOUGHT OF HER WITH MR. CHURCHILL...

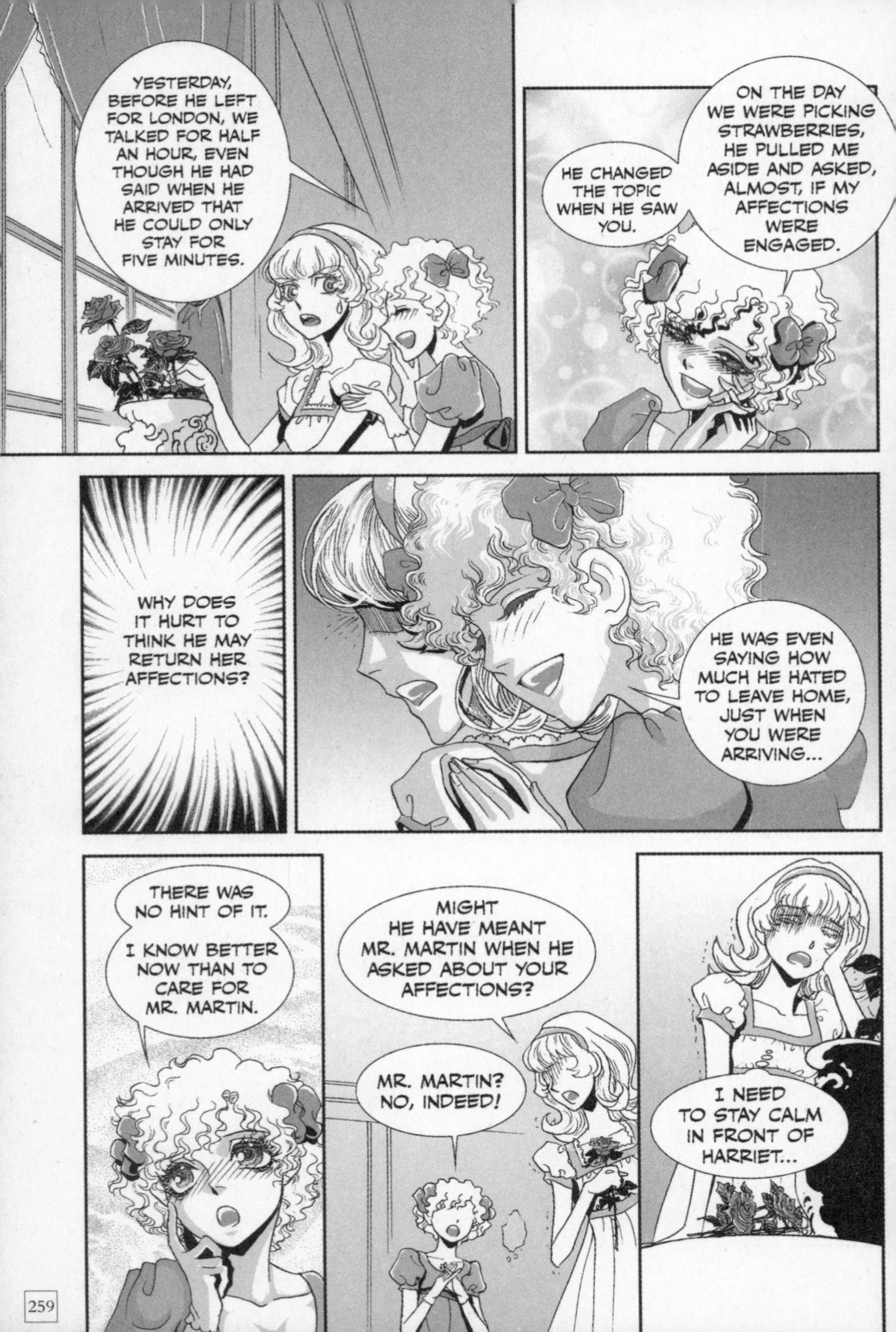
ON THE DAY WE WERE PICKING STRAWBERRIES, HE PULLED ME ASIDE AND ASKED, ALMOST, IF MY AFFECTIONS WERE ENGAGED.
HE CHANGED THE TOPIC WHEN HE SAW YOU.
YESTERDAY, BEFORE HE LEFT FOR LONDON, WE TALKED FOR HALF AN HOUR, EVEN THOUGH HE HAD SAID WHEN HE ARRIVED THAT HE COULD ONLY STAY FOR FIVE MINUTES.
HE WAS EVEN SAYING HOW MUCH HE HATED TO LEAVE HOME, JUST WHEN YOU WERE ARRIVING...
WHY DOES IT HURT TO THINK HE MAY RETURN HER AFFECTIONS?
I NEED TO STAY CALM IN FRONT OF HARRIET...
MIGHT HE HAVE MEANT MR. MARTIN WHEN HE ASKED ABOUT YOUR AFFECTIONS?
MR. MARTIN? NO, INDEED!
THERE WAS NO HINT OF IT.
I KNOW BETTER NOW THAN TO CARE FOR MR. MARTIN.

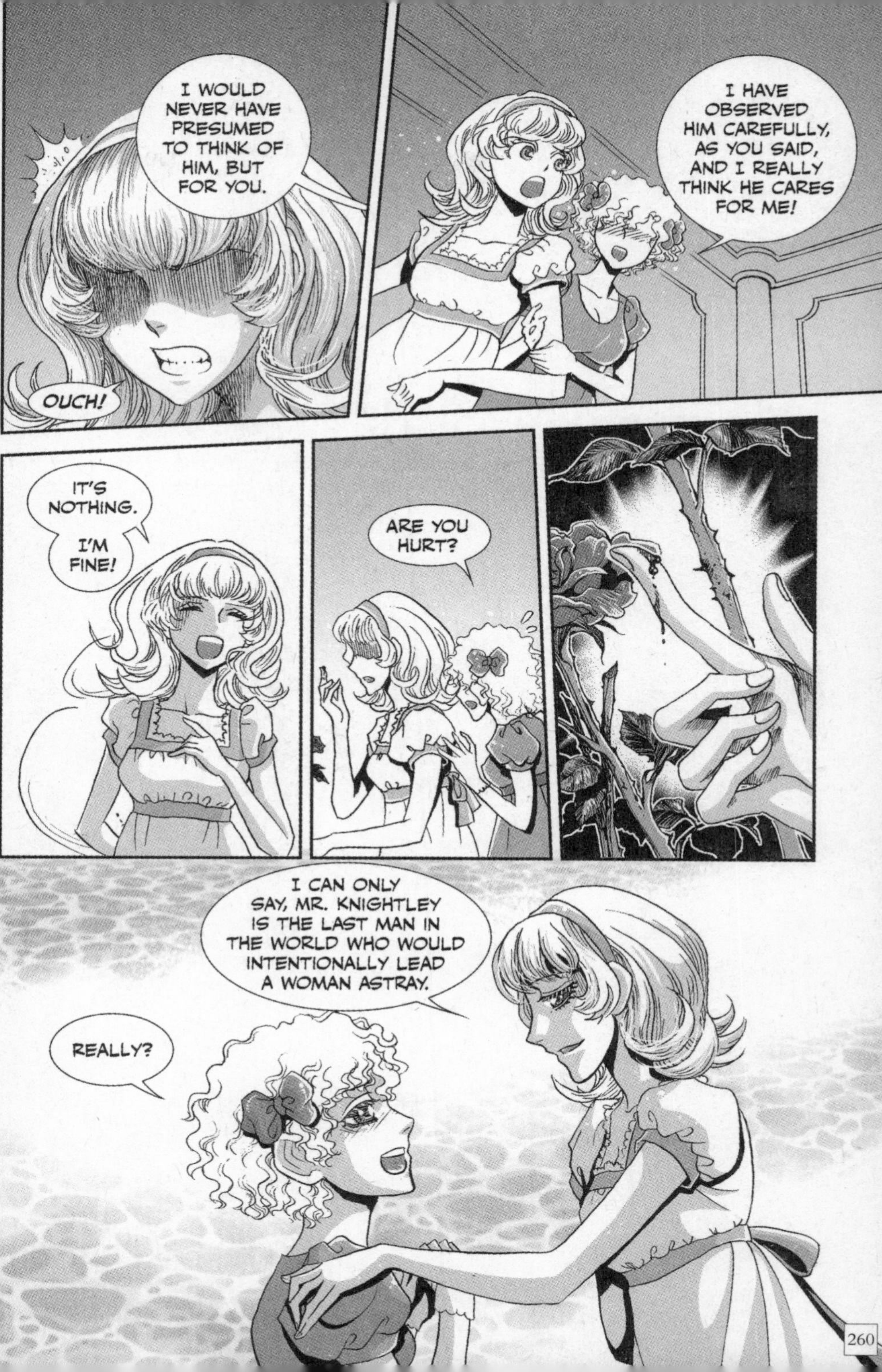
I HAVE OBSERVED HIM CAREFULLY, AS YOU SAID, AND I REALLY THINK HE CARES FOR ME!
I WOULD NEVER HAVE PRESUMED TO THINK OF HIM, BUT FOR YOU.
OUCH!
ARE YOU HURT?
IT'S NOTHING.
I'M FINE!
I CAN ONLY SAY, MR. KNIGHTLEY IS THE LAST MAN IN THE WORLD WHO WOULD INTENTIONALLY LEAD A WOMAN ASTRAY.
REALLY?

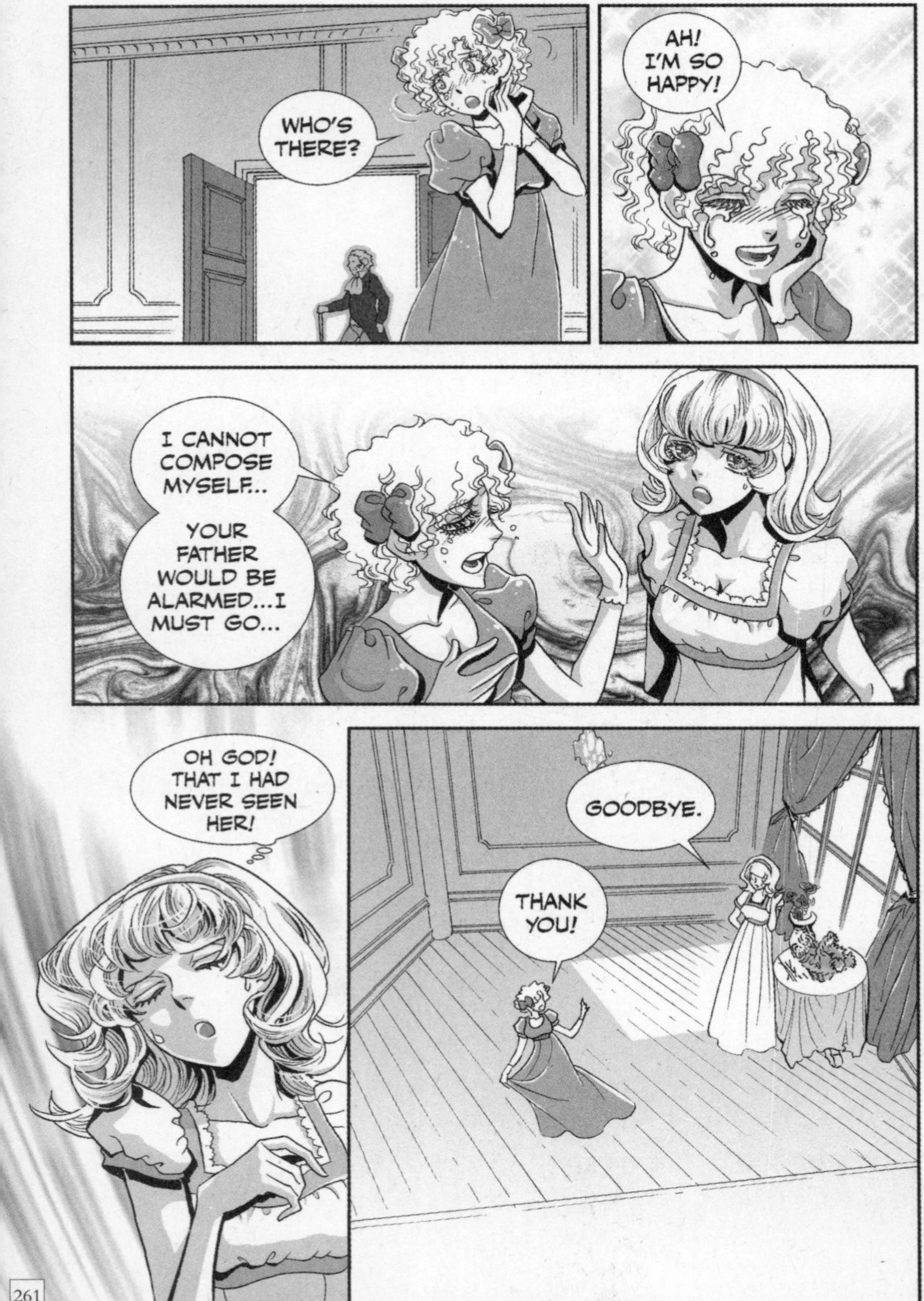
AH! I'M SO HAPPY!
WHO'S THERE?
I CANNOT COMPOSE MYSELF...
YOUR FATHER WOULD BE ALARMED...I MUST GO...
GOODBYE.
THANK YOU!
OH GOD! THAT I HAD NEVER SEEN HER!

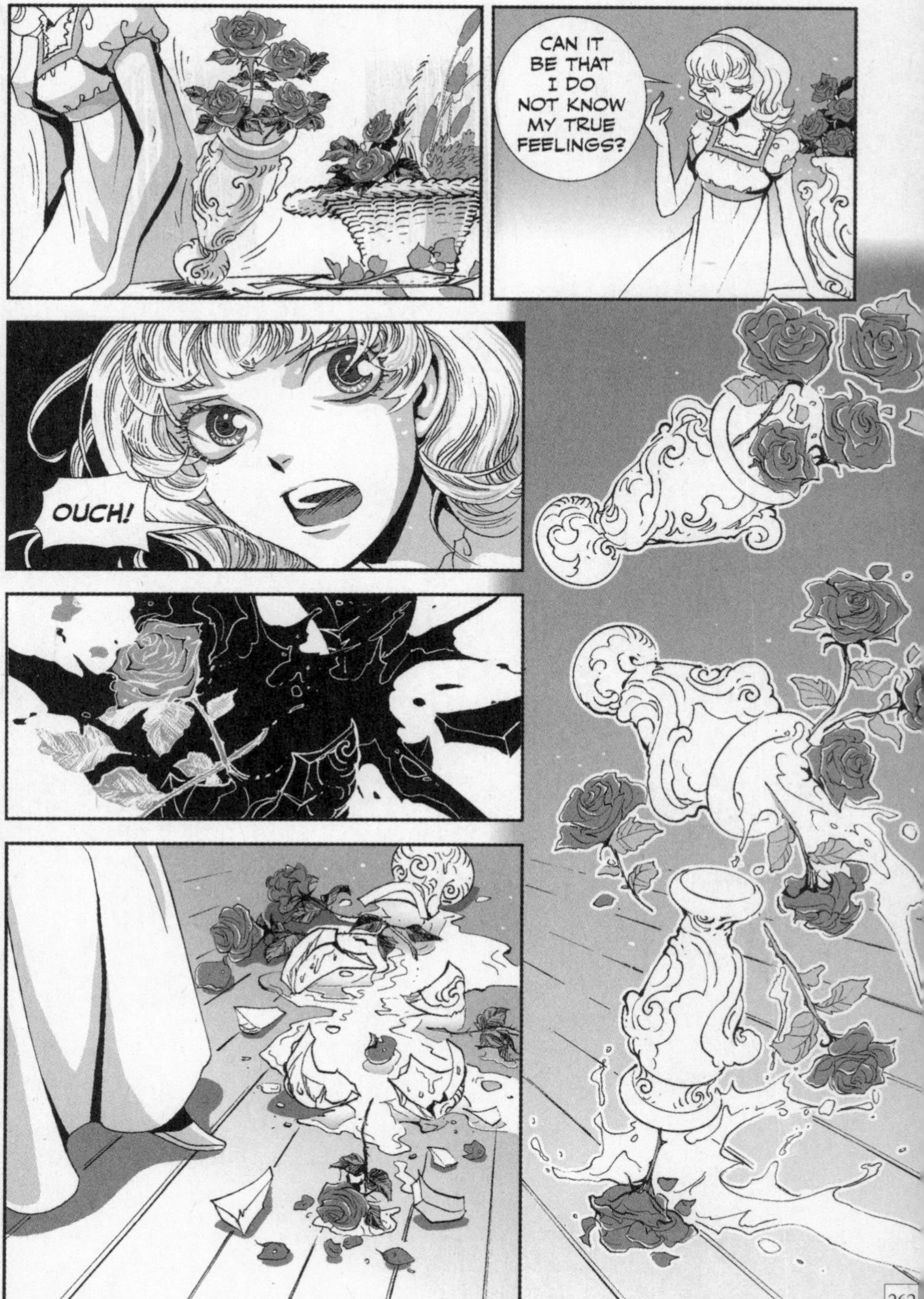
CAN IT BE THAT I DO NOT KNOW MY TRUE FEELINGS?
OUCH!

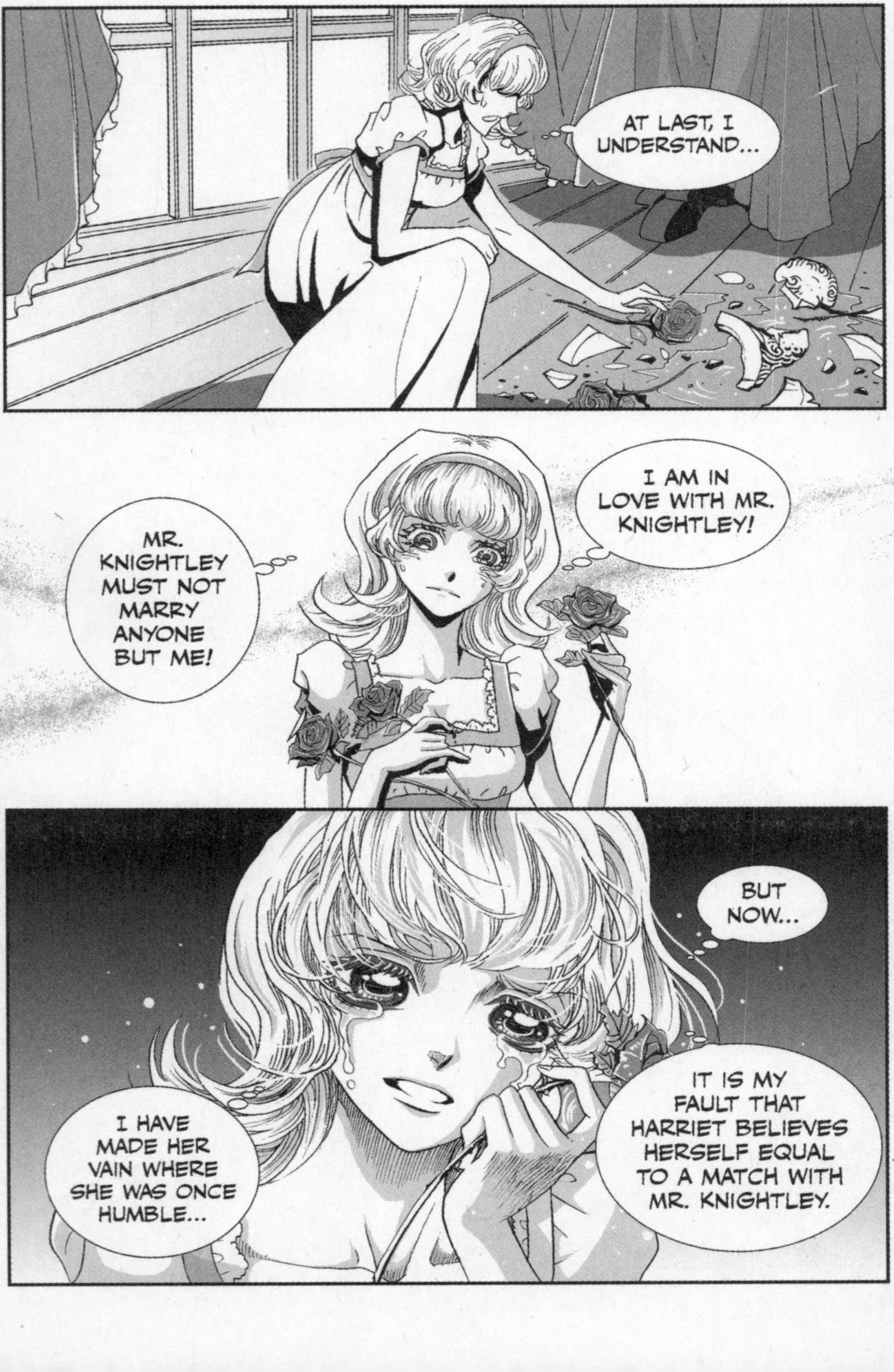
AT LAST, I UNDERSTAND...
I AM IN LOVE WITH MR. KNIGHTLEY!
MR. KNIGHTLEY MUST NOT MARRY ANYONE BUT ME!
BUT NOW...
IT IS MY FAULT THAT HARRIET BELIEVES HERSELF EQUAL TO A MATCH WITH MR. KNIGHTLEY.
I HAVE MADE HER VAIN WHERE SHE WAS ONCE HUMBLE...

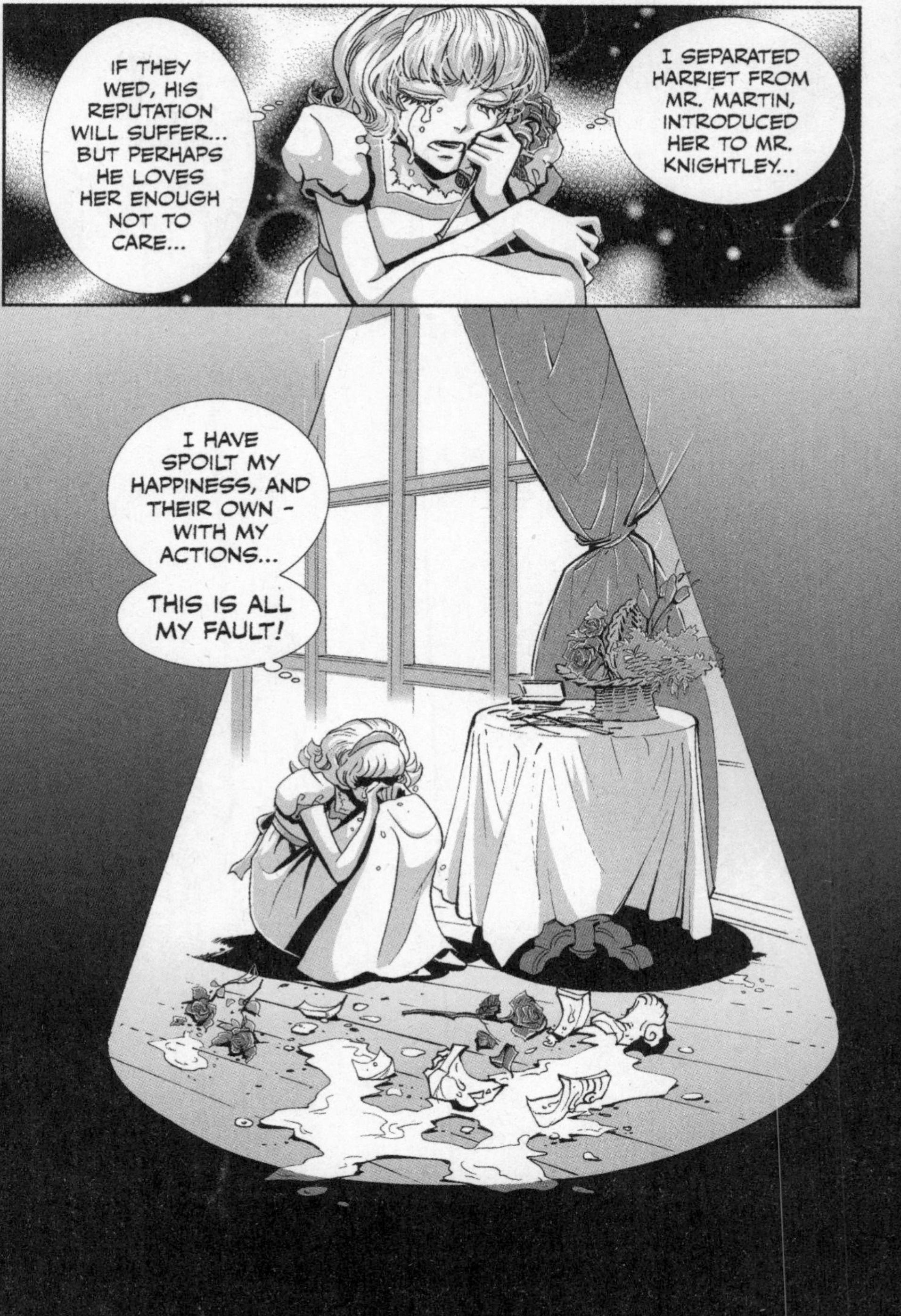
I SEPARATED HARRIET FROM MR. MARTIN, INTRODUCED HER TO MR. KNIGHTLEY...
IF THEY WED, HIS REPUTATION WILL SUFFER... BUT PERHAPS HE LOVES HER ENOUGH NOT TO CARE...
I HAVE SPOILT MY HAPPINESS, AND THEIR OWN - WITH MY ACTIONS...
THIS IS ALL MY FAULT!

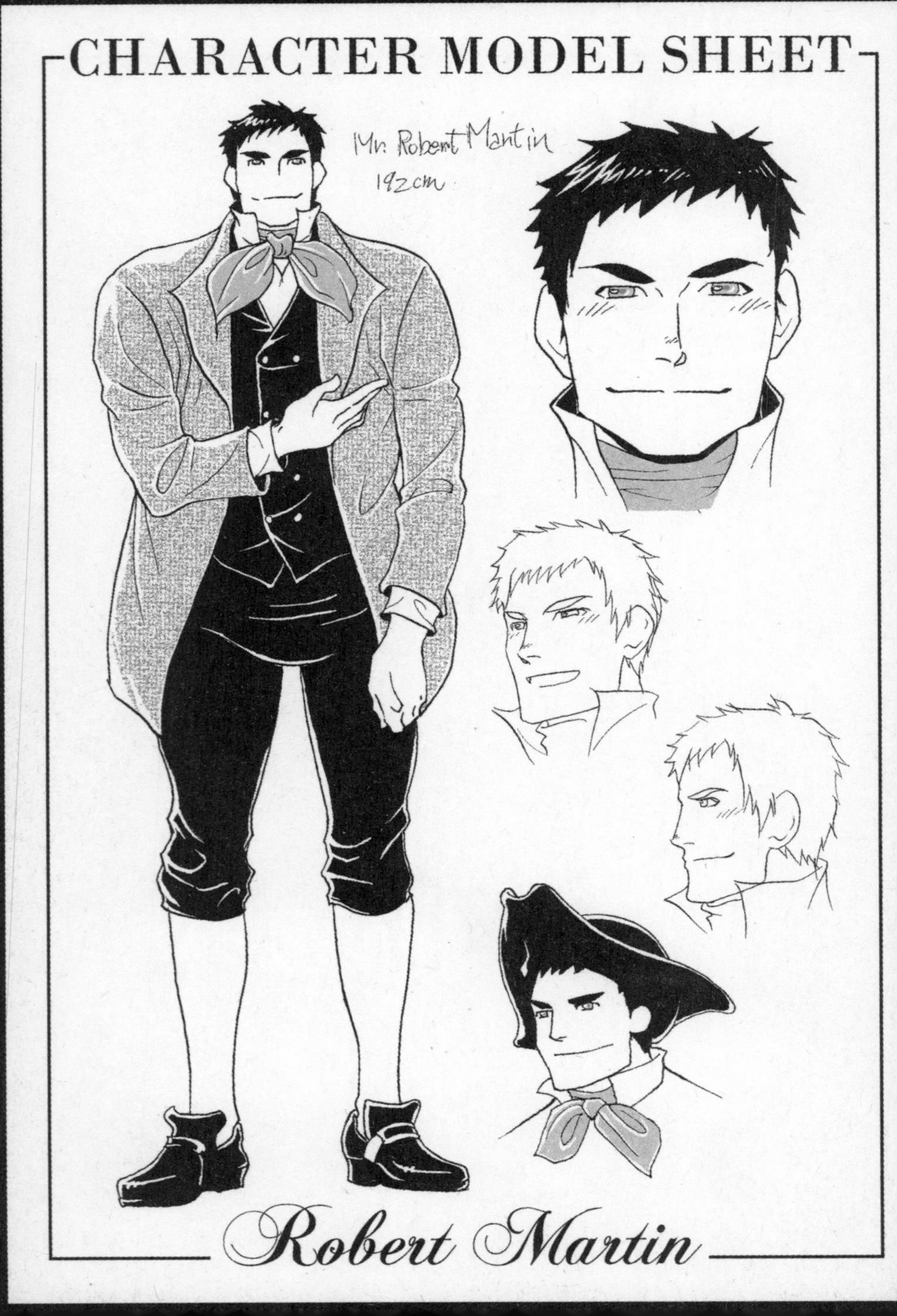
CHARACTER MODEL SHEET
Mr. Robert Martin
192cm
Robert Martin

CHARACTER MODEL SHEET

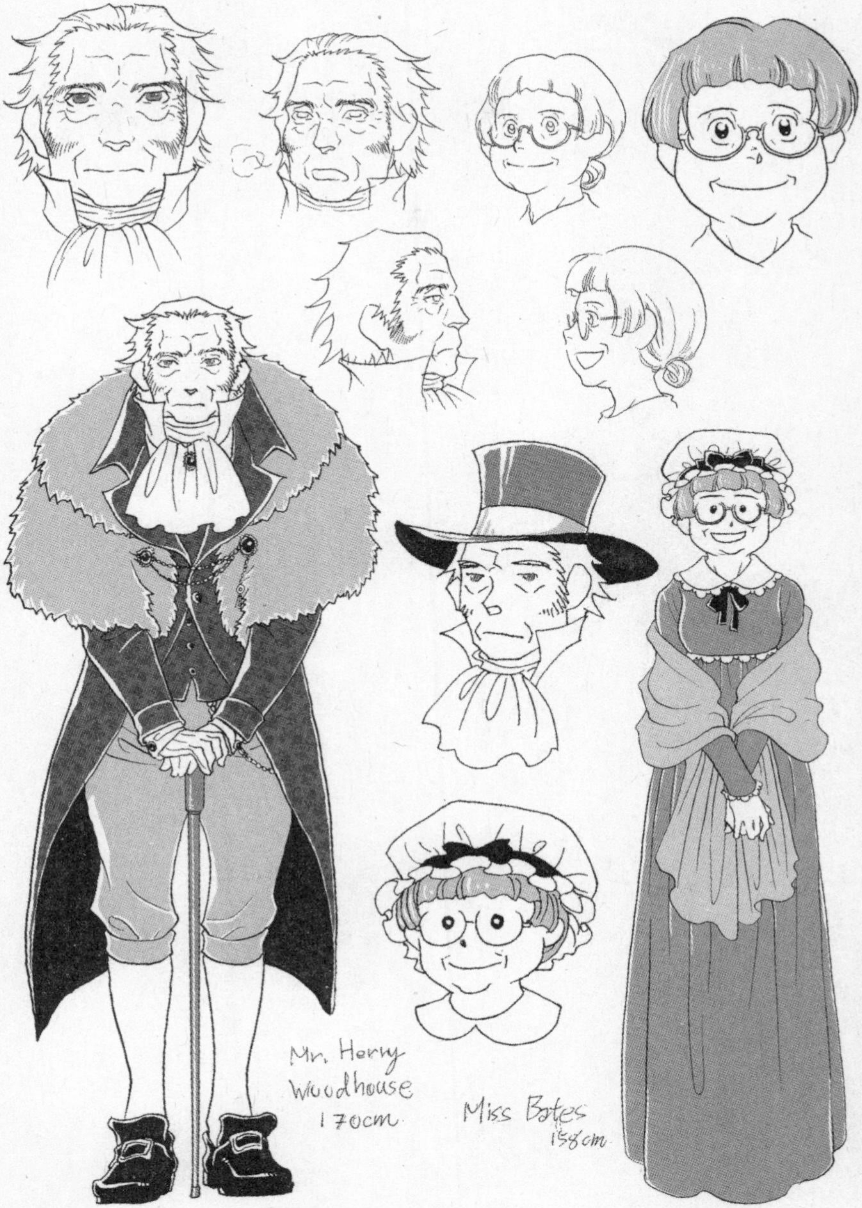
Mr. Herry
Woodhouse
170cm
Miss Bates
158cm

Mr. Woodhouse, Miss Bates

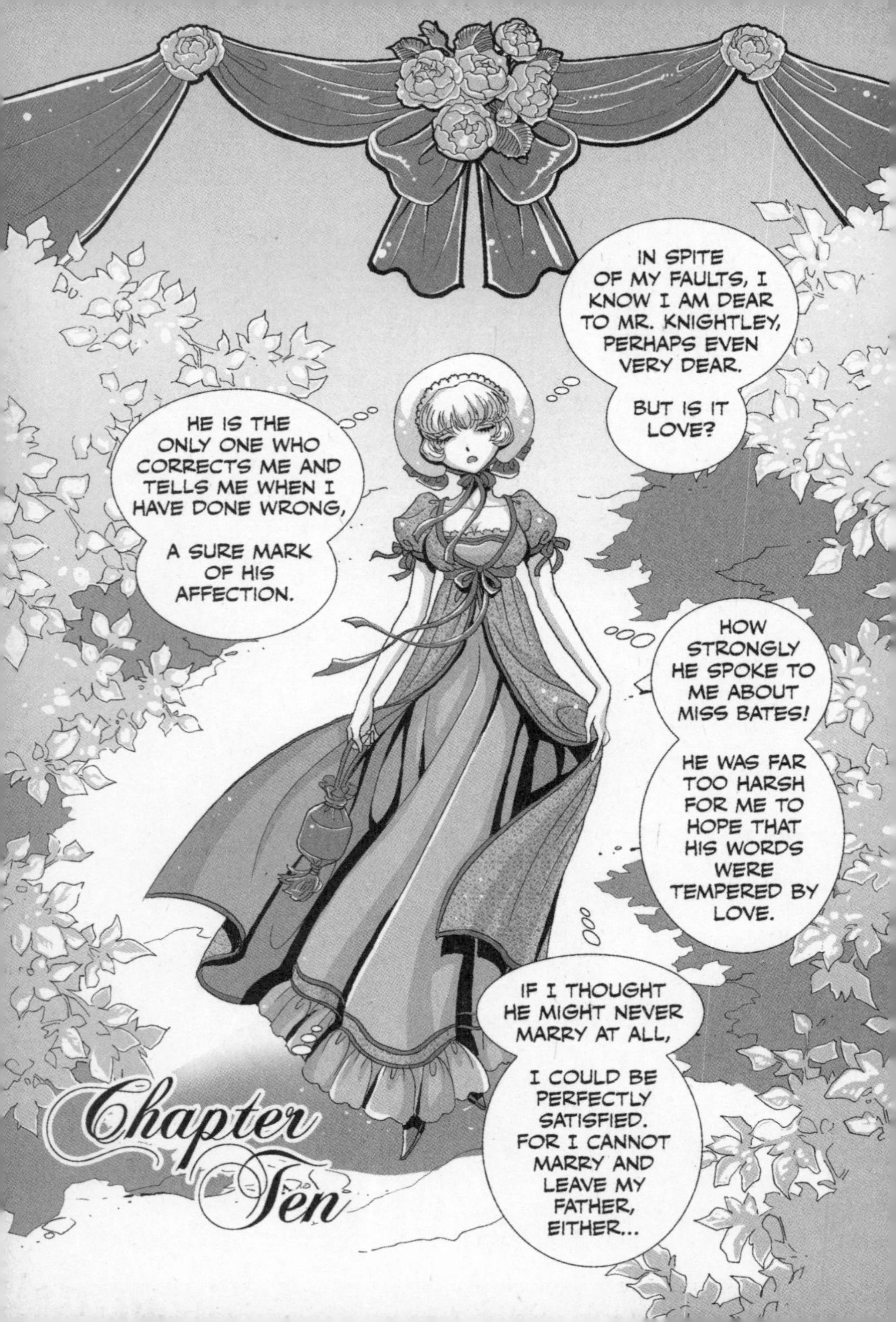
IN SPITE OF MY FAULTS, I KNOW I AM DEAR TO MR. KNIGHTLEY, PERHAPS EVEN VERY DEAR.
BUT IS IT LOVE?
HE IS THE ONLY ONE WHO CORRECTS ME AND TELLS ME WHEN I HAVE DONE WRONG,
A SURE MARK OF HIS AFFECTION.
HOW STRONGLY HE SPOKE TO ME ABOUT MISS BATES!
HE WAS FAR TOO HARSH FOR ME TO HOPE THAT HIS WORDS WERE TEMPERED BY LOVE.
IF I THOUGHT HE MIGHT NEVER MARRY AT ALL,
I COULD BE PERFECTLY SATISFIED. FOR I CANNOT MARRY AND LEAVE MY FATHER, EITHER...
Chapter Ten

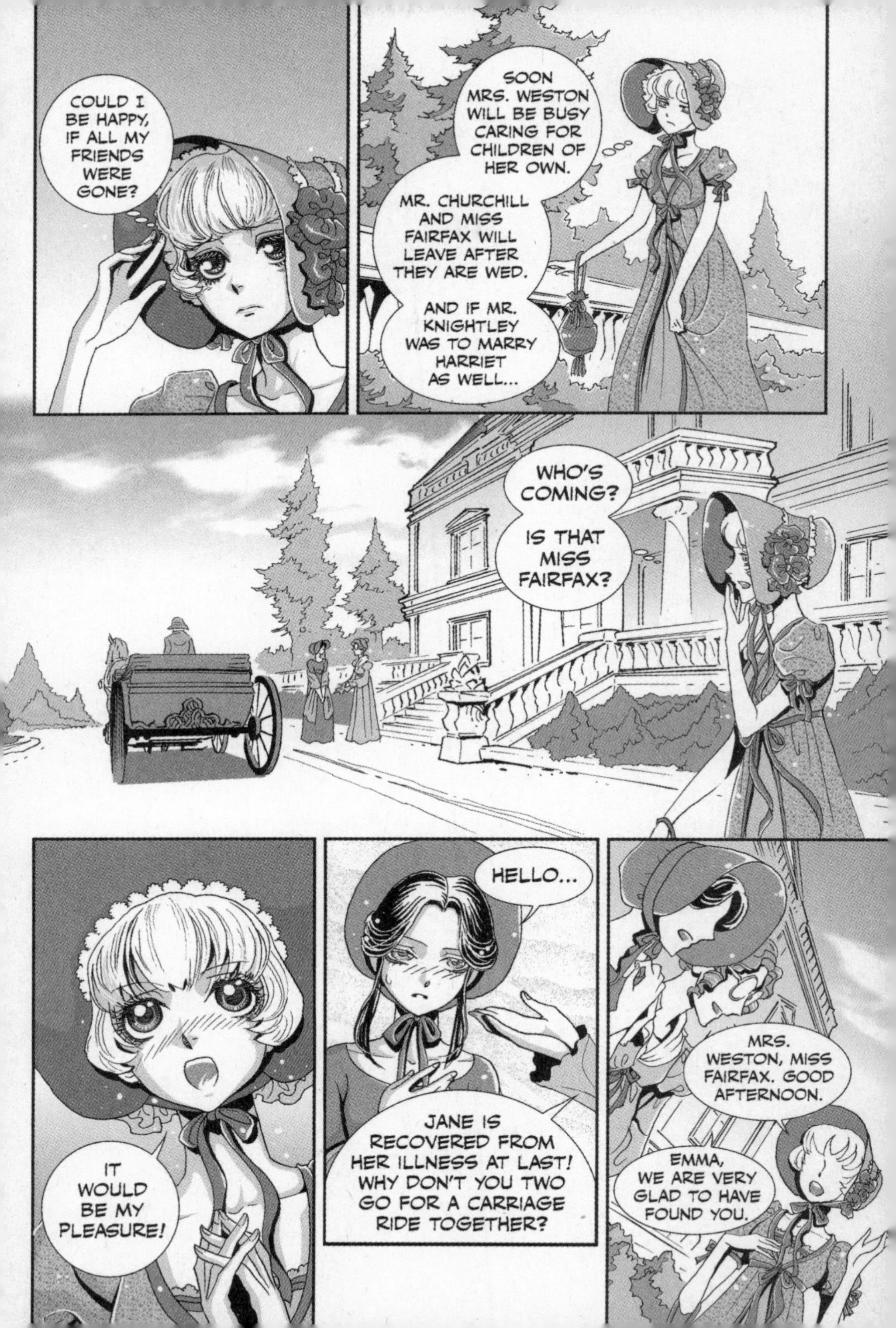
SOON MRS. WESTON WILL BE BUSY CARING FOR CHILDREN OF HER OWN.
MR. CHURCHILL AND MISS FAIRFAX WILL LEAVE AFTER THEY ARE WED.
AND IF MR. KNIGHTLEY WAS TO MARRY HARRIET AS WELL...
COULD I BE HAPPY, IF ALL MY FRIENDS WERE GONE?
WHO'S COMING?
IS THAT MISS FAIRFAX?
MRS. WESTON, MISS FAIRFAX. GOOD AFTERNOON.
EMMA, WE ARE VERY GLAD TO HAVE FOUND YOU.
HELLO...
JANE IS RECOVERED FROM HER ILLNESS AT LAST! WHY DON'T YOU TWO GO FOR A CARRIAGE RIDE TOGETHER?
IT WOULD BE MY PLEASURE!

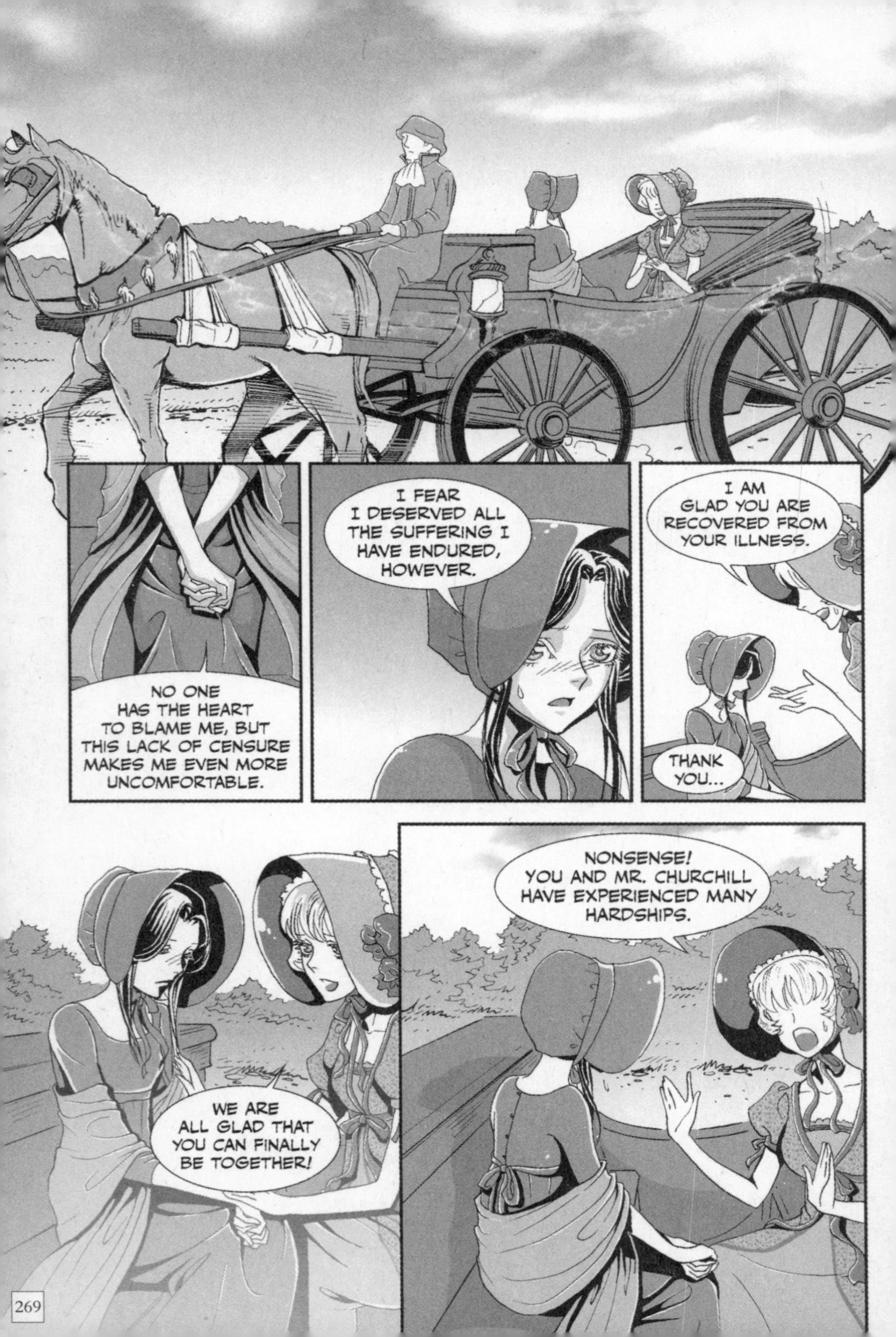
I AM GLAD YOU ARE RECOVERED FROM YOUR ILLNESS.
THANK YOU...
I FEAR I DESERVED ALL THE SUFFERING I HAVE ENDURED, HOWEVER.
NO ONE HAS THE HEART TO BLAME ME, BUT THIS LACK OF CENSURE MAKES ME EVEN MORE UNCOMFORTABLE.
NONSENSE! YOU AND MR. CHURCHILL HAVE EXPERIENCED MANY HARDSHIPS.
WE ARE ALL GLAD THAT YOU CAN FINALLY BE TOGETHER!

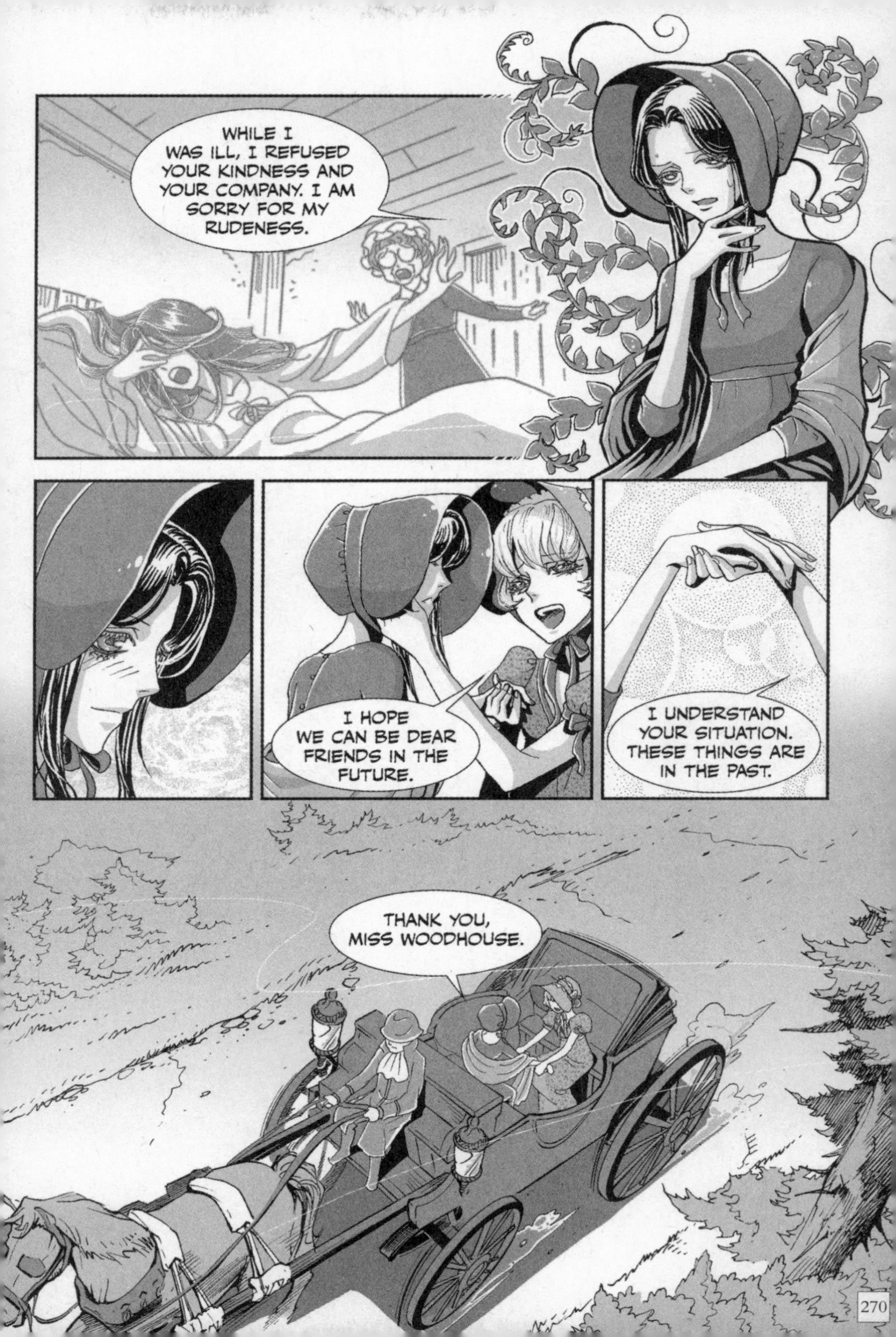
WHILE I WAS ILL, I REFUSED YOUR KINDNESS AND YOUR COMPANY. I AM SORRY FOR MY RUDENESS.
I UNDERSTAND YOUR SITUATION. THESE THINGS ARE IN THE PAST.
I HOPE WE CAN BE DEAR FRIENDS IN THE FUTURE.
THANK YOU, MISS WOODHOUSE.

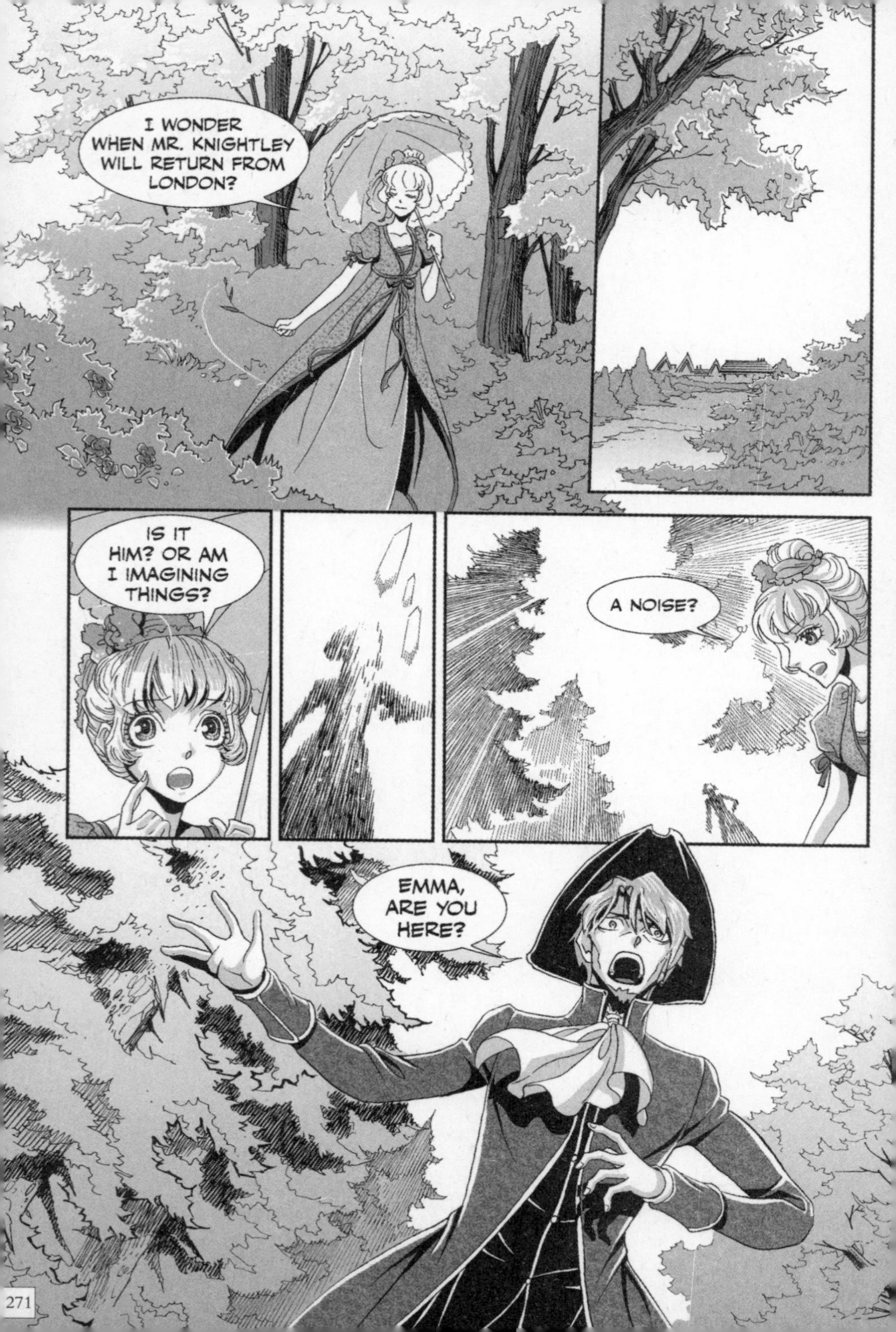
I WONDER WHEN MR. KNIGHTLEY WILL RETURN FROM LONDON?
A NOISE?
IS IT HIM? OR AM I IMAGINING THINGS?
EMMA, ARE YOU HERE?

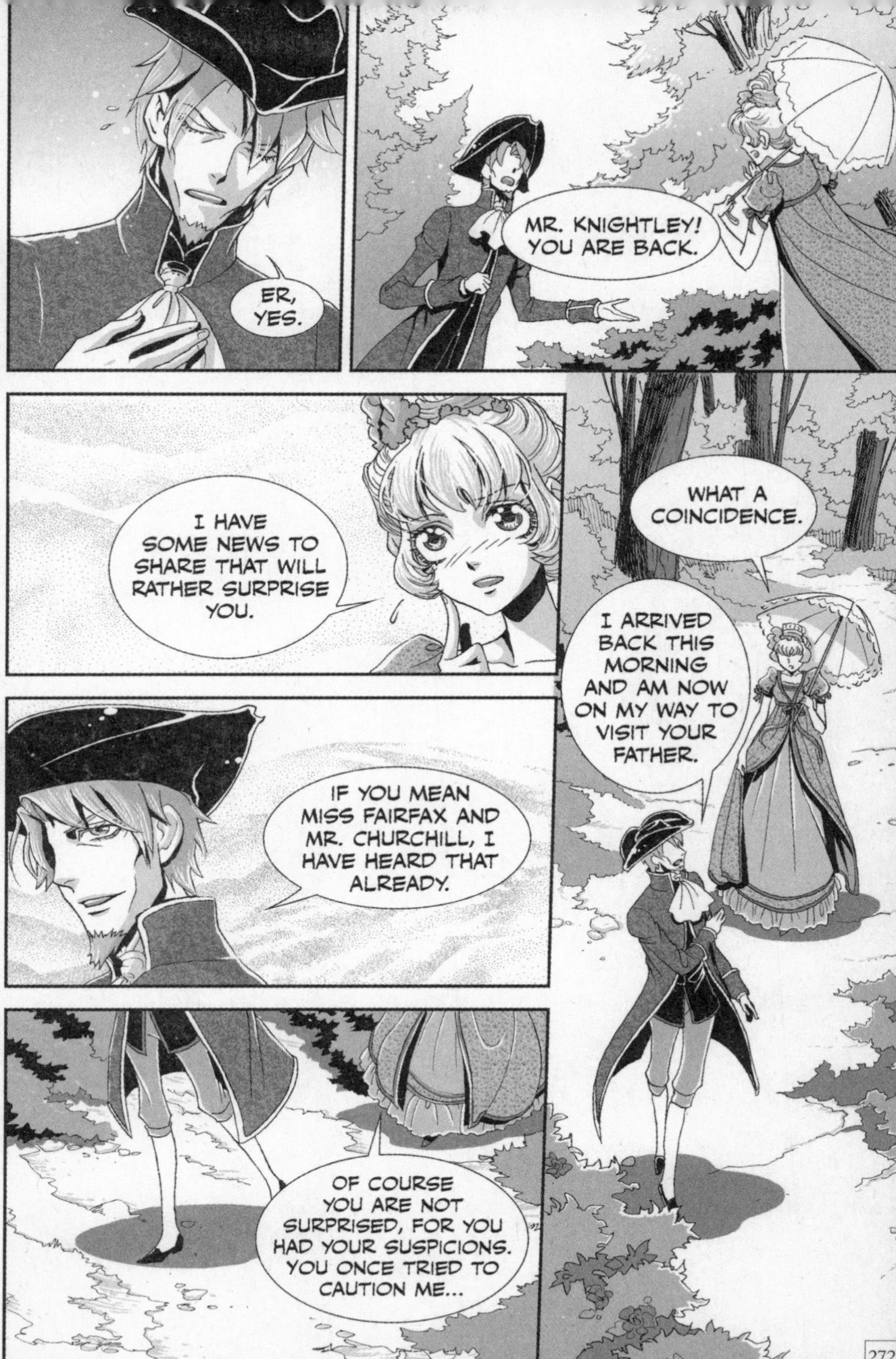
MR. KNIGHTLEY! YOU ARE BACK.
ER, YES.
WHAT A COINCIDENCE.
I ARRIVED BACK THIS MORNING AND AM NOW ON MY WAY TO VISIT YOUR FATHER.
I HAVE SOME NEWS TO SHARE THAT WILL RATHER SURPRISE YOU.
IF YOU MEAN MISS FAIRFAX AND MR. CHURCHILL, I HAVE HEARD THAT ALREADY.
OF COURSE YOU ARE NOT SURPRISED, FOR YOU HAD YOUR SUSPICIONS. YOU ONCE TRIED TO CAUTION ME...

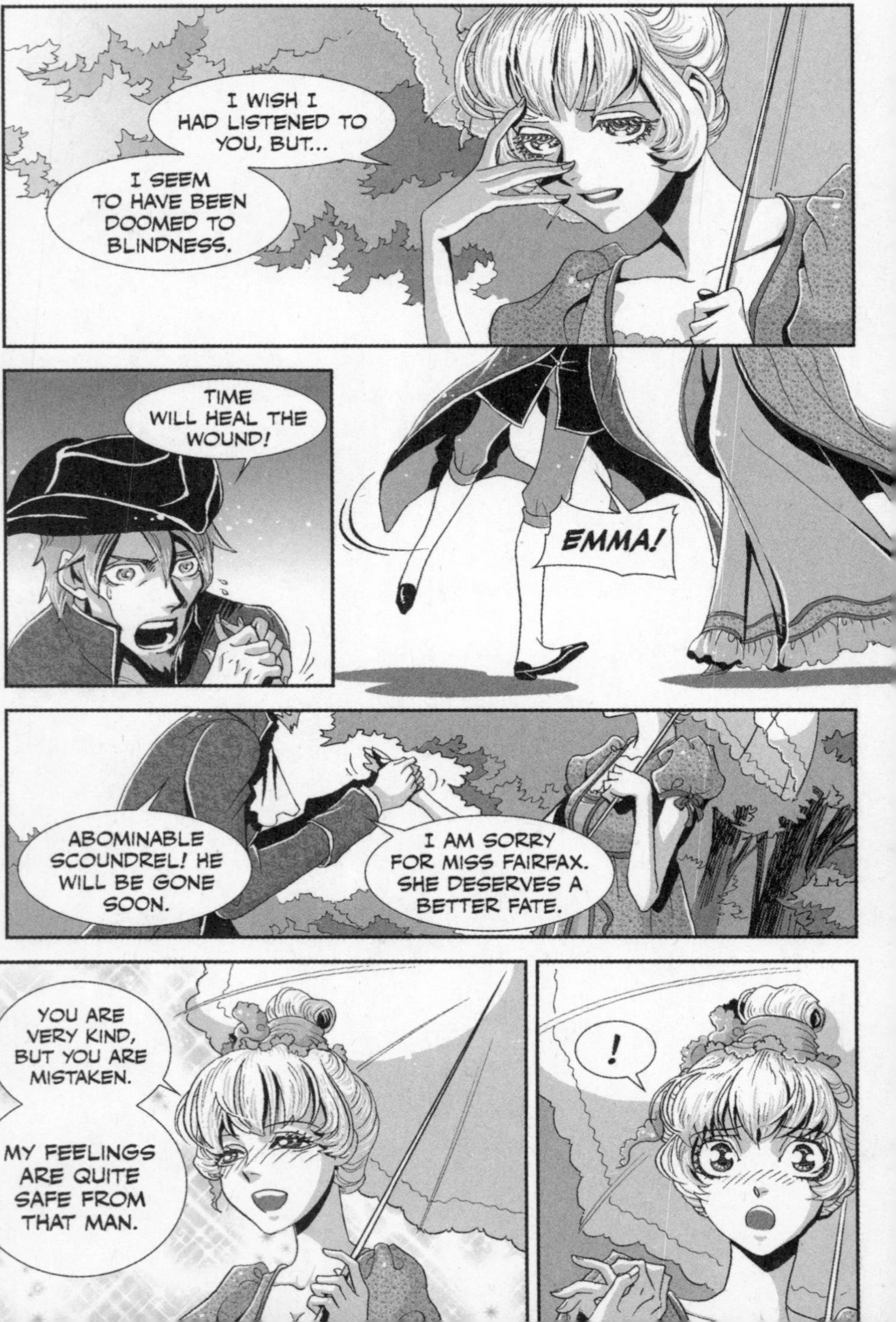
I WISH I HAD LISTENED TO YOU, BUT...
I SEEM TO HAVE BEEN DOOMED TO BLINDNESS.
EMMA!
TIME WILL HEAL THE WOUND!
I AM SORRY FOR MISS FAIRFAX. SHE DESERVES A BETTER FATE.
ABOMINABLE SCOUNDREL! HE WILL BE GONE SOON.
!
YOU ARE VERY KIND, BUT YOU ARE MISTAKEN.
MY FEELINGS ARE QUITE SAFE FROM THAT MAN.

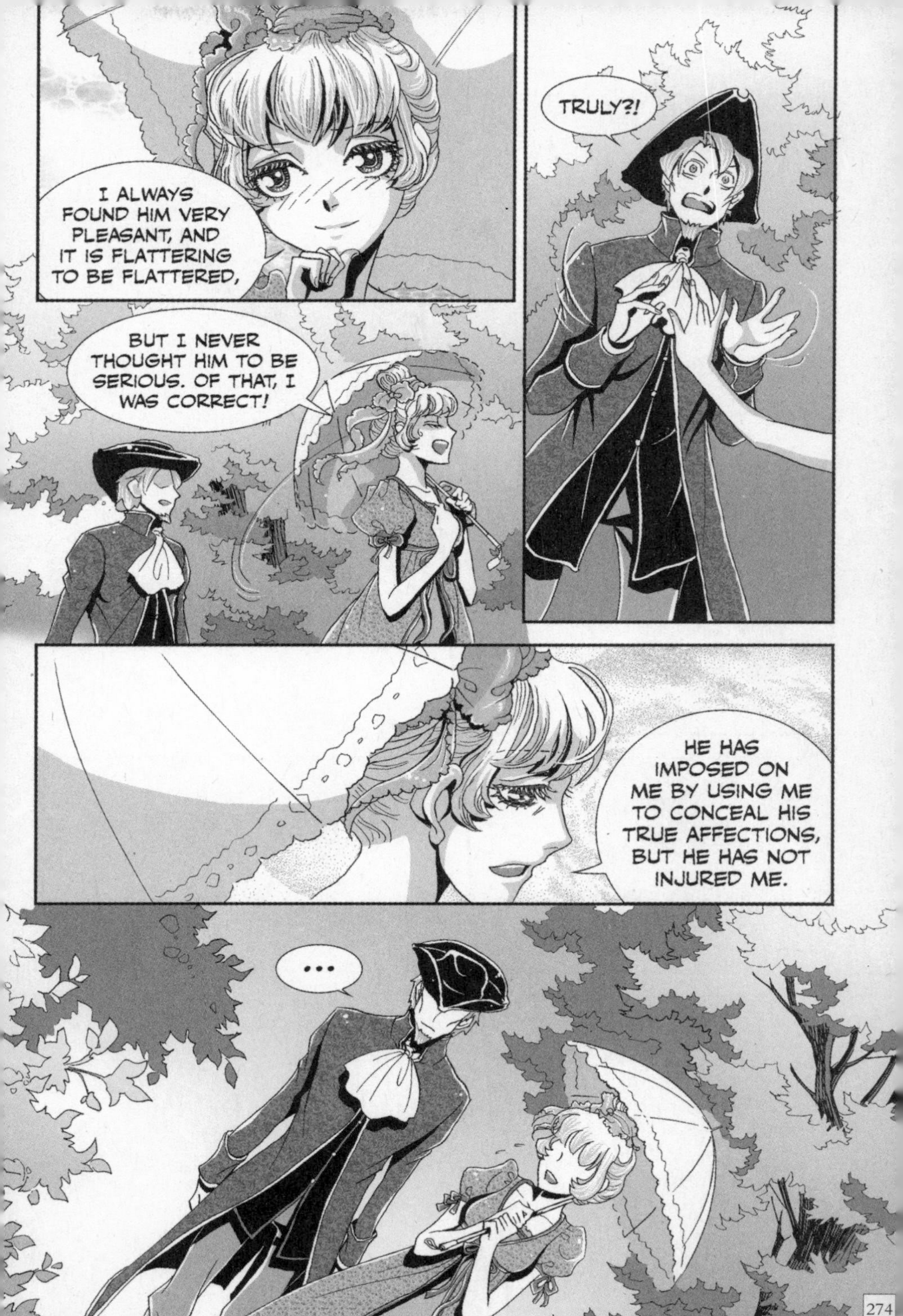
I ALWAYS FOUND HIM VERY PLEASANT, AND IT IS FLATTERING TO BE FLATTERED,
BUT I NEVER THOUGHT HIM TO BE SERIOUS. OF THAT, I WAS CORRECT!
TRULY?!
HE HAS IMPOSED ON ME BY USING ME TO CONCEAL HIS TRUE AFFECTIONS, BUT HE HAS NOT INJURED ME.
...

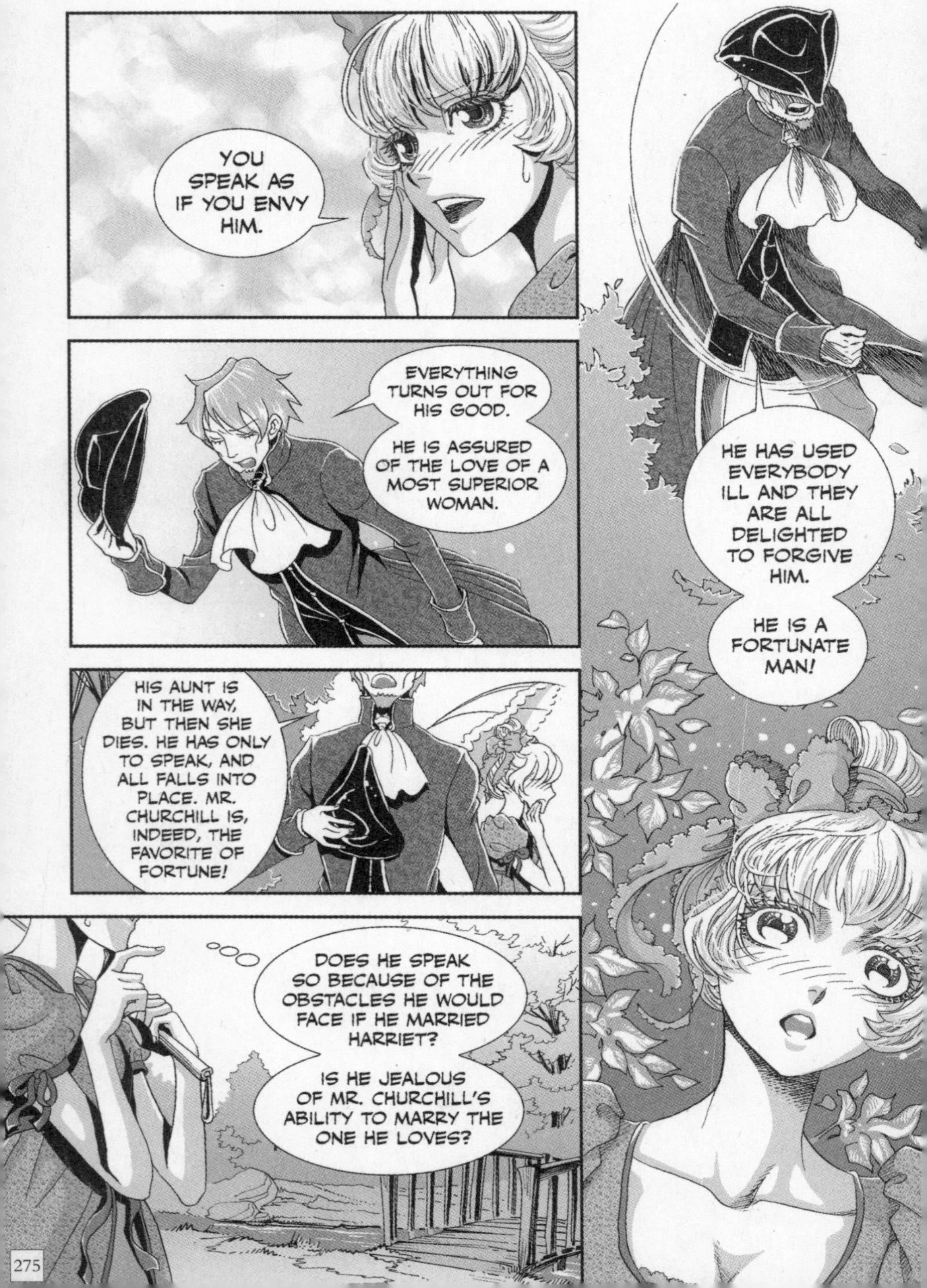
HE HAS USED EVERYBODY ILL AND THEY ARE ALL DELIGHTED TO FORGIVE HIM.
HE IS A FORTUNATE MAN!
YOU SPEAK AS IF YOU ENVY HIM.
EVERYTHING TURNS OUT FOR HIS GOOD.
HE IS ASSURED OF THE LOVE OF A MOST SUPERIOR WOMAN.
HIS AUNT IS IN THE WAY, BUT THEN SHE DIES. HE HAS ONLY TO SPEAK, AND ALL FALLS INTO PLACE. MR. CHURCHILL IS, INDEED, THE FAVORITE OF FORTUNE!
DOES HE SPEAK SO BECAUSE OF THE OBSTACLES HE WOULD FACE IF HE MARRIED HARRIET?
IS HE JEALOUS OF MR. CHURCHILL'S ABILITY TO MARRY THE ONE HE LOVES?

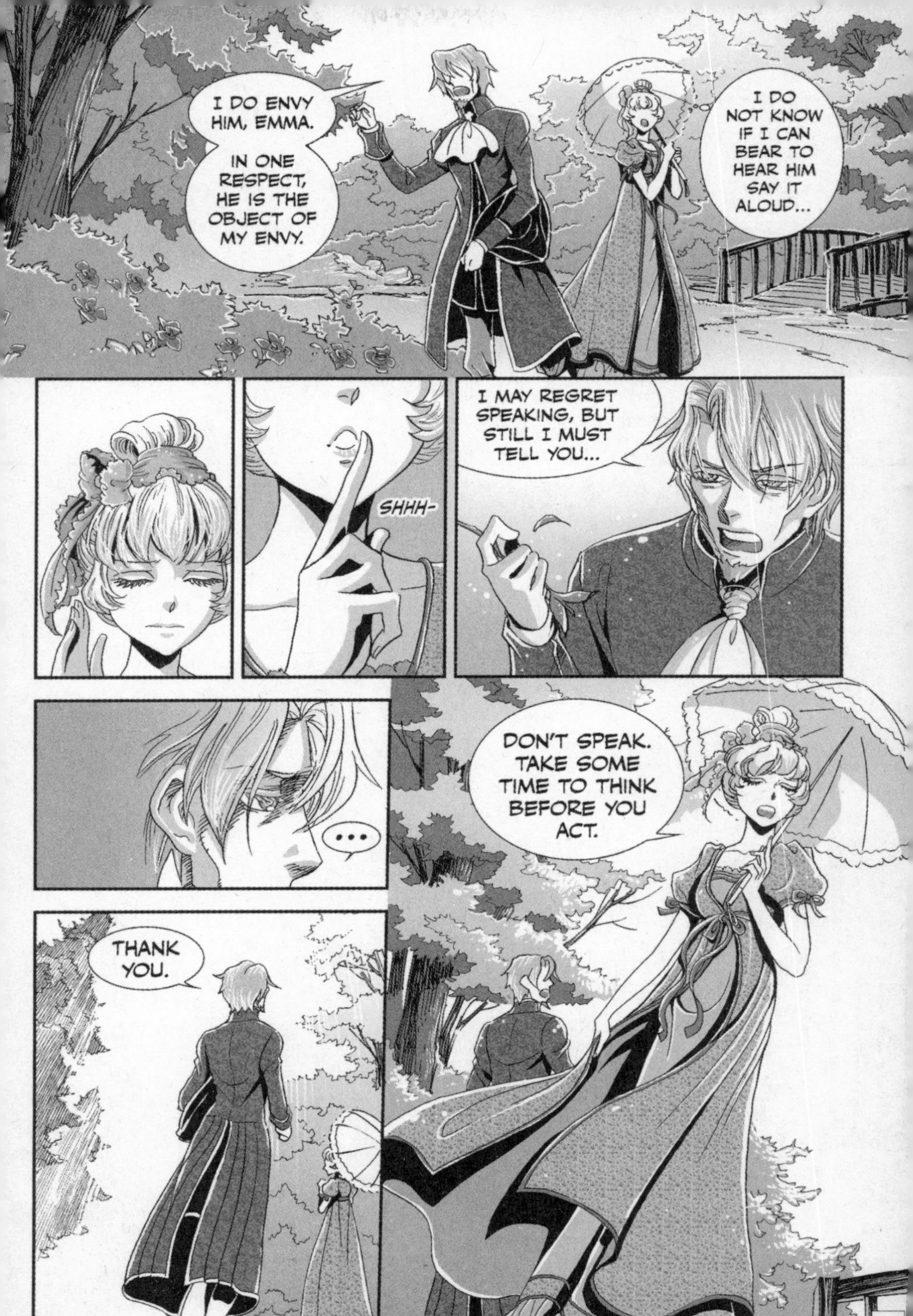
I DO NOT KNOW IF I CAN BEAR TO HEAR HIM SAY IT ALOUD...
I DO ENVY HIM, EMMA.
IN ONE RESPECT, HE IS THE OBJECT OF MY ENVY.
I MAY REGRET SPEAKING, BUT STILL I MUST TELL YOU...
SHHH-
DON'T SPEAK. TAKE SOME TIME TO THINK BEFORE YOU ACT.
...
THANK YOU.

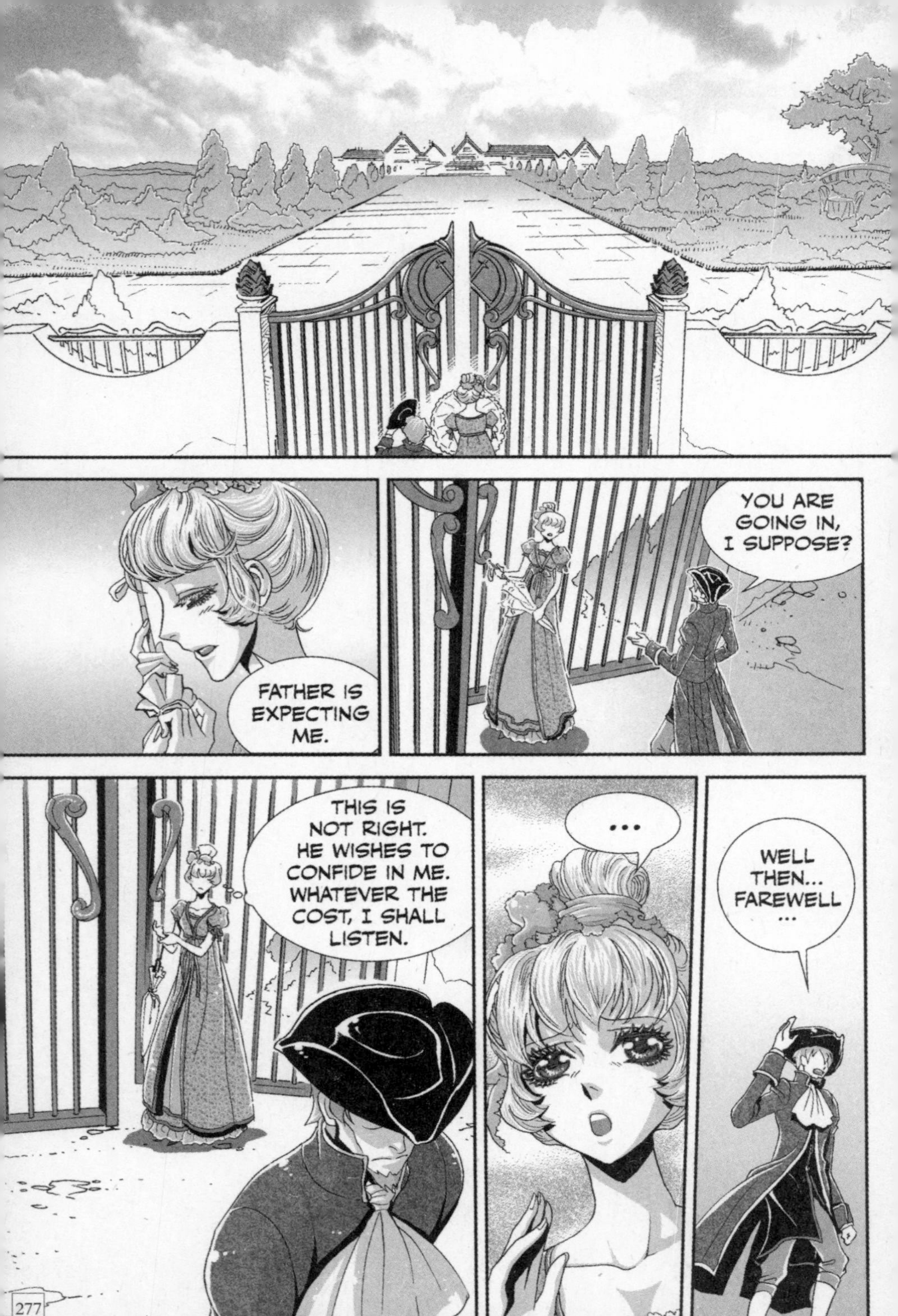
YOU ARE GOING IN, I SUPPOSE?
FATHER IS EXPECTING ME.
WELL THEN... FAREWELL ...
...
THIS IS NOT RIGHT. HE WISHES TO CONFIDE IN ME. WHATEVER THE COST, I SHALL LISTEN.

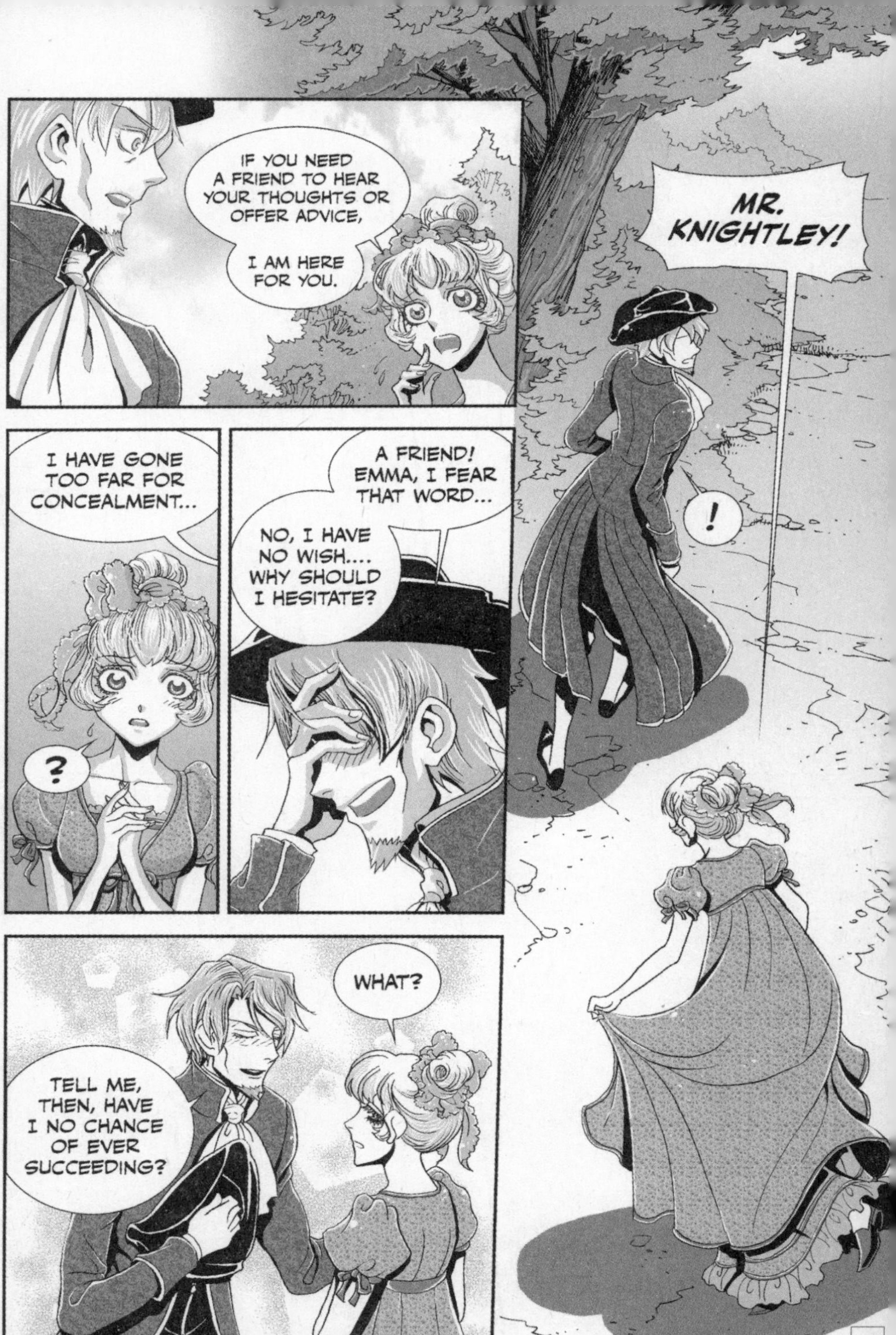
MR. KNIGHTLEY!
!
IF YOU NEED A FRIEND TO HEAR YOUR THOUGHTS OR OFFER ADVICE,
I AM HERE FOR YOU.
A FRIEND! EMMA, I FEAR THAT WORD...
NO, I HAVE NO WISH.... WHY SHOULD I HESITATE?
I HAVE GONE TOO FAR FOR CONCEALMENT...
?
WHAT?
TELL ME, THEN, HAVE I NO CHANCE OF EVER SUCCEEDING?

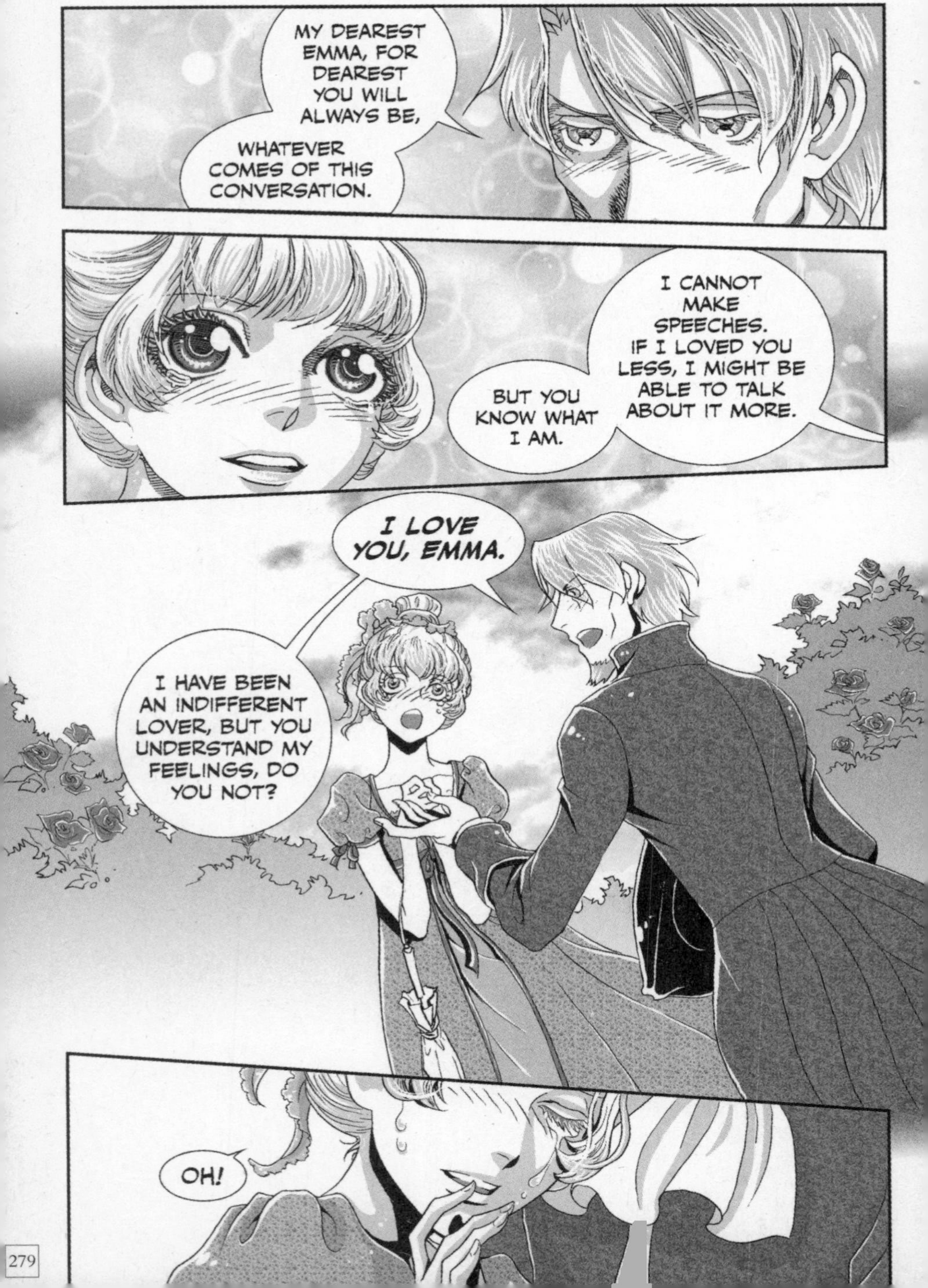

MY DEAREST EMMA, FOR DEAREST YOU WILL ALWAYS BE,
WHATEVER COMES OF THIS CONVERSATION.
I CANNOT MAKE SPEECHES. IF I LOVED YOU LESS, I MIGHT BE ABLE TO TALK ABOUT IT MORE.
BUT YOU KNOW WHAT I AM.
I LOVE YOU, EMMA.
I HAVE BEEN AN INDIFFERENT LOVER, BUT YOU UNDERSTAND MY FEELINGS, DO YOU NOT?
OH!

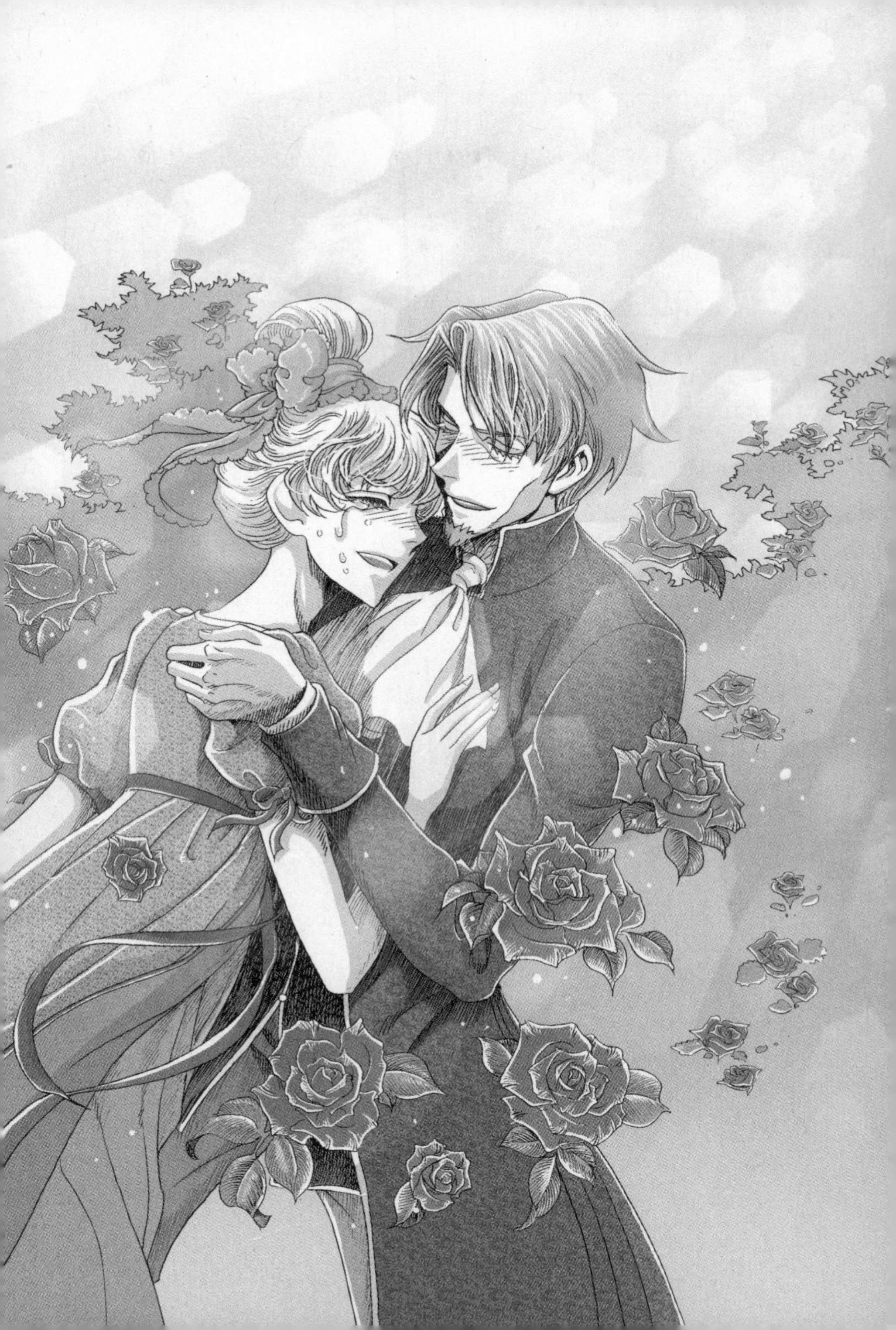

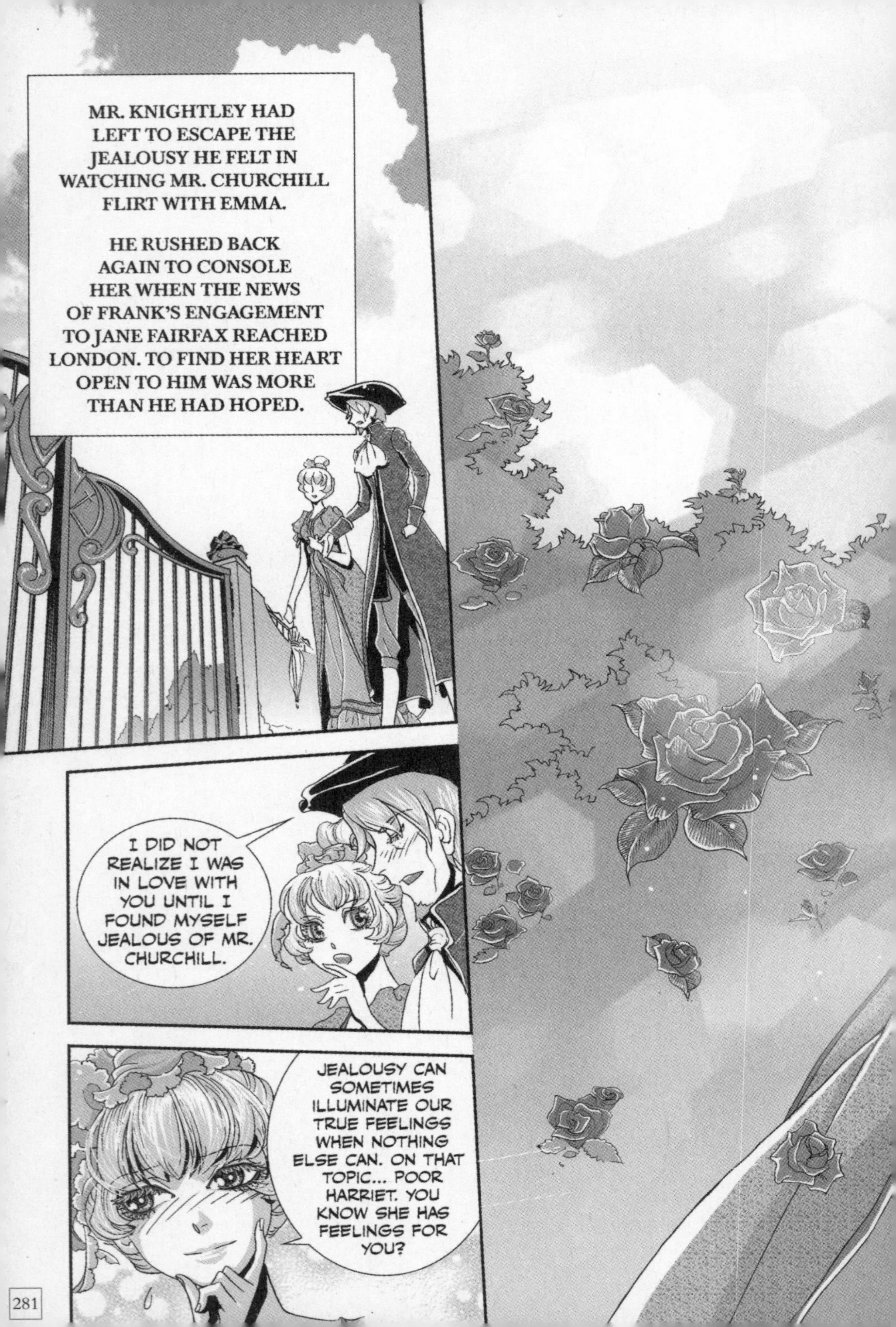
MR. KNIGHTLEY HAD LEFT TO ESCAPE THE JEALOUSY HE FELT IN WATCHING MR. CHURCHILL FLIRT WITH EMMA.
HE RUSHED BACK AGAIN TO CONSOLE HER WHEN THE NEWS OF FRANK'S ENGAGEMENT TO JANE FAIRFAX REACHED LONDON. TO FIND HER HEART OPEN TO HIM WAS MORE THAN HE HAD HOPED.
I DID NOT REALIZE I WAS IN LOVE WITH YOU UNTIL I FOUND MYSELF JEALOUS OF MR. CHURCHILL.
JEALOUSY CAN SOMETIMES ILLUMINATE OUR TRUE FEELINGS WHEN NOTHING ELSE CAN. ON THAT TOPIC... POOR HARRIET. YOU KNOW SHE HAS FEELINGS FOR YOU?

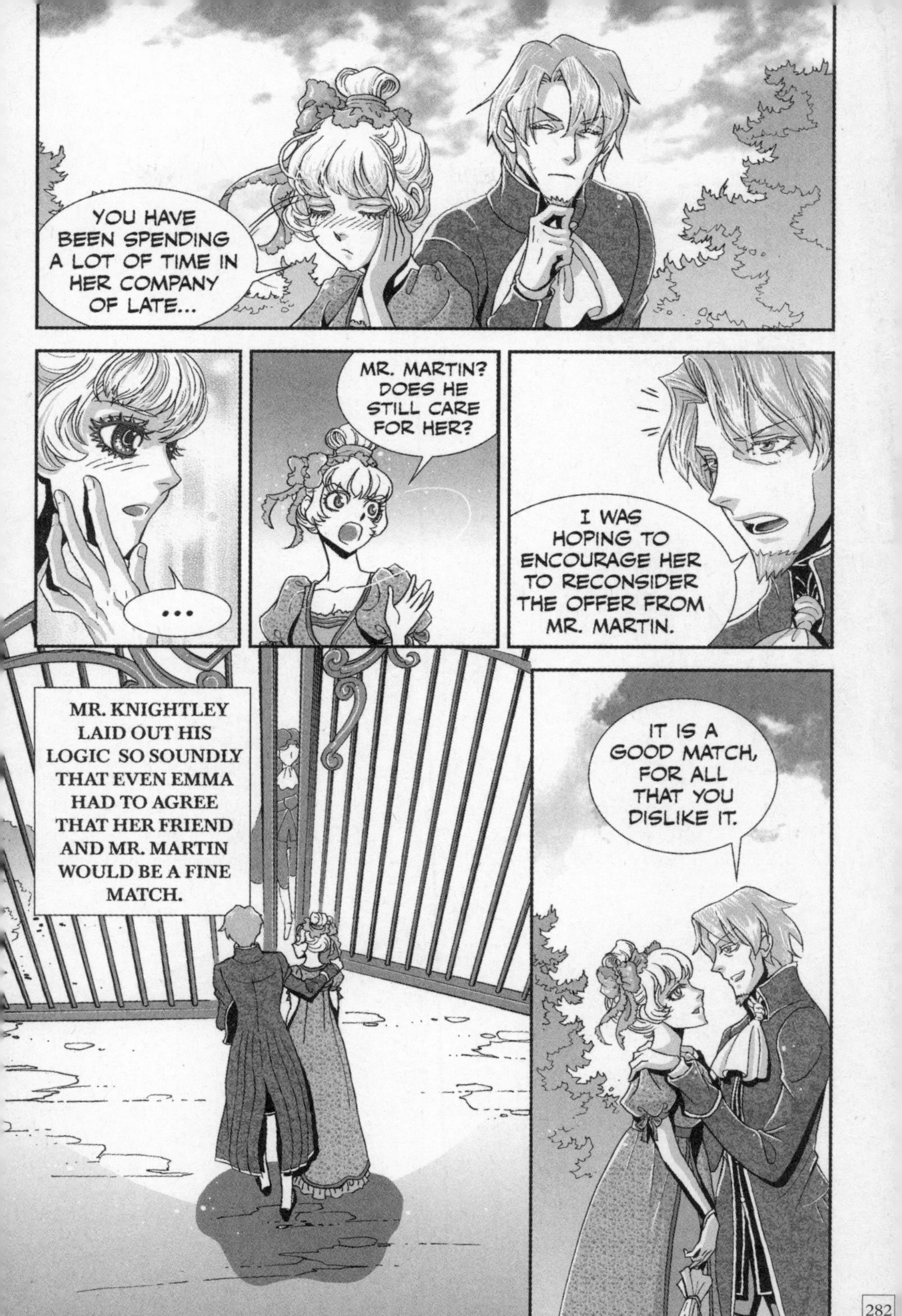
YOU HAVE BEEN SPENDING A LOT OF TIME IN HER COMPANY OF LATE...
I WAS HOPING TO ENCOURAGE HER TO RECONSIDER THE OFFER FROM MR. MARTIN.
MR. MARTIN? DOES HE STILL CARE FOR HER?
...
IT IS A GOOD MATCH, FOR ALL THAT YOU DISLIKE IT.
MR. KNIGHTLEY LAID OUT HIS LOGIC SO SOUNDLY THAT EVEN EMMA HAD TO AGREE THAT HER FRIEND AND MR. MARTIN WOULD BE A FINE MATCH.

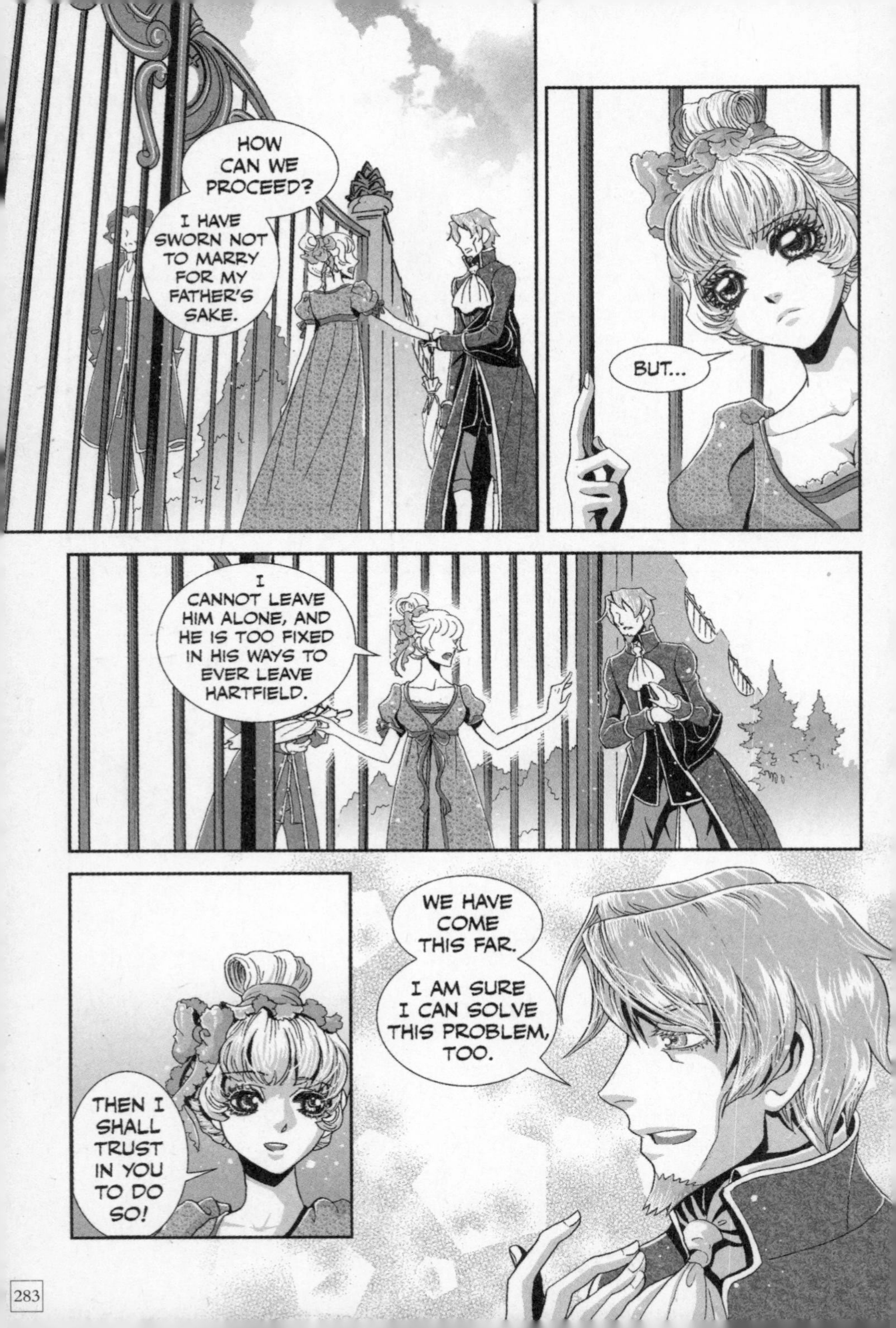
BUT...
HOW CAN WE PROCEED?
I HAVE SWORN NOT TO MARRY FOR MY FATHER'S SAKE.
I CANNOT LEAVE HIM ALONE, AND HE IS TOO FIXED IN HIS WAYS TO EVER LEAVE HARTFIELD.
WE HAVE COME THIS FAR.
I AM SURE I CAN SOLVE THIS PROBLEM, TOO.
THEN I SHALL TRUST IN YOU TO DO SO!

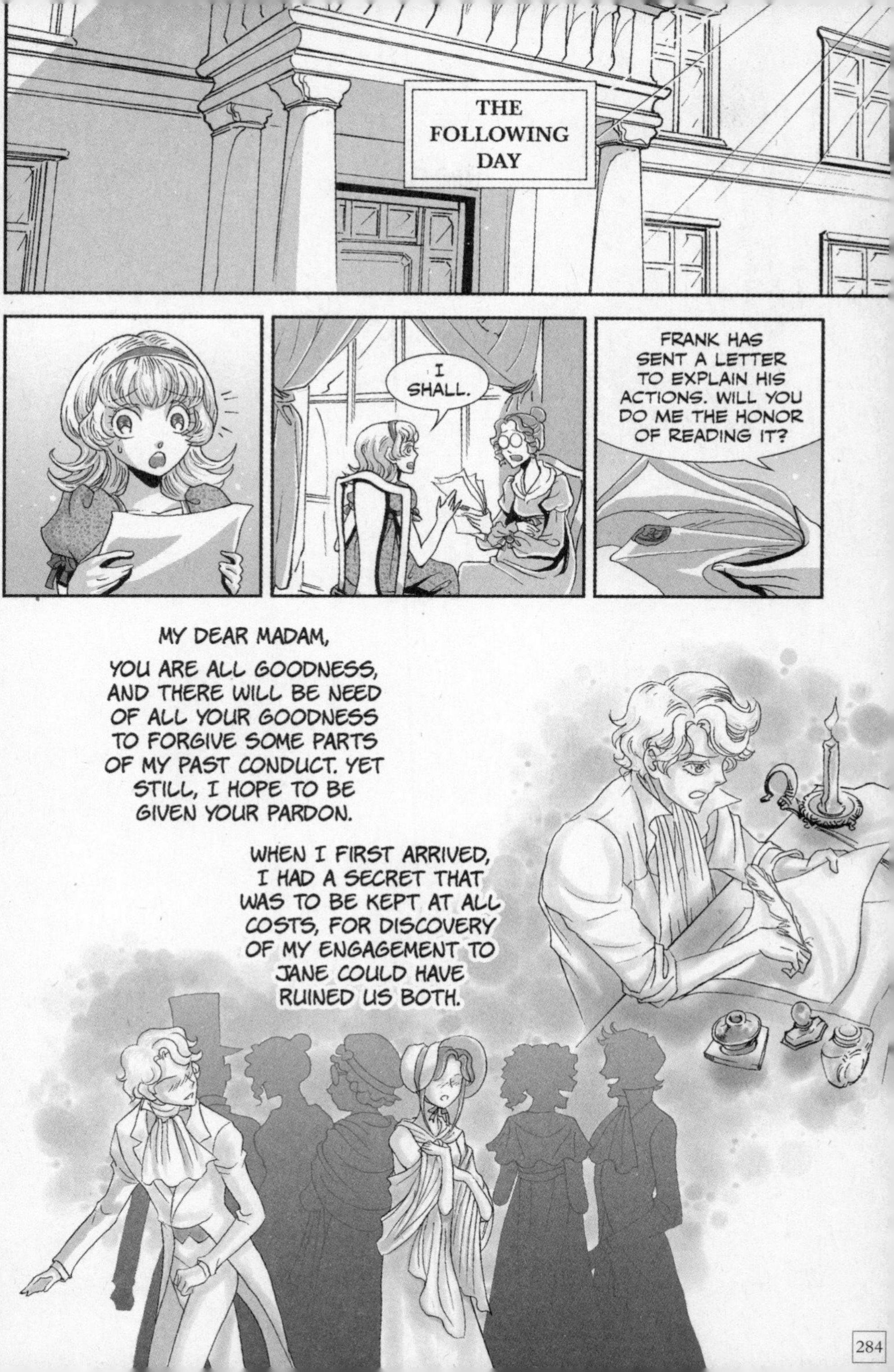
THE FOLLOWING DAY
FRANK HAS SENT A LETTER TO EXPLAIN HIS ACTIONS. WILL YOU DO ME THE HONOR OF READING IT?
I SHALL.
MY DEAR MADAM,
YOU ARE ALL GOODNESS, AND THERE WILL BE NEED OF ALL YOUR GOODNESS TO FORGIVE SOME PARTS OF MY PAST CONDUCT. YET STILL, I HOPE TO BE GIVEN YOUR PARDON.
WHEN I FIRST ARRIVED, I HAD A SECRET THAT WAS TO BE KEPT AT ALL COSTS, FOR DISCOVERY OF MY ENGAGEMENT TO JANE COULD HAVE RUINED US BOTH.

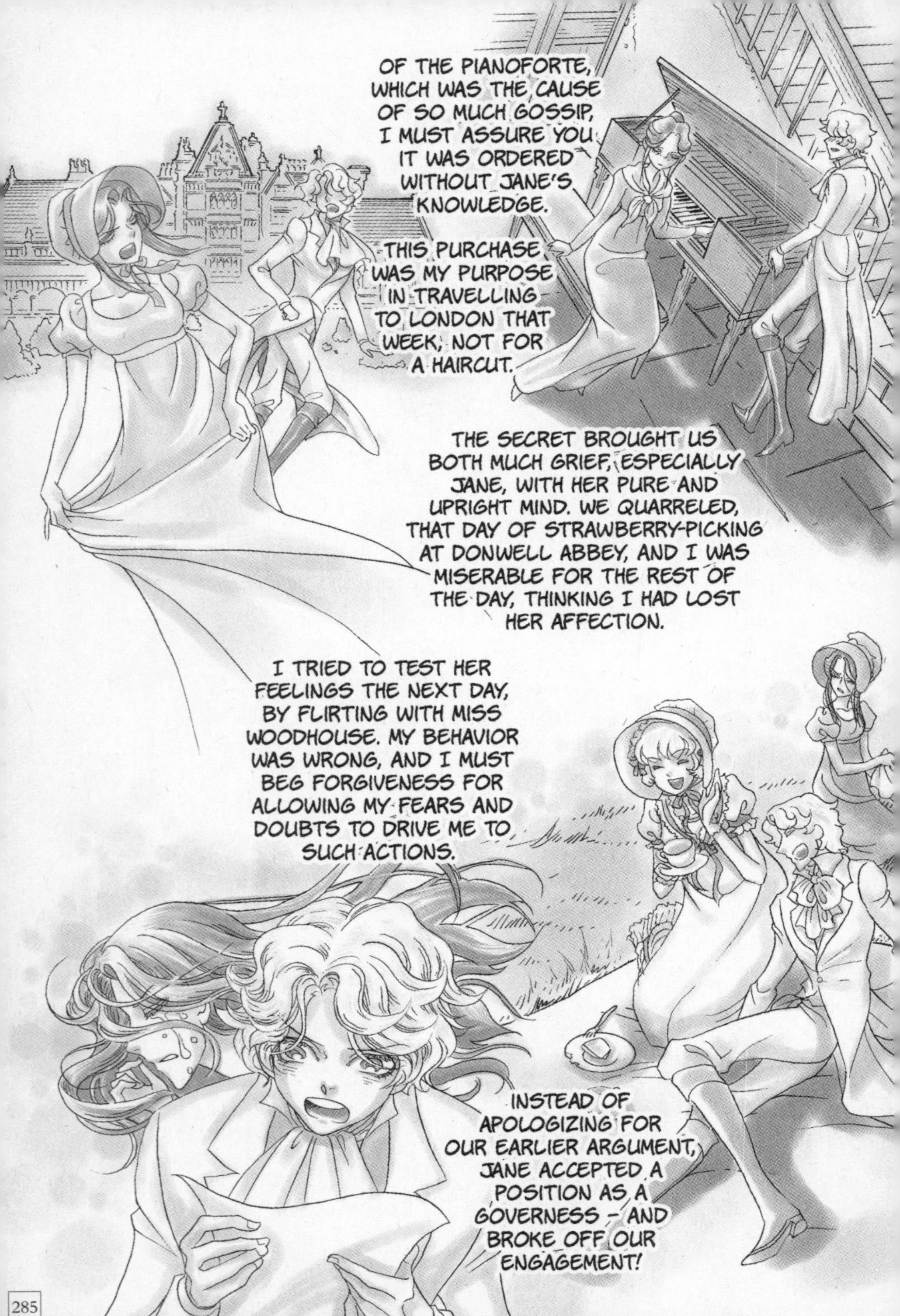
OF THE PIANOFORTE, WHICH WAS THE CAUSE OF SO MUCH GOSSIP, I MUST ASSURE YOU IT WAS ORDERED WITHOUT JANE'S KNOWLEDGE.
THIS PURCHASE WAS MY PURPOSE IN TRAVELLING TO LONDON THAT WEEK, NOT FOR A HAIRCUT.
THE SECRET BROUGHT US BOTH MUCH GRIEF, ESPECIALLY JANE, WITH HER PURE AND UPRIGHT MIND. WE QUARRELED, THAT DAY OF STRAWBERRY-PICKING AT DONWELL ABBEY, AND I WAS MISERABLE FOR THE REST OF THE DAY, THINKING I HAD LOST HER AFFECTION.
I TRIED TO TEST HER FEELINGS THE NEXT DAY, BY FLIRTING WITH MISS WOODHOUSE. MY BEHAVIOR WAS WRONG, AND I MUST BEG FORGIVENESS FOR ALLOWING MY FEARS AND DOUBTS TO DRIVE ME TO SUCH ACTIONS.
INSTEAD OF APOLOGIZING FOR OUR EARLIER ARGUMENT, JANE ACCEPTED A POSITION AS A GOVERNESS - AND BROKE OFF OUR ENGAGEMENT!

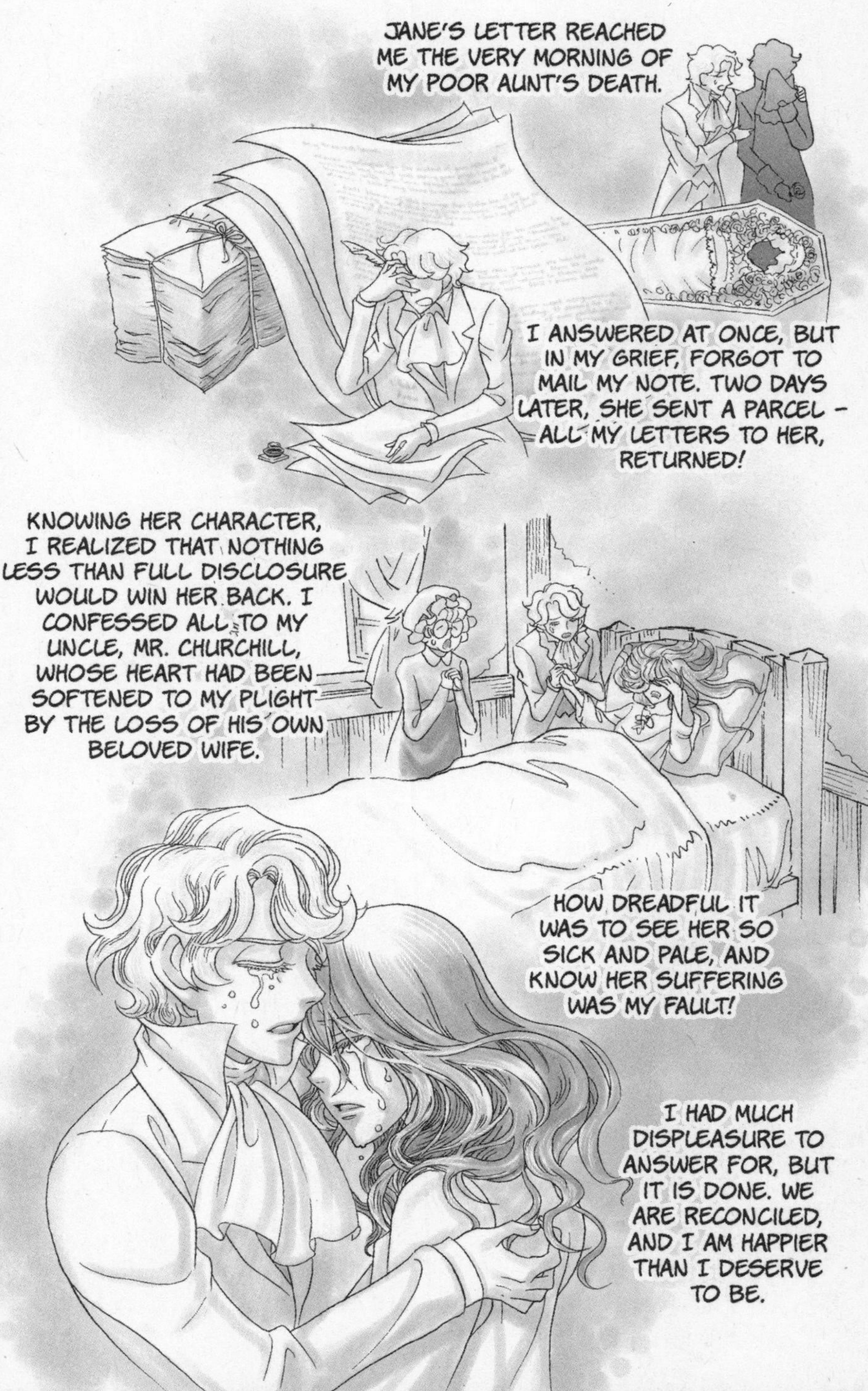
JANE'S LETTER REACHED ME THE VERY MORNING OF MY POOR AUNT'S DEATH.
I ANSWERED AT ONCE, BUT IN MY GRIEF, FORGOT TO MAIL MY NOTE. TWO DAYS LATER, SHE SENT A PARCEL - ALL MY LETTERS TO HER, RETURNED!
KNOWING HER CHARACTER, I REALIZED THAT NOTHING LESS THAN FULL DISCLOSURE WOULD WIN HER BACK. I CONFESSED ALL TO MY UNCLE, MR. CHURCHILL, WHOSE HEART HAD BEEN SOFTENED TO MY PLIGHT BY THE LOSS OF HIS OWN BELOVED WIFE.
HOW DREADFUL IT WAS TO SEE HER SO SICK AND PALE, AND KNOW HER SUFFERING WAS MY FAULT!
I HAD MUCH DISPLEASURE TO ANSWER FOR, BUT IT IS DONE. WE ARE RECONCILED, AND I AM HAPPIER THAN I DESERVE TO BE.

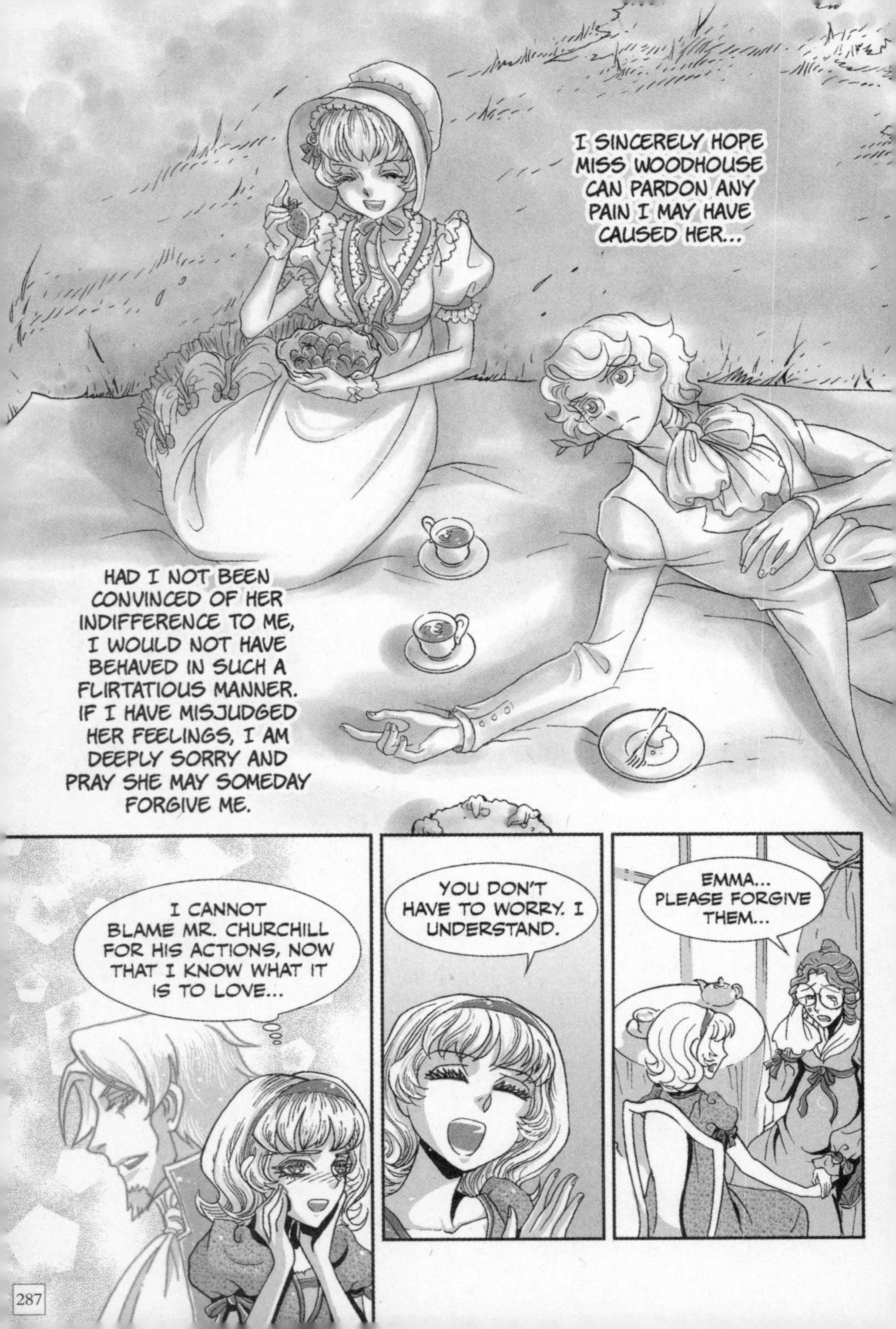
I SINCERELY HOPE MISS WOODHOUSE CAN PARDON ANY PAIN I MAY HAVE CAUSED HER...
HAD I NOT BEEN CONVINCED OF HER INDIFFERENCE TO ME, I WOULD NOT HAVE BEHAVED IN SUCH A FLIRTATIOUS MANNER. IF I HAVE MISJUDGED HER FEELINGS, I AM DEEPLY SORRY AND PRAY SHE MAY SOMEDAY FORGIVE ME.
EMMA... PLEASE FORGIVE THEM...
YOU DON'T HAVE TO WORRY. I UNDERSTAND.
I CANNOT BLAME MR. CHURCHILL FOR HIS ACTIONS, NOW THAT I KNOW WHAT IT IS TO LOVE...

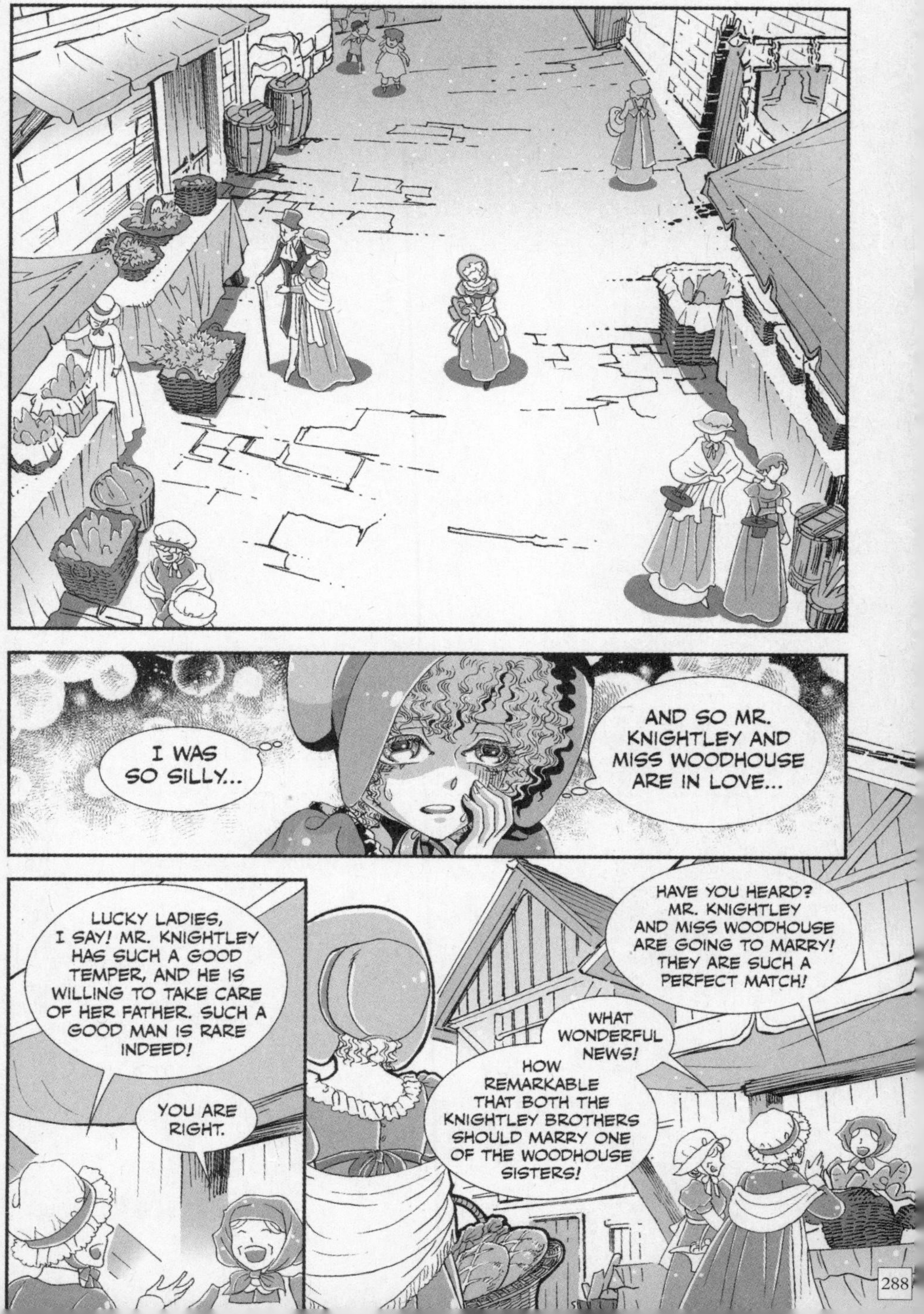
AND SO MR. KNIGHTLEY AND MISS WOODHOUSE ARE IN LOVE...
I WAS SO SILLY...
HAVE YOU HEARD? MR. KNIGHTLEY AND MISS WOODHOUSE ARE GOING TO MARRY! THEY ARE SUCH A PERFECT MATCH!
WHAT WONDERFUL NEWS!
HOW REMARKABLE THAT BOTH THE KNIGHTLEY BROTHERS SHOULD MARRY ONE OF THE WOODHOUSE SISTERS!
LUCKY LADIES, I SAY! MR. KNIGHTLEY HAS SUCH A GOOD TEMPER, AND HE IS WILLING TO TAKE CARE OF HER FATHER. SUCH A GOOD MAN IS RARE INDEED!
YOU ARE RIGHT.

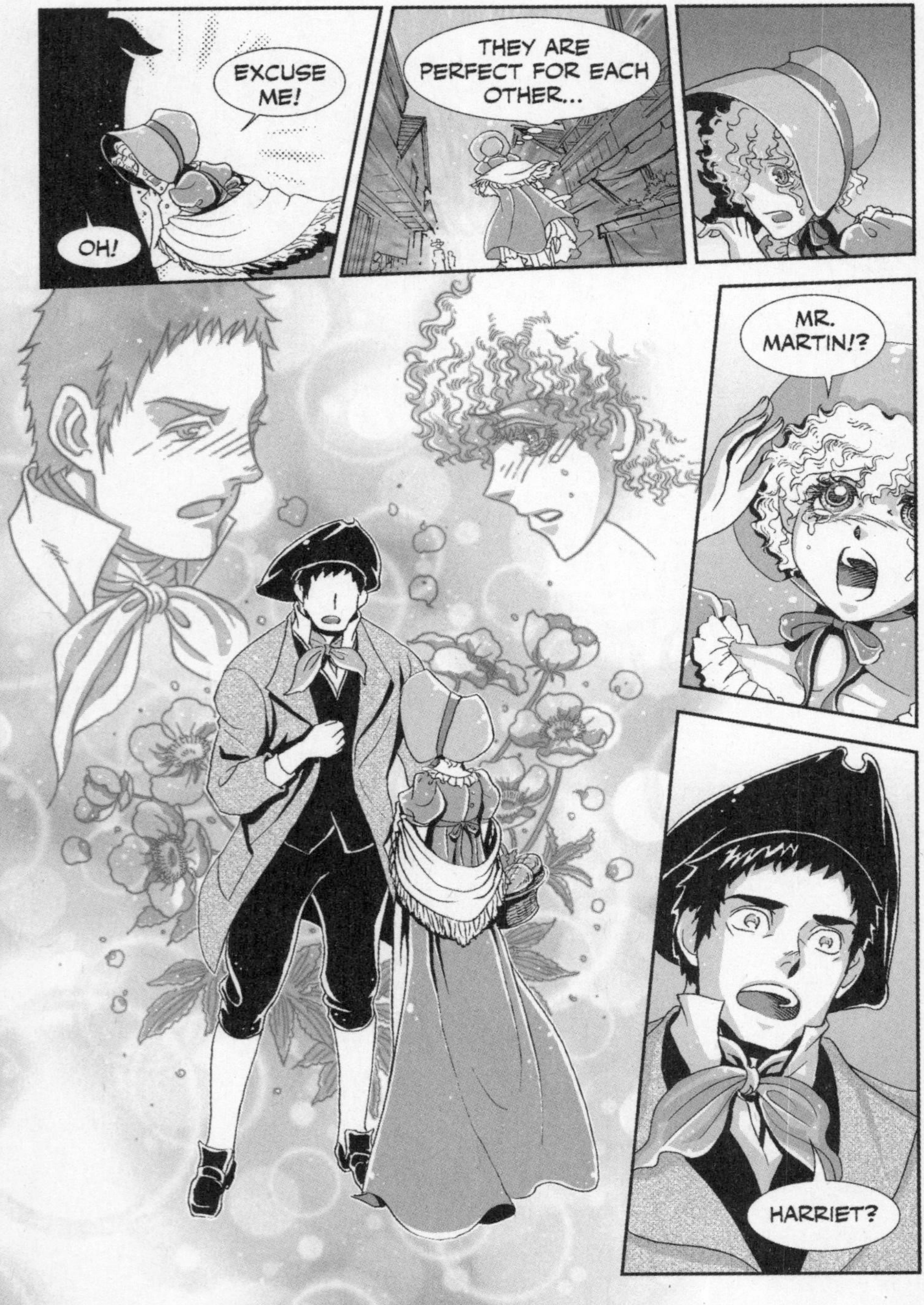
THEY ARE PERFECT FOR EACH OTHER...
EXCUSE ME!
OH!
MR. MARTIN!?
HARRIET?

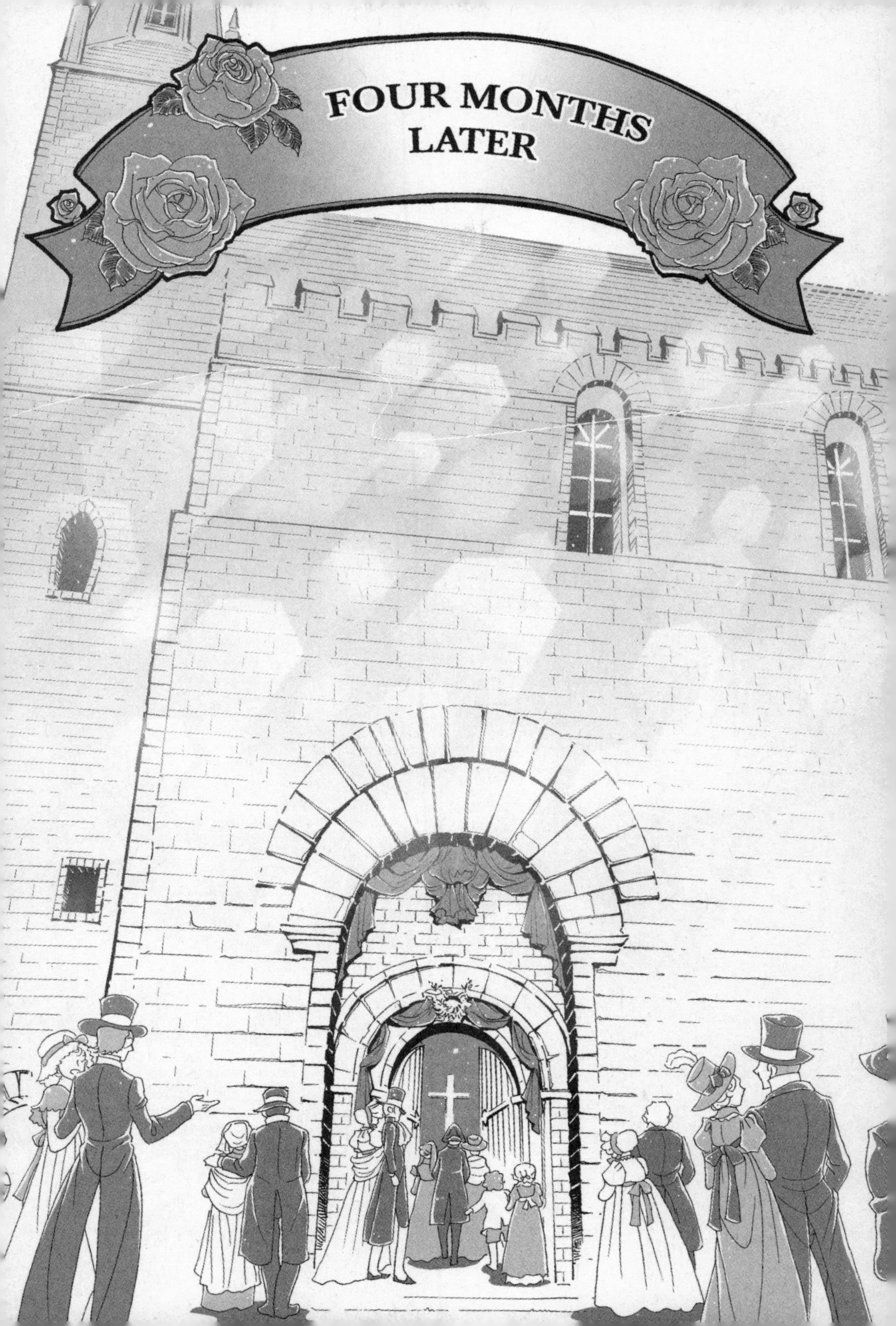
FOUR MONTHS LATER

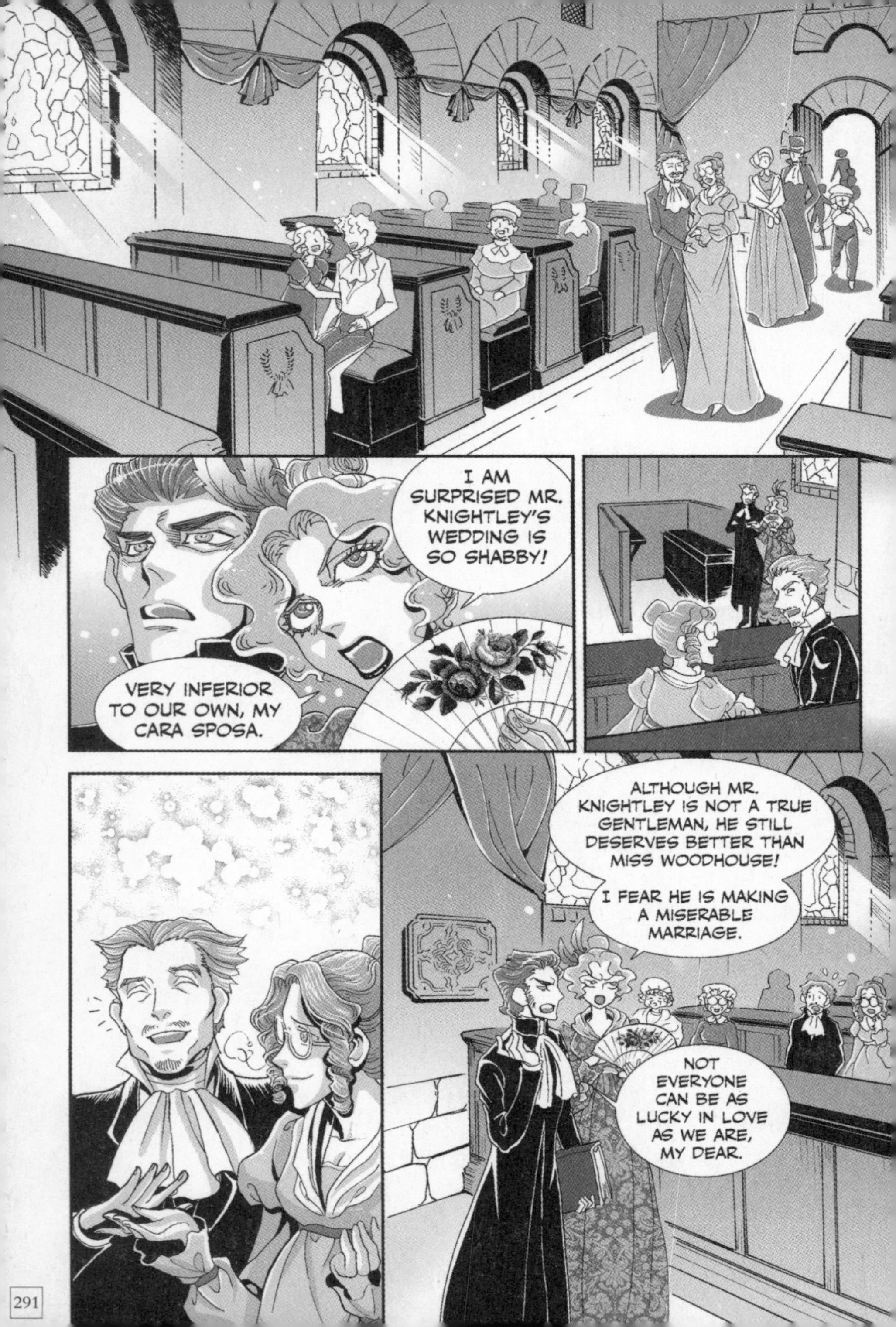
I AM SURPRISED MR. KNIGHTLEY'S WEDDING IS SO SHABBY!
VERY INFERIOR TO OUR OWN, MY CARA SPOSA.
ALTHOUGH MR. KNIGHTLEY IS NOT A TRUE GENTLEMAN, HE STILL DESERVES BETTER THAN MISS WOODHOUSE!
I FEAR HE IS MAKING A MISERABLE MARRIAGE.
NOT EVERYONE CAN BE AS LUCKY IN LOVE AS WE ARE, MY DEAR.

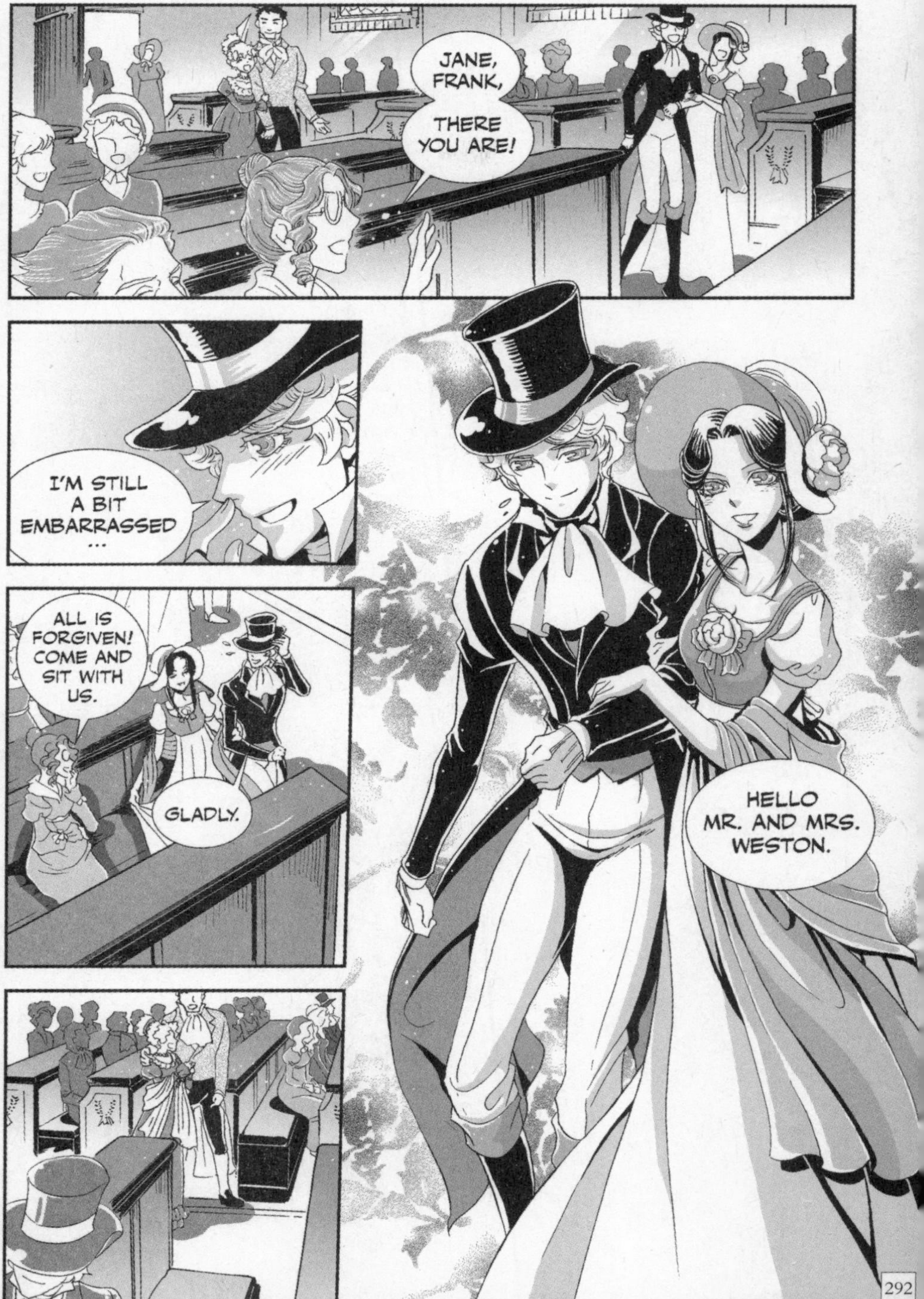
JANE, FRANK, THERE YOU ARE!
HELLO MR. AND MRS. WESTON.
I'M STILL A BIT EMBARRASSED ...
ALL IS FORGIVEN! COME AND SIT WITH US.
GLADLY.

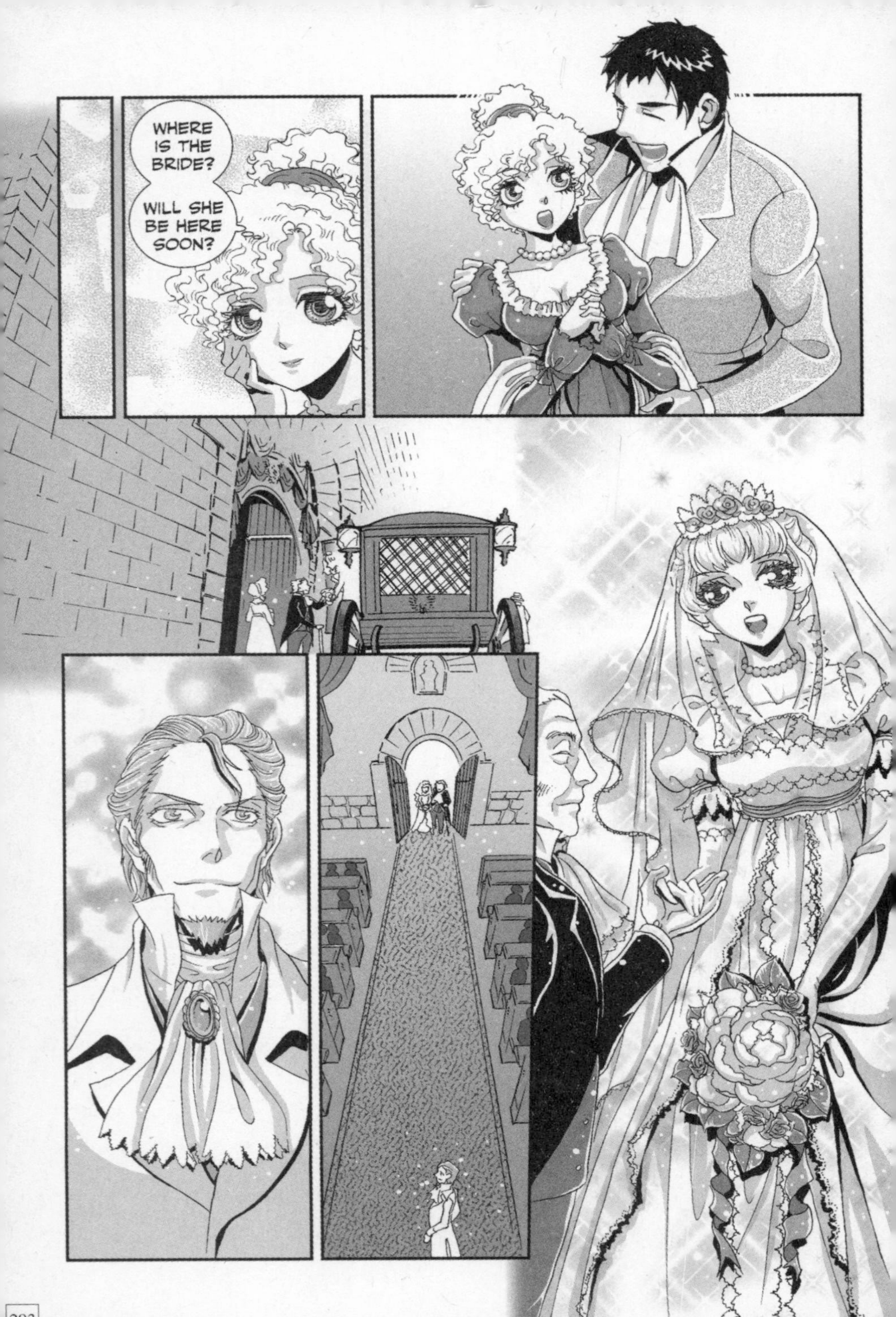
WHERE IS THE BRIDE?
WILL SHE BE HERE SOON?

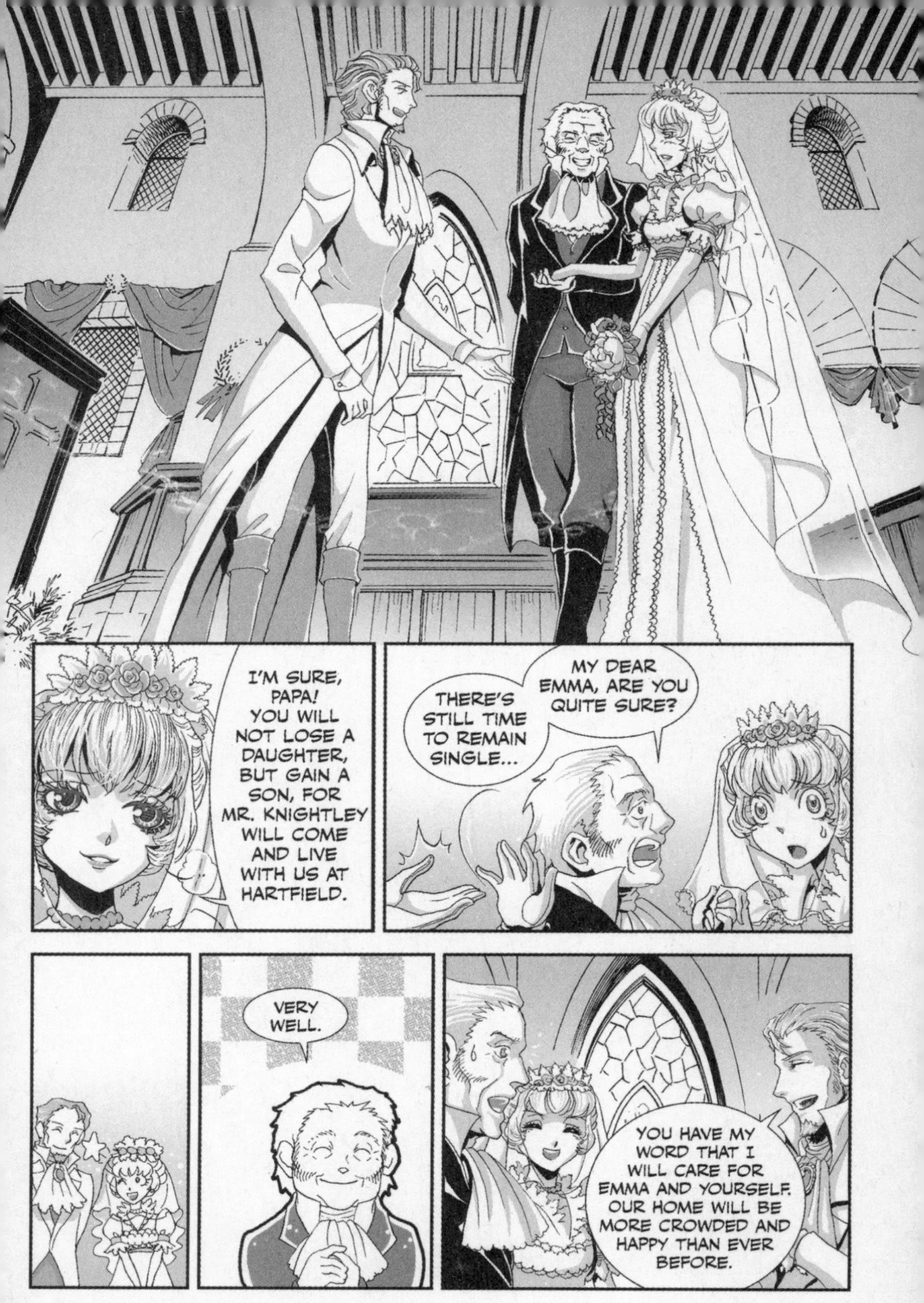
MY DEAR EMMA, ARE YOU QUITE SURE?
THERE'S STILL TIME TO REMAIN SINGLE...
I'M SURE, PAPA! YOU WILL NOT LOSE A DAUGHTER, BUT GAIN A SON, FOR MR. KNIGHTLEY WILL COME AND LIVE WITH US AT HARTFIELD.
YOU HAVE MY WORD THAT I WILL CARE FOR EMMA AND YOURSELF. OUR HOME WILL BE MORE CROWDED AND HAPPY THAN EVER BEFORE.
VERY WELL.

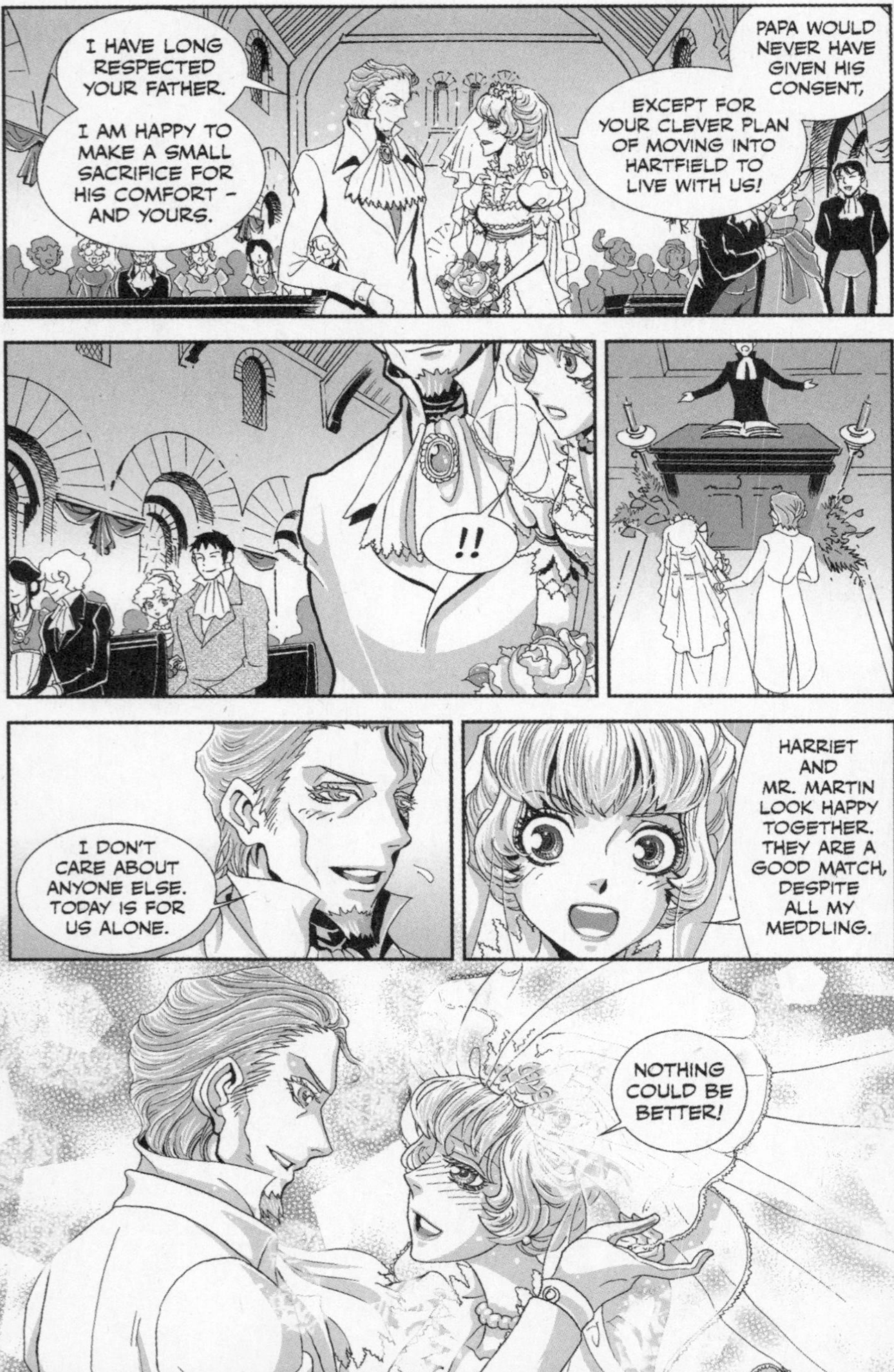
PAPA WOULD NEVER HAVE GIVEN HIS CONSENT,
EXCEPT FOR YOUR CLEVER PLAN OF MOVING INTO HARTFIELD TO LIVE WITH US!
I HAVE LONG RESPECTED YOUR FATHER.
I AM HAPPY TO MAKE A SMALL SACRIFICE FOR HIS COMFORT - AND YOURS.
!!
HARRIET AND MR. MARTIN LOOK HAPPY TOGETHER. THEY ARE A GOOD MATCH, DESPITE ALL MY MEDDLING.
I DON'T CARE ABOUT ANYONE ELSE. TODAY IS FOR US ALONE.
NOTHING COULD BE BETTER!

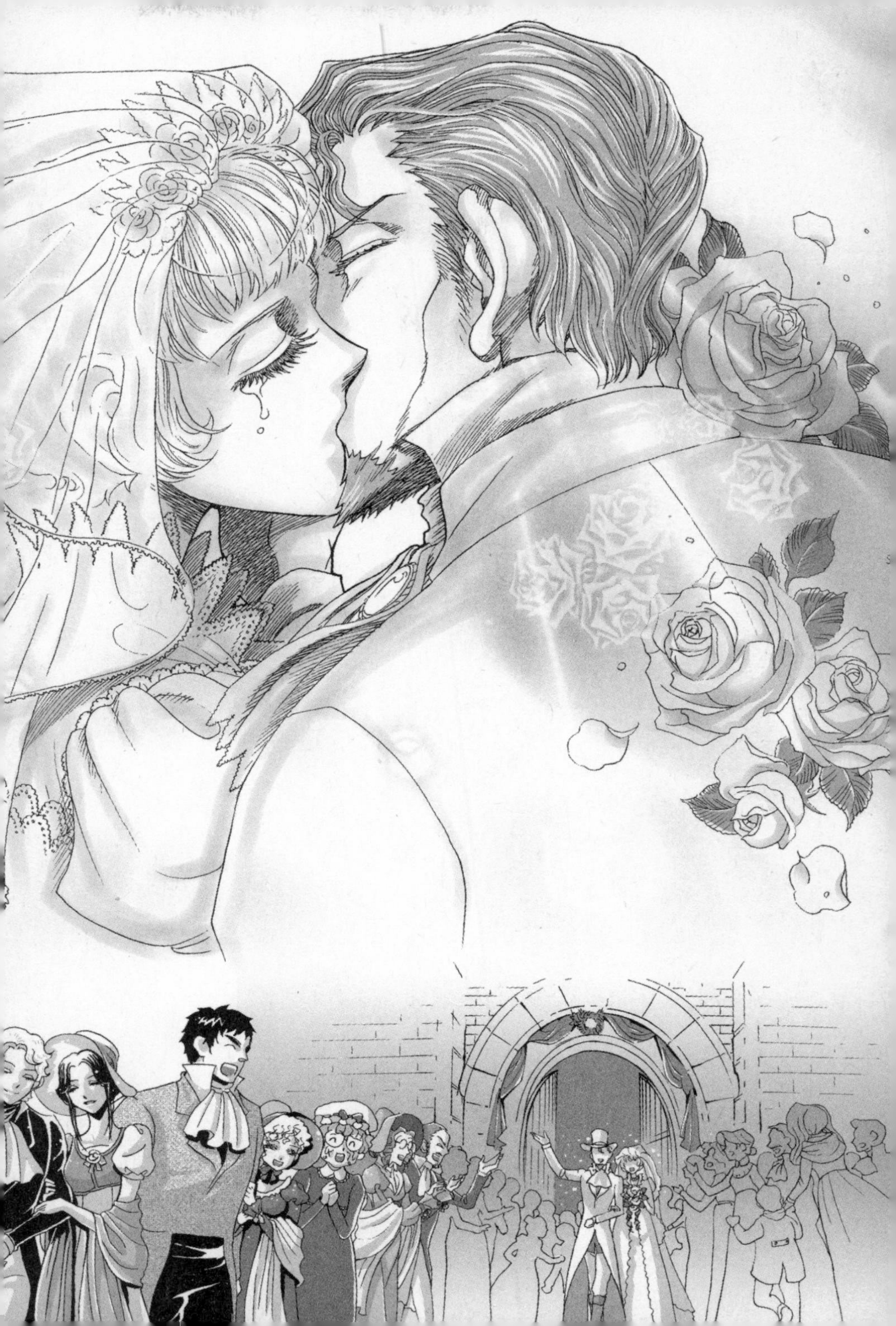

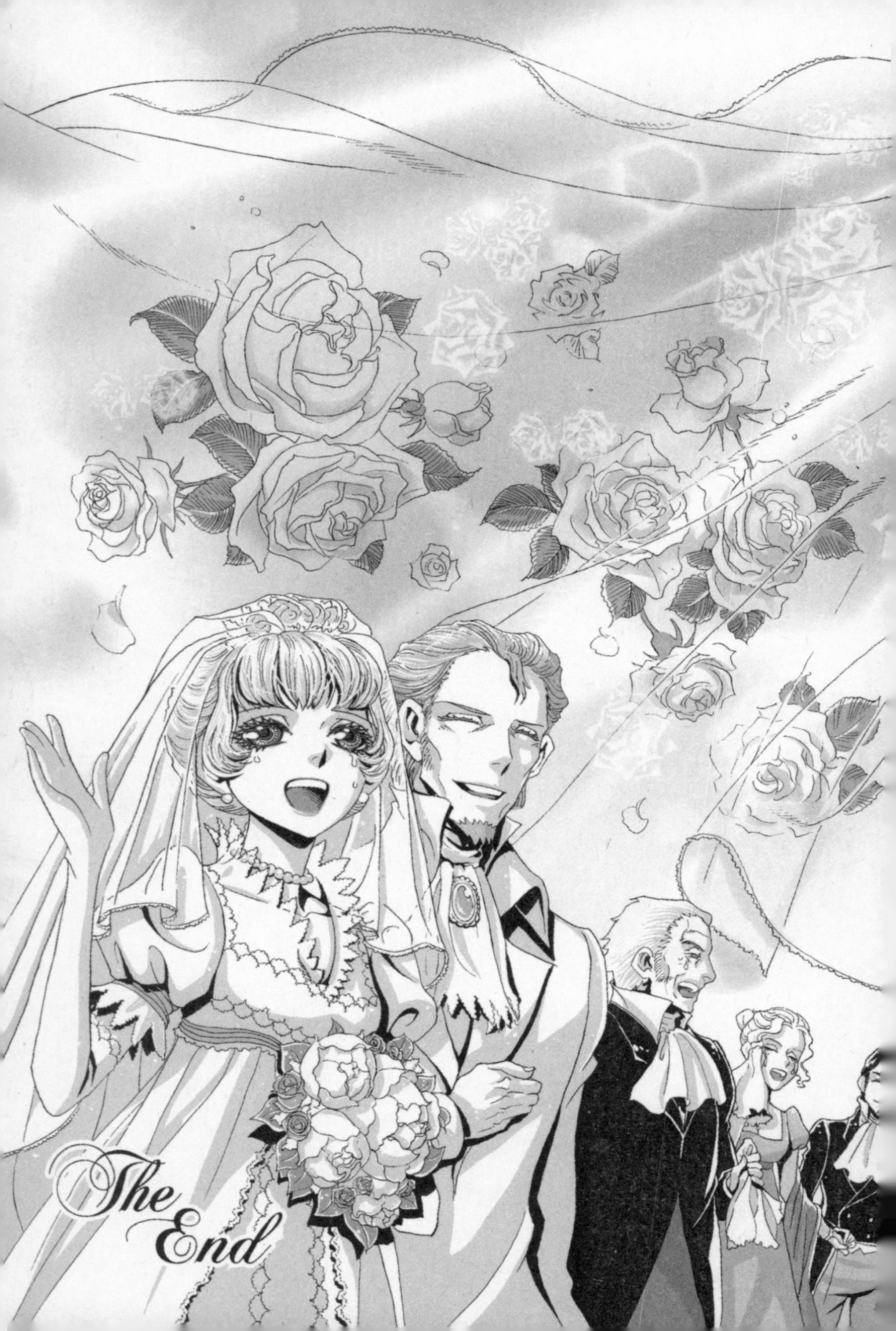
The End

THE SYMBOLS OF LOVE

When arranging the symbolic links, it is not enough to just have dialogue with hidden meanings; scenes that raise readers' suspicions are also required. Taking Frank and Jane as an example once again, I took the vaguest parts of their relationship in the original book and used them to reveal their relationship gradually in the manga, while still maintaining the excitement of unveiling their relationship at the end of the story. You see the first hint of this at Mr. and Mrs. Cole's ball in chapter five; Frank quietly peeks at Jane from a corner, and when Emma catches him doing this, he explains that he was peeking at Jane because of her strange-looking hair. His explanation and the way he acts in this scene are quite far-fetched and suspicious. Emma does not suspect him, however, and also misleads the readers into thinking nothing of his suspicious behavior. In doing so, this obvious clue toward Frank and Jane's unusual relationship is rendered unremarkable. But no matter how hard Frank and Jane try, they ultimately cannot hide the fact that they are in love. In chapter eight, while everyone is playing cards, Mr. Knightley notices Jane and Frank flirting, so he warns Emma to be careful. Since Mr. Knightley is the story's main male character, readers will generally find his point of view convincing, leading them to suspect Jane and Frank once again if they weren't already. On the contrary, Emma disagreeing with Mr. Knightley in this situation acts as a diversion to once again confuse the readers, ultimately encouraging them to wonder and really think about which of them is correct. Also in chapter eight, Emma sees Jane and Frank acting unusual at Donwell Abbey. Jane, who never expresses her feelings, tells Emma in a moment of weakness that she is exhausted in mind and spirit, while Frank – who is usually known to be upbeat and friendly all the time – throws a tantrum in front of Emma. During the outing at Box Hill, Frank and Jane have a rare moment where they talk to each other directly in front of the whole group, and the conversation does not go well. Again, Emma acts in a manner that misleads readers in terms of the mystery behind Frank and Jane, enhancing the story's suspense. There are many more vaguely mysterious points like this in the original book – too many to list, in fact!

AH-HA, THERE YOU ARE!
OH!
WHAT ARE YOU LOOKING AT?

!?

!

THE MYSTERIES OF LOVE

Back when we had just started working on this manga adaptation, the artist actually suggested that we make it clear to readers that Frank and Jane are a pair, with only Emma being clueless about it. In some ways, this was a good idea; thanks to how popular and widely read the original version of *Emma* is, even people who haven't read the book may already know some of the story going into this manga version. The sooner the mystery surrounding Frank and Jane is revealed, the sooner readers will understand the symbolic links hidden in their dialogue. On the other hand, for those readers who know nothing about the story and are going into this manga version fresh, if they re-read it after finishing it, I believe they will experience the fun of discovering the various symbolic links their second time through, so the end result is the same. I discussed this matter with the artist, telling him that the story should be adapted as faithfully to the original book as possible regardless of whether or not the readers know what's going to happen going in, because doing so allows Austen's original craftsmanship to shine through more clearly in our manga version. The prime goal of the Manga Classics series, after all, is to stay true to the original books. I was able to convince the artist of my reasoning, and he agreed. Therefore, every single line of dialogue and all of the plot elements in our adaptation are closely linked to the original story's suspenseful qualities.

...Continues on Page 3

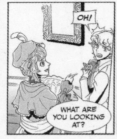

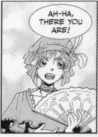

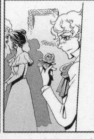

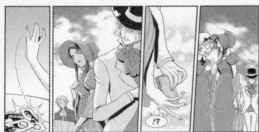

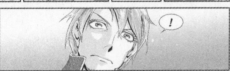

CRYSTAL S. CHAN: ADAPTING EMMA

Note: To avoid reader confusion, *Emma* (in italics) refers to the title of the book; Emma (in plain text) refers to the actual character.

THE LOVE DETECTIVE

Emma was published late in Jane Austen's writing career. As such, it had much better plot arrangement than many of her previous works and it has been said that *Emma* is more a detective story than it is a pure love story. Austen was good at using details to guide readers toward discovering the truth themselves, further enhancing the fun of the love story even after they had experienced the plot's numerous twists and turns. Here, I will discuss how we kept this characteristic intact when adapting *Emma* and also go over some things we had to pay attention to when working on the script.

"*Emma* is a love story. How could it be a detective story?" Good question! Well, let's look at the characteristics of a detective story. Detective stories are particularly attractive because they provide readers with symbolic links to guess at and puzzle over, allowing them to enjoy the fun of painstakingly investigating an exciting mystery, with the eventual answers to the puzzle being unexpected yet reasonable. That last part is vital, as it is important for readers to be surprised by the answers without feeling like they don't make sense. The greatest suspense of a detective story is the person behind everything, while the greatest suspense of a love story is whether the gentleman and the lady will get together in the end. Based on *Emma*'s story structure, it is easy to guess that Mr. Knightley and Emma will end up together, and that fits the general expectation of a love story. On the other hand, the story behind Frank and Jane's relationship as well as the target of Mr. Elton's admiration in the first half of the story both add unmistakable elements of a detective story. Therefore, when I was adapting *Emma*, I added some reasonable yet subtle symbolic links to daily life scenes and dialogue to maintain the characteristics of the original book.

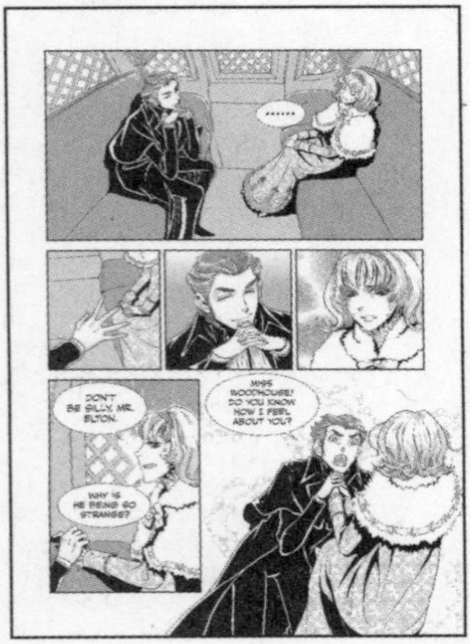
......
MISS WOODHOUSE! DO YOU KNOW HOW I FEEL ABOUT YOU?
DON'T BE SILLY, MR. ELTON.
WHY IS HE BEING SO STRANGE?

Take Frank and Jane as an example; even though we find out at the end of the story that they had been concealing their engagement, I believe most readers will figure it out long before that. For that reason, I tried to keep them distant from each other when they first appear in the story. Like in chapter five, Jane is given a piano and a music sheet by an anonymous person, which raises everyone's curiosity as they try to discover that person's identity. They come to the general conclusion that her foster father Colonel Campbell sent her the present, and only Jane knows that the mystery person is actually Frank. One day in Miss Bates' house, Frank intentionally says to Jane, "Your friends in Ireland will be happy for you to enjoy the piano." "Your friends in Ireland" implies Mr. Dixon, because it is mentioned earlier in the story that Mr. Dixon is in Ireland. On the surface, Frank is trying to test Jane by echoing Emma's point of view. While it seems like Frank is trying to please Emma (and Emma ends up thinking that there is something between Mr. Dixon and Jane), the true purpose of his words is to cover up the fact that he's the one who sent the piano. Then, even though Frank pretends to praise Colonel Campbell for giving Jane the heartfelt gift of the music sheet, he is actually using Campbell's name to express his true feelings toward Jane in front of Emma, while Emma is none the wiser. Frank successfully pleases Jane without anybody knowing and makes Emma believe he's echoing her opinions at the same time, and when this all comes together, it's easy to see that the scene design here is both outstanding and complicated. There are other mysterious or otherwise vague elements in *Emma* that you will not know the full meaning behind until you learn the story's ending. Therefore, adapting the script from the original book required extra care; we had to carefully use symbolic links to convey both the surface and hidden meanings of these complex story elements and character interactions; failing to do this would have wasted the symbolic links and made it impossible for the story to progress.

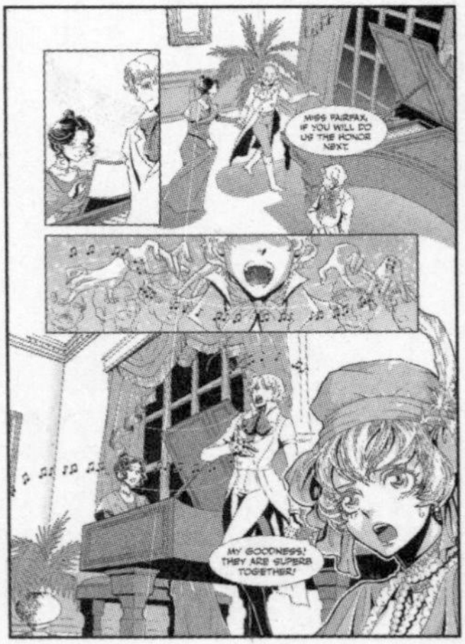
MISS FAIRFAX, IF YOU WILL DO US THE HONOR NEXT.
MY GOODNESS! THEY ARE SUPERB TOGETHER!

THE DETAILS OF LOVE

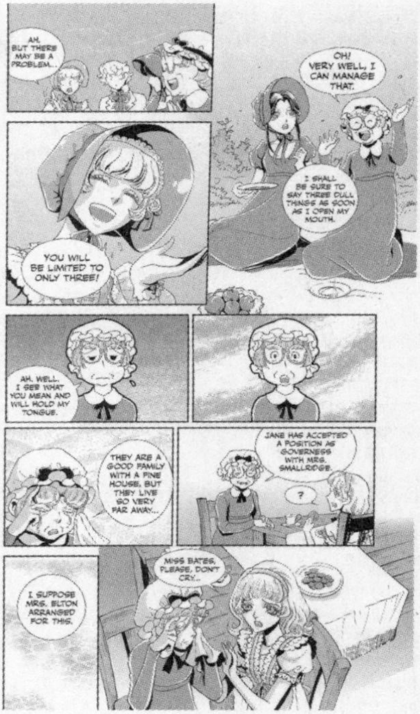
OH! VERY WELL, I CAN MANAGE THAT.
I SHALL BE SURE TO SAY THREE DULL THINGS AS SOON AS I OPEN MY MOUTH.
AH, BUT THERE MAY BE A PROBLEM...
YOU WILL BE LIMITED TO ONLY THREE!
AH, WELL. I SEE WHAT YOU MEAN AND WILL HOLD MY TONGUE.
JANE HAS ACCEPTED A POSITION AS GOVERNESS WITH MRS. SMALLRIDGE.
?
THEY ARE A GOOD FAMILY WITH A FINE HOUSE, BUT THEY LIVE SO VERY FAR AWAY...
MISS BATES, PLEASE, DON'T CRY...
I SUPPOSE MRS. ELTON ARRANGED FOR THIS.

Finally, let me talk about some of the small details we added in order to portray gradual shifts in a character's attitude. At the beginning of the story, Emma dislikes Miss Bates for being too chatty, and she tries to avoid having any unnecessary contact with her. Therefore, when Emma and the others visit Miss Bates' house and she generously offers them some freshly-baked biscuits, Emma is the only one who refuses them, implying that she has negative feelings about Miss Bates in her heart. Much later on in the story, Mr. Knightley scolds Emma for being rude to Miss Bates during the Box Hill outing. Emma then comes to realize that she was wrong to have such an unfairly negative attitude toward Miss Bates, so she visits her in person and apologizes. This time, she tries one of Miss Bates' biscuits and remarks to herself about how delicious it is, implying that she has finally accepted Miss Bates in her heart as well. The purpose of this small pair of scenes is to enhance the reader's understanding of Emma's disposition and how it gradually changes over the course of the story. Since none of this is really related to the main plot, it would not have been suitable to use narration to actively describe her changing attitude, which is why I arranged subtle details like the ones I just described. Besides, when it comes to the main plot, the love between Emma and Mr. Knightley is already portrayed splendidly in the original book, so I was able to spend less effort on adapting that aspect of the story and focus on highlighting smaller plot threads like the relationship between Emma and Miss Bates.

Hopefully, you now see how every single line and scene from *Emma* was carefully adapted for this manga version. It was certainly a rigorous challenge for us, especially when I realized I was adapting a detective story as well as a love story! (laughs) When you read this adaptation, I hope you are touched by the feelings of true love between the main characters while simultaneously experiencing the thrill of uncovering the secrets they are hiding.

Crystal (Silvermoon) Chan

About the Author

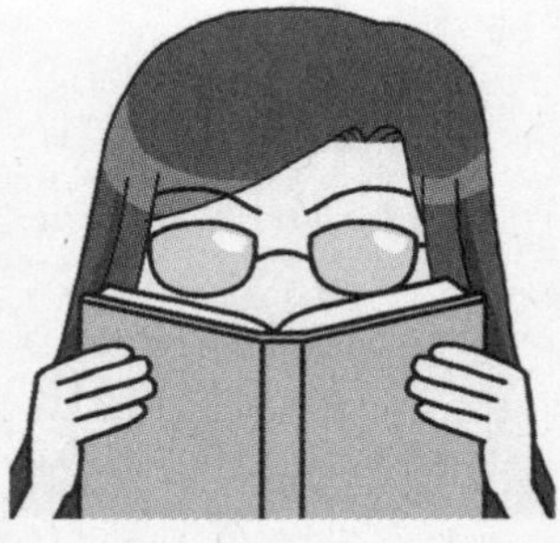

Crystal S. Chan
(aka Crystal Silvermoon)

Crystal has won an Award for Teen Literature and earned a degree in language and literature. She was a professional screenplay writer for TV drama before working as an adapter for the Manga Classics series. She accepts the challenge because of her love in literature and comic. Her background allows her to always find the right balance between preserving the depth of the original piece while keeping up with the taste of the younger generation.

Crystal is a big fan of Sailor Moon. She loves it so much that she once made her alias as Crystal Silvermoon to pay tribute to the author.

...Continued from Page 2

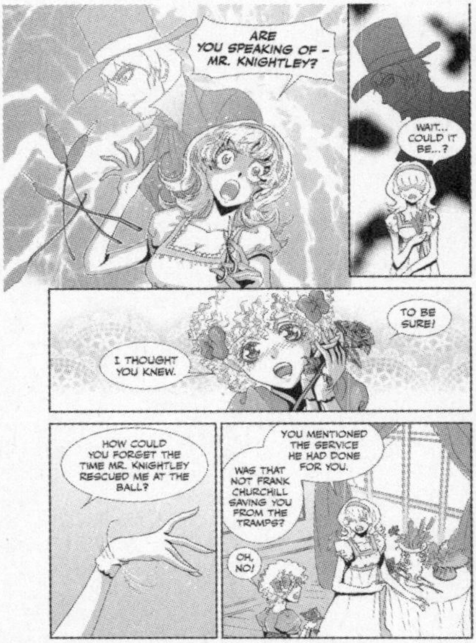
WAIT... COULD IT BE...?
ARE YOU SPEAKING OF – MR. KNIGHTLEY?
TO BE SURE!
I THOUGHT YOU KNEW.
YOU MENTIONED THE SERVICE HE HAD DONE FOR YOU.
WAS THAT NOT FRANK CHURCHILL SAVING YOU FROM THE TRAMPS?
OH, NO!
HOW COULD YOU FORGET THE TIME MR. KNIGHTLEY RESCUED ME AT THE BALL?

Other than the characteristics of a detective story mentioned above, we adjusted other details based on the uniqueness of manga as a format. For example, I devised ways for the characters to express their feelings and thoughts through physical action. Everyone knows how incisive Austen's dialogue is, and that is one of the things that makes reading her novels so pleasurable. With manga, however, there's much less room and opportunity to explain a character's mental state in detail, with conversation taking priority. But when a panel shows characters talking, that sometimes isn't enough to express their innermost thoughts and feelings. Why not just describe a character's mental state right on the page, through more text? This would work for shorter descriptions, but longer ones would take up too much panel space and even cover the characters' faces. At that point, you would just be better off reading the novel! That's why I attempted to express the characters' thoughts and feelings through movement and physical actions instead. A good example of this is in chapter nine, when Harriet tells Emma that Mr. Knightley is the one she admires. Emma goes through a lot of shock here; first, she finds out she was mistaken when she thought Harriet was in love with Frank, and then she learns that Harriet is actually in love with Mr. Knightley. Right after that, Harriet reveals that Mr. Knightley seems to return her feelings, and at that point, Emma realizes that she truly loves Mr. Knightley. The original book focuses on describing the step-by-step changes in Emma's emotional state as she receives gradually worse shocks, culminating in her realizing how she feels about Mr. Knightley. So for this scene in the manga adaptation, I decided to have Emma arranging flowers, which also fits her social status as a lady. By having her knock down the vase, carelessly prick her finger on the rose, and then break the vase altogether by dropping it, I was able to express her increasing levels of shock through visual action, thereby unleashing the manga format's greatest strength: the ability to tell a story through pictures.

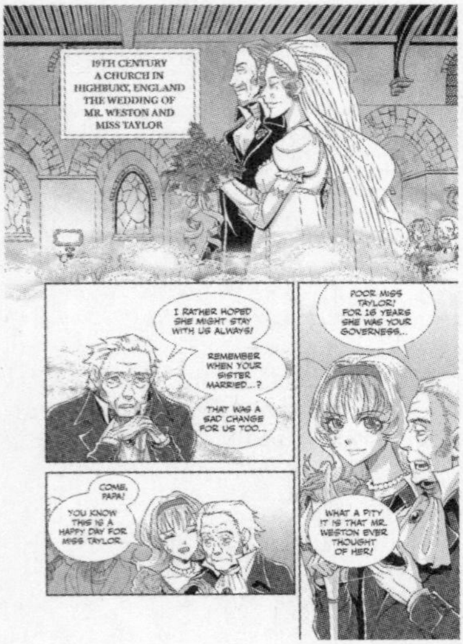
19TH CENTURY
A CHURCH IN
HIGHBURY, ENGLAND
THE WEDDING OF
MR. WESTON AND
MISS TAYLOR
POOR MISS TAYLOR! FOR 16 YEARS SHE WAS YOUR GOVERNESS...
WHAT A PITY IT IS THAT MR. WESTON EVER THOUGHT OF HER!
I RATHER HOPED SHE MIGHT STAY WITH US ALWAYS!
REMEMBER WHEN YOUR SISTER MARRIED...?
THAT WAS A SAD CHANGE FOR US TOO...
COME, PAPA!
YOU KNOW THIS IS A HAPPY DAY FOR MISS TAYLOR.

Otherwise, we also had to heavily adapt some of the original book's narration to fit the manga format. For example, chapter one opens with Miss Taylor and Mr. Weston's wedding ceremony. In the original book, this event is related to the reader through narration, and the thoughts of Emma's father and Emma herself – like how she is fond of playing cupid – are narrated as well. While it would have been fine to narrate all of this in the manga version too, I decided to adapt the wedding into an actual scene in order to allow readers to meet some of the characters and become familiar with their dispositions right off the bat. Those who have watched the movie or television drama versions of *Emma* might ask, "Are you ever worried that this adaptation is too similar to some of those other versions?" To be honest, I once considered researching every single prior adaptation of *Emma* (except for the very oldest adaptations, which are extremely hard to find) precisely because I was concerned about that. But when I started writing the script for our version, I actually found those worries to be quite pointless. That's because a hundred different scriptwriters will portray even the same scenes and characters in a hundred different ways. The only thing I needed to do was write *Emma* as I alone understand it, because my interpretation of it is just as unique as those who came before me.

Early Character Design Sketches

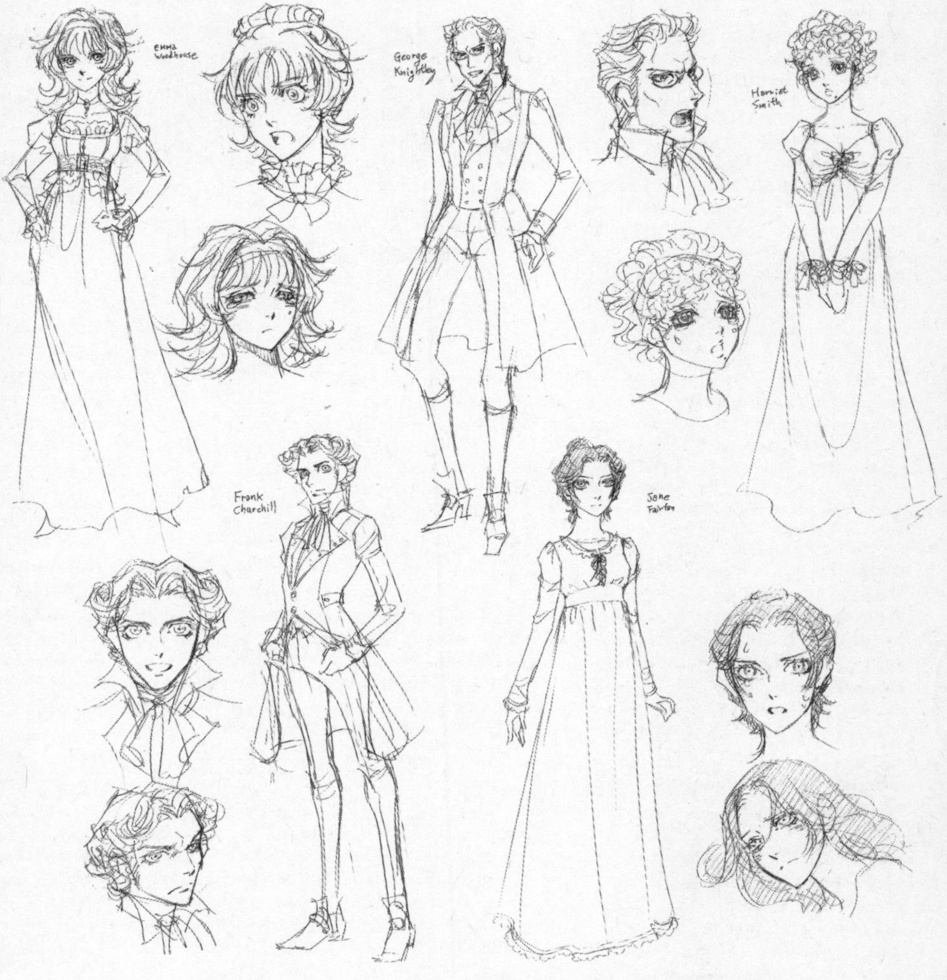
EMMA Woodhouse
George Knightley
Harriet Smith
Frank Churchill
Jane Fairfax

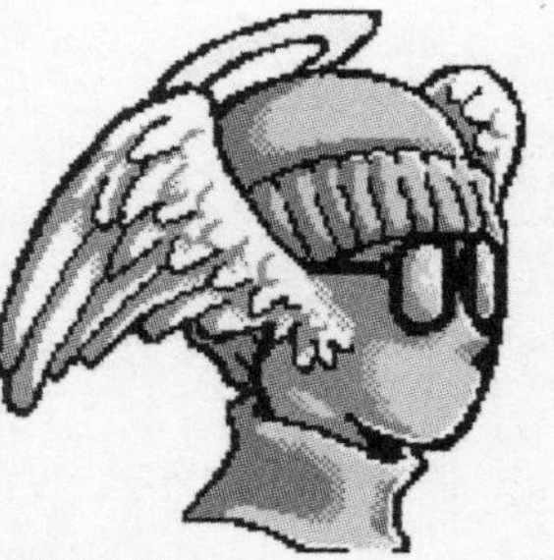

Po Tse (aka Lemon Po)

About the Artist

Po Tse, better known as Lemon Po to his followers and friends, is a veteran in the comic-activists community. His uncanny talent of drawing authentic shoujo style as a male artist has made him a rare breed among his peers. Po's drawing style is inspired by manga artists of the 80's. He may bring the old school genre back to style again with his own unique touch!

Aside from being a shoujo comic artist, Po is a domestic husband who enjoys making desserts to delight his friends and family.

PO TSE:

CREATING THE CHARACTERS

Greetings, Janeites! It's nice to see you here again with this second book in the Jane Austen manga adaptation series (with the first book being "Pride and Prejudice" - make sure to pick up a copy if you haven't read it before!). "Emma" is my favorite of all of Jane Austen's famous works, not only because of the mindful design of the story and the smart, playful lines, but also because the characters are adorable.

First, Augusta and Phillip Elton as the story's villains are very interesting; they are so exaggerated and loveable, and the story is more energetic and lively thanks to them. Mr. Henry Woodhouse is kind and always stays at his luxurious house, but he always murmurs about his health problems... though I think that is just his way of expressing his caring nature to the others and absolutely not hypochondriasis! It's reasonable for Mr. Knightly to respect him! Similarly, though Miss Bates seems to be talkative, this is just her passionate way of treating others; in the end she is happy and satisfied with her circumstances. It's not hard to see why everyone in the book accepts her. Mrs. Anne Weston (AKA Miss Taylor) was optimistic and kind in the original book; it's a pity she doesn't play a bigger role in this adaptation, and I am sorry I wasn't able to make her a more impressive character. John Knightley was bold and frank in the classic book, which provides an interesting contrast to his brother. Also, there's not much written about Robert Martin in the original version of the story, but he seems to be nice based on his friendly interaction with Emma!

Among the main characters, Harriet is wimpy, timid, and a crybaby. Quite a few readers might find her troublesome, but we can see that Mr. Knightley admires her tender and affectionate nature, and later she grows strong thanks to Emma's influence. We can see throughout the book that she tries hard to change herself, but sometimes she just changes herself in the wrong ways. Mr. Frank Churchill, the "womanizer" who can be commonly found in Jane Austen's various works, horribly betrays Emma's love but ends up being the luckiest womanizer around. Not only does he gain forgiveness from everyone, he marries beautiful Jane!~~ It's clear to me that he has learned from his mistakes, and I think he will one day become a good man under Jane's care and influence! Despite being the main male character of this book, George Knightley actually keeps a very low profile, but he is intelligent and righteous. Although he always fights with Emma, his words are quite witty indeed, and that makes their fights more interesting. He was much calmer in the original book, but became relatively harsh this time around due to the dramatic expressions used in this adaptation.

Finally, regarding the two main female characters Emma and Jane, they both have their own outstanding qualities, but personally I like Jane Fairfax the most. She is exactly the type of person I like. It looks like she is devoid of feelings, but the truth is that she's tortured by strong emotions deep in her heart. This shows the beauty in her strength and is one of the highlights of this book! As for Emma Woodhouse, Austen herself said it best: she is "a heroine whom no one but myself will much like." I believe this really sums up my feeling towards our brave protagonist!

Until next time! Read more manga! Read more classics!

Po Tse

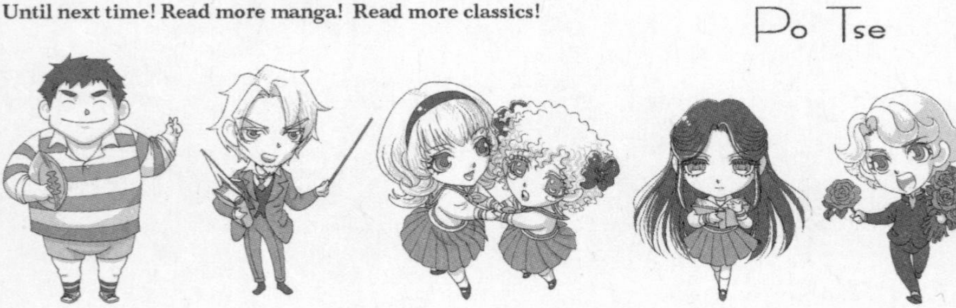

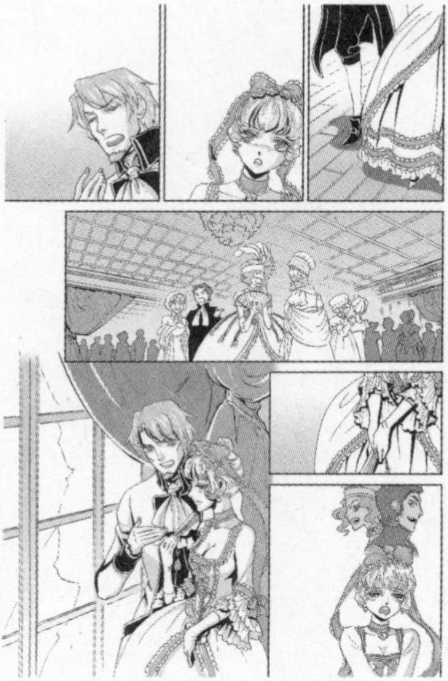

Step 5: Grey tones applied.

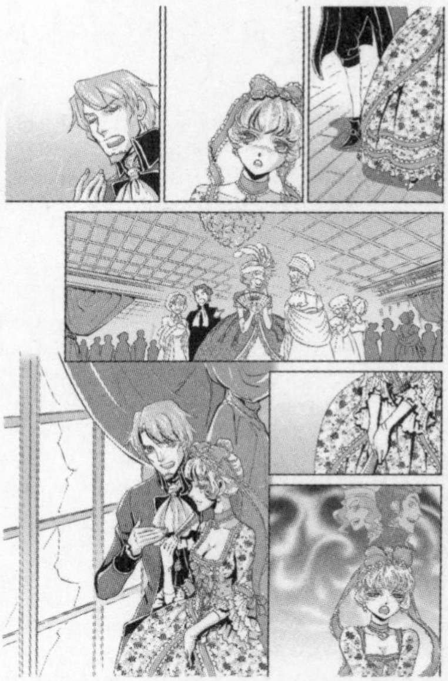

Step 6: Add patterns for cloths and backgrounds

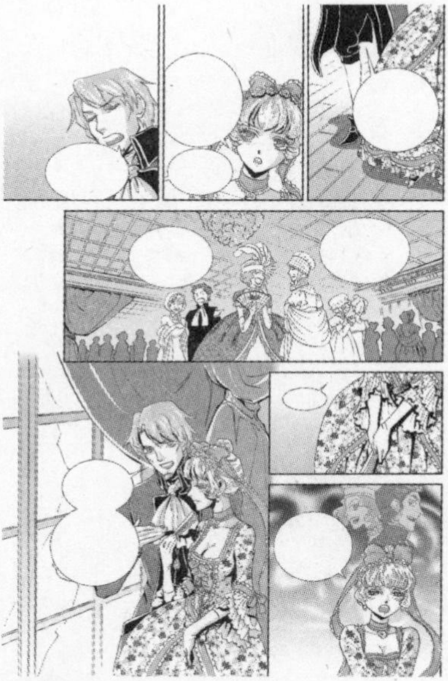

Step 7: Apply word balloons.

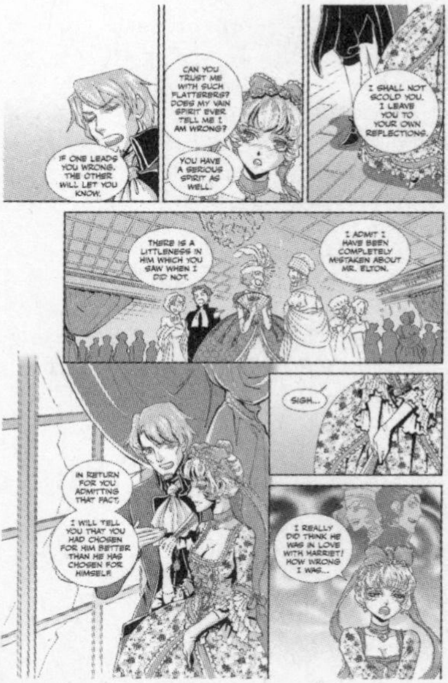
I SHALL NOT SCOLD YOU. I LEAVE YOU TO YOUR OWN REFLECTIONS.
CAN YOU TRUST ME WITH SUCH FLATTERERS? DOES MY VAIN SPIRIT EVER TELL ME I AM WRONG?
YOU HAVE A SERIOUS SPIRIT AS WELL.
IF ONE LEADS YOU WRONG, THE OTHER WILL LET YOU KNOW.
I ADMIT I HAVE BEEN COMPLETELY MISTAKEN ABOUT MR. ELTON.
THERE IS A LITTLENESS IN HIM WHICH YOU SAW WHEN I DID NOT.
SIGH...
I REALLY DID THINK HE WAS IN LOVE WITH HARRIET! HOW WRONG I WAS...
IN RETURN FOR YOU ADMITTING THAT FACT,
I WILL TELL YOU THAT YOU HAD CHOSEN FOR HIM BETTER THAN HE HAS CHOSEN FOR HIMSELF.

Step 8: Put in the dialogue and we are done!

CREATING A MANGA PAGE!

A step by step look at how a page of *EMMA* is made:

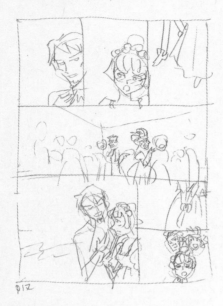

Step 1: Artist did a rough layout of the page.

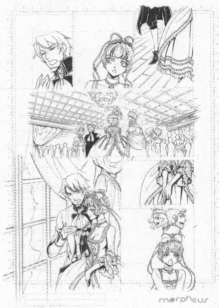

Step 2: Line art is done and scanned in.

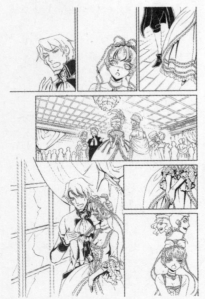

Step 3: Cleaned up final lines.

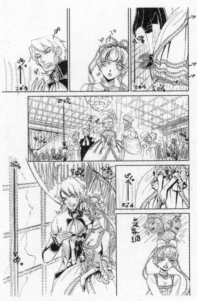

Step 4: Artist did his shading guide.

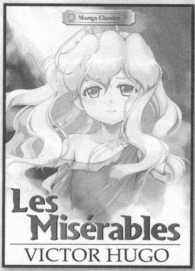
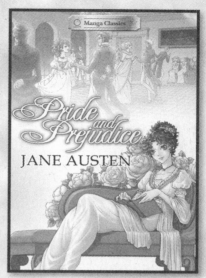
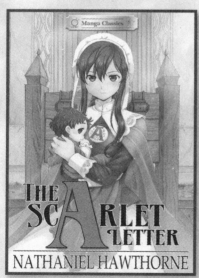
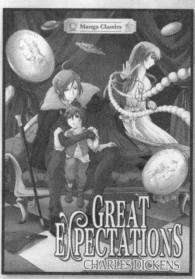

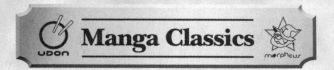
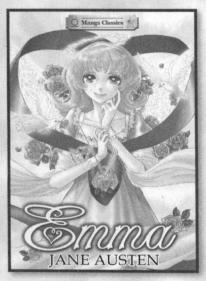

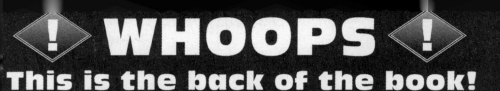

WHOOPS

This is the back of the book!

UDON's Manga Classics books follow the Japanese comic (aka Manga!) reading order. Traditional manga is read in a "reversed" format starting on the right and heading towards the left. The story begins where English readers expect to find the last page because the spine of the book is on the opposite side. Flip to the other end of the book and start reading your Manga Classics!

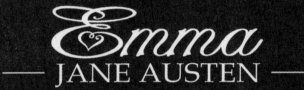

Emma

JANE AUSTEN

Art by: Po Tse
Story Adaptation by: Crystal S. Chan

English Dialogue Adapted by: Stacy King
Lettering: Morpheus Studios
Lettering Assist: Long Vo

UDON STAFF:

UDON Chief of Operations: Erik Ko
Senior Producer: Long Vo
VP of Sales: John Shableski
Senior Editor: Ash Paulsen
Group Editor - Manga Classics: Stacy King
Marketing Manager: Jenny Myung
Production Manager: Janice Leung
Copy Editing Assistant: Michelle Lee
Japanese Liaison: Steven Cummings

MORPHEUS STAFF:

Morpheus Chief: Andy Hung
Production Manager: Tai
Editor : Maygi Lam
Art Assistants: KK, Ashton Touyu, VIP96neko, Mingsin Song, Stoon

Manga Classics: Emma Published by UDON Entertainment Inc. 118 Tower Hill Road, PO Box 20008, Richmond Hill, Ontario, L4K 0K0, Canada. **Printed in Canada**

First Printing May 2015.
Hard Cover Edition ISBN # 978-1-927925-36-2 Soft Cover Edition ISBN # 978-1-927925-35-5
Recommended Age: Young Adult Genre: Manga BISAC Code: CGN004050 / CGN004140 / FIC014000

www.mangaclassics.com

An UDON Entertainment Production, in association with Morpheus Publishing Limited.
www.udonentertainment.com www.morpheuspublishing.com

W9-CRM-604